LAW IN SOCIETY

Canadian Readings

LAW IN SOCIETY
Canadian Readings

Nick Larsen *Brian Burtch*

HARCOURT
BRACE
CANADA

Harcourt Brace & Company, Canada

Toronto Montreal Fort Worth New York Orlando
Philadelphia San Diego London Sydney Tokyo

Canadian Cataloguing in Publication Data

Main entry under title:

Law in society: a Canadian reader

ISBN 0-7747-3605-4

1. Sociological jurisprudence. 2. Law — Canada. I. Larsen, Nick, 1948–. II. Burtch, Brian E., 1949–.

KE3098.L37 1999   340'.115'0971   C98-932169-X

KF385.ZA2L38 1999

Senior Acquisitions Editor: Heather McWhinney
Developmental Editor: James Bosma
Production Editor: Carolyn McLarty
Copy Editor: Barbara Tessman
Cover Design: The Brookview Group Inc.
Interior Design: Opus House
Typesetting and Assembly: Bookman Typesetting Co.
Printing and Binding: Hignell Printing Limited

Cover Art: Rudolf Stussi, *Battleship Toronto* (1995). Oil on linen. 40" × 60". Reproduced with permission of the artist.

Harcourt Brace & Company Canada, Ltd.
55 Horner Avenue, Toronto, ON, Canada M8Z 4X6
Customer Service
Toll-Free Tel.: 1-800-387-7278
Toll-Free Fax.: 1-800-665-7307

This book was printed in Canada.

1 2 3 4 5   03 02 01 00 99

For Irene Seebach, Gilda Gordon, and Claire Culhane.

Brian Burtch

For Simon Verdun-Jones and Phil Wichern — mentors and friends.

Nick Larsen

Preface

It has been exhilarating and challenging to select the articles for this reader. This collection of essays covers a range of topics, including labour law, abortion, obscenity and censorship, the politics of prostitution, illicit drugs, prosecution of corporate crime, and the Aboriginal justice system. We have also selected key articles on gay and lesbian rights and theories of racial or ethnic difference; and in a section on women and law, we focus in on domestic assault, the battered woman syndrome defence in criminal law, and debates over child support, child custody, and property settlements in divorce.

This reader brings forward a distinctively Canadian perspective on law making and legal conflicts. While we also draw on international parallels and examples, for the most part we focus on Canadian examples. This focus allows us to consider examples that are closer to home and to examine how major theoretical perspectives may apply, or not apply, when we consider Canadian circumstances.

Increasingly, social scientists are exploring the impact of specific legislation and key legal decisions as part of their exploration of power and stratification in our society. Similarly, there is a noticeable increase in critical legal scholarship from law students and law professors and practitioners. The authors in this collection are some of the leading scholars in law in society studies. Gender, race, and class have become inescapable in most discussions of law; indeed, we as editors were hardpressed to find scholarship that took an unvarnished liberal or conservative outlook on legal questions. That said, it seems clear that liberal and conservative values are very much part of Canadian political life, of culture, and certainly of the spirit of law making and dispute resolution. Together, we see some overlap between the spheres of law and society, and, as the two spheres are blended, we gain a clearer perspective on law in society.

The essays in this collection draw on the complexity and vitality of rights struggles in Canada. We hope that readers will reflect on instances whereby law has excluded as well as included people, and where it has denied or affirmed legal protections for various groups and individuals. We hope readers will learn from specific facts and cases taken from historical and contemporary cases, and will come to appreciate how there truly are no settled questions, no definite answers to the impact of laws on our social framework. What we do know is that there will be continued emphasis not only on legal decisions as such, but on the social context in which legal

decisions are made. While there are no definitive conclusions about law in society, we believe that using jurisprudence and social science evidence enriches our theoretical and practical understanding of formal social control measures and the informal forces that influence legal structures.

ACKNOWLEDGEMENTS

We have been fortunate to work with the editorial team of Martina van de Velde, James Bosma, and Heather McWhinney of Harcourt Brace Canada. Their support and professionalism were instrumental in bringing this project to fruition. As well, we wish to thank Hal Harder of Harcourt Brace for encouraging us to undertake this project, and for helping us develop the original proposal.

Jack Corse of the Simon Fraser University library assisted with database searches and obtaining information on short notice. As well, the staff of the Lohnlab Centre for On-line Teaching, Centre for Distance Education at Simon Fraser University, provided invaluable help. We also wish to acknowledge the financial assistance provided by Chapman University, which facilitated the collaboration necessary to produce this collection. We wish to thank the staff, faculty, and students in both the School of Criminology and the Department of Women's Studies at Simon Fraser University. Constance Backhouse, Joan Brockman, Mark Carter, and Fiona Kay provided helpful suggestions when we were first formulating this collection. We are grateful to Carol Hird, Leora Burtch, Joe Lelay, and Bonnie Ach for their support throughout this project, and to our parents for their encouragement in our academic pursuits.

Finally, we wish to thank the reviewers for their helpful comments throughout the development of this text: Marilyn Belle-McQuillan, University of Western Ontario; Cathy Fillmore, University of Winnipeg; Fiona Kay, University of British Columbia; Jacqueline Lewis, University of Windsor; Ruth Mann, University of Toronto; and Linda Neilson, University of New Brunswick.

A NOTE FROM THE PUBLISHER

Thank you for selecting *Law in Society: Canadian Readings*, by Nick Larsen and Brian Burtch. The authors and publisher have devoted considerable time to the careful development of this book. We appreciate your recognition of this effort and accomplishment.

We want to hear what you think about *Law in Society*. Please take a few minutes to fill in the stamped reader reply card at the end of the book. Your comments and suggestions will be valuable to us as we prepare new editions and other books.

Contents

x CONTENTS

Restorative Justice

Introduction

Legal conflicts and debates surround us. In the media, legal disputes are an important staple of coverage by television, radio, newspapers and magazines, and, increasingly, the World Wide Web. Politicians, lawyers, judges, and citizens at large are drawn into debates over national standards of child support following separation and divorce, issues of Aboriginal title and land claims, and laws touching on abortion, firearms, the secession of Quebec, and spousal benefits to same-sex couples. Statistics are presented and critiqued, and principles outlined as people try to formulate their version of what is higher ground in law and justice. Law has thus become a vital institution in Canadian society, flanked and pressured by an array of social values and economic interests, as legislators and legal officials seek to create and re-create a sense of justice and purpose in Canada.

Even while laws surround us, it is unclear what to make of particular laws or the overall meaning of legal regulation. One way of expanding our understanding is to apply various theories and to study patterns of legal decisions systematically. This approach helps us explore how power, social inequality, and social change play a part in legal decision making. This approach, which Alan Hunt aptly describes as "the sociological movement in law," gains strength from empirical studies of the legal order and society, as well as theorizing about relationships in law and society. While our space is limited here, we can review some key theoretical frameworks in understanding law and society.

Liberal political theory rests heavily on the notion of individual freedoms and individual rights protected through law by the doctrine of the rule of law. Citizens are thus free to pursue activities, unless these activities are deemed so harmful to other individuals or to society as a whole that they must be prohibited or regulated. Liberalism appeals to many people since it is built around a concept of pluralistic diversity, with the state and other institutions ideally working to preserve our freedoms. Liberalism does not present a revolutionary focus on social and legal change, opting instead for gradual reforms of specific statutes, policies, and cultural life.

Law has also been influenced by conservative political traditions. Conservatives tend to emphasize social order as a higher priority than individual freedoms, which they sometimes see as destructive forms of licence. Examples of conservative influences in law include barriers to liberalized divorce, opposition to spousal benefits, and marriage for gay or lesbian couples. The conservative influence is also evident

in calls for more severe sanctions against young offenders and against criminals generally. Conservatives may also borrow from liberal discourse on individual freedoms, evident, for example, in protests against what is seen as undue interference through gun control and gun registration legislation. Rarely discussed in academic circles, and we think often dismissed as reactionary by some scholars and activists, conservative influences are nevertheless at play when legal sanctions and remedies are considered in a host of conflicts.

Feminist theory and strategies must also be considered in law and legal struggles. Feminism is a diversified enterprise, generally sharing common ground in the assumption that women are disadvantaged in many, if not all, spheres of society. The diversity arises time and again when we consider which policies should be developed to counteract violence against women — for example, wife abuse and sexual assault — as well as achieving justice in family law, labour law, and reproductive decisions.

There has been considerable concern among feminists about relying on legal structures to further women's interests. This concern stems in part from what is seen as a patriarchal legacy in law, reflected in the dominance of men in virtually all aspects of law making and law enforcement, including the judiciary, the legal profession, and Parliament. At the same time, some feminists favour using legal institutions as part of a broader effort to change society. There has been ongoing interest not only in studying the impact of particular laws and measures on women, but in taking a more introspective look at how women are treated within the legal profession and the courts (Kay & Hagan, 1995). In this collection, three contributors explore the impact of measures in the area of female partner abuse, the defence of battered woman syndrome, and new family law initiatives.

The Marxist and neo-Marxist tradition has been often applied to legal issues. Drawing on the Marxist emphasis on broad economic forces at play in capitalist, class-divided societies, some Marxists view law as merely an instrument of the dominant class, a means of disguising social inequality and legal injustices through the mantle of individual liberties and the non-partisan nature of law. In this view, legal officials tend to act on behalf of the dominant class, repressing other classes through criminal law, labour law, and a host of other measures. As with feminism, the Marxist approach generates considerable disagreement over social change, the nature of oppression, and whether law is inherently antagonistic to a movement toward socialism or communism. The issue of social class appears throughout this collection, exemplified in essays that combine social class analysis with issues of race and gender, such as Gordon and Coneybeer's review of corporate crime and related legislation. Toothless legislation directed at corporate offences contrasts with quite punitive law enforcement that is often directed toward an underclass. This approach is also developed in Barry Sneiderman's critique of the war on drugs.

Along with gender and social class issues, there has been considerable work in the critical race studies tradition. This tradition explores ways in which people are categorized into racial or ethnic groups and are subjected to stereotypes, social inequalities, and discriminatory legal treatment. Here, often along with the focus on gender and class noted above, there is great attention to ways in which race and ethnicity become the grounds for discriminatory treatment. From analyses of harassment of people of colour to hiring barriers and myriad forms of discrimination in housing and welfare, theorists bring race and ethnicity into the foreground. Some analysts challenge assumptions of a common Canadian cultural tradition and shared language by pointing to linguistic differences and clashing cultural approaches to dispute resolution. Other scholars explore the subjective experiences of being treated as a visible minority, as well as ways in which laws are unfairly applied to such minorities. The overrepresentation of African Americans in prisons in the United States and of Aboriginal peoples in Canadian prisons are two examples. Legal scholars have also drawn attention to historical examples where racial minorities have been excluded from law schools and legal practice (Brockman, 1995).

Postmodern influences are also evident in law in society studies. Postmodernism generally takes a pessimistic or at least a cautious stance against the Enlightenment ideals of rationality and progress, including how these concepts are fixed in legal ideology. Postmodernists thus contest taken-for-granted assumptions about the desirability of the rule of law, or the steady progress of liberal pluralist policies. Such challenges have led to what has been called postmodern legality, where the effects of law and social control are examined, and new forms of dispute resolution are developed to empower minority groups. Postmodernism is thus linked with attempts to deepen democratic relationships and with the "new social movements" surrounding issues of disability or "ableism," sexual orientation, multinational politics, race and ethnicity, and environmental and peace movements, to name a few (Rosenau, 1992).

The scholarly study of law and social change has matured dramatically in the past generation. We now have specialized journals, texts, and associations exploring how legislation is formed and applied. Specific topics are discussed in considerable detail by some commentators. The rich tradition of sociological approaches to law continues to deepen, with incisive theoretical commentaries on Marxism, feminism, and postmodernism and law (see, for example, Hunt 1993). We now have the benefit of descriptions of how legislation is created, accounts of specific legal decisions on a wide range of issues, and socio-legal theories of law, power, and social change (see, for example, Burtch, 1992; Treviño, 1996; Vago, 1997). This volume brings forward ongoing concerns about law and the treatment of women, racial minorities, gays and lesbians, and people who are generally disadvantaged.

The growing body of texts and resources helps us to approach several key questions about law in society. For example, what is the impact of law on social values and human behaviour? The chicken-and-egg question of whether specific laws can produce social change, or whether legislation actually emerges from changing values and interests in society, is very much alive in this respect. Some legal scholars (Barnett, 1993) argue that legal change tends to lag behind changing social values, exemplified by such topics as euthanasia and abortion. Others argue that law can instil social change, citing benefits of seat belt legislation, occupational health and safety requirements, and stricter regulation of firearms. As we shall see, such assertions of the value of law are constantly open to question. It is wise, we think, to approach issues of law in society with an open mind and more than a pinch of scepticism about broad assertions for or against legal regulation.

Another key question that recurs in the following articles is whether legal regulation is desirable. For liberals, state regulation through law and other institutions is essential, ideally giving individuals a balance of security and freedom of expression. For conservatives, these same ideals may be sought, but often with a greater emphasis on tradition and what is generally called social order. More critical

theorists tend to challenge the legitimacy of the legal order, seeing it as a form of overt or covert domination over citizens, especially people with limited economic means, visible minorities, women, or gays and lesbians. Powerful contributions in the Marxist tradition of class struggle, and the feminist tradition opposing entrenched patriarchal interests, have been joined by postmodernist interpretations of law in society. The overall effect of these challenges leaves a rather unsettled quality to the legal order, with complex arguments mounted for and against efforts to establish aboriginal title or feminist-informed decisions in family law, for example. This collection of essays seeks to present these various theoretical outlooks, even though our selection, like the field of sociology of law in general, is weighted toward more critical outlooks.

REFERENCES

Barnett, L. (1993). *Legal construct, social concept: A macrosocial perspective on law.* New York: Aldine de Gruyter.

Brockman, J. (1995). Exclusionary tactics: The history of women and minorities in the legal profession in British Columbia. In F. Hamar and J. McLaren (Eds.), *Essays in the history of Canadian law: Vol. 4. British Columbia and the Yukon* (pp. 508–561). Toronto: Osgoode Society.

Burtch, B. (1992). *The sociology of law: Critical approaches to social control.* Toronto: Harcourt Brace Jovanovich.

Hunt, A. (1993). *Explorations in law and society.* London: Routledge.

Hunt, A. (1980). *The sociological movement in law.* London: Macmillan.

Kay, F., & Hagan, J. (1995). The persistent glass ceiling: Gendered inequalities in the earnings of lawyers. *British Journal of Sociology 46,* 279–310.

Rosenau, P. (1992). *Post-modernism and the social sciences.* Princeton, NJ: Princeton University Press.

Treviño, A.J. (1996). *The sociology of law: Classical and contemporary perspectives.* New York: St. Martin's Press.

Vago, S. (1997). *Law and society* (5th ed.). Englewood Cliffs, NJ: Prentice-Hall.

PART ONE

Historical Foundations of Law

Modern laws are a legacy of earlier periods. Rooted in long-standing customs, or based on legal precedent, law creation and law enforcement are best understood when we consider the culture and politics at play in earlier periods of our history. We can make parallels between historical laws and contemporary laws, and mark changing opinions about legal freedoms and social controls. Using historical references, we can see how law has served to define us as workers, men and women, visible minorities, and victims of crime.

For some, the law has served to uphold rights of citizens, serving as a dam against the potential for tyranny. Law helps to produce a coherent society, one where common senses of morality and justice are reinforced. Law thus gives all citizens a voice and, through democratic structures, the opportunity to argue against injustices. For others who are more critical of the power of law, the historical role of law has been largely to dominate individuals, to disallow certain expressions, to maintain a status quo of privilege based on gender, social class, and race or ethnicity. We can see how some social movements sought to penalize individuals for breaching norms or strict moral codes, while others rebelled against these social and legal strictures.

These central issues in law and society are brought out in this section. The first essay, "White Female Help and Chinese-Canadian Employers: Race, Class, Gender, and Law in the Case of Yee Clun, 1924," is written by Constance Backhouse, a professor of law at the University of Western Ontario. She shows how a Saskatchewan statute formulated in 1912 barred male employers of Asian descent from hiring "white" women. She uses a specific legal case — *Yee Clun* v. *City of Regina* (1925) — to show how specific interest groups debated the legislation and its impact. Backhouse not only reviews specific examples of successful and unsuccessful prosecutions under this statute, but also draws out the complexities of racial designation. For example, where was the line between white and non-white status? It seems that legislators, lawyers, judges, and the general public often relied on an arbitrary approach to racial status. Not only was there a lack of consensus as to who was Chinese, but authorities also disagreed as to the definition of "white," debating whether eastern European women fell within that category. Backhouse shows how some authorities constructed race as part of a hierarchy in which whiteness was associated with "the civilized European nations."

Backhouse highlights how seemingly straightforward legislation and terminology were subverted in the courtroom. Specifically in the *Yee Clun* case in Regina, lawyers debated the concept of race and questioned the justice of discriminating on the basis of race or ethnicity. This article is also useful in pointing out how seemingly unjust laws can persist. The legislation protecting white women lasted for decades, repealed in Saskatchewan as late as 1969. Backhouse's findings stand in contrast to later formulations providing formal recognition and, to some extent, protections for multicultural groups in Canada.

The second essay, "Illegal Operations: Women, Doctors, and Abortion, 1886–1939," by Angus McLaren, a professor of history at the University of Victoria, concerns abortion and reproductive law in Canada. Moral and legal questions surrounding abortion remain complex and contentious. Although today there is greater access to legal abortion in North America than there was in the past, there are strong divisions of opinion over the issue, reflected in groups lobbying for and against abortion, and, arguably, in a large middle ground of Canadians who are conflicted over ethical aspects of abortion. Angus McLaren sheds considerable light on the abortion debate in nineteenth- and early-twentieth-century Canada. A prolific historian who has written about the politics underlying reproductive law, McLaren covers over 50 years of Canadian history in his chapter, from the late nineteenth century to the start of the Second World War. McLaren argues that for thousands of years, women have sought to control their fertility, using various methods of contraception and abortion. He underscores how abortions became criminalized, with medical practitioners liable to imprisonment if they were convicted of inducing miscarriages unless they were necessary to save the mother's life.

McLaren's essay draws on 100 cases of women seeking abortions in British Columbia between 1886 and 1939. He provides an insightful look at inquest and court records. We are shown how legal codes prohibiting abortion, and moral codes treating abortion as a sin, greatly affected many women's access to the procedure. At the same time, McLaren notes that women did not always passively accept these legal and moral controls. He shows how women resorted to various patent medicines to induce abortion, and when they were blocked from medical assistance in British Columbia, some travelled across the border to Washington State to procure an abortion.

The issue of power is highlighted in this article. The Criminal Code, supposedly applied in an impartial manner to offenders regardless of their occupational status, was often applied in the case of abortion to marginalized practitioners such as midwives and herbalists. Physicians were typically not charged in the criminal courts. Power is also reflected in the symbolic impact of abortion trials of the day, in an attempt to safeguard "the social and sexual status quo."

McLaren's article provides a historical backdrop to ongoing debates over ethical and legal aspects of abortion, including a trend away from abortion as a crime and a sin and toward contemporary arguments for women's right to choose whether or not to terminate a pregnancy. As with Backhouse's essay, McLaren shows how legislation is often resistant to change.

ONE

White Female Help and Chinese-Canadian Employers: Race, Class, Gender, and Law in the Case of Yee Clun, 1924

CONSTANCE BACKHOUSE

INTRODUCTION

Historians and sociologists have come increasingly to recognize the impact that law has had upon the individuals who immigrated from China to settle in

Source: Constance Backhouse, "White Female Help and Chinese-Canadian Employers: Race, Class, Gender, and Law in the Case of Yee Clun, 1924," *Canadian Ethnic Studies* 26, no. 3 (1994): 34–52.

Canada over the course of the late 19th and early 20th centuries. Racist laws inhibited the Chinese from fully participating in Canadian society in the areas of immigration, taxation, the franchise, employment, business, and social welfare (Backhouse, 1992). The trial of *Yee Clun* v. *City of Regina* (*Yee Clun*, 1925) provides one useful illustration, a unique case study permitting us to examine the role of Canadian law and legal institutions in the creation and maintenance of racial stereotypes.

In early October 1924 the Regina City Council voted to deny Yee Clun a licence that would have allowed him to hire white female waitresses to work in his restaurant. It was obvious to all observers that the vote was motivated solely on the basis of Yee Clun's Chinese-Canadian racial identity. The Council ruling followed the 1912 enactment of a Saskatchewan statute, colloquially known as the "white women's labour law," which prohibited the employment of white women by Asian-Canadian males (see Appendix A). Controversy had attended the passage of the statute almost from the outset, and the litigation which ensued from Yee Clun's application continued the tradition in which members of the Asian community challenged the discriminatory measure, attempting to force the Canadian legal system to live up to its rhetorical claims of fairness and equality. The "white women's labour bill" and the consequent dispute surrounding Yee Clun's application constitute a critical moment in the history of Canadian race relations, in which law functioned as a crucible for melting and reforging prevailing perspectives on race, gender, and class.

INITIAL ENACTMENT OF THE LEGISLATION

To appreciate the significance of the Yee Clun case, it is necessary to provide rather extensive detail about the legal context in which the case was heard. First I will discuss the initial enactment of the "white women's labour bill"; second, the earliest, precedent-setting prosecutions under the act; and third, the legislative amendments passed to alter the statute in certain important respects.

The Saskatchewan Liberal government enacted the anti-Asian statute in March of 1912 in response to an intense lobby campaign from a diverse group of constituents (Backhouse, 1993). Small businessmen and male trade-unionists had banded together to protest what they believed to be unfair competition from immigrant Chinese workers, whose long hours and hard work had begun to make inroads into the business profits and wages of white men. Although the legislation did not directly bar Asian entrepreneurs from operating restaurants, laundries, or other businesses, it enjoined them from hiring white women, something which was intended to have significant economic consequences. Due to the gendered nature of discriminatory pay scales, female employees earned less than males in the labour force. One group of less expensive female workers — white women — would now be off-limits to Asian employers.

It would have been difficult for Asian employers to hire women of colour, for they were few in number in the Canadian west at this time. Restrictive immigration laws and the hostile treatment accorded racially diverse newcomers had combined to retard the arrival of Asian and Black women to the area. In addition, systemic barriers constricted the job market for First Nations and Metis women who continued to live in the west. The ban on hiring white women meant that Asian employers were limited to hiring more expensive male workers, at considerable jeopardy to their competitive position (Backhouse, 1993: 7–10).

Protestant moral reformers and middle-class white women's groups also joined the small businessmen and trade unionists who campaigned for the legislation. Clergy and lay members of various "social and moral reform" councils aligned themselves with the National Council of Women, the Regina Council of Women, the Woman's Christian Temperance Union, and the Young Women's Christian Association to support the measure. Concerned about reports (often exaggerated) of Chinese plural marriage and concubinage, they embellished racist stereotypes which depicted Chinese men as addicts of opium and inveterate gamblers. Fearful of the implications of the pronounced sexual imbalance within the Asian-Canadian community, they decried racial intermarriage and fretted over the potential for coercive sexuality that suffused the employment relationship. White women were called into service as the "guardians of the race," a symbol of the most valuable property known to white society, to be protected at all costs from the encroachment of other races (Backhouse, 1993: 10–19). The combined lobby forces of organized labour, business, religion, moral reform, and feminism — all white — crossed class and gender boundaries in their efforts to impede Asian-Canadian men who might have wished to hire white female employees.

Similar coalitions in other provinces resulted in the passage of identical or similar statutes in Manitoba, Ontario, and British Columbia over the next seven years (see Appendix B).

EARLY PROSECUTIONS

The first prosecutions under the Saskatchewan act occurred in May 1912. Quong Wing and Quong Sing, Chinese-Canadian men who operated two restaurants and a rooming house in Moose Jaw, were charged with employing three white women: Nellie Lane and Mabel Hopham as waitresses, and Annie Hartman as a chambermaid. The cases were hotly contested at trial, with defence counsel arguing that it was impossible to know with any certainty what the legislature meant by the term "Chinese." Various witnesses offered suggestions that the designation might relate to birth in China, birth of one's parents in China, physical presence ("standing on Chinese soil"), citizenship, reputation within the community, proficiency in the Chinese language, and visual appearance. The defence lawyer insisted that the absence of any racial definition within the statute rendered it too vague to enforce. He was backed up by the testimony of Nellie Lane, one of the white waitresses, who stubbornly refused to make any racial designation at all of her employer, Quong Wing, insisting tenaciously that "I treat him as myself."

The notion of "race" is not a natural, biological, or trans-historical feature, but a sociological classification situated in a particular time and context (Fryer, 1988; Montagu, 1942; Bolaria and Li, 1988; Davis, 1991; Anderson, 1991; Harris, 1993; Pascoe, 1991). As Anderson (1991: 3–12) notes, "racial" differences cannot be conceptualized as absolute because genetic variation is continuous. Racial categories form a continuum of gradual change, not a set of sharply demarcated types; there are no natural or intrinsic isolating mechanisms between people, and given the geographic dispersion of populations over time, the concept of "pure" human "races" is nonsensical. It is almost impossible to define "Chineseness" as a fixed concept, transported without variation across generations and location, to identify equally a Chinese person in Hong Kong, a Chinese person in mainland China, an immigrant of Chinese origin living in Saskatchewan, a second-generation person of Chinese origin living in South Africa, and a third-generation Canadian of Chinese origin living in Vancouver (Anderson, 1991: 16). Anderson (1991: 18) has used the term "racialization," a concept of greater utility, to refer to "the process by which attributes such as skin colour, language, birthplace, and cultural practices are given social significance as markers of distinction."

The prosecutions in Moose Jaw represented a successful effort on the part of the state to "racialize" Quong Wing and Quong Sing, who were pronounced "Chinese" by the presiding police magistrate without serious consideration of any of the defence arguments. Although the witnesses might have had difficulty articulating what they meant by "Chinese," most were adamant in their observations that the two defendants were such. Rooted in this particular historical context, racial distinctions took on a certain "common sense" quality, an unconscious, often visceral reflection of community assumptions. The magistrate felt so certain of his ground that he felt no need to offer any rationale or analysis of the matter whatsoever in his judgment.

Members of the Asian community were outraged over the new enactment and the verdicts. Many of them had put down permanent roots in Saskatchewan, taking out naturalization papers, converting to Christianity, and investing considerable labour in developing successful business ventures in the province. They were both insulted and economically disadvantaged by the new law which restricted their opportunity to hire female employees. A number of Chinese merchants organized to raise money to finance appeals. Despite their best efforts, the legislation and the convictions were upheld by the Supreme Court of Saskatchewan in 1913 and the Supreme Court of Canada in 1914 (Backhouse, 1993).

An equally significant test case was tried in Saskatoon in August 1912. Charges had been laid against the Asian proprietor of a local restaurant who employed three white waitresses. There were some debates at trial over the racial identity of the defendant, Mr. Yoshi, who had immigrated to Saskatoon from Tokyo with his wife seven months earlier. The Saskatoon *Daily Star* recounted the amusement of observers, who found the entire line of questioning absurd:

> The mirthful side of the case was revealed when Kabayshi, a cook for Yoshi, was in the witness stand. [...] Cross-examined by counsel for the defence, Kabayshi found himself in a Chinese puzzle when asked how he knew that the defendant was a Jap. "He is a Jap because I know he is a Jap," said witness. He then said that Yoshi's wife told him he was a Jap. Finally, amidst much laughter, witness said that another reason why he knew the defendant was a Jap was because he had heard him tell the girls in the kitchen at the restaurant that he was (*Daily Star*, 1912a).

The matter of the "whiteness" of the female employees was settled with less despatch. The question was complicated by the ethnic origins of the women concerned, who were described as "Russian" and "German." Since the statute contained no definition of "white woman," Crown attorney MacKenzie endeavoured to supply one, arguing that the court should "give these words the meaning which is commonly applied to them; that is to say the females of any of the civilized European nations." Professing great confusion, Saskatoon police magistrate Brown reserved on the issue and adjourned the trial (*Daily Star*, 1912b).

Racial visibility, which is politically and socially constructed, can change dramatically over time. People may be seen as objects of racial difference in one place and time, but find themselves shuffled and recategorized, or rendered invisible in others. The divisions in Canada between the English and French, and Jews and Gentiles, now viewed as linguistic, religious, or culturally based, have historically been depicted in "racial" terms. The boundaries of racial designation that seem obvious in one setting become more elusive in another. One witness who testified before the 1902 Canadian Royal Commission on Chinese and Japanese Immigration announced: "I never call Italians white labour." A Saskatchewan historian, writing in 1924, claimed that Slovaks (or Polaks), Germans, Hungarians, Scandinavians, Finns, and Serbians were each discrete groups in a "racial sense" (Hawkes, 1924: 1397–8). In early 20th century Saskatchewan, residents of English or Scottish origin would have been hard-pressed to identify racially with Russian or German immigrants in matters of employment or social inter-mingling. What was at stake in this trial was whether the latter should be "racialized" as "white" in distinction to Asian immigrants, in the context of the "white women's labour law."

Endeavouring to provide some assistance to the court, one Saskatoon resident wrote the following letter to the editor of the Saskatoon *Daily Star*:

> Sir — Having in mind the adjournment of the [Yoshi] case ... I take the liberty of offering enlightenment as to the definition of the term "white" ... Fingier, the famous ethnologist, says that the white races or Caucasians include Europeans, Armenians and Russians, other than Tartars who are included in the Yellow or Mongolian class. The white races as defined above, are opposed to the black or Negroids, the brown Malays, the red or American aborigines, and the yellow or Mongolians, including the Chinese and Japanese.
>
> This information can be readily obtained from any good encyclopedia, and the writer humbly suggests that some reference be supplied the magistrates in this city, as it is deplorable that such culpable ignorance should delay or prevent the dispensation of justice. [...]
>
> ONE WHO HAS LIVED IN CHINA (*Daily Star*, 1912c).

Whether the police magistrate was prompted to reach a decision by the letter or not, he issued his ruling the next day. He had decided to settle the question "by taking his own opinion," he announced, and the names of the waitresses turned out to be key. The names revealed Russian and German nationality, claimed the magistrate, and although "he did not think it necessary to go into the classification of the white race," he was of the view, by way of "illustration," that "Germans and Russians were members of Caucasian race" (*Daily Star*, 1912d). Although the defendant spoke of an intention to appeal his conviction, no further legal records survive. The ruling would stand as a hallmark of the utility of law in consolidating various strains of national groups into a central "white" Canadian identity, constructed in stark opposition to the "Chinese" other.

LEGISLATIVE AMENDMENTS

Within months of the Yoshi trial, pressure from the Japanese government resulted in amendments to the act. An imperial power of relatively greater military and commercial significance than China, Japan was able to convince the legislature to delete all references to "Japanese" or "other Oriental persons" from the text as of 11 January 1913 (see Appendix A; Backhouse, 1993: 20). The Chinese government continued to voice its concern with being singled out in the statute, and as its international stature improved after World War I, the protestations ultimately became more forceful. In 1919, Saskatchewan restructured its "white women's labour law" to disguise the anti-Chinese focus. The new law deleted all explicit reference to Chinese or other Asian employers, leaving it up to individual municipalities to determine whether to license restaurants or laundries in which white women were employed (see Appendix A).

Attorney General Turgeon explained that the bill was necessary because of pressures brought to bear for "the removal of this discrimination on the ground of the racial susceptibility of the Chinese." The change was one of "form" only, he assured his fellow legislators, since the government intended no substantive alteration in policy, but wished to achieve its ends without "singling out" the Chinese (*Morning Leader*, 1919a). George Langley, the member for Redberry and Minister of Municipal Affairs, advised that "it was the hope of those responsible for the bill" that no municipality would "grant the privilege" contained in the new act (*Morning Leader*, 1919b).

THE YEE CLUN APPLICATION

It was late in the summer of 1924 when the Regina City Council found itself faced with an application for a licence from Yee Clun, the proprietor of the Exchange Grill and Rooming House at 1700 Rose Street. Yee Clun, whose name may actually have been "Lee Clun," was identified variously as "Yee Clun," "Yee Klun," "Yee Kuen," and "Yee Klung" by the newspapers and legal authorities, who generally showed a studied indifference to accuracy in the spelling of foreign names (Backhouse, 1993: 77; Harvey, 1991: 127–30). It was undisputed, however, that Yee Clun had been among the first Chinese residents in the area, settling in Regina around 1901, purchasing property, and opening a restaurant which would achieve a reputation as "one of the best" in the city. One of the few Chinese men to live with his wife in Canada, Yee Clun was also widely acknowledged as "the leader of the Chinese community in Regina" (*Morning Leader*, 1924a, 1924b). In 1922, he had been elected president of the Regina branch of the Chinese National party, a fraternal organization with a membership of one hundred and fifty Chinese residents from the city (*Morning Leader*, 1924c, 1924d).

On 6 August 1924, Yee Clun appeared before city council to request a licence allowing him to employ white women in his restaurant and rooming house. According to the newspaper reporters who covered the case with considerable interest, Yee Clun explained that many Chinese restaurateurs required the services of white female employees because "they can't procure boys of their own nationality on account of the tightening up of immigration laws" (*Morning Leader*, 1924a). Asian employers were indeed facing marked labour shortages. Access to Asian women had always been limited due to the sharp gender disparities in the composition of the immigrant population. With the passage of the federal Chinese Exclusion Act in 1923, a virtual stranglehold had been placed upon all Chinese immigration — male and female — which would last for more than twenty years, dislocating families and further drying up the labour pool for Asian employers (Chinese Immigration Act,

1923; Andracki, 1978; Angus, 1937; Li, 1980; McEvoy, 1982). White men, who were not included in the protective legislation, would have been prohibitively expensive employees for marginally profitable, labour-intensive enterprises (Backhouse, 1993). White women had become by necessity the residual group of potential employees.

Yee Clun obviously realized that his application would be received in the nature of a test case, and he had taken care to obtain prior approval from the city licence inspector and the chief constable of Regina. He also received support from Alderman Cooksley, who pointed out Yee Clun's twenty-three-year residency in the city, and stressed that he "had always borne an exemplary character." Cooksley noted that Chinese cooks and waiters were already employed in most restaurants in Regina, where they worked side by side with white women (*Morning Leader*, 1924a).

Alderman Dawson was less impressed. He declared that "there was all the difference in the world between hiring help and being hired help," and charged that it would be "a dangerous precedent" for council to "permit any Chinese to employ white women." Dawson moved that the matter be tabled until the next meeting to give any organization that might be opposed to the proposal "an opportunity to express their views." In an attempt at compromise, the council voted to give preliminary approval to the application, subject to ratification at the next council meeting (*Morning Leader*, 1924a).

Alderman Dawson's delaying tactics were apparently designed to provide local community groups an opportunity to intervene. Many Saskatchewan whites seem to have nurtured deep suspicions about the Chinese, a perspective undoubtedly bolstered by persistent press reports of their gambling and narcotics activities. Chinatowns were alleged to harbour gamblers, murderers, and those who would traffic in liquor and the "abomination" of narcotics (*Morning Leader*, 1924e). When Chinese residents were prosecuted for drug offences, they found their convictions given great prominence in the newspapers, without any apparent recognition of the racially selective enforcement which often led to their detection and capture (Anderson, 1991: 101; see, for example, *Morning Leader*, 1924f). The Regina *Morning Leader* was given to recounting "sordid and revolting" stories about young white women who were introduced to Chinese men in Sunday school classes, only to come "under the influence of the stronger personalities" of the would-be converts and find themselves tragically transformed into "drug fiends" (*Morning Leader*, 1922a).

The gender implications of such racist propaganda, with its focus on the dangers inherent in encounters between Asian men and white women, were not lost on the women's organizations of the time. Some of the most prominent of Regina's organized feminists nurtured particularly virulent anti-Chinese sentiments. Among the first to debate the matter of Yee Clun's application were the executive members of the Woman's Christian Temperance Union (WCTU), whose concerns revolved around racial intermarriage. The executive of the three Regina WCTU branches called a special meeting on 12 August 1924 to discuss the issue. There, various members decried "instances of girls marrying their Chinese employers," insisting that "intermarriage of the races should not be encouraged." There were some voices of dissent, with a few arguing that it was unjust to oppose racial intermarriage when immigration regulations made it virtually impossible for Chinese men to bring Chinese wives and families to Canada. At least one woman spoke out to assert that she would "rather marry some Chinaman than some white men," but the general sentiment of the meeting was that "there was no desire to see the practice common." Barring white women from Chinese employment would deter "close contact" between the races, it was thought. Those who expressed concerns about limiting job opportunities for women were met with brash assurances: "There was other work to be had which was honest and less fraught with danger." At the end of the day, a resolution was passed that "it was not in the best interests of the young womanhood of the city to grant the request of the restaurateur," and a Mrs. Rankin was designated to head the delegation to carry the message to city council (*Morning Leader*, 1924g, 1924h).

The Regina Local Council of Women (LCW) had been on record as actively opposing such licences since 1920, when it first joined with the Regina Trades and Labour Congress in urging the Regina City Council to deny all applications from "Oriental" men (Harvey, 1991: 127). There was some delay in responding to Yee Clun's particular situation, however, since many members of the LCW were absent from the city on vacation over the summer. The group more than made up for its tardiness when the meeting was finally held, with members voting unanimously and without discussion to lobby city council to ensure that no licences ever be issued to Chinese men (*Morning Leader*, 1924g, 1924i). The LCW would schedule a special lecture on racial intermarriage for later in October, at which time Reverend Hugh Dobson advised them that such liaisons were "growing in number in Canada." Although Reverend Dobson would caution that such trends were "nothing to worry overmuch about," the women of the LCW were clearly of a different view (*Morning Leader*, 1924j).

The Regina LCW comprised a coalition of middle- and upper-middle-class women, first founded in 1895. With few exceptions, the members of the LCW were Canadian-born of British heritage, well-educated, Protestant, middle-aged, and not employed outside the home. The group made it its mission to confer frequently with government officials on matters of education, social welfare, and labour law. Well-known as the founders of the first hospital in Regina and the organizers of the children's aid society, reception facilities for immigrant women, and a milk fund for needy children, the LCW women also lobbied for industrial homes and separate courts for women, as well as the appointment of women to hospital and library boards (Harvey, 1991; Griffiths, 1993: 48, 70, 96, 184; Saskatchewan Labour Women's Division, n.d.).

The resolution to oppose Yee Clun's licence seems to have been particularly championed by the LCW president, Mrs. Maude Bunting Stapleford. A native of St. Catharine's, Ontario, Mrs. Stapleford had graduated from Victoria College, University of Toronto, with an honours in modern languages in 1907. That same year, she married Reverend Ernest W. Stapleford, moving with him to Vancouver, where he took up a post as minister and educational secretary of the Methodist Church in British Columbia. In 1915, they moved to Regina when Dr. Stapleford was appointed President of Regina College. The mother of four children, Mrs. Stapleford was one of the pre-eminent club women in the province, serving successively as president of the Women's University Club, president of the Women's Educational Club, president of the Regina Local Council of Women, and president and convenor of laws and legislation of the Saskatchewan Provincial Council of Women. She was active as well with the WCTU, the Regina YWCA, the Victoria Order of Nurses, the Imperial Order Daughters of the Empire, and the Women's Auxiliary of the Regina Symphony Orchestra (*Pioneers*, 1924: 80; Provincial Council of Women, 1955; Harvey, 1991: 56–7). When she urged that a "strong contingent" of LCW members attend the city council meeting in support of the anti-Chinese lobby, Maude Bunting Stapleford spoke with the authoritative voice of one of the most active leaders of the Saskatchewan women's community.

In taking this position, Mrs. Stapleford was behaving well within the bounds of accepted convention within the organized women's movement. Prohibitions on the hiring of white women by Asian-Canadian men had been debated and endorsed by branches of the YWCA, by the Local Council of Women in Saskatoon, and by the federal umbrella group, the National Council of Women. The latter organization would do a full-scale investigation of the problem in the mid-1920s, noting that employment bureaux discouraged white women from taking such positions, advising that social service workers were "emphatic in desiring the bar raised against such employment," and concluding that the legislation was essential for the "protection of white girls" (Saskatchewan Local Council of Women, 1921, 1926–31; National Council of Women of Canada, 1927: 88; 1928: 97; Backhouse, 1993: 11–18).

When city council reconvened on 19 August 1924, more than twenty representatives of women's organizations were present to speak to Yee Clun's application. Those opposed to granting the licence included several new groups such as the Gleaners Ladies Orange Benevolent Association of Saskatchewan, the Sons of England Benevolent Society, and the Salvation Army Women's hostel (*Morning Leader*, 1924k). Most vociferous of all were the spokeswomen from the Regina Women's Labour League.

The Regina Women's Labour League (WLL) was one of a number of left-wing organizations established during the second decade of the 20th century to give women more voice within the labour movement. Loosely affiliated with the Communist Party of Canada, the leagues were primarily made up of middle-aged wives of trade-union men and single career women such as teachers and journalists (Roome, 1989; Prentice et al., 1988: 219, 278; Collette, 1990; *Searchlight*, 1920a). Although the WLL's main focus was the economic exploitation of women, the analysis the organization adopted was suffused with the maternal feminism which marked the beliefs and practices of more middle-class women's organizations. The primary aim of most Women's Labour Leagues was to support the families of striking workers, and their approval of the concept of a "family wage" led them to lobby for prohibitions on the employment of married women and an end to night work for all female employees (Roome, 1989: 98; *Searchlight*, 1920b). Some even advocated compulsory medical examination for "mental defectives" before marriage (*Morning Leader*, 1924i). The Women's Labour Leagues existed on the fringe of the male trade union world, as the September 1924 decision of the Trades and Labour Congress of Canada to deny their federation membership so eloquently illustrated (*Labour Gazette*, 1924: 852). But the anti-Asian sentiments that laced the activities of the male labour movement, which had lobbied so successfully for the enactment of the "white women's labour law" in the first place, seem to have infected the perspectives of the left-leaning women from the WLL as well. Crossing class boundaries, the WLL resolutely joined with middle-class women's organizations to resist employment proximity for Asian men and white women.

On behalf of the Regina Women's Labour League, Mrs. W.M. Eddy gave the opening address to city council on the evening of 19 August 1924, flanked by sister members Mrs. K. Cluff and Mrs. W.J. Vennele. Regina women were proud of the title "Queen City of the West," she announced, and had no wish to see their city be dubbed the "queer city of the west." Employment of white women by Chinese men was "not in the best interests of white women or the community in general," claimed Mrs. Eddy, and if the Chinese required service, "they could get it from men." The Mayor of Regina, a wholesale grocer of mixed Irish, English, and Scottish background named Stewart Coulter Burton, questioned Mrs. Eddy intently at this point, and the following exchange ensued on the floor of the council chamber:

> Mayor Burton: Have you any evidence that conditions are not right in other places where white help is employed by Chinese?
> Mrs.Eddy: We are not here as a court of morals, but to voice our protest from the economic standpoint. Judging by the Chinese laundries, conditions are not as good as they might be, and if it is allowed, we feel there will be an influx of an undesirable class of women into the city.
> Mayor Burton: Your objection is mainly sentimental?
> Mrs. Eddy: Not by any means, Mr. Mayor. We feel this is only the thin edge of the wedge and that if this application is granted, there will be an influx into the city of an undesirable class of girl. Male help might just as well be employed. Employment of white women by Chinese might lead to mesalliances. In a rooming house there are many opportunities of temptation, more perhaps than in a restaurant. (*Morning Leader*, 1924h, 1924k).

There were a few lone voices in support of Yee Clun. Mrs. Reninger and Mrs. Armour, teachers from the Chinese Mission in Regina, had met Yee Clun when he attended the Sunday school classes offered to Chinese residents (Harvey, 1991: 140). The Chinese Mission women declared that they had known Yee Clun as "a very faithful" and "conscientious man," and claimed that "any girl would be safeguarded in his company." Indeed, "more was expected" from the Chinese than "any other nationality," they asserted. The city licence inspector attested that "the women of the city had nothing to fear" from Yee Clun, and promised that he would cancel the licence forthwith if "there was the slightest appearance of wrong" in the future (*Morning Leader*, 1924k).

The most forceful advocate for Yee Clun was Regina City Solicitor, G.F. Blair, K.C. A lawyer with a record of active community service, Blair had some personal connection with Chinese residents of the city. As a teacher at the Chinese YMCA Sunday school, he was reputed to "endeavor to instill in his students the doctrines of Christianity and a love for Western ideals" (*Morning Leader*, 1924l.) In keeping with his mission of acculturation of the Chinese community, Blair seems to have believed firmly in equality under the law. It was Blair's opinion that council was wrong to assume that it could arbitrarily grant or refuse a permit "except on the ground that the applicant is an undesirable character." "Whether the applicant was Chinese, Japanese, Irish or Greek," insisted Blair, "did not enter into the question." His support for Yee Clun's application came as something of a surprise to the Regina *Morning Leader*, which described Blair's position as a "bombshell." Mayor Burton also seemed somewhat nonplussed by this legal advice, and asked pointblank: "If this man is a respectable citizen with a good character recommended by public officials, then we have no right to refuse his application?" Blair retorted, "You have no right in the world to discriminate." If the council ruled otherwise, cautioned Blair, it "would be inviting litigation." With that last announcement, council adjourned the matter until October (*Morning Leader*, 1924k).

When the debate resumed on 7 October 1924, the Local Council of Women took the rather extraordinary step of bringing along legal counsel to put forth their case. The man they selected to represent them was Douglas J. Thom, K.C., a partner with the prestigious Brown, Mackenzie and Thom firm of Regina. The corporate lawyer was no expert on municipal law or Chinese matters, but was probably acting *pro bono* for his friend Maude Stapleford. As the Ontario-born son of a Methodist minister and a long-time member of the Board of Governors of Regina College, Douglas Thom would undoubtedly have had many interests in common with Maude Stapleford (*Leader-Post*, 1959).

The LCW solicitor, Douglas Thom, opened by noting that they were not asking the council "to originate any discrimination against the Chinese." The federal government had taken the lead in this, with its long-standing network of legislation which discriminated against the Chinese with respect to immigration, taxation, and suffrage (for details, see Backhouse, 1992). Thom's argument was overtly and unabashedly racist. "Chinatowns," he asserted, "have an unsavory moral reputation," and "white girls lose caste when they are employed by Chinese." The authority he cited for this proposition was none other than Mrs. Emily Murphy, Canada's first female magistrate and an internationally renowned feminist. Murphy had published an influential anti-narcotics book in 1922, in which she profiled Chinese involvement in drug trafficking, and warned that entrapment was likely to occur in Chinese "chop-suey houses" and "noodle parlors" (Murphy, 1922). In December 1922, Emily Murphy had written a letter to the Regina *Morning Leader* about the rapid spread of the narcotics traffic into Saskatchewan, mentioning the interracial nature of opium and cocaine use amongst both Chinese men and white women (*Morning Leader*, 1922b). Given information such as this, claimed Thom, regardless of Yee Clun's upstanding character references, "the reputation of the city was at stake" (*Morning Leader*, 1924b).

In an attempt to counter the LCW, the Chinese residents of Regina had banded together to retain the services of solicitor A.G. MacKinnon. He appeared on their behalf before the council, but he directed his arguments solely to his client's honourable reputation. Yee Clun was "the leader of the Chinese in Regina, a man of the highest type, and a law-abiding citizen," claimed MacKinnon. In this, Yee Clun reflected his people, whom MacKinnon asserted tended to be convicted in the courts at a substantially lower rate than people of other nationalities. MacKinnon took a more cautious approach than City Solicitor Blair. He did not argue that it would be unlawful for city council to base their decision on race, merely advising that "the city was not bound by any law to discriminate" against Yee Clun, and urging them not to do so (*Morning Leader*, 1924b).

In this context of unprecedented public intervention and media scrutiny, city council was finally called upon to issue its decision. With all but four aldermen opposing the application, council voted to refuse Yee Clun the licence (*Morning Leader*, 1924b). Possibly realizing that he should have taken a more forceful legal position in front of the council, A.G. MacKinnon immediately announced his intention to appeal the ruling to the courts (*Morning Leader*, 1924m).

MacKinnon's resulting lawsuit to void the ruling of city council was not heard by the Saskatchewan Court of King's Bench until 14 November 1925. At the trial, the mayor and various aldermen from Regina's council took the stand to give evidence as to why they had refused Yee Clun a licence. All admitted the decision was based upon racial grounds. "It was because he employed a number of Chinamen on his premises," they testified, "who, owing to the restrictions placed upon them by our federal laws, have not been permitted to bring their wives into this country." The danger, claimed the witnesses, was that "such employees would constitute a menace to the virtue of the white women if the latter were allowed to work on the same premises with them." Yee Clun himself, they conceded, posed no particular threat, given the presence of his wife in Regina and his "excellent" character. His Chinese employees were another matter entirely (*Yee Clun*, 1925: 234).

This logic seemed to defy Saskatchewan judge Phillip Edward Mackenzie, who appears to have been more inclined to take the position advanced much earlier by Alderman Cooksley. Describing the council's argument as "fallacious," Judge Mackenzie concluded:

> [I]t suggests that if the plaintiff, instead of employing Chinamen, had employed an equal number of white men, matrimonially unattached, no member of the council would have considered it, though the menace to the virtue of the white women might well be greater in the latter event, since there would exist no racial antipathy to be overcome between them and the white men.... [I]t is common knowledge that white restaurant keepers do frequently employ Chinamen on their premises, which suggests the seemingly absurd conclusion that when a Chinaman is employed by a Chinaman, however respectable the latter may be, the former is a menace to the white women's virtue, while, when the white man employs him he is not. (*Yee Clun*, 1925: 235).

Recounting the legislative history of the Saskatchewan statute, Mackenzie noted that the 1919 amendment had removed the racial discrimination contained in the original law. Whether he was unaware of the politicians' real motives, or whether he knew but chose to repudiate them, Mackenzie asserted that the legislative intent was to "abolish the discriminatory principle," and added that "it would be strange if the municipalities ... could now go on and maintain the discriminatory principle which the Legislature had been at such pains to abolish." Judge Mackenzie ordered the city council to grant Yee Clun his licence forthwith (*Yee Clun*, 1925: 236–7).

With the decision to impose race-neutral enforcement of the statute, Judge Mackenzie's ruling cut against the prevailing political grain in the province. It departed as well from the earlier court conclusions that the "white women's labour bill" was constitutional in spite of its discriminatory impact. But Mackenzie's judgment was strangely consistent with a string of earlier decisions from British Columbia judges who had struck down anti-Chinese provincial statutes and municipal by-laws in the late 19th century. John McLaren (1991) has argued that the first British Columbia judges were motivated by a concern to "check the excesses of 'responsible' government," foster the economic contribution of the Chinese, and protect the formalistic "rule of law." Others have argued that where judges ruled against racist legislation, they typically did so not to advance equality, but to protect the interests of white capital. Ryder (1991a; 1991b) and Lambertson and Grove (1994) claim that laws which restricted white employers from access to Asian labourers were frequently offensive to judges, while laws which restricted Asians in their rights to vote or carry on business as entrepreneurs were not. Given the impact of the decision in the Yee Clun matter, which protected the business interests of a Chinese employer, it would appear that McLaren's analysis may be more applicable in this case.

Whatever Judge Mackenzie's motivations may have been, the Saskatchewan legislators were clearly of the view that municipalities ought not to be stopped from applying the racially neutral language of the 1919 statute in a racially biased manner. Before more than two months had passed, the legislature voted in favour of a further enactment to shield Saskatchewan municipalities from any judicial review of their licensing decisions. The 1926 statute expanded the scope of the law to encompass lodging houses, boarding houses, public hotels, and cafes, along with the traditional restaurants and laundries. Curiously, this time the off-limit workers were no longer identified by race; the hiring of any "woman or girl" could subject an employer to municipal scrutiny (see Appendix A). Presumably this, too, was a change in form and not in substance, since access to potential employees who were women of colour remained strictly limited.

Although Yee Clun was not mentioned by name, the new enactment explicitly empowered the city council to revoke the court-ordered licence he had been issued. The statute authorized any municipal council to "revoke a license already granted," and admonished that any such revocation "shall be in its absolute discretion; it shall not be bound to give any reason for such refusal or revocation, and its action shall not be open to question or review by any court" (Appendix A).

It is not clear what action, if any, the Regina City Council actually took to revoke Yee Clun's licence. But records indicate that government officials continued to harass Yee Clun for some time after the litigation was over. Prosecuted and convicted for failing to make proper tax returns for his business, Yee Clun would be forced back to court in 1928, seeking judicial review of this ruling as well. Once again, the Saskatchewan King's Bench overturned the initial decision, finding that the authorities who secured the original conviction had failed to follow proper procedures (*Rex v. Yee Clun*, 1928).

The "white women's labour law," promoted by a coalition of interests crossing class and gender boundaries, functioned as a critical tool enabling racially dominant groups to prohibit Chinese men from participating freely in the economic and social communities in which they lived. Requiring rigid boundaries to be drawn between races, the statute illustrated the inherent difficulties of race definition, and encouraged the articulation of racist stereotypes in inflammatory ways. Leaders among the Chinese community actively contested the validity of such laws, and although they occasionally found their claims met with some success in the courts, the legal system as a whole was notoriously deficient in response. Political form soon superseded judicial opinion to reverse any gains obtained in litigation.

The "white women's labour laws" remained in force for years. Manitoba was the first to repeal its act in 1940, with Ontario following in 1947, but British Columbia let the statute stand until 1968. The Saskatchewan statute, veiled in racially neutral language, was not repealed until 1969 (Appendices A & B). Working-class white womanhood had proven to be a stalwart symbol in the forging of political, social, and economic hierarchies. The enforcement of the "white women's labour law," in the context of racist attacks on the economic opportunities and social freedoms of Chinese men, illustrates the powerful influence of Canadian law in the shaping of historical and contemporary understandings of race, class, and gender.

APPENDIX A

Saskatchewan "White Women's Labour Law," 1912
"An Act to Prevent the Employment of Female Labour in Certain Capacities," Statutes of Saskatchewan 1912, chapter 17.

> First reading was held 26 February 1912, second reading on 1 March 1912, and debate and third reading on 4 March 1912: *Journals of the Legislative Assembly*, 1912, at 68. Section 1 provided: No person shall employ in any capacity any white woman or girl or permit any white woman or girl to reside or lodge in or to work in or, save as a **bona fide** customer in a public apartment thereof only, to frequent any restaurant, laundry or other place of business or amusement owned, kept or managed by any Japanese, Chinaman or other Oriental person.

Saskatchewan "White Women's Labour Law," 1913
"An Act to amend An Act to Prevent the Employment of Female Labour in Certain Capacities," Statutes of Saskatchewan 1912–13, chapter 13.

> Royal assent, 11 January 1913. This amendment deleted all references to "Japanese" or "other Oriental persons."

Saskatchewan "White Women's Labour Law," 1919
"An Act to prevent the Employment of Female Labour in Certain Capacities," Statutes of Saskatchewan 1918–19, chapter 85.

> First reading was given on 15 January 1919, second reading on 17 January 1919, and it went through committee of the Whole and received third reading on 21 January 1919. The bill was granted royal assent on 27 January 1919, to come into effect 1 May 1919. Section 1 read: No person shall employ any white woman or girl in any capacity requiring her to reside or lodge in or to work in any restaurant or laundry without a special licence from the municipality in which such restaurant or laundry is situated, which licence the council of every municipality is hereby authorized to grant.

Saskatchewan "Women's Labour Law," 1926
"An act respecting the Employment of Female Labour," Statutes of Saskatchewan 1925–26, chapter 53, sections 3, 4.

> First reading was held 11 January 1926, second reading 20 January 1926, third reading 28 January 1926, and royal assent granted 28 January 1926. Annual licences were required, and section 4 stated:
> The council may grant or refuse a license under section 3, or revoke a license already granted either under *The Female Employment Act*, chapter 185 of *The Revised Statutes of Saskatchewan 1920* or under this Act. The grant, refusal or revocation shall be in its absolute discretion; it shall not be bound to give any reason for such refusal or revocation, and its action shall not be open to question or review by any court.

See also Revised Statutes of Saskatchewan 1920, chapter 185; Statutes of Saskatchewan 1925–26, chapter 53, sections 3, 4; Revised Statutes of Saskatchewan

1930, chapter 257; Revised Statutes of Saskatchewan 1940, chapter 309; Revised Statutes of Saskatchewan 1953, chapter 269.

The act was not repealed until passage of the "Labour Standards Act, 1969," Statutes of Saskatchewan 1969, chapter 24, section 73. See also "An Act to protect Certain Civil Rights," Statutes of Saskatchewan 1947, chapter 35, as amended by "An Act to amend The Saskatchewan Bill of Rights Act, 1947," Statutes of Saskatchewan 1949, chapter 29, which may have offered an impediment to the continuation of a racially based application of the labour statute.

APPENDIX B

Manitoba
"An Act to prevent the employment of Female Labor in certain capacities," Statutes of Manitoba 1913, chapter 19.

The Manitoba statute, passed on 15 February 1913, stipulated that it was only to come into force "upon proclamation of the Lieutenant-Governor-in-Council," and all indications are that it was never actually proclaimed. Revised Statutes of Manitoba 1913, Schedules B and C, list the statute as unproclaimed, and there is no reference to it in the listing of proclaimed Statutes in the yearly volumes of legislation between 1913 and 1940. With respect to the failure to proclaim, see Walker (1989: 7 and 16). See also Lai (1988: 94) claiming that the failure to proclaim resulted from the opposition mounted by the Chinese communities, who united to fight these statutes throughout the late 1920s.

The 1913 statute was not contained in the Revised Statutes of Manitoba 1913, the Consolidated Statutes of Manitoba 1924, or the Revised Statutes of Manitoba 1940. It was expressly repealed in "An Act to repeal certain Enactments which have become Obsolete," Statutes of Manitoba 1940, chapter 35.

Ontario
"An Act to amend The Factory, Shop and Office Building Act," Statutes of Ontario 1914, chapter 40.

Section 2(1), stated: "No Chinese person shall employ in any capacity or have under his direction or control any female white person in any factory, restaurant or laundry." Section 2(2) provided that "subsection 1 shall not come into force until a day to be named by proclamation of the Lieutenant-Governor in Council."

The Toronto *Globe* (1914: 1) noted: "Hon. James Duff's bill to amend factory, shop and office building act passed through Committee and it was agreed to proclaim the clause regarding employment of women by orientals should Privy Council decisions in Saskatchewan case [Quong Wing] be favourable." Despite the fact that the courts upheld the Saskatchewan act as constitutional, actual proclamation in Ontario did not occur until 2 November 1920, with the provision to come into effect 1 December 1920. A copy of the unpublished order-in-council is held by the Ontario Cabinet Office; see also Executive Council Ontario (1928: 193) which lists the section as proclaimed: "Proclamations: Bringing into force section 31. Factory & Shops Act (re employment of white women by Chinese)." The Ontario

Cabinet Order-in-Council proclaiming the section noted that this was "upon the recommendation of the Honourable the Minister of Labour." A lobby from organized labour seems to have been important: see *Labour* (1928) which notes: "Labour has long sought this regulation and it expects the Ontario government to enforce the law."

When the act was reprinted in the Revised Statutes of Ontario 1927, as "The Factory, Shop and Office Building Act," Revised Statutes of Ontario 1922, chapter 275, section 30, the proclamation subsection was no longer included. This seemed to cause some surprise, since few authorities appear to have been aware of the proclamation: see Department of Labour (1928) where various provincial and federal officials, newspapers, and agents of the Chinese consulate state that no proclamation was ever given. Due to strenuous representations from the Chinese Consulate General in Ottawa, the Ontario legislature passed an amendment in 1929, Statutes of Ontario 1929, chapter 72, section 5, reinserting the proclamation requirement, and making it retroactive to 31 December 1927, the day in which the Revised Statutes of 1927 came into force. The provisions were continued in this form by Statutes of Ontario 1932, chapter 35, section 29 and Revised Statutes of Ontario 1937, chapter 194, section 28, unproclaimed; "Table of Public Statutes: Table B, Acts or Parts Thereof Unproclaimed," Statutes of Ontario 1946, at 928. They were repealed in Statutes of Ontario 1947, chapter 102, section 1.

British Columbia

"An Act to amend the 'Municipal Act'," Statutes of British Columbia 1919, chapter 63, section 13.

Patterned after the Saskatchewan act subsequent to its deletion of the clause relating to "Japanese or other Oriental persons," the statute prohibited the employment of "any white woman or girl" in restaurants, laundries, places of business or amusement owned, kept, or managed by "any Chinese person."

In 1923, British Columbia replaced the racially specific terminology with more neutral language, deleting all reference to Chinese employers and leaving it to the discretion of police officials whether white women were to be allowed to work in restaurants and laundries: "An Act for the Protection of Women and Girls in certain Cases," Statutes of British Columbia 1923, chapter 76. The 1923 act, for the first time, also included "Indian" women and girls as "protected" categories of employees: section 3.

See also Revised Statutes of British Columbia 1924, chapter 275; Revised Statutes of British Columbia 1936, chapter 309; Revised Statutes of British Columbia 1948, chapter 366; Revised Statutes of British Columbia 1960, chapter 410; repealed by "An Act to Amend and Repeal Certain Provisions of the Statute Law," Statutes of British Columbia 1968, chapter 53, section 29.

I have as yet been unable to locate any similar American statutes, although Mears (1927: 306–7) notes that the Oregon legislature considered prohibiting the employment of white females in restaurants or grills "owned or operated by Orientals." A bill to this effect, introduced in 1919 by W.G. Lynn, was defeated in the legislature due to the combined forces of Chinese hotel and restaurant proprietors and the press. Concerns about constitutionality were apparently a factor.

QUESTIONS TO CONSIDER

1. Discuss ways in which the labour legislation discussed by Constance Backhouse corresponded to and violated public sentiments concerning race, dignity, and justice. Use the specific examples of those who supported and opposed Yee Clun's challenge to what was popularly known as the "white women's labour law."
2. Trace the tensions between legislators and judges in their interpretation of anti-Chinese legislation. Whose interests were at stake when such legislation was implemented and challenged?
3. In your view, are racial minorities in contemporary Canada no longer discriminated against by race-specific legislation? Are such minorities disadvantaged in economic, social, and political life despite formal equality provisions in law? Use Backhouse's essay and outside readings to support your answer.

REFERENCES

Anderson, K.J. (1991). *Vancouver's Chinatown: Racial discourse in Canada, 1875–1980*. Kingston and Montreal: McGill-Queen's University Press.

Andracki, S. (1978). *Immigration of orientals into Canada, with special reference to Chinese*. New York: Arno Press.

Angus, H.F. (1937). Canadian immigration: The law and its administration. In Norman MacKenzie (Ed.). *The legal status of aliens in Pacific countries* (pp. 58–75). London: Oxford University Press.

Backhouse, C. (1992). Gretta Wong Grant: Canada's first Chinese-Canadian female lawyer. Unpublished manuscript.

Backhouse, C. (1993). The white women's labour laws: Anti-Chinese racism in early 20th-century Canada. Unpublished manuscript.

Bolaria, B.S., & Li, P.S. (1988). *Racial oppression in Canada* (2nd ed.). Toronto: Garamond Press.

Chinese Immigration Act, Statutes of Canada, chapter 38 (1923).

Collette, C. (1990). For labour and for women: The Women's Labour League, 1906–18. *Labour/Le Travail, 26*, 230–231.

Daily Star (Saskatoon). (1912a). What is white woman? Definition puzzled magistrate and lawyers in case of orientals in court. (August 14), p. 3.

Daily Star (Saskatoon). (1912b). Counsel for defence in orientals case questions authority of provincial legislature to pass act. (August 15), p. 3.

Daily Star (Saskatoon). (1912c). The white help question [Letter to the editor]. (August 19), p. 3.

Daily Star (Saskatoon). (1912d). Judge finds law valid in oriental help case and gives decision against Chinamen and Jap which counsel announces he will appeal. (August 21), p. 3.

Davis, F. J. (1991). *Who is Black? One nation's definition*. University Park, PA: Pennsylvania State University Press.

Department of Labour. (1928). Canadian laws governing the employment of women. Undated memorandum appended to correspondence dated 28 September 1928.

Public Archives of Canada, RG 25, Vol. 1524, file 867, Employment of women by Chinese in Canada, correspondence and memoranda.

Executive Council Ontario. (1923). *Consolidated indexes to orders in council formerly titled the Journals of Executive Council Ontario*, Consolidated Index No. 6, p. 193, 1 Nov. 1919 to 15 July 1923.

Fryer, P. (1988). *Black people in the British Empire: An introduction*. London: Pluto Press.

Globe. (April 8, 1914), p. 1.

Griffiths, N.E.S. (1993). *The splendid vision: Centennial history of the National Council of Women of Canada, 1893–1993*. Ottawa: Carleton University Press.

Harris, C.I. (1993). Whiteness as property. *Harvard Law Review, 106*: 1707–1791.

Harvey, J. (1991). *The Regina Council of Women, 1895–1929*. Unpublished master's thesis, University of Regina, Regina, Saskatchewan.

Hawkes, J. (1924). *The story of Saskatchewan and its people*. Vol. 3. Chicago and Regina: S.J. Clarke Publishing Company.

Labour. (1928). Law prohibits working of white girls with Chinese. (September 8).

Labour Gazette. (1924). Resolution refused to Women's Labour Leagues. (October), p. 852.

Lai, C.D. (1988). *Chinatowns: Towns within cities in Canada*. Vancouver: UBC Press.

Lambertson, R., & Grove, A. (1994). Pawns of the powerful: The politics of litigation in the *Union Colliery* case. *B.C. Studies, 103* (Fall).

Leader-Post (Regina). (1959). Lawyer marks 80th birthday. (June 4).

Li, P.S. (1980). Immigration laws and family patterns: Some demographic changes among Chinese families in Canada, 1885–1971. *Canadian Ethnic Studies, 12*, 58–73.

Lindström-Best, V. (1989). Finnish socialist women in Canada, 1890–1930. In L. Kealey and J. Sangster (Eds.). *Beyond the vote: Canadian women and politics* (pp. 196–216). Toronto: University of Toronto Press.

McEvoy, F.J. (1982). A symbol of racial discrimination: The Chinese Immigration Act and Canada's relations with China, 1942–1947. *Canadian Ethnic Studies, 14*, 24–42.

McLaren, J. (1991). The early British Columbia Supreme Court and the "Chinese Question": Echoes of the rule of law. In D. Gibson and W.W. Pue (Eds.). *Glimpses of Canadian legal history* (pp. 111–153). Winnipeg: Legal Research Institute, University of Manitoba.

Mears, E.G. (1927). *Resident orientals on the American Pacific Coast: Their legal and economic status*. New York: Institute of Pacific Relations.

Montagu, M.F.A. (1942). *Man's most dangerous myth: The fallacy of race*. New York: Columbia University Press.

Morning Leader (Regina). (1919a). Municipalities will decide on employment. (January 18).

Morning Leader (Regina). (1919b). Employment agencies to vanish now. (January 22).

Morning Leader (Regina). (1922a). Spreading the drug habit. (April 7), p. 4.

Morning Leader (Regina). (1922b). The narcotics traffic. (December 30), p. 16.

Morning Leader (Regina). (1924a). Allow white female help in Chinese restaurants. (August 8), p. 1.

Morning Leader (Regina). (1924b). Council turns down request of Yee Klung. (October 8), p. 3.

Morning Leader (Regina). (1924c). Chinese National Party reorganizes. (December 29), p. 9.

Morning Leader (Regina). (1924d). Chinese society to move quarters. (December 16), p. 17.

Morning Leader (Regina). (1924e). Chinatown at Vancouver to get cleanup. (October 3), p. 1.

Morning Leader (Regina). (1924f). Seek to have drug peddler deported soon. (November 6), p. 9.

Morning Leader (Regina). (1924g). Protest white girl help in Chinese restaurants. (August 12), p. 1.

Morning Leader (Regina). (1924h). Women object to Yee Clun's application. (August 13), p. 1.

Morning Leader (Regina). (1924i). City women oppose white female help for Chinese. (September 24), p. 9.

Morning Leader (Regina). (1924j). Is not alarmed at inter-marriages. (October 29), p. 2.

Morning Leader (Regina). (1924k). May not treat Chinese apart from others. (August 20). p. 1.

Morning Leader (Regina). (1924l). G.F. Blair taken by death while sitting at desk. (March 2), p. 2.

Morning Leader (Regina). (1924m). Court to decide Chinese rights. (October 22), p. 9.

Murphy, E. (1922). *The black candle*. Toronto: Thomas Allen.

National Council of Women of Canada. (1927). Report of the Committee on Trades and Professions for Women. *The yearbook of the National Council of Women of Canada*. Ottawa: NCWC.

National Council of Women of Canada. (1928). Report on trades and professions. *The yearbook of the National Council of Women of Canada*. Ottawa: NCWC.

Pascoe, P. (1991). Race, gender, and intercultural relations: The case of interracial marriage. *Frontiers*, 12, 5–18.

Pioneers and prominent people of Saskatchewan. (1924). Toronto: Ryerson Press.

Prentice, A., et al. (1988). *Canadian women: A history*. Toronto: Harcourt Brace Jovanovich.

Provincial Council of Women of Saskatchewan. (1955). *History of the Provincial Council of Women of Saskatchewan, 1919–1954*. Regina: Commercial Printers.

Rex ex rel Eley v. Yee Clun and Yee Low. (1928). *Saskatchewan Law Reports*, vol. 23, p. 170.

Roome, P. (1989). Amelia Turner and Calgary labour women, 1919–1935. In L. Kealey and J. Sangster (Eds.). *Beyond the vote: Canadian women and politics* (pp. 89–117). Toronto: University of Toronto Press.

Ryder, B. (1991a). Racism and the Constitution: The constitutional fate of British Columbia anti-Asian immigration legislation, 1884–1909. *Osgoode Hall Law Journal*, 29: 619–676.

Ryder, B. (1991b). Racism and the Constitution: The constitutional fate of British Columbia anti-Asian legislation, 1872–1922. Unpublished manuscript. Copy on file at Osgoode Hall Law School Law Library.

Saskatchewan Labour Women's Division. n.d. *Saskatchewan women, 1905–1980*. n.p.

Saskatchewan Local Council of Women. (1921). *Minute books* Saskatchewan Archives Board, S-B82 I.3. March 21, 1921, pp. 3–4, April 14, 1921, p. 1; April 28, 1921, pp. 1–2.

Saskatchewan Local Council of Women. (1926–31). *Minute books* S.A.B., B-82 I.4. April 3, 1926, p. 24; December 18, 1927, p. 81; April 25, 1930, p. 191; May 27, 1930, p. 193.

Searchlight (Calgary). (1920a). Women's Labour League active. (January 23), p. 4.

Searchlight (Calgary). (1920b). Work of the Women's Labour League in Calgary. (September 4), p. 3.

Walker, J.W.St.G. (1989). "Race" policy in Canada: A retrospective. In O.P. Dwivedi et al. *Canada 2000: Race relations and public policy* (pp. 1–19). Guelph: University of Guelph.

Yee Clun v. City of Regina. (1925). *Saskatchewan Law Reports*, vol. 20, p. 232.

TWO

Illegal Operations: Women, Doctors, and Abortion, 1886–1939

ANGUS MCLAREN

On 9 July 1919 Sarah Robins, mother of three small children, died in Vancouver General Hospital, her septic poisoning the aftermath of a bungled abortion. In the dying declaration which the doctors extorted from her, Robins left an agonizing portrayal of the last days of her life.

> My trouble started with going to a doctor in Vancouver, Dr. Thomas Vernon, Lonsdale Avenue, North Vancouver.... I was told of him by a Mrs. Peters, Denman St., West End, Vancouver. I saw him last Friday week. I told him I was six weeks overdue in menstruation. I asked him if he could do anything for me and if there was any risk. He asked me who my husband was, and said he charged $100 and there was no great risk as he did eight and ten a day. I went home and my husband implored me not to go. I went the next day Saturday with $75 and told him that was all I could afford. He told me he would not do it. I cried to him and eventually he did. I was ill on Saturday night and the Sunday and the Monday I phoned him. He said he did not remember me. When I asked him what to do for the pain in the abdomen, he said "Better get used to it," said "Take a hot soap-suds douche" which I did. Continued sick as ever. I went to see him on Wednesday. He felt my pulse and said I would get

Source: Angus McLaren, "Illegal Operations: Women, Doctors, and Abortion, 1886–1939," *Journal of Social History* 26, no. 4 (1993): 797–816.

along alright. On Thursday at 4 o'clock in the morning my husband phoned him and demanded him out at once. My husband met the six o'clock boat. He came and curetted me and douched me without anaesthetic.[1]

A few days later Sarah Robins was dead.

Women seeking to control their fertility have had recourse, as far back as it is possible to trace, to abortion. Such a "back-up method" of fertility control was essential given that until the 1930s coitus interruptus was the main means of contraception. Demographic historians and historians of the family have gone so far as to speak of an abortion "epidemic" occurring in the western world at the turn of the century, when the rate of induced miscarriages rose to account for perhaps one-sixth of all pregnancies.[2]

Because such risky strategies were labelled "crimes" it is difficult to analyze the obviously important question of why so many women adopted them. The decisive role played by the medical profession in both North America and Britain in the increased restriction of the law on abortion does not have to be pursued here.[3] It suffices to say that the criminalization of abortion in the nineteenth century meant that neither those who sought to induce their miscarriages nor their accomplices wanted their activities made public. Court reports are accordingly especially valuable for researchers attempting to trace the history of such practices, spotlighting as they do the fact that abortions were not carried out in isolation; they were social acts the investigations of which reveal the particular nature of the relationships of women like Sarah Robins with their male partners, their friends, their doctors, and ultimately the judiciary.

The main purpose of this paper is to use legal sources to explore the decision to abort in the last decades of the nineteenth and the early decades of the twentieth century, an era in which the state and the professions took an unprecedented interest in the fertility control decisions of ordinary women and men. As the pressures to limit fertility increased and recourse to abortion rose, the criminal nature of the act necessarily tainted the relationships of women, men, doctors, and magistrates. The fate of women burdened with unwanted pregnancies, whose well-being was most placed at risk by the law, is the chief concern of what follows. A subsidiary preoccupation of this paper is to investigate the law-induced biases inherent in the sources which the historian of abortion necessarily employs — the court records.

The study exploits the strikingly graphic and intimate information generated by inquests and trials concerning one hundred British Columbian women who, between 1886 and 1939, attempted to induce a miscarriage. The woman who merely sought as well the woman who succeeded in inducing her own abortion, those who assisted such women, and anyone who directly procured an abortion were all, according to Canada's Revised Statutes of 1892, guilty of an indictable offense. But the same statutes held that doctors were not liable for inducing a miscarriage that in their opinion was necessary to protect the life of the mother.[4] The same sorts of laws were in force in the United States and Great Britain.

To whom could women turn, in whom could they confide, when a crisis like the need to terminate a pregnancy occurred? How did their female friends, their male partners, their doctors, and finally the courts respond? The great value of legal documentation is that it contains rare accounts of women and men forced to talk of interactions that would normally have been cloaked in silence, hidden from history.

But before plunging into an investigation of such sources, some provisos are in order. The first pertains to the women whose stories we are told. Abortions usually came to the attention of the authorities only when something went tragically wrong; in three quarters of our cases the woman had died. Since courts tended to hear only about unsuccessful attempts at abortion the women whose fates they discussed were usually the most unfortunate, desperate, and unlucky. But such women represented only a small fraction of those who sought to terminate a pregnancy; the many more successful attempts at induction of miscarriage necessarily escaped public scrutiny. It has to be kept in mind that the courts often consciously played up the dangers of abortion with the obvious intention of policing female sexuality. Repeated reports of deaths due to illegal operations served as a chilling reminder to all women — both married and unmarried — of the fate of those who sought to free themselves from an unwanted or unexpected pregnancy.

The second point to be made about the law-induced bias of the sources is that, while they exaggerated the unfortunate fate of women who aborted, they minimized the role of the men involved. The only single men who emerge from the records are those few who, failing to abscond, became entangled in the law. The courts generally refused, for reasons which will be explored, to hold husbands responsible for their wives' abortions.

The third point to be kept in mind is that doctors' involvement in abortion was also likely to escape full judicial scrutiny. For an illegal operation even to be brought to light usually required medical testimony. When a case threatened the reputations of their hospital or their colleagues, many doctors' natural response was to look the other way. Quacks and the occasional maverick physician, who failed to enjoy collegial support, ran the greatest risk of being reported.

One final proviso. Although witnesses swore to tell the truth, the "truth" was only recognized by the court when expressed in a language that it found acceptable. The legal records were written by and for lawyers; all those involved knew or were soon instructed on what they had to say. Only by constantly reading between the lines can one tease out something of the "actual" experiences of the actors from the ritualized assertions recorded in the transcripts.

Turning to our sources, the first question is why did women seek recourse to abortion? Abortion was not the first line of defense against unwanted pregnancies, but evidence came out in court that at the turn of the century reliable contraceptive protection was simply not available for many. Condoms were expensive and unreliable. Peter Adams, who courted Kitty Morris in 1895, knowing she was afraid of becoming pregnant, promised to obtain contraceptives. "I told her I would buy a French protector, I then went to the Doctor and bought one and I showed it to her ... she examined it and said too thin may break and I want none of that."[5] Some women douched with "Zycol" which was, a doctor explained, similar to "Lysol." "It is a disinfectant and women use it as a means of the prevention of conception."[6] If all else failed celibacy could be tried. When in 1901 Sarah MacDonald and her husband decided they could not afford to have any more children, they simply abstained from intercourse.[7] The fact was that prior to World War Two most Canadian couples hoping to contracept employed the age-old method of coitus interruptus. In the absence of reliable means of contraception, "accidents" inevitably occurred and couples intent on limiting fertility then had to contemplate recourse to abortion.[8]

Why would women be so determined to avoid childbearing as to risk the dangers of abortion? Some contemporary commentators accused them of acting irrationally. "Well it is surprising," retorted one doctor, "the number of times it is done by people who have absolutely no reason in the world for doing it, other than the fact that they don't want to have another child."[9] Such middle-class male commentators failed to realize what a burden pregnancy could pose. When it came to listing motives for recourse to abortion, economic need was, for the married, always paramount. Mary Barnett stated in her dying declaration, "My husband and I want to get it done because we were so hard up and we were out of work."[10] "We agreed we did not want any children," declared Henry Diederichs, "because we could not afford it."[11] Rosaria Silletta had three children and did not want any more.[12] Diana Baker had six under the age of twelve.[13] Alice Nixon had lost two children, but still had six living.[14] Some women could not envisage bearing another child; a few had been warned by doctors that it would be dangerous. In 1886 Annie Emberly told a friend, "that she thought she was pregnant and that she was going to take medicine if she could get it by any means ... that she would never have another child as it would kill her."[15] The public tended to imagine that most women seeking abortion were single victims of seduction and abandonment, but the "typical" case which emerges from the early-twentieth-century inquest and court records is that of the married woman in her mid-twenties. Many were already mothers. They turned to abortion, not to postpone having children, but to limit their number.[16]

For the single or separated, abortion was at first glance apparently not so much linked to family planning as motivated by the desire to protect one's reputation. Real desperation was evident in the 1896 case of Sarah Rosenzweig, a divorced mother who, believing herself pregnant, first sought an abortion and then drowned herself.[17] Jennie Quinlan, who died in 1919 as a result of trying to abort with a catheter, was presumably seeking to hide her pregnancy from her overseas husband.[18] Edith Niemi, a single Finnish maid, did not want her employer to know of her condition.[19] Nellie Rae died in 1926 of a miscarriage induced "to relieve herself of a pregnancy produced by a man who had raped her."[20]

The age and marital status of the women seeking abortion have been regarded by researchers as important because from such facts one can infer motive. The presupposition is that a young, single woman would have been motivated by a desire to protect her reputation; a married woman by the need to limit family size. But a close examination of the court files reveals that the motivations of the married and the single could not always be clearly separated. In 1920 Agnes Michaels became pregnant and sought to abort while her husband was away.[21] In 1923 Annie Mulvaney, who was separated from her spouse, sought to terminate her pregnancy.[22] Hazel Snowden, whose husband was an inmate of the New Westminster asylum, took similar action.[23] An unexpected pregnancy could, in short, pose as great a threat to such married women's reputations and well-being as it did to those of the unmarried.

Who provided women with abortions? Women often refused to implicate third parties and despite incriminating evidence insisted that they had induced their own miscarriages. In some cases while admitting the assistance of others, women attempted to protect those who tried to help, feeling that they were not to blame. Margaret Roberts, though dying, refused to give the name of her abortionist because she did not want to be responsible for sending to jail a woman who had three children.[24] But doctors and police were for their part often intent on tracking down accomplices. Keeping in mind that the involvement of others was difficult to trace, the one hundred cases reveal the following: self-induction was claimed in twenty-seven, the aid of an abortionist or supplier of drugs was admitted in fifty-one, and no clear determination was made in sixteen.

Attempts at self-inducement were no doubt common. A nurse was told in 1913 by Nellie Andrews that she had precipitated her own abortion. "She said she'd used a catheter that day and I told her she couldn't do it and do it properly. Then she said I have done it before about a year ago and it brought on an abortion."[25] The use of instruments was by all accounts the leading method of abortion. The woman would squat and with the help of a mirror insert in the cervix a catheter, speculum, sound, pencil, bougie, needle, or crochet or button hook. The second most important method was consumption of pills or drugs containing such irritants and emmena-gogues as quinine, aloes, or ergot; the third, douching by syringe or enema bag with lysol, carbolic acid, turpentine, or simple soap and water; and the fourth, dilation of the cervix by inserting slippery elm or packing the vagina with cotton batten. In 1930 one Canadian researcher found that out of a sample of seventy-one self-induc-tions, forty-seven were by vaginal insertion, twenty by drugs, and four by vaginal douches.[26] Many of the women had previously aborted successfully. A witness tes-tified that Marjorie Coffin, who died in 1935 after employing a hot water douche and slippery elm, said "this is the sixteenth time and someone told me I would do it once too often."[27] All methods practised outside a hospital setting were danger-ous. Infection — either peritonitus or septicemia — accompanied by the tell-tale chills and fever was the primary cause of death. Hemorrhaging due to rupture of the uterus and drug toxicity also took their toll. Vascular accidents — occurring when air or soapy water which, having been pumped into the uterus, penetrated and obstructed an artery — became more common after World War Two.

Coroners consistently used abortion death inquests as occasions to call for tighter restrictions on the sale of patent medicines that could be used to induce mis-carriage.[28] But women could always try common household supplies such as castor oil, Beecham's Pills, and epsom salts which they had at hand before turning to such compounds as "Dr. Hunt's Female Pills," "French Female Pills," and "Nadruco Female Regulating Pills." Dr. F.C. Curtis said of abortifacients: "Anyone can get them, they are patent medicine.... It is said in the advertisement that they are used for reg-ulating monthly flow but really and truly they ... are intended to bring about abor-tion." At the same trial a druggist described the policing of ergot and savin: "They both come under Schedule A of the B.C. [British Columbia] Pharmacy Act and must be signed for by the parties purchasing them.... Under the Act we are entitled to sell them on signature but very few drug stores will sell them even on a signature."[29] Nevertheless a herbalist shop in downtown Vancouver was a well-known outlet for such products.

If self-induction failed, outside help would be sought. Eighteen-year-old Josephine Stearns had learnt of abortion, so her mother reported, from school mates.[30] Single women usually appeared to be especially reliant on their male part-ner's assistance, often not being able to tell friends or family of their predicament. Married women, who enjoyed more extensive networks of support, first turned to relatives and neighborhood female friends.[31] Alice Peters recalled at the 1919 inquest into the death of her neighbor Sarah Robins a conversation they had had two years previous about limiting family size.

... she said "We are not so wise as you." I said "Wise, I don't know I am sure — I have four. I don't know what you call wise," and she said if I did anything and I said nothing whatever. And she said "I am sure you do" ... she told me before the child was born she had been to Seattle to have an operation performed but they wanted far too much, $250. I said to her, "Why I understand that they did these operations right here in Vancouver."[32]

Annie Woodward in 1910, finding herself several weeks late, went to buy ergot pills, "Mrs. Sumner's Remedies," and a package of womb tonic from a shop on Vancouver's Keefer Street. Annie Mason, the clerk, referred Woodward to a Mrs. Matthews who in turn put her in contact with a Richard Beveridge. Beveridge offered to perform an abortion for twenty-five dollars.[33] In 1915 Concuilla Kappel reported her attempts at aborting to a Mrs. Reed, "who told her to take pennyroyal. It did no good and she was scared her people would find out that she was married. Mrs. Reed told her of a doctor in Vancouver who did that sort of thing and gave her a letter written in German."[34] In this fashion Kappel met "Dr." Joseph Kanstrup, a massage parlour operator.

Women had abortionists recommended to them by others who had availed of their services. Sisters and sisters-in-law helped out. Female friends and neighbors knew what was going on and kept tabs on those in distress. In 1920 Harriet Brown testified that she was aware of the five occasions on which Dr. Bamberg had visited Agnes Michaels.[35] When such cases came to court women were in general far more candid than men — more so even than husbands — in admitting to knowing of their neighbors' attempts to terminate pregnancies.

For those who could go further afield the Vancouver newspapers contained advertisements for abortion services in Washington state.

Dr. David Andrews. Women's Disorders Specialty. 25 Years Experience. Suite 400 Pantages Building, Seattle.
Dr. J. Dunn. Women's Disease Specialist. European Hospital Experience. 317 Walter Building, Seattle.
Sound View Hospital. Specialist in Women's Diseases.[36]

Women went across the border to American towns like Sumas and Blaine, and many references were made at trials to operations sought in Seattle. In 1911 Augusta Benn, after reading an advertisement for the services offered in Seattle, went to be operated on by Dr. Catherine Harriman.[37] In 1917 Mary Dawes was sent by her father to the same city for the same purpose.[38] Nineteen-year-old Frances Pike died in 1918 as a result of a Seattle operation; her mother testified she thought her daughter was visiting friends.[39] Nurse Fromm was implicated in the February 1920 deaths of two British Columbia women who were operated on in her 20th Avenue South Seattle clinic on the same day.[40]

Who were the abortionists? Sixty individuals were cited in fifty-one cases; often an accomplice — usually a single woman's male partner — was indicted along with the practitioner.[41] Forty-seven of the sixty could be called abortionists; the other thirteen were accused of supplying medicines, being accessories, or aiding and abetting. Of twenty-eight women named, nine were identified as doctors, nurses, or midwives. Clara Kaufman, a Victoria masseuse, reportedly assisted over a hundred woman for fees of fifty to a hundred dollars each. "You don't have to go to Seattle to get rid of your trouble," she was quoted as saying at her 1917 trial, "I am a woman's friend."[42] In Vancouver, nurse Clara Jesson, despite three trials, enjoyed a reputation as a skilled practitioner, advertising her services for "private maternity cases" at her home, which had four upstairs bedrooms.[43] In the 1930s Mrs. Esther Morris established a similar operation, the "Home Private Hospital."[44] Hazel Dalton advertised in the papers as "Specialist in female remedies."[45] Edith Pierce provided abortions in downtown Vancouver at "Adam and Pierce's Electrical Steam Treatments."[46]

Women received most of their support from other women; recourse to abortion was commonly regarded as very much a woman's means of birth limitation. But where did men figure in all of this? In the case of the married couple living together, the decision to terminate a pregnancy was often obviously a joint undertaking. In 1914 a woman dying in the Vancouver General Hospital explained, "My husband and I want to get it done because we were so hard up and we were out of work."[47] Another stated, "Well, we [meaning her husband and herself] put some slippery elm up the womb."[48] In some instances the abortion was more the husband's idea than the wife's. Phyllis Villeneuve said she went to an abortionist because she believed that her spouse did not want the baby; at the subsequent inquest he was portrayed by witnesses as a wife beater.[49]

When an abortion case resulting in death ended up in the courts, the husband, while admitting knowledge of his wife's attempts to abort, commonly claimed that he opposed recourse to the final deadly operation. Nellie Andrews's separated husband testified: "I knew of her using an instrument known as a catheter.... I was not in favor of it.... She always had one. Whenever she became pregnant she always had all kinds of things to prevent her going her time."[50] Likewise in 1898 one man testified at his wife's inquest: "Up to this time I did not know that she had been taking any medicine to bring on a miscarriage. I knew that she had used natural means to bring on a miscarriage. She put her feet in hot water. I mean by what I said that she had a little flow but that it did not come as she thought it ought to. She asked me to go to the store to get her something to bring on her periods more freely, or to produce a better flow." He said he brought back whiskey, but she had already procured a pill from the druggist. "She said she had taken it to induce the menstrual flow ... she had been passing an instrument into her womb so she told me.... She had several miscarriages before and in one case she had used a lead pencil and I had attended her and she got better."[51] Similarly, Arnott Woods testified that he had accompanied his wife to a pharmacist's to obtain drugs, but opposed the idea of an instrumental abortion. "I would not hear of an operation, and I left them.... When I returned ... my wife was suffering from an attempted abortion."[52] Robert Blatchford stated that he knew his wife was taking "dope" and douching herself, but that he forbad her to go to Seattle, where she had the operation from which she ultimately died.[53]

Some husbands were no doubt kept completely in the dark. Annie Emberly told her friend Mary Jane Drew "that she had been using a syringe on herself; and that I was not to tell Dr. Walker or her husband when they came."[54] When Orlan Gaynor was told of his wife's abortion he replied "that it was possible my wife might have done something to herself."[55] Of course, it was in the man's interest to feign ignorance of his wife's actions. Few husbands probably needed legal counsel to realize that not to do so could possibly lead to their being charged as an accomplice. On occasion such duplicity was publicly revealed. Henry Andrews's testimony that he opposed his wife's abortion was directly contradicted by a female witness who declared that Nellie Andrews "told me that the husband insisted that she have it done and that the husband wanted her to go to Seattle."[56] Mark Baker said of his wife, "She never discussed very much about those affairs or I don't think we would have had so many children," whereas she stated that he had actively assisted in her aborting.[57]

But even when the husband was obviously involved, the authorities would rarely charge him as an accomplice. Bertrand Barnett was initially prosecuted in 1914 for involvement in his wife's abortion death, but the case seems to have been dropped.[58] The general feeling was that to jail a man who had already lost his wife would be a cruel and unnecessarily harsh course of action.

When an abortion involved a married woman the courts tended to downplay her husband's participation; when abortion involved a single woman the police frequently assumed that her male partner had been actively involved. Such a man, it was felt, clearly had much to lose if the woman's pregnancy was not terminated. This presupposition was apparently borne out in 1895 when the court heard that Locksley Lyons, having impregnated his fifteen-year-old sister-in-law, Kate Burns, provided her with medicine. Kate testified that it consisted of "black pills and a dark brown medicine ... there was no name on it but he said he got it from Dr. Sloan living at Ladner. He gave me the pills two at a time; he gave me the medicine night and morning and two pills a day; he gave me three doses of pills."[59] Though the medicine did not work, Lyons was charged with both intent to procure a miscarriage and seduction.

An equally active bachelor was David McHenry, who in 1904 sought the assistance in Vancouver of Dr. Alexander Stewart Murrow, who reported him as saying, "there was a girl who had missed her menses. The girl lived over on Vancouver Island and he wanted to get some medicine to bring her menses on because he said as you know I am engaged to Miss Bolen and I don't want to have any trouble occur before the wedding." Murrow refused but a Vancouver Island doctor proved more accommodating.[60] Often these careless lovers were charged. The court declared a married Agassiz chiropractor, who in 1929 provided his eighteen-year-old nurse with pills, not guilty of abortion; this was hardly surprising since he had in fact failed to abort her. But he was found guilty of her seduction and sentenced to a year in prison.[61]

When a single woman died as a result of an abortion, the courts were likely to prosecute the man, assuming he had taken the initiative in suggesting the operation. In July 1934, noticing that her daughter Veronica had missed her period, Anna Kuzyk asked the local coroner if Carl Schwam, her daughter's boyfriend, had to marry her. Dr. Truax said there was no legal compulsion, but the Kuzyks could talk to Schwam. They apparently forced him into an engagement, but on 11 September Mrs. Kuzyk reported her daughter missing. The police located Veronica Kuzyk in the nearby town of Greenwood a week later in a state of ill health that required her hospitalization. She was released on 25 September but returned to hospital on 28 September. In a dying statement Veronica Kuzyk declared that Carl had given her lots of pills and, those failing, took her to Grietje Sandstrom, a Greenwood midwife.[62] In return for twenty dollars Sandstrom "mixed up some soap and something in a small bottle and put [it] in a glass pump which she put inside me." Six such attempts failing, Sandstrom then "used a button hook."

Schwam initially denied complicity and later admitted only that he had advised Kuzyk on whom to contact and provided money for the operation. He was charged with conspiracy, tried, convicted, and sentenced to five years in prison; Sandstrom was sentenced to a mere twenty-three months.[63] Going a step further, in a 1931 case the police cited the female abortionist as an accessory, but charged the dead woman's fiancé with her abortion.[64]

Single men, when named as accomplices, frequently sought to save themselves by casting all the blame on the woman. Such was the case when William Underwood was charged in 1911 with having supplied his fiancée, Angelica Stagg, with drugs and a syringe with the intent to procure a miscarriage. Underwood's lawyer, by portraying Stagg as an immoral "half-breed" from Lillooet who had wanted the abortion, succeeded in getting Underwood off.[65] But such tactics did not always work. In 1915 Walter Irwin, a separated thirty-four-year-old construction worker, failed to shift the blame onto eighteen-year-old Gladys Bolton. The court responded that "... a woman may be immoral and yet very truthful.... This is not a question of morals."[66]

As far as the man was concerned, the courts made it clear that it was a question of morals. Husbands were rarely charged as accessories, not because they were less likely than single men to bully their partners into abortion or to support a freely made decision, but because the courts tacitly recognized that as married men they had a "right" to be so involved. Bachelors did not have such rights, indeed they were regarded as usurping the parents' right of surveillance of their unmarried daughters. Single men in short were prosecuted as much for their sexual activities as for their involvement in the abortion that made such "immorality" public knowledge. Such prosecutions, in allowing the justice system to present itself as chivalrously punishing unscrupulous males, gave it a rare opportunity of providing those members of the public that might doubt the fairness of the abortion law with badly needed evidence that it was not aimed simply at women.

Of the thirty-five men cited in abortion cases fifteen were physicians. Doctors could legally provide safe abortions, but only for medical reasons. The special nature of abortion in medical practice was spelled out by a physician testifying at a 1920 inquest.

A. Occasionally we sanction the doing of an operation to save the mother's life.
Q. But just to get rid of the child ... is not a legal operation?
A. It is not sanctioned by the medical profession and is an illegal operation.... And the medical Council does not sanction it.[67]

A woman seeking an abortion or assistance in recovering from one could accordingly not expect to receive from her doctor ordinary medical care.

Abortion was one of the rare medical procedures which, save for exceptional cases, was a crime. Doctors on occasion complained about this encroachment by the law on medicine. What they tended to forget was that in Canada, as elsewhere, physicians, in order to eliminate the competition of midwives and irregular practitioners, had been in the nineteenth century the most vocal proponents of the criminalization of abortion.[68] One consequence was that a doctor who did not report an abortion death risked being implicated in it. Some physicians saw themselves obliged to assume the role of police informers. If a woman were dying in hospital as the result of a bungled abortion, a statement was taken if only to protect the doctor and the hospital staff. No doubt many doctors wanted to help track down dangerous abortionists, but some medical personnel showed themselves more interested in protecting themselves than in caring for their patient. In 1922 Dr. Alexander Stewart Murrow cruelly threatened the dying Jennie Young that he would not treat her for septic poisoning if she did not tell him who had performed her operation.[69] Similar pressure was presumably applied to Winnifred Lewis, because her inquest jury was told that her statement was not made voluntarily.[70] When Sarah Robins was dying at Vancouver General Hospital in 1919, the examining physician went so far as to stimulate her with drugs to acquire a declaration that would protect the hospital staff.[71] Such dying declarations had special force in court, having the status of sworn testimony. Accordingly Dr. Boak testified that he was "satisfied" that Mary Dalziel knew she was dying when she made her declaration at Victoria's Jubilee Hospital in 1917.[72]

When a woman entered a hospital showing signs of abortion but her life was not in danger, the examining physician had to decide whether or not to make a report. Marian Noel, who had endured an operation on a kitchen table carried out by a midwife with "some sort of long thing made to prick the womb" and then went to hospital, ended up having to testify in court because the attending physician alerted police.[73] The same thing occurred when nineteen-year-old Isabella Arcand was hospitalized in October 1921.[74] In 1938 twenty-three-year-old stenographer Ann Tandberg passed out after her third visit to nurse Hazel Dalton and was taken to Vancouver General Hospital, where her abortion was completed and reported.[75] Such reports were far from random. The likelihood was that hospital staff would see and report poor women rather than private patients and the single rather than the married.

The extent of reportage also depended on the zeal of the attending physician. The point that many doctors had little appetite for pursuing such enquiries was made in a 1921 inquest.

> Q. Doctor Fuller, it is not really customary to report these cases when they get better?
> A. I don't know. As a matter of fact I guess not many are reported but I thank the Lord I have so few of them [that] I don't know from my experience. I think if a doctor could find any information that would do any good, most of them would be willing and glad to give information, but what is the good of going to a whole lot of expense when you cannot do anything.[76]

In the privacy of their offices, doctors obviously provided some patients with abortions, but naturally enough never admitted in court to carrying out illegal operations. In 1886 Dr. William McNaughton reported that Annie Emberly, who had been cautioned she would never live through another confinement and found herself pregnant, told him that although she wanted an abortion she did not wish to see him in the penitentiary. Presumably she hoped he would courageously offer his services; McNaughton did not.[77] In 1904 Dr. Ernest McLean likewise testified that he had been asked by Jennie Gammon to help her out of her difficulty, but he had refused.[78] Some women felt there was no one else to whom they could turn. After her doctor rejected her request "to do something," Annie Fields ended her life with cyanide of potassium.[79]

As regards their private patients' discussions of abortion, doctors reported that some were too reticent, refusing to say what had befallen them. Other patients were too candid; doctors claimed to be shocked to find that such women insisted on their assistance. Explaining why he provided a patient with ergo-apiol pills one physician whined, "When a patient comes to us like that you have got to do something for her or they get angry with you."[80] The doctors' worse fear was to be "taken advantage of" by their patients. Such apparently was the case in 1922 when Annie Mulvaney visited Dr. Albert Ross and gave him her maiden name, purposely failing to reveal that she was married and separated. When he asked why she did not resolve the problem of her pregnancy by marrying she replied that if her parents knew of her condition they would turn her out of the house. Ross, in return for fifty dollars, accordingly operated on Mulvaney; a few weeks later he found himself charged with performing an abortion and Annie Mulvaney testifying against him.[81]

Courts were repeatedly told that doctors, to protect themselves from being suspected of providing abortions, were duty bound to notify colleagues of any suspicious cases. "Practically every medical man when he gets a case of this kind immediately calls a consultant. He does that for his own protection."[82] Before a legal therapeutic abortion could be carried out, "a consultation of two or more medical men, and in the case of the hospital the heads of the hospital are notified ... that the patient has been notified ... and that the doctor's opinion is corroborated by that of another doctor who is in good standing and so forth.[83] In 1915 an inquest jury found Dr. Samuel Bamberg negligent in not calling in other doctors in consultation in an abortion case and he was finally charged with the woman's death.[84] In 1920 Bamberg was again charged with murder, but again found not guilty.[85] A Vernon doctor tried to have it both ways. Gerald Wilson privately treated a young woman who had been taking abortifacient pills; only when it became clear a week later that she was not going to survive — possibly due to his incompetence — did he call in a colleague for assistance.[86]

The courts frequently expressed the concern that some doctors concealed evidence of inducement of miscarriage. More than one inquest jury recommended that physicians be forced to make public anything they knew of abortion. Suspecting a medical cover-up, in 1919 the Vancouver coroner warned, "It is a very serious matter, you know, this abortion business — criminal abortion — anybody that advises it or tries to cover it up in any way is guilty, and medical men may run themselves into trouble, because if they grant a certificate in a case that should be reported to the coroner it is an offense, and a criminal offense."[87] The cruel irony was that the doctor whom the coroner suspected colleagues were protecting — Dr. Thomas Vernon — was himself the coroner of the neighboring municipality of North Vancouver. Vernon was implicated in Sarah Robins's abortion death in 1919 and Margaret Graham's in 1926, but in neither case were charges ever filed.[88]

Abortion raised the complex issue of who should discipline doctors — the courts or the medical profession. In 1904 Dr. Robert Temple was initially charged with the murder of Hetta Bowes. "I took some pills today that Dr. Temple gave me," she had told a female friend, "and they nearly killed me." Temple was ultimately tried and found not guilty of the lesser charge of manslaughter, but nevertheless was struck off the medical register for unprofessional conduct.[89] He carried on a long campaign for reinstatement and was finally successful. By the 1930s a qualified doctor, so an inquest jury was told, was rarely prosecuted or censured for involvement in abortion: "... there is nothing to it ... because this goes on every day unfortunately."[90]

Before leaving the discussion of what went on in hospital wards and doctors' offices, it has to be noted that many women who had illegal abortions but did not end up in court were nevertheless "punished." Those doctors who saw themselves first as moral guardians and second as care-givers subjected such women to humiliating interrogations, threatened to withhold from them medical treatment, and extorted dying declarations which both publicized the most intimate details of their private lives and incriminated their friends and neighbors.[91] Given that one doctor might discreetly offer desperately needed services whereas another might call the police, women in distress necessarily approached medical professionals with caution.

What treatment could women expect to receive from the courts? An abortion was most likely heard of, as we have seen, when it resulted in a woman's death. Such a calamity could not be ignored; the police and judiciary had to act. But if the medical fraternity did not like abortion cases, the crown also viewed them with distaste. Evidence was difficult to obtain; the key witnesses were usually party to the crime. Consequently few abortion cases ever made it to court. In only thirty-four of our hundred abortions cases were charges filed. And in the even fewer number in which prosecutions were successfully pursued, the sentence levied for procuring abortion was usually no more than a two-year prison term. In a handful of cases, stiffer sentences were given. In 1910 Richard Beveridge was tried and convicted of manslaughter and sentenced to ten years in prison.[92] In 1914 Enid Shelbourne, a mother of an eight year old, was sentenced to seven years for the manslaughter death of Mary Barnett.[93]

If a death had not occurred, the likelihood was that an abortion attempt would come to the police's attention only because an overzealous attending physician had noticed and reported the suspicious causes of a woman's hospitalization. These sorts of cases were inevitably messy. Judges did not like them. Juries often refused to convict no matter how overwhelming the evidence. On occasion the courtroom drama, instead of properly impressing the public by a demonstration of the power and prudence of the law, brought it into disrepute.[94] The 1902 case of Rex versus Bella Howe climaxed in what the local press called a "sensational finish." Bella Howe had been charged in Nelson with attempting to induce her own miscarriage. The attending physician testified that Howe, having been hospitalized, admitted to attempting to abort by inserting a rigid catheter. The medical witness regarded it as pertinent that Howe was a prostitute. "She is pretty tight," he coldly commented, "evidently she has not been in her occupation very long."[95] Such a charge of self-inducement was rare inasmuch as the woman — despite what the law said — was usually regarded by the public as a victim driven by desperation. On this occasion the charge was presumably laid only because the crown thought it could make an example of a woman of the streets who had no family support. But the jury was more sympathetic and followed tradition in refusing to convict a woman of her own abortion. Mr. Justice Martin, outraged that the jurymen should blatantly ignore the testimony of the doctors, the police, and the accused herself, ordered the jury to be locked up overnight to reconsider their verdict; they returned the next morning with the same verdict of "not guilty." The judge was helpless, but before discharging the jury subjected its members to a "whigging," declaring that they had "signally failed to appreciate the responsibilities of [their] office."[96] Of course, it was the crown that had failed to appreciate its duty — that of levelling charges that it was confident that the community would sustain.

Perhaps the most surprising discovery made in the legal records is that the courts offered the opportunity for one or two vengeful women to report their own abortions in order to implicate their male partners. Although the abortion law clearly victimized women, in such cases women sought to turn a bad law to their own advantage.[97] A case in point was revealed in the press's accounts of Sarah McPhee's extra-marital affair with Dr. Peter Van Kampen, which began in Armstrong in 1901. They apparently did not employ effective contraceptives because, according to Sarah McPhee, Van Kampen aborted her in September 1901, November 1902, and February 1903. In late 1903, pregnant again, McPhee left British Columbia for California, where in 1907 she instituted divorce proceedings against her husband. But when the single Van Kampen subsequently refused to marry her, she in revenge successfully pressed charges against him for her earlier abortions.[98]

A similar scenario was played out in 1914 when Phila Marsden, "mistress" of Dr. Charles Maclean, charged him with aborting her against her will. The defense countered that because of the doctor's refusal to marry her she was out to get him.[99] The crown, after the jury had failed on two occasions to come to a decision, eventually stayed the proceedings. Phila Marsden had nevertheless won a victory of sorts. Not only had she dragged Maclean's name through the mud for months in a trial which set a record as the longest in the province's history; she was sympathetically portrayed in press accounts headlined: "Would Forgive Man She Claims Wronged Her. Pathetic Story is Told by Main Witness in Retrial of Local Medico."[100]

What was printed in the columns of the local newspapers represented for some the potentially most damaging punishment. Doctors were naturally frightened at the prospect of the tarnishing of their reputation that the appearance of their names in the news could cause. Women dreaded having their most intimate acts made a subject of public discussion. But more importantly press reports, in dwelling on gruesome deaths, both made an example of the "guilty" woman who had died at the hands of an abortionist and warned off others who might contemplate a similar gamble. Headlines such as "Her Horrible Death," "Young Life Cut Off Very Suddenly," "Illegal Operation Results in Death of Woman and a Charge of Murder" carried the moral that the woman who tried to interfere with nature inevitably paid a terrible price.[101] Such lurid stories made good copy. It could be argued that newspaper editors were not necessarily trying to play up the dangers of abortion, that they were alerted to and reported on only the most tragic cases, but to do so would require crediting journalists with an unlikely ignorance of what was actually taking place in their communities.

The historian is supposed to differ from the journalist in being candid about the shortcomings of his or her sources. In drawing to a conclusion our analysis of abortion we have to recall our opening proviso that inquest and court records tell only part of the story. Because our sources draw primarily from disastrous attempts at abortion we have only had brief glimpses of women — facing the crisis of an unwanted pregnancy — supported by their male partners and their female friends and neighbors. Nevertheless the dogged determination and courage of individual women, often abandoned by those closest to them, is undeniable. Much of what we have reviewed makes for unpleasant reading: married mothers of children dying of septic poisoning, husbands pretending not to know what was going on, young men bullying young women into dangerous operations, doctors refusing to help, and incompetent abortionists demanding money. But we should not forget that almost everyone was victimized by an inequitable and unenforceable law.

What did the law accomplish? Though there was scant evidence that its avowed purpose of protecting fetal life was served, the law did have its uses. Some regular physicians found that it could be employed to shore up their profession's monopolization of the provision of medical services. The abortionists who were convicted were usually not doctors, but midwives, masseuses, and herbalists. When a maverick physician like Dr. John Garden was found guilty of abortion in 1895, it was chiefly because he did not have the support of the medical profession; he himself declared that he was a victim of a conspiracy of doctors.[102] The law similarly extended the reach of the judiciary. The courts, abetted by the press, brandished the accounts of horrific abortion deaths as a warning to all women and so sought to police the morality of both sexes. Abortion trials, which contain potentially disturbing evidence of class and gender inequities, were "turned to account" in defense of the social and sexual status quo.

At best coroners and jurors simply ignored the law. At worst, as was made chillingly clear in 1936, such a statute could blight more than one life. In that year Helen McDonald died as a result of a botched operation, her fiancé — who considered himself responsible — committed suicide, and Edith Pierce, the abortionist, having endured a trial and two appeals, took her own life.[103]

Given the limitations of the sources used here, the claim could never be made that the entire impact of the criminalization of abortion has been surveyed. But this analysis — of the negotiations of husbands and wives, of single men and single women, of doctors and patients, of police and the public — reveals the ways in which the law poisoned relationships which were often already inherently difficult. It is not necessary to argue that people are innately good, to recognize that such laws made many worse than they had to be.

QUESTIONS TO CONSIDER

1. What differences and similarities are evident between historical examples of abortion practices and abortion law presented by McLaren, and these practices and measures in contemporary Canada? Discuss access to abortion, conflicting assessments of abortion (as a right, a sin, a crime), and pressures on the medical profession to perform, or not perform, abortions.

2. Debate whether abortion law should be incorporated under the criminal law, under another form of law, or not regulated at all. Examine benefits to each approach: criminalization, regulation, and removing legal sanctions and powers altogether. Address the question of whether prosecution of abortionists should be avoided on the basis that abortion can be termed a "victimless crime."

3. To what extent was women's economic, social, and political status in the nineteenth and early twentieth century reflected in abortion legislation of the time? Review the role of social movements and social classes in debating the abortion issue in the time period covered by McLaren's essay.

NOTES

1. Attorney General of British Columbia (hereafter AG [BC]) Inquisitions, 1919: 138 (reel 33).
2. Edward Shorter, *A History of Women's Bodies* (New York, 1982), 177–224; James Woycke, *Birth Control in Germany, 1871–1933* (London, 1988), 68–111.

3. James Mohr, *Abortion in America: The Origins and Evolution of National Policy* (New York, 1978); John Keown, *Abortion, Doctors and the Law: Some Aspects of the Legal Regulation of Abortion in England from 1803 to 1982* (Cambridge, 1988).
4. Constance Backhouse, "Involuntary Motherhood: Abortion, Birth Control and the Law in Nineteenth-Century Canada," *Windsor Yearbook of Access to Justice* 3 (1983): 61–130; Shelley Gavigan, "The Criminal Sanction as It Relates to Human Reproduction," *Journal of Legal History* 5 (1984): 20–41.
5. AG (BC) Inquisitions, 1895: 64 (reel 4).
6. AG (BC) Inquisitions, 1933: 176 (reel 65).
7. AG (BC) Court Records, 1901: 103 (v. 129).
8. Angus McLaren and Arlene Tigar McLaren, *The Bedroom and the State: The Changing Practices and Politics of Contraception and Abortion in Canada, 1880–1980* (Toronto, 1986), 32–53.
9. AG (BC) Inquisitions, 1919: 105 (reel 33).
10. AG (BC) Inquisitions, 1914: 255 (reel 23).
11. AG (BC) Inquisitions, 1936: 266 (reel 72).
12. AG (BC) Inquisitions, 1922: 216 (reel 40).
13. AG (BC) Inquisitions, 1928: 260 (reel 53).
14. AG (BC) Inquisitions, 1931: 283 (reel 62).
15. AG (BC) Inquisitions, 1886: 46 (reel 1).
16. Angus McLaren, "Birth Control and Abortion in Canada, 1870–1920," *Canadian Historical Review* 59 (1978): 319–40.
17. AG (BC) Inquisitions, 1896: 110 (reel 5).
18. AG (BC) Inquisitions, 1919: 105 (reel 33).
19. AG (BC) Inquisitions, 1935: 156 (reel 69).
20. AG (BC) Inquisitions, 1926: 316 (reel 49).
21. AG (BC) Inquisitions, 1920: 346 (reel 36).
22. AG (BC) Court Records, 1923: 31 (v. 266).
23. AG (BC) Correspondence, Inquiries, 1924: Vancouver C49-6 (reel 108).
24. AG (BC) Inquisitions, 1921: 249 (reel 38).
25. AG (BC) Inquisitions, 1913: 141 (reel 20); AG (BC) Court Records, 1913: 198 (v. 179).
26. W.A. Dafoe, "Abortion," *Canadian Medical Association Journal* 22 (1930): 793.
27. AG (BC) Inquisitions, 1935: 193 (reel 70).
28. See for example AG (BC) Inquisitions, 1916: 261 (reel 28).
29. AG (BC) Court Records, 1915: 113 (v. 202).
30. AG (BC) Inquisitions, 1933: 92 (reel 64).
31. On Finnish-Canadian women's reliance on each other see, Varpu Lindström-Best, *Defiant Sisters: A Social History of Finnish Immigrant Women in Canada* (Toronto, 1988), 79–83; and for similar findings elsewhere see, Barbara Brookes, *Abortion in England, 1900–1967* (London, 1988), 29–35.
32. AG (BC) Inquisitions, 1919: 138 (reel 33).
33. AG (BC), Inquisitions, 1910: 257 (reel 15).; AG (BC) Court Records, 1912: 8 (v. 155).
34. AG (BC) Court Records, 1915: 27 (v. 197).
35. AG (BC) Inquisitions, 1920: 346 (reel 36).
36. Vancouver *Sun*, 30 October 1922, 13; Vancouver *Sun*, 27 November 1922, 13; Vancouver *Daily Province*, 5 August 1922, 20.
37. Boon died of blood poisoning on her return to Victoria; AG (BC) Inquisitions, 1912: 6 (reel 17); Vancouver *Daily Province*, 3 January 1912, 1.
38. AG (BC) Inquisitions, 1917: 175 (reel 29).
39. Vancouver *Sun*, 9 January 1918, 12; AG (BC) Inquisitions, 1918: 5 (reel 29); and on Edith Watson's death see, AG (BC) Inquisitions, 1920: 330 (reel 36).
40. On Emily Bard's death see AG (BC) Inquisitions, 1921: 46 (reel 370); on Florence Smith's death see AG (BC) Inquisitions, 1921: 55 (reel 37).

41. On a profile of American abortionists convicted in New York between 1925 and 1950, see Jerome E. Bates and Edward S. Zawadzki, *Criminal Abortion: A Study in Medical Sociology* (Springfield, IL, 1964), 202–203.

42. AG (BC) Court Records, 1917: 31 (v. 209).

43. Clara Jesson was tried in 1923 and sentenced to one year in prison. At her establishment the police found speculums and gum elastic catheters; AG (BC) Court Records, 1923: 82 (v. 271). In 1927 she was implicated in one successful abortion and one abortion death. AG (BC) Court Records, 1928: 17 (v. 329); AG (BC) Inquisitions, 1927: 375 (reel 52); Vancouver *Daily Province*, 14 March 1928, 20.

44. In 1931 Morris was charged as an accessory in the death of Agnes Little. Little's sister testified that she also had been aborted by Morris. AG (BC) Inquisitions, 1931: 174 (reel 61); AG (BC) Court Records, 1931: 134 (v. 384). In 1935 Morris was again charged with procuring a miscarriage. AG (BC) Court Records, 1935: 97 (v. 436).

45. AG (BC) Court Records, 1939: 21 (v. 478); AG (BC) Court Records, 1939: 21 (v. 478); *B.C. Reports*, 1939 (v. 54, pp. 134–36).

46. Pierce was in 1935 implicated in two deaths and found guilty of manslaughter. AG (BC) Inquisitions, 1936: 169 (reel 71); AG (BC) Court Records, 1936: 54 (v. 447); *B.C. Reports*, 1937–38 (v. 52, pp. 264–75); *Canada Law Reports: Supreme Court of Canada*, 1938 (pp. 457–58).

47. AG (BC) Inquisitions, 1914: 255 (reel 23).

48. AG (BC) Inquisitions, 1928: 260 (reel 53).

49. AG (BC) Inquisitions, 1936: 173 (reel 71).

50. AG (BC) Inquisitions, 1913: 141 (reel 20).

51. AG (BC) Inquisitions, 1898: 122 (reel 6).

52. AG (BC) Court Records, 1905: 81 (v. 110).

53. AG (BC) Inquisitions, 1921: 46 (reel 37).

54. AG (BC) Inquisitions, 1886: 46 (reel 1).

55. AG (BC) Inquisitions, 1913: 21 (reel 19).

56. AG (BC) Inquisitions, 1913: 141 (reel 20).

57. AG (BC) Inquisitions, 1928: 260 (reel 53).

58. AG (BC) Vancouver *Daily Province*, 3 July 1914, 12.

59. AG (BC) Court Records, 1895: 63 (v. 57).

60. AG (BC), Inquisitions 1904: 102 (reel 9); Victoria *Daily Colonist*, 31 July 1904, 1. On the changing sexual activities of youths, see Veronica Strong-Boag, *The New Day Recalled: Lives of Girls and Women in English Canada, 1919–1939* (Toronto, 1988), 84–90.

61. AG (BC) Court Records, 1929: 31 (v. 347).

62. Victoria *Daily Times*, 29 December 1934; AG (BC) Inquisitions, 1934: 215 (reel 67).

63. Schwam's appeal was turned down by the British Columbia Court of Appeal, but the Supreme Court of Canada, holding that the dying declaration was inadmissible, reversed the judgment and quashed the conviction. *B.C. Reports*, 1935–36, v. 50, pp. 1–18; *Canada Law Reports: Supreme Court of Canada*, 1935, pp. 367–78.

64. AG (BC) Court Records, 1931: 134 (v. 384). The death by septicemia in 1895 of Mary Ellen Jones was followed by the arrest of Harry Crew, her fiancé, as an accessory to murder; he was, along with Dr. John Garden, eventually found guilty of manslaughter. AG (BC) Court Records, 1896: 28 (v. 62); on affirmation of conviction, see *B.C. Reports*, 1895–97, v. 5, pp. 61–66; Backhouse, "Involuntary Motherhood," 106–107.

65. AG (BC) Court Records, 1911: 33 (v. 147); Vancouver *Daily News-Advertiser*, 6 May 1911, 3.

66. AG (BC) Court Records, 1915: 113 (v. 202).

67. AG (BC) Inquisitions, 1920: 346 (reel 36).

68. Mohr, *Abortion in America*; Keown, *Abortion, Doctors and the Law*.

69. Morrow was criticized by the Vancouver coroner for not notifying the authorities of the abortion until after Young's death. Vancouver *Daily Province*, 5 August 1922, 28; AG (BC) Inquisitions, 1922: 208 (reel 40).

70. AG (BC) Inquisitions, 1930: 255 (reel 59).

71. AG (BC) Inquisitions, 1919: 138 (reel 33).

72. Victoria *Times*, 29 September 1917, 17.

73. AG (BC) Court Records, 1916: 9 (v. 203).

74. AG (BC) Courts Records, 1922: 129 (v. 259).

75. *B.C. Reports*, 1939 (v. 54, pp. 134–136).

76. AG (BC) Inquisitions, 1921: 249 (reel 38).

77. AG (BC) Inquisitions, 1886: 46 (reel 1).

78. AG (BC) Inquisitions, 1904: 88 (reel 9).

79. AG (BC) Inquisitions, 1931 (reel 60).

80. AG (BC) Inquisitions, 1922: 108 (reel 39).

81. Victoria *Colonist*, 8 March 1923, 5; AG (BC) Court Records, 1923: 31 (v. 266).

82. AG (BC) Inquisitions, 1920: 346 (reel 36).

83. AG (BC) Inquisitions, 1931: 174 (reel 61); and see also Shelley Gavigan, "On 'Bringing on the Menses': The Criminal Liability of Women and the Therapeutic Exception in Canadian Abortion Law," *Canadian Journal of Women and the Law* 1 (1986): 279–312.

84. AG (BC) Inquisitions, 1915: 352 (reel 26); AG (BC) Court Records, 1916: 30 (v. 204).

85. AG (BC) Inquisitions, 1920: 346 (reel 36); AG (BC) Court Records, 1921: 31 (v. 239).

86. AG (BC) Inquisitions, 1931: 301 (reel 62); and see *Vernon News* clipping in same file.

87. AG (BC) Inquisitions, 1919: 138 (reel 33).

88. AG (BC) Inquisitions, 1926: 313 (reel 49). Vernon also treated Rose Wood, who died of septic poisoning in 1928. AG (BC) Inquisitions, 1928: 353 (reel 54). In 1909 Vernon was tried for abortion, but his argument that the woman who accused him was a black-mailer won him an acquittal. Vancouver *Daily Province*, 3 May 1909, 1; 4 May 1909, 1.

89. AG (BC) Inquisitions, 1904: 102 (reel 9); Vancouver *Daily Province*, 8 November 1905, 1. Temple was also the attending physician of Frances Pike, who died in 1918 as a result of an operation in Seattle. AG (BC) Inquisitions, 1918: 5 (reel 29). Temple was returned to the medical register in 1909.

90. AG (BC) Inquisitions, 1936: 266 (reel 72).

91. For an excellent account of the way "investigative procedures themselves constituted a form of punishment and control," see Leslie J. Reagan, "'About to Meet Her Maker': Women, Doctors, Dying Declarations, and the State's Investigation of Abortion, Chicago, 1867–1940," *Journal of American History* 77 (1991): 1240–64.

92. AG (BC), Inquisitions, 1910: 257 (reel 15); AG (BC) Court Records, 1912: 8 (v. 155).

93. Vancouver *Daily Province*, 24 November 1914, 12.

94. On the theatrical aspects of courtroom ritual, see Paul Craven, "Law and Ideology: The Toronto Police Court, 1850–80," in David H. Flaherty, ed., *Essays in the History of Canadian Law*, vol. 2 (Toronto, 1983), 248–307.

95. AG (BC) Court Records, 1902: 20 (v. 92).

96. *B.C. Reports*, 1900–1903, v. 9, p. 294; *Nelson Daily News*, 10 May 1902, 1.

97. On women's ability to use the law by playing up the role of the "wronged woman," see Ruth Harris, *Murder and Madness: Medicine, Law and Society in the Fin de Siècle* (Oxford, 1989); Mary S. Hartman, *Victorian Murderesses* (New York, 1977).

98. AG (BC) Court Records, 1908: 103 (v. 129).

99. AG (BC) Court Records, 1915: 23 (v. 197); Vancouver *Daily Province*, 20 November 1914, 14; 3 May 1915, 16.

100. Vancouver *World*, 28 November 1914, 16.

101. Vancouver *Daily Province*, 15 August 1898, 8; Vancouver *Daily World*, 25 July 1904, p. 8; Vancouver *Sun*, 3 July 1914, 2.

102. Victoria *Daily Times*, 27 July 1896, 5; Victoria *Daily Colonist*, 28 July 1896, 6.

103. AG (BC) Court Records, 1936: 54 (v. 447). The file on Edith Pierce's suicide — AG (BC) Inquisitions, 1937: C 49-1, (reel 176) — is lost.

PART TWO
Morality and the Criminal Law

The criminal law represents a society's most formal attempt to control the behaviour of its citizens. Although it can be argued that all types of law are ultimately forms of social control, the imposition of criminal sanctions is specifically designed to deal with activities that are considered a threat to the entire society. Although there is general consensus that activities such as murder, robbery, and assault clearly fit this criterion, the criminal law is also used to control activities that do not constitute so clear a threat.

The first three articles in this section focus on the application of Canadian criminal law to three activities that are frequently classed as "victimless crimes": drug use, prostitution, and pornography. Many people argue that these activities involve moral choices and that the application of the criminal law enforces moral values that may not be shared by the participants or by society generally. The fourth article included in this section deals with corporate crime. Although this topic is not usually included in academic discussions of morality and the law, it is included here because many members of the general public appear to consider it a type of "victimless crime." In this respect, much of the public debate about crime focusses on activities such as drug use, prostitution, and pornography, and excludes all but the most sensational examples of corporate crime. Because so many people are unaware of the nature and extent of corporate crime, it is important to understand the harm associated with it and contrast it with the other crimes discussed in this section.

The first article deals with the issue of pornography. In "LEAF and Pornography: Litigating on Equality and Sexual Representations," Karen Busby discusses the position taken by LEAF (the Women's Legal Education and Action Fund) as an intervenor in the *Butler* case. In this case, which arose out of the prosecution of a Winnipeg adult bookstore, the Supreme Court of Canada upheld the constitutional validity of Canada's obscenity law and attempted to clarify the types of sexually explicit material that are prohibited. In explaining LEAF's position, Busby reviews many of the issues that are currently part of the pornography debate. Although the Supreme Court decision generally prohibited portrayals of sexual activity that is violent, dehumanizing, or involves children, it seemed to argue that other types of explicit sex were acceptable. Busby argues that LEAF decided that this decision essentially approved some types of exploitive sexual activity and thus failed to address several issues of extreme importance to many feminists. For example, she argues that much of the pornography created for "white heterosexual males" contributes to women's oppression by perpetuating rape myths and other forms of sexual aggression directed against women and children. She further argues that the actual production of pornography exploits female actors, many of whom come from abusive backgrounds and/or are coerced to perform in these productions. For these reasons, Busby argues that the Supreme Court decision was too narrow in prohibiting only child pornography and pornography that is violent or degrading in actual content.

In addition to discussing the harm toward women and children that is associated with pornography, Busby also reviews several other issues involved in the debate, including freedom of expression and the way in which obscenity laws are frequently used to repress representations of gay and lesbian sexuality. She argues that the question of freedom of expression must be discussed within the context of women's inequality, and that pornography actually denies many women freedom of expression. Although she recognizes that restricting sexual imagery might negatively affect the artistic community, she argues that the law contains ample provisions for a defence based on "artistic merit." Busby concludes her analysis by reviewing how the issues that affect gay and lesbian pornography may be different from those affecting heterosexual pornography. She notes, however, that obscenity laws have frequently been enforced in a discriminatory manner to target pornography made for the gay and lesbian market. She suggests that these practices might continue after the *Butler* decision and argues that all affected groups (gay, lesbian, and feminist) need to participate in a debate aimed at shaping the further interpretation of Canada's obscenity laws.

The second article in this section conducts a critical analysis of the changes to Canada's prostitution laws resulting from Bill C-49 in 1985. In "The Politics of Law Reform: Prostitution Policy in Canada, 1985–1995," Nick Larsen discusses the implementation of Bill C-49 in Vancouver, Toronto, Winnipeg, and Edmonton. Larsen outlines the origins of the bill in the aftermath of the 1978 *Hutt* decision — which had weakened anti-soliciting provisions in the Criminal Code — and criticizes the role of Canadian police in the enactment of this extremely controversial piece of legislation. He notes that the enforcement of the law between 1985 and 1995 was primarily dictated by political expediency, in which the police and local politicians reacted to pressure from different interest groups. This was particularly true in Vancouver and Toronto, where middle-class residents and corporate interests dominated the prostitution control debate to the detriment of working-class residents and other groups. Larsen argues that Bill C-49 was largely ineffective in all four cities, despite concerted enforcement efforts by the police. He notes that the only instance in which the law was relatively successful occurred in the Strathcona area of Vancouver, when police encouraged negotiation between prostitutes and affected residents. Larsen concludes that involving prostitutes in the discussions regarding prostitution control offers the only real hope that the excesses of the prostitution trade can be controlled.

The third article in this section is Barney Sneiderman's discussion of drug enforcement policies. In "Just Say No to the War on Drugs," Sneiderman analyzes the failure of the current drug-prohibitionist policies employed in Canada and the United States. He begins by outlining the origins of the war on drugs in the aftermath of the Vietnam War and traces the development of that policy into a volatile political issue that has seen the United States incarcerate a greater proportion of its citizens than South Africa did during the apartheid era. Using a satirical style that takes the form of conversations between a visiting alien and various Canadian drug experts, Sneiderman critically discusses many of the myths and misconceptions that motivate contemporary drug enforcement policies in Canada and the United States. In addition to questioning the link between drugs and crime, he also criticizes the hypocrisy implicit in the contradiction between the legality of alcohol and tobacco and the criminal status of marijuana. He argues that during the 1920s, prohibition of alcohol in the United States was unsuccessful, and that our current prohibitionist approach to marijuana and other drugs is also doomed to failure. He concludes by arguing for the decriminalization of marijuana, combined with the adoption of a "health model" to deal with other forms of drug abuse.

The final article in this section discusses the role of corporate wrongdoing in Canadian society. In "Corporate Crime," Robert Gordon and Ian Coneybeer argue that the economic history of Canada is filled with examples of corporate wrongdoing, ranging from political scandals to environmental exploitation and consumer fraud on a grand scale. In the contemporary context, Gordon and Coneybeer discuss five categories of corporate crimes: crimes against the economy, against the environment, against consumers, against humanity, and against employees. They argue that the material and physical harm caused by corporate deviance far exceeds that attributed to predatory street crime, but attracts little public attention. For this reason, it appears to constitute a de facto victimless crime, and the participants are rarely censured or stigmatized in the same manner as the participants in street crimes or other "victimless" activities such as drug use or prostitution. Further, much corporate deviance is not clearly illegal, and, in any case, the laws are poorly enforced. Thus, when one compares the enormous social harm caused by corporate wrongdoing to that attributed to such activities as drug use and prostitution, it would seem clear that Canadian society has misapplied its sense of "morality."

THREE

LEAF and Pornography: Litigating on Equality and Sexual Representations[1]

KAREN BUSBY

In August 1987, the Winnipeg police seized the entire inventory of the video store owned by Donald Butler. He and an employee were charged with about 250 offences under the *Criminal Code* obscenity[2] provisions. Most of the seized materials were sexually explicit videos or magazines for heterosexual men; a small number involved gay men. Ultimately, the case proceeded to the Supreme Court of Canada, where the court considered, for the first time, the effect of the *Charter's* free expression guarantee on the obscenity law. The issue *Butler* presented was whether the *Charter* limits or proscribes government power to criminalize the sale of pornographic materials.

The Women's Legal Education and Action Fund (LEAF) intervened in *R. v. Butler*,[3] arguing the *Charter's* freedom of expression guarantee had to be read in light of the *Charter's* equality guarantees, with a focus on pornography's harms to women. While we have been involved in more than 100 cases and other projects, none has come close to generating the widespread controversy created by *Butler*. (Indeed, many people think that pornography is the *sole* issue in LEAF's mandate, even though this is the only obscenity case in which we have participated.) Since *Butler's* release, our position has been simplified, even caricatured, and criticized, sometimes vociferously, by the media, civil libertarians, and some lesbians and gay men. This

Source: Karen Busby, "LEAF and Pornography: Litigating on Equality and Sexual Representations," *Revue canadienne droit et société/Canadian Journal of Law and Society* 9, no. 1 (1994): 165–92.

paper will discuss the obscenity law before and after *Butler*, LEAF's position in the case and how that analysis affects lesbians and gay men, the impact of *Butler* in the artistic community, and how LEAF has been presented in the media since *Butler*. In addition to providing information and responding to some of the criticisms, we also hope to foster continuing dialogue on what position LEAF should take in the future on issues related to equality and sexual representations.

WHAT WAS THE LAW BEFORE *BUTLER*?

Before the Supreme Court of Canada's decision in the *Butler* case, interpretations of the *Criminal Code* obscenity provisions were vague and inconsistent. The *Criminal Code* prohibits the "undue exploitation of sex" and judges had interpreted this as prohibiting materials that the community would not tolerate others seeing. In turn, determination of the "community standard" required a judge to articulate a "general instinctive sense of what is decent and what is indecent."[4] For example, when the Manitoba Court of Appeal considered the *Butler* case, it condemned all sexually explicit imagery as immoral, finding that any deviations from conservative notions of modesty and permissiveness were illegal. The materials were considered inherently undesirable, independent of any harm.

Before the Supreme Court of Canada decision in *Butler*, it was not clear whether sexually explicit imagery, whose apparent purpose was simply to entertain or sexually arouse, or artistic works dealing with sexual themes would violate the test on the basis of "undue exploitation of sex." And it was far from certain that lesbian or gay materials, even where they were not explicitly about sex, or heterosexual representations purporting to represent lesbianism would survive an application of the "community tolerance" test.[5] Any change to these interpretations of the obscenity law had to be an improvement.

WHAT POSITION DID LEAF TAKE IN THE *BUTLER* CASE?

LEAF's mandate is to promote women's equality through challenges to laws and practices that contribute to systemic or institutional inequalities. LEAF is committed to developing arguments designed to promote substantive equality for all women, including women of colour, lesbians, women with disabilities, and economically disadvantaged women. LEAF had four options in the *Butler* case. We could have accepted the law as it had been interpreted; supported a position that would have eliminated any criminal regulation of pornography; asked the court to strike down the *Criminal Code* provisions and to invite Parliament to introduce new legislation; or, asked the court to redefine the rationale for the *Criminal Code* obscenity provisions by focusing on their equality implications for women and children. Each option was assessed in light of its implications for women's equality and its effects on substantive equality claims of men who are part of historically subordinated communities.

The first option, accepting the law as it had been interpreted, was rejected. LEAF argued that moral intolerance, which is the rationale underlying the conservative case for criminal regulation of most, if not all, sexually explicit imagery, should not be the basis for a conviction. It was this rationale that made materials depicting lesbians or gay men vulnerable to prosecution and reduced feminists' political critiques of pornography to disputes about good taste. We stated in our factum that the traditional rationale for obscenity laws contributed to a "... host of problems, weaknesses, and potential legal disabilities ... includ[ing] vagueness, subjectivity, gender bias, potential for abuse as a mechanism for censorship, and difficulties of proof and effective enforcement."

The remaining three options required a more in-depth consideration of how some forms of pornography contribute to women's oppression and whether these are amenable to state regulation.

HOW DOES PORNOGRAPHY CONTRIBUTE TO WOMEN'S OPPRESSION?

Most feminists are concerned about the harms some pornography engenders. As there is a gross distortion of power in our society in favour of heterosexual white men, any cultural forms and practices that may contribute to this distortion need to be examined. Sexual representations of women created by and for these men must be part of this study. In particular, therefore, we need to examine the theoretical and empirical links between pornography and systemic sexual violence.

Some pornography combines sex and the infliction of violence or humiliation, other depictions sexualize racism or the vulnerability of children or women with disabilities. These depictions eroticize sexual and racist aggression and male dominance, and perpetuate rape myths in a culture where sexual violence against women and children is pervasive. Some of the seized heterosexual materials in *Butler* presented women being raped (in one video an actual rape was filmed), in bondage to men, subjected to racist insults, as children (some actually appeared to be children),[6] sadists, and masochists. In a photo layout titled "Dyke Meat," lesbians were presented as rapists and aggressive recruiters to lesbianism. Brother–sister incest was presented. No materials presented safe sex. One video failed to edit out a black woman being revived with an oxygen mask. She had passed out while performing oral sex at the bottom of a pile of five people performing oral sex on each other.

One form of harm that may exist is a connection between pornography use and an increased propensity to, or tolerance of, physical aggression including sexual assault against women. While some researchers have demonstrated a link between use of some forms of pornography and such actions or attitudes, others assert that the connection cannot be supported. The fact is that social scientists are not capable of proving whether there is or is not a *direct* link between pornography and other forms of violence including sexual assault. Clearly there is a need for further study on the causes of pervasive sexual violence, but in the meantime, LEAF chose not to ignore the substantial body of empirical research indicating that pornography is implicated.

Another area of inquiry is to look to women's direct experiences in pornography production. Pornography produced by straight, white men capitalizes on women's social and economic inequality. Some women and children in the pornography industry are sexual abuse survivors. Others living in poverty sell their bodies to survive. Some are coerced or forced into making the materials, or cope with the work through drug use. Some are physically, psychologically, and sexually hurt during production.[7] It is trite to say that employment laws do not protect the participants. A question that should be thought about in relation to every sexually explicit image is: "What did the women and men in the picture have to do so that the producers could get the shot?"

Pornography can also hurt women associated with its users. Some women's partners humiliate or terrorize them into imitating pornographic materials. Susan Cole's study on women staying at a battered women's shelter found that 25% were forced to perform acts their partners saw in pornography.[8] The presence of pornography in some contexts, like workplaces, serves to harass, even exclude, women.

The freedom of expression guarantee, which wrongly presupposes that everyone has equal access to the marketplace of ideas, is meant to facilitate truth seeking, foster social and political decision making, and permit diversity in individual self-flourishing. Some pornography, on the other hand, inhibits women from telling the truth, undermines respect for our words, and is the antithesis of self-fulfillment for most women. In other words, it denies women free expression. Furthermore, it sexualizes bigotry, contempt, and even hatred for every class of people white men have constructed as less than fully human: white women, women of colour, First Nations women, disabled women, lesbians, prostitutes, and feminists, as well as men from subordinated groups. Pornography is a multi-faceted, systemic practice of exploitation and subordination based on sex that differentially and materially harms women. It plays an important part[9] in the social construction of sexual inequality and, in particular, erodes the potential for any serious assertion of equality rights. When seen in this way, our thinking around pornography must involve a serious assessment of its impact on substantive equality, and not just on the unbridled protection of freedom of expression.

In summary, the relationship between heterosexual pornography and violence against women arising from its use and its creation as established by empirical evidence, and the theoretical links between pornography and the denial to women of freedom of expression are serious, present harms that deny women equality. In light of this, LEAF could not support a strategy of inaction. The *Butler* case could not be argued without reference to the equality interests at stake and, as ultimately proved to be so, only LEAF argued the case on the basis of equality.

IS PORNOGRAPHY AMENABLE TO STATE REGULATION?

While feminists share a broadly based consensus that there is a relationship between some pornography and sexual inequality, the issue of which strategies to pursue in the face of these harms is complex. Some advocate finding places for materials on diverse sexualities which do not exacerbate sex and race inequality. Others encourage direct action like picketing or boycotting. Still others emphasize education on the multiple meanings and effects of all media representations of women. But these strategies, which are not mutually exclusive, rely on isolated and often ignored counter-voices attempting to counter a multi-billion dollar business. Their ability to displace a culture of pervasive inequality is minimal.

In addition to these strategies some look to the law to regulate pornography. Since LEAF's mandate is to promote women's equality through legal action, our work on pornography focuses on obscenity law. Every woman working with LEAF recognizes that, at best, the legal arena is a forum where social change can sometimes be facilitated. In spite of law's limitations, we do not accept that women should abandon law while struggling to transform other institutions which contribute to the subordination of women, principally because law is so implicated in shaping and rationalizing these institutions. Furthermore, this forum has the potential to disrupt established social and political norms. Using litigation to accomplish feminist goals holds as much promise and as much risk as any other form of self-help political activism.

Feminist litigation on pornography provides opportunities for expressive moments on (and acts as the catalyst for further analysis of) the relationship between sexual subordination of women, sexual violence, and the laws that legitimate this violence. It can also lead to an exposure of subtle and not-so-subtle discrimination against those who produce and distribute materials — whether about sexuality or otherwise — that do not conform to gender role dictates imposed and enforced by dominant groups. Finally, it is one place to deliver an important social and political message about variously situated women's equality which, in the context of pornography, is a demand that the discourse on sexual representation be shifted from decency to power.

The *Butler* case focused on whether any sexually explicit representations could and should be subject to criminal prohibition. For some feminists, the disadvantages of criminal prohibition outweigh its benefits. While aspects of pornography contribute to all women's sexual subordination, its proliferation especially harms some, including women of colour and poor women. But its regulation poses greater risks to other women, most notably lesbians and artists.[10] Every feminist is concerned about violence against women and we agree that significant psychic energy and financial and other resources must be dedicated to exposing and working against sexual, racial, and homophobic violence, whatever its form. At the same time, there is a concern that over-emphasizing sexuality's oppressive forms eclipses feminist explorations of eroticism[11] both because the message about sexuality that this research reveals seems, at times, hopelessly pessimistic and because the work itself leaves little energy or impulse for desire.

While exploring women's sexualities must be a feminist project, LEAF could not support a position that would have eliminated any criminal regulation of pornography given the pervasive, direct effects of pornography on women's lives. Just as it will not end sexual assault, criminal prohibition will not eliminate harmful pornography. But it might discourage production of its violent forms, require distributors to evaluate what they are distributing, facilitate civil suits against pornographers, in addition to delivering a political message on pornography's contribution to women's inequality. We were reluctant to ask the court to strike down the *Criminal Code* provisions with an invitation to Parliament to introduce new legislation because we feared that the Conservative government would introduce another morals-based law that would have cast a long shadow over gay or lesbian imagery and artistic work without addressing harms to women.

LEAF argued that the existing obscenity law could be interpreted to promote equality, and to the extent that materials are proscribed on any other basis, the law is unconstitutional. The materials that pose the most serious threat to equality include those made from direct acts of coercion or violence. Pornography made from actual assaults is not worthy of protection. Similarly, using children to make sex pictures is a form of child abuse and should not be protected. We then argued that depictions of explicit sex with violence (including threats of violence) lead to an increased risk of sexual violence against women and therefore should be suppressed.

Finally materials that degrade or dehumanize women have been shown, among other things, to contribute to an increased acceptance of women's sexual servitude and increased callousness towards women. Accordingly, we argued that these should be proscribed as well.

Enforcement of obscenity laws rests with state agents including the police, customs officers, Crown attorneys, and judges. If these agents ignore or do not care to understand the equality/harms-based analysis, they will revert to enforcement policies based on moralism. LEAF has been criticized for naively relying on the patriarchal state for protection.[12] Reliance on state power is always an incomplete, imperfect strategy and its use in relation to pornography is no exception. LEAF is simply attempting to force the state to extend its protection in order to fulfil its promise of security of the person for all women. In other words, we want criminal law to work for women. This is an equality argument. Further, the alternative is an unregulated pornography industry and there is little evidence that the other proposed strategies will have much effect on the so-called free market. Therefore, as will be discussed later, LEAF's response to state agents' abuse of an equality analysis is not to reject that analysis, but to expose, explore, denounce and, ultimately, legally censure the abuse.

WHAT IS THE OBSCENITY LAW AFTER *BUTLER*?

The Supreme Court of Canada recognized that the obscenity law interfered with the freedom of expression guarantee. But, in upholding the law, the court recognized that such interference was justified under Section 1 of the *Charter*, as there is a rational connection between the obscenity law and the objectives it sought to achieve, and as the law minimally impairs freedom of expression. The court rejected an approach to obscenity based on moral disapprobation and modesty stating that "... this particular objective is no longer defensible in view of the *Charter*." The court focused, instead, on the likelihood of harm and the threat to equality flowing from circulation of the materials. The court stated that: "[I]f true equality between male and female is to be achieved, we cannot ignore the threat to equality resulting from exposure to audiences of certain types of violent and degrading materials. Materials portraying women as a class worthy of sexual exploitation and abuse have a negative impact on the individual's sense of self-worth and acceptance."[13]

The court recognized that a direct link between pornography and violence was not susceptible to exact proof. But, as the court did in other cases where the link between expression and harm was impossible to prove conclusively (for example, cases on hate propaganda and advertising directed at children), it recognized a connection sufficient to uphold the impugned law. In other words, there was a reasonable basis for an obscenity law. It held that pornography showing sex with violence (including threats of violence) would almost always be prohibited. Explicit sex that is degrading and dehumanizing would be prohibited if the risk of harm is substantial, that is, if it predisposed people to act in an anti-social manner. Finally, sexually explicit materials involving children are prohibited.

Legislation which interferes with a *Charter* guarantee must do so as minimally as possible. The *Butler* decision made it clear that sexually explicit depictions were protected by the *Charter*'s freedom of expression guarantee even if their sole purpose was to sexually arouse, as long as they do not involve sex and violence, degradation, or children. The court stated the obscenity law cannot "inhibit the celebration of human sexuality." In addition, the court stated that artistic work was at the heart of freedom of expression and accordingly was to be protected. Courts are to be "generous" when characterizing work as art and "any doubt must be resolved in favour of expression."[14]

LEAF, like many organizations which view violence against women as a measure and agent of women's inequality, count the court's decision in *Butler* as a feminist breakthrough. It marks an extraordinary shift in the traditional rationale for obscenity laws from a community standard based on a general instinctive sense of what is decent and what is indecent (the *Brodie* standard)[15] to an obscenity law premised on sex inequality and harms to women. While *Butler* still refers to a "community standard," the test has been so altered that resemblance to the pre-*Butler* standard is in name only. The court explicitly recognized that the pre-*Butler* "community standards" test did little to elucidate the underlying question as to why some exploitation of sex falls on the permitted side and some on the prohibited side.[16] The law no longer retains one universal standard of morally acceptable sexual representations.

LEAF believes that this law, *if appropriately applied*, will prohibit pornography's most harmful forms, that is, those that combine sex with violence, degradation, or the depiction of children. It should also curb state repression of books, videos, images, and art historically deemed morally "indecent" or "disgusting" by a heterosexist society.

The *Butler* decision does not say anything specific about depictions of lesbian or gay sexual activity. However, while discussing the moralism which had animated the law, the court stated that:

> To impose a certain standard of public and sexual morality, solely because it reflects the conventions of a given community, is inimical to the exercise and enjoyment of individual freedoms, which form the basis of our social contract. David Dyzenhaus, "Obscenity and the *Charter*: Autonomy and Equality" (1991), 1 C.R. (3) 367 at 370, refers to this as legal moralism, of a majority deciding what values should inform individual lives and then coercively imposing those values on minorities. The prevention of "dirt for dirt's sake" is not a legitimate objective which would justify the violation of one of the most fundamental freedoms enshrined in the *Charter*.[17]

"Minorities" in this context would seem to include lesbians and gay men. Nonetheless, it is frustrating that the court failed to be more explicit about lesbian or gay imagery, especially given the historic suppression of these materials. Their failure will, of course, result in more litigation.

The difficult component of the *Butler* test is, of course, what representations will be considered to be "degrading and dehumanizing." This standard, like any criminal standard, must have stable, clear boundaries. At the same time, as the court recognized, standards which escape precise technical definition are an inevitable part of the law. For some, any reference to sexual activity outside of a loving, monogamous, heterosexual relationship would meet this new standard. These people may also say that depictions of nudity are, in themselves, dehumanizing. However, given the court's comments on the acceptability of sexually explicit imagery, it is clear that this is not what it meant by "degrading and dehumanizing." The court did hold that "the message of obscenity which degrades and dehumanizes is analogous to that of hate propaganda ... obscenity wields the power to wreck social damage in that a significant portion of the population is humiliated by its gross misrepresentations."[18] The court gave some examples of what might come within the standard by quoting from *R. v. Ramsingh*:

> They are exploited, portrayed as desiring pleasure from pain, by being humiliated and treated only as the object of male domination sexually, or in cruel, violent bondage. Women are portrayed in these films as pining away their lives waiting for a huge male penis to come along, on the person of a so-called therapist, or window washer, supposedly to transport them into complete sexual ecstasy. Or even more false and degrading one is led to believe that their raison d'être is to savour semen as a life elixir, or that they secretly desire to be forcefully taken by a male.[19]

The court also went on to say that:

> Among other things, degrading and dehumanizing materials place women (and sometimes men) in positions of subordination, servile submission or humilation. They run against the principles of equality and dignity of all human beings. In appreciation of whether the material is degrading or dehumanizing, the appearance of consent is not necessarily determinative. Consent cannot save materials that otherwise contain degrading or dehumanizing scenes. Sometimes the very appearance of consent makes the depicted acts even more degrading or dehumanizing.[20]

It is useful to work towards articulating a list of what depictions should be included within the degrading and dehumanizing test. This list, which is not carved in stone but is only intended as a starting point for engagement in the interpretative process by all members of equality seeking communities, might include depictions of:

1. sexualized racism (*e.g.,* insatiable Black women, compliant Asian women);
2. sexualized anti-semitism (*e.g.,* Nazi-prisoner scenes);
3. other sexualized vulnerabilities (*e.g.,* women with disabilities, women in prison);
4. incest;
5. child sexual abuse;
6. positive outcome rape and other rape myths;[21]
7. heterosexist stereotypes of lesbians or gay men;
8. penetration with threatening or dangerous objects (*e.g.,* guns, glass bottles);
9. members of historically subordinated groups as naturally masochistic or sadistic;
10. members of historically subordinated groups as attracted to animals.

While *Butler* marks a new era in Canadian obscenity law, interpretations of the law do not end with the *Butler* decision. The entire community of feminists should participate in the debate that will shape the interpretation and enforcement of this law. For, while we may have succeeded in exposing and begun chipping away at the misogyny embedded in the previous standard, a layer of heterosexism and homophobia has also been more clearly exposed, a layer that was always there and one which now needs to be carved out as well.

DID LEAF APPEAL TO HOMOPHOBIA IN THE *BUTLER* CASE?

Some of the seized materials in *Butler* involved sex between men, and some of these materials were extremely violent. The depictions included gay bashing, penetration with a rifle, gang rape scenes, and prison rape scenes. None of the materials portrayed safe sex. One magazine featured a nude teenage boy surrounded by children's toys. LEAF has been criticized for describing, and for how we described, materials involving gay men in our brief. As we were putting forward a harms-based analysis, a review of the materials was essential. Some media accounts have reported that LEAF presented the videos in court, and some have gone further to say that we did this to appeal to invidious homophobia. During discussions on what to present during the court time allotted for oral argument, those working on *Butler* briefly considered showing excerpts from the videos to the judges in open court, including the videos of sex between men, to impress upon the judges just how violent or dehumanizing the material was. For a variety of reasons — including a recognition that we might be unintentionally playing into judicial homophobia — we decided *not* to show the videos.

Some have expressed the view that, perhaps, LEAF should not have taken any position on gay male representations because it is difficult for women, including lesbians, to understand gay male culture. On the other hand, it would have been difficult to say nothing at all about the materials for gay men. We may have been criticized for rendering invisible gay male materials by ignoring them; as advocates we had to prepare an answer to questions about these materials that the court could and should have asked of all litigants in *Butler*, and we could not ignore the role these materials may have, not only within gay communities but also within a broader social context.

LEAF has also been criticized for collapsing an analysis of gay male pornography into the harms-based analysis of heterosexual pornography. This critique is not in accord with any argument we presented to the court. Our argument in support of legal prohibition of pornography is founded on equality principles, in particular harms to women. Any argument that supports freedom of expression, including sexual expression, must be grounded in equality principles, which means that it must take into account systemic inequalities. After a lengthy discussion on pornography's harms to women, the LEAF factum stated that:

> Individual men are also harmed by pornography, although this is exceptional in that this harm does not define the social status and treatment of men as a group. Indeed, there is no systemic data to support the view that men as such as harmed by pornography. However, LEAF submits that some of the subject pornography of men for men, in addition to abusing some men in ways that it is more common to abuse women through sex, arguably contributes to abuse and homophobia as it normalizes sexual aggression generally.

That there is no systemic data on the uses and effects of gay male pornography should be cause for concern. But given this lack of information, we could not say anything more specific as to how it might "contribute to abuse and homophobia." Since the specific issue of lesbian and gay materials inevitably will be addressed by higher courts, we — LEAF, other equality-seeking organizations, and lesbians and gay men — must talk about these contributions to systemic inequalities in more detail before we can plan future strategies.

IS LEAF'S POSITION ON PORNOGRAPHY ANTI-LESBIAN?

For well over a decade, lesbians have divided on whether legal prohibition is a useful strategy for dealing with any pornography. Some lesbians say criminal prohibitions should be pursued given pornography's integral link to systemic sexual inequality and sexual violence, while others have said that regulating pornography poses too great a risk to lesbian self-representation and self-determination. The debate has been made even more complicated for lesbians by the protracted, divisive, and painful feminist discussions on the equality implications of lesbian sadomasochism (s/m). At the risk of over-simplifying, supporters of s/m believe that its practitioners are sex radicals who disrupt social conventions or pursue the cutting edge of sexual freedom. Those who critique the practice see it as modelling or replicating the worst aspects of a sexuality premised on male dominance and female subordination within a systemically unequal culture. Many lesbians who critique s/m practices still object to state censorship of s/m depictions, arguing that this is an issue for lesbian communities to deal with internally. Others see the practice as so damaging to individual women and to communities that the state should censor the materials. Lesbians need to find safe places and ways to continue talking about s/m practices, its imagery, its public manifestations, and its legal regulation.

Reducing lesbian responses to pornography, including s/m depictions, to either "anti-porn" or "pro-sex" is an error. Not only is this an inaccurate rendering of a much more complex debate, but it divides lesbians (and other feminists) against each other, preventing us from sharing and pursuing our commonalities, while leaving misogynists and homophobes to divide the spoils. Further, women, especially perhaps lesbians, in the western world have only recently begun to explore and create sexual representations. This work, too, forces us to reconsider the "anti-porn" and "pro-sex" straightjackets. Teresa de Lauretis suggests a much more fruitful starting point when she describes a tension for lesbians (perhaps better described as a fluidity, depending on place and time, but certainly not a polarity), between the "erotic" drive and the "ethical" drive:

> An *erotic, narcissistic drive* enhances images of feminism as difference, rebellion, daring, excess, subversion, disloyalty, agency, empowerment, pleasure and danger, and rejects all images of powerlessness, victimization, subjection, acquiescence, passivity, conformism, femininity; and an *ethical drive* that works towards community, accountability, entrustment, sisterhood, bonding, belonging to a common world of women or sharing what Adrienne Rich has poignantly called "the dream of a common language."[22]

She goes on to suggest that these two drives underlie and sustain at once both "the possibility of, and the difficulties involved in, the project of articulating a female symbolic." Exploring the equality implications of this tension may move us towards exploring all women's sexualities.

Regardless of individual views on sexual violence or censorship, lesbians' specific, widely shared concerns include that the law will disproportionately impact on lesbian-created imagery and that it will be enforced in a discriminatory way. LEAF, in consultation with members of affected communities, needs to begin developing arguments which address these concerns. More particularly, what might an argument in favour of sexually explicit lesbian imagery that was *also* founded on a systemic (in)equality analysis look like? And what strategies could be pursued to address discriminatory enforcement of obscenity laws by the state?

LESBIAN IMAGERY AND A SYSTEMIC EQUALITY ANALYSIS

In *Butler*, LEAF advanced, and the Supreme Court of Canada accepted, an analysis which renders moral censorship unconstitutional. *Butler*, therefore, makes possible a political argument, one that has been articulated within lesbian and gay communities and that may advance lesbian and gay equality rights without undercutting the substantive equality case law. The argument is that these representations affirm the identities of members of communities systemically vilified and abused on the basis of sexuality, culture, and intimate social arrangements. They claim visibility and celebrate the diversity of, and within, communities whose existence is denied and coercively suppressed. (Imagine, for example, the powerful effect of a billboard presenting a romantic embrace between two teenagers of the same sex.) Sometimes the images may provide information on safe sex practices. These are equality arguments. *Butler* creates legal space — space which did not exist under the former obscenity law — for such arguments to be constitutionally credited.

Lesbians have been, and are, extremely influential in all aspects of the pornography debate, whereas few gay men talk about harms to women or support any form of state regulation. As well, very few materials are made for lesbians, in contrast to widely available materials for gay men, many of which are produced and distributed by those who produce and distribute materials for heterosexual men. Furthermore, as already acknowledged, it is possible that lesbians (and other women) misunderstand gay male culture (and *vice versa*). These differences suggest that lesbian and gay concerns and strategies relating to sexual representations may not always be co-extensive. At the same time, particularly in the face of the AIDS crisis, lesbians have been more willing to create communities of resistance together with gay men to present stronger, more effective political voices. So, while lesbians must decide deliberately and carefully about whether and when to align with gay men on issues touching sexual representations, this paper will assume mutuality of interests.

While *Butler* establishes the equality framework for defending lesbian and gay imagery, that framework rests on the principle that the material to be defended must not, itself, exacerbate social and sexual inequality. Equality arguments must serve the interests of all systemically subordinated communities; arguments founded on individual freedoms are not exempt from this requirement. Accordingly, LEAF cannot join cause with those who champion freedom of expression, including freedom of sexual expression, without regard for institutionalized inequality. Therefore, we need to consider, theoretically and empirically, not only how the materials might offer affirmation and resistance, but also how they might contribute to homophobia or other abuses of lesbians and other women, gay men, and men who belong to other systemically subordinated communities.

Lesbians and gay men are not exempt from expressing or modelling the coercive sexual practices deeply embedded in the gendered, homophobic, and racist culture that has shaped us all. For example, sexually explicit imagery presenting child sexual abuse cannot be justified simply because it is created for lesbians or gay men. Sexual representations that eroticize rape fantasies, feminize or infantilize the violated party, sexualize Nazism, or designate a "bottom" who derives pleasure from being degraded by a "top," may further some individuals' freedom, but it is difficult to see how they meet the criteria of an equality analysis. But as noted earlier, lesbians need to talk about s/m in more detail, including whether and how to make equality arguments specific to s/m and sexual minorities. LEAF will not take a firmer position on lesbian s/m in litigation until a much clearer, systemic equality analysis emerges from lesbian communities across Canada.

Neither the producers nor the consumers of lesbian or gay sexual imagery define or control its use or its cultural meaning in wider society. Cindy Patton talks about the difficulty in creating lesbian imagery "so that even the most recalcitrant heterosexual male cannot help but be disturbed by his exclusion from lesbian-produced representations. The 'don't let men read it' ethos acknowledges that we have not yet produced images that defy colonization."[23] One gay critic commenting on the "Put the Homo Back Into Homicide" advertisement for *Swoon*, a film on the sexual relationship between two male murderers, said that: "This is not to silence those voices among us who want to investigate stereotypes by pushing them to the edge.... But let's not be disingenuous about the times in which we live, or the fact that we are breathing a bubble of freedom that is only 25 years old — historically speaking, a heartbeat. And that nothing we throw into the discourse is without consequence."[24] No one can ensure that the sexualized racism of, for example, gay houseboy scenarios will not be used against men of colour in a racist culture, or that s/m, or sexually violent or submissive materials will not be used against women or gay men in a misogynist, homophobic culture. Again, it is hard to trust that depictions of gay bashing and gang rapes in the context of materials intended to sexually arouse will not foster homophobia.

LEAF is committed to affirming the social and sexual identities of lesbians through law and otherwise. Constitutional arguments protecting sexual imagery can and should be made but these arguments cannot be made at the expense of others. LEAF supports working towards this protection in concert with those who are also willing to ground their analysis on equality principles.

DISCRIMINATORY ENFORCEMENT

Since *Butler* was released, very few *Criminal Code* charges have been laid regarding heterosexual materials, and few cases have proceeded through the courts. Anecdotal evidence suggests that Crown attorneys and the police have made little effort to understand what an equality driven, harms-based analysis means. While Butler himself was convicted on a re-trial,[25] the reasons for decision are disappointing as they do not give any guidance on how the *Butler* test is to be applied. What is outrageous is that state agents are not applying the obscenity law to heterosexual pornography.

To our knowledge, the Toronto police have not laid any obscenity charges regarding heterosexual materials since *Butler*. But before the ink was dry on the *Butler* decision, they seized, in their first raid in years, *Bad Attitude*, a lesbian erotic magazine from Glad Day Bookshop, a gay and lesbian bookstore. The bookstore was eventually convicted as the magazine described a woman stalking another woman in a shower, assaulting her, and then, now with her consent, having sex with her.

While feminists may disagree on the defensibility of this material, it is, nonetheless, impossible to justify why this magazine would be chosen from all the other available pornography and why this store was raided. The police action was clearly discriminatory.

Within weeks of the *Bad Attitude* raid, a trial relating to the Canada Customs seizure[26] of sexually explicit gay male materials, also destined for Glad Day Bookshop, was held. (The shipment, which was from the United States, had been seized a few years earlier but the trial was delayed pending *Butler*.) In reasons for decision which are clearly homophobic, Judge Hayes prohibited all of the materials because he found sex between two men to be, in itself, degrading.[27] He completely failed to undertake any equality analysis of the materials. This decision is on appeal. These two applications of *Butler* against a gay and lesbian bookstore, very shortly after the decision was released, have served to galvanize some members of lesbian and gay communities, particularly in Toronto, against the *Butler* decision.[28] It should be noted however, that, to our knowledge, no other *Criminal Code* charges have been laid regarding lesbian or gay materials in Toronto or elsewhere, although anecdotal evidence indicates that Toronto police continue to regularly enter Glad Day to review its magazines.

While Canadian police forces have been relatively inactive, the same cannot be said for Canada Customs. Customs officials have retained and prohibited entry into Canada of materials on lesbian and gay sexuality and orientation for years.[29] Indeed, it seems that Canada Customs has a practice of targeting these materials and ignoring heterosexual materials. These seizures are much more pervasive, and regulate, often illegally, lesbian and gay materials much more than does enforcement of the obscenity standard under the *Criminal Code*. These practices are not open to public scrutiny and it is difficult to prove the claim of discrimination in the absence of comparative data. For example, Canada Customs does not publish annual or other reports outlining their seizures and no other agency collects this data in the same way as, for example, crime statistics are collected. They will advise if a publication is on the banned list but they will not permit access to the whole list. The seizures are made without the kind of police action inherent in a raid on a commercial outlet and most individuals tangled in the Canada Customs web will forfeit the materials before the internal administrative proceedings are finished and public oral hearings begin. So the general public, even diligent researchers, have little or no direct knowledge of Canada Customs standards and practices.

The charge of discriminatory practices by Canada Customs against lesbians and gay men is, however, supported by other evidence. If materials are seized at the border, the person who was to have received the materials will be sent a form that will have one or more boxes checked off as the reason for refusing entry. "Anal penetration" is a proscribed category which will result in prohibition of virtually all materials for gay men.[30] There is also evidence that Canada Customs has singled out for review and seizure, shipments to lesbian and gay bookstores, and more recently, feminist and alternative bookstores.[31] American book distributors are increasingly reluctant to deal with gay and lesbian bookstores in Canada because of the long delays in processing the books, and because so many shipments are refused entry or are lost or damaged by Canada Customs. These bookstores are now having to make special arrangements that threaten their commercial viability, such as payment in advance for materials rather than on delivery.[32] Finally there is anecdotal evidence from individual lesbians and gay men who have been questioned and searched when entering Canada on the suspicion that they are carrying pornography, or who have had shipments detained and prohibited.

Most information on customs seizures of lesbian and gay materials relates to pre-*Butler* seizures. One would expect that Canada Customs would have revised all of its policies post-*Butler*. However, a *Globe and Mail* article reported a Customs official as saying that it is "business as usual" — guidelines and practices have not changed since *Butler*.[33] Again, it is outrageous that these state agents are failing to properly apply the law. Canada Customs must be pressured to revise its seizure guidelines and practices so they are more open to public scrutiny and in line with the constitutional standards articulated in *Butler*. Some of these issues are being litigated in Vancouver by the British Columbia Civil Liberties Association and Little Sisters Book and Art Emporium,[34] a lesbian and gay bookstore in Vancouver, with financial assistance from the American Booksellers Association. LEAF supports their claim to a declaration that customs legislation has been construed and applied in a manner that discriminates on the basis of the sexual orientation of the authors and readers contrary to the equality rights guaranteed by Section 15 of the *Charter*. The action against Canada Customs is scheduled to go to trial in October 1993.

HOW MIGHT THE *BUTLER* DECISION AFFECT THE ARTISTIC COMMUNITY?

Many artists are preoccupied with religion, politics, or sexuality since it is within these spheres that we, artists and non-artists, experience our deepest desires and our deepest fears. But it is also within these same spheres that the state and other institutions have attempted to restrict or control public dialogue. Artists have always known that their work might provoke negative, even hostile reactions. Susan Sontag once said that artists *seek* to make their work "repulsive, obscure, inaccessible; in short, to give what is, or seems to be, *not* wanted."[35] Paradoxically, since they still want to be able to create their work, artists work within boundaries while at the same time always pushing the outer edges. Some artists and anti-censorship activists express concern about the fear or threat of criminal prosecutions although it is extraordinarily rare for such charges to be laid in Canada. In terms of artists' everyday lives, far more restrictive factors than the criminal law include arts-funding agencies' policies and practices, provincial film censorship and classification regimes, personal concerns or doubts about how the work will be received or understood, and curators, theatres, and galleries who are reluctant to show controversial work. Those who identify the new obscenity standard as the primary source of "obscenity chill" are overshooting the mark.

Moreover, *Butler* makes it clear that "artistic expression rests at the heart of freedom of expression values and any doubt in this regard must be resolved in favour of expression."[36] The court also held that "... materials which have scientific, artistic or literary merit are not captured by the provision ... the Court must be generous in its application of the artistic defence." The constitutional artistic defence is distinct from, and much more encompassing than, the statutory defence of "public good" set out in Section 163 of the *Criminal Code*. For example, the standard does not seem to require that the materials have "serious" artistic purpose — a standard which may be nonsensical when applied to postmodern art. In the context of criminal prohibitions, this is a *clear* improvement over the pre-*Butler* law and should result in a reduction of the obscenity chill for artists.

In rejecting a morals-based rationale for sexual representations, implicitly *Butler* also calls into question the underpinnings of arts funding and film policies based on this rationale. *Butler* arguably requires that the state's participation in art production cannot bring with it considerations of decency. Any suggestion, for example, by the state that it will not fund work by lesbian or gay artists or work on sexuality must be strenuously denounced.[37]

Furthermore, the state has an obligation to protect artists against unlawful censorship and, in some cases, it actually attempts to fulfil this mandate. For example, it has been inaccurately implied in various contexts that the Winnipeg lesbian artist collective, Average Good Looks, has been censored by the state. In fact, the collective has turned to the state for redress and protection against private forms of censorship. They were first censored by the "free" market when Mediacom refused to print a billboard stating "Homophobia is Killing Us." (Mediacom had misread the original copy as stating "Hemophilia is ..."). A sexual orientation discrimination complaint to the Manitoba Human Rights Commission was settled when Mediacom agreed to provide money for materials and art work, as well as billboard space, for more varied and sustained presentations. Then, when the Ku Klux Klan sent collective members threatening telephone messages (and may have been responsible for paint-bombing the "Homophobia" billboard), criminal charges were laid against the Klan members. Unfortunately, sloppy police practices resulted in the charges being stayed half way through the trial. (Note that the Klan's defence was to have been freedom of expression.)

Butler also takes away the excuse of "the work is prohibited" from gallery operators who may be reluctant to show the work for other unarticulated reasons. During the *Festival du Voyeur: A Celebration of Queer Culture* in Winnipeg (January–February 1993), a gallery operator who had agreed to exhibit homoerotic work, subsequently wanted to back out because, he said, the work was prohibited by criminal law. When I told him that the work would be protected by the *Butler* test, it became clear that his real concern was that the institution within which he worked did not want to be associated with the festival. The criminal law excuse had looked like an easy way out of his prior commitment. In the end, the work was exhibited. It is also interesting to note that there was no police presence at any of the festival's more than 20 events, including a performance of "My Queer Body" by Tim Miller.[38] On the other hand, Toronto police presence at art events and the fact that they issue pre-show warnings has a decidedly chilling, if not destabilizing, effect on the artist community in Toronto. The police must be held accountable for this completely unacceptable practice.

Censorship issues for artists are complex and serious. No one at LEAF has ever denied this and LEAF members have worked with artists, artist organizations, and art journalists on censorship issues in the art community both before and since the *Butler* decision.

CONCLUSION

Some discussion issues emerging from this article include:

1. On the obscenity standard:
   a. When should sexually explicit heterosexual materials come within the degrading and dehumanizing standard?

b. How might materials created for lesbians and gay men contribute to homo-phobia and other abuses of lesbians and other women, gay men and men who are members of other subordinated communities? How do these materials function within these communities and wider society? How might these materials be distinguished from heterosexual materials and defended? Does the answer differ depending on the gender of those represented?

c. How can feminists and others move towards articulating and depicting diverse sexualities within an equality analysis framework, that is, without undercutting the substantive equality claims of subordinated communities?

2. On future action:

a. What specific activities can LEAF and others undertake to expose the lack of state response to heterosexual materials since *Butler*?

b. What specific activities can LEAF and others undertake to expose the long term and ongoing discriminatory enforcement by Canada Customs against materials for lesbians and gay men, and police harassment within these communities?

c. What specific activities can LEAF and others undertake to move government actors involved in art production away from criteria founded on decency rather than artistic merit?

While *Butler* recognizes the relationship between pornography and inequality, thereby marking a new era in Canadian obscenity law, no one expected that discriminatory enforcement of the obscenity law would end, or harmful forms of pornography would disappear from Canada the day after the decision was released. Feminists and other equality seekers must participate in the debate which will shape the law's interpretation and enforcement while at the same time pursuing other strategies for considering uses and effects of all sexual representations. LEAF looks forward to continuing this work.

QUESTIONS TO CONSIDER

1. Outline the major criteria regarding obscenity handed down by the Supreme Court of Canada in the *Butler* decision. Critically discuss whether you feel these criteria represent an acceptable approach to pornography in Canadian society.

2. Summarize the reasons why LEAF chose to intervene in the *Butler* decision. Discuss whether or not you feel these reasons are valid and whether you agree with the position taken by LEAF.

3. Identify several major issues involved in the pornography debate and outline the different positions that can be taken on each issue. Select at least two issues and discuss which position you consider most valid regarding each issue.

NOTES

1. The Women's Legal Education and Action Fund (LEAF) is a national organization that, among other things, participates in litigation that may impact on women's equality claims.

2. While the Criminal Code just uses the word "obscenity," this term and "pornography" are often used interchangeably in *R. v. Butler* (1992), 8 C.R.R. (2d) 1 (S.C.C.) and other cases. While some people use the words "pornography" and "sexually explicit" synonymously, for others "pornography" describes materials which are primarily intended to sexually arouse viewers. Many feminists have used "pornography" to describe harmful sexual imagery. Fewer use it in the same sense as the *Butler* court, *i.e.*, as the descriptive term for materials which should be subject to legal regulation. Needless to say, these semantic differences lead to misunderstanding and confusion. In this paper, "obscenity" is used to refer to the criminal standard for proscribed materials. "Pornography" and "sexually explicit" are generally used synonymously. However, the context of the former will often import a sense of harm (*e.g.*, "some forms of pornography").

3. *Ibid.*

4. The community standards test as defined in *R. v. Brodie*, [1962] S.C.R. 681 at 705.

5. Most notoriously, as discussed *infra* (see note 34), Canada Customs used the Criminal Code standard to bar entry of materials on lesbian and gay sexuality or orientation.

6. Obviously, this observation is a guess as to the age of those involved in production. The guess is based on apparent physical development and my reading of the images' coding and text, which seem to focus on the "actors'" actual youth rather than as adults impersonating children. While my observations may not be accurate in this case, it is undeniable that children are involved in making pornography. See, for example, G. Sereny, *Invisible Children and the Shattering Truth of Runaways On Our Streets* (London: Pan, 1986) — a survey on child prostitutes in three countries; *every one* had been asked to make pornography. L. Kelly, "Pornography and Child Sexual Abuse" in C. Itzin, ed., *Pornography: Women, Violence and Civil Liberties* (Oxford: Oxford University Press, 1992): 70-80% of runaways in one study had been involved in making pornography. T. Tate, *Child Pornography: An Investigation* (London: Methuen, 1990) — a description of the "cottage industry" for child pornography, in particular its reliance on amateur creation and distribution systems. See also, *R. v. Robinson* (15 April 1993), 9201-1805-C6 (Alta. Q.B.), Hunt. J. (conviction for making obscene pictures of a 15 year old prostitute) and "Child Pornography Case Stuns Thompson," *Winnipeg Free Press*, 8 April 1993 — a story on the arrest of a man for making sexually explicit films of 10 and 11 year old girls. In 1992, Winnipeger Karl Krantz was found in possession of videotapes of his sexual assaults of approximately 100 aboriginal girls. Convictions were entered on only a small number of the assaults recorded on the tapes as many of the girls could not be identified or found. It was not an offense *per se* to possess the videotapes.

7. For example, Linda (Marchiano) Lovelace was hurt in the production of *Deep Throat* as is clear from the bruises on her body which are visible in the film and her accounts of what happened to her: L. Lovelace, *Ordeal* (New Jersey: Citadel Press, 1980). In spite of this knowledge which, I think, should influence how we read the film, some have argued that *Deep Throat* is not "an unending paean to male dominance" because it shows a woman actively seeking to attain her own sexual pleasure. See L. Duggan, N. Hunter & C. Vance, "False Promises: Feminist Anti-Pornography Legislation in the U.S." in V. Burstyn, ed. *Women Against Censorship* (Toronto: Douglas & McIntyre, 1985) at 139. Even under ideal conditions, the creations of sexual imagery is full of complicated dynamics. For example, the lesbian artist collective Kiss and Tell acknowledges that one reason why they used only two models in the creation of their "Drawing the Line" exhibition on representations of lesbian sexuality was that it was important to collaborate with "...women who had built trust over an extended period of time. It is our history together that has let us explore the often scary dynamics in explicit sexual photography." Kiss and Tell (S. Stewart, photographer, in collaboration

with P. Blackbridge and L. Jones) *Drawing the Line: Lesbian Sexual Politics on the Wall* (Vancouver: Press Gang Publishers, 1991), n.p.

8. S. Cole, *Pornography and the Sex Crisis* (Toronto: Amanita Press, 1989) at 44.

9. Contrary to what some have said, LEAF does not assert that pornography is the *alpha* and *omega* of women's subordination by men or women's inequality. Women are subordinated and materially disadvantaged in multiple and intersecting ways. Most of LEAF's cases have focused on inegalitarian laws relating to employment, reproduction, or sexual violence and the intersection between them.

10. In making this observation, I am not trying to line up women of colour and poor women against lesbians and artists, especially as there are lesbians of colour who are artists and who are poor. Rather, I am trying to encourage serious thinking about the differential impacts of pornography on variously situated women. This paper will consider this issue as it affects lesbians and artists in more detail because members of these communities that have identified this as a priority requested that LEAF do this work.

11. See M. Valverde, "Beyond Gender Dangers and Private Pleasures: Theory and Ethics in Sex Debates" (1989) 15 *Feminist Studies* 237, where she attempts to provide a framework within which to answer the question: "What is the place of sexuality in both our oppression and our project for liberation?" For a superb discussion on the erotic as a source of information and power in women's lives, see A. Lorde, "Uses of the Erotic: The Erotic as Power" in A. Lorde, ed., *Sister Outsider* (Freedom, CA: Crossing Press, 1984).

12. See, for example, T. McCormack, "Keeping Our Sex Safe" (Winter 1993) 25 *Fireweed: A Feminist Quarterly of Writing, Politics, Art and Culture* 25 at 33.

13. Butler, *supra* note 2 at 33.

14. *Ibid.* at 25, 39.

15. See also *supra* note 5.

16. Butler, *supra* note 2 at 24, quoting *R. v. Towne Cinema*, [1985] 1 S.C.R. 494 at 525.

17. Butler, *ibid.* at 30.

18. *Ibid.* at 36.

19. (1984), 14 C.C.C. (2d) 230 (Man. Q.B.) as cited in Butler, *supra* note 2 at 20.

20. Butler, *ibid.*

21. "Positive outcome rape" is depictions or texts of sexual assaults where the woman (or child) initially resists but ultimately "enjoys" the assault. The encounter usually ends with profuse thanks. This scenario was featured in a number of the *Butler* materials. Most notably, however, it was an aspect of *all* the materials involving children or portraying young-looking women as girls (*e.g.,* pigtails, saddle shoes, shaved pubic hair, small hips and breasts). Other rape myths portrayed include women receiving pleasure from pain, being blamed for inciting sexual advances, desiring sex from any and every man, expressing a secret desire to be raped, etc.

22. T. de Lauretis, "Upping the Anti (Sic) in Feminist Theory" in M. Hirsch and E. Fox Keller, eds., *Conflicts in Feminism* (New York: Routledge, 1990), 266.

23. C. Patton, "Unmeditated Lust? The Improbable Spaces of Lesbian Desires" in T. Boffin & J. Fraser, *Stolen Glances: Lesbians Take Photographs* (London: Pandora Press, 1991) at 238.

24. R. Podolsky, critic for the *L.A. Weekly* (17 June 1992) as quoted in M. Merck, *Perversions: Deviant Readings* (London: Virago Press, 1993) at 8.

25. *R. v. Butler* (31 March 1993), 88-01-04647 (Man. Q.B.) Hewak, J.

26. Customs legislation on obscenity referentially incorporates the *Criminal Code* obscenity provisions, *i.e.* the *Butler* standard. Until 1985, customs legislation prohibited any materials that were "immoral and indecent," but this standard was struck down as too vague to be enforced: Re *Luscher and D.M.N.R.* (1985), 17 D.L.R. (4th) 503 (F.C.A.).

27. *Glad Day Bookshop v. D.M.N.R.* (14 July 1992) 619/90 (Ont. Ct J. (Gen. Div.)) per Hayes, J.

28. It is not always clear whether individuals or groups voicing objections to the Hayes decision are against any form of censorship or whether they oppose Judge Hayes' gross misreading of *Butler*.

29. In recent years, in addition to seizing sex manuals and sexually explicit magazines and videos, Canada Customs has also seized books by, *e.g.*, J. Rule, G. Stein, O. Wilde, A. Dworkin, J. Genet, and J. Weeks.

30. Canada Customs has refused entry for educational materials on safe sex for gay men. For years it prohibited entry of *The Joy of Gay Sex*.

31. "Canada Customs Hits Feminist Stores and Others" (March/April 1993) *Feminist Bookstore News* at 11, 21.

32. Presentation by J. Fuller, manager of Little Sisters Bookstore — a lesbian and gay bookstore in Vancouver (address to the National Association of Women and the Law, Vancouver, 20 February 1993) [unpublished].

33. [Toronto] *Globe and Mail* (26 March 1993) A7.

34. *Little Sisters Book and Art Emporium et al.* v. *Minister of Justice (Canada) et al*, File # A901450 (B.C.S.C.).

35. S. Sontag, *Styles of Radical Will* (New York: Farrar, Strauss, Giroux, 1966) at 45.

36. *Butler, supra* note 2 at 25. None of the parties before the court in *Butler* argued that the materials were anything resembling "art," so the artistic merit defence did not directly arise.

37. Such state action is not unprecedented. The infamous Helms amendment to the funding criteria for the American National Endowment for the Arts prohibited funding to artists whose work was homoerotic. See, *e.g.*, S. Rohde, "Art of the State: Congressional Censorship of the National Endowment for the Arts" [1990] Hastings L.J. 353. Litigation by the American Civil Liberties Union (A.C.L.U.) challenged the constitutionality of the amendment on behalf of four artists who lost their funding as a result of this amendment. This litigation was settled in the summer of 1993 when the amendment was repealed, the artists received their funding and damages, and the A.C.L.U. received its legal costs.

38. Tim Miller was one of the four artists represented by the A.C.L.U. in the litigation challenging the Helms amendment. See *ibid*.

FOUR

....

The Politics of Law Reform: Prostitution Policy in Canada, 1985–1995

NICK LARSEN

INTRODUCTION

....

The development and implementation of legal policies frequently involve highly political processes in which different interest groups attempt to manipulate the laws to further their own goals. This political process is particularly evident with

respect to the control of street prostitution in large urban areas. Much of the insti-
gation for the political activity stems from the contradiction between prostitution's
minor legal status and the high degree of public nuisance frequently associated with
street prostitution. In this respect, the fact that most prostitution-related offences
are classified as "summary" offences limits the ability of police forces to deal effectively with street prostitution.[1] This problem is accentuated by the frequent concentration of street prostitution in residential and business areas near city centres,
a practice that creates conflict with the people who live and work in these areas. This
conflict in turn poses a dilemma for police, who must choose between expending
large amounts of resources on what is legally a minor offence, or ignoring the problem and being accused of failing to protect the public and maintain order. Thus,
Canadian police are often caught between liberal civil rights forces, who feel that
street prostitution does not warrant increased police attention, and residents and
business owners who want the problem solved. The involvement of feminist groups
in the debate adds another dimension to an already complex issue, and further
increases the political factors that Canadian police must contend with in attempting to control street prostitution.

The intent of this article is to conduct a comparative analysis of the manner in
which police in Vancouver, Edmonton, Winnipeg, and Toronto implemented 1985
changes to Canada's prostitution laws. Popularly referred to as Bill C-49, these
changes were enacted as a result of public clamour over the rampant street prostitution that developed in Canada's largest cities after the 1978 *Hutt* decision weakened
the previous anti-soliciting provisions contained in the Criminal Code. This discussion will outline the approaches taken in the different cities and attempt to carry out
four major goals: 1) An assessment will be conducted of the degree to which the reaction of politicians and local interest groups was an important influence on the control process. 2) This analysis will attempt to identify any patterns inherent in the
ability of different interest groups to affect the implementation of the law. 3) An
assessment will also be made of the degree to which the police themselves became
political actors and strayed from their intended role as neutral enforcers of the law.
4) Finally, an assessment will be made as to whether any particular political strategy
was more effective than others at minimizing public conflict over street prostitution.

BACKGROUND EVENTS

Prior to December 1985, street prostitution in Canada was covered primarily by
Section 195.1 of the Canadian Criminal Code, which prohibited "soliciting for the
purposes of prostitution." Although this law was considered satisfactory by the
police and most politicians, there were several anomalies that were problematic from
an enforcement perspective. For example, the courts limited the definition of "prostitute" to females only, and thus male prostitutes could not be convicted under the
section. The law also did not apply to customers, and thus police lacked an effective enforcement tool to deter customers from cruising the prostitution strolls. As
significant as these problems were in terms of the police ability to deal with street
prostitution, they were exacerbated by a 1978 Supreme Court of Canada decision
that soliciting was not an offence unless it was "pressing and persistent" (*Hutt v. the
Queen* [1978]). This decision caused an immediate uproar, with the police, politicians, many residents' groups, and even some members of the judiciary arguing that

it gave prostitutes almost unlimited rights to operate wherever they pleased, as long as they didn't actually physically attack potential customers. This argument was probably exaggerated, but there is little doubt that the *Hutt* decision appeared to correlate with a drastic increase in the numbers of prostitutes on the streets of major Canadian cities. Although there is considerable disagreement over the degree to which the increase in prostitution was attributable to the *Hutt* decision,[2] there is little doubt that the decision exerted a profound effect on police behaviour.

Canadian police forces were adamant that the *Hutt* decision deprived them of their ability to control street prostitution, with the most vocal police reaction occurring in Vancouver. Gradually, most police forces ceased attempting to enforce the law as it became obvious that charges could not succeed. It also became apparent that Canadian police forces had embarked on a concerted political campaign to force the federal government to enact much tougher laws for the control of street prostitution. While the police were undoubtedly concerned about the increasing levels of conflict over street prostitution,[3] there is some evidence to suggest that the police were also motivated by pragmatic organizational concerns. Inasmuch as the police traditionally rely on prostitutes as informers, the *Hutt* decision effectively deprived them of this source of information by reducing their power to pressure prostitutes into informant roles. On a more positive note, it also reduced the power of pimps, and many prostitutes began turning their pimps over to the police and agreeing to testify against them in court (Larsen, 1992).

While it is beyond the scope of this article to engage in a detailed analysis of the police role in the post-*Hutt* political debate, it must be noted that the political conflict continued to escalate across Canada, and Ottawa established the Special Committee on Pornography and Prostitution (the Fraser Committee) to study the problem and make recommendations. This committee commissioned original research and held public hearings in 22 cities and towns across Canada. Various officials, politicians, interest groups, and members of the public were invited to make submissions and express their views on prostitution. The testimony was divided almost equally between groups (including the police, residents, and politicians) wanting stricter laws and groups advocating a more decriminalized approach to the problem (Flieschman, 1989). Canadian police forces were virtually unanimous in arguing against any form of decriminalization. The police instead lobbied vigorously for much stricter laws and argued that they would quickly solve the prostitution problem if they had an effective legal tool (Larsen, 1992).

Despite the lobbying efforts by the police, the Fraser Committee ultimately tabled a report in which the nuisance effect was identified as the major problem to be addressed. The committee further advocated that the laws be amended to accomplish the dual goals of minimizing the nuisance to citizens while allowing prostitutes to practise their profession. Specifically, the committee recommended that most prostitution-related activities should be decriminalized, that small numbers of prostitutes should be allowed to operate out of their residences, and that the laws dealing with the exploitation of prostitutes should be strengthened (Fraser, 1985). The committee also recommended that the provinces and municipalities be empowered to regulate prostitution much like any other business, subject to a community decision making process.

The federal government failed to act on any of these recommendations, and instead introduced amendments that significantly strengthened the laws against prostitution. It is against this historical backdrop that the police commenced enforcing the new laws against communicating for the purposes of prostitution. Because the police had lobbied so actively for tougher sanctions against prostitution, they were undoubtedly under enormous pressure to move quickly both to reduce the numbers of street prostitutes and to eliminate the conflict among prostitutes, pimps, and the public that had become almost endemic in Toronto and Vancouver.

THE IMPLEMENTATION OF BILL C-49

Bill C-49 was proclaimed into law on December 28, 1985, amidst some of the most bitter controversy ever engendered with respect to Canadian criminal legislation.[4] The new law effectively criminalized all public communication for the purposes of prostitution,[5] and although most police forces and many residents' and business groups welcomed the new law, many other groups argued that the law was neither necessary nor likely to solve the problems associated with street prostitution. In particular, many civil rights groups expressed fears that the law's draconian provisions would lead to "overkill" and might result in innocent people being convicted on the basis of a "wink or a nod." Although most police forces attempted to reassure all groups that the law would be enforced fairly and effectively, the implementation of Bill C-49 engendered considerable political controversy. In order to facilitate the analytical goals outlined in the introduction, this section will discuss the enforcement policies of the four cities separately before conducting a critical comparison of the relative effectiveness of their approaches.

THE IMPLEMENTATION OF BILL C-49 IN VANCOUVER

The Vancouver police adopted an aggressive approach to the implementation of Bill C-49[6] and conducted several sweeps against prostitutes during the first few weeks of January 1986. The law initially appeared to be working, as both the number of arrests and the number of visible prostitutes remained low throughout January. Although several politicians and community leaders quickly proclaimed the law a "success," it appears that prostitutes had been staying off the streets only until they had a sense of how the Vancouver police would enforce the new law (Marie Arrington, president of the Vancouver chapter of POWER [Prostitutes and Other Women for Equal Rights]). They quickly returned to the streets in greater numbers, and the number of arrests increased. There were several court challenges under the Charter of Rights and Freedoms, and a Provincial Court decision overturning the law further increased the numbers and visibility of the prostitutes (*Vancouver Sun*, May 9, 1986: A3).[7] Although these constitutional challenges were quickly overruled by the British Columbia Supreme Court and the police adopted even tougher measures against prostitutes, the conflict over street prostitution continued to escalate. Prosecutors began routinely asking that area restrictions be made part of probation orders for convicted prostitutes, even though this tactic simply pushed most prostitutes to the edge of the restricted area.[8] The fact that the area restrictions did not apply to customers ensured that there was a steady supply of customers, and many commentators argued that prostitutes would remain on the street as long as there was business. The practice of area restrictions was also criticized by prostitutes' spokespersons and some defence lawyers because it contravened the principle of equal enforcement (Marie Arrington, president of POWER; Tony Serka and Bridget Eider, defence attorneys).

The debate over Bill C-49 continued, and by late 1986 it was clear that the new law was not the definitive solution that many people had expected. Once prostitutes overcame their fear of the law, they quickly developed new strategies to cope with it, including not discussing arrangements until inside the potential customer's car and waiting for the customer to make the first offer (Marie Arrington). Although the Vancouver police appeared satisfied with the law, many community groups were arguing that it was clearly a sham. This was particularly true of the Mount Pleasant area, a working-class neighbourhood near the city centre. The Vancouver police had stopped responding to prostitution-related calls from the area, and many residents became convinced that the police were using Mount Pleasant as a "dumping ground" for street prostitution because of its lower socio-economic status.[9]

In response to these criticisms, the Mount Pleasant Task Force was established to co-ordinate police efforts during the summer months of 1986 to 1988. The task force experimented with harassment tactics aimed at prostitutes, and organized periodic "blitzes" against prospective customers. In addition, it stepped up the frequency of visible uniformed patrols near where prostitutes were working to discourage customers from cruising the area (Staff Sergeant Thompson, Prostitution Liaison Officer for Team 6). Although the task force was reasonably effective, area residents complained that the police rarely consulted them and seemed to resent their attempts to provide feedback (Tim Agg, spokesperson for a Mount Pleasant residents' group). It is also important to note that the task force's tactics were not dependent on Bill C-49 and could have been used before the law was implemented. Further, the activities of the task force displaced large numbers of prostitutes into the Downtown Eastside area, including the working-class area known as Strathcona.[10]

The scenario that developed in Strathcona differed significantly from other areas, largely because both the residents and the police adopted radically different attitudes toward the problem than those evident in other parts of the city. Instead of adopting confrontational tactics, residents and prostitutes negotiated compromise agreements outlining where the prostitutes could work. This approach was reinforced when police suggested that patrol personnel would tolerate some prostitution if the prostitutes stayed away from schools and residential areas (*Vancouver Sun*, April 20, 1988: B5). Although there was some disagreement about the effectiveness of the initial police response, the police remained receptive to public input. Accordingly, a group of dissatisfied Strathcona residents organized the Strathcona Prostitution Action Committee (SPAC) in May 1988 and lobbied the police and city hall. This action quickly resulted in the formation of a Special Police Liaison Committee for Strathcona, which met with the dissatisfied residents and drew up a plan of increased uniformed patrols. Three area prostitutes also attended the meeting and participated in the discussion and negotiations over the problem (City of Vancouver, 1988). The initiatives of the liaison committee appeared to resolve the issue, as there was no further indication of trouble in the area. These tactics were continued by the uniformed patrol team responsible for the district, and follow-up research in 1993 indicated that the police extended their liaison work with prostitutes to include regular consultations with the affected groups.[11] Thus, although significant amounts of prostitution activity remained in the Strathcona area during the 1985–95 period, there was remarkably little conflict after 1988.

In summarizing this discussion of Bill C-49 in Vancouver, it is clear that the new law was not effective in reducing the numbers of street prostitutes in the city (Lowman, 1989: 95). Although it did give the police somewhat greater ability to control the areas in which prostitutes worked, and thus helped quiet public controversy, harassment tactics using traffic codes and other non-criminal laws were far more effective. The most effective solution, however, involved the negotiation and other "political" compromises practised by the police and residents in Strathcona. While these tactics did not appear to reduce the numbers of prostitutes, they did minimize conflict. Unfortunately, such negotiation was limited to the Strathcona area as residents and patrol teams in other areas were unwilling to adopt it.[12] As a result, conflict continued in the Mount Pleasant area, and there was an ongoing media debate regarding the best approach to the problem.

THE COMMUNICATING LAW IN TORONTO

The initial implementation of Bill C-49 in Toronto appeared to involve much more planning and co-ordination than had been evident in Vancouver. After consultation with the prosecutor's office and other groups, the Toronto police announced that they intended to concentrate on customers, and that they would co-operate with social service programs designed to help prostitutes change their lifestyles (*The Toronto Star*, Jan. 26, 1986: A6). The police quickly adopted a pattern of arresting more customers than was the case in Vancouver, and this tactic succeeded in deterring many customers from cruising the strolls. Although the numbers of prostitutes working the streets also dropped drastically,[13] this success was short-lived. Many of the prostitutes who temporarily vacated the streets moved into escort agencies and massage parlours, a move that increased the number of pimps and their ability to dominate the prostitution trade.[14] The police subsequently placed greater emphasis on escort agencies, which forced prostitutes back on the street, where they adopted new tactics to cope with police surveillance. A Provincial Court decision overturning Bill C-49 further increased the numbers of prostitutes and customers returning to the streets. At this point, the police changed their tactics and began concentrating on female prostitutes, but the evidence suggests that their efforts simply displaced many prostitutes to other areas. By August 1986, street prostitution had again become a major problem, and the police conducted a prolonged series of sweeps against female prostitutes. Although Toronto police adopted many of the tactics being used in Vancouver, the increased police activity failed to significantly affect the prostitution trade (*The Toronto Star*, Aug. 22, 1986: A1).

The controversy and conflict regarding street prostitution intensified in 1987 despite much more aggressive enforcement of Bill C-49. The Toronto police formed the Police–Community Prostitution Liaison Committee to facilitate co-operation and information sharing with residents and business owners, the Crown attorney's office, and local politicians. The prostitutes themselves were not included, which may explain why this committee was less successful than the one in the Strathcona area of Vancouver. Further, although the committee likely represented a genuine effort to deal effectively with citizens' concerns, it also was clearly an attempt to appease some of the most vocal groups and to subvert local political activity to serve the interests of the police.[15] In this respect, it was relatively successful at minimizing public criticism of the police and directing public lobbying efforts against politicians. However, it was also criticized by many residents and local politicians for being ineffective at incorporating public feedback in prostitution policies.

Although the police were able to minimize public conflict in the two main strolls located near the city centre, problems developed in the Lakeshore Drive and Queen Street West areas during 1987. The latter area was a working-class housing neighbourhood in West Toronto, which had always contained a small amount of street prostitution. However, the increased police activity in the two main strolls displaced large numbers of prostitutes into this area, precipitating public anger among residents who were convinced that they were being ignored by the police because of their lower socio-economic status. The divisional officers responsible for the area responded with increased patrols, and the problem initially seemed to disappear (Superintendent John Getty, chair of the Police–Community Prostitution Liaison Committee). But this success was also short-lived, and conflict continued to reappear in the area during the period under discussion. Indeed, residents interviewed in 1993 and 1995 maintained that the area was being ignored because of its working-class character.

The Lakeshore area was located along the shores of Lake Ontario in the City of Etobicoke, within the Metropolitan area but not in the City of Toronto. It was an area of middle-class housing and respectable, but reasonably priced, motels and restaurants. During the mid-1980s, many of these motels had been bought by large corporations and were being allowed to deteriorate. Although it initially appeared that the increase in prostitution in the area was simply a displacement effect from the downtown strolls, the events that transpired are interesting because they assumed a conspiratorial character. The residents and business owners lobbied much like the downtown residents, only to be completely ignored by the police and Etobicoke City Council (Ed Gonzalas, motel owner and interest group spokesperson). Although a concerted lobbying and media campaign eventually led to the creation of a special task force, it accomplished little, and Etobicoke Council remained adamant that nothing could be done about either the prostitution problem or the deterioration of the motels.

Yet there is evidence to suggest that Etobicoke City Council, supported by corporate interests, wanted to develop the area along the lake into a high-profile tourist area. (It should be noted that Ontario was planning to introduce legalized gambling casinos in the near future.) Although highly speculative, this suggestion explains the reluctance of Etobicoke Council to support increased prostitution enforcement, since the presence of the prostitutes was an important factor in the corporate redevelopment plans for the area.[16] It is also supported by comments made by a senior Toronto police officer in a 1989 interview about Etobicoke Council's plans to develop the area.[17] In any case, as events transpired, the Ontario government located its casino in another city, and the area was never developed. Although a small amount of prostitution remains in the area, it was not characterized by significant conflict after 1993.

Despite their initial successes on the downtown strolls, the Toronto police were not able to reduce the numbers of prostitutes. In defiance of police's aggressive enforcement of Bill C-49, the numbers of prostitutes on the streets doubled between January and October 1987 (*The Globe and Mail*, Oct.15, 1987: A3). The fact that most of this increase occurred after the police shifted their emphasis from customers to prostitutes underscored the futility of tougher laws against prostitution. Although the police ultimately returned to their previous concentration on customers, there is little evidence to suggest that it was effective. Conviction rates remained high, but so did the number of visible prostitutes (Moyer & Carrington, 1989). Further, public dissatisfaction began to grow to the point where it could no longer be contained by the Police–Community Prostitution Liaison Committee. In order to appear more effective, Toronto police instituted a practice of moving prostitutes from area to area, never allowing them to stay in one district for lengthy periods of time (Staff Inspector Jim Clark, officer in command of Toronto Police Morality Division; Staff Superintendent John Getty, chair of Police–Community Prostitution Liaison Committee). These practices were continued throughout the time period under discussion, and although some prostitution activity was displaced even into Toronto's outer suburbs, this simply spread the nuisance problem over a larger area. The Toronto media continued to debate the prostitution issue, and there were constant reports of conflict between residents and prostitutes. In this respect, it is significant that local politicians quickly began calling for legalized "zones of tolerance" and bawdy houses (*The Globe and Mail*, Oct. 26, 1991: A10).

THE IMPLEMENTATION OF BILL C-49 IN WINNIPEG

The Winnipeg police adopted a more tolerant approach to the implementation of Bill C-49 than occurred in either Vancouver or Toronto. Instituting a short "period of grace" following the proclamation of the law, they announced that they would take a tough stance with all people who contravened it once the grace period expired (Staff Inspector Tony Cherniak, officer in command of the Vice Division). The Winnipeg police were unique in that they initially enforced the law equally against male and female prostitutes as well as customers. They were also unique insofar as they explicitly stated that they were not trying to wipe out prostitution, but rather to "manage" it in order to avoid community conflict and other undesirable side effects. This stated objective allowed them to take a more flexible approach to the issue and consider more creative solutions in consultation with affected groups. The implementation of Bill C-49 was initially successful, and most prostitutes had left the main stroll by the middle of January (*Winnipeg Free Press*, Jan. 14, 1986: 3). This appeared to solve the problem, and most prostitution areas remained quiet in the aftermath of the initial implementation of the bill. However, it is difficult to conclusively attribute this lack of activity to the enforcement of Bill C-49 since there are no reliable statistics regarding the numbers of prostitutes over this period, and prostitution had not been a major issue prior to the law. The majority of the businesses in the main female stroll did not consider prostitution a problem. Further, the general public was not overly concerned about street prostitution, and over 50 percent of the population felt that Bill C-49 was too tough (*Winnipeg Free Press*, Feb. 16, 1986: 3).

Although the prostitution issue remained quiet in the main female stroll,[18] controversy quickly arose in two other areas. The first instance involved complaints from residents of the Hill area about male prostitution activities in the lanes and parking lots surrounding the legislative buildings.[19] The police responded by setting up roadblocks and conducting traffic checks and other harassment activities. Although these measures temporarily alleviated the problem, it reappeared in early fall. Residents renewed their complaints, which precipitated several public meetings involving residents, the police, and the gay community. Numerous possible solutions were discussed, and ultimately the City of Winnipeg installed permanent traffic barriers to prevent motorists from cruising through the area. Although this tactic simply displaced the prostitutes and their customers into a more heavily populated part of the area, changes in attitudes by prostitutes, combined with stepped-up police patrols, apparently solved the problem. There was little further public controversy, and some observers credit the involvement of the gay community for the success of the negotiations (*Winnipeg Free Press*, Sept. 26, 1986: 3).[20]

The success of the police action in the Hill stands in stark contrast to the situation that arose in the "lo-track" area during this time period.[21] In this case, a police attempt to clean up the Main Street strip displaced many prostitutes into the adjacent residential area. This led to conflict with residents, who complained that the police were ignoring the problem because of the neighbourhood's poor economic status (*Winnipeg Free Press*, Oct. 17, 1986: 3). The police responded with a series of sweeps against female prostitutes. Although this crackdown was largely ineffective, it destroyed the police's previously good relationship with the prostitute community. The Winnipeg chapter of POWER quickly condemned the police for ignoring male customers and also accused them of ignoring assaults against prostitutes (*Winnipeg Free Press*, Oct. 19, 1986: 3; Debbie Reynolds, president of POWER). Although the police denied both accusations, their relationship with the prostitutes deteriorated sharply after this point. The situation was exacerbated by the attitudes of area residents and business owners, many of whom exhibited very inflexible attitudes toward the prostitutes (Inspector Ray Johns, officer in command of the Vice Division). Thus, the problem was not resolved, and conflict over prostitution continued in the area during the remainder of the time period under discussion.

In summarizing the application of Bill C-49 in Winnipeg, it is clear that the law was not effective in reducing the amount of street prostitution. Although there is little firm evidence regarding levels of street prostitution before and after the law, most observers agree that there was no significant long-term reduction in the numbers of visible prostitutes (*Winnipeg Free Press*, Nov. 23, 1988: 1). In terms of reducing political conflict, a clear class bias emerged: the police were much more responsive to public concerns from the middle-class Hill area than they were to those emanating from the lo-track area. The police denied such a bias, arguing that they were unable to control prostitution because of the overly lenient attitudes of the courts, and calling for even tougher laws to deal with the issue. There was an ongoing media debate regarding street prostitution, and polls conducted in 1994 indicated that a majority of the public were in favour of legalized red light areas (*Winnipeg Free Press*, March 10, 1994: D8–D9). However, the Winnipeg police argued that they had no intention of tolerating prostitution in any area of the city (*Winnipeg Free Press*, April 25, 1994: C10).

THE IMPLEMENTATION OF BILL C-49 IN EDMONTON

Edmonton had experienced fewer problems with street prostitution in the aftermath of the *Hutt* decision than either Vancouver, Winnipeg, or Toronto. This situation was likely due to the generally tolerant attitudes of the residents and business owners and the restrained approach taken by the *Edmonton Journal* in response to *Hutt*. These attitudes, combined with the willingness of the Edmonton police to negotiate with prostitutes and other groups, led to a search for creative solutions to the problems created by the *Hutt* decision. Thus, there was relatively little public debate as the Edmonton police quietly began enforcing the new law on January 3, 1986. The police adopted a routine approach to the law, concentrating on female prostitutes and eschewing the major sweeps that were taking place in other cities. The new law initially appeared effective in forcing prostitutes off the street, and on February 7, 1986, the police estimated that the numbers of prostitutes working Edmonton's streets on an average night had been reduced from between forty and fifty to six or seven (*Edmonton Journal*, Feb. 7, 1986: B7). It also appeared that the street prostitutes were not being displaced into escort agencies or bars, and the police were generally happy with the law during the first few weeks of its operation.

The initial success of Bill C-49 was short-lived, and by early May the media began to comment on its reduced effectiveness. As the prostitutes became accustomed to police activity under the new law, they began to return to the street in significant numbers. Although the Edmonton police stepped up their enforcement activities, there is little evidence that these tactics exerted any long-term effect (Staff Sergeant Whitton, Morality Squad). Despite the increase in prostitution activities, the police did not become overly concerned until the prostitutes moved into Riverdale, a middle-class residential area adjacent to a working-class stroll. Although there had always been some prostitution on the fringes of the area, the incursion of large numbers of prostitutes into the heart of the area prompted a storm of protest from the residents. The variable of social class was introduced into the situation as the middle-class residents demanded action, and the *Edmonton Journal* began to publish graphic accounts of the problems experienced by the residents. This publicity resulted in an immediate crackdown, in which the police adopted some of the harassment tactics being used in other cities.[22]

The crackdown solved the immediate problem, and the street prostitution issue remained quiet for several months. However, in early July, the Edmonton police came under criticism from residents' groups in the working-class Boyle and McCaully areas located near a stroll adjacent to the main police station (*Edmonton Journal*, July 11, 1987: B1). Again, the familiar class bias appeared. Initially, the police seemed content to allow prostitutes to occupy the two working-class areas, but such inaction led to the development of residents' lobby groups within these areas, which forced the issue onto the public agenda. The Edmonton Police Commission responded by implementing a policy of harassing prostitutes until they moved to "new ground" (*Edmonton Journal*, July 11, 1987: B1). Although this activity temporarily alleviated the problem in the Boyle and McCaully areas, street prostitution was also becoming a problem in a middle-class stroll located in the heart of Edmonton's central business area (*Edmonton Journal*, Sept. 6, 1987: A1). Conflict between prostitutes and business owners transformed street prostitution into a high-profile public and political issue. The police responded by establishing a "storefront" prostitution control office in the heart of the area to provide better co-ordination of the enforcement of Bill C-49 (*Edmonton Journal*, Sept. 5, 1987: B1). Although this initially solved the problem in the business district, it simply pushed the prostitutes back into the working-class areas whose residents remained convinced that they were being ignored because of the working-class nature of their neighbourhood (*Edmonton Journal*, Sept. 8, 1987: A1). Thus, the prostitution problem remained on the political and media agendas for the remainder of the time period under discussion (*Alberta Report*, 1993: 14).

In concluding this overview of Bill C-49 in Edmonton, several important issues need to be emphasized. First, despite public and political pressure, the Edmonton police did not take a particularly hard line in enforcing the law.[23] They publicly stated that prostitution could only be repressed by using huge amounts of police resources, which would detract from more important police operations (*Edmonton Journal*, Sept. 9, 1988: A1). Further, the police intentionally maintained a good relationship with the street prostitutes.[24] Although this policy was partially motivated by the increasingly critical reaction of the media to police crackdowns on prostitution, it clearly assisted the police when they decided to negotiate with prostitutes in an attempt to minimize the nuisance associated with street prostitutes. Although this practice never reached the extent carried out in the Strathcona area of Vancouver, it nevertheless appeared relatively successfully in defusing some of the tensions.[25] Although the overall scope of the negotiation was quite limited, it represents the one tactic that appeared to minimize conflict over the issue.

SUMMARY AND CONCLUSIONS

Several points of similarity can be identified in the manner in which Bill C-49 was implemented in Toronto, Vancouver, Winnipeg, and Edmonton. One of the most obvious and significant points involves the fact that none of the cities adopted a consistent policy regarding the implementation of Bill C-49. While initial crackdowns were instituted in all cities immediately after the law was proclaimed, they were universally short in duration. Moreover, the police in all four cities frequently exhibited considerable ambivalence regarding the specific approaches that they applied to the implementation of the new law. Further, there is absolutely no evidence that the police and municipal governments in any of the cities ever attempted to articulate long-term goals or to develop comprehensive strategies for the control of street prostitution. Inasmuch as police and municipal politicians had extensively lobbied the federal government for tougher laws to control street prostitution, this omission is nothing short of incredible. It suggests that these groups either were not sincere in their calls for tougher legislation or else lacked the ability to implement the law in a coherent fashion. Unfortunately, neither conclusion speaks well for the integrity or competence of the police and local politicians.

The absence of comprehensive strategies for implementing Bill C-49 was further exemplified by the fact that the police in all four cities regarded the law as primarily a "crisis management tool" which they enforced in response to public pressure or specific problems. Thus, Bill C-49 was implemented in accordance with short-term political considerations, in which the police and politicians responded to public pressure based largely on the political clout of the groups demanding action. While this situation was most obvious in Vancouver and Toronto, it was a factor in all cities and contributed to a universal class bias in which street prostitution was "managed" so that it inconvenienced as few middle-class residents and businesses as possible. In many cases, this "management" involved displacing prostitutes into lower-class areas and ignoring them as long as they remained there. It also contributed to the "creeping red district" phenomena in which the police constantly displaced the prostitutes around different areas of the cities in response to public pressure. This tactic failed to solve the problem. Indeed, much of the public conflict in all four cities arose because of police efforts to displace prostitutes out of their traditional strolls.

The final and most significant aspect of the implementation of Bill C-49 centres on the manner in which the respective police forces interacted with the interest groups affected by street prostitution. The Toronto police clearly developed the most proactive policy toward such groups, and this approach contributed to their success in co-opting the local political activity to serve their own interests. On the other hand, while the Vancouver police attempted to establish police liaison committees in the Mount Pleasant area, their effectiveness was often hampered by the refusal of residents and the Vice Squad to participate. Further, although the Winnipeg and Edmonton police also used consultation and negotiation with affected groups, their success was limited by both the attitudes of the affected groups and the failure to include prostitutes in the negotiation process. The most successful example of the consultation approach occurred in the Strathcona area of Vancouver. The drastic difference in outcomes between the Strathcona and Mount Pleasant scenarios clearly suggests that negotiation and compromise can represent a useful tool as long as the police are committed and sincere in their efforts to negotiate with all the different interest groups. Further, the greater success of the "political" solution implemented in Strathcona was also due to the more flexible attitudes of the residents, combined with the inclusion of the prostitutes in the negotiation process.

QUESTIONS TO CONSIDER

1. Outline the factors that motivated the enactment of Bill C-49. Based on this analysis, discuss whether you feel the new law was necessary.
2. Discuss several important factors that influenced the implementation of Bill C-49. From this analysis, does it appear that the police in Vancouver, Toronto, Winnipeg, and Edmonton attempted to control prostitution to protect the rights of *all* citizens?
3. Outline several different enforcement strategies used in Vancouver, Toronto, Winnipeg, and Edmonton. Discuss whether any of these strategies were more "successful" than others. Which variables seem to be crucial in minimizing public conflict over street prostitution?

NOTES

1. For example, summary offences require the police to have direct knowledge that an offence has occurred and preclude laying charges on the basis of "reasonable grounds."
2. For example, Lowman (1986) argues that the Vancouver problems were more closely related to the closure of two nightclubs that catered to prostitutes and their customers. This action drove large numbers of prostitutes onto the street, where they migrated to business and residential areas. Larsen (1992) links the problem to patterns of gentrification occurring in major cities. This process, which peaked during the late 1970s and early 1980s, saw previously rundown houses in prostitution areas bought and renovated by middle-class professionals, who then lobbied for the removal of the prostitutes.
3. In this respect, the police in Vancouver were certainly justified in their concern over the escalating conflict between prostitutes and their pimps on one hand and residents

and business owners on the other. There were almost daily accounts of residents, armed with baseball bats, carrying out "hooker patrols."

4. See Larsen (1992) for an in-depth analysis of the political events surrounding the development of the law.

5. Bill C-49 provisions:

   (1) Every person who in a public place or in any place open to public view: a) stops or attempts to stop any motor vehicle, impedes the free flow of pedestrian or vehicular traffic or ingress to or egress from premises adjacent to that place, or b) stops or attempts to stop any person or in any manner communicates or attempts to communicate with any person for the purpose of engaging in prostitution or of obtaining the sexual services of a prostitute is guilty of an offence punishable on summary conviction. (2) In this section, "public place" includes any place to which the public have access as of right or by invitation, express or implied, and any motor vehicle located in a public place or in any place open to public view.

6. It should be noted that Bill C-49 legally became S. 195.1 of the Canadian Criminal Code once it was proclaimed into law. However, the numbering of the section changed several times during the time period covered by this article, and the term Bill C-49 will be used throughout to avoid ambiguity or confusion.

7. The situation was exacerbated when Mayor Mike Harcourt directed the Vancouver police to move against several bawdy houses and forced even more prostitutes out on the street. (*Vancouver Sun*, March 27, 1986: A3). Considering that the major goal was to keep prostitutes off the street, this action suggests that the Vancouver police and City Council had failed to develop a coherent strategy for dealing with prostitution.

8. In fact, the area restrictions may have exacerbated the problem by expanding the red light area. Referred to by some as the "creeping red light district" phenomenon, it spread the problem of street prostitution over a larger area and actually increased the amount of public outcry.

9. This information was provided by Tim Agg and Phylis Alfeld, leaders of two community organizations that were created by residents to attempt to do something about the prostitution problem in Mount Pleasant. Although these organizations were in fact dominated by professionals moving into the area, there was significant participation from the original working-class residents. In any case, the perception that the area was working class still remained in the minds of police and politicians (Libby Davies, Vancouver alderperson).

10. This area was located along the Vancouver Harbour and near Chinatown. It encompassed skid row, a large area of public housing, some established working-class residential districts, and the trendy restaurant and shopping area known as Gastown. Although the area had always contained significant amounts of prostitution, the transient nature of the population, combined with the preponderance of seedy bars and other transient-oriented businesses, minimized conflict.

11. Constable Griff Simons, Team 3, Vancouver police. In a 1992 interview, Constable Simons stated that he and his partner made a point of developing rapport with prostitutes in their area to facilitate their co-operation. They also attended monthly liaison meetings with prostitutes, residents, and business owners. This approach is apparently working well, and several informants from various organizations in the area expressed satisfaction with the police activity. Further, one community leader informed this writer that they were very satisfied with the willingness of prostitutes to co-operate (Muggs Sigurdson, Strathcona resident, Interview February 1992.)

12. It should be pointed out that the Vice Squad also refused to participate in the type of negotiations that occurred in Strathcona. The fact that the Vice Squad was much less active in Strathcona than in Mount Pleasant also likely contributed to the success of the tactic in Strathcona.

13. In April, the police announced that the numbers of prostitutes had dropped to approximately one-third of their pre–Bill C-49 levels (200–300 against 600–700) (*The Toronto Star*, April 27, 1986: A8). The police claimed that their strategy of going after the customers was effective because middle-class customers (often with families) were much more easily deterred than prostitutes, most of whom already had long criminal records.

14. This was because pimps now found it easier to control their "girls" than when they were on the streets. While a prostitute working the streets could "turn tricks" without giving her pimp his share, this would be more difficult in an agency, where the pimp could monitor all calls without leaving the office. The police were virtually powerless to intervene since it was all underground, and they lacked an effective way of monitoring the activities of the pimps (*The Toronto Star*, April 27, 1986: A8).

15. For example, a senior Toronto police superintendent informed this writer that he regularly used the committee to "make noise" when he wanted to put pressure on city hall.

16. Several informants noted that the presence of street prostitution contributed to the decline of property values and motivated the residents and motel owners to sell out to corporations at much lower prices that they would normally get for their properties. This contributed to an overall decline in the status of the area and made it ripe for redevelopment.

17. There were also persistent rumours related by residents that the Toronto Morality Division was encouraging prostitutes to move from the downtown strolls to the Lakeshore. However, this writer could not verify this directly with any prostitute informants.

18. Referred to as the "hi-track," this stroll was centred on Albert Street, an area of restaurants and boutiques near the downtown and adjacent to city hall and Chinatown. Many of the area merchants welcomed the prostitutes because they attracted street traffic, which was good for business.

19. The Hill area, located near the legislature in downtown Winnipeg, is the centre of the male prostitution trade in Winnipeg. The males were frequently drunk (as opposed to being on drugs) and were very noisy. They also made a practice of turning tricks in full view of apartment windows and passing traffic.

20. It is worth emphasizing that the Hill is noted for a high percentage of gay residents, and that their willingness to negotiate with the prostitutes facilitated a resolution to the issue. It is also significant that the gay community has played a significant role in counselling male prostitutes and that this has helped gain their co-operation.

21. The "lo-track" area is a working-class residential area near skid row. It is used primarily by younger, less expensive female prostitutes and male transvestites.

22. Interestingly, John Geiger, a columnist for the *Edmonton Journal*, asserted that the Edmonton police had "caused" these problems when they harassed the prostitutes out of a rundown area of parking lots and decrepit businesses near the main police station (John Geiger).

23. For example, they often gave out appearance notices to prostitutes charged twice in the same night (*Edmonton Journal*, Sept. 11, 1987: B1). In addition, the practice of seeking area restrictions as probation or bail conditions was never adopted in Edmonton. (Mike Allen, senior Crown attorney, Interview, August 1995.)

24. For example, Anne Dolina, spokesperson for the Alliance for the Safety of Prostitutes (ASP), publicly commended the Edmonton police for their enlightened approach and obvious desire to maintain a good working relationship with prostitutes (*Edmonton Journal*, May 24, 1988: A1). This policy was also confirmed by Staff Sergeant Whitton and Inspector Noel Day of the Edmonton Police Morality Squad.

25. Ruth Gelderman, Telephone interview, August 1989. Ms. Gelderman spoke highly of the work carried out by Community Service Officers, who acted as a liaison between

the police and the public on a wide range of issues. However, she also suggested that they were sometimes undermined by the Morality Squad, who sometimes conducted sweeps while the CSOs were trying to negotiate with the prostitutes.

REFERENCES

City of Vancouver. (1988). *Vancouver city manger's report to council.* (August 26). *Edmonton Journal.* Various issues.

Flieschman, J. (1989). *Street prostitution: Assessing the impact of the law.* Ottawa: Department of Justice.

Fraser, J. (1985). *Report of the Special Committee on Pornography and Prostitution.* Vol. 2. Ottawa: Supply and Services Canada.

Hutt v. the Queen. (1978) 32 CCC (2d) 418.

Larsen, E.N. (1992). The politics of prostitution control: Interest group politics in four Canadian cities. *International Journal of Urban and Regional Research,* 16(2), 169–189.

Lowman, J. (1986). "Street prostitution in Vancouver: Notes on the genesis of a social problem," *Canadian Journal of Criminology,* 28(1), 1–16.

Lowman, J. (1989). *Street prostitution: Assessing the impact of the law — Vancouver.* Ottawa: Department of Justice.

Moyer, S., & Carrington, P. (1989). *Street prostitution: Assessing the impact of the law — Toronto.* Ottawa: Department of Justice.

The Toronto Star. Various issues.

Vancouver Sun. Various issues.

Winnipeg Free Press. Various issues.

FIVE

Just Say No to the War on Drugs

BARNEY SNEIDERMAN

INTRODUCTION

I would like to begin by dedicating this presentation to George Orwell (1903–1950), the renowned English novelist, essayist, and social critic, and that is because of his brilliant and incisive commentary about the perversion of language to serve political goals. Accordingly, I am going to talk about the Orwellian distortion of

Source: Barney Sneiderman, "Just Say No to the War on Drugs," *The Manitoba Law Journal,* 24, no. 2 (1996–97): 497–531.

language under the following headings: *The War on Drugs*; *Drugs*; *Use versus Abuse*; and *Addiction versus Habit*. I also dedicate this presentation to Lady Godiva (who, according to legend, rode naked through the streets of Coventry in the 11th century); to E.T. (that adorable extra-terrestrial); and to that noble bird that, alas, cannot fly: the ostrich. Last but not least, an acknowledgment (dedication seeming inappropriate here) to Dr. Joseph Goebbels, Minister of Popular Enlightenment and Propaganda, Nazi Germany, 1933–1945.

THE WAR ON DRUGS

As the United States was winding down its military commitment in Vietnam, President Richard Nixon replaced one conflict with another by declaring "all out global war on the drug menace."[1] In 1986, President Ronald Reagan and the First Lady redeclared the War on Drugs in a joint television address to the American people, during which Nancy spoke that memorable war cry, "Just say no to drugs." Actually, the word *war* was only spoken once, although in the press secretary's announcement of the address ten days earlier, it appeared six times: e.g., "The President and Mrs. Reagan will address the Nation from their living quarters in the White House on what we, the American family, can do to win the war on illegal drugs."[2] The following are excerpts from the President's opening remarks:

> Drugs are menacing our society. They're threatening our values and undercutting our institutions. They're killing our children.... Drug trafficking is a threat to our national security.... Let us not forget who we are. Drug abuse is a repudiation of everything America is. The destructiveness and human wreckage mock our heritage. Think for a moment how special it is to be an American. Can we doubt that only a divine providence placed this land, this island of freedom, here as a refuge for all those people in the world who yearn to breathe free.[3]

After a few comments along the same line by the First Lady, the President responded that "Nancy's personal crusade [against drugs] ... should become our national crusade." He then went on to use the word *crusade* four more times, while also referring to the "*battle* against this cancer of drugs."[4] In his continuing rhetorical flourish, he proceeded to draw a linkage between World War II and the War on Drugs and then concluded with a stirring appeal to patriotism:

> My generation will remember how America swung into action when we were attacked in World War II. The war was not just fought by the fellows flying the planes or driving the tanks. It was fought at home by a mobilized nation, men and women alike, building planes and ships, clothing sailors and soldiers, feeding marines and airmen; and it was fought by children planting victory gardens and collecting cans. Well, now we're in another war for our freedom, and it's time for all of us to pull together again.... It's time, as Nancy said, for Americans to "just say no" to drugs. When we all come together, united, striving for this cause, then those who are killing America and terrorizing it with slow but sure chemical destruction will see that they are up against the mightiest force for good that we know. Then they will have no dark alleyways to hide in.... We Americans have never been morally neutral against any form of tyranny. Tonight we're asking no more than that we honor what we have been and what we are by standing together.[5]

The First Lady then chimed in with the last word: "Now we go on to the next stop: making a final commitment not to tolerate drugs by anyone, any time, any place. So won't you join in this great, new national crusade."[6]

All in all, it was a brilliant performance, orchestrated by a media star turned president who years earlier had tellingly extolled television's power to shape public perceptions: "Television has the power to shape thoughts, stir emotions, and inspire actions. It teaches, it sells, it entertains, it informs, and it has the capacity to influence powerfully."[7]

He certainly knew whereof he spoke. His "Declaration of War Against Drugs" was promptly embraced by the "liberal" media that right-wingers love to excoriate, and I vividly recall how television responded to the Ron and Nancy Show with a flood of stories about the cocaine menace. Nancy's war cry, "Just say no to drugs," calls to mind another memorable phrase calling the nation to arms — "a date which will live in infamy" — which is how President Franklin D. Roosevelt described the 7 December 1941 attack on Pearl Harbor when he asked Congress on the following day for a declaration of war against Japan. Admittedly, although "just say no" doesn't have the ring to it that "day of infamy" does, Nancy set the tone for a relentless national policy on illicit drugs that continues to the present day.

When his turn came, President George Bush chose "the drug problem" as the theme of his first Address to the Nation. Seven years later, that war continues in full force, and it is perhaps appropriate that President Clinton has recently appointed a retired four-star general as his drug czar. After all, if one is fighting a war, then who else but a general should be waging the campaign dictated by the Commander-in-Chief? Although my purpose is not to catalogue the horrific social costs that have been engendered by the so-called War on Drugs, I must at least give them their due. We tend to associate the War on Drugs with the United States because it is the major player; and it is the very nature of that war that the more vigorously a nation wages it, the more catastrophic are the social consequences inflicted upon itself. We in Canada have suffered less only because we have not pursued the war with the ardor and single-minded determination of the Americans. A capsule summary of the war's impact upon the United States is noted by Nova University law professor Steven Wisotsky in his book, *Beyond the War on Drugs*, where he tells us that it "... has spun a spider's web of Black Market Pathologies, including roughly 25% of all urban homicides, widespread corruption of police and other public officials, street crime by addicts, and subversive narco-terrorist alliances between Latin American guerrillas and drug traffickers as well as wholesale corruption of governments in Latin America and the Caribbean. These pathologies were foreseeable because they are a function of money."[8]

Yet there is even more — in truth, far more — to the debit side of the War on Drugs. The U.S. has long since passed South Africa as the country with the world's highest prison population per capita, and that is thanks to the War on Drugs. It is a war that is flooding the penal system with so many drug offenders that it is necessary to keep building more and more institutions to house these prisoners of war. Moreover, although illicit drug use cuts across racial lines, what is striking is that it is primarily young black males who are being swept off the streets of their ghettos into the correctional system. (In 1989, the newspaper *USA Today* reported that although only 12 percent of those using illicit drugs were black, 38 percent of those arrested for drug violations were black males.[9]) In the federal prison system alone,

62 percent of inmates — 47 000 men and women — are drug offenders. Altogether, more than a third of a million Americans are doing time for violating drug laws, and roughly another million are on probation or parole.[10] Prisons are also the fastest-growing part of many state budgets. The war ties up the courts and diverts the police from dealing with criminals who commit the traditional-type crimes that form the basis of the FBI's annual crime index (crimes against the person and property). In the U.S. the concept of civil liberties has been subverted by the practice of mandatory drug testing, the judicial removal of safeguards for obtaining search warrants in drug cases, and the random search for drugs in high-school students' lockers.

And there are the horrendous civil forfeiture statutes that buttress the so-called "zero tolerance" policy. If, for example, a family member or house guest is found in possession of marijuana in your home, you the home-owner can lose your property to the U.S. government unless you can prove — that's right, you have the burden of proof — that not only were you ignorant of the drug's presence, but also that your ignorance was not the result of negligence. In fact, not even that limited defence was allowed until the *Anti-Drug Abuse Act* (1988) was accordingly amended; before then the mere presence of the drug was sufficient in itself to trigger forfeiture.[11] Last but not least, there is the DEA (the U.S. Drug Enforcement Agency), those noble drug warriors who, in their zeal, have been known to break into homes, terrorizing the occupants, and occasionally killing law-abiding residents who get caught in the confusion. But, then, all wars produce their "friendly fire" casualties.

Not a pretty picture, but then war never is. Furthermore, when one fights a war, one must vilify the enemy because how otherwise can the troops be motivated to fight? After all, if our adversaries are really no different from us, then why should we be warring against them? It has thus happened that those who wage the War on Drugs brand the enemy as diabolical creatures who threaten the lives and well-being of those who do not follow in their wicked ways.

As defined in Webster's Dictionary, *dope* is a slang expression for "any drug or narcotic." Actually, it is a slang expression for illicit drugs; no one refers to alcohol or tobacco as dope but only drugs such as heroin, cocaine, LSD, and marijuana — all of which tend to get lumped together under that pejorative heading. And who are the consumers and purveyors of such drugs — dope addicts, dope fiends, dope peddlers (invariably lurking in school grounds), or simply dopers. If one is using dope, then one is beyond the pale. The very word conjures up images of people who are out of control and behaving like crazed animals who would be pitied except that they have wilfully brought about their own degradation.

Of course, when one is waging a Manichean struggle between the forces of good and evil, one cannot be expected to wage war in accordance with the Marquis of Queensbury's rules of gentlemanly conduct. It is thus that the Reagan/Bush Drug Czar William Bennett has publicly advocated that drug traffickers be beheaded in public squares. He presumably includes those dealing in marijuana, because I heard him proclaim on the NBC Nightly News that "marijuana is the most dangerous drug of them all." (Bennett, America's self-anointed moral philosopher king and author of *The Book of Virtues*, a best-selling anthology of moral tales, is a close political ally of North Carolina Senator Jesse Helms, who aggressively represents the interests of the tobacco industry whenever it comes under threat. Commanding $40 000 per speech on the lecture circuit, Bennett is living proof that virtue is its own reward.) Then there is Newt Gingrich, the Speaker of the U.S. House of Representatives, who has recently called for the mandatory execution of convicted drug smugglers. In introducing a bill to that effect, he said that if we kill enough of them: "it will have a very chilling effect on people bringing drugs into the U.S."[12] On the other hand, Daryl Gates, former chief of the Los Angeles Police Department, would not stop at traffickers. As he testified before the U.S. Senate, casual drug users should be taken out and shot. He explained, "we're in a war!"[13]

Although William Bennett comes across as a bleeding heart compared to Chief Gates, he too is no less adamant in sounding the alarm of a nation imperiled by (illicit) drugs. According to the first National Drug Defense Control Strategy, prepared by the Office of National Drug Control Policy under his direction: "Illicit drug use degrades human character, and a purposeful, self-governing society ignores its people's character at great peril. Drug users make inattentive parents, bad neighbors, poor students, and unreliable employees.... [Using drugs is] a hollow, degrading, and deceptive pleasure ... and pursuing it is an appallingly self-destructive impulse."[14]

In a sense, then, drug use is an atrocious crime, perhaps exceeded only by murder — although in the opinion of Nancy Reagan, "if you're a casual drug user, you are an accomplice to murder."[15] So drugs, after all, ranks with the most serious crime that one can commit. (Though tell me, Nancy, if as your drug czar has said, drug use is an "appalling self-destructive impulse," wouldn't it be better labelled as suicide instead of murder?) In any event, it is no wonder that the propaganda arm of the War on Drugs is waging a relentless campaign to discourage that "self-destructive impulse." At the forefront of the propaganda war stands the Partnership for a Drug-Free America, whose self-avowed mission is to "reduce demand for illegal drugs by using media communications to help bring about public intolerance of illegal drugs, their use, and users."

Hence, for example, the Frying Pan commercial. As butter sizzles in an iron skillet, the announcer intones, "This is drugs." After a sunny-side-up egg appears and sizzles in the pan, he informs the viewer, "This is your brain on drugs. Any questions?" Or the Russian roulette print spot, depicting two fingers loading a hand-rolled marijuana cigarette into the chamber of a revolver. As the caption reads: "The odds are that marijuana won't ruin your life. And that Russian roulette won't kill you."[16] And then there is the video in which a terrified patient cowers in his bed as his hysterically giggling surgeon, puffing away at a marijuana cigarette, asks him, "What's wrong with you — tonsillitis?" He replies, "No, appendicitis," and then — as the anaesthetist (presumably also stoned) installs the face mask — he utters a pitiful "Oh, no." At which point the voice-over asks, "Would you still say marijuana is harmless?"[17]

It is of course the nature of propaganda that it distorts the truth; all that counts is whether the message gets across. It was the Nazi Propaganda Minister, Joseph Goebbels, who expressed the cynical view that if the state incessantly repeats a Big Lie, then people will come to believe it. The Big Lie propounded by the Partnership for a Drug-Free America is that society is divided into two camps: the good people who don't use illicit drugs and the evil others who do, and that the latter must be eliminated by measures, however drastic, just as one resorts to the drastic remedy of chemotherapy to root out cancer. In short, the end justifies the means.

Goebbels also believed that propaganda for the masses had to be simple, aimed at the lowest level of intelligence, and reduced to easily learned slogans repeated over and over. The Frying Pan, Russian Roulette, and Stoned Surgeon scenarios would have been right up his alley. As the old saying goes, truth is the first casualty in war.

By the way, it is not only the Partnership for a Drug-Free America that distorts the truth. Consider, for example, a story on marijuana by reporter Roger O'Neil which appeared on 12 September 1995 on the *NBC Nightly News*. The gist of the story was as follows. Marijuana is a dangerous drug threatening the youth of America. A new study suggests that it is addictive. It impairs learning. Once you use marijuana you then go on to cocaine, from cocaine to heroin, and from heroin to the gutter. When O'Neil delivered that final grim message, he stood next to a bum lying in the gutter of some American ghetto. The implicit message, of course, was that the bum had started down the inevitable road to degradation when he smoked his first joint. As the story faded out, the camera panned to anchorman Tom Brokaw, who had the look of concern and anguish that one would expect after hearing such a terrifying account of the ravages wrought by reefer madness.

It is not only in the realm of propaganda that Joseph Goebbels offers a parallel to the War on Drugs. At the beginning of World War II, Germans were forbidden to listen to the BBC under threat of death or imprisonment; and it was Goebbels who urged members of the Hitler Youth to inform upon their parents and anyone else that they caught listening. In that regard, consider this recent parallel that proves that, as in any war, just about anything goes in the War on Drugs. On November 6, 1991, a story appeared in the *Winnipeg Free Press* under the headline: "Turning in dope dealer pays double in November." As the article opens: "Crime pays — now more than ever. Winnipeg police are counting on the lure of big bucks to get people to turn in their neighbours, friends, or even family for cultivating marijuana.... According to the Winnipeg Police Crime Stoppers co-ordinator, 'If it takes a drug problem off the street, we don't care who makes the phone call.'"[18] So for the month of November, anyone informing on someone growing marijuana, even for his own use, was promised double the normal cash reward. This, by the way, was not the first or the last time that such a policy has been promoted by the Winnipeg Police Department.

In that same article, Winnipeg Police Vice Inspector Ray Johns was quoted as stating that: "[i]t's our belief that young people get their introduction into narcotics through marijuana." (At least, the learned Vice Inspector recognizes that marijuana is not a narcotic, which is more than one can say for our Parliamentarians, who include marijuana as a prohibited drug under the *Narcotic Control Act*.) What Johns is referring to is the so-called "stepping-stone" or "gateway" theory, which is a matter of holy writ for the police in their waging of war against marijuana. The implicit admission behind the theory is that marijuana is not the killer drug it is often made out to be. But it must be vigorously suppressed nonetheless because there is something about the drug — what that is, is never explained — that somehow compels its user to go on to cocaine and heroin, the so-called "hard" drugs. (Recall that this was the theme of that NBC newscast that I earlier referred to.)

With all due respect for the Vice Inspector, the disreputable gateway theory presents a notion of cause and effect that is simply another example of the Big Lie. Firstly, since there are multiples of marijuana consumers for every heroin and cocaine consumer, how can one say that the marijuana user of today is the heroine/cocaine user of tomorrow? It is estimated that as many as 70 million Americans have smoked marijuana at one time or another.[19] Thus, if the gateway theory had any validity, then the total population of Canada would be outnumbered by Americans snorting cocaine and/or shooting heroin! I would think that most consumers of these two drugs have either used or continue to use marijuana. However, it is also true that heroin/cocaine users have also indulged in alcohol, tobacco, and a variety of prescription and over-the-counter drugs.

The fact that a cocaine user has used marijuana no more proves a cause and effect relationship than the fact that before cocaine he experienced tobacco, coffee, or mother's milk. The gateway theory illustrates the logical fallacy called by the Latin phrase, *post hoc, ergo propter hoc* ("after the fact, therefore before the fact"). In other words, the fact that event A occurs before event B does not in itself prove that the former caused the latter. One is thus tempted to conclude that all that is proved by the gateway theory is the muddledness of its proponent. But not quite. What I mean is illustrated by the Dutch policy on marijuana, whereby the government allows its sale in specially licensed and strictly regulated coffee shops. Cultivation for personal use is also tolerated, and consequently there are hydroponic stores that furnish the means for doing so. By adopting this approach, the Dutch government is promoting a principle that it calls the "separation of markets."[20] In other words, if the marijuana consumer does not have to seek out an underworld connection for his drug of choice, he is less likely to be exposed to the so-called hard drugs like heroin and cocaine. In a sense, then, separation of markets acts as a *gateway* against exposure to heroin and cocaine. (By the way, the per capita use of marijuana in The Netherlands is about half what it is in Canada and the United States.)

I'll be returning to the Dutch policy on drugs in my concluding remarks, but suffice it to note that American and Canadian drug warriors treat the Dutch approach with contempt. They remind me of the hawks during the Vietnam War, who kept insisting that the only way to victory was to commit ever more resources to a cause that its critics rightly branded as unwinnable. But the War on Drugs is not being won, and more of the same isn't going to do it either. We can distort language to paint a disastrous social policy as a war that must be fought against the menace of dope, but that does not alter the reality that the war is a losing proposition that makes the social disruption caused by Prohibition — the American war against alcohol that marked the turbulent decade called the Roaring Twenties — pale in comparison.

And now, begging your indulgence, a play in three acts, respectively titled: *Drugs, Use versus Abuse*, and *Addiction versus Habit*. The cast (in order of appearance): E.T., the Police Inspector of Vice (hereinafter called the Vice-Inspector), the Pharmacologist, and the Criminologist.

THE PLAY, ACT I: DRUGS

As in the War on Drugs, The Coalition for a Drug-Free America, Just Say No to Drugs.

An inhabited planet in our galaxy has dispatched an emissary by spaceship to Canada to learn about the War on Drugs. They select someone who has been studying our planet from afar but who admits that he finds our species hard to understand. And so arrives one E.T. whose first appointment is with the Vice-Inspector of the local police force.

E.T.: On my way to your office, we passed a number of Drug Stores and I am wondering what they have to do with the War on Drugs.

Vice-Inspector: Actually, Drug Stores is not what the war is all about. That is because Drug Stores are legitimate businesses selling drugs for medicinal purposes, whereas the War on Drugs is directed against the non-medicinal or recreational use of drugs. I am referring here to such drugs as heroin, cocaine, LSD, and marijuana. In fact, it is because these drugs are so harmful that it is not enough simply to out-law manufacture and distribution. It is also necessary to target the consumer by banning possession for personal use.[21]

Well, so much then for Drug Stores and their drugs. Let us assume at this point that, being a clever fellow, E.T. knows that a police officer is not an expert on the properties of drugs. So he asks to meet with someone who has scientific credentials in the field and can brief him about those dangerous recreational drugs. He is accordingly directed to a professor of phar-macology at a prestigious medical school, who graciously agrees to help him with his inquiries.

E.T.: Since the War on Drugs is a war against recreational drugs, I am wondering what are the recreational drugs that cause the most harm to consumers?

The Pharmacologist: That's easy to answer — tobacco and alcohol. And unfortu-nately, because these are two of the most widely used recreational drugs, the harm they cause is therefore quite substantial.

E.T.: I'm frankly surprised because I have studied the video and print materials produced by the Partnership for a Drug-Free America — and nowhere did I come across any reference to those two drugs.

The Pharmacologist: Well, that is because the Partnership is only concerned with illegal drugs, and alcohol and tobacco are perfectly legal. So what it means by "Drug-Free" is an America free of the use of illicit drugs.

E.T.: I find this puzzling, because I would think that if your society is going to ban certain drugs — a concept unknown in our world — you would ban the drugs that have the most potential to harm consumers.

The Pharmacologist: That's not how it works here. In any event, perhaps a good place to begin your education is by highlighting the harm caused by alcohol and tobacco. To begin with, there is the carnage wrought on the highways by drunk dri-vers and the drug's association with crimes of violence such as spousal abuse. Take a look at this brochure, *Alcohol the Drug*, produced by the Addictions Foundation of Manitoba. As it explains,

> Alcohol like any other drug can be misused. It can be addicting. Statistics cite alcohol as a factor in:
> 64% of all homicides
> 31% of all suicides
> 40% of all hospital admissions
> 50% of all highway deaths
> 34% of all rapes
> 40% of all family court appearances.

Overindulgence can also wreak havoc upon the consumer's physical and mental well-being. And beyond that is the fact that the most preventable cause of mental retardation is the drinking of alcohol during pregnancy. In fact, Fetal Alcohol Syndrome (FAS) is the single leading cause of mental handicap in North America. There are children and adults in our midst with literally holes in their brains because when they were in the womb they were being bathed in alcohol. To add insult to injury, the Canadian liquor industry does nothing to fund programs for these drug victims and it steadfastly opposes labels on their products warning against drinking while pregnant. You will recall that, according to the Partnership for a Drug-Free America, if you use any drug (i.e., any illicit drug), then the drug fries your brain like a pan fries an egg. Yet, that is precisely what alcohol can do to the fetal brain.

By the way, tobacco also takes a fearful toll upon fetal development. According to a 1995 article in the *Journal of Medical Practice*, smoking mothers in the United States annually cause the deaths of about 5000 infants (about 2000 from Sudden Infant Death Syndrome), suffer about 115 000 miscarriages, and give birth to about 50 000 low weight infants (40 percent of whom require neonatal intensive care).[22]

The public generally doesn't think of alcohol and tobacco as drugs; but there is another drug — cocaine — that is illegal, and the cocaine/pregnancy connection is being addressed. In fact, a number of American states prosecute mothers for using cocaine during pregnancy (charging them under drug laws), aided and abetted by physicians informing on their patients. Some have even gone so far as to charge mothers delivering cocaine-affected infants with "trafficking in a controlled substance to a minor." The prosecutions have rested on the dubious theory that cocaine must have passed into the newborn's blood system before the umbilical cord was severed.

No matter that — as a number of American medical and public health organizations have stressed — such practices are likely to drive pregnant women using drugs away from pre-natal care. During his tenure as Drug Czar, William Bennett suggested that pregnant women using cocaine be forced into treatment to avoid the "real catastrophe" of a generation of children with potentially severe learning disabilities. As he explained, "If we stopped the drug problem tomorrow dead in its tracks, we would have this generation of children."[23] Not surprisingly, there is no public record of his expressing concern for the generation of children harmed in utero by alcohol and tobacco.

The Drug Czar's moral blind spot is frankly no surprise. Unfortunately, we can expect no better from the media, even from the best that the media has to offer. When *60 Minutes*, the much heralded CBS TV news program, did a recent segment on what it labelled as a major drug problem — cocaine use during pregnancy — the A and T words (alcohol and tobacco) were never even mentioned. No, all we heard from *60 Minutes* is that the drug-during-pregnancy problem is cocaine. But then of course alcohol and tobacco really aren't drugs, right, whereas cocaine is a drug and there are the drug laws in place to use against women ingesting that drug in pregnancy. But rest assured that, as with alcohol, the *60 Minutes* segment never touched upon the havoc wrought by tobacco consumption in pregnancy. Ironically, *60 Minutes* is no friend to the tobacco industry as it has done a number of highly critical segments about its practices. But still, it just never made the alcohol/tobacco connection to the hazards of mixing drugs and pregnancy.

E.T.: Given what you have told me about the effects of tobacco on fetal development, I wonder what it does to those who smoke this drug.

The Pharmacologist: I can't help but smile when you call tobacco a drug. That it certainly is, although like alcohol the public doesn't think of it as a drug. To put it bluntly, the more we learn about tobacco, the more lethal it looks, the protestations of the tobacco companies to the contrary. In fact, the most preventable cause of death is smoking; if everyone stopped smoking, our mortality and morbidity rates would plummet. But there is Joe Camel, that lovable advertising figure who has captured an impressive share of teenage smokers for his parent company; there are also cigarette ads in American fashion magazines that show anorexic models and convey the message that smoking is the way to stay slim. In fact, there is a brand of American cigarettes called Virginia Slims that is marketed particularly for women and whose slogan is, "You've come a long way, baby." Women have indeed come a long way. More are being killed by lung cancer than by breast cancer,[24] and teenaged girls are taking up smoking to a significantly greater extent than their male peers.

Twenty-five years ago, journalist Thomas Whiteside published a book called *Selling Death*,[25] subtitled *Cigarette Advertising and Public Health*. Nothing has really changed since then except that we know now that cigarettes are even more lethal than we assumed a quarter century ago. That title — *Selling Death* — is certainly an apt description of what the tobacco industry is all about. To that industry the cigarette is conceived as a nicotine delivery system. As the public is well aware from extensive media coverage, there have been recent revelations that cigarette companies have been manipulating nicotine levels in order to fine-tune the drug's impact on smokers.

By the way, cigarettes kill about 400 000 Americans and 40 000 Canadians per annum — which is roughly the number of Americans and Canadians killed during all of World War II — and all the deaths from all illicit drugs amount to only a tiny fraction of the cigarette mortality toll.[26] In 1995 the World Health Organization went out of its way to castigate tobacco companies for ignoring death and suffering in their pursuit of profits. According to the UN agency: "Every year, tobacco is responsible for the deaths of three million people around the world, one death in every 10 seconds." It also noted that one-third of tobacco-related deaths occur in developing economies where teens and women are special targets of cigarette advertising. And these dismal figures are steadily going up, not down.[27]

Here in Winnipeg as elsewhere, there are liquor stores and cigarette vending machines that make these drugs readily available to consumers. The drugs are heavily taxed, which means that the government has a vested interest in their sale. In fact, in Manitoba, it is the government that directly runs the trade in alcohol; in other words, the same government that wages the War on Drugs is the province's major drug trafficker.

As E.T. raises his four eyebrows in surprise, the Pharmacologist smiles and continues.

Well, the thinking goes like this. For one thing, about 90 percent of those who drink are so-called social drinkers who don't harm themselves or others, so why punish them because of the 10 percent who do cause harm because of excessive drinking. Besides, just about everyone drinks. The drug is so deeply ingrained in our culture that it would be impossible to enforce even a marginally effective ban against it.

From 1920 to 1933 — a time frame called the Prohibition Era — the United States engaged in such an act of folly. If you were to advocate Prohibition as a response to the ravages wrought by that drug, a liquor industry spokesperson would doubtless refer to that era of lawlessness and social chaos as an historical precedent against criminalization. I would agree, although one would be curious to know if he would make the same connection to cocaine. As is the case with alcohol, most consumers of cocaine are not harmed by its use (roughly the same percentage of consumers abuse cocaine as abuse alcohol). Still, the cocaine front is the major battleground of the War on Drugs, and cocaine is to the Drug Warriors as the Eastern Front was to the German Army in World War II — an unmitigated disaster.

There is, by the way, a derivative of cocaine called crack cocaine, which certainly has a high harm potential. The irony is that crack cocaine is a stepchild of the War on Drugs. Because of the grossly inflated black market price of cocaine, crack was developed as a cheap alternative. But that's another story.

Regarding cigarettes, an interesting point is that — unlike any of the illicit drugs, or alcohol for that matter — there is little casual use. In other words, once you begin to smoke, the odds are quite high that not only will you smoke every day, but also that you will smoke multiple cigarettes every day. You will smoke year in and year out, and unless you muster the awesome amount of willpower required to quit the drug, you run the risk of dying of cancer or heart disease. But if we ban cigarettes we would create a black market of nightmarish proportions (which is bad enough as it is with cheaper cigarettes flowing across the American border). Besides, does it really make any sense to treat someone as a criminal just because he or she is a cigarette smoker? Better to try to educate the consumer about the health consequences of smoking; and in Canada we have been getting the message across and consumption has been dropping, except unfortunately among our teenaged population (especially girls).

E.T.: True enough, but if your society had banned alcohol and tobacco way back when, isn't it fair to say that you wouldn't now be experiencing the widespread harm caused by those two drugs?

The Pharmacologist: Not likely. That is because of what Nova University law professor Steven Wisotsky so aptly calls *black market pathologies*, which are an ineradicable byproduct of the War on Drugs.

After explaining Wisotsky's phrase — see Part I of this chapter — she continues.

Can you imagine the nightmare that would be created by the criminalization of these two recreational drugs? Given the enormous demand for alcohol and tobacco, the law that would ban them would not cause the demand to vanish. Simply put, the criminal law is not a magic wand; it cannot work miracles. Instead, what would happen is the emergence of a black market to satisfy the demand. That is the way it is with the currently illegal drugs, and that is the way it would be with the outlawing of alcohol and tobacco.

Still, we are making a dent on tobacco and that is by educating consumers with the straight goods. If you keep stressing the high harm potential of the drug, then many consumers will get the message and either quit smoking — no mean achievement given the addictive properties of the drug — or never start. Regarding alcohol, it is true that most who indulge are responsible consumers; but a problem with that drug is our culture, a culture that out of one side of its mouth preaches moderation but from the other side glamorizes the drug and fails to instill inhibitions against its destructive effects. We are, after all, a booze culture, and how do you deal with that?

E.T.: Although I am endowed with a superintelligence that has no equal on your poor planet, I admit that I am still befuddled. What, then, is the War on Drugs all about? What determines which drugs are legal and which are not?

The Pharmacologist: If you'll excuse me for a minute, I can help you to a quick understanding of the War on Drugs after I make a quick trip to the Roman Catholic Church next door.

E.T. scratches his pointed green head with wonderment but waits patiently until she returns with two bowls of water.

One of these bowls is filled with ordinary tap water and the other with holy water, which means that it is sanctified by the Church. How can you determine which is which?

E.T.: I would think that chemical testing would answer that.

The Pharmacologist: That certainly is an intelligent answer, but it is not the right answer. The truth is that both would test chemically as ordinary tap water; the difference between them is ceremonial.[28] And that, my extraterrestrial friend, is what you have to know to begin to understand the War on Drugs — that it is not the inherent properties of a drug that determine whether it is legal or illegal, that to try to understand the War on Drugs by studying the effects of the drugs themselves would make as much sense as trying to understand the difference between tap water and holy water by comparing samples of each under a microscope. The War on Drugs is really an exercise in ceremonial chemistry.

To illustrate the point, take a look at this book. It is titled *Licit and Illicit Drugs*, and its subtitle is: *The Consumers Union Report on Narcotics, Stimulants, Depressants, Inhalants, and Marijuana — including Caffeine, Nicotine, and Alcohol*.[29] Published in 1972 by the consumer watchdog organization the Consumers Union, it remains a valuable, comprehensive, and objective study of its subject matter.

Given his superbrain power, E.T. is able to digest the 600-page book in 30 minutes. She then continues.

Do you now understand why I said that the holy/tap water demonstration would help explain what the War on Drugs is all about?

E.T.: Yes, I do, because as the book makes clear, there is no correlation between the harm potential of a drug and its legal classification. I was also struck by the comment that "no drug is safe or harmless at all dosage levels or under all conditions of use."[30] In that regard, the authors note that "caffeine can be a dangerous drug," which I suppose would surprise most people who wouldn't even think of their morning cups of coffee as a drug. They also have this to say about coffee, which I imagine is equally applicable to tobacco and alcohol: "By keeping coffee legal, society has avoided extortionate black-market prices that might otherwise bankrupt coffee drinkers and lead them into lives of crime. And coffee drinkers are not stigmatized as criminals, driven into a deviant subculture with all that criminalization entails."[31]

The Pharmacologist: You certainly catch on fast. There is, by the way, a voluminous body of literature that echoes the findings reported in 1972 by the Consumers Union. I won't belabour the point, but consider this statement by the U.S. National Commission on Marijuana and Drug Abuse. It dates from 1973 but is as true today as it was then:

> The imprecision of the term "drug" has had serious social consequences. Because alcohol is excluded, the public is conditioned to regard a martini as something fundamentally different from a marijuana cigarette, a barbiturate capsule or a bag of heroin. Similarly, because the referents of the word "drug" differ so widely in the therapeutic and social contexts, the public is conditioned to believe that "street" drugs act according to entirely different principles than "medical" drugs. The result is that the risks of the former are exaggerated and the risks of the latter are overlooked.[32]

E.T.: I still don't get what the War on Drugs is all about. But I'm beginning to think that what may explain it is that you earthlings are even stranger than I thought.

The Pharmacologist: I can't comment on that, but I can help you understand why the War on Drugs is not about the drugs that have the most harm potential. Rather, what determines whether a particular drug is criminalized is not its inherent properties and/or potential for social harm but rather the kinds of people associated with its use. Since this takes us outside my field of expertise, I have taken the liberty to ask a colleague in the Department of Criminology to join us. He specializes in the area of Drug Control, and here he is now.

After the introductions, the Criminologist tells E.T. that he can understand his confusion and that he will do his best to clear it up. He continues.

The Criminologist: What we have learned is that the behaviour in which people indulge is often less important than the social category assigned to them. Why do certain drugs get labelled as deviant whereas others do not? Well, it is necessary to understand that the drugs of choice of the so-called "moral centre" — the so-called solid citizens, the professional and business classes, the police, politicians, etc. — don't get criminalized. It is only the drugs whose primary indulgers are the so-called "morally susceptible" that are placed beyond the pale. Of course, these so-called deviants also use alcohol and tobacco, but the fact that these are also the drugs of choice of the moral centre ensures that they remain legal.[33]

E.T.: Excuse me for interrupting, but isn't this concept of the "moral centre" contradicted by the notorious American experience with Prohibition?

The Criminologist: Good point, but not really. The so-called Prohibition Era — the banning of alcohol in the United States from 1920 to 1933 — is simply the exception that proves the rule. Prohibition was a product of the moral fervour engendered by World War I — that a nation couldn't fight the Germans if its soldiers and armaments workers were soused with booze. Although, admittedly, also at play were the so-called Temperance Societies, which had been lobbying for the banning of alcohol for years because of its horrific social costs. But still, it was the entry of the United States into the war that made Prohibition a politically viable measure. Compared to the long drawn out War on Drugs, Prohibition was a short run experiment. The reason that it was repealed was that the "moral centre" could not abide the continued criminalization of its preferred recreational drug.

It is particularly instructive to study the history of drug criminalization in the United States and Canada — the reasons why particular drugs were banned. Indeed, as I've said, what one finds is that the currently illegal drugs were criminalized because of the people associated with their use.[34] In fact, it was the Canadian Parliament that set the precedent for the Americans, banning trafficking in opium for nonmedicinal purposes in the *Opium Act* (1908), followed by a ban on possession in the *Opium and Narcotic Drug Act* (1911). The legislation reflected the anti-Oriental sentiment of the day and was directed at the "heathen" Chinese consumers of the drug, even though there was no evidence that their recreational opium use was a social problem.[35] (Incidentally, the Americans did not adopt a criminal law model of drug control until 1914, when Congress passed the *Harrison Narcotic Act*.) In 1923, marijuana was added to the schedule of prohibited drugs in the *Opium and Narcotic Drug Act* and was approved by Parliament with no discussion whatsoever.[36] (Once again, Parliament was one step ahead of Congress, which did not outlaw marijuana until the 1937 enactment of the *Marijuana Tax Act*; it is pertinent to note that at that time the drug's consumers in the United States were primarily Mexicans, blacks, and jazz musicians.) The 1923 amendment had been prompted by a series of sensationalist articles that were published in *Maclean's Magazine* in 1920 and whose stated purpose was to pressure the government to enact stricter drug laws.

Written by Emily Murphy, a champion and spokesperson for various social causes (including women's suffrage), the articles were published in book form in 1922 under the title *The Black Candle*.[37] Her writings on the subject of drugs reek of "popular racial bias, fables, and sensationalism."[38] But her views were widely publicized and endorsed in newspaper editorials across the country. Her chapter titled "Marijuana — A New Menace" is replete with "documented" cases reported by police officials of the most horrific crimes committed by crazed marijuana addicts. Most of the horror stories involved Mexicans, although none was said to have happened in Canada. Still, *The Black Candle* was of sufficient influence to lead to the banning of the drug in Canada.

Regarding marijuana, the drug was not that popular until the 1960s, and it is clear that the current war on marijuana, which is conducted with even greater intensity in the United States than here, is a war against the 1960s! The war against marijuana is a war against the 1960s because no drug is more associated with that era of political dissent, hippies, and alternative life-styles. What other explanation is there for the continued criminalization of a drug whose ill effects pale in comparison to those of alcohol and tobacco? Why else would William Bennett call it the most dangerous drug of them all? The answer is simple — holy versus tap water. It is true, of course, that there are marijuana smokers who harm themselves by overindulgence in the drug. But, as you know, one can say that about virtually any drug — whether licit or illicit. Aspirin, for example, is truly a wonder drug, but it can do you serious, even life-threatening, harm. As the Consumers Union Report explains, there is virtually no drug — legal, illegal, prescription, over-the-counter — that is harm free. Two years after the publication of *Licit and Illicit Drugs*, that point was underscored when the distinguished medical authors of a book called *Pills, Profits, and Politics* reported that an estimated 130 000 deaths occurred annually in the United States from adverse reactions to prescription drugs![39] The figures are even higher now but are never connected to the so-called drug problem, and William Bennett would no doubt respond that these are medicinal drugs and that somehow this makes the difference.

So, now you have a clear understanding of the term "ceremonial chemistry," which might also be called "political pharmacology" or "Calvinist pharmacology." In short, it is not the inherent pharmacological properties of drugs that determine their legal status. It is rather at the political level that these decisions are made.

The Pharmacologist: There is an important point that I should reiterate. Over time the public has been so brainwashed that most people do not even think of alcohol and tobacco as drugs, a mindset illustrated by that oftspoken phrase, "alcohol and drugs" — as in, "Such-and-such a community is having problems with alcohol and drugs." Its explicit meaning is that although alcohol may be a problem, it is not a drug problem. In the early 1970s, a "substances regarded as drugs" survey was conducted in the United States. When asked which substances on a list were drugs, regarding alcohol only 39 percent of adults and 34 percent of minors said Yes, and regarding tobacco only 27 percent of adults and 16 percent of minors said Yes.[40] Is there reason to think that the brainwashed public is any less misinformed today than two decades ago? I think not.

Although alcohol is far and away the major drug problem affecting our youth, one hears time and time again that young people do not regard alcohol as a problem because, after all, it is not a drug! I recently watched a Detroit television news programme, in which some teenagers were deploring the effects of alcohol on many of their peers and were saying, "Just because it's not a drug doesn't mean that it can't harm you."

What could be more absurd than to watch a baseball or football game on TV where an anti-drug commercial is followed by a beer commercial, the latter extolling the connection between beer and being a real man. In a 50-page booklet titled *Myth, Men and Beer*, even as respectable an organization as the AAA (Automobile Association of America) has called for the banning of beer commercials. As the booklet (published in 1988) states: "Beer is represented as an essential element in masculinity, so that one cannot be attained without the other. In our view, this is a distorted and dangerous message to broadcast to young people."

The Criminologist: The only thing I'd like to add is that all those Drug Warriors — the Reagans, George Bush, William Bennett, Newt Gingrich, Daryl Gates, and their Canadian allies — are quick to bemoan government intrusion into the private lives of the citizenry. Get government off the backs of the people, they have all said. But, hey, drugs are different, right?

E.T.: Thank you both for enlightening me, but I still find this somewhat confusing. I suppose that if I were not a stranger to your planet and in particular to your species, I would have a better understanding of what you call the War on Drugs. But as it is I still find it difficult to grasp why you earthlings would pursue such a mindless policy.

The Pharmacologist: I have the same trouble. All I can say is that it might help you get a handle on the War on Drugs by reading this book. It is called *Alice in Wonderland*.

THE PLAY, ACT II: DRUG USE VERSUS DRUG ABUSE

The Pharmacologist: In any event, continuing with your education, let me tell you about the "use" and the "abuse" of drugs. When I use the term "drug abuse," I mean that the consumer is being harmed by the drug (either in the physical and/or psychological sense or in his relationships with others — family, friends, workmates, even strangers). In other words, what abuse means is that for the user the burdens stemming from consumption have exceeded its benefits. For example, as used non-medically in our society, alcohol is taken occasionally and in moderation with few undesirable side effects by the great majority of users. But then there is abuse, and I am here referring to those who get into trouble with the drug: impairing judgment and coordination sufficient to cause an auto accident, increasing aggressiveness that results in crimes of violence (more often than not against one's spouse), or causing irreversible damage to the brain, liver, and other body parts. So much, then, for the distinction between drug use and drug abuse.

However, when a drug is criminalized, there is no use but only abuse. If you smoke a joint on the weekend as part of a social evening with your friends — if the drug is one aspect of a good time had by all — then you are a drug abuser simply because there is no legally recognized use of illicit drugs. Even if you are smoking marijuana for its medicinal properties — for example, to combat the nausea of chemotherapy — you are still considered a drug abuser! In any case, I know that my colleague would like to pick up this theme of use versus abuse.

The Criminologist: Students of criminal law are familiar with two Latin terms: *malum in se* and *malum prohibitum* (wrong in itself and wrong by the force of law). On the one hand, there are such traditional crimes as murder, robbery, kidnapping, and assault, which regardless of any particular penal code would be universally regarded as wrong in themselves: i.e., *malum in se*. Consider, on the other hand, offences such as carrying open liquor in your vehicle, an act which is not wrongful in itself (e.g., an unsealed bottle of whiskey on the back seat that is just sitting there). It is wrongful because the act is so defined by law: it is *malum prohibitum*.

In summary, then, one must understand that when a drug is criminalized, whether the drug harms the user is beside the point. By definition, then, one cannot use an illicit drug. One can only abuse, and surely abuse is wrong in itself. In other words, the public at large has been conditioned to accept illicit drug use as *malum in se*.

THE PLAY, ACT III: DRUG ADDICTION VERSUS DRUG HABIT

The Pharmacologist: Finally, a word about drug addiction and the tobacco habit. In the War on Drugs, addiction is a term that is used all too lightly. If you use heroin or cocaine, then you are an addict. But the evidence is that the majority of those who use heroin and cocaine do not do so on a day in, day out basis. I am certainly not saying that these drugs cannot be addictive, but since most users are not addicted, it is the properties of the drug combined with the psychosocial makeup of the user that determine whether a person becomes hooked.[41] But, still, we do know that there is one drug for which casual use is a rarity — that most of those who start using it will wind up consuming it compulsively over time. And quitting it is harder than quitting heroin, and that drug is nicotine! Consider the following excerpt from a chapter in the Consumers Union Report, titled "Nicotine as an Addictive Drug":

> One hallmark of an addicting substance is the fact that users seek it *continuously* day after day. If they can take it or leave it — take it on some days and not be bothered by lack of it on other days — they are not in fact addicted. Judged by this standard, nicotine is clearly addicting; the number of smokers who do not smoke every day ... is very small. The typical pattern of nicotine use, moreover, is not only daily but hourly. Nearly four male smokers out of five and more than three female smokers our of five consume 15 or more cigarettes a day — roughly one or more per waking hour.... No other substance known to man is used with such remarkable frequency. Even caffeine ranks a poor second.[42]

By the way, tobacco shows stunning parallels with heroin in terms of its addictive power. But the point is that we talk only about the tobacco habit. If we were to call it what it is — an addiction — then we might have to admit that it is, after all, a drug. On the other hand, if you are an infrequent user of heroin or cocaine — in other words, if you can take it or leave it — you are still at risk to be labelled a drug addict.

Be that as it may, the tobacco industry not only continues to assert that there is no scientific proof that their product is harmful but also heatedly denies that it is addictive. The industry has transformed its stance of wallowing in righteous indignation into an art form, as illustrated by an Associated Press release on 4 April 1988. When the then U.S. Surgeon-General C. Everett Koop stated that nicotine was addictive, the vice-president of the U.S. Tobacco Institute responded that: "It is apparent that anti-tobacco zeal has overtaken common sense and good judgment." In a comment that can be described only as pure unadulterated *chutzpah*, he added: "To imply that the 55 million American tobacco-smokers are drug-abusers is to subvert and divert attention from the nation's war on illicit drugs. It is a trivialization of the country's urgent concerns with hard drugs and verges on irresponsibility."

So endeth the extraterrestrial's lesson on the subversion of language to serve a political agenda. As he prepares to leave our planet, E.T. telepathically dispatches the following message to home:

"I have encountered earthlings. They have a bizarre and nonsensical custom. They proudly call it the War on Drugs. I regret to report that my mission has failed — we have yet to discover intelligent life elsewhere in the universe."

THE OSTRICH AND THE NAKED EQUESTRIENNE

In December 1993, Jocelyn Elders, the then U.S. Surgeon-General, publicly stated that it was time to consider whether legalizing drugs might help fight crime. I heard former Drug Czar William Bennett's response on CNN: "She's morally obtuse, nutty, just plain nutty." And President Clinton reacted quickly to disassociate his administration from her comment, authorizing the White House communications director to inform the media that "it's nothing we would ever entertain." Clinton himself announced that he had no intention of reviewing the War on Drugs agenda of Ronald Reagan and George Bush. Like them, he is content to bury his head in the sand whilst the war continues to wreak its havoc upon a beleaguered public. Still, the ostrich cannot fly and neither can the War on Drugs. The difference is that the ostrich accepts nature's will whereas the Drug Warriors remain unshaken in the mad belief that a war that by its very nature is unwinnable is actually winnable. John Cleese of Monty Python fame could capture the essence of the War on Drugs in a two-minute routine. His gangly body covered with feathers, he jumps out a window, furiously flapping his arms and chanting a "Just Say No to Drugs" mantra. Not surprisingly, he plummets to the ground, landing on John Q. Public and crushing him like a bug. Cleese gets up, brushes himself off, and says, "I'll get it right next time" — and with a look of grim determination, he leaps up the stairs on his way back to the same window. Repeat the scene *ad nauseam* and one has a capsule history of the War on Drugs.

It may well be that President Clinton is not a true believer in the holy drug crusade. But he is a shrewd politician, who no doubt fears that questioning the legitimacy of the War on Drugs is politically the kiss of death. During the Cold War, there were politicians who profited by accusations of "soft on Communism" levelled against their political opponents, and Clinton knows that the accusation of being "soft on drugs" would provoke the same kind of backlash. In welcome contrast, there are a number of public figures with solid conservative credentials who have expressed the same view as Dr. Elders, including free market economist Milton Freedman, Reagan's Secretary of State George Schultz, and William F. Buckley, conservative media pundit and editor of the magazine *National Review*.[43]

What they have come to recognize is that the criminalization of drugs carries in its wake social costs that typify efforts to stamp out so-called consensual crimes; and that the greater the zeal invested in the process — as in the War on Drugs — the more the havoc that is wreaked. To know what the War on Drugs is really all about is to know the nature of the society that pursues it with such grim determination. Of course, I am referring to the United States. I suggest to you that the War on Drugs is really about scapegoating, about the need to conjure up enemies with whom to wage battle. It is about a characteristic of American society that dates back to the Salem witch trials of 1692 and that carries an unbroken thread through the Red Scare of the early 1920s, the McCarthy Era of the 1950s (the so-called Communist witchhunts), the War on Drugs, and the recent spate of cases involving unfounded allegations of ritual sexual abuse of children (particularly notorious are the cases involving day care centres). In short, the War on Drugs is as American as apple pie.

It is a war waged by a country whose tobacco industry has found prosperous new markets in third world countries, and whose tobacco farmers benefit from generous government subsidies to promote their lethal product overseas. By the way, keep in mind that the reason for one of Canada's drug smuggling problems — tobacco — is that the Americans won't use the taxing power to discourage consumption as we do. What I'm talking about is hypocrisy, about a war that wallows in it up to its red-white-and-blue eyeballs.

I'm talking about an America whose black ghettoes are awash with crack cocaine; and instead of confronting the socioeconomic breeding grounds for crack, it mounts what is in effect a race war against the drug's consumers. About a country that invades Panama to get rid of one drug trafficker (formerly on their payroll) — killing hundreds of innocent people in the process — and then quickly pulls out its troops, in effect guaranteeing that the illicit drug business would continue as usual. Panama was President Bush's doing; he called it Operation Just Cause. Good old George, as a Drug Warrior he stood as tall in the saddle as his mentor, Ronald Reagan.

I am here reminded of that 19th century Mexican general who lamented, "Poor Mexico, so far from God, so near the United States." I won't comment on the theological aspect of his remark, but regarding the geographical, all I'll say is, poor Canada. It is true that we have not embraced the war with the singleminded fanaticism of the Americans, but being neighbours, we cannot escape the taint of their unrelenting Drug War rhetoric. Yet it is equally true that Canada, no less than the United States, embraced the Police Model of drug control early in this century; and that, albeit we do not enforce the law with the same rabid intensity of the Americans, we are still committed to the pursuit of a bankrupt and shameful policy that has caused far more harm than any good that it has sought to accomplish.

Of course, the War has been good — good for the politicians who garner votes by showing that they are not soft on drugs, good for those in the business of building and running prisons, good for bloated bureaucracies like the DEA, good for people in the burglar alarm business because of all the break-ins committed by those who steal to get the money to pay the inflated black market price for their drugs of choice, and finally, last but not least, good — hey, wonderful — for organized crime.

Is there another way? Is there anything to learn from elsewhere? I have referred to the principle of *separation of markets* that informs Dutch drug policy. It operates in tandem with another principle: what the Dutch call *harm reduction*.[44] Although Dutch law prohibits the possession and sale of cocaine and narcotic drugs such as heroin, the provisions against possession are in effect not enforced. The rationale is as follows. If the person's use of an illicit drug is not dysfunctional, then there is no reason for state intervention. However, if the drug use is dysfunctional, then the arm of the state that should be involved is not law enforcement but rather public health. And why not? If someone is having a drug problem, what do we accomplish by labelling him a criminal? In any event, we would much sooner get him into treatment if the state treats him as a patient — as one with a health problem — rather than as a criminal. In short, if drug use, then it is not the state's business; if drug abuse, then it is the business of public health, not criminal justice.

What we have to recognize is that the pursuit of pleasure through recreational drugs — whether licit or illicit — is part and parcel of the human condition. In his insightful book, *Intoxication: Life in Pursuit of Artificial Paradise*, Dr. Ronald Siegel, a renowned professor of psychopharmacology at UCLA, refers to recreational drug use as the "fourth drive."[45] Exhibited by both animals (e.g., cats and catnip) and humans, the pursuit of intoxication, according to Dr. Siegel, is as natural and powerful a drive as sex, hunger, and thirst. His thesis probably explains why anthropologists have yet to discover a society that has not featured the non-medical use of drugs. In other words, it is human nature that we are talking about, and the notion of a society rid of recreational drug use is an impossible dream. The War on Drugs is a war on the biological and social nature of our species; it is a civil war, a war on our own people, those who do not use the right drugs. As Pogo says, the enemy is us.

The era of the compact disk is no place for that old fashioned and terribly outdated record player that keeps grinding out the message that a drug is either legal or illegal, and if it is illegal, then that means War. A century ago, Queen Victoria referred to the women's suffrage movement (women seeking the right to vote) as a "mad wicked folly." That it surely wasn't, but if ever there was a social policy that deserved that label — a "mad wicked folly" — it is the War on Drugs.

So, where do we go from here? Are there feasible alternatives to a social policy that wallows in hypocrisy and moral bankruptcy? The Drug Warriors and their allies have buried their heads in the sand because they cannot abide a different way; but the point is that we'll never know of alternatives until we come up for air and start looking. For those who are prepared to extricate their heads (and brains) from the sand, I suggest the following points to ponder.

There is a need to guide the public policy of drug control according to the harm principle. Each drug, regardless of its label as licit or illicit, must be considered on its own merits. What is the particular drug's relative potential for both personal and social harm? And what can we do to minimize the harm? In other words, we need a policy that is tailor-made for each particular drug. For example, in Canada we have done a fairly good job along that line with regard to tobacco, as a combination of public education and high taxes has served to decrease consumption. But we must keep in mind not only that every drug has the potential to cause harm but also that what determines any drug's impact upon the consumer and society is not simply the chemistry of the drug. It is rather the interaction between the drug and the consumer. As the authors of the Consumers Union Report explain in their introduction: "Readers who traditionally think in terms of the effect of a drug will learn here that even the simplest (psychoactive) drugs have a wide range of effects — depending not only on their chemistry but on the ways in which they are used, the laws that govern their use, the user's attitudes and expectations, and countless other factors."[46]

Marijuana is a case in point. Recall my reference to the reefer madness NBC news item and the statement that the drug impairs learning. What I object to is its presentation as a categorical statement: marijuana impairs learning. Actually, the reference was to a study suggesting that even if they have not smoked marijuana for a day, some heavy smokers may have trouble performing simple tasks that involve sustaining and shifting attention. Still, that is a far cry from saying that the drug inevitably produces that result. Furthermore, to say that a drug "impairs learning" is more ominous than to say that it affects attention. But I'll say once again that there are no totally harmless drugs. After all, even that wonder drug aspirin can cause gastric bleeding, mental confusion, blood clotting, and a host of other unpleasant and sometimes life-threatening side effects.[47] The solution is not to criminalize those who have a drug problem but rather to formulate nonpunitive strategies to deal with their dysfunctioning. It makes no sense to treat alcohol and tobacco abusers as criminals, just as it makes no sense to treat marijuana, cocaine, and heroin abusers as criminals.

I am encouraged by the recent news that a number of Canadian Senators have publicly called for the decriminalization of possession of small amounts of marijuana and hashish.[48] I applaud their sentiment, albeit I would go further as I believe it unconscionable to criminalize the possession of any drug for personal use. I simply cannot accept the concept that a person becomes a criminal because of what she ingests into her own body, whether it be marijuana, tobacco, cocaine, alcohol, or a steady diet of cream puffs, cheese blintzes awash in sour cream, and Big Macs. To my mind, the very notion of the crime of possession of drugs for personal use invokes the spectre of the state as Orwellian Big Brother. If the substance leads the consumer to batter his spouse or cause an auto accident, then prosecute him for the substantive offence. But otherwise leave him alone, although offer him help if his drug consumption proves dysfunctional. But that is of course a far cry from branding him as a criminal. I am here reminded of what Dr. Helen Nowlis, a renowned drug researcher, has aptly called "the drug problem problem" — the harm caused by the manner in which society has approached the question of drug control.[49]

By the way, the possession of alcoholic beverages for personal use was not criminalized during the Prohibition Era. Rather the law was directed against manufacture, sale, and importation. So at least the tragic social costs of Prohibition were not compounded by grinding ordinary consumers into the jaws of the criminal justice system.

Way back when, I read a marvelous book, a true classic, called *The Limits of the Criminal Sanction*, by Stanford law professor Herbert Packer.[50] Packer outlines six criteria as "a benchmark for the optimal use of the criminal sanction."[51] The final one — which he suggests is the most important — is that, with regard to the conduct in question: "There are no reasonable alternatives to the criminal sanction for dealing with it."[52] I would suggest that this ground alone furnishes sufficient reason to decriminalize possession for personal use. Surely, a Health Model that truly distinguishes between use and abuse and seeks to help, not criminalize, abusers is a far preferable mechanism of social control than the Police Model. Another criterion that Packer weighs heavily is that "the conduct ... is not condoned by any significant segment of society."[53] Aside from those who do not use marijuana but who don't mind that others do, there are an estimated 2 000 000 marijuana smokers in Canada, who in one fell swoop are branded as criminals. I personally deplore a system of criminal law that brands such sizeable numbers of its subjects as outlaws not because they commit crimes against persons or property but because they choose to ingest a particular drug. In Victorian England over a hundred years ago, the renowned philosopher John Stuart Mill published his memorable book-length essay, *On Liberty*, in which he had this to say about the limits of criminal sanctions: "The principle is, that the sole end for which mankind are warranted ... in interfering with the liberty of action of any of their members is self-protection. That the only purpose for which power can be rightfully exercised over any member of a civilized community against his will is to prevent harm to others. His own good, either physical or moral, is not a sufficient warrant."[54]

Those were wise words then and they are wise words today. Would that those who rant and rave about "getting government off the backs of the people" come to make that connection to the War on Drugs! Of course, it is true that there are consumers of illicit drugs whose drug use directly leads to crimes committed against persons and property. But that is a byproduct of the war itself — the artificially inflated black market cost of drugs that are criminalized is bound to drive abusers to commit crimes for the money, to afford that cost. That aspect of the War on Drugs is, I suggest, as bizarre and nonsensical as anything that Alice ever stumbled upon in Wonderland.

In any event, I can well imagine a loud chorus of angry voices protesting that decriminalizing possession for personal use sends the wrong message — that it would encourage the use of illicit drugs. I doubt that. It is fanciful to believe that there are hordes of solid citizens who have thus far shied away from illicit drugs but who would somehow be prompted to indulge if possession were decriminalized. (Bear in mind that when a number of American states drastically reduced penalties for marijuana possession in the 1970s, there was no discernible increase in consumers.) I rather think that my proposal would be sending the right message — that the time has come to seek a new way and that, in the meantime, the least we can do is to proclaim an armistice in the war against those who possess illicit drugs for personal use. That is the first step, but who can say at this juncture where we will end up? But at least that would be a good beginning.

But beyond that one small but needed step, we must seek to devise a model of drug control that is markedly different from the Police Model framework of the War on Drugs. In the quest for a new way, I suggest that we see what there is to learn from the Dutch drug control policy, what one could call an integrated Health/Police Model. Its two overriding principles — *separation of markets* and *harm reduction* — are health-oriented, albeit the Health Model rebounds to the benefit of the Police Model because the latter is ill-equipped to suppress consumer demand for drugs. As Professor Ethan Nadelman, the director of the Lindesmith Center, a drug policy research institute in New York City, sums up the Dutch experience:

> American drug warriors like to denigrate the Dutch, but the fact remains that Dutch drug policy has been dramatically more successful than U.S. drug policy. The average age of heroin addicts in the Netherlands has been increasing for almost a decade; HIV rates among addicts are dramatically lower than in the United States; police don't waste resources on non-disruptive drug users but, rather, focus on major dealers or petty dealers who create public nuisances. The decriminalized cannabis (marijuana) markets are regulated in a quasi-legal fashion far more effective and inexpensive than the U.S. equivalent.[55]

Dutch drug policy reflects two aspects of the Dutch national character: a tolerance for diversity coupled with pragmatism (if one cannot suppress an activity — e.g., drugs or prostitution — then bring it out into the open and regulate it). There is much to be said for that philosophy. Our way has been different, ever since Canada embraced the Police Model in 1908 and the United States did likewise in 1914. But it is incumbent upon us to seek a new way, one that inevitably will proceed by bumps and starts, requiring fine tuning as we learn from our mistakes along the road to developing a social policy that minimizes the harm caused by dysfunctional drug use (i.e., drug abuse). That hope was expressed two years ago by Barbara Ehrenreich in a thoughtful essay, "Kicking the Big One," in which she indicted drug prohibition as "an evil [that] grips America, a life-slapping, drug-related habit" and proposed that, "It's not necessary to quit cold turkey. Consider starting with marijuana, then easing up on cocaine and heroin possession, concentrating law enforcement on the big-time pushers. Take it slowly, see how it feels. One day at a time."[56]

I agree with Ehrenreich that the place to begin is with marijuana but that drug law reform cannot end there. It is thus my fervent hope that, if Senators are prepared to question the criminalizing of small amounts of marijuana, they will go on to question the very legitimacy of the war itself.[57] There is a voluminous body of literature — both American and Canadian — presenting alternatives to the Police

Model of drug control, and all that it takes to seek new paradigms is the moral courage to just Say No to the War on Drugs. A good place to start the quest for a new way is by reading the cover story in the 12 February 1996 issue of William Buckley's magazine, *National Review*. Titled "The War on Drugs Is Lost," it contains seven articles (the first by Buckley himself) that prove the point. The final article is by Yale Law Professor Steven Duke, co-author of *America's Longest War: Rethinking Our Tragic Crusade Against Drugs*. I'll leave you with Duke's final paragraph — the cover story's last word: "The only benefit to America in maintaining prohibition is the psychic comfort we derive from having a permanent scapegoat. But why did we have to pick an enemy the warring against which is so self-destructive? We would be better off blaming our ills on celestial invaders flying about in saucers."[58]

Unfortunately, that "psychic comfort" is very much in evidence in the 1996 U.S. presidential campaign, as the incumbent and his opponent strive to outdo one another in their commitment to the War on Drugs. The President stood as a true Drug Warrior when he proclaimed "I hate drugs" during his renomination speech before his party's national convention. He reiterated that war cry in the first televised debate with Senator Dole. But he is not to be outdone by the Senator, who by the way is a staunch defender of the tobacco industry and who has informed the American public that cigarettes really aren't addictive (although he has recently backtracked from that position, saying that since he is not a doctor, he cannot say for certain). The Senator has called for more police and more prisons to combat the menace of drugs. When asked if he would implement a "zero tolerance" policy, he replied that it would be "zero, zero, zero, zero tolerance." And he has managed to blame the President for the recent upsurge in illicit drug use by teenagers.

Yet, the inescapable truth bears repeating: that more of the same — more police, harsher penalties, and more prisons — is not going to win a war that by its very nature is unwinnable. That is because of the Black Market Pathologies referred to earlier; there are such enormous amounts of money to be made that the market in illicit drugs is virtually unstoppable. As the author of a recent magazine article titled "The Phony Drug War" expressed it: "Putting a murderer in jail means one less murderer on the street. Putting a dealer in jail creates a job opening."[59] Simply put, law enforcement efforts to suppress the importation and cultivation of illicit drugs have a *push down, pop up* effect. If one hydroponic marijuana operation is uncovered, then another simply pops up in its place. If cocaine production were to vanish overnight in Colombia, it would soon flourish elsewhere in South America. And if it stopped throughout South America, it would thrive in Asia. And if not Asia, then Africa. Alas, one can also say the same about heroin.

In a telegram to Prime Minister Chrétien, an organization of concerned parents — who describe themselves as "volunteers working to stop substance abuse by children" — expressed its impassioned opposition to the relaxation of criminal penalties for marijuana. As it asked the Prime Minister, "What do you want for Canada, a drug-free society or a drug-filled society?"[60] But the truth is that we will never have a "drug-free" society. Recreational drugs are here to stay; as I have been told by more than one high school and junior high school teacher, marijuana is available to virtually any student who wants it.

I too as a parent share the concern of those parents who worry about children abusing drugs. But what reason is there to believe that we have no choice but to persevere in a rigid commitment to a policy that has done such a dismal job of keeping children (and adults) away from drugs? If a business conducted an enterprise with the dismal track record of the War on Drugs, its board of directors would long since have been turfed by outraged shareholders. Is there a better way? The point is that we'll never know until we begin to look, to expand our horizons beyond the limited vision of the Drug Warriors. I have suggested that at the very least we consider the *decriminalization* of illicit drug use: that whatever the drug, possession for personal use fall outside the ambit of the criminal law. As the distinguished American criminologist Elliott Currie has commented: "decriminalization is not a panacea; it will not end the drug crisis, but it could substantially decrease the irrationality and inhumanity of our present punitive war on drugs."[61]

Since decriminalization is only a halfway measure, should we go all the way to *legalization*: a free market in which illicit drugs are made as legally available as tobacco and alcohol? Professor Currie says no, at least as regards heroin and cocaine, and as he explains, his view is coloured by the nature of American society:

> Evidence ... confirms that much (though, of course, not all) of the harm caused by endemic drug abuse is intrinsic to the impact of hard drugs themselves (and the street culture in which drug abuse is embedded) within the context of a glaringly unequal, depriving, and deteriorating society. And it affirms that we will not substantially reduce that harm without attacking the social roots of the extraordinary demand for hard drugs in the United States. Just as we cannot punish our way out of the drug crisis, neither will we escape its grim toll by deregulating the drug market.[62]

On the other hand, he also acknowledges that "there is a strong argument for treating marijuana differently from the harder drugs."[63] Professor Currie is but one of many thoughtful critics who have argued against the call for escalation of the War on Drugs on the grounds that "more of the same [won't] do the job."[64] But if we don't simply want more of the same, then we must do what we are supposed to do in a democracy on contested issues of public policy: proceed in a calm and measured fashion to talk and listen and debate the merits of conflicting views.

I am pleased to report that this kind of debate is already happening on Parliament Hill. The House of Commons Health Committee is currently holding hearings on Canada's drug policy, as a follow-up to the recent enactment of *The Controlled Drugs and Substances Act* (not yet proclaimed). The new *Act*, which replaces the *Narcotic Control Act* and sections of the *Food and Drug Act*, embodies the Police Model and, if anything, is even more punitive than the old law. When the *Act*, originally called Bill C-7 and then Bill C-8, was before the Senate Legal and Constitutional Affairs Committee, it drew the ire of the Canadian Bar Association. In expressing its strong opposition to Bill C-7, the CBA's National Criminal Justice Section rightly noted that, "[T]he criminalization approach to drug control has proven ineffective for decreasing drug use, reducing crime, or improving health status in the general population."[65] The brief then went on to make the startling admission that: "To recommend diminishing the prohibitionist approach ... is in direct contradiction to the self-interests of lawyers, in that any decriminalization would ultimately mean less work for lawyers.... However, the National Criminal Justice Section takes the position against continued prohibition, contrary to the economic self-interests of lawyers, because we firmly view that position to be in keeping with our professional responsibility to advance the public interest."[66] In its later submission to the Senate against Bill C-8, the CBA reaffirmed its stand: "We submit that it is in the public interest to take the harm-reduction approach rather than the criminalization approach. It will mean, of course, less work for lawyers."[67]

Wonder of wonders — that an organization of lawyers has advocated against the profession's own economic interests! The CBA's principled stand is a clarion call that I hope will inspire the House's Health Committee to take a critical look at what we have wrought by our single-minded devotion to the War on Drugs.

Finally, a word to Nancy and Ronald Reagan, George Bush, Bill Bennett, Newt Gingrich, Daryl Gates, their newest ally, Bill Clinton, and all the other Drug Warriors, American and Canadian, who keep telling us that what we require is more of the same: more drug police, harsher punishments, more prisons, and more education on the evils of illicit drugs. You remind me of the story of the emperor strutting around in what he believed was a splendid new cloak, and all save a small boy were too embarrassed to tell him the truth: that he was wearing nothing but the suit he was born with. So to all of you cloaked in the mantle of the War on Drugs — surprise, it's made of see-through glass, and if you glance in the mirror, you'll discover that you too have the look of Lady Godiva on that memorable day in Coventry so long ago. But at least she could hold her head proudly. Yours should be bowed down with shame.

QUESTIONS TO CONSIDER

1. Summarize several important points Sneiderman makes about the impact of the War on Drugs. Do you agree or disagree with his arguments?
2. Outline the reasons why drugs such as opium, marijuana, and cocaine were criminalized in Canada and the United States. Does this discussion support or refute the argument that drugs are criminalized because they are dangerous?
3. Is the War on Drugs "winnable"? Discuss the steps that would be necessary for Canada to eliminate illegal drug use. Also discuss whether these steps would be acceptable in Canadian society.

NOTES

1. S. Duke, "The War on Drugs Is Lost" *National Review* (12 February 1996) at 47.
2. Administration of Ronald Reagan (4 September 1986). National campaign against drug abuse: Statement by the principal press secretary to the president announcing an Address to the Nation by the President and Mrs. Reagan. *Weekly Compilation of Presidential Documents*, 22 (38) at 1138–39. Cited in W.N. Elwood, *Rhetoric in the War on Drugs: The Triumphs and Tragedies of Public Relations* (Westport: Praeger, 1994) at 28.
3. Ronald Reagan (14 September 1986). National campaign against drug abuse: Address to the Nation. *Weekly Compilation of Presidential Documents*, 22 (38) at 1183–87. Cited in Elwood, *supra* note 2 at 28–29.
4. *Ibid.* at 1187. Cited in Elwood, *supra* note 2 at 30.
5. *Ibid.* at 1186–87. Cited in Elwood, *supra* note 2 at 31.
6. *Ibid.* at 1187. Cited in Elwood, *supra* note 2 at 32.
7. *Ibid.* at 1183–87. Cited in Elwood, *supra* note 2 at 28–29.

8. S. Wisotsky, *Beyond the War on Drugs* (Buffalo: Prometheus Books, 1990) at xx.
9. Elwood, *supra* note 2 at 99.
10. R. Reynolds. "Hooked on the Drug War" *The Hartford Advocate* (26 January 1995) 14.
11. S. Duke & A.C. Gross, *America's Longest War* (New York: Putnam's Sons, 1993) at 135–45.
12. "Gingrich Urges Death Penalty for Illegal Drug Smugglers" *Washington Post* (27 August 1995) 3.
13. J.D. McNamara, "The War on Drugs Is Lost" *National Review* (12 February 1996) 42.
14. Office of National Drug Control Policy, Executive Office of the President, National Drug Control Strategy (1989) at 7 and 9.
15. Duke & Gross, *supra* note 11 at 106.
16. *Supra* note 2 at 84–85. Chapter 4 (81–101) presents a fascinating account of the Partnership for a Drug-Free America.
17. The Stoned Surgeon video appears in a PBS documentary, *Altered States*, that was broadcast in April 1995.
18. *Winnipeg Free Press* (6 November 1991) A17.
19. E.A. Nadelman, "The War on Drugs Is Lost" *National Review* (12 February 1996) 38.
20. J.H. VanVliet, "Separation of Drug Markets and the Normalization of Drug Problems in the Netherlands: An Example for Other Nations?" (1990) 20 *Journal of Drug Issues* 463.
21. As an aside, if E.T. pursued his inquiry elsewhere, he would learn about the role of pharmaceutical companies in promoting the use of drugs that are a mixed blessing: drugs that harm as well as benefit consumers; drugs that are grossly overused because of aggressive market promotion and over-prescribing by physicians. That, by the way, is the theme of a study by J. Lexchin, M.D., *The Real Pushers: A Critical Analysis of the Canadian Drug Industry* (Vancouver: New Star Books, 1984).
22. J.R. DiFranza & R.A. Lew, "Effect of Maternal Cigarette Smoking on Pregnancy Complications and Sudden Infant Death Syndrome" (1995) 40 *Journal of Medical Practice* 385.
23. "Bennett Suggests Forced Treatment" *Winnipeg Free Press* (18 June 1989) A21.
24. "Women's Lung Cancer Deaths Up" *Winnipeg Free Press* (2 September 1992) A8.
25. T. Whiteside, *Selling Death* (New York: Liveright, 1970).
26. "Smoking Accounts for 20% of Deaths, Study Suggests" *Winnipeg Free Press* (11 October 1991) A5. See also J. Urschel, "Want a War on Drugs? Let's Take 'Em All On" *USA Today* (14 December 1993) A7.
27. "WHO Hits Tobacco Firms Over Death Rate" *Winnipeg Free Press* (31 May 1995) A7.
28. Alas, the very clever holy/tap water metaphor is not mine but that of the renowned psychiatrist and social critic, Dr. Thomas Szasz. See T. Szasz, *Ceremonial Chemistry* (New York: Anchor Press/Doubleday, 1974).
29. E.M. Brecher *et al.*, *Licit and Illicit Drugs* (Toronto: Little, Brown & Co., 1972).
30. *Ibid.* at 536.
31. *Ibid.* at 206.
32. National Commission on Marijuana and Drug Abuse, *Drug Abuse in America: Problem in Perspective*, 2d report (1973) at 11.
33. T. Duster, *The Legislation of Morality* (New York: The Free Press, 1970) at 247–48.
34. J. Helmer, *Drugs and Minority Oppression* (New York: Seabury Press, 1975); M. Green. "A History of Canadian Narcotics Control" (1979) 37 *U.T. Fac. L. Rev.* 42.
35. S. Small, "Canadian Narcotics Legislation, 1908–23: A Conflict Model Interpretation" in W. Greenaway & S. Brickey, eds., *Law and Social Control in Canada* (Scarborough: Prentice-Hall, 1978) 28.
36. At the present time, marijuana is a prohibited drug under the *Narcotic Control Act.* Parliament has chosen to classify marijuana as a narcotic, although botanically it is

not. In section 2, the *Act* broadly defines "trafficking" as including "to manufacture, sell, give, administer, transport, send, deliver, or distribute...." Thus, if you *give* a joint to a friend, then — *in the eyes of the law* — you are a narcotics trafficker!

37. E. Murphy, *The Black Candle* (Toronto: Thomas Allen, 1922).

38. B. Anthony & R. Silverman. "Introduction" in E. Murphy, *The Black Candle* (Toronto: Coles Publishing Company, 1973) [reprint] at 3.

39. M. Silverman & P.R. Lee, *Pills, Profits, and Politics* (Berkeley: University of California Press, 1974) at 264.

40. *Supra* note 24 at A10.

41. Note that genetic predisposition may also be involved; it is certainly a contributing factor in some cases of alcoholism.

42. *Supra* note 29 at 223.

43. *Supra* note 11 at xviii.

44. *Supra* note 20. As indicated by his article's title, VanVliet also uses the phrase "normalization of drug problems" as another description of "harm reduction."

45. R. Siegel, *Intoxication: Life in Pursuit of Artificial Paradise* (New York: E.P. Dutton, 1989).

46. *Supra* note 29 at xi.

47. M.J. Rodman & D.W. Smith, *Pharmacology and Drug Therapy in Nursing* (Toronto: J.B. Lippincott Company, 1968) at 163.

48. "Senators High on Legalizing Marijuana" *The Toronto Star* (17 May 1996) 3.

49. *Supra* note 29 at 521.

50. H. Packer, *The Limits of the Criminal Sanction* (Stanford: Stanford University Press, 1968).

51. *Ibid.* at 296.

52. *Ibid.*

53. *Ibid.*

54. Quoted in N. Morris & G. Hawkins, *The Honest Politician's Guide to Crime Control* (Chicago: University of Chicago Press, 1969) at 4.

55. *Supra* note 19 at 39.

56. B. Ehrenreich. "Kicking the Big One" *Time* (28 February 1994) 60.

57. I would also couple the decriminalization of possession for personal use with the legal availability of marijuana for medicinal purposes: e.g., for cancer (reducing the nausea caused by chemotherapy), for multiple sclerosis (easing pain), for glaucoma (reducing pressure on the eyeballs), and for AIDS (stimulating appetite). There is no more cruel aspect of the War on Drugs than the denial of the drug to those who can benefit from its medicinal properties and for whom there are no adequate legal substitutes.

58. *Supra* note 1 at 48.

59. J.W. Shenk, "The Phony Drug War" *The Nation* (23 September 1996) 11.

60. Lambton Families in Action for Drug Education, Inc. telegram to the Right Honourable Jean Chrétien, 7 June 1994.

61. E. Currie, "Towards a Policy on Drugs" in H.T. Wilson, ed. *Drugs, Society, and Behavior* (Guilford, CT: Dushkin Publishing, 1996) at 216.

62. *Ibid.*

63. *Ibid.*

64. *Ibid.* at 214.

65. National Criminal Justice Section of the Canadian Bar Association, *Submission on Bill C-7* (May 1994) at 1.

66. *Ibid.* at 19.

67. (28 March 1996) 3 Proceedings of the Standing Senate Committee on Legal and Constitutional Affairs at 3.5.

SIX

Corporate Crime

ROBERT M. GORDON AND IAN T. CONEYBEER

Questionable activities of business corporations in Canada have a long, fasci-nating, but underexplored history. As Naylor (1973) has pointed out, the sources of some of the great Canadian fortunes, and the origins of some well-known Canadian businesses and banks, can be traced to such activities as the notorious commodity and currency dealings of British army contractors in New France, the system of extortion and human and environmental exploitation known as the fur trade, the processing of goods and the laundering of currency acquired through piracy in Nova Scotia and on the Great Lakes, and the practice of seizing and hoard-ing land and blocking settlement.

The economic history of Canada is filled with examples of corporate wrongdo-ing: exploitation of human and natural resources; pollution of the environment; con-spiracies and scandals involving politicians and corporate interests; the formation of illegal monopolies and price-fixing cartels; stock frauds and manipulations; and the illegal use of child labour (Carrigan, 1991; Snider, 1988).

Despite this rich history and the burgeoning international body of research and literature addressing the nature, scope, and impact of corporate criminality (Clinard and Yeager, 1980; Ermann and Lundman, 1982; Geis, 1982; Simon and Eitzen, 1990; Wickman and Dailey, 1982), few studies had been completed by Canadian criminologists until the late 1970s, when Professors Goff and Reasons published their landmark analysis of Canadian anticombines legislation, *Corporate Crime in Canada* (1978). They traced the origins and evolution of federal legislation ostensi-bly aimed at preserving a competitive, free-enterprise system, identified officially recorded corporate criminality in the period between the early 1950s and the early 1970s, and critically analyzed the federal government's dismal enforcement record.

The results stimulated a growing body of research aimed at describing, analyz-ing, and explaining Canadian corporate criminality (McMullan, 1992; Snider, 1993). Studies have included examinations of the links between corporate deviance and profitability (Glasbeek, 1984; Henry, 1986); analyses of the nature and impact of crimes against consumers and employees (Goff and Reasons, 1986; Reasons, Ross, and Paterson, 1981); a review of the content and enforcement of municipal, provin-cial, and federal laws that protect consumers and the labour force (Snider, 1988; West and Snider, 1985); a further study of the origins of anticombines legislation (Smandych, 1985); and an exposé of the nature, scope, and impact of corporate vio-lence against women (DeKeseredy and Hinch, 1991). We can draw a number of gen-eral conclusions about corporate criminality in Canada:

Source: Robert M. Gordon and Ian T. Coneybeer, "Corporate Crime," chapter 13 in *Canadian Criminology: Perspectives on Crime and Criminality*, 2nd ed., ed. Margaret A. Jackson and Curt T. Griffiths (Toronto: Harcourt Brace, 1995), 399–423.

1. Corporate criminality is widespread and may be categorized in five ways: crimes against the economy, crimes against the environment, crimes against consumers, crimes against humanity, and crimes against employees.

2. Corporate crime results in considerable material loss or damage and physical injury. It affects large numbers of Canadians, and the aggregate impact is greater than traditional, predatory street crime. Although street crime attracts considerable public and state attention and condemnation, the same is not true of corporate crime. Corporate victimization of, for example, consumers is frequently diffuse, indirect, and of low visibility; consequently, there is less public awareness of, and concern regarding, harmful illegal actions. In addition, activities are masked by an ideological screen that explains and excuses corporate transgressions as the unfortunate but unavoidable by-product of a commonly beneficial economic system.

3. Inappropriate behaviour is rarely defined and regulated through the medium of the criminal law, and violators are usually dealt with outside the criminal-justice system. Improper activities are defined in separate legislation and handled by special government departments and bodies in a "regulatory" and mediatory, rather than "punitive" manner. The system of regulation and mediation may include government schemes for the protection, compensation, and appeasement of victims.

4. Laws prohibiting forms of corporate behaviour are poorly enforced. Governments provide only limited resources for investigation and prosecution, and this reflects the purely symbolic nature of legislation and enforcement.

5. Laws governing corporate behaviour are often constructed by the state in conjunction with corporate interests. The latter influence the process of identifying and defining inappropriate conduct, specifying the procedures for investigation and prosecution, and determining the kinds of punishments or other dispositions that may be applied to offenders.

6. There is a gap between official, state expressions of illegality and public sentiment, but there exists a set of universal human values — a higher morality — that transcends state and corporate perceptions and statements of improper conduct. Corporate activities may be quite legal but offend universal human values, fundamental human rights, and basic conceptions of justice.

7. The causes of corporate criminality are three-dimensional and involve a complex interplay between individual, organizational, and social structural factors. Illegal/immoral actions are planned and executed by individuals within and on behalf of their organization, in order to achieve both personal and corporate goals. Corporate goals are determined by the structure and logic of the prevailing economy and, within a capitalist economic system, are generally characterized by one primary consideration: maximization of profits.

8. Criminological investigations of corporate transgressions are impeded by a variety of methodological problems — notably, limited research funding, access to data, and the complexities of corporate ownership.

We now turn to a review of the five categories of corporate criminality. One of these — crimes against employees — is selected as a medium through which to explore briefly the general conclusions and some of the issues and problems.

CATEGORIES OF CORPORATE CRIMINALITY

Corporate criminality has been conceptualized, categorized, and analyzed in different ways, and the field of inquiry is characterized by an often confusing array of terms; for example, the phenomenon is variously described as white-collar crime, suite crime, commercial crime, elite deviance, crimes of the powerful, upperworld crime, economic crime, organizational crime, and corporate crime. Generally, however, the illegal, criminal, and immoral actions of corporations can be categorized in five main ways: crimes against the economy, crimes against the environment, crimes against consumers, crimes against humanity, and crimes against employees.

In each instance, the category describes the type of person or physical entity upon which the corporate behaviour has a negative impact, and the categories involve a certain degree of overlap. For example, where a crime against the environment (e.g., water pollution) involves the destruction or waste of resources (e.g., fish), it might also constitute a crime against the economy. It is not possible, therefore, to always draw clear distinctions between the categories of crime, and the intention is merely to provide a typology that brings some order to the field and thereby aids analysis and understanding. The word *crime* is employed to characterize the behaviour but, in some instances, the irresponsible and damaging actions of corporations do not attract a formal designation as "criminal"; the word is used, therefore, in a nonlegal sense.

CRIMES AGAINST THE ECONOMY

The term "crimes against the economy" encompasses corporate actions that contravene federal and provincial statutes designed to express, implement, and buttress state economic policies and strategies. These policies and strategies shift in accordance with national and international economic developments, and the types of conduct to be prohibited or regulated will change accordingly. Economic crimes include breaches of national and international patent law (i.e., legislation established to protect innovative ideas and inventions, and prevent product piracy), violations of the rules and regulations governing the stock market and designed to prevent unfair and destabilizing practices (e.g., market manipulations aimed at enhancing the value of shares), and breaches of statutes aimed at protecting competition. The best-known example of this type of legislation is the federal Competition Act: a statute (formerly, the Combines Investigation Act) that is ostensibly aimed at preserving a competitive, free-enterprise, capitalist economic system by, among other matters, regulating the extent to which economic power becomes concentrated in the hands of large, national, multinational, or transnational corporations.

The statute makes provision for the "general regulation of trade and commerce in respect of conspiracies, trade practices and mergers affecting competition" (s. 18), and the official purpose is

> to maintain and encourage competition in Canada in order to promote the efficiency and adaptability of the Canadian economy, in order to expand opportunities for Canadian participation in world markets while at the same time recognizing the role of foreign competition in Canada, in order to ensure that small and medium-sized

enterprises have an equitable opportunity to participate in the Canadian economy and in order to provide consumers with competitive prices and product choices. (s. 19)

The extent to which the statute will accomplish these objectives and the corporate interests that have influenced its content are the subjects of a debate that cannot be examined here (Snider, 1993). For our purposes, it is sufficient to note that the statute both amends and preserves some provisions of the former Combines Investigation Act, and that it does so in accordance with new, state economic policies. The act either prohibits various forms of business activity or requires that these be subjected to review by a competition tribunal that may either approve or prohibit the behaviour. The activities include: (1) conspiracies, combines, and agreements that limit production and trade, increase prices, or restrict competition; (2) restrictive trade practices such as "refusal to deal" (e.g., refusing to supply products to another business) and "abuse of a dominant position" (e.g., an "anticompetitive act" involving the use of fighting brands introduced temporarily and selectively to discipline or eliminate a competitor); and (3) corporate mergers that prevent or lessen competition. Violations of the various provisions of the Competition Act and the decisions of the competition tribunal (e.g., prohibition orders) attract penalties and constitute crimes against the economy.

CRIMES AGAINST THE ENVIRONMENT

The term "crimes against the environment" encompasses corporate actions that result in a general or specific pollution of land, air, and water; the contamination of both human beings and the sources of human nutrition; the depletion or destruction of species of fauna, flora, and marine and aerial life; and the wanton destruction and waste of valuable resources. Pollution, depletion, and destruction may be the consequences of the actions of an individual corporation (e.g., the discharge of toxic-waste substances into a river system), the outcome of an accumulation of industries in one particular area (e.g., acid rain), or the collective effect of global industrial activity (e.g., the global warming trend known as the "greenhouse effect" and the erosion of the ozone layer). Regardless, the impact on the human and natural environment is immense, and the consequences of 200 years of industrial growth and uncontrolled pollution and destruction are now appearing (World Commission on Environment and Development, 1988). As David Suzuki has pointed out:[1]

> In 30 years, all the curves indicate that there will be no wilderness left on the planet … it will all have been destroyed or put into tiny little parks.... In ten years, there will be no coastal rain forest left in British Columbia.... In 150 years, 50 percent of all plant and animal species will be extinct, and in 200 years, 80 percent will be extinct.
>
> … [E]very politician, every businessman, every economist will say, "We must have growth" … it is the demand for growth and the steady increase in consumption that is destroying this planet, and yet we demand we have more.

The issue of crimes against the environment points, therefore, to an interesting contradiction. Pollution, the destruction of species, and the rapid consumption of nonrenewable resources are the by-products of corporate activity within an economy dominated by the logic of profit maximization and the associated principle of endless consumption. Growth results in both the steady destruction of the environment that sustains the life necessary for consumption (economic growth ceases when there are no humans left to purchase commodities) and the rapid depletion of the resources necessary for production.

To resolve this contradiction, in the interests of continued economic growth and maximization of profits, the state must take action to control the activities of corporations. In addition, there is little doubt that governments are under mounting pressure to address the issue of environmental damage and that they cannot hope to retain legitimacy if they fail to respond to, in particular, the arguments and evidence presented by individual environmentalists. Just as human- and civil-rights issues became a major concern during the 1960s and 1970s, and resulted in significant and lasting social reforms, so environmental protection and environmental rights will likely become major social and economic issues during the 1990s and into the next century.

There are already signs of a shift in policy at the federal and provincial levels, the objective being to ensure "environmentally sustainable economic growth." The Law Reform Commission of Canada has recommended a formal "criminalization" of actions that damage the environment and proposed that provision be made for "crimes against the environment" in the Criminal Code (Law Reform Commission, 1985). Others argue for a regulatory, rather than punitive, approach to environmental protection (Brown and Rankin, 1991; Law Reform Commission of Canada, 1988), and new federal legislation — the Canadian Environmental Protection Act — reflects an attempt to find a compromise among the different factions. At the provincial level, there are some signs that governments are willing to prosecute blatant offenders and that the courts are prepared to hand down stiff sentences. As Emond (1984) has pointed out, however, the thrust of most provincial legislation in this area is to regulate and legalize, rather than to prohibit, industrial pollution, and this may be a product of the difficulties faced by the state in introducing statutes that interfere with economic growth and short-term profitability (see also Rankin and Finkle, 1983).

As many observers have noted (Caputo, 1989; Schrecker, 1989), the nation's environmental-protection strategy is incoherent and uncertain; expressed through a complex body of statutes, regulations, policies, and principles; and implemented by a confusing variety of regulatory bodies that lack the resources necessary to enforce laws. This is changing as the public demand for the prohibition of environmental pollution and destruction mounts (see, for example, British Columbia, 1993). Still, corporations will likely continue to dump their wastes in oceans and rivers, discharge pollutants into the atmosphere, and engage in other forms of environmental damage (see Box 6.1). Indisputably wrong, such behaviour is a prime example of corporate wrongdoing that should perhaps be defined as "criminal."

CRIMES AGAINST CONSUMERS

Crimes against consumers include price-fixing, price-gouging, deceptive and misleading advertising, and the production and marketing of defective or dangerous products. Price-fixing agreements among "competitors" to keep the price of a product artificially high, price-gouging (e.g., using contrived or real shortages of raw

BOX 6.1 POLLUTION AND CRIME

In January 1989, Inco Ltd. was fined $80 000 for releasing 2 tons of sulphur trioxide into the atmosphere from the Copper Cliff refinery in Ontario. The contaminant combined with water vapour to form a cloud of sulphuric-acid mist 1 km long and 0.5 km wide. This cloud drifted over residential and summer resort areas. Those caught in the mist experienced coughing, choking, vomiting, and burning eyes and noses, and 150 people were treated in hospital. The release was due, in part, to the failure of three safety systems, one of which had been deliberately by-passed during an earlier, routine plant shutdown. In addition to paying the fine, Inco publicly apologized for the incident.

In February 1989, researchers announced that nursing mothers in northern Quebec had dangerously high levels of toxic polychlorinated biphenyls (PCBs) in their breast milk. The mothers were inadvertently contaminating their infants. The levels of PCBs were higher than those recorded anywhere else in the world and were the result of the consumption of fish and fat from marine life: foods in which PCBs tend to concentrate. The toxins descended with the rain and snow and probably came from industrial areas in the south.

In March 1989, a secret report compiled by Environment Canada was leaked to the press. This report indicated that 83 of the 149 pulpmills in Canada were dumping toxic chemicals (i.e., organochlorines, including the poison dioxin) into waterways at a rate and level higher than national pollution standards allowed. Fish and other marine life were being contaminated. The worst offenders were pulpmills in British Columbia and Quebec.

In March 1989, an Environment Canada study of pollution in Vancouver harbour was released. High levels of lead, chromium, and petroleum hydrocarbons were found on the seabed, and bottom-feeding fish (notably sole) were found to have precancerous liver lesions or tumours. The pollution appeared to originate with the chemical works and petroleum refineries along the shoreline.

As these examples demonstrate, the harm may be immediate and direct, as in the cloud of sulphuric acid released from the Inco refinery. The harm may be long-term and indirect and involve the contamination of water that then affects one source of human food (e.g., fish), and consequently the people who eat it.

Although pollution can cause severe physical harm to humans, it is not treated in the same way as other physically damaging acts. It is not defined as a "crime" in the Criminal Code, although there is growing public sentiment that it should be, particularly where the pollution is willful or reckless.

A vast array of federal and provincial "antipollution" legislation exists, and penalties may be imposed on corporations that fail to comply with pollution "standards." The objective, however, is not to stop pollution but merely to contain it within "acceptable" boundaries. Corporations are granted permits to pollute: they are allowed to deliberately contaminate the environment

(continued)

and will only be restrained if they exceed the "safety" limits prescribed by government departments.

The validity of these "safe limits" has been challenged by environmentalists who point to, for example, the failure to account for the long-term, cumulative effects of continuous pollution. In addition, there is evidence that the permit system is ineffective. For example, studies of the enforcement of the waste-management permit system in British Columbia have demonstrated that companies were persistently exceeding allowable pollution limits but were rarely prosecuted for doing so. Even if prosecution does occur, the penalties are minor. Indeed, it is cheaper to pollute and pay the fines than it is to install pollution-control equipment. Fortunately, some provincial governments are moving to change their environmental protection laws and to strengthen the enforcement process, and courts appear to be imposing stricter penalties on corporate polluters.

materials to increase the price of products), and misleading advertising — all result in some form of material loss. The impact on *individual* consumers may be minimal since, for example, a price-fixing cartel in the petroleum industry may cost a consumer only a fraction of a cent per litre at the gas pump. The *aggregate* impact, however, will be massive and can result in enormous profits for the corporations involved. Defective or dangerous products (e.g., inadequately tested drugs, poorly designed automobiles, faulty aircraft parts, and adulterated foodstuffs such as canned tuna) can cause physical harm and will often become evident at the individual and aggregate levels as a result of deaths, foetal deformities, injuries, and sickness. As DeKeseredy and Hinch (1991) point out, women consumers appear to have been the targets of a great deal of corporate violence. This violence includes the production and sale of improperly tested and harmful drugs (e.g., thalidomide), faulty intrauterine devices (e.g., the Dalkon Shield), and silicone-gel breast implants (see Box 6.2).

Consumers are supposedly protected by legislation governing business activities, and, at the federal level, the provisions of statutes such as the Competition Act, the Food and Drug Act, and the Hazardous Products Act prohibit misleading advertising and packaging and the sale of unfit, harmful, or dangerous foods, drugs, cosmetics, and other products. The provinces have also introduced consumer-protection legislation governing such matters as the licensing and regulation of some businesses (e.g., those dealing in securities), the form and use of agreements to purchase goods, the disclosure of the full cost of borrowing money to buy a product (e.g., a new automobile), and advertising practices (Snider, 1993).

An impressive array of federal and provincial legislation is, therefore, in existence, and corporations that violate the provisions of the statutes face both fines and the payment of redress to victims. In some instances, individual employees can be imprisoned. As many studies have shown, however, enforcement is minimal, the penalties imposed are usually weak and ineffective, and the primary target of government agencies appears to be small- or medium-sized businesses, rather than the large corporations.

BOX 6.2   CANADIAN WOMEN FILE SUIT AGAINST NINE BREAST IMPLANT FIRMS

A Vancouver lawyer has filed separate law suits on behalf of 53 Canadian women who claim they suffered injury as a result of receiving breast implants.

Joe Fiorante said he filed the suits Friday as an agent for a Charleston, S.C., law firm. One of the Canadian complainants is from Ontario, another is from Alberta, and the balance are from British Columbia.

Fiorante said the writs were filed to ensure the matter is on record in the B.C. Supreme Court.

He said the Charleston lawyer, Blair Hahn, acts for several hundred women, including the Canadians.

Each of the three-line writs filed by Fiorante states: The plaintiff's claim is for damages suffered as a result of being implanted with breast implants containing or consisting of silicone, silicone gel and/or an elastomer of silicone. The damages were caused by the negligence of the defendants.

Named as defendants are Dow Corning Canada Inc. and eight U.S. companies: Inamed Corp., CUI Corp., Medical Engineering Corp., Bristol-Meyers Squibb and Co., American Heyer-Schulte Corp., Baxter Healthcare Corp., Baxter International Inc., and McGhan Medical Corp.

Source: Karen Gram, *Vancouver Sun*, February 19, 1994, p. A6.

CRIMES AGAINST HUMANITY

The term "crimes against humanity" encompasses a range of corporate activity that is quite legal (indeed, it may be encouraged by governments) but that violates universal human values — that is, a "higher morality." Corporate activities may be legal because they are not deemed *mala prohibita* (wrongs that are recognized and prohibited by the law) but, nevertheless, may be deemed *mala in se*: acts that are wrong in themselves but not recognized as such in law.

To use a well-known example: during the early 1940s, the German chemical manufacturing company I.G. Farben used slave labour from concentration camps to construct factories for the production of synthetic oil and rubber. The prisoners were, literally, worked to death or reduced to the point of death. Along with other "useless" prisoners, the spent labourers were then placed in gas chambers where they were killed with Zyklon B, a substance manufactured by a company that was partly owned by I.G. Farben. The bodies then became a resource — hair for mattresses, fat for soap (Borkin, 1978). An exceptional case, perhaps, but one that conveys the main point: the activity was perfectly legal according to the laws in force in Germany at the time (it was not *mala prohibita*), but it violated an overriding set of universal human values, or "higher morality," which, regardless of the content of laws, views enslavement and genocide as wrong (*mala in se*).

A major problem arises, however, in regard to classifying less outrageous and more contemporary forms of corporate activity as "crimes against humanity." It can be argued that the "warfare industry" — the multibillion-dollar business of manufacturing and selling equipment and weapons for the waging of war — is a crime against humanity since it results in death and destruction.

Activities of many corporations could be classified as "crimes against humanity," but the process of designation involves a value-laden interpretation of the tenets of a "higher morality." Corporate practices of dumping unsafe products and irresponsibly marketing products in Third World countries have attracted widespread condemnation. Examples of unsafe products that have been dumped by American corporations include the Dalkon Shield, a contraceptive substance known as Depo-Provera, various medicinal preparations, pesticides, and baby pacifiers and teething rings (Simon and Eitzen, 1990). The best-known example of irresponsible marketing involved the sale of baby formula to the inhabitants of poverty-stricken nations. The sale of baby formula by at least one company — Nestlé — was alleged to have caused the death of 10 000 babies per year because their parents were mixing formula with impure water. Millions of cases of infant starvation and diarrhea also allegedly occurred because parents who were unable to afford supplies of formula were diluting the product (Simon and Eitzen, 1990). This particular practice ceased as a result of an international boycott of the offending corporations, organized by the Interfaith Center on Corporate Responsibility, a body that justified its actions by reference to a "higher morality."

CRIMES AGAINST EMPLOYEES AND THE ISSUES AND PROBLEMS IN THE FIELD OF CORPORATE CRIMINALITY

Crimes against employees fall into three main groups: actions that result in material loss, actions that result in physical harm, and actions that interfere with the legitimate organization of labour (i.e., unions). Material loss can occur when employers effectively steal from their workers by violating provincial legislation or employer/employee agreements governing working conditions and the payment of the minimum wage. Violations of working conditions involve practices such as requiring that an employee work excessive hours; refusing to pay for overtime; refusing pregnancy leave; arbitrary dismissal; discrimination; and unreasonably withholding vacation pay, termination pay, or outstanding wages (West and Snider, 1985). Physical harm may result from violations of occupational health-and-safety legislation, rules, or standards. Corporate interference with the organization of labour may occur when deliberate efforts are made to obstruct union participation and related activities. Arguably, a fourth type of "crime" also exists when employees are directed to engage in other categories of corporate wrongdoing — for example, dumping toxic waste into a river and thereby causing environmental pollution. Sexual and other forms of harassment would constitute a fifth type of corporate crime in situations where a corporation encouraged or condoned such harassment among its personnel. The focus of our discussion will be on crimes that result in physical harm to employees.

Corporate activities that result in illnesses, diseases, injuries, and death can be divided into two categories: pollution in the working environment and operating practices that create workplace hazards that endanger employees. A report by the Law Reform Commission of Canada (1986) provides an excellent review of the issues and problems in the area of workplace pollution.

Workplace pollution is caused by physical and chemical agents that have an immediate or long-term impact on the health of employees. Pollutants that have a long-term impact include silica particles (silicosis); asbestos fibres (asbestosis); and coal dust ("black lung").

The list of physical and chemical pollutants to which employees may be exposed is growing as researchers isolate the causes of work-related illnesses, diseases, and death. In addition to respiratory diseases, pollutants have been shown to cause (or are believed, with high levels of probability, to cause) cancers, sterility, birth defects, damage to the brain and nervous system, and many other ailments (Law Reform Commission of Canada, 1986).

Employees, particularly in the manufacturing, construction, and resource-extraction industries, may be killed or injured as a result of unsafe working conditions (McMullan, 1992; Reasons, Ross, and Paterson, 1981; Snider, 1993). Examples include:

- malfunctioning machinery in manufacturing industries;
- mine and quarry explosions, cave-ins, and fires;
- improper felling of trees and handling of logs, and overloading equipment and cables;
- construction-site incidents; and
- oil-drilling incidents caused by improper or inadequate rig maintenance, the best-known example being the Piper Alpha rig disaster in the North Sea.

Workplace pollution and unsafe working conditions result in considerable physical harm to employees. As the Law Reform Commission points out: "In 1982, there were 854 fatal on-the-job accidents in Canada, and more than half a million cases of disabling accidents or work-related illnesses. Between 1972 and 1981, more than 10 000 Canadians died from injuries received on the job" (1986, p. 5).

The risk of being killed at work is greatest in the primary industries, particularly forestry and mining. In British Columbia, forestry is the most hazardous industry; 144 loggers were killed between 1984 and 1988 (Farrow, 1988; Salisbury et al., 1991). Nationally, the fatality rate in forestry in 1986 was 104 deaths per 100 000 employees, and the industry has the highest rate of recorded work time lost due to injury (Salisbury et al., 1991). These are conservative figures.

Estimates of the rates of sickness, disease, and injury cannot be determined accurately because of underreporting (injuries may be concealed by employers in order to protect their workers' compensation assessments) and, with ailments caused by some forms of pollution, because of the long period of time between exposure and the appearance of a disease or sickness (Law Reform Commission of Canada, 1986). Some workers may not be covered by workers' compensation and, therefore, may not be represented in official data. Nevertheless, estimates of the rate of sickness, injury, and death have been made and compared with the rate of injury and death caused by traditional, predatory street crime.

Reasons (1987, p. 7) argues that, on average, every working day, an employee is killed every two hours, and an injury occurs every six seconds. Reasons, Ross, and Paterson (1981) point out that, although Criminal Code assaults in 1979 numbered 103 391, work-related "assaults" totalled approximately 1 296 121. Forty-six percent of these workplace assaults were categorized as "disabling." Boal (1985) points out that in 1982 the actions of impaired drivers in British Columbia resulted in 6221 injuries. There is widespread acceptance of this behaviour as a "crime," and therefore it is worthy of considerable government attention. In the same year, there were 67 655 work-related injuries and 176 confirmed fatalities in British Columbia alone, and at least twice this number die each year from unacknowledged diseases originating in the workplace.

The Law Reform Commission of Canada (1986) estimates that approximately 135 000 employees in Ontario are directly or indirectly exposed to ten different types of hazardous workplace pollutants, including cadmium, chlorine, formaldehyde, and nickel. Many other hazards (e.g., asbestos and silica particles) exist, but the number of workers affected is unknown. It is estimated that 200 000 to 500 000 workers throughout Canada are needlessly exposed to radioactive materials and chemical pollutants each year (Casey, 1985).

In the United States, it has been estimated that 100 000 workers die and 390 000 are disabled each year as a result of occupational disease, and that five times as many people die each year from work-related disease and injury as are murdered by all street criminals (Simon and Eitzen, 1990). American researchers have predicted 5000 deaths per year for the next 30 to 35 years as a result of exposure to asbestos fibres (Henry, 1986). In short, corporate crimes may cause greater destruction, loss, and physical harm than all the activities that fall within the purview of the criminal-justice system.

The various statistics and associated projections are helpful but are open to dispute, and a valid and reliable picture of "violence" in the workplace has yet to be fully developed. Nevertheless, three general conclusions can be drawn:

1. Workplace pollutants and unsafe working conditions result in alarming rates of death, injury, disease, and sickness.
2. Unsafe working conditions have an adverse impact on productivity; for example, in 1986, more than 1.9 million workdays were lost as a result of workplace injuries and diseases in British Columbia alone.[2]
3. Unsafe working conditions are more costly in human and economic terms than is traditional, predatory street crime, and employees are more likely to be victims of "assault" in the workplace than on the streets (see Box 6.3).

Deaths and injuries in the workplace are often attributed to either the carelessness or the incompetence of workers, or unavoidable accidents (Snider, 1988; West and Snider, 1985), and there is little doubt that this is sometimes true. Deaths, injuries, disease, and sickness also arise from the practices of employers, however — particularly a failure to minimize risks in the workplace by, for example, properly maintaining or guarding machinery, or, as the following cases demonstrate, protecting employees from the dangerous and known effects of pollutants.

In 1982, a millwright employed at the MacMillan-Bloedel Alpulp operation in Port Alberni, British Columbia, died, seventeen days before his retirement, while repairing a leak in a pipe. Although the Canadian Paperworkers Union had protested the work conditions eighteen months before the worker's death, the individual was exposed to 45 times the "allowable" limits of methyl mercaptan, 320 times the "safe" limit of hydrogen-sulphide gas, and an undetermined amount of dimethyl-sulphide gas. When an inquest was held, it was discovered that workers were left to rely on

BOX 6.3 THE SYSCO CASE: A CRIME AGAINST THE ENVIRONMENT, EMPLOYEES, AND HUMANITY

Since the mid-1980s, the Sydney Steel Corporation of Sydney, Nova Scotia, has been associated with one of the most dangerous chemical dump sites in Canada. The corporation began to manufacture steel in the early 1900s and, for more than 80 years, engaged in the practice of depositing waste in "tar ponds" in the area surrounding the plant. The site, close to the downtown Sydney area, contains 700 000 tons of black, toxic material.

In spring 1988, the major source of the pollutants — a battery of obsolete, open-hearth coke ovens — was permanently closed for economic reasons. Before this closure, Sysco coke-oven workers had been regularly exposed to a toxic combination of contaminants.

After considerable pressure was exerted by environmentalists and steel workers in the mid-1980s, a $34-million clean-up operation was arranged by federal and provincial environmental-protection agencies. Little appears to have been accomplished, however, and once the operation begins, it seems likely that some contamination may be overlooked. The sediment on the bottom of Sydney harbour has not been deemed worthy of attention. Although the Nova Scotia environmental-protection authorities discounted the possibility of PCB concentration in the tar ponds, the Steelworkers Union contended that enormous quantities of the transformer coolant had, for generations, been indiscriminately dumped on the site. The local lobster fishery was closed in the early 1980s because of pollution caused by tar-pond leakage.

The predominantly working-class community in the vicinity of the Sysco plant and its dump site has been affected by a higher-than-average cancer rate. An unpublished report, issued by the director of the federal Bureau of Chemical Hazards in August 1985, indicated that coke-oven pollution could be expected to result in increases of morbidity and mortality in the coke-plant workers and probably in the residents of Sydney.

Two Environment Canada reports, both classified as "restricted" and intended only for internal circulation, revealed that the coke- and steel-making operations violated the provisions of the federal Clean Air Act. The emissions were between 2800 and 6000 percent higher than "allowable" standards. Workers had been advised that paper masks provided adequate protection from pollution, and residents in the neighbourhoods surrounding the Sysco plant were told to consume greater quantities of broccoli in order to counter the high incidence of cancer.

The closure of the coke ovens resulted in the layoff of 125 employees (some with 40 years' service), with no severance pay, workers' compensation benefits, or pensions for the widows of deceased coke workers. An investigation organized and funded by fired employees resulted in the formation, in 1987, of Coke Oven Workers United for Justice. This organization found that of 103 worker deaths over a 25-year period, 64 died of cancer – a frequency almost six times the national average. Despite these and other findings, Sysco

(continued)

refuses to recognize that workers were exposed to pollutants and denies that the work site was hazardous. For example, when one eighteen-year veteran of the coke ovens, with a 41 percent loss of lung function, applied for compensation, Sysco's superintendent of personnel services advised the Nova Scotia Workers' Compensation Board that the corporation was not aware that the claimant had been exposed to a hazardous working environment.

The willingness of workers to tolerate the dangerous working conditions may seem puzzling but can be easily explained: there was little, if any, choice. In an area historically high in unemployment, workers dared not complain about working conditions because the fear of being without a job, when there was no hope of obtaining another, outweighed any risk to health. In addition, Sysco continually reassured workers that they had no cause for concern. Industrial blackmail kept coke-oven workers quiet for decades. With the ovens closed and the jobs gone, the blackmail is no longer effective.

In the view of the Steelworkers Union, the behaviour of Sysco warrants criminal prosecution. This, however, seems extremely unlikely despite the evidence of the serious physical harm caused to the environment, employees, and the people living and working in the city of Sydney.

their olfactory senses or a portable gas sniffer that no one was sure was properly calibrated or even worked at all. When the dead millwright was admitted for autopsy, the chemical odour was so overpowering that the door of the autopsy room had to be left open for ventilation.[3]

In October 1986, employees of Stelco — an Ontario-based steel manufacturer — underwent blood tests for polychlorinated biphenyl (PCB) contamination, after a plant electrician was found to have three times the "safe" level of contamination. PCBs have been linked to cancers of the skin, liver, and digestive system, as well as to birth defects and neurological damage. Some 800 workers in Stelco's electrical division were regularly exposed to PCBs during the servicing of transformers, and cases of cancer have been discovered among these workers. In addition, PCB coolant was being poured on the ground outside the plant's transformer compound and, on occasion, sprayed on company parking lots to control dust during the summer months.[4]

Despite the availability of information concerning the dangers associated with asbestos, every ferry acquired by or constructed for the B.C. Ferry Corporation between 1961 and 1975 contained extensive quantities of the material. As a result of union agitation and a report by an independent company, a decision was made to remove the asbestos. A contractor, hired to complete the work, threatened to lay off workers if the company was required to comply with safety regulations during the abatement operation.[5]

During the construction of the Four Seasons Hotel in the Pacific Centre in Vancouver, crews were applying a spray while other workers were required to remain in the vicinity. The spraying occurred in underground areas, and workers could see particulate matter in the air every day. Repeated inquiries were made of the employer and the Workers' Compensation Board. Workers were simply told the job site was "safe." Two years later, the painter-foreman stated that representatives of both the employer and the Workers' Compensation Board had told him to "keep his mouth shut" about the asbestos in the spray.[6]

In November 1987, it was discovered that employees at the McDonnell-Douglas plant in Toronto had been exposed to the carcinogenic chemical Alodine. The chemical manufacturer had warned the corporation of the danger, but the chemical was stored in vast, open vats at various locations around the plant. Employees were told that the substance might cause ulceration of mucous membranes, but many of those who handled the chemical developed serious skin and respiratory ailments.[7]

The Farmworkers Union has discovered that at one of the largest farms in the Fraser Valley in British Columbia, workers are being required to undertake between ten and twelve hours of continuous pesticide application, every day, without protective apparel. The clothing of workers becomes soaked, and the union reports at least one case of an individual who is suffering from permanent neurological impairment, which manifests itself as a sense of intoxication, nausea, blurred vision, and the "shakes." In 1982, another worker was caught in a pesticide-spray drift — a common occurrence — and, within two months, died from organophosphate insecticide poisoning.[8]

Thus the responsibility for deaths, injuries, diseases, and sickness cannot always be laid at the door of the work force. It is not valid simply to "blame the victims." Many corporations and employers seem more concerned with the protection of machinery and equipment than their labour force.[9] For example, when new IBM computer systems are installed in pulpmills, they require a controlled environment that is airconditioned and free of dust, corrosion, and vibration.

Two questions arise: Why do preventable deaths, injuries, diseases, and sickness occur? Why is corporate wrongdoing in this area not defined and dealt with as "crime"? An answer to the first question can be secured by examining a general, three-dimensional, explanatory model that may be used to explain all forms of corporate "crime." An answer to the second question requires an examination of the relationship among corporate interests, the prevailing economic system, and government — the body that constructs and enforces legislation.

THE CAUSES OF CORPORATE CRIME

Canadian and international researchers studying corporate "crime" suggest that an explanation lies within three interlocking areas: the behaviour of individuals; the nature and imperatives of the organizations (corporations) within which individuals work; and the structure and imperatives of the economic system within which corporations operate (Keane, 1991; McMullan, 1992; Snider, 1993; see also Figure 6.1). We shall examine each of these areas and demonstrate how, in combination, they provide a comprehensive explanation of corporate actions that cause physical harm to employees. The utility of the model for explaining other categories of corporate criminality (e.g., crimes against the environment) should become evident.

The individual level is of importance in understanding corporate criminality since it is people — owners, executives, managers, and supervisors — who implement and sometimes plan corporate wrongdoing. Why do they do it? Can the motivation for the behaviour be reduced to "need" (i.e., material gain to meet personal requirements or commitments), "greed" (i.e., material gain to satisfy particular personal goals), and "opportunity" (i.e., the availability of chances to satisfy need and greed)?

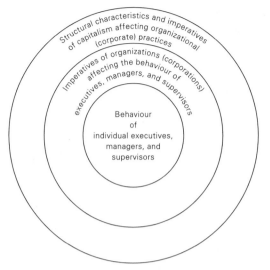

FIGURE 6.1

Corporate Crime: A General Explanatory Model

....

These factors cannot be discounted, but they do not entirely explain the behaviour of those who, often deliberately, endanger the lives of others. In this regard, the famous American pioneer of studies of "white-collar crime," Edwin Sutherland, used his general theory of "differential association" to explain the behaviour of errant business people, and this theory includes some persuasive and empirically verified propositions. Of particular importance is Sutherland's claim that individuals within corporations carry out illegal or improper actions as a consequence of learning (through association with others) both the ways of actually committing an act (i.e., the techniques involved) and the rationalizations necessary to override or "neutralize" moral constraints on behaviour (e.g., that it is improper to break the law or put others at risk) (Sutherland, 1949).

Sutherland's theory may help to explain the actions of the individuals who commit "crimes" against employees. Those responsible for exposing employees to hazards learn (from other managers or supervisors) not only the tactics necessary to persuade workers to carry out dangerous tasks but also the ways of justifying such behaviour. Managers or supervisors might learn how to rationalize their actions by persuading themselves that although workers are endangered, they receive high wages and are therefore compensated for taking unavoidable risks. Alternatively, an employer might mobilize the notion of "choice," the idealistic conception that any worker is always free to leave and seek employment in another industry if he or she does not wish to be exposed to hazards. As the Law Reform Commission of Canada suggests, these are common but ill-founded rationalizations for endangering the lives of workers (Law Reform Commission, 1986).

Sutherland's theory is compelling, and may help to explain the actions of individuals. At the same time, the theory has limitations; for example, it is concerned more with explaining *how* improper actions can be carried out than with *why* they are committed in the first place. To understand the latter, it is necessary to shift to the next sphere of analysis: the nature and imperatives of organizations.

As most analysts point out, a full understanding of corporate crime requires an analysis of the behaviour of individuals within the context of an organization. Improper actions may be planned and carried out in order to achieve personal goals, but these are usually linked to the body that can satisfy these objectives: the organization (e.g., a corporation) that employs the individual. The corporation is the source of material and psychological rewards (e.g., a higher salary and promotion) for those who comply with or facilitate organizational objectives and, although the latter may be perfectly legitimate, the means by which they are accomplished may not be. Ambitious employees may engage in illegal or improper behaviour in order to be rewarded, and it is in this sense that the organization is the cause of transgressions by individuals.

A corporation may place direct and indirect pressure on an executive, manager, or supervisor to "cut corners" and take risks to achieve organizational goals (e.g., increased productivity or the timely completion of a contract) for which he or she may be rewarded. The owners of, or senior personnel within, an organization may direct that certain actions take place and threaten subordinate managers or supervisors with dismissal if they fail to comply. Senior personnel may conceal the illegal or improper nature of practices from subordinates, or they may be the direct or indirect source of the rationalizations necessary to facilitate, for example, violations of occupational health and safety legislation, rules, or standards. A corporation may encourage a manager or supervisor by assuring the individual that deaths and injuries are a regrettable but unavoidable feature of working in an inherently dangerous industry, or indirectly allow the individual to transfer responsibility to the organization (e.g., "It is the fault of the system" or "Higher-ups told me to do it"). The permutations are vast, largely unexplored in the Canadian context, and, in some industries, complicated by subcontracting practices that, as the following example demonstrates, obscure organizational boundaries and distribute responsibility in favour of large corporations.

In 1987, approximately 70 percent of the fatalities in the forest industry occurred in nonunion operations. These operations constitute less than 20 percent of the entire industry, and a disproportionate share of fatalities therefore occurs in this setting. Large companies involved in the forest industry in British Columbia "contract out" to smaller operators, and the latter are under considerable pressure to increase production. A failure to do so could result in a contract not being renewed.

Often, experienced fallers will refuse to work under the conditions specified by some unscrupulous contractors, with the result that younger, less experienced workers are employed. In some cases, fallers with *no* experience are given a chainsaw and directed to cut trees, with predictable results. For example, in one case, a worker was killed felling his first tree. In another case, a worker lasted less than two hours before being struck and killed by a "widow-maker" (a loose branch dislodged from the treetop) (Salisbury, et al., 1991).

Large forest companies are apparently aware of these practices and consequent fatalities but, by contracting out, they are not held to be directly responsible. At the same time, the corporations benefit from the high levels of productivity achieved at the expense of workers. It is the contractor who is blamed, and when an "unacceptable" number of fatalities or injuries occurs, the larger corporations can simply refuse any further contracts, hire another contractor, and thereby allow the cycle to begin again.[10]

The organizational dimension (e.g., both the pressures placed on executives, managers, and supervisors, and the way in which an industry is organized) is, therefore, an important component in the explanatory model. But the activities of corporations (i.e., their owners and senior personnel), in turn, require explanation. In this regard, it is necessary to shift to the final sphere of analysis: the structure and imperatives of the economic system within which corporations operate.

Capitalism is an economic system with a number of interlocking, structural characteristics and imperatives:

- Private ownership of the means whereby things are produced — for example, the manufacturing and resource-extraction industries, the financing of business activity, and agriculture.
- Appropriation, by private owners, of the profits created by labour and technology, for the purpose of private accumulation of wealth or reinvestment.
- A labour system whereby those who do not own the means of production but work for the people who do are paid wages according to the value of their work, as determined by private owners, often in conjunction with labour organizations.
- Flexibility and durability. Capitalism has passed through several periods of change (i.e., the mercantile and industrial periods) and is currently entering the "monopoly" phase. The system has flourished despite challenges, problems, and major crises.
- Maximization of profits as the primary motivating factor and, therefore, one of the major "forces" of production.
- A strain toward consolidation, amalgamation, and monopolization, to maximize profit. This is particularly evident in the current phase of capitalism (monopoly capitalism) and is reflected in the constant process of corporate "takeovers" and mergers.
- Perpetual growth, expansion, and technological improvement to maintain or increase production, consumption, and profitability. This involves a constant hunt for, and stimulation of, the consumers of products (e.g., identifying and developing new markets for goods) and a constant search for both cheap raw materials and ways of reducing labour costs.
- A belief in the virtues of competition, free enterprise, and limited direct government intervention in the routine operations of the economy.
- Structural contradictions that create problems and periodic crises and that, consequently, require constant attention and management. For example, although the concentration of industry (e.g., the creation of a monopoly) maximizes profitability, it also results in a concentration of labour and thereby increases the power of labour to secure a larger share of profits. Technological developments may increase productivity and therefore profitability; however, they may displace the labour force, who consume goods, and thereby result in a crisis of overproduction (too many products chasing a reduced number of consumers). Perpetual growth is necessary to maintain or increase profit, but this may result in the rapid consumption and loss of the finite, nonrenewable resources on which production is based. In short, capitalism contains the seeds of its own destruction.

The foregoing provides a picture of the larger context within which corporations operate and, therefore, the structural factors that might account for corporate crime.

In the case of, for example, "crimes" against the environment, the imperative of maximization of profits and the associated systemic characteristics (i.e., perpetual growth, expansion, consumption, production, and competition) create organizational pressures that are passed down to, and may account for the behaviour of, executives, managers, and supervisors. Corporations find it cheaper to dump poisonous wastes into rivers or oceans, or to allow toxic emissions, than to pay for the processing or safe storage of wastes or the installation of emission scrubbers that prevent atmospheric pollution — measures that affect profitability (McMullan, 1992; Snider, 1993; Tataryn, 1979).

Maximization of profits and other characteristics and imperatives bear on the issue of "crimes" against employees, and Carson's (1982) analysis of the process (and human cost) of extracting oil from the North Sea provides a good example of their impact. In the late 1970s and early 1980s, Britain was facing severe economic difficulties that were affecting the general rate of profit and that could have been eased by the availability of North Sea oil. The resource had to be tapped quickly, and the process of drilling, extraction, and production was occurring while the construction of rigs and equipment was still taking place. For companies such as British Petroleum and Shell Oil, the rapid retrieval of oil (a profitable activity given the so-called global energy crisis) took precedence over all other considerations, and, in Carson's view, the labour force was consequently placed at risk. The "political economy of speed" reduced the lives of workers to one variable in a corporate cost/benefit calculation and accounted for the Piper Alpha rig disaster in which 160 workers were killed. Considerable pressure had been placed on the rig crew to increase production, the workers had no time to undertake proper maintenance, and, in the view of the platform superintendent, the rig was a "time bomb" that eventually exploded (Carson, 1982). House's (1986) analysis of the 1982 Ocean Ranger disaster in the Hibernia oil fields off Newfoundland suggests that similar factors were at work and that the political economy of speed and the concomitant social organization of the oil-rig workplace have a significant impact on the frequency and severity of injuries in the industry (see also McMullan, 1992).

It will be interesting to see whether similar dynamics contributed to the Westray mine disaster in Nova Scotia in May 1992. The initial claims of miners suggest that the massive underground explosion that killed 26 men was caused by a variety of safety violations such as ignoring high methane levels in the mine and the use of acetylene torches underground.

Given the limited enforcement and weak punishments, the costs of engaging in illegal behaviour may be outweighed by the benefits (Barnett, 1981; McMullan, 1992; Snider, 1993). As Henry (1986) points out, a failure to provide a clean and safe work environment may result in low fines, and it is more profitable to violate than comply with legislation and regulations. Two Canadian examples illustrate the importance of maximization of profits in understanding both the willingness to expose employees to harm and the reluctance to either remove dangers or protect workers once the risks are known.

Despite harm caused to both workers and the environment, pesticides are used extensively in Canadian agriculture to increase productivity and profitability. This practice benefits growers and, equally importantly, the companies that manufacture the chemicals. Little effort is made to minimize the harm caused to workers by providing protective clothing and equipment, since this expenditure would not necessarily improve productivity.[11]

In spring 1987, two workers were killed and three injured on a Toronto high-rise construction site. A personnel elevator that could have been carrying up to 35 workers rocketed from the ground floor, at a speed of 100 km/h, and smashed into barricades on the forty-fourth floor. The cause of the incident was identified as a broken gear shaft in the elevator-hoisting mechanism. When the shaft broke, the braking mechanism failed to operate, and the counterweight fell more than 40 floors, dragging the elevator upwards. The elevator had a history of breakdowns and malfunctions, including excessive vibration, stopping at the wrong floor, and stopping altogether for no apparent reason. Each time, there had been long delays in obtaining approval for service and repair. Commenting on deaths on construction sites generally, one Ontario Ministry of Labour safety officer stated that only two priorities existed on sites: the first, to finish the current project; the second, to start another one.[12]

In fairness, there are limits to corporate wrongdoing, particularly in the context of crimes against employees. A corporation cannot be concerned solely with, for example, maximizing profits if the associated practices result in death, injuries, and sicknesses that either drastically deplete or reduce the profitability of its skilled work force. Corporate activities may result in a problem or crisis of legitimacy — that is, a company may experience widespread public condemnation and a boycott of its products. An errant company may encounter stiff union opposition in the form of strikes, which stop production. The state may investigate, prosecute, and penalize a corporation for breaches of occupational health and safety legislation, regulations, or standards. In other words, whereas a structural imperative such as maximizing profits may be an important variable in explaining corporate transgressions, this does not imply that such practices are inevitable and the problems irresolvable. For example, if all the companies in an industry were required to comply with standardized, international environmental protection or worker-safety measures, a company's "competitive edge" — one source of increased sales, and hence, profitability — might not be eroded.

One limitation affecting corporate practices — the possibility of government intervention — raises a question that has a bearing on the entire field of corporate criminality: why are many forms of corporate behaviour that result in extensive material loss and serious physical injury not formally defined and treated as crimes? Why, for example, are the deliberate or negligent actions of corporations that result in the death, injury, or sickness of employees not investigated and prosecuted as murder, manslaughter, criminal negligence, or assault — crimes that attract severe punishments capable of deterring corporate wrongdoing? The answer can be found in the relationship among the entities that define and deal with crime (the levels of government), the dominant economic system (capitalism), and the corporate interests that flourish within that system (McMullan, 1992; Snider, 1993).

CORPORATE CRIMINALITY AND THE STATE

In "crimes" against employees, both the state and business interests go to considerable lengths to shift the blame to the victims of corporate practices. When this fails, efforts are made to ensure that corporate wrongdoing is defined as a regrettable but unavoidable by-product of a commonly beneficial economic system, and is best dealt with through one component of the welfare state — workers' compensation schemes — rather than the criminal-justice system. The provinces have introduced legislation — workers' compensation acts — and compiled regulations governing occupational health and safety that specify standards and create systems of workplace inspection. Governments thus deal with corporate wrongdoing through a regulatory system focussed on mediation and compensation rather than prosecution and punishment (Brown and Rankin, 1991; Snider, 1993).

On the one hand, this approach may be viewed as providing better protection for workers; just and speedy compensation for death, injury, or sickness; and an effective way of resolving conflicts between companies and workers, thereby ensuring better management/labour relations and industrial peace. On the other hand, critics of the system point to a number of deficiencies: the inadequate nature of occupational health and safety legislation and regulations; an insufficient number of fully trained and experienced inspectors to enforce regulations; ineffective penalties for wrongdoing that fail to deter corporations; the process of exempting work sites from health and safety standards; the length of time involved in securing compensation and the often inadequate amounts awarded to victims; the difficulties involved in gaining access to information held by workers' compensation boards; and the apparently close ties between boards and corporate interests (Law Reform Commission, 1986; Livesay, 1988; Paterson, 1985; Reasons, Ross, and Paterson, 1981). In short, the "welfarization," rather than "criminalization," of corporate practices may have been based on a laudable vision of justice and fairness for workers; in practice, however, this approach may benefit corporate, rather than labour, interests.

Studies of the origins of both workers' compensation schemes and occupational health and safety legislation challenge the claim that they were a product of state and corporate kindness (Coneybeer, 1990). Statutes regulating mines and factories first appeared in the late nineteenth and early twentieth centuries: a time when there was growing labour unrest as a consequence of deaths and injuries in the workplace, an increasing organization of labour, and clear signs of international revolutionary activity. The "wounded soldiers of industry," and their unions, were creating a number of problems for the state and corporations and, where civil litigation was pursued by casualties, the courts began to rule in favour of labour and award substantial damages. As Gough (1979) points out, action was taken to address the situation and, in most capitalist nations, the victims of industrial accidents became the first to receive social-security benefits; Canada was no exception (Coneybeer, 1990). More important, both the state and corporations recognized the value of a system of insurance and compensation that would distribute and minimize the costs of death and injury, avoid stigmatizing criminal prosecution and costly civil litigation, allow the state to administer the scheme and assume the task of caring for disabled workers and their families, and, equally important, appease labour. The latter abandoned their right to sue employers — a costly, cumbersome, and unpredictable process — but secured guaranteed, no-fault stipends to be paid in the event of workplace injury (Coneybeer, 1990).

Workers' compensation was one solution to the growing problem of maintaining order in an increasingly militant and unionized workforce, and it may be argued that the various schemes that emerged also enhanced the legitimacy of both the state and capitalism. Labour was controlled through an ostensibly benign set of actions, and there was no disruption to the process of reproducing the social, economic, and ideological conditions necessary for capitalism to continue. The interests of the capitalist class were well served, rather than threatened, by both legislation governing working conditions and workers' compensation schemes (Casey, 1985; Coneybeer, 1990; Gough, 1979).

Both the role of the contemporary workers' compensation system and the practices of this component of the welfare state can be better understood in the light of this brief historical sketch. From the outset, occupational health and safety laws and regulations, and compensation schemes, primarily served corporate interests, and this continues to be true.

1. Corporate violence against employees that cannot be screened as accidents or worker error is defined as a problem for the welfare, rather than criminal-justice, apparatus of the state, and, as a consequence, offending companies are not subjected to criminal prosecution.
2. State-administered compensation schemes channel and resolve disputes and generally appease labour, thereby removing one possible source of management/labour conflict that could lead to industrial unrest, lost production, and diminished profits.
3. Companies can avoid expensive civil litigation and the payment of damages (both of which affect profitability) by paying insurance premiums, the cost of which can be routinely built into the price of products and, therefore, passed on to consumers.
4. Occupational health and safety regulations apply equally to all competing companies within an industry, but they are inadequate and weakly enforced. Penalties are minimal and do not seriously affect profitability. This allows flexibility in the interpretation and application of standards and allows periodic, deliberate transgressions that may be necessary in order to ensure continued productivity and profitability.
5. The system of legislation and compensation is generally viewed as an example of benevolent state and corporate action, and this helps to legitimate and preserve the popularity of both the state and capitalism.

At the same time, however, workers continue to be exposed to risks, sometimes with the knowledge and even the assistance of workers' compensation boards, and often as a result of board inaction. For example, repeated variances (modification or exemption) for engineering inspection of concrete forms before any pouring of concrete are granted to the construction industry by the Workers' Compensation Board in British Columbia — an action that is seen as indicative of the board's willingness to accommodate an employer so that production is not disrupted.[13]

In 1989, board regulations specified that workers in high lead-hazard areas were entitled to the time necessary to take a protective shower at the end of a shift. Workers employed at the Cominco lead-zinc smelter in Trail, British Columbia, were denied this entitlement by the company since it would mean a production slow-down, but the board refused to take action.[14]

The use of a chemical wood preservative (TCMTB) in British Columbia pulp-mills became a cause for concern in early 1988. Employees at one mill had suffered sicknesses after being exposed to the chemical. Information was requested about the "safe levels" of exposure (the measurement of which is viewed with scepticism [Law Reform Commission, 1986]), but it was several months before the Workers' Compensation Board considered undertaking a study.[15]

The strategy used by governments to define and manage violence in the workplace surfaces in other areas of corporate criminality. Crimes against the economy, consumers, and the environment are, in the main, defined in federal and provincial legislation, which is separate from the criminal or quasi-criminal law. The "crimes" are viewed as problems best dealt with through regulation and mediation, and more appropriately managed by government agencies and administrative bodies that lie outside the criminal-justice system (e.g., the Competition Tribunal).

Why have the federal and provincial levels of government responded to corporate criminality in this manner? The state constructs laws and undertakes investigations and prosecutions but also plays a key role in protecting and advancing the interests of capitalism (Glasbeek, 1984; McMullan, 1992; Snider, 1993). This is not to suggest that the federal and provincial governments are merely the faithful servants, or "instruments," of a particular social class — the corporate elite — that dictates policy in the area of, for example, corporate "crime." Close ties exist between senior levels of government and business corporations (Clement, 1975, 1977; Olsen, 1980), but this does not mean that governments and their administrative apparatus (e.g., the bureaucracy and the justice system) act at the behest of one social class, factions within that class, or individual capitalists. It is evident that the state has some independence (i.e., autonomy), but that this autonomy is, nevertheless, relative to the requirements of capitalism as a whole. The state plays a particular "managerial" role that is built into the structure of capitalism and has the relative autonomy to exercise and attempt to synchronize three potentially contradictory "cardinal functions": (1) maintaining order; (2) preserving legitimacy of the state, the government of the day, and the capitalist economic system; and (3) reproducing the conditions necessary for capitalist economic activity to continue (McMullan, 1992; Snider, 1993).

As Canadian political economists and sociologists have demonstrated, problems and crises of, for example, maintaining order and preserving legitimacy periodically arise, and the process of exercising and attempting to synchronize all three cardinal functions can account for a wide variety of government practices and policies (Panitch, 1979; Ratner and McMullan, 1987). The construction of anticombines legislation is no exception (Smandych, 1985), and this "structuralist" theory may explain government responses to the different categories of corporate wrongdoing.

The "order maintenance" function of the state involves the use of various components of the government apparatus (e.g., the justice system and the welfare system) in an attempt to ensure peace and harmony in society, in the interests of capitalism as a whole. This task may extend to maintaining "order" in the economy, where conflicts between different and competing capitalist factions may threaten the common capitalist endeavour. To this end, governments are empowered to "discipline" particular corporations or even an entire industry. For example, governments may intervene in conflicts between corporations involved in resource extraction and those involved in secondary manufacture, or act to prevent one industry (e.g., pulp and paper) from polluting and destroying the natural resources essential to another (e.g., fishing and canning).

In fulfilling this "managerial" role, however, governments must take account of the need to preserve legitimacy (i.e., popular support) and ensure that there is no disruption to capitalist economic activity as a whole. Laws can be introduced and enforced to deal with a problem, but in so doing, governments must avoid the use of harsh and repressive measures that might attract the criticism of capitalist interests. Conversely, governments cannot hope to retain popular support if serious corporate wrongdoing is exposed but ignored; and where the actions of a corporation or corporations threaten the legitimacy of both a government and capitalism as a whole, disciplinary action may follow. Good examples of this can be found in the area of environmental pollution, where governments are working hard to at least appear to be addressing public concerns.

State practices aimed at maintaining order and preserving legitimacy are constrained by the third "cardinal function": producing and reproducing the social conditions necessary for capitalist economic activity to continue. Governments cannot tackle a problem of maintaining order or maintaining legitimacy by introducing repressive measures that might deter all forms of capitalist endeavour and thereby disrupt the general process of production, consumption, and accumulation of profits.

Governments must perform a complex, managerial "balancing act" in regard to their cardinal functions within the structure of capitalism. If a problem or crisis emerges in regard to, for example, popular support (i.e., legitimation), the state's response is conditioned by the need to ensure that order is maintained and that the general social conditions necessary for capitalist economic activity are preserved. Governments have the autonomy to deal with these problems or crises by using disciplinary or other measures and are not necessarily influenced by particular capitalists or capitalist factions. The autonomy of the state, however, is not absolute; it is relative to the common interests and requirements of capitalism as a whole.

So how might this "structuralist" theory of the nature and role of the capitalist state explain government strategies and policies in the area of corporate criminality? In particular, how might it explain the failure to define and deal with corporate wrongdoing as "crime"? How does the theory help us to understand the state's apparent reluctance to use the full weight of the resources (i.e., the criminal law and the criminal-justice system) available to fulfil its order-maintenance function?

Arguably, the answers lie with the government's role in ensuring legitimation and reproducing the conditions necessary for capitalism to continue (Barnett, 1981). The use of strong, repressive measures to combat corporate wrongdoing could result in a loss of popular support for capitalism. The appearance of the captains of industry in the docks of criminal courts might well discredit corporations and create widespread public doubt about the propriety of the prevailing economic and social system. Similarly, there would almost certainly be a disruption in capitalist economic activity as corporations were impelled to abandon, for example, the imperative of relentless maximization of profits. This might be replaced by, for example, the imperatives of environmental and worker protection, which, though laudable, might have an adverse impact on production, growth, international competitiveness, and investment, and hence the nation's economy. This, in turn, might create a crisis for the government as economic stagnation emerged and unemployment became widespread.

The discussion of crimes against employees was offered as a way of exploring some of the key issues and problems in the entire field of corporate criminality. That task is now completed. The conclusion gives a brief examination of the areas where research should be conducted by Canadian criminologists in order to generate a clear picture of the nature, scope, impact, and causes of corporate criminality, as well as the relationship among the state, the economy, and corporate interests.

CONCLUSION

Canadian criminologists have been unduly preoccupied with traditional, predatory street crime. This is hardly surprising, since the bodies that in the main fund criminological research in Canada (i.e., the various levels of government) are also preoccupied with the topic.

Criminologists who seek to explore corporate criminality will, however, encounter some difficulties (Casey, 1985; Snider, 1988, 1993). Research funds may not be available from state and corporate sources unless the topic happens to be one that may assist a government in resolving a growing problem of maintaining order or legitimacy (e.g., crimes against the environment). The information available from official data sources is sparse, and a researcher may wish to seek access to more detailed government and corporate records. Although cooperation might be forthcoming from government departments, corporate assistance is unlikely. A researcher could turn to interviews with "whistle-blowers," anonymous informants working within corporations, corporate employees who have been convicted of wrongdoing, workers and their unions, or independent "watchdog" agencies that have been accumulating information on corporate activity, and this might produce valuable data (Snider, 1993). The process of unravelling the complexities of corporate ownership may pose some difficulties, but, as Clement (1975, 1977) has demonstrated, these difficulties are not insurmountable. Generally, then, various methodological problems exist, but an enthusiastic and tenacious researcher should be able to accomplish his or her goals.

The field of corporate criminality is vast, and there is no shortage of topics to be studied. Canadian political economists and historians have already provided a framework for historical studies of corporate criminality (Carrigan, 1991; Naylor, 1973), and work in this area could yield important empirical and theoretical insights. There is a pressing need for studies in the largely untapped areas of corporate criminality — notably, crimes against the economy (e.g., patent violation and product piracy). Forms of corporate wrongdoing that have already been subjected to some examination (crimes against consumers, the environment, and employees) need intensive and rigorous examination, and among these is the issue of corporate violence against women (DeKeseredy and Hinch, 1991). In each case, empirical studies should be theoretically informed, and a researcher may choose to focus on either a testing of the three interlocking components of the general causal model set out in this discussion or the theories that might account for the state's response to corporate crime.

QUESTIONS TO CONSIDER

1. Outline several conclusions Gordon and Coneybeer make regarding corporate crime in Canada. What do these conclusions suggest about the manner in which Canadian society is organized?

2. Select two of the five categories of corporate crime identified by Gordon and Coneybeer, and discuss in detail the harm associated with them. What measures do you think are appropriate in dealing with these two categories?

3. Discuss whether Gordon and Coneybeer feel that the state attacks corporate crime in the same way that it attempts to repress street crime. What

theoretical approach do Gordon and Coneybeer argue best explains how the government deals with corporate crime?

NOTES

1. On *Newscience*: CHEK 6 Television, Victoria, B.C., October 30, 1987.
2. Data supplied by the Workers' Compensation Board of British Columbia.
3. Case reported in the *Alberni Valley Times*, March 15–17, 1983.
4. Case reported in the *Toronto Star*, October 18, 1986; the *Vancouver Sun*, October 20, 1986; and *The Globe and Mail*, December 12, 1986.
5. Bennie et al. (1987); interview with Mr. B. Redlin, Canadian Union of Public Employees, Burnaby, B.C., April 26, 1988.
6. Interview with Mr. W.C. Denault, Director, B.C. Construction Health and Safety Council, Burnaby, B.C., April 22, 1988.
7. Case reported in the *Toronto Star*, November 20, 21, and 27, and December 23, 1987; *The Globe and Mail*, November 20, 21, and 27, and December 7, 1987.
8. Interview with Mr. S. Boal and Mr. M. Fleming, Canadian Farmworkers Union, Burnaby, B.C., May 5, 1988.
9. Interview with Mr. B. Payne, Canadian Paperworkers Union, Vancouver, B.C., April 25, 1988.
10. Interview with Mr. B. Patterson, Safety Director, International Woodworkers of America/Canada, Local 1-71 (Logging), Vancouver, B.C., May 6, 1988.
11. Boal and Fleming interview.
12. Incident reported in *The Globe and Mail*, May 21, 1987; the *Sunday Star*, August 30, 1987; the *Calgary Herald*, August 30 and September 1, 1987; the *Toronto Star*, August 31, 1987.
13. Denault interview.
14. See British Columbia *Hansard* (Debates of the Legislative Assembly), May 15, 1980.
15. See British Columbia *Hansard* (Debates of the Legislative Assembly), March 21, April 21, and April 28, 1988.

REFERENCES

Barnett, H.C. (1981). Corporate capitalism, corporate crime. *Crime and Delinquency, 27*, 5–23.

Bennie, R., Oram, T., Brewin, J., & Brewin-Marley, J. (1987). *Report on asbestos and the B.C. ferries: Years of neglect, years of pain*. Victoria: B.C. Ferry & Marine Workers Union.

Boal, S. (1985). *Presentation to the B.C. Federation of Labour's inquiry into the Workers' Compensation Board*. Burnaby, BC: Canadian Farmworkers Union.

Borkin, J. (1978). *The crime and punishment of I.G. Farben*. New York: Free Press.

British Columbia. (1993). *Forest Practices Code*. Victoria: Queen's Printer.

Brown, R., & Rankin, M. (1991). Persuasion, penalties, and prosecution. In M.L. Friedland (Ed.). *Securing compliance: Seven case studies* (pp. 323–353). Toronto: University of Toronto Press.

Caputo, T. (1989). Political economy, law and environmental protection. In T. Caputo, M. Kennedy, C.E. Reasons, and A. Brannigan (Eds.). *Law and society: A critical perspective* (pp. 161–172). Toronto: Harcourt Brace Jovanovich.

Carrigan, D.O. (1991). *Crime and punishment in Canada: A history*. Toronto: McClelland & Stewart.

Carson, W.G. (1982). *The other price of Britain's oil: Safety and control in the North Sea*. Oxford: Martin Robertson.

Casey, J. (1985). Corporate crime and the state. In T. Fleming (Ed.). *The new criminologies in Canada* (pp. 100–111). Toronto: Oxford University Press.

Clement, W. (1975). *The Canadian corporate elite: An analysis of economic power*. Toronto: McClelland & Stewart.

Clement, W. (1977). *Continental corporate power: Economic linkages between Canada and the United States*. Toronto: McClelland & Stewart.

Clinard, M.B., & Yeager, P.C. (1980). *Corporate crime*. New York: Free Press.

Coneybeer, I.T. (1990). *The origins of workmen's compensation in B.C.* Burnaby, BC: School of Criminology, Simon Fraser University.

DeKeseredy, W., & Hinch, R. (1991). *Woman abuse: Sociological perspectives*. Toronto: Thompson.

Emond, D.P. (1984). Co-operation in nature: A new foundation for environmental law. *Osgoode Hall Law Journal, 22*, 323–348.

Ermann, M.D., & Lundman, R.J. (1982). *Corporate deviance*. New York: Holt, Rinehart & Winston.

Farrow, M. (1988), August 27. Chopper forestry rules found lax. *Vancouver Sun*, p. A12.

Geis, G. (1982). *On white collar crime*. Toronto: D.C. Heath.

Glasbeek, H.J. (1984). Why corporate deviance is not treated as a crime: The need to make "profits" a dirty word. *Osgoode Hall Law Journal, 22*, 393–439.

Goff, C.H., & Reasons, C.E. (1978). *Corporate crime in Canada: A critical analysis of anti-combines legislation*. Scarborough, ON: Prentice-Hall.

Goff, C.H., & Reasons, C.E. (1986). Organizational crimes against employees, consumers, and the public. In B. Maclean (Ed.). *The political economy of crime* (pp. 204–231). Scarborough, ON: Prentice-Hall.

Gough, I. (1979). *The political economy of the welfare state*. New York: Macmillan.

Henry, F. (1986). Crime: A profitable approach. In B. Maclean (Ed.). *The political economy of crime* (pp. 128–203). Scarborough, ON: Prentice-Hall.

House, J.D. (1986). Working offshore: The other price of Newfoundland's oil. In K.L.P. Lundy and B. Warme (Eds.). *Work in the Canadian context*. Toronto: Butterworths.

Keane, C. (1991). Corporate crime. In R.A. Silverman, J.J. Teevan, & V.F. Sacco (Eds.). *Crime in Canadian society* (4th ed.). (pp. 223–232). Toronto: Butterworths.

Law Reform Commission of Canada. (1985). *Crimes against the environment*. Working Paper No. 44. Ottawa: Law Reform Commission of Canada.

Law Reform Commission of Canada. (1986). *Workplace pollution*. Working Paper No. 53. Ottawa: Law Reform Commission of Canada.

Law Reform Commission of Canada. (1988). *Pollution control in Canada*. Ottawa: Law Reform Commission of Canada.

Livesay, B. (1988). Dying for a living. *This Magazine, 21*(7), 22–26.

McMullan, J.L. (1992). *Beyond the limits of the law: Corporate crime and law and order*. Halifax: Fernwood.

Naylor, T. (1973). The history of domestic and foreign capital in Canada. In R. Laxer (Ed.). *(Canada) Ltd.: The political economy of dependency* (pp. 42–56). Toronto: McClelland & Stewart.

Olsen, D. (1980). *The state elite.* Toronto: McClelland & Stewart.

Panitch, L. (Ed.). (1979). *The Canadian state: Political economy and political power.* Toronto: University of Toronto Press.

Paterson, C. (1985). W.C.B. deficiencies. *The Facts,* 7(1).

Rankin, M., & Finkle, P. (1983). The enforcement of environmental law: Taking the environment seriously. *University of B.C. Law Review 17*(1), 35–57.

Ratner, R.S., & McMullan, J. (Eds.). (1987). *State control: Criminal justice politics in Canada.* Vancouver: UBC Press.

Reasons, C.E. (1987). Workplace terrorism. *The Facts, 9*(3), 6–11.

Reasons, C.E., Ross, L.L., & Paterson, C. (1981). *Assault on the worker: Occupational health and safety in Canada.* Toronto: Butterworths.

Salisbury, D.A., Brubaker, R, Hertzman, C., & Loch, G.R. (1991). Fatalities among British Columbia fallers and buckers, 1981–7. *Canadian Journal of Public Health 82*(1), 32–37.

Schrecker, T. (1989). The political context and content of environmental law. In T. Caputo, et al. (Eds.). *Law and society: A critical perspective* (pp. 173–205). Toronto: Harcourt Brace Jovanovich.

Simon, D.R., & Eitzen, D.S. (1990). *Elite deviance* (3rd ed.). Boston: Allyn & Bacon.

Smandych, R. (1985). Re-examining the origins of Canadian anticombines legislation, 1890–1910. In Fleming, T. (ed.). *The new criminologies in Canada* (pp. 87–99). Toronto: Oxford University Press.

Snider, L. (1988). Commercial crime. In V.F. Sacco (Ed.). *Deviance, conformity and control in Canadian society* (pp. 231–283). Scarborough, ON: Prentice-Hall.

Snider, L. (1993). *Bad business: Corporate crime in Canada.* Scarborough, ON: Nelson.

Sutherland, E. (1949). *White collar crime.* New York: Holt Rinehart & Winston.

Tataryn, L. (1979). *Dying for a living.* Toronto: Deneau & Greenberg.

West, W.G., & Snider, D.L. (1985). A critical perspective on law in the Canadian state: Delinquency and corporate crime. In T. Fleming (Ed.). *The new criminologies in Canada* (pp. 138–169). Toronto: Oxford University Press.

Wickman, P., & Dailey, T. (Eds.). (1982). *White-collar and economic crime.* Lexington, MA: D.C. Heath.

World Commission on Environment and Development. (1988). *Our common future.* Oxford: Oxford University Press.

PART THREE
Minorities and the Law

The treatment of minority groups can be considered a test of the overall fairness inherent in any legal system. Although most contemporary legal systems embody principles of legal equality that advocate the equal treatment of all citizens, there is little doubt that many, if not most, legal systems also contain systematic biases that exclude or discriminate against certain groups. Thus, discrimination based on race, gender, class, culture, and sexual orientation continues to be embodied in both the structures and the application of many legal systems. The Canadian legal system is no exception. The articles in this section deal with three minority groups that have become more prominent in demanding changes to the Canadian legal system to accommodate their needs.

The first article deals with the many issues involved in the increasingly vocal demands being made by Canada's aboriginal peoples for greater autonomy over their legal affairs. In "Alternative Paradigms: Law as Power, Law as Process," Russel Barsh and Chantelle Marlor provide an interesting analysis of the debate regarding possible separate aboriginal legal and criminal justice systems. The authors distinguish between the "power paradigm" of the law, in which a judge or arbitrator imposes a decision from above, and the "process paradigm," which involves redress, peacemaking, and other forms of negotiated justice. The power paradigm is commonly associated with Western legal systems and tends to rely on punishment to deter conflict and antisocial behaviour. It is generally argued that "tribal" law more closely approximates the process paradigm, and that aboriginal people consider the power paradigm alien to their values. Although Barsh and Marlor agree that tribal law is a type of process-oriented law, they question the commonly articulated assumption that developing separate aboriginal legal systems based on aboriginal cultural values would necessarily reduce conflict within aboriginal communities.

Barsh and Marlor start their analysis by arguing that the process paradigm has never been properly evaluated, and that it is unclear whether the use of concepts such as redress, peacemaking, and mediation can effectively reduce conflict. In terms of aboriginal people, they raise several more specific concerns. Although aboriginal people are clearly overrepresented in the Canadian criminal justice system, Barsh and Marlor suggest that this tendency may be caused by factors other than conflict with an alien, power-oriented legal system. They raise several questions about the use of "healing circles," which currently constitute the most widely implemented means of conflict resolution among aboriginal peoples. First they suggest that healing circles are a fairly recent innovation, and it is unclear whether they devolve from traditional aboriginal values. Further, they argue that it is unrealistic to expect healing circles to reduce conflict in communities when the communities themselves may be dysfunctional due to economic marginality and other problems. Finally, Barsh and Marlor argue that the healing circles may actually be oppressive insofar as they place pressure on victims and offenders to accept mediation and ultimately may silence legitimate dissent within the community. They conclude that further research is necessary before it can be definitively argued that aboriginal-controlled legal and criminal justice systems represent a major solution to the oppression faced by aboriginal people.

The second article in this section discusses important issues in the debate over gay and lesbian rights. Douglas Sanders argues that increasing violence against gay and lesbian people, combined with a resurgence of anti-homosexual lobby groups, makes it imperative that new protections for lesbians and gay men be enshrined in

Canada's legal system. Sanders adds that although gay and lesbian rights have finally been taken seriously by many segments of the public, they remain controversial in the minds of many politicians and community leaders. He acknowledges that there is considerable debate within the gay community regarding the best way to frame their claims for increased rights. He notes that although the "right to privacy" argument was originally used to instigate the repeal of statutes that criminalized homosexual activity, the same argument has also been used against gays and lesbians by Canadian courts to deny them spousal benefits. Sanders discusses the possibility of using the equality provisions of the Charter of Rights and Freedoms to justify claims for equal treatment and protection from violence. Such claims are predicated on the twofold argument that homosexuality is not a chosen lifestyle and that sexual orientation neither justifies differential treatment nor constitutes a basis for denying gay men and lesbians rights available to heterosexuals.

Sanders concludes that, although considerable progress has been made by the courts and legislatures in Canada to increase the protections afforded lesbians and gay men, the Charter of Rights and Freedoms still fails to include sexual orientation as a prohibited basis for discrimination. Furthermore, most legislatures that have chosen to specifically protect gay rights have also included statements affirming that they were not condoning homosexuality. Sanders discusses many arguments against equality rights for homosexuals and notes that most of the progress toward equal rights has been made in the areas of decriminalization and protection from job-related discrimination, where an employee's homosexuality is considered a private matter of no concern to the employer. Several other areas, including spousal benefits and other types of family rights, have proved much more resistant to change, since legislation in this area would involve publicly acknowledging gays and lesbians as a legitimate group and would, in the minds of many people, implicitly condone homosexual activity. Sanders concludes his discussion by assessing several specific issues, including child custody rights for gay parents, the discrimination practised by Immigration Canada regarding the sponsorship of same-sex partners, and the legality of same-sex marriages.

The final article in this section takes a much broader approach to the entire question of minority group rights. In "Justice between Cultures: Autonomy and the Protection of Cultural Affiliation," Denise Réaume discusses the philosophical underpinnings associated with the protection of minority groups, as well as the reasonable limitations that may be placed on the unique cultures of such groups. Réaume starts her analysis by noting that contemporary societies are increasingly characterized by the melding of different racial, ethnic, and cultural groups, and that this cultural diversity necessitates the development of principles for dealing with intergroup conflict. Réaume identifies two extreme responses to the problem of cultural conflict and argues that neither is satisfactory. The *philosopher's model* attempts to develop universal principles of human interaction and posits that different groups should give up cultural practices that do not conform to the universal standard. She argues that this approach negates the importance of minority cultural values by collapsing them into a "universal morality" that could potentially oppress some groups. The second model, which she labels the *extreme nationalist model*, seeks to eliminate cultural conflict by isolating the groups and allowing each to conduct its affairs without interference from others. She argues that this approach is also unsatisfactory because most societies are so culturally heterogeneous as to preclude the isolation of different cultural groups, and also because it ignores the possibility of individual dissidents within cultural groups.

Réaume develops a model of intergroup relations that provides for justice between cultures while also protecting individual autonomy. She argues that individual (or personal) autonomy is always interwoven with cultural practices, and that the protection of minority cultural practices within a larger multicultural society cannot be separated from the protection of individual rights. Thus, the protection of minority cultures has implications for individual rights, and any attempt to protect minority groups must constantly guard against the potential abuse of individual autonomy, both within the minority group and within mainstream society. In this respect, the rights of minority cultures and of individuals may not be defensible if they unduly threaten or restrict the rights of other groups or mainstream cultural values. Nevertheless, Réaume concludes by arguing that diversity is a positive value and that outsiders should be careful about interfering in the internal practices of minority groups. She adds that the co-existence of two or more cultures "requires the development of a political culture which sees good in diverse social forms," and that tolerance of diversity by all groups will ultimately reduce the abuse of individual rights because serious conflicts over values will be less common. This conclusion is interesting because it can be applied to virtually any minority culture or subculture, including the rights of lesbians and gay men that were discussed earlier in this section.

SEVEN

Alternative Paradigms: Law as Power, Law as Process

RUSSEL LAWRENCE BARSH
AND CHANTELLE MARLOR

In his theory of history, written in the final days of the Roman Republic, Lucretius argued that a peaceful social order cannot be maintained without *positive law* — that is, a body of legislated rules applied by coercive authority. As an Epicurian, Lucretius assumed that the purpose of human life is the pursuit of individual happiness, which leads to the need for institutions capable of managing conflicting human desires peacefully.[1] The importance of positive law in maintaining social order re-emerged a millennium and a half later in the writings of Jean Bodin, John Locke, and Thomas Hobbes as a fundamental tenet of liberal social theory (Unger, 1975). In our own times, the "rule of law" became a slogan of the Western struggle against communism and repressive regimes (Hutchinson & Monahan, 1987; United Nations, 1996).

Anthropologists have meanwhile concluded that tribal peoples also have law, albeit of a fundamentally different nature. Early studies that tried to synthesize codes of rules from observations of tribal disputes acknowledged the flexibility with which rules were applied and the importance of wide community participation (e.g., Schapera, 1938; Llewellyn & Hoebel, 1941; Pospisil, 1958). By the 1960s, there was wide agreement that tribal peoples tend to favour mediation and negotiation in conflict situations, with the aim of "making the balance" among the parties (Nader, 1969). When articulated at all, beliefs about proper conduct constitute broad talking points rather than enforceable prescriptions (e.g., Bohannan, 1957; Fallers, 1969; Gluckman, 1955). Outcomes are determined largely by social relations among the participants, including the "judges," with relatively little concern for objective proof of what had transpired between the principal disputants. Restoring peace takes priority over the enforcement of rules.

Positive law and tribal law reflect two different paradigms for understanding and resolving social conflicts. Positive law, which we will refer to in this chapter as the *power paradigm*, is based on the assumption that conflicts arise from differences in individuals' desires and in the ways they pursue their desires. Conflict can accordingly be minimized by standardizing behaviour, while permitting people to pursue their individual desires within collectively acceptable limits. Standardization can be achieved by adopting explicit rules, monitoring compliance with the rules, and mobilizing state power to detect and punish any incidents of non-compliance. Rule-making and rule-enforcing institutions in contemporary Western societies include governments, the boards of directors of corporations, the administrative tribunals of trade unions and professional associations, and disciplinary committees of universities.

In theory, rules reduce conflict in two ways. Collectively undesirable activity is prohibited, and human behaviour as a whole is rendered more predictable. For example, most countries have adopted rules prescribing whether one drives on the left side or right side of the road. Without this arbitrary rule, drivers would face uncertainty and potential conflict each time they approached another car.

A basic assumption of the power paradigm is that punishing non-compliance increases compliance. Yet controlled experiments indicate that rewarding compliance ("positive reinforcement") is more effective than punishing non-compliance, and that punishment must be immediate and consistent to have a significant effect on behaviour (see generally Walters & Grusec, 1977). Immediacy is unattainable except in an Orwellian world of pervasive electronic surveillance, and consistency would require perfect surveillance as well as perfectly precise, unambiguous rules covering every possible situation. As long as conflicts involve disputes over what actually occurred, and rule makers have to struggle with the imprecision of human languages and an inability to foresee the future, the conditions for effective behaviour modification will not exist outside of highly controlled experimental settings.

The assumption that punishment increases compliance is not supported by empirical observations. Naturalistic experiments in American cities concluded that even increases in the speed and certainty of arrest and detention had little deterrent effect (e.g., Ross, McCleary, & LaFree, 1990; Sherman et al., 1992). Historical statistics suggest a correlation between property crime and economic cycles (Neustrom & Norton, 1995), which may be independent of changes in the certainty and severity of punishment. In addition, there have been distressing revelations about violence in prisons and the impact of imprisonment on strengthening inmates' anti-social attitudes and beliefs (e.g., Rideau & Wikberg, 1992).

In Canada, a number of public inquiries have drawn attention to the dispro-portionate number of Aboriginal people[2] in prisons (e.g., Hickman, Poitras, & Evans, 1989; Cawsey, 1991; Hamilton & Sinclair, 1991). In the United States, the overrepresentation of American Indians in prisons has been overshadowed by the vastly disproportionate incarceration of African Americans (Grobsmith, 1994). Prison statistics have fuelled demands by Native North Americans and African Americans for decriminalization and for greater community control of policing and sentencing. Community control has become a major tenet of anti-racism and civil-rights advocacy in the United States, while in Canada it has figured increasingly as an objective of Native nationalism.

THE SEARCH FOR ALTERNATIVES

Doubts about the efficacy of the power paradigm have led to increased interest in alternative conflict-management approaches, such as redress, restorative justice, and peacemaking (e.g., Cragg, 1992; de Haan, 1990; Pepinsky & Quinney, 1991). Like tribal law, these alternatives reflect a *process paradigm* in that they rely on flexible, facilitated give-and-take among the parties to reach an agreement that the parties themselves consider appropriate and mutually beneficial. There are some rules of procedure but very little in the way of enforcing substantive rules of behaviour; as much as possible is left for negotiation. Unlike adjudication or arbitration, where the proceedings are managed by a power-figure who makes the final disposition of the matter,[3] mediation and other process-centred alternatives are managed by a trust-figure who encourages the parties to communicate freely and engage in joint problem solving. Participation in alternative approaches is generally voluntary, which proponents argue ensures that the parties are committed to co-operation and achieving "integrative" or win-win results.

The process paradigm has been embraced by two contemporary reform move-ments: alternative dispute resolution (ADR), which has grown increasingly popular among lawyers in Western countries since the 1970s and includes family mediation, criminal diversion schemes, and multistakeholder consensus building in environ-mental disputes; and healing circles or sentencing circles, promoted by indigenous peoples in Canada and New Zealand since the 1980s. Although the proponents of healing circles purport to draw upon traditional cultural practices that are philo-sophically opposed to Western liberal jurisprudence (e.g., Dumont, 1993), they share with the proponents of ADR a faith in the efficacy and empowering nature of facilitated negotiations. We will accordingly refer to both ADR and healing circles in this chapter as manifestations of a contemporary appeal for *negotiated justice*, to dis-tinguish them from positive law as well as from the legal systems of tribal peoples.

Advocates of negotiated justice promise that it will render the criminal law more equitable and less onerous for the poor and marginalized and will make civil dis-pute resolution more accessible, affordable, and adaptable to the needs of the indi-vidual parties (e.g., Dukes, 1993; Pruitt & Carnevale, 1982). Negotiated justice has been advocated as a strategy for managing conflicts ranging from contract disputes, marriage breakdowns, and youth delinquency to environmental controversies, eth-nic violence, and war.

NEGOTIATED JUSTICE IN THEORY

The recent popularization of negotiated justice has led to the publication of many "cookbooks" for resolving conflicts (e.g., Fisher & Ury, 1991). However there continues to be a paucity of coherent theory or systematic testing of claims. (Scimecca, 1993; Druckman, Broome, & Korper, 1988). Theorists and practitioners of negotiated justice do not even agree on the definition of the term *conflict*, which is applied to situations ranging from overt threats and violence to the mere perception, by the parties, that their needs or goals are incompatible (e.g., Ford, 1994). If we cannot agree on the point at which a potential or perceived incompatibility becomes a conflict, we cannot agree on the point at which a conflict *ceases* to be a conflict. This ambiguity is a serious obstacle to testing theories.

Most proponents of negotiated justice nevertheless generally agree that all conflicts fall along a continuum from *competitive*, in which the parties' interests are unavoidably incompatible, to *co-operative*, in which the parties erroneously perceive that their interests are irreconcilable (Druckman, 1993). By definition, relatively competitive conflicts are impossible to resolve fully. The tactics usually recommended by ADR practitioners, such as "logrolling" (asking each party to sacrifice its less important needs in order to win concessions on more important ones) and "expanding the pie" (placing new items on the table that are not directly related to the conflict), are derived from experiences with labour relations and contract negotiations (see Pruitt & Carnevale, 1993, pp. 36–37). They are designed to achieve a mutually beneficial agreement *without* completely satisfying the parties' original concerns.

By comparison, the tactics ordinarily recommended for use in co-operative conflicts draw on concepts and methods of individual psychotherapy and group counselling. If conflicts arise from the parties' misunderstandings of their respective needs, and failure to recognize the compatibility of their interests, then conflicts can be eliminated by reformulating the parties' cognitive schema. Practitioners contend that cognitive change can be fostered by building a relationship between the parties so that they can begin to communicate effectively (Greenhalgh & Chapman, 1995; Clark, 1993); helping the parties identify their needs precisely and explore their beliefs critically (Deutsch & Shichman, 1986); separating ideas that are associated by convention rather than necessity ("unlinking" — see Pruitt & Carnevale, 1982);[4] and encouraging the parties to think creatively about alternatives ("problem-solving"). The facilitator has been compared to a trickster or Zen master, who challenges and educates the parties without exerting authority over them (Benjamin, 1995).

While the competitive–co-operative continuum seems plausible and intuitively appealing, it is not a simple matter to classify particular conflicts. A majority of conflicts are described as "mixed-motive," or having competitive and co-operative elements. Full disclosure by the parties, knowledge of the history of the conflict, and an awareness of all possible alternatives would be required before the facilitator could reliably assess the extent to which a conflict is fundamentally irreconcilable, or involves misunderstandings and misperceptions that can be corrected. If facilitators lack enough wisdom or information to make accurate assessments, they may choose ineffective tactics. Furthermore, if a large proportion of the world's conflicts are competitive, negotiated justice has little hope of improving social order.

Proponents of negotiated justice avoid these questions by focussing on those aspects of conflicts that involve differing cognitive schema rather than differences of power and interests (e.g., Fisher, 1994; Wilson & Canter, 1993; Pruitt & Carnevale, 1993, pp. 84–91; Hewstone, 1988; Klar, Bar-Tal, & Kruglanski, 1988; Condor & Brown, 1988, p. 14). This core assumption, however, has never been satisfactorily tested.

MOTIVATION AND COMMITMENT

Advocates of negotiated justice concede that co-operative problem solving also depends on the motivation of each party to resolve the conflict and the commitment of each party to abide by the process (Lawler & Ford, 1995; Rabbie, 1991; Rubin, 1991). There are many reasons why these conditions are often lacking. For example, some parties actually benefit (or perceive that they are benefiting) from the perpetuation of the conflict. A party that controls a disputed resource, and can continue to benefit from its use as long as the dispute remains unresolved, may agree to facilitated negotiation simply as a way of reducing friction with other parties and avoiding escalation. There may also be disincentives for parties to commit themselves to the process. The parties may believe that they can achieve better results in the courts, may feel too much anger toward the other parties to engage them face to face, or may find it easier to avoid dealing with the conflict altogether (Pruitt & Carnevale, 1982). Prospects for successful problem solving in such cases are poor.

Practitioners generally agree that facilitated negotiation is more likely to lead to agreement and compliance if the parties have a long-term beneficial relationship to protect (Zubek et al., 1992; Wissler, 1995; Greenhalgh & Chapman, 1995). Relationships imply the existence of some trust, concern, and empathy between the parties, as well as an understanding of each other's specific needs and interests. Trust may be a condition for the parties to share information that could be used against them later (Deutsch, 1973, pp. 143–176; Feger, 1991), and empathy may lead to efforts by the parties to understand each other's cognitive schema (Deutsch, 1994; Fisher, 1994; Feger, 1991).

The existence of a conflict suggests that any pre-existing relationships between the parties have broken down and are no longer mutually perceived as beneficial. Practitioners purport to rebuild relationships through the venting of hostile emotions relating to the conflict (catharsis), which they claim fosters healing (Montville, 1993). It is difficult to understand how catharsis can rebuild feelings of trust and mutual benefit in conflicts that have their origins in an inequality of power and resources between the parties. Many proponents of negotiated justice nonetheless seem to embrace a blind faith that mediated confrontations can be "transformative" of power imbalances (e.g., Burgess & Burgess, 1996).

NEGOTIATED JUSTICE AND STATE AUTHORITY

The distinction between positive law and negotiated justice is more clear in theory than in contemporary practice. Mediation and diversion schemes, including healing circles, continue to be subservient administratively to the state legal system. Parties retain the option (or face the threat) of adjudication if mutual commitment to the negotiation process wavers. State legislation generally limits the scope of facilitated negotiations, possible outcomes, and eligible participants. In criminal diversion, for example, the accused must admit guilt and be selected as eligible for diversion by state prosecutors. Negotiations are restricted to legislatively specified forms of punishment and redress, the accused faces the threat of renewed prosecution if negotiations break down, and the facilitator rather than the victim tends to do most of the negotiating (e.g., Dignan, 1992).

As a result, "alternative" institutions tend to be hybrids of the power paradigm and the process paradigm, with the former retaining its dominance. Although negotiated justice is routinely justified as a moral advance that returns power to the people (Nergård, 1993; McElrea, 1994), critics contend that the original motive for its promotion in the 1970s was containing the growing cost of adjudication to the state. The cost of adjudication has meanwhile been contained by reforms in court administration, but negotiated justice continues to be promoted by a self-interested industry of professional facilitators (Scimecca, 1993; Dezalay & Garth, 1996).

To the extent that conflicts in contemporary society arise from differences in power rather than differences in cognitive schema, it seems unlikely that negotiated justice will have much impact on the frequency and severity of conflicts. Indeed, the growing popularity of negotiated justice has arguably increased the power of professionals rather than the power of people. It is difficult to reject these pessimistic hypotheses because it is difficult to test the claims of practitioners and theorists.

PROBLEMS OF EVALUATION

Our ability to compare the efficacy of negotiated justice and positive law under different conditions depends initially on our ability to define and measure the desired outcome. Once we have constructed a valid and reliable way of measuring outcomes, we can also determine whether facilitated negotiation requires similar conditions, and leads to similar results, at all levels from individual disputes to international conflicts (Milburn, 1996).

We begin by defining *conflict* as a situation in which people conclude that their needs are incompatible, and one or more of them has the power to satisfy their needs without the consent of the others (Greenhalgh & Chapman, 1995, p. 167). In the absence of unequal power, there is merely a difference of opinion. Conflict may periodically manifest itself in physical violence, but it exists, influences behaviour, and gives rise to perceived injuries whether or not the more powerful parties actually exercise their power in words or deeds. Oppression based on race or gender is frequently passive and silent, for instance; it is enough that the victims know that they are disfavoured and lack power.

What is the desired outcome of intervention in a conflict? Terms such as conflict resolution, dispute resolution, redress, and healing imply that the conflict and its consequences for the victims can be made to vanish forever. We prefer "peacemaking," which implies the management of conflicts and mitigation of their most disruptive manifestations, without necessarily eliminating the underlying causes, reversing the damage, or banishing painful memories.[5] Peacemaking can also extend to the wider process of fostering mutually beneficial relationships throughout society. Mass media, the arts, schooling, and religion can be involved in peacemaking, although they do not ordinarily engage in "conflict resolution." Peacemaking thus has a short-term goal (mitigating the symptoms of conflict) and a long-term goal (equalizing power and strengthening relationships in order to reduce the frequency of conflict).

In the sense we use it here, peacemaking is fundamentally opposed to "social control." Social control is about the use of power to manipulate individual and collective behaviour. It may lead to the appearance of greater orderliness and to an absence of violence in the short term, but arguably it merely represses and intensifies feelings of injustice and deprivation, which may erupt in other forms over the longer term. Social control is therefore merely symptomatic relief, whereas peacemaking attempts to address the root causes of conflict as well. As such, social control and peacemaking take opposing viewpoints on the distribution of power in society. Social control accepts the status quo and appeals to those with power to use their privilege for the (purported) good of all. Peacemaking aims to redistribute power through building relationships that involve sustainable balances of power — or, in the terms indigenous peoples use, building relationships based on *respect* rather than domination.[6]

It is difficult to define the desired outcome of peacemaking with sufficient precision to form a basis for hypothesis testing. Peacemaking is ultimately a long-term proposition, potentially involving changes in the structures of institutions and personal relations (compare Dukes, 1993). The marginal effect of any one intervention, such as a single mediated agreement, is not likely to be very large, either on the parties or on their communities. We should expect to see only a gradual decline in the symptoms of conflict and a gradual decrease in perceptions of powerlessness or inequality.

From this viewpoint, researchers in the field of negotiated justice generally look for too little and expect too much. They tend to choose readily observable phenomena as outcome measures: keeping appointments, reaching an agreement, and complying with the agreement in the short term (rarely more than one year, e.g., Wissler, 1995; Raisner, 1997); how closely the written agreements match parties' self-reported goals (e.g., Maxwell, 1992; Zubek et al., 1992; LaFree & Rack, 1996); and parties' satisfaction with the agreement at the time it was made (e.g., Dignan, 1992; Wissler, 1995). Similarly, students of communal and international conflicts typically rely on short-term, observable measures such as a six-month cessation of hostilities (Regan, 1996; see Kleiboer, 1996 for a critical review of the international literature).

Short-term measures are inherently problematic when they are used to infer future states. We cannot assume that compliance or satisfaction with a negotiated agreement at the end of, for example, one year will persist for another five years or longer. Short-term measures also fail to detect short-term changes if these changes are very gradual and involve very small increments.[7]

The validity of compliance and satisfaction as measures of success is doubtful as well (compare Barsh, 1993a). Compliance and satisfaction with an agreement are not necessarily associated with improvements in the parties' overall treatment of each other or in their behaviour toward others. Even if negotiated justice were more effective than positive law at achieving agreements in individual cases, it does not follow that negotiated justice will reduce the level of violence or frequency of disputes in society or improve the quality of human relationships.

Even seemingly straightforward measures may be fraught with problems of validity and reliability. The obvious candidate for a simple and objective measure of success in criminal diversion schemes, for example, might be *recidivism*: the likelihood that an accused wrongdoer subsequently re-offends. Which subsequent activities must we count, and how should non-identical activities be weighed for the purpose of comparison? Does it matter whether the victim is the same? How long should we wait before we cease counting? Consider a physical assault on a domestic partner by a young man. He is diverted to a program that arranges for him to engage in conciliation with the victim and perform several hours of community service. Over the next five years, he moves in with another woman, has a shouting match with an unrelated man over a parking space, recklessly runs over a dog on the street, and writes several letters to newspapers complaining that the mayor is openly gay. He does not strike anyone again during this period.

Government statistics would not treat any of these incidents as recidivism, while a psychotherapist might consider *all* of them symptoms of unresolved personal issues involving insecurity about gender, among other things. Using recidivism as a measure, then, the subject has been "healed" by his experience in diversion, but a broader analysis of his behaviour suggests that he has merely relocated his insecurity and aggression. Of course, we also have no way of determining what mischief he might have caused had he *not* been in diversion. Conviction and imprisonment might have made him even more insecure and violent.

Testing the efficacy of negotiated justice has been further complicated by the inherent ambiguity of the claims made by some of its advocates. Claims related to catharsis, forgiveness, and confession have been gaining recent prominence in the descriptive and prescriptive literature of negotiated justice, for instance. Expressions of anger, pain, and remorse enable the victims to "let go" of their injuries, proponents contend, and enable wrongdoers to internalize the norms they have violated (George, 1995; Levine, 1988). Claims for the healing power of catharsis find parallels in studies of Western psychiatry and tribal psychotherapy (Jilek, 1993; Dow, 1986; Kosmicki & Glickauf-Hughes, 1997), and may have roots in Christian theology, which makes virtues of forgiveness, atonement, and suffering (Hurley, 1996; Baker, 1992). This philosophical approach raises especially troublesome issues in relation to the victimization of women, who have long been persuaded to suffer in silence and to see virtue in acceptance (LaRoque, 1997).

Catharsis was originally used by psychoanalysts to describe an outburst of repressed emotions, the culmination of a cycle of the accumulation and release of tension. Catharsis was therefore conceived to be a major *cause* of, rather than cure for, violence, but this conception has been widely criticized (e.g., Goldstein, 1992; Kumagai & Strauss, 1983; Saunders, 1977). However, neither the causative nor curative models of catharsis have been tested systematically. The powerful appeal of the notion of catharsis in North America and Europe is more likely due to its Christian resonances than to the results of scientific study.

The curative model of catharsis finds current application in "reintegrative shaming" — formal ceremonies in which the wrongdoer is denounced by respected representatives of the community, then permitted to offer redress and apologize in exchange for symbolic re-inclusion in society (Braithwaite, 1989). There are parallels in the use of humiliation in hazing rituals, "brainwashing," and other practices that tend to produce conformity in individuals' loyalties and beliefs. As yet there have been no demonstrations that shaming ceremonies result either in long-term satisfaction or long-term compliance. Braithwaite and Mugford (1994) dismiss the relevance of such tests, suggesting that the process itself has inherent social value as an alternative to retribution (see, too, McElrea, 1994).

Negotiated justice holds out the promise that wrongdoers can be rehabilitated effectively and inexpensively without cruelty or punishment. This is a comforting faith, particularly against the contemporary media backdrop of global warfare, terrorism, random shootings, and high levels of violence and recidivism in prisons. However, diversion schemes in criminal matters have begun to draw public and professional criticism for being too protective of the offender and for giving low priority to the needs of victims (Dignan, 1992). Failure to establish claims of efficacy more persuasively has paved the way for a backlash; indeed, support for negotiated justice has been waning since the 1980s (Clairmont, 1996).

RESULTS OF EVALUATION RESEARCH

Assuming that we could construct valid and reliable measures of the desired outcomes of negotiated justice, we could construct and compare stratified samples of individual conflicts dealt with by the courts and conflicts diverted to some form of facilitated negotiation. Assuming furthermore that we could obtain detailed comparable longitudinal follow-up data on the behaviour of the two groups of subjects, we could estimate the comparative efficacy of the courts and negotiated justice in changing the specified kinds of undesirable behaviour. Unfortunately, there are many practical problems with conducting naturalistic experiments of this nature. Negotiated justice programs are highly selective with respect to the kinds of conflicts and kinds of wrongdoers they will accept, targetting the individuals they believe they can change the most. Since programs are biased in favour of success, there is no way of assembling a genuine control group for comparison.

There have nevertheless been a few attempts at quantitative research on negotiated justice. Hughes and Schneider (1989) sent self-assessment questionnaires to 240 criminal mediation programs in the United States and concluded that there was no satisfactory evidence of their effectiveness. Wooldredge et al. (1995) could detect no significant difference between court-ordered probation and community diversion in the likelihood that juvenile offenders would re-offend within a year. One-fifth of the Norwegian youth brought before conference boards for vandalism did not re-offend within a year (Nergård, 1993), but this was based on self-reports by offenders, which cannot be considered reliable. Stead (1995) claimed that criminal diversion had reduced recidivism in Regina, Saskatchewan, but his data are biased by the fact that diversion was limited to minor offences and targetted offenders considered to be low risks by prosecutors. In a comparative study of court-supervised and independent family-mediation cases in the United Kingdom, Yates (1990) found little difference in participants' satisfaction with the process or in short-term (eighteen-month) compliance with agreements. Wissler's (1995) comparison of mediation and adjudication in Boston small-claims court found that while the parties who chose mediation expressed greater satisfaction with the process, there was no appreciable difference in outcomes (measured by compliance with agreements). A parallel study conducted in New Mexico found that there were greater ethnic and gender disparities in outcomes (measured by the size of monetary settlements) in mediation than adjudication (LaFree & Rack, 1996). In other words, mediators were more likely than judges to allow stronger parties to direct the process. The beneficiaries of mediation were white males and "repeat players" — individuals who knew the mediation process from previous experiences as participants.

In a survey of 161 environmental mediations, Bingham (1986) focussed on identifying factors that increased the likelihood of achieving an agreement, such as the kinds of parties and nature of the issues involved. She was unable to confirm that mediation had cost the parties less than adjudication, or had saved them time, and she noted that potential litigation was a factor that might have encouraged consensus in some cases and discouraged consensus in others. In a study of 81 environmental mediations that *failed* to produce agreements, Buckle and Thomas-Buckle (1986) found that the parties in many cases felt they had gained useful ideas from the process. The authors argued that this educational outcome justifies mediation. In a critical overview of environmental mediation in Hawaii, however, Modavi (1996) argues that environmentalists have actually been demobilized and delegitimized by participating in mediation, while the power of industry has been strengthened and legitimized.

Qualitative surveys of community justice projects in North America emphasize the need to address power inequalities through structural changes or "transformation" but fail to produce any evidence that negotiation leads to such changes (e.g., Merry & Milner, 1993; Milner, 1996, critiquing Bush & Folger, 1994; Dukes, 1993). Managing individual disputes and mitigating expressions of conflict through conciliatory processes that are essentially voluntary in nature may simply re-affirm existing power relations, setting the stage for a continuation of the underlying conflict.

Practitioners agree that the establishment of sentimental attachments or relationships among the parties is an important step in coming to an agreement (Lovaglia & Houser, 1996; Shelly, 1993). Unlike the courtroom, facilitated negotiation can elicit strong feelings of guilt, shame, and empathy, which are said to be the psychological mediators of individual self-control (Wall & Callister, 1995). However, frequent offenders may be offending precisely because they have difficulty feeling or expressing such emotions. In particular, men's sexual violence is associated with low self-esteem, low empathy, and feelings of victimization and frustration (Osland, Fitch, & Willis, 1996; Marshall & Maric, 1996; Scully, 1988). Low empathy and normlessness are predictors of adolescent violence regardless of ethnicity (Kingery, Biafora, & Zimmerman, 1996). Empathy-building exercises can lead to more prosocial behaviour among children (e.g., Roberts & Strayer, 1996), but the results of similar interventions with convicted offenders have been equivocal (e.g., Schewe & O'Donohue, 1996). Negotiated justice is therefore unlikely to produce much change with violent offenders.

Contrition may be effective at rehabilitating offenders only under special conditions, such as when all of the parties have a stake in long-term beneficial relationships within a community of shared beliefs. Becker (1976) found that contrition was usually accepted as full settlement of disputes in Renaissance Florence. But when greater social mobility eroded the solidarity and collective liability of Florentine families, the use of punishments became more frequent and severe. Communal and family solidarity are relatively weak in contemporary Western industrial societies. Indigenous peoples stand alone in claiming that they satisfy this condition for the maximum effectiveness of negotiated justice — an issue to which we will return below.

Practitioners agree in only the most general terms that the personality, skills, approach, and authority of facilitators can play a large role in the outcome of negotiated justice. Studies of facilitators' personalities and strategies have not produced consistent findings. For example, mediator empathy has been a positive factor in some studies (e.g., Zubek et al., 1992) and a negative factor in others (e.g., Bartos,

1989). The effects of mediators' style undoubtedly depend greatly on the nature of the caseload. Recent studies in Asia report that mediators used an empathetic style in family disputes and a more rationalistic approach in commercial disputes (Wall et al., 1995; Wall & Sohn, 1993). There is also inconsistent evidence regarding the effect of gender on facilitators' effectiveness. Some research suggests that women secure greater compliance with settlements, especially in emotionally charged cases (Maxwell, 1992), while other research suggests that women are less effective at overcoming inequalities of power between the parties (LaFree & Rack, 1996).

In conclusion, there is thus little evidence to support claims that negotiated justice is more effective than the courts at reducing conflict or transforming society. Yet it is significant that, regardless of its objective short-term efficacy, participants tend to express more satisfaction with negotiated justice than with adjudication (Rudd, 1996; Wissler, 1995; Zubek et al., 1992). Negotiated justice is therefore more successful than positive law in terms of legitimizing itself as a regime and of contributing through that perceived legitimacy to people's general feelings of living in a just society. What long-term effect this trend might have on conflict reduction is unknown.

As a whole, the field of negotiated justice is dominated by appeals to cultural values such as democracy, equality, and respect for the individual and for individual freedom of choice, rather than the use of empirical evidence to show that there are better ways of reducing conflict, violence, or crime in society. Studies that advocate negotiated justice tend to avoid comparisons with positive law. Instead, they claim to have proven the efficacy of negotiated justice by showing a "high" (greater than 50 percent) level of short-term satisfaction or short-term compliance among the participants. This implies that negotiated justice should be preferred as long as it is no less effective than positive law in reducing conflict.

INDIGENOUS INITIATIVES: A SPECIAL CASE?

The cultural values that characterize contemporary advocacy of negotiated justice as a whole tend to overlap with many of the core values asserted by indigenous peoples (Barsh, 1995a). At one level, this tendency explains the success of indigenous peoples in Canada, Australia, and New Zealand in securing public support for healing circles. At another level, it raises questions about claims that healing circles are culturally distinctive or are inherently opposed to Western jurisprudence.

Indigenous peoples should provide the strongest case for the advocacy of negotiated justice because, in principle, they retain collective solidarity, participate in strong kinship networks, and value harmonious, egalitarian, non-authoritarian social relations (Ross, 1996; Ryan, 1995; Dumont, 1993). Although European intervention has admittedly disrupted indigenous cultures and institutions to some extent, proponents assume that pre-existing social relations will re-emerge once the legal processes in indigenous communities have been "indigenized" (e.g., Tomaszewski, 1997).

Is there evidence that healing circles — regardless of their authenticity in relation to precolonial ideals or practices — are likely to liberate Native communities from state manipulation, or to help them "heal," reconcile, and reunite themselves internally? What is the likelihood that healing circles will transform power relations within Native societies, and between Native peoples and the state? Or will healing circles simply enforce existing power relations in new forms?

Contemporary Native communities represent a great diversity of ancestral cultures, as well as great variation in factors such as the incidence of violence and the degree to which communities internalize responsibility for violence (e.g., Auger et al., 1992; LaPrairie & Diamond, 1992). "The aboriginal justice discourse remains ... primarily at the political and jurisdictional levels and assumes a communal, egalitarian ethos in communities" (LaPrairie, 1995, p. 523). On the contrary, most Native communities have experienced several generations of resettlement, missionization, integration into capitalist markets, bureaucratic interference in their internal affairs, extreme poverty, coercive assimilation programs such as residential schools, and, most recently, the cultural impacts of television and mass advertising. The beliefs and distribution of power within Native communities have arguably been affected to the extent that social harmony is no longer possible (Depew, 1996; Nielsen, 1991).

Native scholars have drawn attention to three kinds of "new" divisions and inequality in Native communities: gender, religion, and class. Women have become targets of violence, intimidation, and neglect, even in societies where they once held considerable economic, political, and ceremonial power (LaRocque, 1997; Monture-Angus, 1995). In societies where women remain influential, it is often only through unofficial, informal means (e.g., Fowler, 1982, pp. 270–272). The erosion of women's status has been attributed to government programs aimed at training them to be "civilized," and to colonial-era diplomacy, warfare, and trade, which augmented the economic and political contributions of men (Carter, 1996; Devens, 1992; Shoemaker, 1995; Gonzalez, 1981).

Native communities have also experienced class formation due to the introduction of competitive market capitalism, as well as the emergence of Native leadership elites that control political resources such as access to federal bureaucrats (Boldt, 1993, pp. 118–147; Barsh, 1987; LaPrairie, 1995). Native communities are usually also divided between traditional ceremonialism and Christianity. This division has become confounded with class because Christians tend to be more aggressive in seeking elected offices and administrative positions (e.g., Fowler, 1987; Alfred, 1995). Native economies tend to be dominated by discretionary federal aid administered through locally elected councils. Local elections can play a significant role in the distribution of employment, housing, scholarships, and other benefits, and families compete with each other electorally in what has been described as a rotating political spoils system (Barsh, 1993b). Electoral competition increases the tensions and jealousies associated with cultural and social differences among families.

Hence there is great inequality not only between communities and the state, but within communities as well. Some commentators have concluded that, under these circumstances, political mobilization and empowerment are impossible without actively forging a new moral consensus within Native nations (e.g., Boldt, 1993, pp. 195–196). Others contend that Native communities have become Westernized or statelike in their organization and institutions to the extent that they cannot secure internal justice or stability without the adoption of Western-style checks and balances, such as protection of individual rights (Barsh, 1995a; LaRocque, 1997).

One consequence of increasing social divisions within Native communities has been the growing reliance of women and dissenters on external agencies such as the courts for protection (LaPrairie, 1995, p. 531). In Canada, Native women's organizations have opposed the devolution of power to Native governments on the grounds that this would result in greater oppression of women (LaRocque, 1997).

Under these circumstances, at least two important conditions for effective negotiated justice may be lacking: a community of shared values and valued relationships, and widely respected and trusted individuals who can serve as the facilitators.

At the same time, it must be asked whether any process aimed at "healing" the psychological and social scars of oppression can succeed while the oppression continues. Achieving internal unity will depend on strengthening self-confidence, trust, and optimism. If Native communities continue to be subjected to discrimination, capricious state policies, and external economic forces that are perpetuating poverty and inequality, it is difficult to see how these communities can be reunited except, perhaps, by a millennial movement that persuades people to overlook each others' acquired social status and share their property. As Depew (1996) observes, expecting healing circles to heal oppressed communities is not only unrealistic, it trivializes the oppression.

Descriptive studies of healing circles in Canada (Canadian Bar Association, 1996; Ross, 1996; Ryan, 1995; Mandamin, 1993), New Zealand (McElrea, 1994; Consedine, 1992), and Hawaii (Wall & Callister, 1995) reveal a number of shared features: a special setting rich in traditional symbolism such as a tepee or *marai*; an opening ceremony, such as prayers using the pipe and sweet grass, that draws attention to participants' spiritual responsibilities; circle seating according to participants' status and function; and several rounds of talk supervised by a trust-figure (elder, judge, police officer). In principle, conflict, its wounds, and its underlying causes are addressed simultaneously. Accordingly, no distinction is drawn between conflict resolution and therapy (compare Watson-Gegeo & White, 1990), and healing circles often do not involve specific disputes or victims. Healing circles are frequently only one part of a larger program of activities aimed at promoting "spirituality" through cultural teaching, individual and group religious activities such as purifying sweats and pipe ceremonies, and individual counselling by Native elders.

Most Native healing initiatives focus on violent, addicted, or incarcerated adults. There have been some qualitative studies of healing projects in prisons, which agree that inmates attach great value to learning about their cultures, developing positive self-imagery, and praying (Waldram, 1997; Nechi Institute & KAS Corporation, 1995; Grobsmith, 1994). Inmates describe new feelings of security, empowerment, and responsibility toward others. The extent to which these self-reported personality changes result in behaviour change is uncertain. Individuals who achieved education and employment after prison frequently attribute their success to cultural renewal and spirituality, but there have been no studies comparing inmates who participated in healing programs with those who did not.

According to its promoters, healing circles are effective at two levels, which we will call situational and intergenerational. In terms of situational justice, the healing circle restores good relationships among the parties (individuals as well as their families) to the immediate conflict or dispute. Intergeneration justice applies to those situations where the healing circle purportedly also terminates the bequeathal of pain and anger from victims to their children, breaking the "cycle of violence" in communities. The situational and intergenerational goals of healing circles parallel the short-term (agreement and compliance) and long-term (transformative) goals embraced by the non-Native proponents of negotiated justice.

The extent to which healing circles achieve their goals will depend not only on the social resources of individual communities, such as shared values, strong relationships, and widely respected and trusted facilitators, but on the nature of the root causes of violence within Native communities. As a preliminary matter, the notion of a cycle of violence should be approached with caution. The validity of statistical studies comparing the careers of violent offenders with those of their parents or children is subject to question (Widom, 1989). Most studies purporting to demonstrate a cycle of violence are actually evidence of a cycle of criminalization (e.g., Rowe & Farrington, 1997). By using criminal charges or convictions as measures of violence, they fail to account for police profiling and targetting of particular families, neighbourhoods, and ethnic or racial groups, which create higher ratios of criminal charges to actual violent events (Jackson, 1989). They also fail to take account of differences in behaviour that tend to expose particular cultural groups to a greater likelihood of detection (e.g., Barsh, 1995b). Public drinking and fighting attracts more attention and results in more charges than consuming drugs at home or breaking surreptitiously into homes.

Most research on the causes and manifestations of violence in Native communities have stressed distinctive cultural factors, such as a value system that extols physical bravery (e.g., Bachman, 1991). It was similarly argued for many years that distinctively African-American values were responsible for the disproportionate levels of violence and criminalization in American inner cities; however, a recent study found that African Americans tend to view violence much *less* favourably than other Americans (Cao, Adams, & Jensen, 1997). Machismo may simply be a highly visible element of youth subcultures that assumes particularly violent manifestations in conditions of extreme poverty, discrimination, and frustration.

An alternative model of the cycle of violence draws upon the works of indigenous and Third World scholars on the psychology of oppression (Duran & Duran, 1995; Nandy, 1983; Memmi, 1973; Fanon, 1967). In this model, the oppressed are said to internalize their oppression, seeing themselves with the eyes of their oppressors. The experience of discrimination and marginalization is thereby transformed into self-contempt and expectations of failure. The cycle of violence is symptomatic of a deeper psychological cycle of self-rejection, perpetuated within family relations. Parents have low esteem for themselves and expect their children to fail. Emotional commitment is tentative and encouragement weak. While some children may react violently in frustration, the predominant symptoms predicted by this model are inaction and mistrust.

Applying the psychology of oppression to healing circles in Native communities, it may be asked whether people experiencing self-rejection and mutual mistrust can "heal" through a process of trying to share these feelings with each other. Proponents of healing circles generally claim that "healing" has occurred when the participants have expressed anger, pain, and grief through words and tears (Clairmont, 1996). The participants may not only feel a temporary emotional release, but believe that emotional outbursts reduce the risk of repressed feelings causing violence (compare Russell & Arms, 1995). Yet by venting feelings of grief and rage, participants relive their experiences of oppression and abuse. Without effective resolution of some kind, then, the venting of feelings of victimization may actually make the participants feel more aggrieved and powerless. The meaning and therapeutic management of expressed emotion vary considerably cross-culturally (Jenkins & Karno, 1992), and it is unclear what the facilitators of healing circles are doing other than formally acknowledging the feelings that are expressed.

Intervention and confrontation can make some abusive men more violent (Sherman et al., 1992), giving rise to justifiable concerns for the safety of Native women.

The circle format itself is a powerful metaphor, and it can be argued that the living symbolism of community members sharing their fears and hopes in this way can be therapeutic. Metaphors are a familiar tool of both traditional healing and contemporary psychiatry (Kirmayer, 1993; Florsheim, 1990; Watson-Gegeo & White, 1990). The message conveyed by the circle metaphor will depend not only on how people are seated, but on what they say and how they interact. Pavlich (1996) has criticized negotiated justice generally as a "confessional ritual" in which participants exert strong emotional pressure on the victim and wrongdoer to redefine the conflict and themselves. Accepting the will of the group is not necessarily the same as "healing."

There is a tendency in group decision making for the majority to silence dissent and enforce consensus (Michener & Wasserman, 1995). Healing circles seek to mobilize a large cross section of the community, and the "public" may greatly outnumber the victim and wrongdoer. Laboratory and naturalistic studies suggest that pressures on individual participants to conform are greatest when the group is isolated, under stress, relatively cohesive, or very dependent on the personality of a strong leader — conditions that, arguably, characterize many Native communities. There is a danger, then, that victims' needs will be subordinated to group goals, as well as a danger that the accused will express contrition only to satisfy the group's demand for consensus. The healing circle may therefore only appear to restore harmony, while the parties leave the circle with their underlying negative feelings unresolved.

Two forms of victimization are most often raised as healing issues by Native communities in Canada: the institutionalization and abuse of Native children in missionary "residential schools" and (more recently) foster care, and the physical and sexual abuse of Native women and children by family members. Are healing circles an appropriate setting for Native people to confront the priests, bureaucrats, and kinfolk who victimized them? As noted earlier, empathy-building exercises do help sex offenders to better understand their victims' feelings, but the impact on offenders' subsequent behaviour is unclear (Schewe & O'Donohue, 1996). Moreover, being involved in empathy building with offenders may be extremely stressful and destructive for the victims (LaRocque, 1997).

Confessional rituals such as "truth commissions" and the use of mediation as an empathy-building exercise have been advocated as tools for resolving ethnic conflicts (Steiner, 1997; Ryan, 1996; Montville, 1993), but the efficacy of these strategies has yet to be demonstrated. A confessional format may be *more* applicable to cases of collective oppression than to individual-level conflict. Kelman (1973) has argued persuasively that states cannot mobilize citizens to inflict massive collective abuses on their neighbours without first blocking empathy through a process he describes as authorization, routinization, and dehumanization. In such cases, restoring the human feelings of the victims and the victimizers through direct, personal, emotionally charged contact is plausible. But there is no evidence yet that negotiated justice has this effect.

Recent work by non-Western psychotherapists on the causes of distress and illness in communitarian, kinship-oriented societies suggests that individuals "heal" when they understand and accept their responsibilities to others (e.g., Doi, 1973; Sow, 1980). The task of the healing process, according to this therapeutic model, is to re-integrate the individual into a web of responsibilities, rather than to achieve individual autonomy. Native people have been exposed to mainstream schooling and advertising to a great extent, and at least some members of Native communities are attracted by competitive individualism and consumerism. One therapeutic model based on communal solidarity may no longer be effective in communities with mixed and opposing motivations and social orientations.

In this context, it is interesting that healing circles have gained considerable appeal among Native prison inmates as a tool for addressing anger, victimization, and addiction. Inmates are geographically and socially isolated from their communities, and their healing circles draw eclectically on the spiritual beliefs and practices of different Native nations (Waldram, 1997). Under these circumstances, "healing" may reinforce inmates' individual self-esteem and self-control, but without rebuilding their family and community relationships. Inmates' feelings of alienation and frustration could conceivably increase after they return home to face the collective expectations of their communities.

The healing-circle movement focusses on resolving negative feelings and conflict among adults as a means of ending the cycle of oppression and violence. Recent research on child development suggests that focussing on the learning environment of young children could be more effective. In a longitudinal study of Native Hawaiian children, Werner and Smith (1992) identified a number of "protective factors" that increased the likelihood of children's emotional survival and productive, non-violent adulthood. Chief among these protective factors were childhood emotional anchoring to one or more supportive adults, and strong ethnic or religious values and identity. Unfortunately, subsequent studies of child survival have relied on readily acquired developmental statistics such as physical health and standardized intelligence tests (e.g., Stattin, Romelsjö, & Stenbacka, 1997), rather than investigating childhood social relationships. However, cross-cultural studies confirm a correlation between child-rearing patterns and the acceptability and prevalence of violence in adulthood (e.g., Fry, 1992; Briggs, 1978; for current theory see Evans, 1997). If childhood social relationships are effective at breaking the intergenerational transmission of self-rejection and violence in Native communities, initiatives such as cultural immersion and the involvement of elders in schooling may be more effective than adult healing and law reform in reducing conflict in communities.

The punishment or therapy meted out to men who abuse women may be ineffective as long as children continue to develop their gender identities within a web of patriarchal relationships at home, in school, and in the administration of their communities (Snider, 1998). In view of the exposure of Native parents to mainstream media and parenting models such as residential schools, it should not be assumed that Native children are already being socialized in culturally distinct, appropriate ways.

Although couched in distinctively Native cultural terms, the healing circle project is suspiciously transcultural. It employs the same symbols and protocols throughout North America, and to a large extent, overlaps with the wider project of negotiated justice in Western countries. Whether or not they are effective in reducing conflict in or reuniting Native communities, healing circles seem to represent the "invention of tradition," as Dickson-Gilmore (1992) argues in the case of the Kahnawake Mohawk Nation. Establishing a "traditional court" within the longhouse may be a new structure, but it draws on old principles and represents an important symbolic achievement of Mohawk nationalism.

Like negotiated justice generally, healing circles cannot be fully disengaged from state systems of positive law. The courts refer cases to healing circles and usually participate directly in the cases they have referred. Healing circles are financed by state agencies and must achieve some form of acknowledgement or accreditation before they can secure the co-operation of police, judges, and other state officials. Critics of healing circles in Canada and Australia contend that state supervision and financing of healing circles have increased the presence of the state within indigenous communities and are responsible for the high level of standardization of the protocols adopted by different communities (Blagg, 1997; Depew, 1996).

It may be more accurate to say that the state is competing with Native people over the design of healing circles, and that the courts and healing circles are competing with each other for legitimacy and caseloads. In India, forum-shopping by litigants placed British-style courts in competition with village councils or *panchayats*, with the result that the weaker institution began to adopt the structures of the stronger (Galanter, 1968). We may accordingly expect healing circles to grow more standardized and courtlike. Indeed, healing circles were arguably really a state project from the outset, like the systems of tribal courts in the United States and much of Africa (Moore, 1992; Barsh & Henderson, 1976) and the programs for achieving Native "self-government," which ultimately increased state bureaucrats' control over communities' decision making (Barsh, 1995b).

CONCLUSIONS

There is little evidence that negotiated justice terminates individual conflicts, reduces the overall level of conflict in society, or is more effective than positive law in modifying the way people treat each other in the long term. At best, it can be stated with confidence that people who participate in negotiated justice tend to feel that it is preferable to adjudication. With regard to Native communities, healing circles are compatible with Native conceptions of a just social order at the level of theory. The actual conditions in contemporary Native communities, such as power differentials between families, seem incompatible with the use of negotiated justice to achieve social harmony.

The movement for negotiated justice has been criticized for medicalizing problems that arise from power, rather than from illness or miscommunication (Depew, 1996). It may be comforting to think that people who abuse their power can be "healed" through speech and empathy building with their victims, but there is no evidence that power differentials are transformed by such means. Parties that engage in constructive co-operation are far more likely to be satisfied with the results of negotiated justice than those that act competitively or aggressively (Rudd, 1996; Zubek et al., 1992), but it seems obvious that parties will be happy if the process is consistent with their personal values. The parties' satisfaction with the process does not necessarily reflect behavioural changes. Furthermore, the parties most likely to work co-operatively may be those who already enjoy a balance of power or share a culture of egalitarianism.

Proponents of negotiated justice often appear to be arguing from the perspective that nothing could be worse than the current system of positive law, especially the criminal law (e.g., Avison, 1994). The failures of positive law are abundantly evident; the comparative advantages of negotiated justice remain hypothetical. It is incumbent upon social scientists to devise more precise and testable theories relating to the cause and reduction of conflict so that citizens can truly make informed choices. Otherwise, the flight from positive law, however much it may be justified, may lead simply to new forms of social control disguised as popular justice.

QUESTIONS TO CONSIDER

1. Distinguish between the "law as power" and "law as process" models discussed by Barsh and Marlor. Outline and critically assess several criticisms that they raise regarding the law as process model.
2. Outline several criticisms that Barsh and Marlor raise regarding the current rush to implement a process-oriented criminal justice approach to Aboriginal people. Do the authors necessarily accept that the use of measures such as healing circles will lower conflict in Aboriginal communities?

NOTES

1. *De Rerum Natura*, 5, 1136. The other great school of classical Greek and Roman philosophy, Stoicism, attributed social order to self-awareness, self-discipline, and unselfishness.
2. "Aboriginal" is used in Canada's Constitution Act, 1982, to refer collectively to "the Indian, Inuit, and Métis peoples of Canada." It is not popular as a term of self-identification in Canada, however, and is not used in the United States. We will use the more general terms "Native American" or "Native" to refer to the indigenous peoples of North America.
3. Arbitration differs from adjudication chiefly to the extent that the parties, rather than the state, select the judge. The arbitrator may encourage negotiation but retains the ultimate authority to impose a resolution on the parties.
4. Loggers may associate environmentalism with preservationism — that is, with the complete removal of people from forests. Yet many environmentalists support sustainable commercial harvesting. Unlinking of ideas can lead to the parties' realization that their interests are not necessarily in conflict at all.
5. We borrow from Mohawk jurist Patricia Monture-Angus (1995, pp. 255–256 and her discussion of the Mohawk conception of "fitting nicely together," which has parallels in the jurisprudence of other North American indigenous peoples.
6. It should be noted that critics of negotiated justice regard it as a form of social control because it is based on untested theory (e.g., Scimecca, 1993).
7. The nul hypothesis is that negotiated justice is as effective as (but no more effective than) positive law. Failing to confirm that desirable outcomes persist beyond a year may result in erroneously rejecting the nul hypothesis. Seeking only short-term effects of a long-term process may result in erroneously accepting the nul hypothesis.

REFERENCES

Alfred, G.R. (1995). *Heeding the voices of our ancestors: Kahnawake Mohawk politics and the rise of Native nationalism*. Toronto: Oxford University Press.

Auger, D.J., Doob, A.N., Auger, R.P., & Dribben, P. (1992). Crime and control in three Nishnawbe-Aski Nation communities: An exploratory investigation. *Canadian Journal of Criminology* 34(3–4), 317–338.

Avison, D. (1994). Clearing space: Diversion projects, sentencing circles and restorative justice. In R. Gosse, J.Y. Henderson, and R. Carter (Eds.). *Continuing Poundmaker and Riel's quest* (pp. 235–240). Saskatoon: Purich.

Bachman, R. (1991). The social causes of American Indian homicide as revealed by the life experiences of thirty offenders. *American Indian Quarterly* 15(4), 469–492.

Baker, B.M. (1992). Penance as a model for punishment. *Social Theory and Practice* 18(3), 311–331.

Barsh, R.L. (1987). Plains Indian agrarianism and class conflict. *Great Plains Quarterly* 7(2), 83–90.

Barsh, R.L. (1993a). Measuring human rights: Problems of methodology and purpose. *Human Rights Quarterly* 15(1), 87–121.

Barsh, R.L. (1993b). The challenge of Indigenous self-determination. *University of Michigan Journal of Law Reform* 26(2), 277–312.

Barsh, R.L. (1995a). Indigenous peoples and the idea of individual human rights. *Native Studies Review* 10(2), 35–55.

Barsh, R.L. (1995b). Native justice in Lethbridge. *Journal of Human Justice Critical Criminology* 6(2), 131–139.

Barsh, R.L., and Henderson, J.Y. (1976). Tribal courts, the Model Code, and the police idea in American Indian policy. *Law and Contemporary Problems* 40(1), 25–60.

Bartos, O.J. (1989). Agreement in mediation: A sociological approach. *Peace and Change* 14(4), 425–443.

Becker, M.B. (1976). Changing patterns of violence and justice in fourteenth- and fifteenth-century Florence. *Comparative Studies in Society and History* 18(3), 281–296.

Benjamin, R.D. (1995). The mediator as trickster: The folkloric figure as professional role model. *Mediation Quarterly* 13(2), 131–149.

Bingham, G. (1986). *Resolving environmental disputes: A decade of experience.* Washington, DC: The Conservation Foundation.

Blagg, H. (1997). A just measure of shame? Aboriginal youth and police conferencing in Australia. *British Journal of Criminology* 37(4), 481–501.

Bohannan, P. (1957). *Justice and judgment among the Tiv.* London: Oxford University Press.

Boldt, M. (1993). *Surviving as Indians: The challenge of self-government.* Toronto: University of Toronto Press.

Braithwaite, J. (1989). *Crime, shame, and reintegration.* Cambridge: Cambridge University Press.

Braithwaite, J., & Mugford, S. (1994). Conditions of successful reintegration ceremonies: Dealing with juvenile offenders. *British Journal of Criminology* 34(2), 139–171.

Briggs, J.L. (1978). Inuit management of aggression. In Ashley Montagu, (Ed.). *Learning non-aggression: The experience of non-literate societies* (pp. 54–93). New York: Oxford University Press.

Buckle, L.G., & Thomas-Buckle, S.R. (1986). Placing environmental mediation in context: Lessons from "failed" mediations. *Environmental Impact Assessment Review* 6(1), 55–70.

Burgess, H. & Burgess. G. (1996). Constructive confrontation: A transformative approach to intractable conflicts. *Mediation Quarterly 13*(4), 305–322.

Bush, R.A.B., & Folger, J.P. (1994). *The promise of mediation: Responding to conflict through empowerment and recognition.* San Francisco: Jossey-Bass.

Canadian Bar Association. 1996. *Contemporary Aboriginal justice models: Completing the circle.* Ottawa: Canadian Bar Association.

Cao, L., Adams, A., & Jensen, V.J. (1997). A test of the Black subculture of violence thesis: A research note. *Criminology 35*(2), 367–379.

Carter, S. (1996). First Nations women of Prairie Canada in the early reserve years, the 1870s to the 1920s: A preliminary inquiry. In C. Miller & P. Chuchryk (Eds.). *Women of the First Nations: Power, wisdom, and strength* (pp. 51–75). Winnipeg: University of Manitoba Press.

Cawsey, R.A. (1991). *Justice on trial: Report of the Task Force on the Criminal Justice System and its Impact on the Indian and Metis People of Alberta.* Edmonton: Government of Alberta.

Clairmont, D. (1996). Alternative justice issues for Aboriginal justice. *Journal of Legal Pluralism and Unofficial Law 36*, 125–157.

Clark, M. (1993). Symptoms of cultural pathologies: A hypothesis. In D.J.D. Sandole & H. van der Merwe (Eds.). *Conflict resolution theory and practice: Integration and application* (pp. 43–54). Manchester: Manchester University Press.

Condor, S., and Brown, R. (1988). Psychological processes in intergroup conflict. In W. Stroebe, A.W. Kruglanski, D. Bar-Tal, & M. Hewstone (Eds.). *The social psychology of intergroup conflict: Theory, research and applications* (pp. 3–26). New York: Springer-Verlag.

Considine, J. (1992). *Restorative justice: Healing the effects of crime.* Lyttelton, New Zealand: Ploughshares.

Cragg, W. (1992). *The practice of punishment: Towards a theory of restorative justice.* London: Routledge.

De Haan, W. (1990). *The politics of redress: Crime, punishment, and penal abolition.* London: Unwin Hyman.

Depew, R.C. (1996). Popular justice and Aboriginal communities: Some preliminary considerations. *Journal of Legal Pluralism and Unofficial Law 36*, 21–67.

Deutsch, M. (1973). *The resolution of conflict: Constructive and destructive processes.* New Haven, CT: Yale University Press.

Deutsch, M. (1994). Constructive conflict resolution: Principles, training, and research. *Journal of Social Issues 50*(1), 13–32.

Deutsch, M., & Shichman, S. (1986). Conflict: A social psychological perspective. In M.G. Hermann (Ed.). *Political psychology* (pp. 219–250). San Francisco: Jossey-Bass.

Devens, C. (1992). *Countering colonization: Native American women and Great Lakes missions, 1630–1900.* Berkeley: University of California Press.

Dezalay, Y., & Garth, B. (1996). Fussing about the forum: Categories and definition as stakes in a professional competition. *Law and Social Inquiry 21*(2), 285–312.

Dickson-Gilmore, E.J. (1992). Finding the ways of the ancestors: Cultural change and the invention of tradition in the development of separate legal systems. *Canadian Journal of Criminology 34*(3–4), 479–502.

Dignan, J. (1992). Repairing the damage: Can reparation be made to work in the service of diversion? *British Journal of Criminology* 32(4), 453–472.

Doi, T. (1973). *The Anatomy of dependence*. Tokyo: Kodansha International.

Dow, J. (1986). Universal aspects of symbolic healing: A theoretical synthesis. *American Anthropologist* 88(1), 56–69.

Druckman, D. (1993). An analytical research agenda for conflict and conflict resolution. In D.J.D. Sandole & H. van der Merwe (Eds.). *Conflict resolution theory and practice: Integration and application* (pp. 25–42). Manchester: Manchester University Press.

Druckman, D., Broome, B.J., & Korper. S.H. (1988). Value differences and conflict resolution: Facilitation or delinking? *Journal of Conflict Resolution* 32(3), 489–510.

Dukes, F. (1993). Public conflict resolution: A transformative approach. *Negotiation Journal* 9(1), 45–58.

Dumont, J. (1993). Justice and Aboriginal people. In *Aboriginal peoples and the justice system* (pp. 42–85). Ottawa: Royal Commission on Aboriginal Peoples.

Duran, E., & Duran, B. (1995). *Native American post-colonial psychology*. Albany: State University of New York Press.

Evans, T.D., Cullen, F.T., Burton, V.S. Jr., Dunaway, R.G., & Benson, M.L. (1997). The social consequences of self-control: Testing the general theory of crime. *Criminology* 35(3), 465–504.

Fallers, L.A. (1969). *Law without precedent: Legal ideas in action in the courts of colonial Busoga*. Chicago: University of Chicago Press.

Fanon, F. (1967). *Black skin, white masks*. New York: Grove Press.

Feger, H. (1991). Cooperation between groups. In R.A. Hinde and J. Groebel (Eds.). *Cooperative and prosocial behavior*. New York: Cambridge University Press.

Fisher, R.J. (1994). Generic principles for resolving intergroup conflict. *Journal of Social Issues* 50(1), 47–66.

Fisher, R., and Ury, W. (1991). *Getting to yes: Negotiating agreement without giving in* (2nd ed.). New York: Penguin.

Florsheim, P. (1990). Cross-cultural views of the Self in the treatment of mental illness: Disentangling the curative aspects of myth from the mythic aspects of cure. *Psychiatry* 53(3), 304–315.

Ford, R. (1994). Conflict and bargaining. In M. Foschi and E.J. Lawler (Eds.). *Group processes: Sociological analyses* (pp. 231–256). Chicago: Nelson-Hall.

Fowler, L. (1982). *Arapahoe politics, 1851–1978: Symbols in crises of authority*. Lincoln: University of Nebraska Press.

Fowler, L. (1987). *Shared symbols, contested meanings: Gros Ventre culture and history, 1778–1984*. Ithaca, NY: Cornell University Press.

Fry, D.P. (1992). "Respect for the rights of others is peace": Learning aggression versus nonaggression among the Zapotec. *American Anthropologist* 94(3), 621–639.

Galanter, M. (1968). The displacement of traditional law in modern India. *Journal of Social Issues* 24(4), 65–91.

George, K.M. (1995). Violence, solace, and ritual: A case study from island southeast Asia. *Culture, Medicine and Psychiatry* 19(2), 225–260.

Gluckman, M. (1955). *The judicial process among the Barotse.* Manchester: University of Manchester Press.

Goldstein, A.P. (1992). Aggression reduction strategies. *Peace Review* 4(3), 14–18.

Gonzalez, E.B. (1981). *Changing economic roles for Micmac men and women: An ethnohistorical analysis.* Canadian Ethnology Service Paper No. 72. Ottawa: National Museum of Man.

Greenhalgh, L., and Chapman. D.I. (1995). Joint decision making: The inseparability of relationships and negotiation. In R.M. Kramer & D.M. Messick (Eds.). *Negotiation as a social process* (pp. 166–285). Thousand Oaks, CA: Sage Publications.

Grobsmith, E.S. (1994). *Indians in prison: Incarcerated Native Americans in Nebraska.* Lincoln: University of Nebraska Press.

Hamilton, A.C., & Sinclair, C.M. (1991). *The justice system and Aboriginal people: Report of the Aboriginal Justice Inquiry in Manitoba.* Winnipeg: Queen's Printer.

Hewstone, M. (1988). Attributional bases of intergroup conflict. In W. Stroebe, A.W. Kruglanski, D. Bar-Tal, & M. Hewstone (Eds.). *The social psychology of intergroup conflict: Theory, research and applications* (pp. 47–71). New York: Springer-Verlag.

Hickman, T. A., Poitras, L.A., & Evans. G.T. (1989). *Royal Commission on the Donald Marshall, Jr., prosecution: Commissioners' report.* Halifax: Province of Nova Scotia.

Hughes, S.P., & Schneider, A.L. (1989). Victim–offender mediation: A survey of program characteristics and perceptions of effectiveness. *Crime and Delinquency* 35(2), 217–233.

Hurley, M. (1996). Reconciliation and forgiveness. *The Jurist* 56, 465–486.

Hutchinson, A.C., & Monahan, P. (Eds.). (1987). *The rule of law: Ideal or ideology?* Toronto: Carswell.

Jackson, P.I. (1989). *Minority group threat, crime, and policing: Social context and social control.* New York: Praeger.

Jenkins, J.H., & Karno. M. (1992). The meaning of expressed emotion: Theoretical issues raised by cross-cultural research. *American Journal of Psychiatry* 149(1), 9–21.

Jilek, W.G. (1993). Traditional healing against alcoholism and drug dependence. *Curare* 16(3–4), 145–160.

Kelman, H.C. (1973). Violence without moral restraint: Reflections on the dehumanization of victims and victimizers. *Journal of Social Issues* 29(4), 25–61.

Kingery, P.M., Biafora, F.R., & Zimmerman, R.S. (1996). Risk factors for violent behaviors among ethnically diverse adolescents: Beyond race/ethnicity. *School Psychology International* 17(2), 171–186.

Kirmayer, L.J. (1993). Healing and the invention of metaphor: The effectiveness of symbols revisited. *Culture Medicine and Psychiatry* 17(2), 161–195.

Klar, Y., Bar-Tal, D., & Kruglanski, A.W. (1988). Conflict as a cognitive schema: Toward a social cognitive analysis of conflict and conflict termination. In W. Stroebe, A.W. Kruglanski, D. Bar-Tal, & M. Hewstone (Eds.). *The social psychology of intergroup conflict: Theory, research and applications.* New York: Springer-Verlag.

Kleiboer, M. (1996). Understanding success and failure of international mediation. *Journal of Conflict Resolution 40*(2), 360–389.

Kosmicki, F.X., & Glickauf-Hughes, C. (1997). Catharsis in psychotherapy.
Psychotherapy 34(2), 154–159.

Kressel, K., Pruitt, D.G., & Associates (Eds.). (1989). *Mediation research: The
process and effectiveness of third-party intervention.* San Francisco: Jossey-Bass.

Kumagai, F., & Strauss, M.A. (1983). Conflict resolution tactics in Japan, India,
and the U.S.A. *Journal of Comparative Family Studies 14*(3), 377–392.

LaFree, G., & Rack. C. (1996). The effects of participants' ethnicity and gender on
monetary outcomes in mediated and adjudicated civil cases. *Law and Society
Review 30*(4), 767–797.

LaPrairie, C. (1995). Community justice or just communities? Aboriginal communities in search of justice. *Canadian Journal of Criminology 37*(4), 521–545.

LaPrairie, C., & Diamond, E. (1992). Who owns the problem? Crime and disorder in James Bay Cree communities. *Canadian Journal of Criminology 34*(3–4),
417–434.

LaRocque, E. (1997). Re-examining culturally appropriate models in criminal jus-
tice applications. In M. Asch (Ed.). *Aboriginal and treaty rights in Canada:
Essays on law, equity, and respect for difference* (pp. 75–96). Vancouver: UBC
Press.

Lawler, E.J., & Ford. R. (1995). Bargaining and influence in conflict situations. In
K. Cook, G.A. Fine, & J.S. House (Eds.). *Sociological perspectives on social psychology.* New York: Allyn & Bacon.

Levine, M. (1988). How self-help works. *Social Policy 19*(1), 39–43.

Llewellyn, K.N., & Hoebel, E.A. (1941). *The Cheyenne way: Conflict and case law in
primitive jurisprudence.* Norman: University of Oklahoma Press.

Lovaglia, M.J., & Houser, J.A. (1996). Emotional reactions and status in groups.
American Sociological Review 61(4), 867–883.

McElrea, F.W.M. (1994). Restorative justice — the New Zealand Youth Court: A
model for development in other courts? *Journal of Judicial Administration 4*,
33–54.

Mandamin, L. (1993). Aboriginal justice systems: Relationships. In *Aboriginal
peoples and the justice system* (pp. 275–308). Ottawa: Royal Commission on
Aboriginal Peoples.

Marshall, W.L., & Maric. A. (1996). Cognitive and emotional deficits in child
molesters. *Journal of Child Sexual Abuse 5*(2), 101–110.

Maxwell, D. (1992). Gender differences in mediation style and their impact on
mediation effectiveness. *Mediation Quarterly 9*(4), 353–364.

Memmi, A. (1973). *Portrait du colonisé.* Paris: Payot.

Merry, S.E., & Milner, N., (1993). *The possibility of popular justice: A case study of
community mediation in the United States.* Ann Arbor: University of Michigan
Press.

Michener, H.A., & Wasserman, M.P. (1995). Group decision making. In K. Cook,
G.A. Fine, & J.S. House (Eds.). *Sociological perspectives on social psychology*
(pp. 336–361). New York: Allyn and Bacon.

Milburn, T.W. (1996). What can we learn from comparing mediation across
levels? *Peace and Conflict Studies 3*(1), 39–52.

Milner, N. (1996). Mediation and social theory: a critique of Bush and Folger. *Law and Social Inquiry* 21(3), 737–759.

Modavi, N. (1996). Mediation of environmental conflicts in Hawaii: Win-win or co-optation? *Sociological Perspectives* 39(2), 301–316.

Monture-Angus, P. (1995). *Thunder in my soul: A Mohawk woman speaks*. Halifax: Fernwood.

Montville, J.V. (1993). The healing function in political conflict resolution. In D.J.D. Sandole & H. van der Merwe (Eds.). *Conflict resolution theory and practice: Integration and application* (pp. 112–127). Manchester: Manchester University Press.

Moore, S.F. (1992). Treating law as knowledge: Telling colonial officers what to say to Africans about running "their own" Native Courts. *Law and Society Review* 26(1), 11–46.

Nader, L. (1969). Styles of court procedure: To make the balance. In L. Nader (Ed.). *Law in culture and society* (pp. 69–91). Chicago: Aldine.

Nandy, A. (1983). *The intimate enemy: Loss and recovery of self under colonialism*. Delhi: Oxford University Press.

Nechi Institute & KAS Corporation Ltd. (1995). Healing, spirit and recovery: Factors associated with successful integration. Aboriginal Peoples Collection No. 11. Ottawa: Corrections Branch, Solicitor General of Canada.

Nergård, T.B. (1993). Solving conflicts outside the court system: Experiences with the Conflict Resolution Boards in Norway. *British Journal of Criminology* 33(1), 81–94.

Neustrom, M.W., & Norton, W.M. (1995). Economic dislocation and property crime. *Journal of Criminal Justice* 23(1), 29–39.

Nielsen, M.O. (1991). Criminal justice and Native self-government in Canada: Is the incorporation of traditional justice practices feasible? *Law & Anthropology* 6, 7–24.

Osland, J.A., Fitch, M., & Willis, E.E. (1996). Likelihood to rape in college males. *Sex Roles* 35(3–4), 171–183.

Pavlich, G. (1996). The power of community mediation: Government and formation of self-identity. *Law and Society Review* 30(4), 707–733.

Pepinsky, H.E., & Quinney, R. (Eds.). (1991). *Criminology as peacemaking*. Bloomington: Indiana University Press.

Pospisil, L. (1958). *Kapauku Papuans and their law*. Yale University Publications in Anthropology, No. 54. New Haven, CT: Yale University Press.

Pruitt, D.G., & Carnevale, P.J.D. (1982). The development of integrative agreements. In V. Derlega & J. Grzelak (Eds.). *Cooperation and helping behavior: Theories and research* (pp. 151–181). New York: Academic Press.

Pruitt, D.G., & Carnevale, P.J. (1993). *Negotiation in social conflict*. Pacific Grove, CA: Brooks/Cole.

Rabbie, J.M. (1991). Determinants of instrumental intra-group cooperation. In R.A. Hinde & J. Groebel (Eds.). *Cooperation and prosocial behavior* (pp. 238–262). New York: Cambridge University Press.

Raisner, J.K. (1997). Family mediation and never-married parents. *Family and Conciliation Courts Review* 35(1), 90–101.

Regan, P.M. (1996). Conditions of successful third-party intervention in intrastate conflicts. *Journal of Conflict Resolution* 40(2), 336–359.

Rideau, W., & Wikberg, R. (1992). *Life sentences: Rage and survival behind bars.* New York: Times Books.

Roberts, W., & Strayer, J. (1996). Empathy, emotional expressiveness, and pro-social behavior. *Child Development 67*(2), 449–470.

Ross, H.L., McCleary, R., & LaFree, G. (1990). Can mandatory jail laws deter drunk driving? The Arizona case. *Journal of Criminal Law and Criminology 81*(1), 156–166.

Ross, R. (1996). *Returning to the teachings: Exploring Aboriginal justice.* Toronto: Penguin.

Rowe, D.C., & Farrington, D.P. (1997). The familial transmission of criminal convictions. *Criminology 35*(1), 177–201.

Rubin, J.Z. (1991). Changing assumptions about conflict and negotiation. In R.A. Hinde & J. Groebel (Eds.). *Cooperation and prosocial behaviour* (pp. 268–280). New York: Cambridge University Press.

Rudd, J.E. (1996). Communication effects on divorce mediation: How partici-pants' argumentativeness, verbal aggression, and compliance-gaining strategy choice mediate outcome satisfaction. *Mediation Quarterly 14*(1), 65–78.

Russell, G.W., & Arms, R.L. (1995). Canadians' beliefs in catharsis. *Social Behavior and Personality 23*(3), 223–228.

Ryan, J. (1995). *Doing things the right way: Dene traditional justice in Lac La Martre, N.W.T.* Calgary: University of Calgary Press.

Ryan, S. (1996). Peacebuilding strategies and intercommunal conflict: Approaches to the transformation of divided societies. *Nationalism and Ethnic Politics 2*(2), 216–231.

Saunders, D.G. (1977). Marital violence: Dimensions of the problem and modes of intervention. *Journal of Marriage and Family Counselling 3*(1), 43–52.

Schapera, I. (1938). *A handbook of Tswana law and custom.* London: Oxford University Press.

Schewe, P.A., & O'Donohue, W. (1996). Rape prevention with high-risk males: Short-term outcome of two interventions. *Archives of Sexual Behavior 25*(5), 455–471.

Scimecca, J.A. (1993). Theory and alternative dispute resolution: A contradiction in terms? In D.J.D. Sandole & H. van der Merwe (Eds.). *Conflict resolution theory and practice: Integration and application* (pp. 211–221). Manchester: Manchester University Press.

Scully, D. (1988). Convicted rapists' perceptions of self and victim: Role taking and emotions. *Gender and Society 2*(2), 200–213.

Shelly, R.K. (1993). How sentiments organize interaction. *Advances in Group Processes 10*, 113–132.

Sherman, L.W., Schmidt, J.D., Rogan, D.P., Smith, D.A., Gartin, P.R., Cohn, E.G., Collins, D.J., & Bacich, A.R. (1992). The variable effects of arrest on criminal careers: The Milwaukee domestic violence experiment. *Journal of Criminal Law and Criminology 83*(1), 137–169.

Shoemaker, N., (Ed.). (1995). *Negotiators of change: Historical perspectives on Native American women.* New York: Routledge.

Snider, L. (1997). Towards safer societies: Punishment, masculinities, and violence against women. *British Journal of Criminology 38*(1), 1–39.

Sow, A.I. (1980). *Anthropological Structures of madness in Black Africa*. New York: International Universities Press.

Stattin, H. Romelsjö, A., & Stenbacka, M. (1997). Personal resources as modifiers of the risk for future criminality: An analysis of protective factors in relation to 18-year-old boys. *British Journal of Criminology 37*(2), 198–223.

Stead, D.G. (1995). The effectiveness of criminal mediation: An alternative to court proceedings in a Canadian city. *Great Plains Sociologist 8*(1), 48–61.

Steiner, H. (Ed.). (1997). *Truth commissions: A comparative assessment*. Cambridge, MA: Harvard Law School Human Rights Program.

Tomaszewski, E.A. (1997). "AlterNative" approaches to criminal justice: John Braithwaite's theory of reintegrative shaming revisited. *Critical Criminology 8*(2), 105–118.

Unger, R.M. (1975). *Knowledge and politics*. New York: Free Press.

United Nations. 1996. *Resolution adopted by the General Assembly: Strengthening of the rule of law*. UN Document A/RES/50/179.

Waldram, J.B. (1997). *The way of the pipe: Aboriginal spirituality and symbolic healing in Canadian prisons*. Peterborough, ON: Broadview Press.

Wall, J.A., Jr., & Callister, R.R. (1995). Ho'oponopono: Some lessons from Hawaiian mediation. *Negotiation Journal 11*(1), 45–54.

Wall, J.A., Jr., & Sohn, D.-W. (1993). Community mediation in South Korea. *Journal of Conflict Resolution 37*(3), 536–543.

Wall, J.A., Jr., Sohn, D.-W., Cleeton, N., & Jin, D.-J. (1995). Community and family mediation in the People's Republic of China. *International Journal of Conflict Management 6*(1), 30–47.

Walters, G.C., & Grusec, J.E. (1977). *Punishment*. San Francisco: W.H. Freeman.

Watson-Gegeo, K., & White, G.M., (Eds.). (1990). *Disentangling: Conflict discourse in Pacific societies*. Stanford: Stanford University Press.

Werner, E.E., & Smith, R.S. (1992). *Overcoming the odds: High risk children from birth to adulthood*. Ithaca, NY: Cornell University Press.

Widom, C.S. (1989). Does violence beget violence? A critical examination of the literature. *Psychological Bulletin 106*(1), 3–28.

Wilson, M., & Canter, D. (1993). Shared concepts in group decisionmaking: A model for decisions based on quantitative data. *Journal of Social Psychology 32*(2), 159–172.

Wissler, R.L. (1995). Mediation and adjudication in the small claims court: The effects of process and case characteristics. *Law and Society Review 29*(2), 323–258.

Wooldredge, J., Hartman, J., Latessa, E., & Holmes, S. (1995). Effectiveness of culturally specific community treatment for African American juvenile felons. *Crime and Delinquency 40*(4), 589–598.

Yates, C. (1990). The Conciliation Project Report: A study of non-judicial dispute resolution in family cases. *Journal of Social Welfare Law 1990*, 33–44.

Zhang, S.X. (1995). Measuring shaming in an ethnic context. *British Journal of Criminology 35*(2), 248–262.

Zubek, J.M., Pruitt, D.G., Pierce, R.S., McGillicuddy, N.B., & Syna, H. (1992). Disputant and mediator behaviors affecting short-term success in mediation. *Journal of Conflict Resolution 36*(3), 546–572.

EIGHT

Constructing Lesbian and Gay Rights

DOUGLAS SANDERS

In spite of changing social attitudes, lesbians and gay men continue to be stigmatized minorities. Most homosexuals stay "in the closet" at work and with extended family members. Staying in the closet is a stressful choice that makes lasting relationships more difficult to sustain. Lesbian and gay leaders talk of increasing levels of violence. Being visible and on certain streets at certain hours can be risky. The hope of gradual progress towards acceptance or accommodation has been challenged by the rise of active anti-homosexual lobbies in the United States and Canada.[1]

Controversies on lesbian and gay issues have divided major Canadian religious denominations and political parties.[2] The Progressive Conservative government of Prime Minister Brian Mulroney (1984–1993) had an anti-homosexual backbench "family caucus" which fought reform and once publicly broke with the government. Since the election of 1993, the family caucus has been replaced by the anti-homosexual Reform Party and a couple of vocal dissenters within the Liberal caucus.[3]

The public debates over lesbian and gay rights indicate how fundamentally everything has changed. Thirty years ago there were almost no references to the existence of lesbians and gay men. The silence was the most oppressive aspect of Canadian society. Now the rights of lesbians and gay men are part of a public human rights discourse. Since 1986, every Federal Minister of Justice has pledged to add "sexual orientation" to the *Canadian Human Rights Act*. There are now lesbian and gay spokespeople in all parts of Canada, though often few in number. Certain politicians court the lesbian and gay vote.[4] Federal Justice Minister Kim Campbell, Vancouver Mayor Gordon Campbell, and two provincial Social Credit MLAs were on the podium for ceremonies at the international "Gay Games" held in Vancouver in 1990. The Canadian government endorsed equality rights for lesbians and gay men in both the public and private sessions of the United Nations World Conference on Human Rights held in Vienna in June 1993.[5] The major university presses in North America are now publishing scholarly works on lesbian, gay, and bisexual issues.[6] "Spousal" employment benefits are now frequently extended to same-sex partners in both the public and private sectors. And Canadian courts have ruled, in a series of cases, that lesbians and gay men are protected from discrimination by the equality provision in the *Canadian Charter of Rights and Freedoms*.

Not surprisingly, there are disputes over exactly how claims for lesbian and gay rights should be framed. There are controversies whether lesbians and gay men should argue sameness or difference. In practice both arguments are used. And both

Source: Douglas Sanders, "Constructing Lesbian and Gay Rights," *Revue canadienne droit et société/Canadian Journal of Law and Society* 9, no. 2 (1994): 99–143.

are used in rebuttal. There are controversies whether lesbians and gay men simply want access to the institutions of the larger society or whether the recognition of sexual diversity will involve some transformation of society as a whole, something beyond arguments for equality.

This chapter attempts two projects. As a gay legal academic, I am trying to describe the different ways in which lesbian and gay rights claims are presented. Secondly, as part of the discussion of equality arguments, I recount how equality rights have come to be recognized in the last decades in Canadian law and the current controversy over equal access to spousal benefits.

PRIVACY

An old argument asserted a right to be homosexual without arguing for a right to be involved in sexual activity. This approach tried to put a positive cast on the fact that criminal laws had focused on homosexual acts, not the status of being homosexual.[7] This approach was largely displaced by the idea that society should tolerate "private" homosexual activity. As long as the partner was an adult and consented, sexual activity could be permitted when it happened in the privacy of a bedroom. The pioneering formulation is found in the 1957 Wolfenden report in the United Kingdom, which argued that there was a sphere of private morality that should not be regulated by the criminal law.[8]

In Canada, the decriminalization of homosexual acts in 1969 was linked to privacy. Prime Minister Trudeau made his famous comment that the "State has no place in the bedrooms of the nation."[9] Since that time, privacy arguments have played a very limited role in Canadian discourse. After the Toronto police raids on gay steam baths in 1976, activists formed the Right to Privacy Committee to support those charged under the *Criminal Code*.[10] In 1988, Svend Robinson, a New Democratic Party member of the Canadian Parliament, publicly confirmed that he was gay. Other federal politicians called this a "private" matter. They seemed to resent being forced to comment on a subject they normally relegated to silence.[11]

Privacy was a winning argument before the European Court of Human Rights in the *Dudgeon*, *Norris*, and *Modinos* cases, which struck down anti-homosexual criminal laws in Ireland, Northern Ireland, and Cyprus.[12] In a similar case, *Toonen* v. *Australia*, the United Nations Human Rights Committee ruled against a criminal law in the State of Tasmania.[13] The United States Supreme Court rejected a privacy argument in *Bowers* v. *Hardwick*, upholding an anti-homosexual criminal law largely because the court had come under strong public criticism for its privacy-based ruling on abortion.[14] In 1992 and 1993, courts in Kentucky and Texas ruled that anti-homosexual criminal laws were in violation of provisions on liberty, equality, and privacy in state constitutions.[15] Privacy remains a major argument in the United States and other jurisdictions where criminal law issues are still important.[16] The major problems in Canada have been social attitudes, not criminal laws, making U.S.-style privacy arguments largely irrelevant.

A recent Canadian judicial decision argued that lesbian and gay equality rights were "premised on an unarticulated right to privacy," with the result that homosexuals could not assert spousal benefits claims. Such assertions would take the courts inside "the bedrooms of the nation."[17] Privacy was to be imposed on homosexuals — but not on heterosexuals, who could still assert their relationships to qualify for spousal benefits. The ruling was wrong to see privacy as the foundation of lesbian and gay rights in Canada. The basic theme is equality, not privacy.

In United States discourse, "privacy" is actually used to refer to values of autonomy and liberty. As a result, "privacy" absorbs what otherwise might be a separate libertarian argument. This merging of terminology can be seen in a statement of United States Supreme Court Justice Ruth Bader Ginsburg describing "personal autonomy" as one aspect of a right of privacy: "The government shall not make my decisions for me. I shall make as an individual uninhibited, uncontrolled by my government the decisions that affect my life's course."[18]

Privacy or libertarian arguments are very limited bases for supporting rights of lesbians and gays. They focus on ending state involvement, not recognizing or affirming important parts of people's lives. The privacy arguments are so transparent that the actual discussions in *Bowers* v. *Hardwick* and the other United States privacy cases are not about privacy. Rather, they discuss the significance of sexual relationships in people's lives.

Part of the appeal of privacy and libertarian arguments is the fact that they can be linked to statements that depreciate homosexuality. A clear anti-gay endorsement of privacy rights came from an activist in Oregon: "We all know that the militant gays have pushed their agenda beyond the right to privacy and it's time to draw the line."[19] He was the author of a proposed amendment to the state constitution, which would have prohibited anti-discrimination laws for lesbians and gay men and which called on the schools to teach youth that homosexuality was "abnormal, wrong, unnatural, and perverse." His comments demonstrated the implicit message in much privacy discourse — that homosexuals are to be tolerated on the condition that they stay in the closet. Privacy is linked to invisibility and silence. The constitutional initiative was defeated by voters in November 1992.[20]

PROTECTION AGAINST VIOLENCE

Lesbian and gay leaders often argue that homosexuals suffer discrimination, hostility, and increasing levels of violence.[21] This has led to campaigns for better police protection and inclusion in any laws dealing with "hate crimes." In 1994, the Canadian Minister of Justice announced his intention to enact legislation giving guidelines for the sentencing of individuals whose crimes were motivated by hatred based on race, religion, or sexual orientation.[22] Lesbian and gay lobbyists in the United States succeeded in having lesbians and gays included in the federal *Hate Crimes Statistics Act*.[23] The Metropolitan Toronto Police Department began reporting on hate-motivated crimes in 1993, including crimes aimed at lesbians and gay men.[24] Laws prohibiting the incitement of hatred against lesbians and gays have been enacted in Ireland and the Australian State of New South Wales.[25]

Is violence against lesbians and gays increasing? There have been some extraordinary acts of violence: serial killings of homosexuals in cities in Australia, Canada, Colombia, Mexico, and the United Kingdom.[26] These events have strong parallels to attacks on prostitutes, transvestites, refugees, and ethnic minorities. They remind even the most privileged homosexuals of their potential vulnerability.

What of the day-to-day life of most lesbians and gay men in Canada? Violence against homosexuals was under-reported by victims in the past and is probably still under-reported. That makes a statistically accurate assessment of change impossible. But some things are clear. There are increased numbers of complaints by victims. "Gay bashing" not only continues but has become a familiar, commonly understood form of violence in North American life. The message may be that greater visibility has made it easier to target lesbians and gay men.

If deterrence works in this area, those who attack lesbians and gays now face institutions which are less tolerant of such violence than in the past. There are now open lesbians and gay men on police forces and sometimes special recruitment policies.[27] In parts of the United States there are openly lesbian and gay judges. The Vancouver police force was embarrassed in September 1992 by a large protest demonstration alleging an inadequate police response to "gay bashing." An initial denial of the accusations was quickly followed by promises of reform and plans for special training for police officers.[28]

There is a debate in feminist, lesbian, and gay circles over political strategies based on assertions of victimization. The privileged dislike "the passive role of perpetual victim."[29] They have job security and safe space. Many others find Canadian society physically threatening. That must be remembered.

The threat of violence and other forms of discrimination has been recognized in the context of refugee law. Decisions in Canada, the United States, Australia, and several European states have found that individual lesbians and gay men qualify as refugees because they, as individuals, have a well-founded fear of persecution in their country of origin because of their sexual orientation.[30]

EQUALITY

THE CLAIM TO EQUALITY

Claims to privacy and protection from violence are aspects of a larger lesbian and gay claim to equality. The equality claim is based on the assertion that sexual orientation does not justify differential treatment. In the classic discourse on this subject, being homosexual is equivalent to being red-headed or left-handed.[31] Homosexuality has no inherent meaning or significance.

In the post-Wolfenden years, it became generally accepted that anti-homosexual laws could not be based on moral or religious concerns alone. This left open the question whether there were medical bases for differential treatment. Studies established that psychological testing could not differentiate homosexuals from heterosexuals.[32] That finding led the psychiatric associations in the United States and Canada to remove homosexuality from the category of psychiatric illnesses in 1973.[33] In 1991, the World Health Organization deleted homosexuality from the International Codex of Diseases.[34] The passing of moral and medical arguments has laid the basis for the acceptance of equality claims.

The Supreme Court of Canada has brought its concern with a "purposive" interpretation of the *Charter of Rights and Freedoms* to its rulings on equality rights. In this process, "formal equality" and the "similarly situated test" have been rejected in favour of seeing categories of people "in the context of the place of the group in the entire social, political, and legal fabric of our society."[35] It is not enough that members of the group are denied equality; the denial must be discriminatory. "A finding that there is discrimination will, I think, in most but perhaps not all cases, necessarily entail a search for disadvantage that exists apart from and independent of the particular legal distinction being challenged."[36]

And so it becomes relevant to ask if the category of people involved (women, non-citizens, homosexuals) is a vulnerable group. Perhaps the group is vulnerable as a "discrete and insular minority." One can look to "indicia of discrimination such as stereotyping, historical disadvantage, or vulnerability to political and social prejudice."[37]

The cases do not always reflect this analysis. In many situations, a formal equality construction seems to establish a clear case (for everyone knows that homosexuals are victims of discrimination).[38] The rejection of the spousal benefits claim in *Egan* on the basis that it had been presented as a formal equality claim is a warning of the willingness of some judges to use a purposive analysis against lesbian and gay claims. A number of judicial decisions have been careful to describe patterns of disadvantage or discrimination apart from the discrimination in issue in the case at hand and to describe equal recognition as having a positive impact on the lives of lesbians and gay men and their children.[39]

THE RELEVANCE OF CAUSATION

In discussing the issue of equality, is it relevant to ask whether homosexual orientation is a matter of choice, socially constructed, or biologically determined?

Recent public debate in the United States has focused on the question of choice versus biological determinism. Perhaps a decade ago, gay men began to describe their homosexuality as a "life style," in an apparent strategy of appealing for acceptance as just another group within a plural society. Some lesbians identified lesbianism with feminism, suggesting that lesbianism was a political or ideological choice. "Choice" and "life style" became central terms in arguments against lesbian and gay rights in the early 1990s in the United States.[40] In contrast, supporters of lesbian and gay rights drew analogies between sexual orientation and race and sex, classic "immutable characteristics," beyond personal control.[41]

This debate cannot be taken literally. The formulations used by opponents convey ideas of blame, difference, and wilful perversity.

Why is there such concern with causation? Any parallel debate on the causes of racial or gender characteristics would be suspect. As Kosofsky Sedgwick has said, there is no "unthreatening theoretical home for a concept of gay and lesbian origins."[42] If the question of causation is raised, it is almost always because homosexuality is viewed as a problem. If the cause is choice, that choice should not have been made. If the cause is biological, perhaps homosexuality can be prevented. Homosexuals are often highly suspicious about the dominant society's interest in the issue of causation. Such suspicion of motivation is typical of minorities in their interaction with majorities.

The debate also seeks to label homosexuals as different from heterosexuals. If you ask a heterosexual whether his or her sexual orientation is a "chosen life-style," you can expect an immediate denial in virtually all cases. To apply the idea of "chosen life-style" to homosexuals is to construct homosexuals as fundamentally different from heterosexuals. Homosexuals choose. Heterosexuals do not. Fundamental difference calls into question the entitlement of the other category to equal treatment. Homosexuals fail on a "sameness" test.

Are opponents of homosexual rights simply arguing that if individuals make choices about their lives they cannot expect the larger society to support or endorse those choices? Such an approach has problems. What of the choices of religious and political belief? They are respected. And why does society give legal recognition and protection to heterosexual relationships and heterosexual marriage? Heterosexuals choose to establish relationships and they are recognized and respected by the legal system and society. Some choices are recognized and some are not. The real message is that a homosexual choice is bad, and a heterosexual choice is good.

The debate on origins has been so pervasive that homosexuals have necessarily been drawn into it. Gay men, in general, seem comfortable with the idea that their sexual orientation is immutable. Many lesbians state that they have chosen to be lesbians. Feminist insights are particularly important for lesbians. The lesbian tendency to assert choice may reflect the general rejection of bio-determinist arguments which have been used against equality for women.[43] As well, certain feminists developed a political goal of "women-identified women." This gave lesbianism a positive political meaning for some women.[44]

Bisexuals are routinely ignored in this debate. Perhaps most bisexuals would see bisexuality as a "normal" not "chosen" state. The fact that bisexuals have a choice of gender partners says nothing about whether bisexuality itself is chosen, social constructed, or biologically determined.

I think that lesbians, gay men, and bisexuals would agree that changing sexual orientation would be either an impossible or a highly oppressive demand.

The question of choice versus biological determinism is highly misleading, for it suggests two polar explanations for two polar categories. It treats "choice" of sexual orientation as equivalent to deciding between holidays in Florida or Europe. To the extent that choices may be made, they seem analogous to choices of religious or political belief. A group of intervenors in the *Mossop* case made that analogy.[45] In *Watkins* v. *United States Army*, the Court was prepared to treat as effectively immutable characteristics which could only be changed with great difficulty or which would involve an inherently coercive change of an autonomous person's identity.[46]

The black historian Henry Louis Gates, Jr. argues that there is no "simple comparison" between lesbians and gay men on the one hand, and blacks or women on the other, for prejudices "come with distinctive and distinguishing historical peculiarities." He has described a paradox: "Most people think of racial identity as a matter of (racial) status, but they respond to it as behaviour. Most people think of sexual identity as a matter of (sexual) behavior, but they respond to it as status.... Disapproval of a sexual practice is transmuted into the demonization of a sexual species." Gates comments that "in many ways, contemporary homophobia is more virulent than contemporary racism."[47] He urges a focus on prejudice, not on precise analogies to other biases. His suggestion of focusing on acts of prejudice recognizes the existence of homosexuals and identifies the basic social issue as discrimination.

What have been the concerns of Canadian courts on this question? The most striking fact is that lesbian and gay rights cases in Canada do not reflect this debate. The arguments of the lawyers and the reasoning of the judges implicitly accept that sexual orientation is basic to the lives of individuals, usually without discussing the issue. One judge noted different "levels of immutability" characterizing the different grounds of discrimination expressly prohibited in section 15 of the *Charter* and concluded that "sexual orientation would fit within one of these levels of immutability."[48]

Another cited psychiatric evidence that the strongest explanation of homosexuality is biological and "not a deliberate choice."[49] Mr. Justice LaForest in the *Andrews* case referred to "immutability" in the context of section 15, but clearly not as an equivalent of "unchangeable," for he was dealing with citizenship. He equated "immutable" characteristics to those that could only be changed with "unacceptable costs."[50]

Rather than focus on the causes of homosexuality, it is much more logical to focus on the causes of homophobia. Why should a different sexual orientation trigger such a strong reaction in many people? Diversity is such a basic characteristic of human life that it is irrational to pick out sexual variation as particularly problematic. This approach links racism, sexism, and homophobia as essentially similar phenomena.

The substantial progress now achieved on equality rights for lesbians and gay men represents a clear rejection of the pathological assumptions that have been present in the public debates on homosexual rights. We can move to a review of that story.

THE EXPERIENCE WITH ANTI-DISCRIMINATION LAWS

The federal and provincial jurisdictions in Canada all have human rights laws aimed at ending discrimination in employment, accommodation, and many publicly available services. These laws list specific grounds on which discrimination is prohibited — grounds such as sex, race, marital status, or family status.

Over the years, courts and tribunals have interpreted these human rights laws restrictively when they have been invoked by homosexuals. "Sex" has been limited to gender.[51] "Family status" has been limited to heterosexual relationships.[52] This negative pattern of decision-making lay behind the campaigns of lesbian and gay activists to have "sexual orientation" added to the statutory lists of prohibited grounds of discrimination. For two decades, lesbians and gay men sought recognition with this demand.[53] Most Canadian jurisdictions have now made the change.

In 1973, the City of Toronto barred discrimination on the basis of sexual orientation in city employment.[54] In 1977, without public controversy, Québec enacted the first law at a provincial or state level in North America, prohibiting discrimination on the basis of sexual orientation.[55] There were bitter fights over similar reforms in Ontario (1986), Manitoba (1987), and Yukon (1987).[56] More recently, reform came without significant controversy in Nova Scotia (1991), New Brunswick (1992), British Columbia (1992), and Saskatchewan (1993).[57] Reform was promised at the federal level in 1986, but repeatedly delayed.

In the United States, eight states, the District of Columbia, and around 100 cities ban discrimination in employment on the basis of sexual orientation.[58] In Australia, discrimination against lesbians and gay men is prohibited in South Australia, New South Wales, Queensland, the Northern Territory, and the Australian Capital Territory.[59] New Zealand added "sexual orientation" to its human rights law in 1993. Discrimination on the basis of sexual orientation is banned in four cities in Brazil, including Saõ Paolo and Rio de Janeiro.

THE *CHARTER OF RIGHTS AND FREEDOMS*

When Canadians debated the content of the *Charter of Rights and Freedoms* between 1978 and 1982, equality rights for lesbians and gay men were not on the agenda.

With virtually no discussion, "sexual orientation" was not included in the list of prohibited grounds of discrimination in section 15. But, unlike the pattern in human rights statutes, the list was non-exclusive. The section was "open-ended." It was possible that lesbians and gay men would be protected as unenumerated but analogous groups.

Section 15 did not come into force for three years to allow governments to bring their laws into line with its requirements. The delay reflected a widespread belief among politicians and others that section 15 would bring major changes to the Canadian legal system. The high expectations for section 15 put considerable pressure on governments to systematically review their laws. Statutory "audits" were done in this period by governments and by women's organizations.

In January 1985, just months before section 15 came into force, the federal government issued a discussion paper on equality rights. A brief section on "sexual orientation" did nothing more than defend the ban on homosexuals in the military.[60]

The government document was considered by a special Parliamentary Committee on Equality Rights. The submission of the Canadian Bar Association argued that lesbians and gay men would be covered by the open-ended wording of section 15. The committee report cited the CBA position and unanimously concluded that lesbians and gay men were entitled to equality under the *Charter of Rights and Freedoms*.[61] The report was a major breakthrough. It called for an ending of discrimination in the military and the RCMP and endorsed adding "sexual orientation" to the *Canadian Human Rights Act*.[62]

The government had to respond to the committee report. On March 4th, 1986, John Crosbie, the Minister of Justice, rose in the House of Commons and tabled the government's response.[63] He announced that the Department of Justice had advised the government that "sexual orientation" was covered by section 15 of the *Charter of Rights and Freedoms*. Crosbie promised to bring federal laws into line with the *Charter*. His statement prompted a back-bench revolt by members of the "family caucus." But John Crosbie spoke for the government and had the backing of the Prime Minister.[64]

John Crosbie's statement was a pivotal event. His statement meant that there was an official, legal, "rights" analysis supported by the national government. Crosbie said he was acting on legal advice. He was no progressive reformer, no "red tory." He had introduced strong laws against prostitution and pornography. The views of the Department of Justice, the report of the special parliamentary committee, and increased public and media support were the developments which had pushed the government to a recognition of equality rights for lesbians and gay men. The opposition, coming largely from within the Progressive Conservative caucus, was an embarrassment to the Conservative leadership.

The courts confirmed the government's interpretation of the *Charter*. In 1989, in *Veysey* v. *Canada*, Dubé J. of the Federal Court, Trial Division, ruled that sexual orientation was covered by section 15 of the *Charter of Rights and Freedoms*, citing the 1985 Parliamentary Committee report and the legislative reforms in Québec, Manitoba, and Yukon.[65] In 1990, Coultas J., of the British Columbia Supreme Court, made the same ruling in *Brown* v. *British Columbia*.[66] On the appeal of *Veysey*, the point was conceded by the federal government.[67] In *Knodel* v. *British Columbia*, the provincial government conceded the point, and the judgment cited *Veysey* and *Brown* as authorities. Lawyers for the federal government conceded the point in the

Ontario Court of Appeal in *Haig* v. *Canada*. Krever J., for the court, noted the concession. Since it was a concession on a point of law, Krever specifically ruled that the concession was rightly made.[68] Again the lawyers for Canada conceded the point in the Federal Court of Appeal in *Egan* v. *Canada*, and again there were rulings that the concession was rightly made.[69]

In *Haig* v. *Canada*, the Ontario Court of Appeal concluded that the *Canadian Human Rights Act* violated section 15 of the *Charter of Rights and Freedoms* by excluding "sexual orientation" from the list of prohibited grounds of discrimination. To remedy this deficiency, the court ruled that the *Human Rights Act* had to be applied as if "sexual orientation" was included. Justice Minister Kim Campbell did not appeal the decision. Human rights commissions in almost all Canadian jurisdictions began accepting complaints of discrimination based on sexual orientation, whether or not their legislation expressly included the phrase. The *Haig* ruling has been followed in Alberta in *Vriend* v. *Alberta*.[70]

There has been another interesting development. As noted, early decisions refused to locate discrimination on the basis of sexual orientation within discrimination on the basis of sex. Two recent decisions have departed from that tradition. In 1993, in *Baehr* v. *Lewin*, the Supreme Court of Hawaii ruled that the denial of legal marriage to same-sex couples was discrimination on the basis of gender.[71] In 1994, in *Toonen* v. *Australia*, the United Nations Human Rights Committee held that the prohibition on discrimination on the basis of sex in the International Covenant on Civil and Political Rights, to which Canada is a party, included discrimination on the basis of sexual orientation.[72]

With the opinion of the Department of Justice and the various judicial rulings, Canada became one of the few countries in the world in which the national Constitution protects lesbians and gay men from discrimination by governments.[73] The rulings in *Haig* and *Vriend* required the equal protection of lesbians and gay men in human rights statutes which apply to the private sector. This means that the Constitution has the effect of prohibiting discrimination in those parts of the "private" sphere covered by such laws, unless governments are prepared to repeal their human rights statutes. These are striking developments, but they simply confirm the statement made by the Progressive Conservative Minister of Justice John Crosbie in the House of Commons on March 4th, 1986.

The Canadian Constitution protects lesbians and gay men from discrimination by the interpretation of an "open-ended" equality provision. The new interim constitution of South Africa is the first constitution in the world to expressly prohibit discrimination on the basis of sexual orientation.[74] The African National Congress had long supported such a provision.

PATTERNS OF DISCRIMINATION

Are there strong patterns of discrimination against lesbians and gay men in employment? Most lesbians and gay men still hide their sexual orientation from employers, and most would still not fight a discriminatory firing. A recent European book comments that "it is in the workplace that lesbians and gay men face the most widespread and economically devastating discrimination" but cites no studies.[75]

It is striking that we know very little about current patterns of employment discrimination. The Alberta Human Rights Commission did an impressionistic study on the question.[76] The Québec Human Rights Commission held public hearings on violence and discrimination against lesbians and gay men, reporting in June 1994.[77] Massachusetts held hearings on problems faced by lesbian and gay youth in 1993, leading to legislation prohibiting discrimination against lesbian and gay students in public schools.[78] We need more such investigations because we have virtually no data on actual patterns of discrimination. The "closet" creates unique problems for public responses to discrimination on the basis of sexual orientation.

Openly discriminatory laws and policies have been ending. The ban in the *Immigration Act* on the admission to Canada of lesbians and gay men was repealed in 1976. The Royal Canadian Mounted Police ended discrimination in hiring and promotion in 1988.

The military has been a special case. Most European states have no ban on lesbians or gay men serving in the military.[79] The United Kingdom still has a ban and people are discharged, though homosexuals can now obtain security clearances.[80] The bureaucracy in the Canadian Department of National Defence wrote the section on "sexual orientation" for the 1985 federal government White Paper on equality rights. The paper defended the military ban on homosexuals, arguing, among other things, "majoritarian values."[81] The military objections were rejected by the Parliamentary Committee on Equality Rights in October 1985.[82] In March 1986, John Crosbie promised change but failed to act.

In 1991, the federal government decided to end the ban on lesbians and gay men in the military. Canada informed the United States government of the impending change because of the NATO and NORAD defence links. Both *The Globe and Mail* and *The New York Times* ran stories that the announcement would be made the next day.[83] But there was no announcement. The back-bench "family caucus" had blocked the reform by threatening to break caucus solidarity on the issue. The government was left with a military policy that it believed was legally indefensible.

Michelle Douglas had taken the government to court challenging the military ban. The litigation became the occasion for the much delayed change in military policy.[84] In October 1992, the case was settled in five minutes. Federal lawyers conceded that "sexual orientation" was protected under section 15 of the *Charter of Rights and Freedoms* and conceded that the discrimination could not be justified under section 1 of the *Charter*. The judge signed a consent order. Within hours, the Department of National Defence announced the end of the anti-homosexual policy. Then Conservative member of Parliament Donald Blenkarn, a member of the "family caucus," had lost a fight but saw the victor as the courts, not the Minister of Justice. He said with resignation: "There comes a point when you can't keep fighting lawsuits."[85]

Australia ended its ban in 1992, a change also triggered by a complaint brought by a lesbian. During the 1992 United States election campaign, Bill Clinton pledged to end the military ban. Ending the ban became the main policy controversy of the first six months of the Clinton presidency. In July 1993, Clinton announced a compromise under which homosexuals would not be asked about their sexual orientation, could not reveal their sexual orientation, and could not engage in sexual activity. Under this "Don't ask, don't tell, don't pursue" policy, homosexuals were to be tolerated so long as they remained in the closet. Litigation has already challenged the constitutionality of this new policy, with its clear limitations on freedom of speech, association, and conduct.[86] Meanwhile, in December 1992, the Federal

Bureau of Investigation ended discrimination on the basis of sexual orientation in employment with the agency.[87]

THE LIMITATIONS ON EQUALITY

As with privacy and libertarian arguments, an anti-discrimination position can be coupled with anti-homosexual statements. When John Crosbie said that he would add sexual orientation to the *Canadian Human Rights Act*, he made it clear that he was not condoning homosexuality. "Far from it," he said.[88] When Manitoba added sexual orientation to its human rights law, it included a legislative statement that the province was not condoning or condemning any "beliefs, values, or lifestyles" listed in the legislation.[89] The United Kingdom passed legislation in 1988 prohibiting the promotion of homosexuality, including teaching that homosexuality was acceptable as a "pretended family relationship."[90] Finland, Austria, and Liechtenstein prohibit the promotion or encouragement of homosexuality.[91] Austria and Liechtenstein prohibit organizations which promote homosexuality, though, in fact, such organizations function openly and publish, at least in Austria.[92] Criminal law reforms in the Australian states of Victoria and Western Australia had preambles stating the laws were not condoning homosexual activity. United States President Clinton, in the debate on the military ban, said the government must not appear to be promoting or endorsing a "gay life style."[93]

The standard response of politicians who are accused of being pro-gay is to say that they are against discrimination. The person avoids suggesting that homosexuality is a good thing. Such disclaimers would never occur about race, gender, religion, or ethnicity. There is a clear double standard. Heterosexuality is embraced. Homosexuality is "not condoned."

A second, pervasive problem, generally not touched by the recognition of equality rights, is the blocking out of what should be the routine acknowledgement of the existence of lesbians, gays, and bisexuals in our societies. The formal legal order, state programs, and public media continuously reinforce the virtual exclusivity of heterosexual narratives. We all know the basic heterocentric plot line: "boy meets girl, boy loses girl, boy gets girl back again." The story plays hundreds of times every day on television, in movie theatres, in print. "The dawning realization that themes of homophobia and heterosexism may be read in almost any document of our culture means that we are only beginning to have an idea of how widespread those institutions and accounts are."[94]

A headmistress in London, England, refused free tickets for her students to a ballet performance of *Romeo and Juliet*, calling it a blatantly heterosexual work. She objected to her students being exposed to exclusively heterosexual presentations of the world. The local director of education called for her dismissal, but governors of the school voted to retain her.[95] When New York City schools adopted a "rainbow curriculum" designed to deal with racial, cultural, linguistic, and sexual diversity in the family experiences of students, there was a major public political fight and a retreat.[96]

The result is to turn acceptance of "equality" into a refurbished concept of "privacy." Homosexuals can have "equality" so long as their lives are "not condoned" and their presence in the society is not forced into the consciousness of others.

EQUALITY FOR SAME-SEX RELATIONSHIPS

THE ISSUE

It is simple logic that discrimination against same-sex couples is discrimination on the basis of sexual orientation. But this simple logic is contested.

The stated reasons for drawing a distinction between the recognition of individual equality and equality for same-sex couples is almost always the procreative potential of heterosexual relationships. Social policy goals concerned with the care of children are relied on to justify a special recognition of heterosexual relationships, resulting in the non-recognition of same-sex couples. But when the particular benefits, rights, or obligations in question in particular cases are considered, the argument does not make sense in terms of the stated policy objective of aiding children.

The essential reason for drawing the distinction is quite different. Equality for individual homosexuals can be endorsed by those who want to keep lesbians and gay men in the closet, who do not want to "condone" homosexuality, who do not want to have to acknowledge that lesbian and gay people are part of their societies. In contrast, equality for same-sex couples involves a public recognition of homosexuals, equal to the public recognition the state and society accord to heterosexuals by the recognition of heterosexual relationships. The image is no longer the protection of individual victims of job discrimination, a situation in which sexual orientation is irrelevant and should be ignored by employers. The image is of lesbians and gay men in publicly recognized relationships.

Public recognition of homosexuals undermines the phenomenon of the "closet." Public recognition has the effect of stabilizing and normalizing homosexual lives.[97] Public recognition is occurring most effectively, at the moment, in the debates over "spousal" benefits. Equality for same-sex couples is, therefore, not a peripheral or add-on issue, even when the benefits in question are minor.[98] Because of its challenge to the closet, the recognition of same-sex relationships emerges as the most important equality issue for lesbians and gay men at this point in time.

The recognition of relationships is also important in challenging the stereotype of gay males as unstable and promiscuous. The image of promiscuity is very pervasive in anti-homosexual argumentation. It has a perverse logic, for the various forms of discrimination against homosexuals make the achievement of stable relationships difficult.

The issue of spousal benefits is being won in practice in the workplace, with significant help from judicial and administrative decisions.

THE STATUTES

The Québec *Human Rights Charter* exempts organizations providing social benefits from coverage, allowing discrimination in benefits against same-sex couples.[99] When the province of Ontario added "sexual orientation" to its Human Rights Code in 1986, it left in place a definition of "spouse" which only covered heterosexual relationships.[100] The Manitoba amendment of 1987 added "sexual orientation" but permitted special regulations to govern permissible distinctions for employee benefit plans.[101] When Nova Scotia amended its *Human Rights Act* in 1991, it added "sexual orientation" and a new clause defining "marital status" to only include heterosexual relations.[102] The more recent amendments in New Brunswick, British Columbia, and Saskatchewan had no wording which would restrict partner benefits.

Conservative Justice Minister Kim Campbell introduced amendments to the *Canadian Human Rights Act* in 1992 which would have added "sexual orientation" while defining "marital status" in heterosexual terms. Campbell denied that the definition would undercut spousal benefits for same-sex couples.[103] Campbell's amendments were widely criticized by lesbian and gay spokespersons, and the bill was never debated in the House of Commons. Liberal Minister of Justice Allan Rock has promised to introduce legislation adding "sexual orientation" to the *Canadian Human Rights Act* with no restrictive definition of marital or family status.[104]

In 1994, Ontario introduced legislation to amend 56 provincial laws to equate same-sex couples with heterosexual couples.[105] This was the first North American attempt to move from *ad hoc* changes to systematic reform. The Québec Human Rights Commission urged similar legislation in Québec.[106] The Ontario bill was defeated by nine votes on second reading in June 1994.[107] There were mixed messages. It was a clear defeat, coming after more than two decades of incremental gains. The provisions on the adoption of children and the definition of "marital status" were the most controversial, but not the most substantive, elements of the package. The issues will continue to be pursued in the courts.

A review of the use of terms such as "spouse" and "family" in federal law has been under way. The federal Minister of Justice has suggested reforms that would recognize a broad category of dependent relationships beyond heterosexual and homosexual partners. It is too early to sense whether federal reforms will proceed along those lines.

JUDICIAL AND QUASI-JUDICIAL DECISIONS

The pioneering decision on family benefits for same-sex couples in the United States is *Braschi v. Stahl*, upholding survivor rights to a rent-controlled apartment.[108] The second leading United States decision is *In Re Guardianship of Sharon Kowalski*, where, after a long fight, a lesbian was given guardianship of her partner, who had suffered severe brain damage and other injuries in an automobile accident.[109]

Some of the Canadian cases on spousal benefits have been lost. In *Vogel* and *Mossop*, discrimination on the basis of "family status," invoking anti-discrimination statutes, was argued unsuccessfully.[110] In *Egan*, a *Charter* case, the Federal Court of Appeal denied a "spousal" pension under the *Old Age Security Act*, saying the denial was not on the basis of sexual orientation but on the basis that the same-sex partner was not a spouse.[111]

Many cases have now been won. In *Veysey*, the plaintiff successfully sought same-sex conjugal visiting rights in a federal prison.[112] In *Knodel*, the British Columbia Supreme Court extended medicare coverage to same-sex partners, declining to follow an earlier Ontario decision.[113] In *Morrissey*, a Canadian lesbian claimed the right to sponsor her partner as an immigrant under "family class" sponsorship provisions. Canadian immigration officials gave the foreign partner permanent residency as an individual applicant, reversing a previous decision, an action which avoided *Charter* litigation.[114] *Carrott*, a second *Charter* case on the immigration issue, was also resolved out of court after immigration formulated new guidelines for handling applications involving same-sex partners.[115] In *Leshner*, an Ontario human rights tribunal upheld "spousal" survivor benefits under a pension plan.[116] In the decision, the board held that the section in the Ontario *Human Rights Act* limiting "spouse" to heterosexual partners was in conflict with the guarantee of equality in the *Charter of Rights and Freedoms*. To remedy this conflict, the board struck out the limitation in the definition. A number of cases have recognized same-sex relationships in the context of applying a constructive trust analysis to the division of what for heterosexuals would be "marital" property.[117] In *Holmwood*, the Workers' Compensation Board of British Columbia recognized a lesbian partner for survivor benefits.[118] In *Lorenzen,* an adjudicator with the Canadian Public Service Staff Relations Board recognized same-sex relationships for family-care leave provisions in a collective agreement.[119] In *Clinton*, a human rights tribunal required a private medical insurer to extend spousal benefits to same-sex partners.[120] In *Jeffs*, an Unemployment Insurance Commission appeals board recognized a lesbian relationship as giving a proper cause for the claimant to leave her job and relocate.[121] In *Guèvremont*, a labour arbitrator ruled that Canada Post had to extend spousal benefits to gay and lesbian employees.[122]

Litigation continues. In an Ontario case, a lesbian is seeking spousal support payments from her former partner. The provincial Attorney-General has conceded that the exclusion of same-sex spouses from the relevant provisions in the *Family Law Act* is unconstitutional.[123]

CHANGES IN ACTUAL COVERAGE

There have been numerous employers who have extended benefits without being taken to court. Benefits were extended to the same-sex partners of public servants in Yukon in 1990, Ontario in 1991, British Columbia in 1992, and New Brunswick in 1993.[124] Various cities or municipalities have extended benefits, including Calgary, Edmonton, Ottawa-Carleton, Toronto, and Vancouver. The Toronto Board of Education extended dental benefits in 1993, settling a human rights complaint.[125] The Toronto and Ottawa YMCAs have extended family membership rates to same-sex couples. Air Canada will now transfer Aeroplan mileage points to a surviving same-sex spouse, settling a human rights complaint.[126] A business page story in June 1994 noted the extension of benefits by London Life Insurance, Levi Strauss (Canada), Mutual Group, Northern Telecom, IBM Canada, and BC Telecom.[127] Certain trade unions have been significant supporters on the benefits issues, taking cases like *Andrews*, *Knodel*, and *Lorenzen* to boards or courts and promoting non-discriminatory benefits provisions.[128]

There are, apparently, no financial arguments against extending benefits; evidence to date indicates that the actuarial consequences are insignificant.[129] Even if costs are involved, the benefit schemes are contributory or tax-funded. Lesbians and gay men will be paying for the programs in the same ways that heterosexuals pay for them. Same-sex couples have been financially penalized by the denial of access to the programs in the past.

ARGUMENTS BASED ON THE DIFFERENCE IN PROCREATIVE POTENTIAL

In *Egan and Nesbit* v. *Canada*, Robertson J.A. ruled that Nesbit was not a "spouse." This ruling was accomplished by limiting "spousal" relationships to those with procreative potential.[130] There are two categories: spouses, restricted to heterosexual couples, and non-spouses, which include homosexual couples and all other non-spousal couples. It is remarkable that this ruling was made in the context of a "spousal" allowance that had no relationship of any kind to dependent children.

Robertson J.A. noted that the plaintiffs had proven that they were "similarly situated," that they met the "formal equality" test. But, he said, that test had been rejected by the Supreme Court of Canada in *Andrews* in favour of a "purposive" analysis.[131] Using the purposive test, Robertson ruled against the benefits claim. Robertson's logic could have led to the claim being rejected on either basis. He made no attempt to see lesbians and gay men in the "social, political, and legal fabric" of Canadian society, as required by the *Andrews* decision.[132]

The hardest part of Robertson's analysis for lesbians and gay men to digest is the grouping of lesbian and gay couples with couples not involved in any sexual relationship. To Robertson, lesbian and gay couples do not exist as discrete categories. They are just another run-of-the-mill non-reproductive grouping. They could be tennis partners who share an apartment. Lesbians and gay couples, as such, are rendered invisible.

For years, reproductive difference has been used as an argument against equality for women.[133] In the context of discrimination on the basis of sex, the argument is now understood as rationalizing discrimination. In a parallel way, reproductive difference is now being used as a basic argument for denying equality to lesbian and gay couples.

It is true that homosexual sexual activity, on its own, cannot impregnate a female. This is an extremely limited point of difference when it is seriously examined. The difference does not prevent same-sex couples from forming. Such relationships serve basic goals of erotic and emotional fulfillment. Many heterosexual couples do not have children, often by choice. Most heterosexual intercourse is non-procreative. No one denies family benefits to heterosexual couples in childless relationships. No one denies family status to adopted children. No one argues that reproduction is the only purpose of sexual relations.

It is also not uncommon for same-sex couples to raise children. Usually the children are from a previous heterosexual marriage of one of the partners, but often a lesbian couple will have a child using alternative insemination techniques. Individuals and non-sexual couples will often raise children as well, confirming that social programs aimed at children should not be based on a requirement of any particular kind of family unit, but on the fact of a dependent child.[134]

The *Andrews* medicare case sought family coverage for a lesbian partner and the child who the couple were raising. The court held that the couple were not spouses. After the ruling, Ontario abolished premiums and moved to individual coverage. Any differential treatment of children based on the nature of the family unit ended.[135] There have been two Canadian cases on immigration sponsorship. One involves a childless couple. The other was brought by a couple raising two children.[136] Current immigration practice allows the non-Canadian to be admitted on "compassionate and humanitarian" grounds, a discretionary decision. If the non-Canadian has children, the children will gain residency as dependants of the non-Canadian. The "spousal allowance" in issue in the *Egan* case, in contrast to medicare and immigration claims, has no potential implications for children. It requires a means test and is designed to smooth the transition from full salary to the old age security pension for a couple. Since it targets individuals in their 60s, it was formulated without concern for dependent children. Yet in *Egan*, where children do not feature in the logic of the benefits scheme, the rulings have focused on the non-procreative potential of homosexual relationships in order to deny eligibility.[137]

In most cases, it will be better to formulate benefits schemes on the basis either of individual coverage or actual dependency. But, to the extent that we continue to use kinship criteria for certain rights, obligations, and benefits, it is discriminatory to limit those criteria to heterosexual relationships. The denial of "spousal" status in *Egan* is a transparent rationalization of discrimination on the basis of sexual orientation.

DENYING BENEFITS BY CONSTRUING THEM AS PRIVILEGES NOT RIGHTS

If a particular benefit is available only to a limited and defined group, then it is sometimes argued to be a "privilege" and not a "right," and therefore outside *Charter* protection. This argument has been put forward repeatedly by Immigration Canada to deny claims of lesbian and gay Canadians to sponsor their non-Canadian partners, a sponsorship available to heterosexual Canadians. "The Immigration Act and Immigration Regulations offer a preferential treatment to applicants legally married to a sponsor who is a Canadian citizen or a permanent resident of Canada. All other applicants for immigration in Canada, except members of the family class and refugees, are subject to selection criteria. Therefore, the treatment of spouses is a distinction in favour of a group, not against a group."[138] This argues that family class sponsorship, being limited to legally married heterosexuals, is a privilege or preference or favour. The norm is non-sponsorship, and that is all that can be claimed by any group or category of people. This argument is inconsistent with the decision of the Supreme Court of Canada in *University of British Columbia* v. *Berg*, where benefits given only to a limited group of people were held to be claimable, rejecting at least part of the logic of the earlier Supreme Court of Canada decision in *Gay Alliance* v. *Vancouver Sun*.[139]

ARE THERE SPECIAL CONSIDERATIONS ON ISSUES OF CUSTODY AND ACCESS TO CHILDREN?

The emotional attachment to children is often much stronger than the attachment between partners. The love of children is commonly seen as a major factor in sustaining relationships. Any denial of access, custody, or adoption on grounds of race, sex, or sexual orientation is a highly discriminatory act.

Of course our law favours the "best interests of the child." It is sometimes suggested that same-sex couples will have a different impact on the children they raise than a heterosexual couple. There are fears that children raised in homosexual households (a) will become homosexual (seen as a bad thing), or (b) may be victimized by discrimination against the family unit.

Current data suggest that children raised in homosexual households are no more likely to be homosexual than children raised in heterosexual households.[140] This logic should be obvious, since almost all lesbians and gay men are raised by heterosexuals. There are some positive factors, as well. Homosexual households are guaranteed to let a child know that there are homosexuals, heterosexuals, and bisexuals in this world. That information is important to the healthy development of children.

On the second concern, if we seek to end discrimination against lesbians and gay men, we cannot allow existing patterns of discrimination to be confirmed and endorsed by depriving lesbians and gay men of access, custody, or adoption because of general social attitudes.

This area remains very sensitive. The Ontario government offered to remove the provisions on adoption by same-sex couples from their package of family law reforms in June 1994, hoping to reduce opposition. The Danish and Norwegian "registered partnership" laws equate same-sex registered partnership with legal marriage for almost all purposes but state that registered partners are not to be considered spouses for the purposes of adoption laws.[141] Two states in the United States specifically prohibit adoption by same-sex couples: Florida and New Hampshire. Six states specifically allow such adoptions.[142] Decisions in Massachusetts and Virginia have ruled that homosexuality is irrelevant in custody cases.[143] There are also some restrictions in Europe on lesbian access to alternative insemination, though alternative insemination has become quite common among lesbians in North America.[144] Two lesbians have brought a human rights complaint against a doctor in British Columbia for the refusal to provide alternative insemination to lesbians.[145]

SHOULD SAME-SEX COUPLES HAVE ACCESS TO LEGAL MARRIAGE?

THE LEGAL SIGNIFICANCE OF MARRIAGE
While marriage remains the paradigm of spousal rights and obligations, its legal significance has been sharply reduced in recent decades. On the one hand, many "spousal" rights, obligations, and benefits have been extended to unmarried heterosexual couples and, increasingly, to same-sex couples. On the other hand, there have been trends to move from kinship-based benefits programs to universal coverage, eliminating the need to assert intimate relationships of any kind.

With the ending of the centrality of marriage in organizing rights, obligations, and benefits, it might have been thought that lesbians and gay men would seek legal equality on substantive issues such as spousal benefits, access to children, support, and division of property, but not be concerned with the symbolism of marriage. Perhaps the *Charter* is not available for symbolic issues. Perhaps it should be.

THE RELIGIOUS OR CULTURAL SIGNIFICANCE OF MARRIAGE
If the concern with access to marriage has a religious component, it must be recognized that there are now denominations, congregations, and clergy that will perform religious ceremonies for same-sex couples.[146] Little more can be expected, for Western legal systems are not going to order unwilling religious institutions to perform same-sex marriages.

It seems that marriage is sustained more by social or cultural attitudes than by law or religion. Marriage is understood as a heterosexual institution, though that understanding does not give any reasoned explanation for its denial to homosexuals. There may be assumptions that homosexual relationships are different than heterosexual relationships. It is sometimes suggested that homosexuals are more promiscuous than heterosexuals, making access to legal marriage inappropriate. There are two problems with that argument. Promiscuity is common among both heterosexuals and homosexuals. Secondly, if promiscuity is seen as a bad thing, it might be advisable to make marriage available to homosexuals to discourage promiscuity.

We are in trouble whenever we speak of "traditional" marriage or "heterosexual" norms. Marriage has changed dramatically over time in Western Judeo-Christian history, and has enormous cross-cultural variations. To refer to a particular model as "traditional" is to make an ideological, not a factual, statement.[147] To refer to a pattern as "heterosexual," apart from the gender of the parties, is equally to make an ideological statement.

THE POLITICS OF THE CLAIM TO MARRIAGE

The religious, legal, and social images of marriage make any lesbian and gay claims to marriage both radical and conservative. Access to marriage would be an unqualified recognition of equality by the larger society. But such recognition would come with the most cultural baggage.[148]

There are some lesbians and gay men who aspire to an ideologically "traditional" marriage and want both church and state involved in the recognition of their relationships. In contrast, there are heterosexuals who want both the church and state to stay out of their relationships (though the state is no longer giving that option as freely as it once did). This is the context in which certain lesbians and gay men have been demanding access to legal marriage, while other lesbians and gay men regard marriage as a major symbol of inequality, sexism, and heterosexism and want nothing to do with it.[149]

In spite of earlier cases rejecting same-sex access to legal marriage, there have been major test cases in a number of jurisdictions in recent years. Thirty same-sex couples applied for marriage licences in Portland, Oregon, in December 1991.[150] Two hundred and fifty same-sex couples applied for marriage licences in 50 German cities on August 19th, 1992.[151] In *Layland and Beaulne*, the Ontario Divisional Court in 1993 rejected a claim to access to marriage by a gay couple.[152] The majority limited legal marriage to heterosexuals on the basis of procreative potential. A dissent talks of the policy goals of supporting same-sex relationships and reducing discrimination against children raised in such units. Robertson J.A. found the spousal benefits argument in *Egan* to be "an indirect challenge to the common law and statutory concept of marriage...."[153] Much of the federal government's strategy in arguing the appeal had been to describe the claim as leading logically to access to marriage for same-sex couples. Hawaiian activists organized around the marriage issue and won a major victory in 1993 when the Hawaiian Supreme Court in *Baehr v. Lewin* required the state government to show "compelling state interest" for its discrimination against homosexuals in marriage laws, a standard it almost certainly will not be able to meet.[154] Activism on the issue continues: a male couple were refused a marriage licence in Moscow in April 1994.[155]

COMPROMISE SOLUTIONS

The reasonable Scandinavians went for a practical compromise. Denmark, Norway, and Sweden now have laws making registered partnerships available to same-sex couples. The registered partnerships have all the consequences of legal marriage except they do not require the state church to perform the ceremony and they do not establish the couple as a family for the purposes of adoption laws. There is an additional difference from heterosexual marriage; one party must be both a citizen and resident of the country. A second type of registered partnership exists, limited to creating a formal public record of the relationship without conferring any legal rights or obligations. The record can establish eligibility for any benefit schemes which are otherwise available to same-sex couples. Such registration systems exist in the Netherlands at the municipal level and in over 20 cities in the United States. The registration laws in the Netherlands are generally open to both homosexual and heterosexual couples.

In June 1993, the Law Reform Commission of the State of Queensland, Australia, published a report, "De Facto Relationships," recommending the recognition of both unmarried heterosexual and homosexual relationships. In the same month, the government of the Australian Capital Territory released a discussion paper on possible "Domestic Relationship Legislation" which would apply to heterosexual and homosexual couples. In November 1993, the Ontario Law Reform Commission recommended the establishment of a registration system in that province available to heterosexual and homosexual couples for purposes of rights to marital property, support, and survivor claims.[156] The report was followed by the bill to recognize same-sex couples in areas of provincial family law. The bill was defeated on second reading in June 1994.

The governments in both Spain and the Netherlands indicated in 1994 that they would introduce legislation to recognize unmarried heterosexual and homosexual couples.[157]

CHOICES

There seem to be around seven choices in the current debates on how to recognize same-sex couples.

a) The extension of benefits and obligations to unmarried heterosexual or homosexual couples, as is happening at present, without legal marriage or any system of registered partnerships. The relationship will be established by evidence of the relationship, not by rebuttable presumptions based on legal marriage or registration. Exact criteria for recognition of unmarried relationships (self-description, one year together, two years together) will vary from law to law (something already accepted in practice for unmarried heterosexual relationships). This approach has the strength of focusing on substantive benefits and obligations, and not on symbolism.[158]

b) The creation of a registration system for same-sex couples. If such a system is limited to same-sex couples, it has the problem that it will be seen as a second-class version of legal marriage. It has the additional problem that if benefits are tied to registration, homosexuals will be required to register their relationships to get benefits, while heterosexuals generally now do not have to marry or register to be eligible. Again, there would be discrimination. A third problem is the assumption that lesbian and gay couples would be willing, in the present climate of public opinion, to register. Some will and some will not. It cannot be expected, given social attitudes, that a registration system will work in the same way for homosexuals as choices of marriage and registration would for heterosexuals. For this reason, the scheme could also be held to be discriminatory.

c) A registration system for heterosexual and homosexual couples. This would be more satisfactory, but would still have some of the problems described above.

d) A registration system for heterosexual, homosexual, and other relationships which the parties wish to be legally recognized for various family law purposes.

The common element would be interdependency. Such a system would not limit registration to sexual relationships.

e) A registration system for heterosexual and homosexual couples, with provision that existing patterns of establishing the fact of a relationship by evidence, without marriage or registration, would continue to be available to couples.

f) The availability to heterosexual and homosexual couples of marriage, registration, or evidentiary proof of their relationships. This establishes equality, but it involves extending the important symbolism of "marriage" to same-sex couples.

g) Withdrawal by the state from marriage, leaving marriage to non-legal religious or secular authorities, while making registration or evidentiary proof of relationships available to homosexual or heterosexual couples.

This debate is far from over.

MINORITY RIGHTS

Is equality enough? Cultural minorities seek more than equality. They want to survive and develop as distinct collectivities. First Nations communities seek social, cultural, and political autonomy within Canada. Other minorities, with less distinctiveness, seek more limited control over aspects of their lives. At present, lesbians and gay men have a number of distinct cultural characteristics. We have our own organizations, neighbourhoods, media, slang, issues, politicians, holidays, parades, histories of struggle, and fights over political strategies. The Queer Nation slogan "we're here, we're queer, get used to it!" is a classic, if abrasive, formulation of a minority rights demand for the recognition of difference.[159]

Lesbians and gay men emerged as visible minority groups, in the sense we are now talking about, only in the last couple of decades. Gay residential and business areas are now familiar parts of the major cities in Canada and the United States. There are lesbian and gay caucuses within various political parties in both countries. A separate lesbian and gay law association was recognized as an affiliate by the American Bar Association in August 1992, giving it a voting seat in the ABA House of Delegates.[160] A lesbian and gay rights section was established within the British Columbia branch of the Canadian Bar Association in 1993. Separate organizations of lesbians and gay journalists have been established in both the United States and Canada.[161] There are lesbian and gay studies programs, following the models of black studies, women's studies, Native American studies. These programs are concerned with lesbian and gay issues and are staffed by lesbians and gay men.

There was an effort to get lesbians and gay men to vote as a block in the 1992 United States presidential election.[162] Republican Party Chairman Haley Barbour referred to Clinton's pledge to end the ban on homosexuals in the military as "a political payoff to a powerful special interest group."[163] It was heartening to be labelled a "special interest group" in a country in which special interest groups are seen as powerful.

Lesbians and gay men now expect representation in the various institutions of the state. Various U.S. states and cities have openly homosexual officials charged with liaison with the lesbian and gay communities. President Clinton redeemed his campaign pledge to have open lesbians and gay men in his administration.[164] Various police forces recruit homosexuals, as the RCMP in Canada recruits First Nations people and other visible minorities.

When Svend Robinson disclosed his homosexuality in 1988, Ed Broadbent, the New Democratic Party leader, and other members of Parliament described Robinson's homosexuality as a private matter.[165] They did not say that it was a good thing to have lesbians and gay men represented in the institutions of government, though they believed it desirable to have women, visible minorities, First Nations people, and the disabled represented. They did not welcome a "pluralism" or "diversity" which included lesbians and gay men.

The fact that lesbians and gay men organize as minorities does not mean that the goal is the recognition of homosexuals as cultural minorities. Both cultural minorities and equality seeking groups organize in much the same way, though their end goals differ. The key question is whether there are lesbian and gay subcultures which are expected to endure.[166] Are lesbian and gay subcultures simply cultures of oppression and resistance? If lesbians and gay men achieved real equality and acceptance, would any lesbian and gay culture continue? This question, put to lesbians and gay men, usually produces uncertainty or a reluctant "no." Its highly theoretical character flows from the fact that none of us actually believe that we will personally experience a situation of full equality and acceptance. Almost all minorities face some continuing tensions and sense of marginalization in their relationships with dominant populations. Even if tolerance or acceptance become the norm, homophobia might return.[167] Sexual minorities are not going to assimilate to dominant patterns, so a minority ethos will continue to characterize the lives of lesbians and gay men. It follows that we do have to have some separate space, some special representation. We have to hold on to elements of the subcultures we have built.

Some litigation can be properly seen as concerned with lesbian and gay minority rights. In March 1994, the Tokyo District Court awarded damages against the Tokyo Metropolitan Government for its refusal to allow a lesbian and gay organization to use a public lodge owned by the city.[168] The harassment by Canadian Customs of materials going to lesbian and gay bookstores is not simply problematic in terms of overly broad censorship powers and a lack of proper procedures, but also as an attack on important institutions of the lesbian and gay communities.[169] Customs actions threatened the economic survival of these businesses by delaying whole shipments addressed to the stores. These businesses cannot be seen in purely economic terms. They affirm the legitimacy of being lesbian and gay by giving access to the broad literature now available, including newspapers, magazines, fiction, new books by specialized presses, and new books by the major North American university presses. When the function of these businesses is seen in minority terms, then meaningful analogies can be drawn. A similar interference with the functioning of Christian Science Reading Rooms would be immediately understood as an attack on a minority. Little Sisters Book Store in Vancouver brought an action against Canadian Customs, which went to trial in October 1994, after three adjournments at the request of the federal Department of Justice.[170]

The 1979 decision *Gay Alliance Towards Equality* v. *Vancouver Sun* involved an attempt by a "gay liberation" newspaper to place an advertisement in a major newspaper.[171] Obviously the lesbian and gay newspapers that now exist in all major centres in Canada are important institutions in the individual and collective lives of lesbians and gay men. The Supreme Court of Canada ruled that classified advertisements in newspapers were not a service generally available to the public and therefore were not a service covered by the particular anti-discrimination law. This odd ruling was justified as protecting freedom of the press. Majority press freedom was used as a rationale for inhibiting an emergent minority lesbian and gay press.

In October 1994, the Colorado Supreme Court struck down an amendment to the state constitution, enacted by referendum, which prohibited laws protecting lesbians and gay men from discrimination. The court held that the amendment singled out one form of discrimination and "removed its redress from consideration by the normal political process." Political action, expected of any minority, had been made more difficult for lesbians and gay men, who would have to seek an amendment to the state constitution.[172]

The Coalition for Lesbian and Gay Rights in Ontario prepared a number of 30-second "public service announcements" advocating spousal rights for same-sex couples. The announcements had been categorized by the Telecaster Committee of Canada, a private regulatory body of broadcasters, as "public service announcements," clearing their way for free airing under publicly sanctioned community service broadcasting. But television stations refused to broadcast the announcements.[173] Equal media access was denied (as in *Gay Alliance*), inhibiting minority political action (as in the Colorado case).

The construction of lesbian and gay infrastructures — organizations, businesses, media — is an important way of responding to oppression and marginalization. Such institutions are essential to the political activity aimed at ending discrimination and serving the needs of lesbians and gays as minorities.

RECOGNITION OF DIVERSITY

Many lesbians and gay leaders see equality and minority rights arguments as misdescribing lesbian and gay realities, as implicitly denying the diversity of lives and identities within the lesbian and gay communities. They argue that lesbians and gay men must not be fitted into role models made by heterosexuals for themselves and refitted as criteria for heterosexual acceptance of homosexuals.

A logical extension of this position is to argue for the recognition of the diversity of sexual identities and sexual arrangements within society as a whole. A recognition of lesbians and gay men that does not remake them in standardized heterosexual images seems to require a change in how everyone understands patterns of sexuality. The alternative is to see lesbian and gay communities as fundamentally unlike heterosexual communities.

At the moment, lesbian and gay self-presentation involves an assertion of sexual diversity that is unsettling to many people, both inside and outside those who identify as lesbians or gay men. The large North American lesbian and gay pride parades have men dressed as nuns and women on motorcycles. There are transvestites, transexuals, bisexuals, and sadomasochists. The only open organizations of pedophiles are composed of gay males, and they are sometimes represented in the parades. Individuals living with HIV or AIDS march as well. Videos of pride parades have been used by anti-homosexual lobby groups to portray a threatening image of the "gay agenda."[174]

But bisexuality, transvestism, transexualism, pedophilia, sadomasochism, and HIV/AIDS are not lesbian or gay. This is indisputable. There are far more heterosexual transvestites than homosexual transvestites. Transexuals are usually seeking to establish anatomically heterosexual relationships. The dominant mode of HIV transmission worldwide is heterosexual intercourse.[175] Yet lesbian and gay pride parades and lesbian and gay media reinforce over and over again stereotypical associations with homosexuality. In doing so, they portray lesbian and gay communities in ways that the larger society finds unsettling. What is going on?

The dominant heterosexual society clearly represses the acknowledgement of sexual diversity within itself and within society as a whole. We can begin with how amazing the denial of the existence of lesbians and gay men has been. People still say that they have never met a lesbian or gay man, indicating a startling blindness to the people living around them. United States media in May 1993 recounted the story of a marine colonel who learned, five days before he was to testify before the Senate Armed Services Committee in support of the ban on homosexuals, that his 24-year-old son was gay.[176] The media stories never suggested that the father should have known, suspected, or at least recognized the possibility that his son was gay. There was no hint of blame on the father for his ignorance. Such blindness is expected. It is "normal."

Lesbian and gay invisibility is not normal in any sense. It is socially constructed and socially constructed by the dominant society, which prefers to avoid the recognition of sexual variance. The "closet" is not created by homosexuals. We would be incapable of avoiding detection if the dominant society chose to be observant.

Over 40 years ago, Kinsey described sexual orientation as different points on a continuum. There were not two categories: homosexual and heterosexual. There were not three categories: homosexual, bisexual, and heterosexual. Life was not that neat and orderly. We were all at different points on a continuum between exclusive heterosexuality and exclusive homosexuality. That basic information has still not been accepted in North American society. This avoidance of recognizing diversity is pathological. It does harm to us all.

Because the dominant society represses recognition of the existence of bisexuals, transvestites, transexuals, and sadomasochists, those people can only find a public home in the institutions of the lesbian and gay communities. The bisexuals, transvestites, and transexuals are refugees from a dominant culture which denies sexual diversity. Lesbian and gay society is probably no more sexually diverse than heterosexual society, but as marginalized groupings, lesbian and gay communities had fewer mechanisms of exclusion. Acceptance was not always there, for many lesbians and gay men sought to escape marginality by asserting sameness and denying what appeared to be differences (but were not). This ambivalence meant that it was only with considerable hesitation that lesbian and gay organizations have become supportive of bisexuals, transexuals, and others.[177] The Gay Games, held every four years, have taken this strategy one logical step further. They are open to all.

How are anti-diversity arguments put? One formulation involves warnings of the consequences of "permissiveness," and finds its classic, if now comic, formulation in dark references to the decline and fall of the Roman Empire. A recent account of legislative debates on lesbian and gay issues in the British Parliament was interesting in reminding readers of the now-dated use of warnings about the slide further into a "permissive society." Some argue that tolerance of homosexuality will lead logically to acceptance of consensual pedophilia and polygamy.[178] An extreme version of the argument appeared in an Italian neo-fascist newspaper: "If homosexuality is elevated to a right, then rape, incest, and bestiality can be regarded as rights as well."[179] These statements ignore the need to balance assessments of harm against claims to liberty.

The fact of diversity has not yet been translated into legal argument. Privacy or libertarian arguments can be used to support particular forms of sexual expression. The *Brown* decision of the House of Lords in 1993 sentenced men to jail for consenting, private sadomasochistic activity, discovered because it had been videotaped for use by the participants.[180] The case is to go to the European Human Rights Commission on privacy grounds. Transexual operations have become widely accepted as legitimate medical procedures which can be covered by state medical insurance programs. The European Court of Human Rights has now required state facilitation of the new gender identity of transexuals.[181]

Considerable diversity is now tolerated in practice, though a decision like *Brown* indicates how fragile it may be in individual cases when judges are unfamiliar with the context.

A FINAL WORD

Three decades ago, in 1964, the first lesbian and gay rights organization was established in Canada.[182] Decriminalization came in 1969, not as a result of lesbian and gay visibility or political work, but as an elite reform, reflecting international trends. The first anti-discrimination laws came in 1973 and 1977. In 1986, the federal government, for political and legal reasons, accepted that lesbians and gay men were protected from discrimination by the equality provision in the *Charter of Rights and Freedoms*. That conclusion has been confirmed by the courts. In the 1970s and 1980s, lesbians and gay men constructed a new kind of visible social infrastructure in Canada, with community centres, newspapers, churches, counseling services, and sports leagues. With the onslaught of AIDS in the early 1980s, this infrastructure had to be extended. The epidemic altered gay male patterns, reducing promiscuity and directing energies into care-giving organizations. AIDS significantly enhanced both the image and visibility of gay men in North America. The recognition of feminism in various academic fields has led to a new recognition of lesbians, separately from the recognition of gay males.

After the issue of individual equality rights for lesbians and gay men had largely been won, the issue of the recognition of same-sex relationships came onto the public policy agenda. In the last decade, the progress on same-sex partner benefits has been remarkable. One can look to the completion of this normative shift before the end of this decade.

None of these gains have come about without controversy. None have been embraced with enthusiasm by any political party. There remain controversies over strategies and goals. It is impossible to predict the outcome of some of the disputes. Will marriage be extended to same-sex couples, or will some Scandinavian compromise be established in its place? Will social acceptance really produce a situation in our lifetime when being lesbian or gay will truly be "no big deal," when minority rights strategies will cease to be necessary?

Two major Canadian events of the 1980s were John Crosbie's statement in the House of Commons in 1986 and Svend Robinson's "coming out" in 1988. Both events promised significant change. Crosbie promised to change federal laws. He never did. When Svend Robinson came out, commentators expected a number of other national figures to acknowledge their homosexuality. They never did. In each case, the event did not trigger immediate changes. When change occurred, it took place in different ways than expected. Crosbie's promise has largely been implemented, but more by the courts and provincial governments than parliament. And Robinson's lead is being followed by new political candidates, rather than incumbents, and more at the municipal level than the provincial or national levels.[183]

Change did not come in exactly the ways expected, but now we can see that the changes have been cumulative. Canada has made great progress in recognizing the rights of lesbians and gay men, in ways more positive and less divisive than in the neighbouring United States. We can be a little surprised. We can be somewhat proud.

QUESTIONS TO CONSIDER

1. Outline some of the limitations discussed by Sanders regarding using the "right to privacy" argument to achieve increased rights for gay men and lesbians. Why does Sanders feel that using the equality provisions of the Charter of Rights and Freedoms might offer several advantages over privacy arguments?

2. Discuss several specific areas identified by Sanders in which lesbians and gay men are denied important rights and outline how he wishes to remedy them. Also discuss the extent to which you agree or disagree with Sanders's arguments.

NOTES

1. A United States formulation, that equality rights for homosexuals and same-sex couples involve "special" rights or privileges, has begun to appear in Canada. The phrase was attributed to Alberta Community Development Minister Diane Mirosh, who later was said to have "backed off the statement": M. Cernetig, "Why Alberta Moves Slowly on Gay Rights" *The [Toronto] Globe and Mail* (5 February 1993) 7; M. Hays, "Alberta Minister Attacks Gay Rights" *Xtra Supplement* (lesbian, gay, bisexual newspaper published in Toronto) (March 1993) 7; "Homophobe or Heroine?" *Alberta Report* (18 January 1993) (cover story on Diane Mirosh). It is also used by REAL Women; P. Hannan, "Twisted Sisters" *Xtra* (1 April 1994) 1.

2. M. Riordon, *The First Stone: Homosexuality and the United Church* (Toronto: McClelland & Stewart, 1990); J. Ferry, *In the Courts of the Lord* (Toronto: Key Porter, 1993).

3. M. Cernetig, "Preston Manning and his Faith" *The [Toronto] Globe and Mail* (2 December 1991) 1, quotes Reform Party leader Preston Manning as saying: "I really believe homosexuality is destructive to the individual, and in the long run to society." Manning stated he would re-instate the ban on lesbians and gay men in the Canadian military: "Reform's Manning Riles Gays by Calling for a Ban in Military" *The [Montreal] Gazette* (17 June 1993). On the "family caucus," which opposed initiatives on lesbian and gay rights by the Conservative government of Prime Minister Mulroney, see "The Revolt of the Tory Right" *Western Report* (17 March 1986) 12; G. York, "At Odds on Gay Rights" *The [Toronto] Globe and Mail* (18 April 1992) 5; "Plan to Protect Gays Splits Tory Caucus" *Vancouver Sun* (20 April 1992); G. York, "Tory Politicians Form Family Compact" *The [Toronto] Globe and Mail* (3 June 1992) 1; B. Ries, "'Family Caucus' Fighting to Preserve Traditional Values" *Vancouver Sun* (9 June 1992) 8. On the development of an equivalent grouping in the Liberal caucus of the Chrétien government, see E. Greenspon, T. Thanh Ha, "Dissident Liberals Balk Over Hate Bill" *The [Toronto] Globe and Mail* (27 October 1994) 1.

4. Prime Minister Campbell's constituency office sold T-shirts during the 1993 election campaign which read: "Gays for Kim — Get Used To It," phraseology borrowed from the radical Queer Nation organization.

5. An address by the Honourable Barbara McDougall, Secretary of State for External Affairs, to the United Nations World Conference on Human Rights, delivered by Dorothy Dobbie, Member of Parliament, Vienna, Austria, 16 June 1993 (Statement, External Affairs, 93/48). In the drafting committee a Canadian government representative proposed wording which would have added "sexual orientation" to a list of prohibited grounds of discrimination in the conference's final statement. In the end, the wording of the section was altered to omit any list in favour of an open-ended endorsement of equality.

6. Both Columbia University Press and Duke University Press have established a series of publications on lesbian, gay, and bisexual issues. Columbia had 13 titles in November 1993. Other university presses publishing in the area are California, Chicago, Harvard, Indiana, Massachusetts, Minnesota, Princeton, Stanford, Temple, and Yale. Specialized law journals now exist: Australasian Gay and Lesbian Law Journal (Federation Press, New South Wales); Law and Sexuality (Tulane University School of Law); Lesbian/Gay Law Notes (Lesbian and Gay Law Association of Greater New York).

7. A current revision of the Roman Catholic catechism includes a statement that homosexuals should be treated with respect, but homosexual acts avoided: "Revising Catholicism Became a Matter of Faith" *The [Toronto] Globe and Mail* (17 November 1992) 1. The position of the United States government in its 1993 position on lesbians and gay men in the military is similar. The Supreme Court of Canada decision in *R. v. Klippert* (1967), S.C.R. 822, made being homosexual a crime, though a conviction for an act had to precede the determination of "dangerous sexual offender" status.

8. U.K., "Report of the Committee on Homosexual Offences and Prostitution," Home Office (1957).

9. See G. Kinsman, *The Regulation of Desire* (Montreal: Black Rose, 1987) 164.

10. *Ibid.* at 206; D. Berwick, "Mass Arrests, Massive Response" *Xtra* (18 March 1994) 21.

11. "Robinson's Sex Life Called his Own Affair by Most MPs" *Vancouver Sun* (26 February 1988) 6; "MP's Sexuality Private Issue, NDP Says" *The [Toronto] Globe and Mail* (26 February 1988) 8; E.K. Fulton, "Gay and Proud; Canada's Only Publicly Gay MP Tells his Story" *Maclean's* (16 May 1994) 36. Members of Parliament had an odd privacy on the issue of Robinson's homosexuality. There was constant heckling of Robinson as gay in the House of Commons, but those remarks were excised from the record of debates and deliberately not reported by the media. The ability of members of Parliament to "correct" the transcript of debates is well established. The media censorship of the heckling was benevolent in intention, but hid open homophobia in a major national institution. After Robinson "came out," the heckling ceased, perhaps because the media censorship would no longer be practised.

12. *Dudgeon v. United Kingdom* (1981), 5 E.H.R.R. 149; *Norris v. Ireland* (1988), 13 E.H.R.R. 186; see T. O'Malley, "*Norris v. Ireland* — An Opportunity for Law Reform" *Irish Law Times* (December 1988) 279.

13. The case invoked the provisions of the International Covenant on Civil and Political Rights: "U.N. Prods Tasmanian Devils" *Advocate* (lesbian, gay, bisexual magazine published in Los Angeles) (17 May 1994) 18.

14. 478 U.S. 186 (1986).

15. The 1992 decision in *Commonwealth of Kentucky v. Wasson* is discussed in "Recent Cases" (1993) 106 Harvard Law Review 1370. Three cases in Texas are discussed in "Refusal to Rule" *Advocate* (22 February 1994) 24.

16. Twenty-seven states and the District of Columbia have repealed their "sodomy" laws since the first repeal in 1961 by the State of Illinois. C. Bull, "Green light district" *Advocate* (2 November 1993) 37. Criminal laws in other jurisdictions are often not enforced, but may be used to justify discrimination against lesbians and gay men.

17. *Egan v. Canada* (1993), 103 D.L.R. (4th) 336 at 392, Robertson J.A. (F.C.A.).

18. A statement in confirmation hearings; "Quote/Unquote" *International Herald Tribune* (23 July 1993) 3.

19. M. Campbell, "Gay Rights Trigger Verbal War" *The [Toronto] Globe and Mail* (29 October 1992) 1.

20. "Polls Failed to Allow for Anti-gay Vote Blush Factor" *Vancouver Sun* (6 November 1992) 13.

21. "Anti-gay Violence Rises in 6 Cities, Study Finds" *The New York Times* (7 March 1991) 16; C. Bull, "Group's Survey Says Hate-crime Reports Rose in Six Areas" *Advocate* (19 April 1991) 14. A study by the National Gay and Lesbian Task Force indicated 14% fewer recorded incidents of harassment and violence in 1993 than in 1992: "Antigay Violence in America" *Advocate* (19 April 1994) 15. Coultas J., in *Brown v. British Columbia* (1990), 66 D.L.R. (4th) 444 at 457 suggested that discrimination against lesbians and gay men had become more severe since the onset of AIDS.

22. "Rock to Beef Up Hate-crimes Law" *The [Toronto] Globe and Mail* (11 June 1994) 4.

23. R. Harding, "Capitol Gains" *Advocate* (27 March 1990) 8. Some religious conservatives were horrified when President Bush invited lesbians and gays to the White House for the signing ceremony. The Southern Baptist Convention withdrew its invitation to President Bush to speak at its annual meeting because of the incident: G. Wills, "The Born-again Republicans" *New York Review of Books* (24 September 1992) 9. The Canadian Radio-television and Telecommunications Commission has enacted regulations barring abusive comments about lesbians and gays. The policy was a response to a religious program which suggested that AIDS was a punishment by God against homosexuals: D. Claveau, "On-air Bashing is Not Okay" *Angles* (lesbian, gay, bisexual newspaper published in Vancouver) (December 1991) 3. An account of two state-level hate crimes statutes is found in T. Kogan, "Legislative Violence Against Lesbians and Gay Men" (1994) *Utah Law Review* 209.

24. "Hate Crime" *Xtra* (15 October 1993) 17.

25. See the Irish *Incitement to Hatred Act*, mentioned in J. Annetts, B. Thompson, "Dangerous Activism?" in K. Plummer (Ed.), *Modern Homosexualities: Fragments of Lesbian and Gay Experience* (London: Routledge, 1992) 227 at 235. The *Anti-Discrimination (Homosexual Vilification) Amendment Act 1993, No. 97* was passed in New South Wales in October 1993.

26. See "Serial Killer Stalking London's Gay Community" *The [Toronto] Globe and Mail* (18 June 1993) 7; "Gays, Police Meet in Wake of Murders" *The [Toronto] Globe and Mail* (11 December 1993) 5.

27. The chair of the Kanata Police Commission in Ontario, Alex Munter, is openly gay: "Munter Re-elected Kanata Police Commission Chair" *Goinfo* (lesbian, gay, bisexual newspaper published in Ottawa) (March 1994) 2.

28. K. Griffin, "Homosexual Community Plans Demonstration Against Violence" *Vancouver Sun* (3 September 1992) 1; B. Janoff, "Darkness at the Edge of Town" *Vancouver Sun* (12 September 1992) D4; "Police Liaison Committee Finally Making Headway" *Angles* (October 1992) 3; J. Lee, "Police Get Orders on Gay-Bashing: Chief vows sensitivity training" *Vancouver Sun* (16 September 1992) 1; B. Morton, "Sensitivity Training Applauded" *Vancouver Sun* (17 September 1992) B4.

29. C. Paglia, "Review of Farrell, *The Myth of Male Power*" *International Herald Tribune* (6 August 1993) 8.

30. These decisions involve a holding that being homosexual constitutes membership in a particular "social group," an interpretation supported by the U.N. High Commission for Refugees. The Canadian decision receiving the most publicity was the granting of refugee status to Jorge Inaudi of Argentina in 1992 (decision of the Immigration and Refugee Board, 9 April 1992, case number T91-04459): E. Oziewicz, "Homosexual Granted Status as Refugee" *The [Toronto] Globe and Mail* (11 January 1992) 1; C. Farnsworth, "Homosexual Is Granted Refugee Status in Canada" *The New York Times* (14 January 1992) 5. On United States decisions, see J. Brooke, "In Live-and-Let-Live Land, Gay People Are Slain" *The New York Times* (12 August 1993) (on the granting of refugee status to a man from Brazil); D. Johnston, "Ruling Backs Homosexuals on Asylum" *The New York Times* (17 June 1994) 6 (describing a general order by Attorney General Janet Reno on the question). On Australia see "Australia" *Advocate* (5 May 1992) 29, dealing with a refugee claim by two gay men from China.

31. Robertson J.A., in *Egan v. Canada, supra* note 17 at 392, suggested that because "sexual orientation" must be treated as irrelevant it cannot be the basis for a claim to equal benefits, only to claims for protection from personal disentitlement.

32. This was established by the pioneering work of Dr. Evelyn Hooker; see E. Hooker, "Male Homosexuality in the Rorschach" (1958) 22 Journal of Projective Techniques 33; E. Hooker, "The Adjustment of the Male Overt Homosexual" (1957) 21 *Journal of Projective Techniques* 18.

33. The expert report of Dr. Michael Myers, entitled "A Psychiatric Approach to Homosexuality," 9 May 1991, 27 pp., submitted to the British Columbia Supreme Court in the case of *Knodel v. B.C.* [1991] 6 W.W.R. 728, noted the ending of the classifications and concluded that homosexual people were no more prone to the range of psychiatric illnesses than heterosexual people. Copy in possession of the author.

34. "WHO Deletes Homosexuality from Disease Codex" *Passport* (gay magazine published in San Francisco) (April 1992) 4. Homosexuality had been listed as a form of sexual deviance along with bestiality and pedophilia.

35. Wilson J. in *Andrews v. Law Society of British Columbia* [1989] 1 S.C.R. 143 at 152.

36. Wilson J. in *R. v. Turpin* [1989] 1 S.C.R. 1296 at 1332.

37. *Ibid.* at 1333.

38. Madam Justice Russell in *Vriend v. The Queen* (Alta. Q.B.) [unreported], 12 April 1994, took judicial notice of patterns of discrimination against homosexuals, in the absence of specific proof by expert testimony.

39. See *Knodel v. British Columbia, supra* note 33; Mr. Justice Linden in dissent in *Egan v. Canada, supra* note 17; Mr. Justice Greer in dissent in *Layland and Beaulne v. Ontario* (1993), 104 D.L.R. (4th) 214.

40. See P. Gomes, "Back in the Military Closet" *The New York Times* (May 22 1993) 15. Former United States Vice President Dan Quayle came out for choice, arguing that homosexuality represents a choice of lifestyle that should not be accepted as a valid alternative: "Quayle Contends Homosexuality Is a Matter of Choice, Not Biology" *The New York Times* (14 September 1992) 15.

41. The American Civil Liberties Union, in a full page advertisement in the *The New York Times* (15 December 1992) 11, quoted both the then current version of the ban on homosexuals and a ban 50 years earlier on blacks, noting the similarity in the formulations.

42. E. Kosofsky Sedgwick, "How to Bring Your Kids Up Gay" in M. Warner, *Fear of a Queer Planet* (Minneapolis: University of Minnesota Press, 1992) 69 at 79.

43. This linkage is suggested in S. Ash, "Not in Bed Together: Lesbians and Gay Men" [Vancouver] *Outcomes* (publication of the OutRights Conference) (1993) 9. I am not aware of a literature on the extent to which lesbians assert choice over immutability.

44. Lillian Faderman locates this idea in the 1970s; see Chapter 7 of her book, *Odd Girls and Twilight Lovers* (New York: Columbia University Press, 1991).

45. A common factum was submitted by EGALE (Equality for Gays and Lesbians Everywhere), the Canadian Disability Rights Council, the National Association of Women and the Law, the Canadian Rights and Liberties Federation, and the National Action Committee on the Status of Women.

46. Ninth Circuit Court of Appeals, 847 F. 2d 1329.

47. H.L. Gates, "Blacklash" *New Yorker* (17 May 1993) 42.

48. Dubé J., in *Veysey v. Canada* [1990] 1 F.C. 321, 39 Admin. L. R. 161, 29 F.T.R. 74.

49. Rowles J., in *Knodel v. British Columbia, supra* note 33.

50. *Andrews v. Law Society of British Columbia, supra* note 35. Immutability was described as an important feature of many of the listed grounds in section 15 but not an essential one in *Leroux v. Cooperators General Insurance* (1991), 83 D.L.R. (4th) 694.

51. *University of Saskatchewan v. Saskatchewan Human Rights Commission* [1976] 3 W.W.R. 385 (Sask. Q.B.).

52. *Canada v. Mossop* (1993), 100 D.L.R. (4th) 658 (C.S.C.). See M. Eaton, "Patently Confused" (1994) 1 Review of Constitutional Studies 203. *Mossop* is an ambiguous decision. It implicitly confirms that "sex" is limited to gender and expressly holds that "family status" does not apply to homosexuals on the basis of legislative intent. The majority emphasized strongly that the decision was not based on the *Charter*, which had not been argued.

53. One account is David Rayside, "Gay Rights and Family Values: The Passage of Bill 7 in Ontario" (1988) 26 *Studies in Political Economy* 109.

54. E. Jackson, "Our First Win" *Xtra* (1 October 1993) 17. This story indicates that Windsor and Ottawa "soon followed Toronto's example."

55. Statutes of Québec, 1977, c. 6, s. 1.

56. Statutes of Ontario, 1986, c. 64, s. 18(1); Statutes of Manitoba, 1987–88, c. 45, adding section 9(2); Statutes of Yukon, 1987, c. 3, section 6(g). See "Voters Oppose Bill on Homosexuals, Tory MPPs Contend" *The [Toronto] Globe and Mail* (28 November 1986) 5; M. Maychak, "Fierce Lobbying Swamped MPPs: Furor Made Ban on Extra-billing Appear 'Mild in Comparison'" *The Toronto Star* (3 December 1986) 18; G. York, "Public Outcry, Caucus Defections Endanger Manitoba Gay Rights" *The [Toronto] Globe and Mail* (14 July 1987) 5; "Bigotry in the Yukon" *Maclean's* (6 January 1986) 58.

57. Statutes of Nova Scotia, 1991, c. 12; Acts of New Brunswick, 1992, c. 30; Bill 63, *Human Rights Amendment Act*, British Columbia (1992).

58. California, Connecticut, Hawaii, Massachusetts, Minnesota, New Jersey, Vermont, and Wisconsin are the states; J.B. Stewart, "Gentleman's Agreement" *New Yorker* (13 June 1994) 74 at 76. J. Schmalz, "Gay Politics Goes Mainstream" *The New York Times Magazine* (11 October 1992) 18 at 21.

59. New South Wales prohibits discrimination on the basis of "homosexuality," and Queensland prohibits discrimination based on "lawful sexual activity." The laws in Queensland and the Northern Territory exempt jobs involving responsibility for children.

60. Department of Justice, *Equality Issues in Federal Law: A Discussion Paper* (1985) 65 pp.

61. Parliamentary Committee on Equality Rights, *Report: Equality for All* (Ottawa: Queen's Printer, October 1985) (Chairman: J. Patrick Boyer, M.P.) 176 pp. M.P. Svend Robinson was a member of the committee.

62. The perception of issues in the report was limited to acts of discrimination against individuals. The recognition of equality issues relating to same-sex couples had to wait for progress on individual equality issues.

63. *Toward Equality: The Response to the Report of the Parliamentary Committee on Equality Rights* (Ottawa: Supply and Services Canada, 1986) 65 pp.

64. Information on backbench opposition can be found in D. Jenish, "The Revolt of the Tory Right" *Western Report* (17 March 1986) 12; P. Gessel, "An Activist in Justice" *Maclean's* (5 May 1986) 10; M. Rose "Altering the Contours of Society" *Maclean's* (17 March 1986) 61 (which indicates that Prime Minister Brian Mulroney made it clear to the "dissidents" that there "would be no moving backward" on the issue).

65. *Veysey v. Canada, supra* note 48.

66. (1990), 42 B.C.L.R. (2d) 294 at 310.

67. (1990), 109 N.R. 300 at 304.

68. *Haig v. Canada* (1992), 94 C.L.R. (4th) 1 at 7.

69. *Supra* note 17 at 340 (Mahoney J.A.) and 381 (Robertson J.A.).

70. (1994) 6 W.W.R. 414 (Alberta Queen's Bench).

71. 5 May 1993.

72. CCPR/C/50/488/1992, views given 31 March 1994.

73. Article 1 of the Constitution of the Netherlands is an open-ended rejection of discrimination and has been interpreted by Parliament and the Courts as prohibiting discrimination on the basis of sexual orientation: P. Tatchell, "Equal Rights For All" in Plummer, *supra* note 25 237 at 247, footnote 4. A recent article said that "the French constitution in theory forbids discrimination on the basis of sexuality, though nobody has ever invoked this theoretical right."; S. Watney, "Gai et Français" *Gay Times* (lesbian, gay, bisexual magazine published in the United Kingdom) (March 1994) 20.

74. Section 8 of the interim constitution, which will govern the country for five years, has a general affirmation of equality and a general prohibition of discrimination. A non-exclusive list of prohibited grounds of discrimination names "race, gender, sex, ethnic or social origin, color, sexual orientation, age, disability, religion, conscience, belief, culture, or language." E. Cameron, "Sexual Orientation and the Constitution" (1993) 110 *South African Law Journal* 450 at 465.

75. K. Waaldijk and A. Clapham, *Homosexuality: A European Community Issue* (Boston: Nijhoff Publishers, 1993) 21.

76. M. Cernetig, "Why Alberta Moves Slowly on Gay Rights" *The [Toronto] Globe and Mail* (5 February 1993) 7.

77. M. Hays, "Québec Rights Commission Launches Inquiry" *Xtra* (9 July 1993) 17; "Hearings" *Xtra* (15 October 1993) 17.

78. C. Bull, "Hetero Heroes: William Weld" *Advocate* (16 November 1993); S. Rimer, "Gay Rights Law for Schools Advances in Massachusetts" *The New York Times* (8 December 1993) 10.

79. "Gay Soldiers Cut the Mustard Abroad" *The New York Times* (22 November 1992) E16, describing a study by the U.S. General Accounting Office on the issue.

80. Information in 1994 indicated that 260 lesbians and gay men had been discharged from the forces since 1990. This discrimination may be challenged in a case to the European Court of Justice; D. Smith, "Campaigners Consider Landmark Job Bias Appeal to European Court of Justice" *Gay News* (lesbian and gay magazine published in the United Kingdom) (September 1994) 27.

81. Canada, Department of Justice, *Equality Issues in Federal Law: A Discussion Paper* (Ottawa: Queen's Printers 1985) 65 pp.

82. Canada, Parliamentary Committee on Equality Rights, *Report: Equality For All, Report of the Parliamentary Committee on Equality Rights* (Ottawa: Queen's Printer, October 1985) c. 4, 31.

83. T. Appleby, "Military Policy on Homosexuals to End" *The [Toronto] Globe and Mail* (10 October 1991) 4; C. Farnsworth, "Canada Ending Anti-Gay Army Rules" *The New York Times* (11 October 1991) 3; S. Bindman, "Ottawa Backs Off on Lifting of Gay Curbs" *Vancouver Sun* (11 October 1991) 4; G. Fraser, "Ottawa Delays Decision on Gays" *The [Toronto] Globe and Mail* (11 October 1991) 4.

84. *Douglas v. Canada* (1992), 98 D.L.R. (4th) 129. While the matter was decided on the basis of a consent order, the judge later issued written reasons for the decision.

85. T. Claridge and G. York, "Forces Agree to End Anti-gay Policies" *The [Toronto] Globe and Mail* (28 October 1992) 1.

86. For an account of the fight over the military ban, see D. Osborne, "Betrayed" *Advocate* (25 January 1994) 50.

87. I. Molotsky, "F.B.I. Bias Protection Expanded to Cover Homosexual Employees" *The New York Times* (3 December 1993) 13.

88. *Maclean's* (5 May 1986) 10.

89. Section 9(5), *Human Rights Code*, Statutes of Manitoba, 1987–88, c. 45. The model might have been a draft anti-discrimination law for New York City, which included a statement that "it is not the function of this civil rights statute to promote a particular group or community" and that it shall not be construed to "endorse any particular behavior or way of life." See "Protecting, Not Endorsing Homosexuals" *The New York Times* (14 March 1986) 26 (editorial).

90. S. Jeffery-Poulter, *Peers, Queers and Commons* (London: Routledge, 1991) c. 11.

91. A group deliberately challenged the law in a public protest in which they called out slogans encouraging homosexual activity. A Finnish court upheld the law, but imposed no penalty. See "Finland" *Angles* (October 1992) 7. The law had earlier been challenged in a communication to the United Nations Human Rights Committee in *Hertzberg v. Finland*, communication 61/1979, views of 2 April 1982. The references to Austria and Liechtenstein are taken from A. Duda, "Comparison of the Legal Situation of Homosexuals in Europe" reprinted in Euro-Letter, No. 18 (8 August 1993), published by the National Danish Organization for Gays and Lesbians.

92. The organization Hosi Wien was convicted of promoting homosexuality, though it continues as a legally registered organization with a social centre in Vienna and a monthly magazine.

93. Excerpts from "Clinton's Question-and-Answer Session in the Rose Garden" *The New York Times* (28 May 1993) 10.

94. M. Warner, "Introduction" in M. Warner, *Fear of a Queer Planet* (Duluth, Minnesota: University of Minnesota Press, 1993) at xiii.

95. "No Suspension" *Bangkok Post* (27 January 1994) 10.

96. In February 1993, New York City schools chief Joseph Fernandez agreed to revision of the "Children of the Rainbow" curriculum. In March 1993, he was dismissed from his position; see "Yearbook" *Advocate* (25 January 1994) 36.

97. A strategy of normalizing homosexual lives is only occasionally articulated. A Lutheran Bishop, reflecting on Denmark's 1989 law allowing same-sex registered partnerships, saw that goal as having been advanced: "There was a tendency of demonstrating every-where and every time. But, to the contrary since then, there is no sensation. They are quite normal." L. Ingrassia, "A Marriage Made in Denmark" *The [Toronto] Globe and Mail* (9 June 1994) 9. A conservative defence of same-sex benefits attributed "the more flamboyant aspects of the gay lifestyle" to social marginality, adding: "If you want peo-ple to join the mainstream, you have to let them in first." A. Coyne, "Squawk About Same-Sex Benefits and You Can't Squawk About Quotas" *The [Toronto] Globe and Mail* (13 June 1994) 16. Some lesbian and gay activists object to "assimilationist" strategies.

98. The actual benefits are frequently minor. In *Mossop* the issue was one day's pay. In both *Knodel* and *Egan* the Crown proved that the couple were financially better off to avoid recognition of the relationship because of eligibility rules for social assistance. In both cases the court recognized that the claim was for the recognition of rights, not an actual financial benefit.

99. A committee reporting to the Québec Human Rights Commission recommended the repeal of Article 137, which contains the exemption: Hays, *supra*, note 77.

100. S.O. 1986, c. 64, 2. 18(1) added "sexual orientation." The 1986 amendments left in place section 10(1), which defined "spouse" as it had since S.O. 1981, c. 53.
101. *Human Rights Code*, S.M. 1987–88, c. 45, s. 9(2) includes "sexual orientation." S. 9(5) allows for regulations on employee benefit plans.
102. *An Act to Amend the Human Rights Act*, S.N.S. 1991, c. 12. The new section 5(1) included "sexual orientation." The definition of "marital status" was in new section 3(1). The earlier statutes were not aiming to curtail same-sex spousal benefits, for that issue had not emerged on the public policy agenda.
103. S. Magee, "Campbell's Rights Act Under Fire" *Vancouver Courier* (13 December 1992) 4, reported Campbell's views as follows: "Many same-sex couples enjoy these benefits already, and where there are disputes they will continue to be resolved on a case by case basis in the courts or in front of human rights tribunals," she said. "But we've drawn the line at the definition of marriage — something very consistent with Canadian public opinion and what happens in other jurisdictions." Campbell described the amendments as a "compromise" which had been necessary to prevent a split in the caucus: November 1992, meeting with representatives of the Lesbian and Gay Immigration Task Force in Vancouver.
104. S. Bindman, "Liberals Pledge to Overhaul Law on Youth Crime" *Vancouver Sun* (23 December 1993) 4.
105. M. Mittelstaedt, "Gay-couple Package Would Affect 56 Laws" *The [Toronto] Globe and Mail* (20 May 1994) 8; M. Mittelstedt, "Same-sex Bill Called Model of Tolerance" *The [Toronto] Globe and Mail* (2 June 1994) 4.
106. R. Mackie, "Benefits for Gays Urged in Quebec" *The [Toronto] Globe and Mail* (2 June 1994) 5.
107. "Ontario Bill on Gay Rights Defeated" *The [Toronto] Globe and Mail* (10 June 1994) 1.
108. 74 N.Y. 2d 201 (1989), 543 N.E. 2d 49 (1989) (Ct. App.). The United Kingdom in 1993 began recognizing same-sex survivor rights to public housing; "Yes, We Have a Home Today" *Angles* (July 1993) 6.
109. 478 N.W. 2d 790 (Minn. Ct. App. 1991); see M. Cameli, "Extending Family Benefits to Gay Men and Lesbian Women" [1992] 68 *Chicago–Kent Law Review* 447.
110. *Vogel v. Manitoba* (1992), 90 D.L.R. (4th) 84; *Canada v. Mossop, supra* note 52.
111. *Supra* note 17.
112. *Veysey v. Commissioner of Correctional Services* (1989), 44 C.R.R. 364 (F.C.T.D.); 47 C.R.R. 394 (F.C.A.). The trial ruling was substantive, but the Appeal Court confined the reasoning to an administrative law point.
113. *Knodel v. British Columbia, supra* note 33. The earlier Ontario decision was *Andrews v. Ontario* (1988), 49 D.L.R. (4th) 594 (High Court of Justice).
114. The case of *Morrissey and Coll v. Canada* was filed in Federal Court in January 1992. In September 1992, immigration gave Bridget Coll permanent residence status as an independent applicant.
115. See M. Davidson, "Processing of Same Sex and Common Law Cases" (Hull: Department of Immigration, ORDO150) (3 June 1994). This fax instructs immigration officials in embassies and consulates to handle "family class" applications involving same-sex or common law spouses as independent applications, and indicates that such cases may be appropriate cases for humanitarian and compassionate consideration, allowing the waiver of normal selection criteria.
116. *Leshner v. Ontario* (1992), 16 C.H.R.R. D/184 (Ontario Board of Inquiry).
117. The major reported case is *Anderson v. Louma* (1986), 50 R.F.L. (2d) 127 (B.C.S.C.). A claim for maintenance was refused on the basis that maintenance was dependent upon statute and was limited, by statute, to heterosexual couples. In the judgment, constructive trust principles were applied to divide marital assets in the same manner as the courts have done with unmarried heterosexual couples. Two recent decisions

dividing the marital property of same-sex couples are *Brunet* v. *Davis* (Ontario Court, General Division) [unpublished] (April 1992), described in "Judge Finds Constructive Trust to Compensate Gay Partner" *The Lawyers Weekly* (12 June 1992) 6, and *Forrest* v. *Price* (B.C.S.C.) (3 November 1992) (Boyd J.). In a more recent case, Ontario has conceded that its *Family Law Act* discriminates against same-sex couples by only recognizing heterosexual "common-law" couples and is, for that reason, in breach of the *Charter*. The case involves marital property and maintenance: E. Brown, "Ontario Admits Discrimination" *Xtra* (14 May 1993) 11.

118. Decision of 9 November 1992, on the claim of Shirley Petten in relation to the death of Beverly Holmwood, by Mr. N. Gallagher, Director, Disability Awards, Workers' Compensation Board. Mr. Gallagher ruled that section 17 of the British Columbia *Workers' Compensation Act*, R.S.B.C. 1979, c. 437, which refer to married or common law spouses, must be taken to include same-sex spouses.

119. M. Philp, "Gay Employee Wins Family Leaves" *The [Toronto] Globe and Mail* (2 October 1993) 3. The federal government decided against an appeal: M. Philp, "Ottawa Acquiesces on Gay Spousal Leave" *The [Toronto] Globe and Mail* (15 April 1994) A1.

120. The tribunal decision was reversed by the Ontario Divisional Court in *Clinton* v. *Ontario Blue Cross* (3 May 1994) (Carruthers, Dunnet, Adams JJ.), but exclusively on the grounds that constitutional notice had not been given to argue section 15 of the *Charter of Rights and Freedoms*.

121. E. Brown, "These Two Women Are Spouses" *Xtra* (7 January 1994) 1. The decision is being appealed.

122. "Another Victory for Same-sex Spouses" *Goinfo* (May 1994) 1.

123. M. Battista, "Lesbian Files for Alimony" *Xtra* (1 April 1994) 17.

124. The single exception in the Ontario extension was the pension scheme in issue in the *Leshner* case. The delay with the pension scheme resulted from problems with federal tax law. Ontario had decided to lobby the federal government to change the *Income Tax Act* before it extended spousal pension benefits: D. Boyce, "Gay Partners Approach Equality in Ontario" *Advocate* (3 November 1992) 33; E. Brown, "The Leshner Decision Is a Significant But Tiny Victory, Lawyer Says" *Xtra* (18 September 1992) 9. J. Pegis, "NB Extends Same-sex Spousal Benefits" *Xtra* (14 May 1993) 13. The benefits involved include health and dental plans and life insurance but not pensions or long-term disability.

125. "Healthy Teeth" *Xtra* (29 October 1993) 17.

126. "Air Canada's Yes" *Xtra* (29 April 1994) 13.

127. M. Bigg-Clark, "More Firms Offer Same-sex Benefits" *The [Toronto] Globe and Mail*, *Report on Business* (7 June 1994) B1. See also T. Stewart, "Gay in Corporate America" *Fortune Magazine* (16 December 1991) 42 at 50; Bureau of National Affairs, "Recognizing Non-traditional Families," BNA Special Report #38, Special Report Series on Work and Family, February 1991, 32 pp; J. Gallagher, "Benefits for the Fringe" *Advocate* (25 January 1994) 56.

128. A special kit on same-sex benefits for lesbian and gay employees and their families is available from the Canadian Union of Public Employees, Equal Opportunities Department, 21 Florence Street, Ottawa, K2P 0W6. The British Columbia Federation of Labour, 4279 Canada Way, Burnaby, B.C., V5G 1H1, publishes an information kit, "Ending Workplace Discrimination Against Lesbians and Gay Men." CUPE gave backing to Karen Andrews in her case for medicare benefits. The Hospital Employees Union of British Columbia took the *Knodel* case on behalf of one of its members. Brian Mossop's grievance over bereavement leave was made with the "approval and support" of his union according to the judgement of L'Heureux-Dubé in *Mossop, supra* note 52. The Canadian Labour Congress convention in May 1994 approved a program to fight homophobia, to encourage lesbian and gay participation in unions, and

to negotiate same-sex benefits: M. Battista, "Planes, Trains and Automobiles: The Labour Movement Is Taking Up the Same-sex Benefits Battle" *Xtra* (10 June 1994) 15.

129. There was evidence in both *Knodel* and *Egan* that the consequences were actuarially insignificant. See also M. Gibb-Clark, "Gay-couples Ruling Won't Break the Bank" *The [Toronto] Globe and Mail, Report on Business* (7 September 1992) B4; "No Problems Seen in Extending Benefits" *Vancouver Sun* (3 September 1992) 7; M. Gibb-Clark, "More Firms Offer Same-sex Benefits" *The [Toronto] Globe and Mail* (7 June 1994) B1.

130. Robertson adopted the trial judge's statement on the centrality of reproduction, which referred to heterosexual units which have "traditionally been treated as the basic unit of society upon which society depends for its continued existence."

131. *Egan v. Canada, supra* note 17 at 390.

132. Wilson J., in *Andrews v. Law Society of British Columbia, supra* note 35.

133. The classic example in Canada was the decision of the Supreme Court of Canada in *Bliss v. A.G. Canada* [1979] 1 S.C.R. 183, stating that discrimination on the basis of pregnancy was not discrimination on the basis of sex. That decision was reversed in *Brooks v. Canada Safeway* [1989] 1 S.C.R. 1219.

134. Attorney General Marion Boyd, in the debates in the Ontario Legislature in June 1994, invoked the beloved Canadian novel, *Anne of Green Gables*, in which the orphan Anne was raised by a brother and sister, certainly a "non-traditional family"; R. Sheppard, "Storybook Anne and Same-sex Benefits" *The [Toronto] Globe and Mail* (8 June 1994) 25.

135. *Andrews v. Ontario* (1988), 49 D.L.R. (4th) 584 (High Court of Justice).

136. Anna Carrott and Andrea Underwood began a court case in February 1992, seeking the right for the Canadian partner, Underwood, to sponsor the non-Canadian partner, Carrott. They are raising two children from Anna Carrott's previous marriage.

137. *Egan v. Canada, supra* note 17.

138. Letter of J.G. Boissoneault, Departmental Assistant–Immigration, Office of the Minister of Employment and Immigration (23 July 1992) to the author. The immigration policy reflected in the letter has changed; see note 115, *supra*.

139. Judgment dated 19 May 1993.

140. A summary of the findings of 30 studies of the children of lesbian and gay parents was published in the October 1992 issue of the journal *Child Development*. It concluded that the studies were nearly unanimous in their findings that the children had developed normally.

141. Section 4(1) of the Danish law provides: "The provisions of the Danish Adoption Act regarding spouses shall not apply to registered partners." This is taken from an "unofficial translation" supplied by the Royal Danish Embassy, Ottawa. The Norwegian law has a similar provision. The text of the Swedish law was not available at the time of writing. In Denmark at least, adoption is restricted to married couples.

142. "Mom Loses Bid to Get Son Back from Gay Couple" *Bangkok Post* (13 April 1994) 9, notes that six states, including Washington State, allow adoptions by same-sex couples.

143. "Court Grants Parental Rights to Mother and Lesbian Lover" *The New York Times* (12 September 1993) 21; "Homosexuality Does Not Make Parent Unfit, Court Rules" *The New York Times* (22 June 1994) 8.

144. A major issue in the Netherlands has been equal access of lesbians to artificial insemination services provided as part of the national health system. Section 13(5) of the United Kingdom's 1990 *Human Fertilization and Embryology Act* provides that a woman shall not be provided with services "unless account has been taken of the welfare of any child who may be born as a result of the treatment (including the need of that child for a father) ...," see D. Cooper & D. Herman, "Getting 'the Family Right': Legislating Heterosexuality in Britain, 1986–1991" (1991) 10 *Canadian Journal of Family Law* 41.

145. R. Banner, "Lesbians Refused AI" *Angles* (July 1993) 1.
146. See A. Priest, "Next Best Thing" *Vancouver Sun* (27 October 1990) C1; "'Gay' Church Holds Rite for Blessing Relationships" *Vancouver Sun* (18 February 1992) 6. J. Kennedy, "Gays Feel Same-sex Unions Merit Equality With Heterosexual Ties" *Vancouver Sun* (4 June 1992) 4, indicated that Ottawa's First United Church offers a "blessing and commitment" ceremony for same-sex couples. The Metropolitan Community Church gave evidence in *Layland v. Ontario* that the denomination had performed 10 000 same-sex ceremonies of "holy union."
147. In the *Layland* case the Attorney General of Canada submitted the affidavit of Dr. Charles Hobart, which noted homosexual marriages in ancient China and during the last period of the Roman Empire. On China see B. Hinsch, *Passions of the Cut Sleeve* (Berkeley: University of California Press, 1990). A more recent study by the Yale University historian John Boswell, *Same-Sex Unions in Premodern Europe* (New York: Villard Books, 1994) uncovers examples of same-sex marriage in Christian Europe.
148. A presentation of opposing arguments can be found in companion articles by two leading lesbian and gay activists and commentators: Thomas Stoddard, "Why Gay People Should Seek the Right to Marry" and Paula Ettelbrick, "Since When Is Marriage a Path to Liberation?" in S. Sherman (Ed.), *Lesbian and Gay Marriage* (Philadelphia: Temple University Press, 1992) at pp. 13 and 20.
149. An excellent discussion of many of the issues can be found in N. Duclos, "Some Complicating Thoughts on Same-Sex Marriage" (1991) 1 *Law and Sexuality* 31.
150. "Gay Couples Apply for Marriage Licenses" *San Francisco Sentinel* (lesbian, gay newspaper) (12 December 1991) 9.
151. "German Gay Couples Demand Marriage Licenses" *Xtra Supplement* (November 1992) 4. One of the couples was Hella von Sinnen, a very popular television personality, and her partner Cornelia Scheel, daughter of former West German President Walter Scheel.
152. *Layland v. Ontario, supra* note 39.
153. *Egan v. Canada, supra* note 17 at 389.
154. *Baehr v. Lewin* (Supreme Court of the State of Hawaii) (5 May 1993) [unpublished]. A domestic partnership law is being discussed and a commission to investigate the issue may be established by legislation: J. Gallagher, "The Wedding Is Off" *Advocate* (17 May 1994) 24.
155. "Around the World: Russia" *Advocate* (17 May 1994) 22.
156. Ontario Law Reform Commission, *Report on the Rights and Responsibilities of Cohabitants under the Family Law Act* (1993) 74 pp.
157. F. Williams, "Spain Set to Recognize Gay Partnerships" *Gay Times* (September 1994) 36.
158. Two recent marriage cases were actually about immigration rights. A case went to the highest court in Switzerland seeking immigration rights via an entitlement to legal marriage. The court rejected the argument, while suggesting that the status of the non-citizen could be handled on humanitarian grounds. The *Layland* case involved a Canadian and non-Canadian who hoped that access to legal marriage would resolve the non-Canadian's immigration status. While the case received considerable publicity in Canada, the immigration aspect was not noted.
159. See A. Stanley, "'Gay' Fades as Militants Pick 'Queer'" *The New York Times* (3 April 1991) 9.
160. "ABA Grants Affiliation to National Lesbian and Gay Law Association" *NLGLA News* (11 August 1992) 1.
161. There is a lesbian and gay caucus within the Canadian Association of Journalists and a National Lesbian and Gay Journalists Association in the United States: P. Hannan, "Journalists Are Slowly Coming Out" *Xtra* (10 December 1993) 20.
162. P. Byron, "Meet Mixner the fixer" *Out Magazine* (lesbian, gay, bisexual magazine published in the United States) (Fall 1992) 51 at 52.

163. J. Lawrence, "Payoffs or Principles?" *Bangkok Post* (9 February 1993) 4.

164. Roberta Achtenberg, a lesbian, was nominated and confirmed as Assistant Secretary of Housing and Urban Development: C. Krauss, "Senators Attack Housing Nominee" *New York Times* (21 May 1993) 13. That appointment was followed, without controversy, by appointments of a federal patent commissioner and a federal judge: R. Gordon, "The Point Is I Won, Gay Mandarin Says" *Vancouver Sun* (18 June 1994) B12.

165. "MP's Sexuality, Private Issue, NDP says" *The [Toronto] Globe and Mail* (26 February 1988) 8; "Robinson's Sex Life Called his Own Affair by Most MPs" *Vancouver Sun* (26 February 1988) 6.

166. Two recent books arguing that separate cultures exist are F. Browing, *The Culture of Desire* (New York: Crown, 1993), and G. Herdt, *Gay Culture in America* (Boston: Beacon Press, 1992). Neither volume deals with the question whether lesbian and gay cultural differences will endure.

167. J. Boswell, in *Homosexuality in the Western Christian Tradition* (Chicago: University of Chicago Press, 1980), argues that considerable acceptance existed in Western Europe, but the acceptance was reversed in the 13th century, when Jews, Muslims, heretics, and homosexuals were targeted. Germany had a significant homosexual rights movement in the inter-war period, indicating a climate of tolerance which was reversed under Hitler, when homosexuals were sent to the death camps.

168. Reuters, "Court Backs Gays in Landmark Ruling" *Bangkok Post* (31 March 1994) 9.

169. J. Kirchhoff, "A Sad Chapter in 'Homophobia'" *The [Toronto] Globe and Mail* (14 July 1990) C2; D. Fagan, "Gays Win a Round" *The [Toronto] Globe and Mail* (23 March 1987) 1; S. Lyall, "At Canada Border: Literature at Risk?" *The New York Times* (13 December 1993) 6; R. Hough, "Degrading Customs" *The [Toronto] Globe and Mail* (12 February 1994) D-1.

170. A. Wilkinson, "The Never-ending Book Trial" *The [Toronto] Globe and Mail* (17 December 1993) 23.

171. [1979] 2 S.C.R. 435.

172. "Democracy Triumphs in Colorado" (editorial) *The New York Times* (14 October 1994) 18; R. Bernstein, "When One Person's Civil Rights Are Another's Moral Outrage" *The New York Times* (16 October 1994) E6.

173. S. Campbell, "Television Stations Reject Spousal-rights Commercials" *Xtra* (24 December 1993) 14.

174. See R.K. Herrell, "The Symbolic Strategies of Chicago's Gay and Lesbian Pride Day Parade" in G. Herdt, *Gay Culture in America* (Boston: Beacon Press, 1992) 225. A guest columnist wrote that she was ashamed of the "freak show" presented in the parades: C. Chellew, "The Naked Truth" *Advocate* (6 September 1994) 5.

175. A study by the United States Centers for Disease Control and Prevention reported homosexual transmission at 46.6% in the United States in 1993, still the largest single category in that country: "AIDS Infection of Heterosexuals Picking Up Speed" *The [Toronto] Globe and Mail* (11 March 1994) 8. Transmission in Africa and India, the major crisis areas internationally, is primarily through heterosexual intercourse.

176. E. Schmitt, "Father–son Drama Over the Gay Ban" *The New York Times* (13 May 1993) 9; F. Clines, "Surprised by the Limelight, a Colonel's Gay Son Shines" *The New York Times* (17 May 1993) 1.

177. In the last decade, numerous organizations have changed their names to include a reference to bisexuals as well as lesbians and gay men. The 1993 march on Washington was in the name of lesbian, gay, bisexual, and transgendered people, the last term seen as inclusive of transvestites and transexuals. Consensual sadomasochism, often referred to as the "leather" scene, is interesting in including homosexuals and heterosexuals. The National Leather Association in the United States describes itself as a "pansexual organization": see advertisement, *The Leather Journal* (October 1993) 8.

178. Stockwell Day, Minister of Labour and Government House Leader in Alberta, was reported as telling local media after the equality decision in the *Vriend v. King's College* case, that "the decision would give licence to pedophilia." See A. Edelson, "Queen's Bench Corners Alberta Tories" *Xtra* (29 April 1994) 17.

179. "Italian Neo-fascist Fini Disputes Rights for Gays" *The [Toronto] Globe and Mail* (1 June 1994) 6.

180. *R v. Brown* (1993), 2 All. E.R. 75. See L. Bibbings & P. Alldridge, "Sexual Expression, Body Alteration, and the Defence of Consent" (1993) 20 *Journal of Law and Society* 356; G. Rogerson, "Consent no defence for sm" *Xtra Supplement* (May 1993) 6.

181. *B. v. France* (1992), 16 E.H.R.R. 1, departing from much of the spirit of *Cossey v. U.K.* (1990), 13 E.H.R.R. 622.

182. The Association for Social Knowledge was formed in Vancouver in 1964. The writer was the second president of the organization.

183. In 1993, five openly lesbian or gay candidates ran for federal or provincial office. At the end of 1993, there were openly gay men on city councils in Vancouver, Edmonton, Winnipeg, Toronto, Kanata, and Montréal. In September 1994, Réal Ménard, Bloc Québécois member of Parliament, stated that he was homosexual, as part of his response to anti-homosexual statements made by Liberal member Roseanne Skoke: P. Hannan, "Second MP Comes Out" *Xtra* (14 October 1994) 13.

NINE

Justice between Cultures: Autonomy and the Protection of Cultural Affiliation

DENISE G. RÉAUME

The reconciliation of the conflicting needs and interests of different racial, ethnic, and cultural groups has become one of the most urgent concerns of our time. The co-existence of such groups has, of course, been a fact for thousands of years, but a phenomenon of modern times — the ease with which people and information can be moved about the globe — has heightened the urgency of designing principles for the conduct of intergroup relations. The greater the contact between groups, the greater the potential for conflict; hence the greater the need for principles to regulate that conflict.

Two extreme responses to the problem of intergroup relations can be identified. The first we might call the *philosopher's model*. It strives to work out a set of principles for the governance of human interaction which is perfectly universal. Such a proposal would eliminate the problem by eliminating distinguishable groups themselves.

Source: Denise G. Réaume, "Justice Between Cultures: Autonomy and the Protection of Cultural Affiliation," *UBC Law Review* 29, no. 1 (1995): 117–41. © Denise G. Réaume, 1995.

Accepting this ideal entails that a single set of practices or rules should apply to all and that we should each be persuaded to give up any cultural practices that do not conform. It would therefore be justifiable to respond to groups who refuse to conform with coercion, just as it would be with an individual who violates a justified rule. Institutionally, this approach leads to an argument for world government.

The second model is that of the *extreme nationalist*. It seeks to eliminate the problem of conflict between groups by eliminating contact between groups. Treating cultural and ethnic difference as a given, it recommends that each group, in isolation from the others, be free to conduct its affairs however it wishes. The nation-state ideal may be regarded as the closest institutional approximation to this model ever proposed.

The philosopher's model leaves no room for attributing value to particular cultures. Culture is collapsed into universal morality and mores, making culture itself a redundant concept. By contrast, the nationalist model treats culture and ethnicity as naturally and unquestionably good. Justice between cultures becomes a simple matter of leaving one another alone. I want to explore the middle ground between these two positions. I assume that the nation-state model is not feasible, if it ever was. Cultural heterogeneity is overwhelmingly the norm in modern states. In this context, we face the question of the appropriate reach of universal rules applicable to all groups and the amount of room available for the free play of cultural difference. This requires us to provide a normative account of what the nationalist treats as natural: cultural affiliation. In trying to do this, I will argue in favour of some scope for the autonomy of cultural groups. It follows that the philosopher's model, considered as a comprehensive ideal, is an unattractive one. However, the group autonomy for which I shall argue is not unlimited either *vis-à-vis* other groups or a group's own members.

I want to consider these questions as they arise in two related contexts. The first assumes solidarity within each of the groups: the Big-Enders of Lilliput uniformly break their eggs at the big end, and the Small-Enders uniformly break theirs at the small end. To what extent is each entitled to the other's non-interference in their practices? From here, we move on to the situation in which intra-group solidarity is missing; controversy within one group about what practices should be followed has led to a fracturing of the group. Dissident Big-Enders, asserting that the appropriate end for breaking should be left to the conscience of the individual, appeal outside their own group for help in implementing or enforcing that principle. We must distinguish two such cases: first, that in which the dissidents seek to transform (some of) their own group's practices; and second, that in which the dissidents seek outside aid in order to relinquish their membership in their own group.

These reflections about the appropriate principles of justice between cultures implicate several classic questions in political theory. Most centrally, they recall the debate between liberals and communitarians about the ideal of political neutrality, which is itself connected to the debate about the relative priority of the right and the good. Arguably, as well, a particular view about equality is either implicit in, or follows from, the answers one provides. I do not propose to explore all these connections here. Instead, I will focus on another classic aspect of the debate — the value of autonomy — and argue that we can derive from a sufficiently rich understanding of autonomy, and the conditions that make it possible, principles to regulate relations between cultural communities as well as between individuals. I will argue that concern for personal autonomy dictates that we pay attention to the role of cultural forms — which are inherently social — in people's lives. Doing so requires us to develop a conception of group autonomy with respect to culture. At the same time, the cases of internal disagreement outlined above do raise questions concerning the degree of compatibility of some social processes of cultural development with personal autonomy, and require establishing some priority between cultural and personal autonomy when they conflict.

I begin by bracketing two of the ways one might go about arguing for the normative significance of a community's particular cultural practices. The first has an aesthetic flavour to it. Diversity is a good in itself simply because it is a manifestation of the scope of human creativity. We should therefore encourage and protect it.[1] This may in fact be true, but I want to bracket it because it gives the participants in a particular form of human creativity no special claim — that is, no claim special to them — for the protection of their culture. Instead, it argues that we all have an interest and the same interest in the protection of each culture. This kind of idea may well ground some protections for culture, but it is unlikely to go far enough.

The second type of account would seek to make culture a constitutive part of the self, so that a failure to protect culture is tantamount to the most serious kind of violation of the person imaginable. In recent argument, this kind of account is traceable to Michael Sandel[2] and has achieved some popularity with communitarian writers. Without arguing the case here, let me just say that I find this conception of the self implausible as well as politically abhorrent. Cultural identity is important, but it should not be elevated to the level of metaphysics or epistemology.[3] Once more, I want to explore the territory between two extremes. Is there an account of the importance of culture that is capable of grounding particular claims by one group against others but understands culture as less than a totally seamless web leaving no room for individual deviation?

"Culture" is one of the most indeterminate concepts in the political and philosophical lexicon.[4] The same is true of any particular version, such as "Canadian culture" or "Aboriginal culture" (even "Haida culture"). It seems likely that both in the generic and in the particular, the concept of culture is essentially contestable and therefore incapable of definition. Nevertheless, it is important that I provide at least a general sense of how I employ the term. By culture I mean the entire web of social practices, rules, beliefs, and ways of doing things that constitute and structure a group's understanding of itself as a group. This explication makes plain, I hope, the complexity and richness of the phenomenon it describes. Culture is an essentially fluid and organic phenomenon, the product of the conscious and unconscious activities of many people on many levels. It admits of degrees of scope, so that we can speak of the (close to) comprehensive culture of a group bound by ethnic heritage, language, religion, tradition, and a shared history from time immemorial, but we can also speak of corporate culture or sports culture. In what follows, when I speak of two different cultures trying to co-exist, I have in mind two groups that can be placed near the comprehensive end of the spectrum, each group bound together by shared history and traditions, by religion and perhaps by language.

My object is to begin to establish a framework for thinking about justice between cultures. I imagine two cultures, that is, two sets of social forms which comprehensively structure the significance of the everyday behaviour, goals, and projects of their members, which are stable and longstanding, and which have developed each in their own way in relative isolation from the other. Questions of justice arise when two or more such groups are brought together in a single political framework (whether that be international or domestic). The outcome of what was once an apparently natural process of internal development that might have been as invisible as the air we breathe now must be considered only one option amongst others requiring some justification. This is certainly so if others are to be persuaded to adopt a particular set of practices, perhaps even to justify retaining them in the face of challenge from the other culture. My argument proceeds through three stages. First, I outline the connection between culture and autonomy, that is, the ability to pursue a conception of the good. I argue that this account must incorporate the significance of particular cultures to their participants, not just culture considered generically. Next, I argue that the presence of value indeterminacy both helps account for the existence of cultural diversity and gives us a moral framework within which a degree of cultural autonomy accorded to groups makes sense. Finally, I consider the implications of this framework for the position of dissenters within a particular community.

AUTONOMY AND CULTURE

THE IMPORTANCE OF CULTURE TO INDIVIDUAL AUTONOMY

Although it is often thought that the affirmation of the value of autonomy results from and reinforces a highly individualistic moral and political theory, recent liberal accounts, such as those of Raz and Kymlicka,[5] have given a more nuanced account of personal autonomy which disputes this characterization. In particular, these accounts pay special attention to the social preconditions of autonomy. The ideal of personal autonomy has a long history, at least in Western thought. Raz states it simply as the idea that people should make their own lives;[6] Kymlicka, drawing on Rawls and Dworkin, says that people have an essential interest in being able to devise and revise their own conception of the good.[7]

However, human beings do not live, grow, dream, imagine, or plan in isolation from one another. This much is obvious. But it is not merely the case that it is convenient or useful or more fun to have others around to share one's dreams and plans. Rather, the very possibility of planning a life — the significance or meaning one's plans have — is predicated upon human interaction. Raz recognizes this in arguing that our most significant decisions — the ones that allow us to claim authorship of our lives — typically require *social* institutions of a variety of sorts.[8] The meaning and therefore value of "being a lawyer" or "being a monk," for example, is conditioned by the existence of suitable "social forms," that is, the "shared beliefs, folklore, high culture, collectively shared metaphors and imagination, and so on" which characterize a society.[9] Add religion (which might already be considered part of shared beliefs) and language, and the set of these social forms that characterizes a particular society or subset thereof is what I mean by culture.

In another attempt to render liberal theory less atomistic, Kymlicka argues, "Different ways of life are not simply different patterns of physical movements. The physical movements only have meaning to us because they are identified as having significance by our *culture*, because they fit into some pattern of activities which is culturally recognized as a way of leading one's life" (emphasis in original).[10]

From this, he concludes that what he calls the "cultural structure" of a community deserves protection.

Both of these accounts acknowledge that meaning is socially, not individually, created, so that an individual must rely, to some extent, on socially given meaning in choosing a life plan. The individual's ability to choose a path for herself is dependent upon the options made available, and the meaning assigned those options, by her culture. One cannot be a married philanthropist if one's culture does not formally sanction semi-permanent domestic unions or socially organize charitable giving. Nor can one be a medicine man in a society that does not recognize and support the sacred and ceremonial uses of certain plants, or a prophet in a society in which God is conceived of as too aloof from human affairs to speak to human beings through a human intermediary.

I want to take up and develop this line of argument in order to help ground an argument for affording some protection to minority cultural practices within a multicultural environment. I will argue that neither Raz nor Kymlicka accounts fully for the value of particular cultures such as to ground protection for one community's practices against another. In particular, both demonstrate that autonomous decision-making must rely upon some socially rooted structures and practices but do not provide a complete defence for the protection of any particular set of structures and practices. Without the latter, minority cultural communities remain vulnerable to assimilationist measures. At the same time (and I will come back to this later in this chapter), I do not want to erase the "personal" from the ideal of personal autonomy by making autonomy hinge entirely on participation in phenomena that are exclusively under communal control.

FROM THE GENERIC TO THE PARTICULAR: GROUNDING PROTECTION FOR PARTICULAR CULTURES

In adopting the view that social forms give meaning to behaviour, Raz constructs an argument that makes an important contribution to our understanding of social forms considered generically, that is, abstracting from the differences that characterize the social forms of different communities. However, in *The Morality of Freedom*, he is not primarily concerned with conflicts between communities holding to different social forms, so he says very little about the importance of the social forms of one's own community in making autonomy possible. In other words, his argument shows that *some* social forms are necessary in order for personal autonomy to be possible but not necessarily the *particular* social forms that characterize one's own community. The argument largely assumes cultural homogeneity. More recently, Raz has addressed the multicultural context, reiterating the argument that because life choices depend upon culture, "it is in the interest of every person to be fully integrated in a cultural group."[11] But again, this only goes so far as to establish that it is important for a person to belong to some culture, not that her particular culture should be protected.

More importantly, one important aspect of Raz's analysis of social forms would appear to limit the protection that can legitimately be claimed by minority cultures. For Raz, one of the key implications following from the social preconditions of personal autonomy is that individuals do not have a right to the provision of any particular social forms.[12] Although governments have some obligation to (help) create the conditions of autonomy, this does not extend to the obligation to create any particular set of conditions. I, as an individual, have no right to the formal recognition of my domestic relationship if the society in which I live does not acknowledge the social form that marriage is. It would seem to follow that members of a minority culture within a larger culture that does not recognize marriage also have no right to support for this social form. If a minority cultural community is to be treated merely as a collection of individuals, it is hard to see how it can have any more claim against the majority to support for its social forms than can a lone individual. If the majority can validly argue that its own practices provide adequate conditions for an autonomous life, members of the minority cannot claim that their autonomy is infringed by social policies designed to assimilate them into the majority culture.

This bleak conclusion may, however, be tempered by Raz's invocation of two principles that limit state power to regulate social forms. These principles go some way to establishing the importance of the protection of particular cultural practices rather than just culture in the abstract. Some minority cultural practices may warrant protection within Raz's framework because he supports the harm principle: that coercion not be used against individuals except to prevent harm.[13] Thus, a state politically controlled by members of one cultural community could not use coercion to enforce its social forms against a minority if the minority's practices do no harm. Similarly, some protection for particular minority practices would stem from Raz's argument that it would be an infringement of autonomy to eliminate a life option for someone who was already deeply committed to it because it would be harder for such a person to substitute another life plan for the one denied.[14]

Raz explicitly uses both of these sorts of arguments in the service of minority cultures in "Multiculturalism: A Liberal Perspective." He argues that one aspect of many people's life plan to which they are deeply committed involves intergenerational relationships grounded in the kind of understanding that requires a common culture. Thus, parents want "to understand their children, to share their world."[15] For this reason, "a policy that forcibly detaches children from the culture of their parents"[16] is wrong. Here, the argument against disturbing existing commitments and that against the use of coercion come together. Raz also argues that because cultural membership contributes to a person's sense of identity, "[s]lighting my culture, holding it up for ridicule, denying its value, and so on, hurts me and offends my dignity."[17] All these arguments purport to justify some form of protection for the particular culture a person happens to be committed to, the culture that happens to constitute her identity. However, the amount of protection they justify is unclear. There are many ways that a majority culture can affect the minority's ability to live according to different social forms without using coercion to create a gulf between parents and their children. Much more subtle and gradual pressures toward assimilation may have the effect of eliminating a minority culture without running afoul of these protective principles. Further, these principles provide little support for positive state action in support of a minority's maintenance of its practices. Thus, these arguments provide only an imperfect defence of particular cultures. They also sit uneasily with that aspect of Raz's political theory that denies the viability of individual claims of right in the context of the pursuit of particular social forms.

The argument against an individual right to the existence or protection of particular social forms is compelling, but it does not tell against the possibility of there being a group right. Elsewhere,[18] I have agreed with Raz that there are no individual rights in this context but argued that he puts too much emphasis on the fact that social forms are publicly produced, that is, they require the participation of many in their production. More important, in my view, is that their value lies precisely in their being shared with others, in the participation with others that produces them. These are not individualizable goods and therefore cannot be claimed as of right by individuals. But this does not preclude an argument that there may be a group right to such goods.[19] My argument here against an individual right is a conceptual one. Without knowing anything about the importance of the good in issue or the impact on others of imposing duties on them to provide it, we can say that an individual right is not possible. This conceptual barrier does not apply to a claim of group right. Such a claim can only be made if there is a group, that is, a number of people participating in the production and maintenance of a certain social form sufficient to sustain it at some minimal level. If a group exists, there is no conceptual argument against it making a claim of right for the protection of its social forms as against the members of another group. The good in issue is enjoyable by the group as a whole.

As long as we think exclusively in individual terms, there is some doubt whether Raz's analysis of the importance of social forms is capable of grounding protection for minority cultural communities. This difficulty might be resolved by contemplating the possibility of a minority holding a group right as against the majority group. Whether the minority can have such a right depends on whether the interest of the minority group in maintaining its social forms justifies the imposition of duties on others. If such an argument can be made, it will yield a right to protection for particular cultures as long as there exist groups with different social forms. I will return to the question of grounding this group interest below. First, I want to turn to Kymlicka's defence of minority rights to show why it fails.

Kymlicka very clearly situates his argument in the context of a multicultural society and recognizes the need to address the degree of protection to be offered membership in a particular culture: "[p]eople may require a cultural structure to make sense of their lives, but it doesn't follow that we ought to be concerned about their own culture."[20] He argues that membership in a particular cultural community is a good because "[p]eople *are* bound, in an important way, to their own cultural community. We can't just transplant people from one culture to another, even if we provide the opportunity to learn the other language and culture. Someone's upbringing isn't something that can just be erased; it is, and will remain, a constitutive part of who that person is. Cultural membership affects our very sense of personal identity and capacity" (emphasis in original).[21] However, he rejects the idea that personal identity may be bound up with existing community practices. He distinguishes between two senses of "culture": the character of a historical community, by which he means its particular norms and values and their attendant institutions;[22] and cultural structure itself. It is cultural structure, and not the character of a community, that deserves protection. Because people are bound to a particular cultural structure, because it is constitutive of who they are, membership in *that* cultural structure must be recognized, not merely the need for some cultural structure.

The notion of cultural structure is elucidated in two quite different ways by Kymlicka. The first analyzes it as "a context of choice," the good of which lies "in its capacity of providing meaningful options for us and aiding our ability to judge for ourselves the value of our life-plans."[23] The second articulation defines it "in terms of the existence of a viable community of individuals with a shared heritage."[24]

I shall try to show that both versions attempt to abstract from the particular practices of a community and that this undercuts the claim that particular cultures should be protected because cultural structure is constitutive of personal identity. But the abstract conception of cultural structure is important to the liberal character of his argument and cannot be readily abandoned. Ultimately, I shall suggest that it is the claim that culture is constitutive of identity that should be jettisoned in favour of a very different basis for the recognition of the value of particular cultures.

Kymlicka's analysis of cultural structure as "a context of choice" itself ambiguously wavers between including particular practices and abstracting from them. When first introduced, culture as a context of choice is described as a range of options from which we choose a way of life.[25] A "range of options" here seems to refer to a set of concrete practices among which we may choose. Later, he argues that the good of a context of choice lies "in its capacity of providing meaningful options for us, and aiding our ability to judge for ourselves the value of our life-plans."[26] We still have here the options themselves, in the sense of the actual concrete practices, but now he has also added the idea that this context of choice aids our ability to judge these options. Still later, context of choice is equated with the "ability to examine the options that [the] cultural structure [makes] meaningful."[27] Note that now the ability to judge the worth of options has become the core of the idea of context of choice rather than the options themselves from which choices are made. In other words, the ability to evaluate dominates the context or the choices offered. But if the idea of protecting membership in a particular cultural community is to make any sense, the actual context, the concrete choices presented by a culture, cannot be made to disappear altogether. A context of *choice* is still, after all, a *context* of choice. This, in fact, is apparent in Kymlicka's own defence of the need to protect membership in particular communities. In arguing that we cannot simply transplant people from one culture to another, he has to make reference to particular concrete practices such as use of a particular language. The "upbringing" that cannot just be erased must be knowledge of, and commitment to, particular concrete practices. If what we are bound to were simply the abstract ability to make choices, this would not justify protection for particular cultures.

Kymlicka's aim is to rescue liberalism from the charge of atomism by acknowledging that individuals cannot manufacture a conception of the good from whole cloth on their own. Certain options are given meaning by the culture in which one finds oneself, and these are the raw materials out of which the individual creates a life for herself. At the same time, Kymlicka wants to defuse arguments like those of fundamentalists of a variety of stripes, religious and secular, who seek to fossilize certain practices as the only true representation of the group's culture, without which they will be plunged into chaos and disintegration if not eternal damnation.[28] This kind of argument is a familiar, conservative rhetorical ploy which seems to be unavoidably part of every debate of any significance. I share Kymlicka's suspicion of these arguments. However, they cannot be legislated out of existence through a conceptual distinction, at least not without compromising the argument for the protection of particular cultures.

Kymlicka's second conceptualization of cultural structure construes it as "the existence of a viable community of individuals with a shared heritage (language, history, etc.)."[29] Although the notion of the existence of a community appears to abstract from concrete practices, if interpreted this way, it will not bear the weight it must in his argument. To see why, let us look at his claim that although a great many of the traditional social practices of the Québécois were significantly altered through the process of the "Quiet Revolution," the *existence* of the Québécois — and therefore their cultural structure — was not threatened.[30] What would jeopardize the existence of Québec culture?

Imagine that after a process of deliberation about their key social practices, the consensus in Québec had been to resist the siren call of modernization and to reassert the traditional role of the Church and the agrarian way of life. Suppose further that English-speaking Canada had been ill disposed toward this decision and had introduced measures designed to thwart it and to force Québec to modernize. Some of the social forms the Québécois had chosen would have been replaced with different ones more in line with the wishes of English-speaking Canadians. Would this be consistent with the continued "existence" of Québec culture? If it is, it is hard to see how anything short of genocide will interfere with the existence of a community. The protection of the existence of the culture must embrace the protection of the concrete practices the community has chosen to adopt, adapt, or reaffirm — hence the continual focus on the protection of the *French* language in Québec, not merely on people's need for some language base as a tool in the pursuit of a conception of the good. The participants in a culture do not think of their culture as merely an abstract decision-making procedure; they experience it as well as the concrete decisions they have made. But it is precisely these concrete choices that Kymlicka wants to exclude from the concept of culture as merely the present "character" of the community.

Kymlicka's mistake is to think that in coming to terms with the importance of one's own culture, we can entirely separate the particular concrete practices of a culture — the actual options it presents to its members — from the abstract ability to judge the worth of options that any genuine context of choice presupposes. In order to dismiss the idea of the character of a community as adequate to inform the concept of culture, he interprets character entirely statically. Character is existing practices and meanings frozen in time. While it is true that fundamentalist rhetoric often appears to be arguing for the freezing of certain practices for all time, in fact there is no such thing as a culture that does not allow for change and development of its practices in some measure. Any set of practices that was frozen would be mere dead ritual. A culture is both a vaguely described set of particular practices and meanings and an equally vague process of change and elaboration of those practices and meanings. Within the processes of change incorporated into cultural practices, there exists some room for individuals to question the worth of the status quo. But while unavoidably present in all cultures, the scope for such questioning will vary widely from culture to culture and may fall far short of the kind of freewheeling examination Kymlicka clearly thinks is desirable. Any account of why and the extent to which particular cultures should be protected from incursions by others must take account of both aspects of culture: the particular practices observed and the internal process of change incorporated into those practices.

In both these versions of "cultural structure" Kymlicka's attempts to abstract from the actual practices of a particular community undermines his defence of minority rights as grounded in the constitutive importance of one's particular culture to personal identity. Without incorporating actual practices, Kymlicka's conception of culture supports only a claim to the protection of *some* context of choice for members of a community, not *their* context of choice. If we incorporate actual practices, whatever they may be, we may have an argument for the protection of particular cultures but only at the expense of liberal ideals, since illiberal cultures must be as much constitutive of the personal identities of their members as liberal cultures are.

Any account of the normative basis for the protection of particular cultures must, at some point, take account of what makes a particular culture particular. To at least some extent, it must provide a foundation for protecting a given culture, whatever its content is. Nothing short of this will provide room for a multiplicity of cultures in a context in which there is competition for scarce resources. This suggests that we focus on the argument that culture is constitutive of personal identity in order to find a way out of the dilemma Kymlicka's account creates.

This claim might be construed in any number of ways. Clearly Kymlicka cannot mean to imply either that it is somehow impossible for an individual to stand outside of his culture in order to evaluate it or that it is wrong for him to try.[31] Either of these positions would be inconsistent with Kymlicka's professed liberalism. We might, instead, interpret the claim much more loosely as simply that some degree of identification with a particular community and its practices is of special importance to people. Some story along these lines could be told consistent with the ability and even desirability of individual evaluation of the community's practices. This kind of account is consistent with Raz's pro-multiculturalism arguments that are grounded in the harm of familial disruption and loss of self-esteem.[32] However, the argument outlined above against the possibility of individual rights to goods like the social forms that characterize a particular culture casts doubt on the effectiveness of this strategy. There can be no doubt that an individual's culture is important to her, but because it is not an individualizable good, this importance cannot ground any kind of individual claim of right to its protection. It therefore provides the wrong kind of starting point to ground protections for particular cultures. This suggests that a better strategy would be to provide an account of the interest that a group as a whole has in the secure enjoyment of its culture. Such an account is plausible if we take note of the indeterminacy of value that characterizes much of the moral context within which particular cultures develop and distinguish themselves from one another. I turn now to an exploration of that context.

VALUE INDETERMINACY, CULTURAL DIVERSITY, AND AUTONOMY

Value, in particular the concept of the good life, is indeterminate in two important ways. First, there is indeterminacy with respect to the means of achievement of any particular good. Any complex moral value admits of many paths toward its fulfilment. I can be a faithful friend by sharing particular important interests of my friend, or by being the one with whom she shares her troubles, or by being a sounding board for her deliberations about important decisions, or by trading with her frank views on everyday events. All of these are equally worthy forms of friendship, and people who find themselves in one of these sorts of friendship ought not to envy or criticize those who participate in a different sort. Second, moral value is plural. There is more than one kind of pursuit that gives life value, and the pursuit of one value may be inconsistent with the pursuit of others. We recognize this when we allow, for example, that a life dedicated to literary pursuits is neither better nor worse than, simply different from, one dedicated to the cultivation of one's physical talents through involvement in sports or a life of spiritual commitment.

This understanding of moral value opens the door to attributing a particular role to choice in assessing our own actions and those of others. As Raz argues in the context of an individual's life plan,

> Having embraced certain goals and commitments, we create new ways of succeeding and new ways of failing. In embracing goals and commitments, in coming to care about one thing or another, one progressively gives shape to one's life, determines what would count as a successful life and what would be a failure. One creates values, generates, through one's developing commitments and pursuits, reasons which transcend the reasons one had for undertaking one's commitments and pursuits. In that way, a person's life is (in part) of his own making. It is a normative creation, a creation of new values and reasons.[33]

By embracing a certain path, we make indeterminate goals determinate,[34] thus giving ourselves new reasons for action. Where, once upon a time, more than one way of achieving a valuable goal may have been open, or the choice between the pursuit of several goods unconstrained, after a certain decision has been taken, options previously open become foreclosed. Had one of the earlier decisions been different, current options might well be different. Over the course of a life, as these individual decisions build upon one another, a particular path may be revealed which is right for that individual, even though it might not have been chosen and therefore would not be right for someone else. Thus, in the face of indeterminacy, it is our choices that create value, that confer worth on the next step, that make certain decisions the right ones.

Although groups do not choose in exactly the way individuals do, it can nevertheless be said that the social processes that give a group its culture create value or new reasons for action in the same way that an individual's choices do.[35] Thus, the adoption of certain social forms in the past gives each group reason to continue on its particular path, rather than abandoning it in order to adopt another group's. A group's path is formed through a complex social process in which the choices of individuals play a part, but no one such choice is decisive. The process is deliberative. Growth and development, change or reaffirmation of tradition arise out of debate and reflection within the group about the best forms of life for the members of the group. A path is set, even if there is no decisive moment of the sort that constitutes the paradigm case of choosing. With each question that arises for discussion within the group about the adequacy of its social forms, the community faces a deliberative enterprise very similar to that engaged in by an individual assessing her life plan. There is more than one way socially to organize familial relationships or the workplace or the care of the aged, or to recognize the spiritual dimension of human experience. In addition, there are different virtues that may be pursued. It is unlikely that a comprehensive culture will fail to recognize opportunities for the pursuit of many, if not all, of the virtues; nevertheless the emphasis placed on each and the precise mix may differ from culture to culture. Thus, a decision can be right for this group, because of its history, that would not be right for — certainly that might not be the outcome of an organic process of decision-making within — another group.[36]

Culture in a generic sense is simply the upshot of a basic human need to impose order and meaning on the world. Particular cultures represent the instantiation of this generic impulse, conditioned by contingency. Particular cultures are the by-product of historical circumstances that are contingent and themselves lacking in normative significance. Culture grows organically out of the interaction over sub-stantial periods of time of large numbers of people. The existence of a plurality of cultures is the result of different groups embarking on this process in relative isola-tion from each other and subject to different material and social conditions. The more richly we describe the concept of culture and the greater the period of time during which the groups are apart, the greater the variation we can expect between any two cultures. Indeed, this can be true even where there is a common cultural root between the communities.

This kind of process can be witnessed in microcosm and with greater clarity in the development of languages having a common root, such as French, Italian, and Spanish. Over the centuries, each of these language communities, starting from the same basic material, has gone its own way, developing its language in distinctive directions so that the three languages are now mutually unintelligible. This is dif-ference born of historical contingency.[37] We can see a similar phenomenon in the development along different lines of legal systems originally drawn from the same source. In the absence of a requirement to maintain conformity of the common law in Canada with that of England, the two systems have developed, incrementally and organically, along different lines, leading in some cases to quite dramatic differences of ethos and outcome. Similarly, the Canadian and American common law legal sys-tems differ even more significantly, their isolation from one another having been even more pronounced, both in degree and in length, than that between the Canadian and English systems. As with languages and legal systems, so cultures in the larger sense develop in different directions under different conditions.

Any set of social forms constituting a comprehensive culture is bound to be richly textured. Each will provide an array of options for its members within which they can plan their lives. The options may well be very different in any two cultures, the differences having developed simply as a result of generations of building upon and elaborating initial "decisions" about the social forms most conducive to the achievement of the good life. In the face of indeterminacy in the realm of moral value, it is a community's choice of social forms, accomplished through its devel-opment and elaboration of its culture, that confers value on those particular social forms and makes certain next steps right for them even though they might not be right for other communities.

This account of the role of choice in conferring value must have consequences for those who might have preferred that a different choice had been made. The group's actual choices must be respected. To take this view is to argue for a degree of cultural autonomy for groups to decide their own future and carry through with their choices. This idea of group autonomy is necessary to make sense of Kymlicka's intuition that the changes wrought by Québec's Quiet Revolution did not threaten its cultural structure. Kymlicka must have in mind a formal definition of cultural structure, abstracting at one level from particular practices but also using an unar-ticulated decision-making procedure for settling upon particular practices. Québec culture seems to be whatever those who have traditionally spoken French and have a particular past *decide* to make of it. Since the Québécois have chosen to change their practices in particular ways, the integrity of their cultural structure presumably depends upon their ability to carry through with those changes without interference from outside sources. What is important to the existence of their culture is the integrity of their exercise of choice, not the change or lack thereof itself; in other words, not the content of their choice.

Suppose, again, that Québec had decided to resist modernization. Just because English Canada might have already made various modernizing choices which were the right thing for it to do does not necessarily make these same choices the right ones for Québec. Differences in history and tradition between the two groups might well lead each community to different conclusions. The decision for Québec has to be made from the perspective of Québec culture and its development. And while it is in principle possible for an outsider to enter into such a debate in the proper spirit — leaving behind the differences her own cultural background might make — this is very likely to be difficult. Even if the outsider succeeds in addressing the question from the Québécois point of view, the fact of moral indeterminacy at this decision-making stage may mean there is no one right answer. These kinds of decisions are ones about which reasonable people can disagree. If the selection of a certain path gives that path value for the community that chooses it, others can have no right to impose a different choice. The attempt to do so can only be interpreted as a denial of respect for the other cultural community.

This focus on autonomy at the group level provides the ingredient that was missing from Kymlicka's account — the ingredient needed to justify protections for particular cultures without relying on the existing character of the community in any static sense that might buy into fundamentalist argument. To say that a cultural community has a right to decide for itself what the future development of its basic social forms should be is to provide a content-independent analysis capable of general application that is given bite in the service of particular cultures by filling in the particular choices of a particular culture. The indeterminacy of moral value provides the framework for such an argument. When there is no single right answer available, what is right for *this* community depends upon what *it* has decided.[38] This in no way strengthens the fundamentalist's hand because it leaves it entirely open to those within the community to have a full discussion on the merits, but it does say that outsiders should respect the decision made, even if they disagree with it. It should be noted that the scope of this justification of group autonomy is limited. It extends only to those areas in which there is more than one right answer. It remains to be explored whether autonomy is sufficiently valuable that it should have some weight in protecting wrong choices, that is, choices that do not pursue the good, but I leave this task to another day.

The fact of moral indeterminacy makes the universalism of the philosopher's model, at least conceived of as a comprehensive one, unattractive. Its unacceptability is intuitively clear if we postulate the coming together of two cultural communities of equal size and power. (We can see an approximation of this in the debates about the movement toward greater European political unity, especially between Britain,[39] France, and Germany, three cultural communities used to dealing with others from a position of strength.) In deciding how to organize a co-ordinated life it is inconceivable that any powerful community would agree to give up its own social forms and be assimilated into another's. The creative process of having developed its social forms over many generations gives them value for those whose forms they are. To expect their abandonment is to deny that value.

In actual societies, what is more common is an imbalance of power between groups, with one having a numerical advantage or otherwise having achieved a position of dominance. Typically, this results over time in many social institutions being given characteristics exclusively befitting the social forms of the dominant group. Whenever one group has greater political power and there is an absence of respect toward the cultures of other groups, basic social institutions can easily be created in the cultural image of the dominant group. Let me illustrate with an example drawn from the context of the debates about language policy which have racked this country since before Confederation but from which we still seem to have learned little. From the time of the First World War and until very recently, the public school systems in the predominantly anglophone provinces were organized so that catchment areas were defined geographically, mixing students of different mother tongues. Then, unilingual materials were prescribed and unilingual teachers hired. In this way, a key social form of one group — the English language — was imposed on all other language groups in a context that is crucial, at least in the modern world, to the ability of all groups to maintain and elaborate their own linguistic heritage. Similarly, until very recently, the anglophone majority had organized governmental structures, including Parliament and the civil service, on the assumption that participants would speak English. When it is more important for the minority to be able to understand what members of the other group are saying than *vice versa*, incentives are created for the minority to abandon its language. The more options are foreclosed to the minority by the majority, the more corrosive the impact will be on the integrity of the minority community over time. The imprinting of these major institutions with the social forms of one group denies all others the ability to pursue their own cultural path.

IMPLICATIONS FOR THE REGULATION OF INTRA-GROUP CONFLICT

OUTSIDERS AND THE DEFENCE OF THE INTERNAL DISSIDENT[40]

So far we have focussed on the possibility of conflict between groups and the regulation of that conflict in a context of intra-group solidarity. Now let us turn to a context in which there is dissension within one of the groups. My analysis of the relationship of culture to autonomy, both personal and group, also has implications for this type of case. Here, both the relationships between communities and those between groups and their members are in issue. More attention to the collective nature of certain social forms leads to the conclusion that there are cases in which the individual's claim against the group deserves no vindication, at least at the hands of outsiders.

Imagine someone who identifies himself as a Catholic, yet comes to the view that Jesus Christ was not the Son of God. We'll call him Jude, after the patron saint of lost causes. Jude wishes to try to persuade others of his view and acts in certain ways in conformity with his new views. In any complex social practice, there is overwhelmingly likely to be a great variety of ways in which the dissident will in fact be free to communicate his views and act on them, to find space to advocate his reconceptualization of community practice. If he speaks of his new understanding of his religion to his friends and acquaintances, there will be no repercussions beyond the personal reactions of these individuals. Even if he turns up at the meetings of a local Bible study group proclaiming his views, writes op-ed pieces in the newspaper, or goes on radio, the Church is likely to take little notice, is certainly unlikely to organize a response.

But what if, while attending mass, he begins to interrupt the priest during the celebration of the Eucharist in order to correct him about the true significance of that wafer of bread. Or he approaches the altar to receive communion, having announced that he takes it to be symbolic of communal provision of the basic necessities of life rather than of Christ's sharing of his body and blood with the disciples at the Last Supper. At this point, the Church is likely to react, perhaps by expelling Jude from the premises because he is disrupting mass — certainly by refusing to allow him to participate in communion. Suppose now that Jude brings a legal action against the Church in battery for having forcibly removed him and seeks an injunction requiring the priest to administer communion to him, that is, Jude appeals to outside authorities to arbitrate this dispute. I think the intuitive reaction to these legal claims is that they would and should fail.

This example raises a particular version of the call for help by an individual against his community: that of a dissident who wants to remain within the group. We might label him an "internal dissident." That is, he continues to consider himself a Catholic and wants other Catholics to share his conception of the status of Jesus Christ. He therefore wants to continue to participate in the religious practices of the group such as the celebration of mass and the Eucharist. In other words, he has a competing interpretation of the meaning of Catholicism. So understood, it becomes clear that the request for intervention is a request that outsiders enforce the dissident's interpretation of the community's religious practices against the rest of the community.

To require the Church to tolerate the intervention of someone who refuses to accept the community's practice and to allow him to participate in that practice in a manner inconsistent with the group's understanding comes perilously close to requiring the group to accept the dissident's interpretation. But this, of course, involves Jude and his defenders in a contradiction: if Jude has a right to revise his conception of the good so as to come to the conclusion that Jesus Christ is not the Son of God, other Catholics have a right to reaffirm that part of their conception of the good that asserts that He is. The Church cannot be compelled to continue to treat the dissident as a member in good standing consistently with the latter right. There comes a point at which the group must be allowed to say, "if that is what you believe, you are not one of us." The claims of the two sides are inherently competitive: they both lay claim to *the* correct interpretation of Catholicism. But the meaning of Catholicism, like any social form, is collectively formed; no individual can hijack that collective process.

This problem arises precisely because at least some social practices are constituted by a belief system. But, as I argued above against Kymlicka, we should not understand these aspects of culture in a static and rigid way. Any belief system capable of uniting and keeping together a substantial group of people in a complex social practice is bound to be fluid and constantly changing as a result of internal debate about the best understanding of the group's practice. This, as we have seen, is an organic process which cannot be precisely mapped out. Nevertheless, while the idea that a social practice is constituted by certain beliefs necessarily means that membership criteria are also determined by acceptance of those beliefs, it does not necessarily follow that such social practices provide no room for internal dissent. It does mean, however, that the integrity of the practice requires at some point that decisions be made about whether a dissident's or group of dissidents' behaviour is such as to violate the practice itself. Culture is not static, but neither are there no bounds to the choices that can be made by members consistent with remaining members. If outsiders intervene in disputes between internal dissidents and the rest of the group, they are usurping the power to decide the ultimate membership criteria of the group. It interferes with the autonomy of the group to determine for itself its cultural direction. Autonomy must include the power to reject change as much as to embrace it.

If this analysis is right, it means that there is a certain way that internal dissent must be pursued, namely, internally. Someone who wishes to challenge the prevailing wisdom about the meaning of a group's practices must do so according to the group's own rules about the expression and limits of dissent — at least if he wishes to remain a member of the group. This raises the question of exit. If the group determines that the dissident has overstepped the legitimate bounds of internal disagreement, it has the right to expel him. Does the dissident have the right to leave?

THE DEFENCE OF THE RIGHT TO EXIT

This leads us to our final scenario, that of the justifiability of interference in another group's practices for the sake of vindicating a dissident's right to leave. What if the group continues to claim the dissident as member and also seeks to compel conformity to the prevailing conception of the group's practices? This is a very complex question which cannot be fully debated here. I confine myself to elaborating the implications for it of my argument about the relationship between culture and autonomy.

Short of an argument that individuals are so defined by their communal identity as to be incapable of exercising individual judgment, denying the right to exit would embroil the group's defenders in a mistake that is the mirror image of that made by the internal dissident claiming the power to determine the meaning of the group's practice. This argument flows from the analysis I have provided of culture and its development. Any particular culture is essentially contestable. Although there may be some reasonably fixed points, even key practices will be indeterminate, allowing room for discussion and debate about their interpretation and significance. This indeterminacy creates space for each member of the group to make an individual contribution to debate. She can do this only by formulating her own interpretation to be offered for consideration by the others. Indeed, it is important to remember that although group decision-making is a collective process, that process relies ultimately on the application by individuals of their own powers of judgment. That the group rejects a particular individual contribution does not render it meaningless or worthless. The individual may continue to hold to it so strongly that she feels compelled to change her cultural affiliation. Although she cannot compel the group to adopt her views, she is entitled to her own (new) beliefs. Living her life fully according to these new views may not be feasible insofar as they require the existence of alternative social forms if there is no other community within which she can pursue them. However, if these social forms or compatible ones already exist in another group, cultural emigration is possible. If the internal dissident is not able to protect herself from the power of the group to penalize her for her beliefs, she is entitled to call upon outside assistance.

Thus, the same fluid and open-textured conception of culture that grounds the group's right to protect the integrity of its practices requires extending some protection to the individual who comes to find herself out of tune with the rest. In fact, any account of culture that would not leave at least this much scope for individual autonomy would, again, treat culture as dead ritual. If there is to be room for growth and development, there must be room for individuality. But this will sometimes give rise to dissension rather than a new consensus.

Let me conclude this partial vindication of the rights of individuals against groups with a warning. Along with the tendency to see "alien" cultures as static and incapable of rich internal debate that is part of the demonization of other cultures goes the assumption that these groups are naturally inclined to use coercion against their members. The potential for the abuse of group power is not to be denied. However, to the extent that some groups seem disturbingly ready to coerce continued membership as the means of preserving the group's practices, we should wonder how much this has to do with the threat to their cultural integrity caused by their inability to enforce the valid duties of other groups, rather than to a natural tendency to ride roughshod over the conflicting claims of individual members. In the face of intransigence by another group, particularly a larger, more powerful one, it is not surprising that a minority should turn its attention to the only people it does have some control over, namely, its own members. This tendency does not justify the infringement of individual members' rights, but it does make it more understandable. It also suggests that before a majority leaps to criticism of the minority for its treatment of individual members, it should first examine whether it — the majority — is fulfilling all of its duties toward the minority.

CONCLUSION

The idea of group autonomy over the practices that constitute its culture is worrisome because of the potential for abuse. But outsiders should not be too quick to jump to the conclusion that every practice that deviates from their own constitutes such abuse. Until proven otherwise, every culture should be presumed rich enough to create internal space for dissent and creative debate about its future. Those who represent embattled causes within their own community and yet resent external interference testify to this richness. The Catholic who thinks divorced teachers should not be fired from separate schools, and yet thinks the fired teacher is wrong to bring unjust dismissal proceedings; the Aboriginal woman who knows at first hand about sex discrimination within her community and yet is against making self-government subject to the *Charter* — each demonstrates her faith in the internal capacity of her community to permit fair and free discussion and deliberation of these issues. Outsiders may facilitate such discussion where possible, but they should not interfere to determine the outcome of the debate.

The co-existence of two or more cultures requires the development of a new political culture that is more open to seeing the good in diverse social forms. I would venture to speculate that this would do more to reduce the chances of abuse of individual rights — by eliminating the perceived need for defensiveness — than any

other strategy. The coming together of cultures has usually been attended by impe-
rialistic impulses, which result from the combination of the nationalist demagogue's
conception of culture as natural and unquestionable and the philosopher's drive to
uniformity. This impulse leads to a willingness to impose cultural uniformity wherever one can get away with it and a corresponding intransigence among those upon
whom the imposition is attempted. We cannot do worse, and we stand to do a great
deal better by cultivating a political culture that acknowledges a plurality of goods
and the autonomy of different communities to pursue the different paths each has
forged through the workings of its creative energies on its particular historical circumstances. This is the starting point for a theory of justice between cultures.

QUESTIONS TO CONSIDER

1. Distinguish between the philosopher's model and the extreme nationalist
   model as responses to the problem of cultural conflict. Discuss why Réaume
   considers both models unsatisfactory, and briefly outline the main points of
   the approach that she advocates as a better approach to the problem of cultural conflict.
2. Discuss why Réaume argues that the protection of minority cultures cannot
   be separated from the question of individual rights. Why does she believe
   that respect for diversity among all groups will ultimately protect individual
   rights as well?

NOTES

1. S. Wolf, "Comment" in A. Gutman, ed., *Multiculturalism and "The Politics of
   Recognition"* (Princeton: Princeton University Press, 1992) at 75.
2. *Liberation and the Limits of Justice* (Cambridge: Cambridge University Press, 1982).
3. For a more detailed argument against accepting this kind of relationship between
   culture and identify, see A. Gutman, "The Challenge of Multiculturalism in Political
   Ethics" (1993) 22 *Philosophy & Public Affairs* 171 at 182ff.
4. See C. Geertz, *The Interpretation of Cultures: Selected Essays* (New York: Basic Books,
   1973) ch. 1.
5. J. Raz, *The Morality of Freedom* (Oxford: Clarendon Press, 1986); W. Kymlicka,
   Liberation, Community, and Culture (Oxford: Clarendon Press, 1989); see also N.
   MacCormick, "What Place for Nationalism in the Modern World" in *In Search of New
   Constitutions*, Hume Papers on Public Policy 2(1) (Edinburgh: Edinburgh University
   Press, 1994) at 81ff.
6. Raz, *ibid.*
7. Kymlicka, *supra* note 5 at 33, 48.
8. Raz, *supra* note 5 at 310. Raz's precise claim is that an autonomous life requires the
   choice of "comprehensive goals" which in turn require that there be social forms to
   support them.
9. *Ibid.* at 311.
10. Kymlicka, *supra* note 5 at 16.
11. J. Raz, "Multiculturalism: A Liberal Perspective" (1994) *Dissent* 67 at 71.
12. Raz, *supra* note 5 at 410-11.
13. *Ibid.* at 412ff.
14. *Ibid.* at 411.
15. Raz, *supra* note 11 at 71.

16. *Ibid.*
17. Kymlicka makes a similar argument, to which I will return below.
18. D.G. Réaume, "Individuals, Groups, and Rights to Public Goods" (1988) 38 U.T.L.J. 1. For an argument very different from the one presented here, one that seeks to ground protections for minority cultures in the individual right to association, see C. Kukathas, "Are There Any Cultural Rights?" (1992) 20 *Political Theory* 105.
19. Although Raz argues that his analysis in "Multiculturalism: A Liberal Perspective," *supra* note 11 at 72, recognizes that "[c]ultural, and other, groups have a life of their own," it remains unclear whether he would recognize the possibility of a group right.
20. Kymlicka, *supra* note 5 at 173.
21. *Ibid.* at 175.
22. *Ibid.* at 166.
23. *Ibid.*
24. *Ibid.* at 168.
25. *Ibid.* at 164–65.
26. *Ibid.* at 166.
27. *Ibid.* at 167.
28. See Kukathas, *supra* note 18 at 120–22.
29. Kymlicka, *supra* note 5 at 168.
30. *Ibid.* at 167.
31. Chapter 4 of Kymlicka's *Liberalism, Community, and Culture, supra* note 5, is devoted to arguing against a strongly communitarian conception of the relationship between culture and identity.
32. This line of argument is also consistent with Kymlicka's most recent work in which the emphasis is on how difficult it is for people to move from one culture to another successfully: W. Kymlicka, *Multicultural Citizenship: A Liberal Theory of Minority Rights* (forthcoming, Oxford University Press) c. 5.
33. Raz, *supra* note 5 at 387.
34. *Ibid.* at 189.
35. Without a formal decision-making structure, determining what a group's choices are will obviously be more complicated than determining what choices an individual has made. I leave consideration of these complexities for another day.
36. This argument from indeterminacy for group autonomy differs from that offered by Gutman, *supra* note 3 at 193ff, against "comprehensive universalism" as a response to intercultural conflict. Gutman rejects comprehensive universalism because "it overlooks those cases of moral conflict where no substantive standard can legitimately claim a monopoly on reasonableness or justification" (at 194). This seems to place the emphasis on our inability, at any one point in time, to comprehend fully the requirements of justice, rather than on the co-existence of competing moral foundations for action. Gutman's approach leads her to suggest a largely procedural means, which she labels "deliberative universalism," to resolve disputes. The upshot of her approach is the production of a single standard applicable to all but arrived at after deliberation taking into account the competing perspectives of all participant cultural communities.
37. This is not to say that such processes are not susceptible to deliberate political manipulation. See, *e.g.*, E.J. Hobsbawm's demonstration of the role of the state in the creation of distinct languages, as in Italy, in *Nation and Nationalism Since 1780: Programme, Myth, Reality* (Cambridge: Cambridge University Press, 1990).
38. Raz's argument that individuals should not have options to which they have become deeply *committed* foreclosed trades on the same notion that the fact of having made this commitment is what gives it value. My argument seeks to build upon whatever sort of claim individuals can make to the protection of their choices and commitments,

by extending the argument to groups to allow a claim of group right by a minority against the majority.

39. Or perhaps I should say England, since Britain also consists of the distinct national communities of Scotland, Wales, and Northern Ireland, although many would argue that the "British" posture in dealing with other member states of the European Union reflects more of English values than those of Britain's other national groups.

40. I am grateful to Arthur Ripstein for several discussions which helped me work out my thinking on the problem of the internal dissident.

PART FOUR

Women and the Law

The status of women in law has become central to social activism and scholarly activity in Canada. Only recognized as legal persons with respect to Senate eligibility in 1929, women in Canada have challenged gender discrimination on many fronts. Increasingly, advocates of new rights for women, or greater enforcement of these legal rights, draw on women's experiences before the law and on broader statistical evidence of gender discrimination. Even with advances in the status of women, many scholars point to ongoing studies of patterns of discrimination against women within the legal profession in North America, as well as documentation of gender discrimination in work and other spheres.

The point remains, is law an effective means of remedying gender discrimination? Liberal-minded and more critical feminist scholars disagree over specific applications of law, with the former more inclined toward reform of existing legal and social structures, and the latter frankly sceptical of the power of law to move past its patriarchal roots. This section explores three key issues concerning women and law: legal and social policies on female partner abuse; battered woman's syndrome as a legal defence for women charged with injuring or killing their partners; and how women's status is affected by legal procedures addressing issues of child custody, child support, and property division following separation or divorce.

Mark Drumbl provides a detailed, balanced discussion of developments in domestic assault. In "Civil, Constitutional, and Criminal Justice Responses to Female Partner Abuse: Proposals for Reform," he reviews how widespread such abuse is in Canada and the United States, and points out that the issue is in the forefront of social activism and legal reactions concerning women's safety. Drumbl argues that where such violence occurs, women are reduced to "second-class citizenship." His essay offers a valuable overview of the toll of female partner abuse: sexual assault, psychological damage, hospitalization for injuries, and even death. This essay increases our understanding of various legal options, including civil, constitutional, and criminal approaches to female partner abuse.

Drumbl's article adopts a comparative approach, contrasting official reactions and social resources available for victims of domestic violence in Buffalo, New York, and Toronto and London, Ontario. One interesting finding is that, unlike in Canada, women in Buffalo may increasingly seek civil redress through the family court, rather than relying on public prosecution through the criminal court. But there are several difficulties with what amounts to an either-or choice for victims. For example, they have only 72 hours to elect one of these options, and they may not be informed of possible outcomes, including the likelihood of a more lenient disposition for a civil course of action. The trade-off is that civil cases are resolved more speedily than criminal actions. In Canada, domestic assault cases are conventionally managed through the criminal courts. A key shortcoming in Canadian cases is the often ineffectual restraint order, only theoretically barring the abusive spouse from harassing or contacting the injured spouse. Drumbl focusses on London, Ontario, which was the first municipality in Canada to establish mandatory arrest policies for spousal abuse. Drumbl discusses the impact of such policies, including the prospect of police officers — who may be subject to discipline for not arresting alleged offenders — making arrests "without reasonable grounds."

While Drumbl is alert to possible violations against men accused of domestic assault, he argues that some prosecutors and judges act in ways that generate lenient attitudes toward wife battering. For example, in Metropolitan Toronto, it was reported that nearly two-thirds of those prosecuted for simple assault receive either a conditional discharge or a suspended sentence or are placed on probation. Drumbl is expressing a majority opinion about the importance of taking decisive action when domestic violence is alleged. To do otherwise is to tacitly condone women being deprived of psychological and physical security and having their civil rights violated. The traditional view of family relationships and the family home as being a private sphere, out of the reach of official intervention, is thus challenged in this essay.

In her article, "The Battered Woman Syndrome Revisited: Some Complicating Thoughts Five Years after *R. v. Lavallee*," Martha Shaffer, a professor at the University of Toronto, reviews implications of using battered woman syndrome (BWS) as a defence for women who have killed, or tried to kill, their abusive partner. She shows how early interpretations of this syndrome allowed women to draw on a history of brutality by spouses as an explanation of their eventual recourse to violence for self-protection. As a point of departure, she uses the 1990 Supreme Court of Canada landmark decision in *Lavallee*, where the judge ruled that evidence of abuse could be incorporated into a self-defence argument in court cases involving murder or serious injury to abusive spouses.

For some observers, BWS is welcome, as it allows the court to consider the seriousness of women's victimization and may explain and excuse what may otherwise be seen as random violence. Other analysts are not so positive. Some detractors contend that BWS excuses women's violence, possibly without clear evidence that the defendants were in fact in serious danger at the time of the incident. In cases where the alleged victimizer is dead, it is possible that the surviving spouse's evidence can be distorted, even fabricated. Some feminist scholars and activists fear that using BWS as a defence strategy may undermine women's status as willful agents. Furthermore, BWS terminology can "medicalize" women's problems, with medical experts joining social scientists and legal experts in assessing the merits of particular cases. This can empower the medical profession and other experts, with the woman's voice and motivations appropriated by these specialists.

Shaffer takes up these themes, cautioning that there is a danger of treating the victimized woman as pathological and possibly losing sight of the cruelty and control exercised through earlier beatings and even torture endured by abused women. She is also critical of attempts to create a stereotype of battered women, a narrow approach that would possibly discount forms of abuse suffered by some women. This essay thus takes us into the heart of legal interventions that can dramatically affect how women are viewed as legal subjects, as well as in society at large. Shaffer's research also complements other work exploring how patterns of physical, sexual, and psychological abuse can work to women's disadvantage, including imprisonment of many women who have been thus abused.

The final essay of this section is "Private Troubles, Private Solutions: Poverty among Divorced Women and the Politics of Support Enforcement and Child Custody Determination." Professor Jane Pulkingham of Simon Fraser University examines a topic that is also relevant to many of us. Separation and divorce have become much more common in Canada, with dramatic increases in divorce in the past 30 years and clear changes in the nuclear family ideal, as the number of single-parent families, stepfamilies, and same-sex parents has grown. Divorce rates have increased since divorce law was liberalized in the late 1960s, but there have been ongoing debates over gender bias in family law. On the one hand, it is argued that, in general, women suffer disproportionately in financial terms after separation, that the threat of separation places some women at risk of spousal assault or even murder, and that men are advantaged through the courts. There are serious concerns about abusive men intimidating their partners after separation and even bullying women through unfounded custody proceedings and unfair maintenance agreements. On the other hand, some observers argue that family law norms are biased against fathers. These commentators point to ongoing patterns of awarding sole custody to mothers as evidence that women are privileged in family law, while fathers are disinherited with respect to day-to-day parenting. They point out that not all fathers fit the stereotype of abusive husbands or of "deadbeat dads" who refuse to support their children financially. Women are rarely ordered to pay child support, with men standing as the vast majority of those ordered to make support payments. Some family law norms are thus called into question, with a movement toward "shared parenting" as distinct from the term sole or even shared custody, terms that imply ownership of, and control over, children.

Jane Pulkingham offers an insightful assessment of debates in family law, examining changes in social policy and legislation that affect families undergoing separation or divorce. She re-examines the "feminization of poverty" among many single mothers and the difficulties of custodial mothers in securing adequate child support payments from their former spouses. Drawing upon recent studies, statistics, and varying perspectives on gender, power, and the family courts, she assesses the merits of various theories of family law and social justice, accepting some aspects of feminist criticisms of existing policies, but pointing out the pitfalls of others. In particular, she rejects the notion that awarding custody to the "primary caregiver" and enforcing child support payments will cure women's poverty. Pulkingham's essay provides a comprehensive, free-thinking approach to family law cases and implications of specific theoretical outlooks and legal doctrines surrounding family law. Pulkingham refutes the myth that mothers are losing sole custody to their former spouses, pointing out that approximately three-quarters of divorce actions lead to sole maternal custody. Pulkingham adds that clinging to this norm of maternal custody may, ironically, deepen women's dependency on ex-partners or the welfare state.

We could add to these concerns the importance of bringing forward other studies on the value of joint custody decisions, or joint parenting arrangements, thus reviving the legal doctrine of the best interests of the child. Clearly sympathetic to many feminist contributions in the area of child custody and support, and wary of the potential for further subordinating women's rights and resources, Pulkingham nevertheless expresses concerns about a privatized approach. This approach places blame on some parties and relies on stepped-up state enforcement of maintenance obligations that often obscure wider social obligations and possibilities of increasing men's obligations as fathers.

These three articles touch on fundamental issues identified by feminist scholars and allow the reader to weigh the extent to which legal structures can work toward women's equality before the law or other goals of the women's movement. These articles should also serve to generate discussion about the many ways in which social and legal relations are "gendered," drawing on changing formulations on what it is be to male or female, to be victimized, and to rely on legal resources. Pulkingham's essay, together with the other articles in this section, illuminates trends in legal regulation and legal ideologies, and shows the complexities of using legal powers to appreciate gendered differences in society and to reverse patterns of gender inequality.

TEN

Civil, Constitutional, and Criminal Justice Responses to Female Partner Abuse: Proposals for Reform

MARK ANTHONY DRUMBL

INTRODUCTION

Domestic violence is an endemic reality in North America.[1] As such, the silence surrounding it must be broken. Womanbeating[2] must no longer be hidden behind curtains and doors. Its ugliness must be pushed out into the open so that it can be squarely judged for what it is: a public health issue intimately tied to patriarchy.

This paper shall compare the response of the law, the police, and social services to domestic violence in New York (Buffalo) and Ontario (Toronto and London). References will also be made to other Canadian jurisdictions, most notably British Columbia. Attention shall be focused on the nature of arrest policies for batterers as well as the type of remedies available to victims within these jurisdictions. This comparison is particularly useful since, unlike Toronto or London, Buffalo does not have a pro-arrest policy[3] yet allows for battered women to use a wide array of civil remedies against the abuser as well as the police. This paper shall investigate whether the availability of these "two-tracks" make the New York response to domestic violence more effective.

This comparative approach is not an end in itself. Its purpose is instrumentalist in nature: to lay the groundwork for a substantive analysis of how the needs of battered women in Canada can be better addressed. Can the criminal justice system play a preventative role? Would it not be more effective if integrated into a wider and more comprehensive response? These questions raise the broader issue as to what extent we should rely on the criminal law in order to deter crime and enforce socially acceptable behaviour. In effect, this paper posits that the criminal justice system, although capable of promoting social change, only has a limited ability to do so.

Source: Mark Anthony Drumbl, "Civil, Constitutional, and Criminal Justice Responses to Female Partner Abuse: Proposals for Reform," *Canadian Journal of Family Law* 12 (1994): 115–69.

The fight against womanbeating is central to the struggle towards gender equal-ity more generally. Gender-based violence relegates women to a form of second-class citizenship. The pervasive nature of family violence is such that the legal system — unless consciously working against it — contributes to its perpetuation.

The right of a woman to be safe in her own home shall thus be perceived as a civil rights issue. This conceptual approach animates the reforms proposed by this paper. Although not guaranteeing a solution to a complex problem, these reforms can propel us in new directions.

RETHINKING TERMS AND ATTITUDES

This paper propounds the use of "female partner abuse" as an appropriate term to describe violence against women in the household, although "domestic violence" remains in full operative use. The drawback with the designation "domestic vio-lence" is that it is gender-neutral and thus implicitly denies the fact that violence within the family is overwhelmingly committed by men. In fact, women are assaulted by men in 97% of inter-spousal violence.[4] Moreover, "domestic violence" provides an image of "mutual combat" in relationships that is fundamentally incor-rect.[5] Gender-neutral definitions have serious implications: if the police and the courts believe that battering relationships are characterized by reciprocal violence, why should they be expected to provide greater protection for female victims?

Similarly, the term "wife assault" is also conceptually inadequate. It semantically limits the violence to married couples, denying the extent of "girl-friend abuse" as well as the fact that divorced and separated women together constitute 75% of all battering victims.[6] To this end, the term "female partner abuse" better describes the dynamic of violence within the home since it emphasizes the gendered nature of the harms as well as the fact that they are often inflicted outside of marriage.[7]

Our understanding of the term "abuse" also needs to be rethought. Being "abused" involves more than just being slapped or punched. Roughly 60% of all women murdered in Canada are victims of domestic violence.[8] This rate is double that found in the United Kingdom and Japan. One-third of battered women in Canada are hurt to the point that medical care must be sought.[9] Domestic violence occasionally involves physical torture. It can also include being raped after a beat-ing.[10] Underlying the physical harm is the underpinning of emotional betrayal.[11] Children who witness female partner abuse often bear deep emotional scars. They also run a significant risk of being beaten, as studies reveal that wife batterers are highly likely to abuse their children.[12]

Female partner abuse does not take the form of a one-shot incident. It is repeated. The London Battered Women's Advocacy Clinic estimates that, on aver-age, a woman is battered thirty-five times before she begins to seek help. The unusu-ally high rate of recidivism in female partner abuse distinguishes it from other crimes.[13] American estimates reveal that as much as 80% of all incidents of domes-tic violence involve womanbeaters with prior spousal assault records or evidence of prior police involvement.[14]

This paper adopts the hypothesis that there are no classes or subsets of women that are "more likely" to be beaten nor certain groups of men who are "more likely" to beat.[15] This view conflicts with the conclusion of certain scholars that "the most consistent risk markers [of domestic violence] are youth and low income."[16] Others, members of what can loosely be labelled the "demographic school," view female partner abuse as tied to ethnicity and culture. These scholars feel it essential to target these "high risk" groups in order to develop a more precise police and legal response to family violence. Nevertheless, as pointed out by Rosemary Tong, the fact that there are more women of colour and poor women in shelters does not indicate that they are more victimized, just that they have fewer options of where to go in the event of domestic violence. Violence among poor people and minorities is simply more likely to become a police matter: "Lower-class people are denied privacy for their quarrels: neighborhood bars, sidewalks, and crowded, thin-walled apartments afford little isolation. The privacy of the middle-class lifestyle preserves an illusion of greater domestic tranquility; but it is, apparently, only an illusion."[17]

The "demographic" approach to womanbeating creates a context in which misogynist violence is seen as "normal" among certain groups of people yet "deviant" among others. Ironically, the criminal law, punishing only "deviant" behaviour, does not respond to the needs of the groups signalled out as being "high risk" in the first place.[18]

It seems futile to attempt to tie womanbeating to class and nationality when its origins are rooted in patriarchy and sexism. A civil rights approach to womanbeating directly addresses this reality. Violence against women must be perceived as deviant and unacceptable behaviour in all cases.

RESPONSES TO FEMALE PARTNER ABUSE: A COMPARATIVE ANALYSIS

BUFFALO (NEW YORK)

THE POLICE RESPONSE

Buffalo (population: 357 870) is the only city with over 100 000 inhabitants in all of New York State whose police force has neither a mandatory arrest nor a pro-arrest policy.[19] Police are not instructed to arrest, yet merely "not to refrain from arresting" solely due to the "domestic nature of a dispute between married couples."[20] The only obligation on the Buffalo police is to "provide information" about the availability of support services and, if an assault has occurred, to give the victim a "warrant card" entitling her to engage in legal proceedings if she expresses to the police a willingness to do so. A warrant card will not protect the woman from the batterer after the police leave without him. A further problem is that, due to the absence of policy guidelines, the police do not take charge of the situation and sometimes put pressure on the woman to decide whether or not they should arrest. This increases the vindictiveness of the abuser towards the woman, as she is deemed "responsible" for having him charged. If this discretion were taken out of the hands of the victim, then the state would bear the responsibility for charging the womanbeater.

Table 10.1 reveals how the response of the Buffalo Police Department to "domestic calls" is inadequate. A ratio of .002 arrests per call (1990) is hardly effective. This compares to a 34.3% arrest per call ratio for arson, 159% for prostitution [sic] and 6.7% for general assault.[21] The statistics for 1986 reveal that, out of nearly 14 000 calls, in only 394 cases were men arrested (an arrest per call ratio of 3%). The overwhelming majority of arrests were for simple assault, the least serious of the offences in the "assault family."

TABLE 10.1 *Female Partner Abuse in Buffalo: Response of the Buffalo Police Departments*

	1986		1990
Domestic Calls	13 930		19 026
Arrests:	*Men*	*Women*	
Aggravated Assault	72	16	
Simple Assault	280	7	
Violation of Orders	42	1	
	394	24	
Total:	418		40

Source: Statistics from the *Buffalo Police Department Annual Report:* Volumes 25 and 26 (1990) and from B. Paskoff, *Preliminary Needs Assessment of Spouse Abuse Services* (Buffalo: Man-to-Man Counselling Services, 1991). Women's shelters in Buffalo (Haven House and the YWCA) receive 2500 calls annually.

Between 1986 and 1990, the number of domestic violence calls increased significantly, yet the number of arrests plummeted. The arrest per call ratio in 1990 was only 7% of the 1986 rate. Sue Tomkins of the Domestic Violence Clinic of the University of Buffalo School of Law attributes this reduction in the number of arrests to the fact that officers are increasingly instructing victims to file civil complaints in Family Court or lay private charges in Criminal Court.[22]

Contrasting Table 10.1 with Table 10.2 (Toronto) and Table 10.3 (London) indicates that there are more arrests in jurisdictions in which the police operate under mandatory arrest directives. Nevertheless, several caveats must be drawn. One reason why the arrest rate is so low in Buffalo is that "domestic calls" are defined broadly to include domestic disputes as well as disturbing the peace, arguments with neighbours, and barking dogs.[23] In Toronto, during the same time period, there were roughly one-third the number of "domestic calls," despite the fact that Toronto's urban population is eight times the size of Buffalo's. The more limited scope of the "domestics" category used by the Metro Toronto Police Force (family violence only) could help account for this difference. Nevertheless, if the 2500 calls annually received by women's helplines and shelters in Buffalo are roughly indicative of the number of domestic violence situations (and let us generously assume the police would have been called in approximately half of these incidents), the arrest rate in Buffalo is increased to 30% in 1986 and 3% in 1990, still below Toronto's (65% in 1991) and considerably below London's (89% in 1990). Although many batterers are the subject of private criminal or civil proceedings, it is clear that the absence of an arrest policy in Buffalo allows fewer batterers to be publicly accountable to the state for their actions.

THE VICTIM'S CHOICE

In New York State, a victim of domestic violence has a choice of two remedies: (1) proceeding criminally; or (2) launching a civil action in Family Court. Even when the police arrest, it is up to the victim to elect how to proceed.[24] These remedies are not concurrent. The victim has seventy-two hours from the time of the filing of the first complaint (criminal or civil) to "make up her mind" and definitively choose in which court to proceed.[25] There is also no affirmative duty on the police or court clerks to explain to the victim the differences involved in proceeding civilly or criminally. This is unfortunate, since punishments in Family Court are generally less severe than those in Criminal Court, although they may be obtained more expediently.[26]

Fully 90% of all spouse abuse cases are seen in Family Court. Family Court workers claim that this is largely due to the fact that victims prefer the private nature of the proceedings and the speed with which a hearing is granted. However, the overwhelming tendency for spousal abuse cases to be heard in Family Court must also be tied to the fact that the police often do not bother pressing charges or filling out reports and simply shuffle the victim to Family Court. Abusers may also pressure the woman into proceeding civilly in cases where the bodily harm they inflict would be significant enough to result in criminal culpability. This highlights a major shortcoming in this non-concurrent "two-track" system: female partner abuse is effectively decriminalized.

PROCEEDING CRIMINALLY

If the victim chooses the "criminal" option, she loses control of the case to the prosecutor. The vast majority of domestic violence cases in Criminal Court are prosecuted under the assault provisions found in paragraph 120 of the *New York Penal Law*.[27]

Paragraph 220.10 of the *New York Penal Law* is extensively used to plea bargain 90% of all criminal charges for female partner abuse cases. If the accused does not plea bargain and enters a "not-guilty" plea, guilt must be proven beyond a reasonable doubt through the use of criminal rules of evidence. Depending on the severity of the offence, trial may be by jury.

There is a wide spectrum of criminal remedies.[28] Depending on the class of felony, a custodial sentence may be given. Paragraph 530.13 of the *Criminal Procedure Law*[29] empowers the Court to issue an order of protection in addition to any other disposition. These orders can be longer than those issued by Family Court — their length varies according to the seriousness of the offence: usually from one to three years. Section 65.10(2)(d) of the *Penal Law* permits a judge to order psychiatric treatment. In practice, however, criminal sentences are light. Small fines or poorly enforced orders of protection are the most frequent dispositions. A common interlocutory remedy is the Adjournment in Contemplation of Dismissal (ACD), which involves mediation before trial. If this "mediation" is successful (or even appears to be successful), the charges may in fact be dropped.

If the police refuse to lay charges, the victim can do so herself. However, after the complaint enters the criminal justice system, the prosecutor, barring extraordinary circumstances, will take charge of the case. Thus, although a victim can choose to proceed criminally, the ultimate success of her complaint (or even its introduction in court) is almost always dependent on prosecutorial discretion. If the charges are dropped anywhere along the criminal process, the victim can then proceed with the case in Family Court. Nevertheless, her chances of success are low since the fact that the charges were previously dropped is generally introduced as mitigating evidence by the defendant in the civil trial.

PROCEEDING CIVILLY

Article VIII of the *New York Family Court Act* (the "family offenses" section) is specifically intended to provide a remedy in cases of both family violence and spousal assault. Paragraph 821 provides that criminal conduct is required to trigger this civil remedy:

1. A proceeding under this article is originated by the filing of a petition containing the following:
    (a) An allegation that the respondent assaulted or attempted to assault his or her spouse, parent, child, or other member of the same family or household or engaged in disorderly conduct, harassment, menacing or reckless endangerment toward any such person.

Unlike the criminal provisions, paragraph 812 limits the applicability of the *Act* to certain classes of women: those legally married to or divorced from[30] their abuser as well as those women who are not legally married but who have children with their abuser. There is no civil remedy for those women battered by common-law partners with whom they do not have children. Women in this situation must go to Criminal Court and, hence, are effectively denied any statutory civil remedy.[31]

The major advantage of the civil cause of action is the speed with which it proceeds. For instance, a judge can hear a complaint within twenty-four hours of the filing of the application in Family Court. The abuser may be given a summons to appear at the trial hearing (para. 825), and arrest may result from a failure to appear. Paragraph 841 empowers the judge with a wide range of dispositions, some of which can be given *ex parte*. Although she cannot order jail, she can place the respondent on probation for a period not exceeding one year. She can impose an "order of exclusion" upon the aggressor, thereby precluding him from entering the family home. Orders of exclusion are awarded on an infrequent basis; to this end, it is generally the woman, the victim, who is obliged to leave the home, often with her children, for the simple reason that she has been beaten and continues to fear the batterer. Paragraph 841(c) permits the batterer to be ordered to attend treatment in an "educational group." This is a fairly regular sentence, although domestic violence workers in Buffalo would like it to be an obligatory part of any disposition. In other cases, a fine can be levied or an order of protection issued. Although Family Court cannot grant a divorce, paragraph 817 empowers it to order that the abuser make support payments to the woman and children. Paragraph 842(h) allows the court to order the batterer to pay the medical bills and compensation for the injuries he has caused.

Orders of protection were placed upon 852 men brought before Buffalo Family Court in 1986. There are two types of orders: temporary orders of protection (TOP) and regular orders of protection. There is a great deal of arbitrariness in the types of orders given as well as the decision to issue one in the first place. Domestic violence caseworkers in Buffalo note that whereas some Family Court judges are sensitive to issues of domestic violence, others remain callous.[32]

The power to grant a temporary order of protection derives from paragraph 828 of the *Family Court Act*. If the victim is requesting a temporary order, the hearing is usually scheduled for the same day. The abuser is phoned and asked to attend. If he cannot be present, the hearing can take place *ex parte*. In order to obtain a TOP, the victim must "show cause": she must convince the judge that she is "desperate and in need of immediate protection."[33] In certain rare cases, the Family Court judge may give the victim a warrant for the womanbeater's arrest. In order to demonstrate the need for this, the judge will consider whether the batterer will obey a summons or whether the safety of the woman/children is in danger. The temporary order of protection will normally only be valid until the scheduled trial date. Treatment in an educational group cannot be ordered; the TOP normally only provides for the man to cease and desist the assaultive behaviour. It is often the case that the woman will have been so poorly treated by the system in her quest for a TOP that, even if she obtains one, she will not return on the scheduled trial date to ask for a permanent order of protection or financial compensation. This is unfortunate, since the temporary order of protection has the potential to play an instrumental role in the protection of battered women. It can address the woman's safety needs from the incident up to the date of the trial. A common problem in pro-arrest jurisdictions such as Ontario and British Columbia is that even if a man is arrested, he may be set free several hours later. It is not uncommon that such abusers then further harass the victim.

It is a good deal more complicated to obtain a permanent order of protection in Family Court. After having met with an intake worker, the victim attends at the "legal department" to meet with a law clerk. A date is then set up when both the victim and the womanbeater are to return for a hearing. It is then the responsibility of the petitioner to serve the documents on the abuser at least twenty-four hours before the court date. If the batterer then fails to appear in court on this date, one of three things can happen: (1) an order can be issued *ex parte*; (2) an arrest warrant can be issued; (3) a new court date is set, and the victim will once again have to serve the documents and reappear in court.[34]

The hearing proceedings are bifurcated. There is a "fact-finding hearing" and, if the allegations in the petition are established, there is a dispositional hearing. The facts must be proven on a "fair preponderance of the evidence."[35] Section 842 provides that the order can be issued for up to one year. No criminal record can ensue from any Family Court ruling except in cases of a breach of a court order.

Another possible outcome is that the judge may award a mutual order of protection. This is a court order indicating that both parties are equally to blame for the assault. These orders ignore the general dynamic of the battering relationship and can further victimize the woman: "I got the same thing he did and I didn't do anything except get beaten up."[36]

Even if the victim succeeds in obtaining a stringent order of protection, its effectiveness hinges on the extent to which it is perceived by the batterer to be legally binding.[37] To this end, adequate enforcement is critical. Such enforcement appears to be lacking in Buffalo, since 266 of the 852 orders of protection issued in 1986 were subsequently violated by the batterers. If the victim notifies the police about the breach of an order and the police response is inadequate, she can return to Family Court and file a new petition called a "Violation of an Order of Protection." A new summons must then be handed to the batterer. In theory, up to six months' imprisonment (for contempt of court) can be ordered for the "willful" violation of an order of protection (para. 846a); in practice, however, such a disposition is rare. The court will generally just issue a new order or levy a small fine. In the end, such leniently enforced orders of protection do not eliminate the threat of reprisal.

Despite these shortcomings, over 1300 women in Erie County sought relief under Article VIII of the *Act* in 1990.

TORONTO AND LONDON (ONTARIO)

In Canada, matters related to female partner abuse are usually treated as criminal offences. Many of Canada's police forces require officers to lay charges in cases where there are reasonable and probable grounds to believe an assault has occurred. If the

TABLE 10.2 *Domestic Violence in Metro Toronto*

	July 1, 1985 to June 30, 1986	1991*
Domestic violence calls	3,047	5,100
Charge per call ratio	40%	65%
% of victims told to lay private charges	11%	n/a
% of victims getting a peace bond	30%	n/a
% of the victims female	96%	95%
% reporting previous violent incidents	90%	90%

12% had a prior conviction for female partner abuse.

*1991 STATISTICS FROM "NEW POLICE POLICY ON DOMESTIC VIOLENCE PRAISED" *GLOBE AND MAIL* (5 JULY 1991) A9, AND PERSONAL INTERVIEW WITH B. PASKOFF, 2 NOVEMBER, 1992.

Source: Statistics from B. Leighton, *Spousal Abuse in Metropolitan Toronto: Research Report on the Responses of the Criminal Justice System* (Toronto: Ministry of the Solicitor General, 1989) and B. Farge & B. Rahder, *Police Response to Incidents of Wife Assault* (Toronto: Assaulted Woman's Helpline, 1991), both reproduced in J. Mosher, *Wife Abuse: Assessing the Interventions of Law and Social Work* (University of Toronto, 1992) at 256 and 251 respectively.

police do not lay charges, the woman may go to a Justice of the Peace and "lay an information" (a private charge). Layings of private informations are fairly infrequent.

The civil remedies are much narrower in scope than those in New York. Neither Ontario nor any other province has yet enacted a statute similar to the *Family Court Act*. Aside from common law battery actions, family law legislation offers the only means to launch civil claims. These statutory causes of action are limited. For example, the Ontario *Family Law Act*[38] permits a woman to obtain a restraining order ordering her spouse to stop threatening her. Section 36.1 of the British Columbia *Family Relations Act*[39] allows the court to make an order restraining any person from molesting, annoying, harassing, or communicating with the spouse. Nevertheless, neither *Act* permits treatment to be part of such orders. Section 24(3)(f) of the Ontario *Family Law Act* allows the Court to award a wife[40] an order for exclusive possession of the matrimonial home.[41] Violence on the part of the man can be considered in making such an order. Nevertheless, these orders offer only illusory protection, since they prevent the man from entering the home yet not from approaching the victim in person once she leaves the home. These inadequacies are not surprising given that this legislation was not intended to deal with issues of domestic violence in the first place.[42]

PROCEEDING CRIMINALLY IN CANADA

The Canadian *Criminal Code*,[43] in a manner similar to the *New York Penal Law*, divides all offences into categories. But this is done in a much simpler fashion as there are only three groups: summary offences, hybrid offences, and indictable offences. Summary offences are the least serious, whereas indictable offences are the most serious. Hybrid offences occupy the middle ground. For this category, it is up to the Crown prosecutor to decide (based on the circumstances of the crime) whether to proceed summarily or by indictment. As in New York, except in cases of murder or attempted murder, the vast majority of cases of female partner abuse are prosecuted under the simple assault provisions of the *Criminal Code*.[44]

If an incident of female partner abuse involves coerced sexual activity, it can be prosecuted as a sexual assault. Sexual assault is dealt with in three sections of the *Code*. Section 271 is the general prohibition against sexual assault. As with simple assault, the Crown can proceed either summarily (6 month maximum jail sentence) or by indictment (10 year maximum).[45] The importance of the wide discretion awarded Crowns should not be underestimated. In the past, the widely accepted belief that the "domesticness" of an assault was a factor mitigating its severity induced many Crowns to proceed summarily in cases where they might otherwise have proceeded by indictment. An inappropriate election to proceed summarily could trivialize the offence and bind the hands of the court if it seeks to impose a just sentence.

In the mid-1980s, Crowns dropped, on average, about one-third of all wife assault charges.[46] This is significantly lower than the 75% attrition rate in New York State. The disparity can be partially explained by the fact that, unlike in Ontario, New York Family Court operates as a stop-gap mechanism. Buffalo prosecutors might thus be more willing to drop charges since this does not necessarily mean that the abuser is completely absolved of any responsibility. As of 1985, the Ontario Attorney General's office began to introduce "no-drop" policies mandating Crowns to prosecute all allegations of domestic violence, yet not precluding the possibility of plea bargaining. In practice, spousal assault charges are frequently plea bargained from aggravated assault to general assault. Although, in theory, the victim is to be consulted after a plea bargain is suggested, this usually takes place only moments before the trial. Moreover, the Barbra Schlifer Woman's Clinic (Toronto) reports that, in Ontario, the Crown often perseveres with a plea bargain even if the victim does not agree to it.[47]

THE POLICE RESPONSE

The first mandatory arrest directive in Canada was introduced in London, Ontario, (population: 280 000) in May 1981: "Commencing immediately, charges are to be laid by our Force in all cases where there are reasonable and probable grounds to believe that an assault has taken place. The practice of instructing the victim to lay private informations is to cease."[48] Research indicates that several years after the introduction of the directive, the number of arrests in domestic violence calls rose by 2500%.[49] This generally benefits the victim: the London Family Court Clinic found that Ontario courts tend to be "tougher" on offenders when police, rather than victims, lay charges.[50] The early success of the London policy induced the federal Solicitor-General to issue a directive in 1982 to all police forces to lay charges in wife assault cases similar to the way charges are to be laid in other incidents of assault.[51] This directive has not been universally followed.

From 1982 to 1991, Metro Toronto had a pro-arrest policy in which the decision of an officer not to arrest or charge was not reviewable by internal or external administrators.[52] In 1988, police laid charges in 51% of domestic violence calls;[53] in 1991, that figure rose to 65%.[54] Although significantly higher than the Buffalo results (due to the existence of a policy in the first place), the arrest rate is lower than in London, where the decision of an officer not to arrest is reviewable.[55] In 1990, London police laid charges in 89% of wife assault cases compared with 3%

TABLE 10.3 *Arrest Per Call Ratios in London: Female Partner Abuse*

	1987	1988	1990
Percentage of calls in which the police laid a charge	65	71	89.9

in 1979, when there was no arrest policy.[56] Metro Toronto, in 1992, modified its policy so as to allow for the disciplining of officers who fail to lay charges in domestic violence cases where "probable cause" existed. This should further increase the number of arrests.[57] However, these policies could also augment the likelihood that the police officer, fearful of the consequences of a decision not to arrest, will take into custody an alleged batterer without reasonable grounds to arrest in the first place. This is clearly an undesirable result. Any attempt to increase the number of abusers brought into the justice system must not violate the rights of the accused (or even the suspected). However, a balance can be struck. One potential way to maintain this equilibrium is to provide the police with clear guidelines as to when to take the alleged abuser into custody. These guidelines would include the existence of physical evidence of an assault, any prior history of conjugal violence, statements of witnesses, and the opinion of the victim.

Another area of concern is the speed with which the police respond to domestic violence calls. In Metro Toronto, the Assaulted Woman's Helpline estimates that in 24% of all calls, the police took between 30 minutes and one hour to respond; in 7% they took between one and two hours to arrive at the scene.[58] It is clear that improving these response times should form an essential part of any plan to ameliorate the police's reaction to female partner abuse.

Arrest can potentially have the advantage of ensuring the woman's immediate safety. Nevertheless, the mere fact that the police lay charges does not mean that they always take the batterer away with them. "Charging" can also mean issuing a summons or appearance notice. The police can also investigate the matter and return to arrest the abuser later. If the police's only action is to issue a summons, this means the woman might have to spend the night with her aggressor. This can have serious repercussions. For example, in Metro Toronto, 23% of women reporting a domestic assault were further beaten after the police left.[59] Half of these repeat assaults occurred within three hours of the police's departure. To this end, more aggressive police departments such as those in Duluth, Minnesota, do not leave the scene of the assault unless one of the parties (usually the man) vacates the premises. Furthermore, the members of the Duluth Domestic Abuse Intervention Project successfully lobbied the police to include "no-contact" orders as an essential part of every batterer's release conditions. This order prohibits the man from coming into contact with the woman until after the disposition of the case in trial. Ontario jurisdictions (as well as those across Canada) should investigate the implementation of these provisions, given that many victims are harassed or further battered in the period after arrest and before trial.

SENTENCING
The most stringent mandatory arrest and no-drop policies will be ineffective unless accompanied with a results-oriented sentencing scheme. Although judges are

demonstrating a greater willingness to view battering as criminal behaviour, much ground still has to be covered before the sentencing of womanbeaters can be deemed to be effective. Part of the problem is that, unlike in New York, the *Criminal Code* sets few fixed minimum sentences. Section 717 of the *Code* accords Canadian judges wide discretion in sentencing. This creates the risk that, even if a man is convicted, he will be given a light sentence.

In Metro Toronto, 15% of all charges actually brought before a judge are dismissed absolutely, and a further 16% are settled with the payment of a small fine, usually $250.00.[60] Widespread prosecution of female partner abuse under simple assault has led to a situation in which 65% of all convicted batterers receive one of three sentences: conditional discharges, probation, or suspended sentences. These are rarely joined with a restraining order and, if so, they are usually inadequately enforced. Another common sentence is the issuance of a recognizance to keep the peace (a "peace bond," found in section 810 of the *Code*), which does not by itself give the abuser a criminal record. A breach thereof can, however, be punishable as a criminal offence with up to twelve months imprisonment. Nevertheless, peace bonds are both difficult to enforce and rarely stop men who batter.[61] The fact that the Canadian justice system considers incarceration as the appropriate disposition for a serious crime indicates that female partner abuse is rarely, if ever, viewed as serious since only 5% of all offenders are imprisoned.[62] In order to be jailed, one is likely to have killed, to have engaged in very grievous assault, or to have a prior criminal record (often in an unrelated area).

Toronto lags behind Buffalo in terms of the accessibility of services to victims and offenders. This is most notable in the case of treatment for offenders. Whereas New York judges regularly order a man into treatment after the woman files civilly or criminally, this remedy is rarely used in Ontario (with the exception of London). Although counselling is awarded in roughly one-third of all dispositions in Toronto, only in 20% of these cases was the counselling geared towards batterer's therapy.[63] This means that roughly 6% of all convicted perpetrators are sent to batterer's counselling, and, unlike in Buffalo, attendance at these sessions is often not mandatory. The comparative unwillingness of the Ontario Provincial Division judges to order treatment is unfortunate, since many women do not want their partners to go to jail.[64] These women may be fearful of the stigma that incarceration may have on their husbands, upon whom they are often economically dependent. Research has indicated that over 80% of women would be more likely to involve the police if treatment would be part of the sentence.[65]

STACCATO VOICES: THE CHANGING ATTITUDES OF THE CANADIAN JUDICIARY

In recent years, Canadian courts have demonstrated a growing sensitivity to domestic violence, although, as suggested earlier, this has generally not translated into more effective sentencing policies. A clear example of this is found in the 1984 decision of the Ontario Court of Appeal in *Regina* v. *Petrovic*.[66] The accused, Pera Petrovic, had abused his wife over a long period of time. During the evening on which he was eventually charged, he repeatedly slapped the victim across the face, humiliated her in front of a common friend, then "pushed her away." Ms. Petrovic went to the apartment's balcony and jumped over the railing. She died from a fractured skull and internal injuries caused by the fall.

Lacourcière J.A., writing for the court, noted that the appellant's conduct formed part of a "callous [and] long-standing pattern of physical abuse."[67] He also underscored the "necessity of general deterrence in cases involving ... repeated acts of violence against a vulnerable victim belonging to a class requiring this court's protection."[68] Nevertheless, Lacourcière J.A. did not specify that battered women fall into this class.[69] In the end, the Court reduced the accused's sentence to two years.

The *Petrovic* decision was affirmed in 1989 in *R. v. Inwood*.[70] In this decision, the Ontario Court of Appeal held that the "domesticness" of an assault should no longer be a mitigating factor in sentencing.[71] The accused, Kirby Inwood, repeatedly assaulted his wife, Tanya Sidorova, as well as their one-year-old child, Michael. Howland C.J.O., speaking for the Court, accepted the submissions of the Crown that sterner policies be accepted towards domestic violence: "Domestic assaults are not private matters, and spouses are entitled to protection from violence just as strangers are."[72] Nevertheless, in a manner similar to that found in *Petrovic*, the Court merely imposed a three-month custodial sentence for the offences along with a three-year probation period. The Crown's submission that a 12-month reformatory term be imposed was rejected. The Court did, however, mandate treatment for alcoholism and violence against women as part of the terms of probation.

High Courts in other Canadian provinces, although condemning acts of female partner abuse, have not attempted to develop effective measures to deter such conduct. For example, the Supreme Court of Nova Scotia, in *Publicover v. The Queen* (1986), sentenced the accused to an intermittent sentence of 80 days for "non-permanent" injuries inflicted on his wife. In spite of the fact that he awarded this lenient sentence, MacDonald J.A. still concluded that: "Incidents of wife-beating appear to be more prevalent in our society than at one time believed. The courts have an obligation to show society's denunciation of such conduct."[73]

The most sweeping pronouncement on the seriousness of domestic violence was made by the Supreme Court of Canada in *R. v. Lavallee*.[74] A victim of domestic violence was tried for the murder of her abuser. In allowing the accused to avail herself of the self-defence provisions of the *Criminal Code*, Wilson J., speaking for the Court, introduced Lenore Walker's theory of the "battered wife syndrome" into Canadian law. Walker's research revealed that battering victims suffer from a "learned helplessness" characterized by low self-esteem, physical disabilities, stress, depression, and constant fear. This "helplessness" makes it most difficult for the victim to leave the relationship, seek external support, or confront the batterer directly.[75]

In some cases, lower courts have used decisions such as *Lavallee* to justify the imposition of serious sentences and constructive treatment on womanbeaters. In one recent case, Steven Beckwith was sentenced by Mr. Justice Cole of the Ontario Court (Provincial Division) to 11 years in prison for the aggravated assault of his wife on their wedding night.[76] *The Globe and Mail* reported that the abuser broke his wife's jaw in two places and smashed her nose and cheekbones. Cole J. stated that " ... courts must do their part to send out a message that spousal assault is ... a serious crime."[77] In another case, a man who, in an attack that may have lasted for hours, beat his wife (in her sixth month of pregnancy) to death with his fists, a coat-hanger, and a broomstick, was sentenced to life imprisonment without parole for 10 years.[78]

Nevertheless, despite all of the steps forward, there are others occasionally taken backwards. Mona Brown's 1991 *Report on Criminal Justice* found that: "Comments from the bench can have the effect of downplaying the seriousness of an incident of wife assault. Characterizing the injuries of the victim as modest or trifling, or making inappropriate comments about the accused ... are examples of ways in which judges demonstrate an inability or unwillingness to treat wife abuse as seriously as other crimes of violence."[79]

An example of this is found in a recent decision of Mr. Justice John Murphy of the Ontario Court (Provincial Division). Murphy J. gave an absolute discharge to a man accused of severely battering his wife.[80] He concluded that there had been an assault, yet held that " ... it takes two to tango, and there were two tangoing here."[81] He went on to hold that "both parties went a little bit overboard": this despite the fact that the husband, Stephen Smart, "only had nail scratchings on his right ribs and on his left shoulder," while his wife had injuries commensurate with her being hit, pushed, and slammed face-first into the floor.[82] The danger in a finding of mutual assault is that it assumes equal responsibility and fault for the violence, which is rarely the case.

Certain judges from other jurisdictions in Canada have also demonstrated less than exemplary behaviour when faced with complaints of female partner abuse in their courtrooms. For instance, Judge Frank Allen (Manitoba Provincial Division), in *R. v. Peter Ashley Tavares*, instructed the accused that " ... the trouble with women is that you can't live with them and you can't live without them ... but I can tell you from 60-odd years' experience there isn't any woman worth the trouble you got yourself into." A colleague of Allen J., Manitoba Provincial Court Judge Ken Peters, is on record as affirming that " ... sometimes a slap in the face is all that she needs and might not be such unreasonable force after all."[83] In November 1993, Quebec Court Judge René Crochetière, while presiding over a preliminary hearing in which a man was charged with uttering death threats to his common-law spouse, muttered to the victim that he " ... wouldn't lose any sleep if she was to be killed by her husband."[84] Nevertheless, the fact that disciplinary action was taken in all three cases indicates that the judiciary as a whole does not tolerate such conduct on the part of its members.

KEY AREAS OF CONCERN

TWIN MYTHS: "KEEPING THE FAMILY TOGETHER" AND "A MAN'S HOME IS HIS CASTLE"

Many judges and law enforcement officials are reluctant to charge a man with a criminal offence out of fear that doing so will "break up the family." These attitudes are rooted in the belief that any "broken family" is a bad one. Such an approach fails to acknowledge the fact that a troubled family "kept together" may even be more damaging to its individual members. In any case, why should the perpetuation of this "family unity" become the goal of the court? Such an attitude further imprisons a woman and her children in a violent relationship.

The perception that a "man's home is his castle" implies that whatever transpires within the "castle walls" is not of concern to public authorities. This perception can have deleterious effects. It creates a "neutrality of non-interference" in which the failure to intervene in turn fails to stop a man from battering. The protection of this right to privacy can " ... carve out an island of violence"[85] as well as challenge the courts to use their creativity to develop a wide array of excuses to justify woman-beating in the home instead of safeguarding the victim.

MANDATORY ARREST

Mandatory arrest takes two forms. In its more absolute sense, "mandatory arrest" means that in every call of domestic violence where the police witness an assault or have "reasonable and probable grounds" to believe an offence has happened, they are required to arrest the abuser. Under such a policy, the arrest will occur regardless of the victim's opinion, and she may thus be forced to be involved in a lengthy criminal procedure when all she may have originally wanted was immediate protection. The second variant is usually called the "pro-arrest policy": there is a "presumption of arrest," which allows a police officer *not* to arrest when she has "probable cause" to believe that such an arrest would be counterproductive.

The principal drawback with an absolute mandatory arrest policy is that it disempowers both the victim as well as the officer from exercising their individual judgments. It seems fair to say that some discretion should be allowed the officer as to whether or not to arrest.[86] Nevertheless, this discretion should not be unfettered. If no arrest is made, then the officer should be obliged to prepare a written report on the events explaining the rationale behind the decision not to arrest. A copy of this report should be given to the victim (perhaps to use in *ex post* civil litigation) and another copy kept in the police department's records. Police departments ought to develop a clear, workable definition of "probable cause" and state it in their pro-arrest directives. Factors such as injuries, witnesses, evidence of a fight in the room, as well as the statements of the victim should all be considered in determining whether or not to arrest. The police should fulfill a preventative role and remove the man if they feel that there is a chance that an assault will occur after they leave. The London Police Department seems to have developed a good balance: although there is a high arrest rate, police used their discretion not to arrest in 4% of all calls, often relying on the victim's wishes.[87]

Many individuals oppose both mandatory and pro-arrest policies. Their reservations stem from the legitimate observation that domestic violence is different than other crimes. As such, the victim and the police should be allowed a total discretion to press charges or not. Although it is true that female partner abuse is significantly different than other criminal activity, the Buffalo experience indicates that the complete absence of any arrest policy is a non-solution. It is also no answer to oblige the victim to lay the charges herself: this has been proven to perpetuate the cycle of violence. Moreover, an Ontario survey revealed that 88% of the women who laid charges themselves would have preferred the police to do so.[88] It is the state's responsibility to prosecute those engaging in what is deemed to be criminal activity, and womanbeating is such an activity. Pro-arrest thus sends a message that society no longer approves of female partner abuse as acceptable behaviour.

As discussed earlier, the London, Ontario, experience demonstrates that complaints are taken more seriously when the police lay the charge than when a private information is laid.[89] Although incarceration is still infrequent, overall sentences are stiffer.[90] The credibility of the charge is important given the fact that an abuser often files counter-charges against the victim after he finds out that criminal action has commenced. The purpose of such behaviour is to induce the Crown prosecutor to plea bargain the case or to persuade the judge to find offsetting assaults. The victim may also feel more confident if the police have laid the charge. Research by Jaffe and

Burris reveals that assaulted women are twice as likely to follow through on charges laid by the police than on charges they originally laid themselves.[91]

However, there are other shortcomings to mandatory arrest policies. For example, although resulting in more arrests, these policies could very well inhibit many women from calling the police in the first place. Many women just want immediate protection and an end to the violence, not incarceration for their husbands. To this end, they may be dissuaded from calling the police out of fear that their husbands will be jailed. Nevertheless, creative sentencing policies that emphasize the treatment of the batterer may reduce this reluctance to call. In fact, research demonstrates that, in Duluth, the pro-arrest policy did not increase victim's reluctance to call the police, due to common knowledge that the court would attempt to be responsive to the needs of the victims in sentencing.

Alternately, many women fear that, if they report violence in their home and the police are under orders to arrest, their children will be taken away from them and placed in "non-violent" foster homes. Public education can help dispel these fears by emphasizing that the established practice stipulates that, unless it is the mother who is violent, the child will not be taken away from her, providing that either they (mother and child) or the batterer leave the ordinary place of residence. Children's Aid Societies across Canada should be clearly instructed to separate the battering victim from her children only in extenuating circumstances. For the mother, separation from the children can amount to a double victimization. Separation is also detrimental to the children since they, in their own way, are also victims of the battering. Allowing the mother and the child to remain together in the post-battering phase can provide a critically important element of stability.

Many battered women are economically dependent on their spouses. As such, they are financially disadvantaged should he spend any time in jail. Moreover, since a criminal record can *de facto* exclude a person from retaining or obtaining employment, many women face the potential of long-term economic loss by calling the police:

> I've thought many times about calling the police. But I always figured it would do more harm than good. My husband works as a security guard. Right in his contract it says he can't have a criminal record. So I call the police, and bang, he's out of a job, and jobs aren't so easy to come by here. Then where are we at? Things'll just get worse. We'll have no money. He'll start drinking more. He'll be even more angry at me and he'll hit me more. So where's the sense in calling the police?[92]

A potential solution is to redesign sentencing policy so as to have the convicted batterer continue to work and require him to contribute to the family's finances. He would work during his normal hours and spend the rest of his time at a treatment centre until his therapy is completed. Alternatively, if the batterer is incarcerated, he could be permitted to attend at his regular place of employment through the use of a day pass. If the batterer leaves the place of work in an attempt to harass the victim, such conduct would be deemed to violate the victim's right to protection and would automatically entail state retribution against the batterer. If a batterer is unemployed (or too dangerous to be allowed to leave the treatment centre), he could be required to complete supervised public service. He would be given a stipend for this service; part of this sum would, in turn, be passed on to the family according to its needs. Women who fear that a criminal record will hinder their spouse's chances for employment in the future should also be able to benefit from civil remedies (similar to those found in New York) through which protection orders can be acquired without the stigmatizing effects of a criminal record.[93]

In short, the disparity between the number of charges laid in Buffalo and Toronto/London indicates that a pro-arrest policy certainly seems to increase the number of abusers brought into the justice system.[94] However, the London experience reveals that mandatory arrest policies attain their goal while sharply decreasing the number of private charges that are laid.[95] This is a positive development given the fact that private charges are treated less seriously by the courts than are police-laid charges. There is also evidence that the introduction of pro-arrest policies constructively affects police attitudes towards womanbeating more generally.[96]

Nevertheless, although mandatory arrest certainly increases the number of charges laid by the police, it is unclear whether it operates as an effective *deterrent* to female partner abuse.[97] In the first thorough study[98] on the deterrence effects of arrest, American sociologists Sherman and Berk found that arrested abusers (of all backgrounds and social classes) manifested significantly less subsequent violence than those who were just "ordered to leave" or merely "advised on the situation."[99]

However, the Sherman and Berk findings are not conclusive. For example, they only measured recidivism over a six-month period, and thus leave unanswered the question whether these men were still violent one year or ten years later. Furthermore, these findings have been contradicted by the 1992 research of Hirschel *et al.*, who found that arrest failed to deter spousal violence at all.[100] Nevertheless, it should be noted that Hirschel *et al.*'s research took place in Charlotte (North Carolina), where significant racial tensions increase the arbitrariness of arrest and a lack of constructive treatment programs reduces its effectiveness.

Perhaps the most comprehensive research on the subject has been conducted by Steinman, who, in a 1990 analysis of female partner abuse in Lincoln (Nebraska), found that arrest produced *more* abuse *except* when it was tied to other sanctions such as treatment.[101] Thus, even if arrest does not on its own reduce recidivism, it clearly is a necessary condition to the inclusion of more offenders into the justice system. If these individuals are constructively sentenced, they could then learn to become less violent. Steinman's findings were echoed in a study commissioned by the London Family Court Clinic, which found that the mandatory arrest policy in place since 1981 helped reduce violence in families since it was linked to anti-recidivism therapy programs.[102]

Nevertheless, even if not conclusively proven to deter wife assault, arrest clearly has positive effects in ensuring the immediate protection of the victim for a period long enough for her to get out of the house before the abuser is released on bail. The simple fact that pro-arrest policies have rough edges does not mean they should be jettisoned, especially given the deleterious effects of *not* having a policy at all. The real challenge is thus to render these policies sufficiently flexible and contextual so that they can effectively meet the needs of the victim as well as of society more generally. A pro-arrest policy with clear guidelines and *some* narrow discretion might be an optimal compromise. Although we should not blindly jump on the "mandatory arrest bandwagon," it is clear that a carefully designed policy could play a pivotal role in the struggle against womanbeating. Moreover, those still unwilling to proceed criminally could still acquire protection if civil causes of action similar to those found in New York State were introduced into Canadian law.

"NO-DROP" POLICIES

Formerly, in both New York State as well as Canadian jurisdictions, both police and prosecutors would frequently drop the charges if asked to do so by the victim. This usually disadvantaged the victims since they were often coerced by their abuser to request that the charges be dropped. In recent years, the growing awareness of the dynamics of the battering relationship has been parallelled with a drive to implement "no-drop" policies. In 1985, the Ontario Attorney-General passed a "no-drop" directive applicable to all Crown prosecutors. The Barbra Schlifer Clinic in Toronto reports that, at present, Crowns " ... will not withdraw charges in cases of wife assault except in exceptional or unusual circumstances."[103]

It is true that any deterrent effect of the threat of arrest is minimal if the claim is not followed through the judicial system. The question arises, however, if all prosecutorial discretion should be dropped at all stages of the criminal trial process. This would create a separate standard for female partner abuse crimes in which the prosecutor is denied a right she can exercise for all other offences.

The major benefit of the "no-drop" policy is that a victim cannot be "blamed" for the fact that her abuser is on trial. The major drawback is that the victim loses control over the case. As with mandatory arrest, a certain element of discretion should be retained just to permit the system the flexibility needed to deal with a complex crime. This could be attained through a "probable cause not to prosecute" standard similar to that found in pro-arrest policing practices. Moreover, the decision of a Crown to drop a charge should be open to both internal and external review in order to ensure accountability.

WOMEN OF COLOUR AND WOMEN OF THE FIRST NATIONS

Just as contemporary social norms are sexist, so too are they racist. Women of colour are in a particularly vulnerable position when it comes to domestic violence. Categorical rules such as mandatory arrest as well as "no-drop" policies can have a harsh impact on women of colour. Fear of having to face an unfriendly and overwhelmingly white criminal justice system might inhibit many women of colour from calling the police in the first place. The case of Aboriginal women is particularly revealing: it is estimated that 75% of Native women in Ontario have suffered abuse at the hands of an intimate partner, yet it is precisely these women most in need that are the least likely to access the system.[104]

According to Rosemary Tong, the legal system must recognize that the intersection of sex and race discrimination leaves black women and other women of colour even more prone to excuse their husbands' violent behaviour: "All battered women have a tendency to blame themselves for provoking their husbands, for not being kind, patient, and long-suffering enough, but this tendency is more marked in Black women, who know only too well that in this society, life is harder for Black men than for White men ... [but] like the White man's privileges, the Black man's burdens constitute neither an excuse nor justification for woman-battering."[105]

Tong also concludes that there is a likelihood that, if a black woman's complaint is not dismissed on account of her gender, it will be dismissed on account of either her race or her class.[106] Caroline Forell further develops these themes in a submission to the *Berkeley Women's Law Journal*.[107] She notes that, at first blush, mandatory arrest would appear to benefit disadvantaged groups by reducing the amount of discretion awarded to individual police officers as to whether or not to arrest. Nevertheless, Forell notes that even the limited discretion available in a pro-arrest system can still disadvantage women of colour. However, a study released by the Duluth Minnesota Domestic Abuse Intervention Project indicates that if coherent guidelines are established (and if these are legally binding upon police officers), minorities are treated *more* fairly under a pro-arrest policy. In Duluth, under a "no-policy" approach, minority males were arrested in 33% of all cases; under a probable cause pro-arrest policy, more minority males were arrested, yet they only accounted for 8.5% of the total arrests, much more in line with the actual percentage of minorities in the overall population.[108] In sum, pro-arrest policies, by establishing clear working guidelines, can reduce the arbitrary impact of prejudice and stereotype yet still offer enough flexibility to relieve the harshness occasioned by a categorical application of the law.

COMPELLING THE VICTIM TO TESTIFY

It is clear that a victim's testimony is critical to a successful prosecution: the Seattle Battered Woman's Project found that the conviction rate when victims did not testify was only 30% of that when they did.[109] Nevertheless, does this mean that prosecutors should be empowered to force the victim to testify at the trial of her abuser? What happens if the victim refuses to take the stand? In Canada, some judges have charged victims of wife assault with contempt of court for refusing to testify against their batterers. Linda MacLeod, a leading Canadian researcher on domestic violence, describes such conduct as demonstrating a "glaring lack of sensitivity."[110] She cites a shelter worker:

> We can't become too purist about the effectiveness of criminal justice system intervention, or the criminal justice system will simply become a major way to victimize women. For example, the current trend in some jurisdictions to charge women with contempt of court if they refuse to testify is victimizing women. I can see why it is necessary from a purist point of view. It's necessary to leave an impression on the women as well as on the men that wife-battering is a crime, and that it's not alright to drop charges in wife battering cases, any more than it is alright to drop charges in other criminal cases. But wife-battering cases aren't just like other cases.[111]

Forcing victims to testify might not be necessary if the police prepared detailed reports during the investigation of the alleged assault, since these reports could be introduced as evidence demonstrating the nature and severity of the assault. Laws of evidence could be flexibly applied so as to also render admissible statements made to the police by the victim before the trial. On a related note, if sentencing policies were better suited to the needs of victims, then battered women might be more likely to take the stand willingly.

PROPOSALS FOR REFORM: WHERE SHOULD WE GO?

This paper suggests that the governing paradigm orienting any future reforms to society's response to female partner abuse ought to be an interdisciplinary one. To this end, a comprehensive approach is proposed, linking the law, social services, and educational programs. The fusion of these various elements can help provide a more coordinated response to an endemic problem.

REFORMS TO THE JUSTICE SYSTEM

The first step in this analysis is to determine whether the criminal justice system is a worthwhile place to address the needs of women beaten by their intimate partners. Authors have suggested that the criminal justice response, even if ameliorated, will only marginally reduce violence against women in the household.[112] The arbitrary way with which the criminal law has dealt with beaten women in the past gives credibility to such a point. The adversarial nature of the criminal justice system, as well as the fear of facing gender discrimination in the courts, dissuades many women from proceeding criminally.[113] As noted by MacLeod: "No more than 30% [of battered women] felt they would ever seriously consider using the criminal justice system and only 20% believed they would use it in the future. As one woman said, 'I've been living with fights for the past 15 years. As far as I can tell, taking him to court is another fight. I just want to put all those battles behind me.'"[114]

Should we then look outside the criminal justice system to respond to the needs of battered women? Clearly, yes. However, this does not mean that the criminal justice system cannot be part of an overall response. This paper shares MacLeod's optimism that the criminal justice system has the potential to be an important ally in deterring wife battering.[115] Female partner abuse must be regarded as criminal activity. However, a mere tinkering with existing provisions is not what is needed. The reforms must not be a matter of degree, but of kind. The criminal justice system has the responsibility to present itself as an accessible and user-friendly option. Victims must not only know they can go to court, they must have some expectation that the court is willing and able to act to reduce their danger.[116]

The criminal justice system (as well as the entire law) is the product of a patriarchal society which has, up until very recently, legitimated violence against women in the household. Violence against women, especially by that woman's partner within the home, is still not universally viewed as "criminal" behaviour. Many people approve of a man slapping his spouse to "discipline" her or "keep her in line"; crimes involving intimates are often rated as less serious than crimes committed by strangers.[117] As long as womanbeating in the home is somehow viewed as "normal," our society shall not adequately respond to it. Conjugal violence must be characterized as unacceptable behaviour in all cases. Restructuring the criminal law can both indicate as well as contribute to these attitudinal changes. Catherine Cerulli of the Domestic Violence Clinic of the University of Buffalo School of Law echoes this point: "The criminal justice system cannot change a societal ill; however, it can send a message that family violence is a crime — and will no longer be tolerated."[118]

This paper explores seven areas in which the criminal law can be reformed so as to better meet the needs of beaten women. These reforms involve amending the

Criminal Code, introducing the concurrent availability of civil remedies, restructuring sentencing policy so as to increase its rehabilitative effects, as well as redesigning the setting in which, and procedures by which, female partner abuse complaints are to be heard. Many of these proposals emerge from the results of the comparative analysis of the Ontario and New York responses to female partner abuse.

AMENDMENTS TO CRIMINAL LEGISLATION:
RECOGNIZING THE CIVIL RIGHTS ISSUES INVOLVED

"Crimes against women" penal provisions This paper suggests that the *Criminal Code* be amended to include a separate category of offences entitled "crimes against women." These would include domestic violence, sexual assault, as well as femicide. Within the context of conjugal violence, these provisions would allow different penalties to be meted out for female partner abuse than for male–male violence. For example, a presumption could be created that female partner abuse is to be prosecuted as aggravated and not simple assault. Additionally, sentences for female partner abuse — as opposed to those for general assault — would ordinarily include mandatory treatment for the abuser. In short, all things being equal, a man would be differently punished for assaulting his spouse than for assaulting a stranger in a pool-hall. Is it not logical, given the distinctive nature of the harms engendered in intimate assault as opposed to stranger assault, that the law respond differently to both crimes? Conjugal violence, as discussed earlier, is characterized by rates of recidivism much higher than stranger assault. Victims generally do not have the opportunity to simply "leave" the relationship and subsequently "disappear" from the life of the aggressor — economic and emotional dependence, responsibilities towards children, as well as the effects of the "battered wife syndrome" often induce the victim into remaining intimately involved with the batterer. Within the context of acquaintance and stranger assault, the lives of the victim and the aggressor are not intertwined. These considerations, combined with the fact that it is often extremely easy for the aggressor to determine the whereabouts of the victim even after the law has intervened, underscore the need for protection orders to be readily available and consistently enforced.

Major constitutional issues would arise if such provisions were introduced in Canada. For example, it could be argued that these provisions violate the equality guarantees of the *Canadian Charter of Rights and Freedoms* since they would punish a man more severely for assaulting a female partner than they would punish a woman for assaulting an intimate male partner. Although the "crimes against women" provisions do create a distinction on the basis of sex — an enumerated ground listed in s. 15 — it must be kept in mind that s. 15 has been consistently interpreted to allow certain individuals to be treated unequally in order to provide greater overall equality.[119] It is clear that domestic violence — overwhelmingly committed by men against women — reinforces and perpetuates the disadvantaged status of women as a group.[120] The purpose of the "crimes against women" provisions is to fight against this collective disadvantage. A 1993 decision of the Supreme Court of Canada — *Conway* v. *Attorney General of Canada* — can be used to uphold the constitutionality of the "crimes against women" provisions. In *Conway*, La Forest J. held that: "The jurisprudence of this court is clear: equality does not necessarily connote identical treatment and, in fact, different treatment may be called for in certain cases to promote equality.... The reality of the relationship between the sexes is such that the historical trend of violence perpetrated by men against women is not matched by a comparable trend pursuant to which men are the victims and women the aggressors."[121] A compelling argument can thus be made that crimes against women should be treated more seriously because their gendered nature renders them discriminatory and in violation of the victim's personal integrity as well as the civil rights of women as a collectivity.

Alternatively, it could be suggested that the "crimes against women" amendments are discriminatory due to the fact that they could punish male–female intimate violence more severely than male–male intimate violence,[122] thereby potentially treating violence within same-sex couples less seriously than within heterosexual couples. This would clearly be an undesirable result, given the fact that battering is a fact of life in many same-sex relationships. However, the mere fact that the "crimes against women" provisions direct their attention towards heterosexual violence does not necessarily mean that intimate violence in same-sex couples shall be neglected. In fact, many of the recommendations proposed by this paper can be useful in developing a more effective response to reduce the extent of intimate violence in same-sex couples. One potential element in this response could be the amending of the *Criminal Code* to punish male–male and female–female violence differently depending on whether the parties to that violence were strangers or intimately involved in a relationship.[123]

Lastly, an argument can be made that these provisions violate section 15 of the *Charter* due to the fact that they create a discriminatory distinction between assaulters of intimate partners and assaulters of strangers or acquaintances. Nevertheless, it is unclear as to whether the distinction between men who assault intimate partners and men who assault strangers is one that would even be caught by section 15 in the first place.[124] The *Criminal Code* establishes a plethora of distinctions among offences based on the extent to which society disapproves of the particular conduct in question and the need of the potential class of victims to be protected. According to the section 15 jurisprudence, these distinctions shall only be in violation of the *Charter* if they directly or indirectly disadvantage groups facing historical or structural discrimination or groups deemed to constitute "discrete and insular minorities."[125] It seems problematic that the class of men who assault intimate partners qualifies as such a group.

In sum, entrenching these provisions within the civil rights context would convey a powerful message: female partner abuse is not merely a crime against a particular individual, but a form of discrimination that, on a systemic level, constitutes the most blunt tool in the subordination of women. If we have recognized sexual harassment as a human rights issue, as in section 7 of the Ontario *Human Rights Code*, why not do the same for domestic violence, especially since it is a more extreme point on the same continuum of misogyny?

Placing womanbeating within this constitutional context could also justify more stringent restraining orders on batterers as well as tougher sanctions for their violation. Certain American courts have already moved in this direction. For example, a 1990 Pennsylvania decision, *Coffman v. Wilson Police Department*, held that a protection order gave its holder a constitutionally protected "property interest" in police enforcement due to the fact that it created a "special relationship" between the holder and the police.[126] Other courts have gone one step further and held that the failure to adequately enforce protection orders is a violation of the civil rights of the class of women protected by them.[127] A more liberal reading of either the Fourteenth Amendment or section 1983 of the *Civil Rights Act* could perhaps support a claim that a failure to adequately punish an abuser constitutes discrimination against a disempowered group (women more generally) and a failure to accord them their "property interest" in equal benefit of the law. This, in turn, could justify the inclusion of more stringent conditions into protection orders in situations of womanbeating. A similar argument could be made in Canada. In fact, the *Charter's* substantive theory of equality, as opposed to the "formal equality" embedded in the American Constitution, gives Canadian advocates greater chances of success in arguing for these separate and more stringent provisions.

Advocacy groups could also use section 7 of the *Charter* to ensure that restraining orders, peace bonds, and orders of protection are adequately enforced. In Canada, the police are under a public duty to preserve the peace, prevent crimes, and apprehend offenders. As public authorities, they are bound to act in a manner consonant with the *Charter*. A failure to adequately award or enforce protection orders arguably results in a denial of a victim's right to the security of her person not made in accordance with fundamental justice. The "spirit" of sections 7 and 15 of the *Charter* could also encourage the creation of a new type of joint civil/criminal order of protection specific only to female partner abuse cases. This would eliminate the present confusion (there are at least three or four types of orders a woman can acquire) as well as sclerosis within the system (a probation officer may not know if a civil order had previously been awarded).

Aside from the constitutional considerations, there are other legitimate concerns involved in the creation of a separate series of offences for womanbeating in Canada. In many ways, most successful attempts to reverse the law's neglect of female partner abuse have come from demonstrating that violence in the home is *just as serious* as violence outside of it. By categorizing such abuse separately, as was formerly the case, will the crime of wife assault once again become trivialized? In response to this concern, it would have to be conceded that the creation of separate categories can often lead to marginalization. But the purpose of carving out a separate category in this case would be to make male crimes against women *more serious than* "men against men" crimes. This would help extract the courts from the "vicious circle of precedent" that presently exists in the domestic violence context and limits the severity of punishments.

Provocation "Provocation" should be given less weight as a mitigating factor in sentencing. At present, provocation-style defences reduce sentences in two-thirds of femicide and general spousal assault cases.[128] The judicial definition of provocation is very wide, going beyond what was intended in the *Criminal Code*. It can cover a woman yelling at a man for hours.[129] A woman's wearing of a T-shirt showing polar bears engaged in sexual acts has also been deemed to be "provocative."[130] This T-shirt permitted the batterer of this woman to be acquitted of assault and merely fined one thousand dollars. Such a liberal application of provocation as a mitigating factor denies fundamental justice to the victims of domestic assault.[131] Physical violence is simply not acceptable behaviour, barring truly extenuating circumstances.[132]

Drunkenness A large number of domestic violence incidents occur when the abuser is intoxicated. Although, in Canada, drunkenness is not a defence to general intent crimes such as simple assault, it is a defence to crimes of specific intent such as aggravated assault. It is clear that the special context of female partner abuse, its cyclical nature, and the high incidence of repeat offences should not consistently allow drunkenness in the one particular incident brought to the attention of the court to permit the abuser to be prosecuted only under the less serious crime of simple assault.

Bail and no-contact orders All Justices of the Peace should be instructed that bail must be awarded only if the abuser agrees to a no-contact order. Moreover, in all cases when the abuser is released on bail, the victim should be immediately notified of the timing and conditions thereof. To this end, probation officers must also become involved in the process so as to ensure that a batterer out on bail is held responsible for any violation of a no-contact order.

INTRODUCTION OF A CONCURRENT CIVIL REMEDY FOR WOMAN BATTERY

The comparison of the responses to female partner abuse in New York and Ontario indicates the potential advantages of a rapidly and easily accessible civil remedy to victims of domestic violence. It permits the victim to quickly access safety and compensation, as well as to avoid the potential drawbacks of a criminal trial. By expanding their options, such a remedy may induce beaten women to file a complaint without fearing that the batterer will be incarcerated or be burdened with a criminal record.

Serious thought should be given to the implementation of such a separate system in Canada. However, the bar of mutual exclusivity found in New York must be lifted. A woman should be able to file civilly while the state presses criminal charges. Rules against double jeopardy would preclude "double punishment" yet would permit the woman to seek full relief through criminal compensation boards as well as civil remedies. Other victims can seek civil relief or injunctions against acts which have been deemed to be criminal. Why not battered women? Ostensibly, in order to guard against unjust enrichment, any award from a Criminal Compensation Board would be reduced by the size of the civil award, if any. A major shortcoming of a "criminal-only" approach (such as Ontario's) is that it makes it more difficult for the victim to personally vindicate her rights or obtain any compensation. Although all Canadian provinces have Criminal Compensation Boards as well as "Victim Assistance Programs," many crime victims have difficulty obtaining financial reparations. Creating a civil remedy might mitigate these problems, as well as reduce the pressure on the taxpayers' purse. Granted, there is always the risk that the batterer will be impecunious. In order to respond to this possibility, a special compensation fund could be created from which battered women could obtain their civil damage awards.

The existence of a complementary civil remedy can help stop the gaps that any criminal remedy, no matter how well-designed, will leave.[133] A criminal trial will normally take place several months after the charge has been laid, and there is limited protection available to women during this time period. It is here that a civil remedy such as a temporary protection order can be used if such an order did not form part of the original criminal probation or bail terms.

Any breach of a civil order of protection or an order of no-contact should be criminalized and entail the immediate issuance of an arrest warrant against the perpetrator. Section 127 of the *Criminal Code*, providing for conviction by indictment and imprisonment for up to two years for breach of a court order, could be purposively used to ensure compliance.

MacLeod found that many battered women are more comfortable with civil proceedings and believe that such proceedings better meet their needs.[134] The fact that the victim has a good deal of control over the case creates a feeling of empowerment and a sense that one is vindicating one's rights. The introduction of the civil remedy could prompt more women to report their assaults and use the justice system in a proactive way.[135]

TREATMENT AS THE FOCAL POINT OF SENTENCING POLICY

In both criminal and civil actions, the preferred disposition should involve some form of treatment for the abuser. Treatment, although far from ideal, appears to be more effective than jail. As discussed earlier, combined use of both has been demonstrated to be the most effective available deterrent.[136] Treatment addresses not only physical abuse (the tip of the iceberg) but also the psychological and emotional abuse with which it is inextricably linked. MacLeod's research in Ontario reveals that most women felt that mandatory counselling sessions would be effective.[137] Mandatory batterer's counselling is not expensive. Cerulli estimates that a "model intervention" of arrest, temporary jail-time, and therapy would cost two thousand sixty dollars (U.S.) per incident.[138] This cost is nominal when compared to the human and economic toll of female partner abuse in Canadian society.[139]

The treatment should focus on the batterer's violence. The programs should stress awareness of violent behaviour, the constructive channelling of emotions, and instil a greater accountability for one's actions. Although many incidents of battering occur when the aggressor is under the influence of alcohol, sending that person to alcoholism rehabilitation (as is often the case) is not a solution to his misogyny. All that such treatment might produce is a sober batterer. If drug dependence caused family violence, the enormous discrepancy between the number of male and female perpetrators of such violence would simply not exist.

The argument that batterers' therapy ought to be central to the fight against womanbeating is not without its critics.[140] These individuals feel that batterers' treatment directs resources away from women's shelters and places the attention of the state on the offender as opposed to the victim. These critics legitimately point to the fact that treatment has not proven itself to be wholly effective. Another point is that treatment will not help those who are unreceptive to it; in fact, forcing someone to attend therapy sessions against his will could just increase his vindictiveness.[141]

Nevertheless, this paper places considerable emphasis on the potential of batterers' treatment. It is encouraging that some counselling programs report success rates of over 60%.[142] Therapy is especially important since female partner abuse is often a learned phenomenon. It is estimated that 40% to 60% of violent men witnessed womanbeating as children and were thus socialized into believing that hitting one's partner is a proper way for a man to deal with his anger.[143] It is clear that the reduction of criminal activity in society invariably requires that some resources be directed towards offenders. In any case, incarceration in and of itself is a costly process. Clearly, any expenditure of resources on batterers' therapy should not come at the undue expense of any allocations made to shelters and victims' housing. Rather, society should strive to develop an optimal allocation of resources through which both the victim and batterer can be helped.

Obligatory therapy through civil proceedings raises important constitutional issues. The *Charter* rights of the accused could be infringed by the fact that he could be forced to attend therapy sessions (thereby having his s. 7 right to liberty of the person interfered with) merely on a civil standard. It could be argued that the interference with a person's liberty engendered by placing that person in a mandatory therapy program can only respect fundamental justice if it is meted out pursuant to a finding of criminal intent beyond a reasonable doubt. However, there are also persuasive arguments supporting the constitutionality of these provisions. In Canada, there are a wide array of statutes that permit incarceration (a larger interference with one's liberty than attendance at therapy sessions) pursuant to the commission of civil public welfare offences. In some cases, the constitutionality of these statutes has been upheld even if they operate on a reverse onus strict liability basis.[144] Finally, if this new civil cause of action is based on the New York *Family Court Act*, then the standard of proof is much more than a simple balance of probabilities. In fact, the petitioner must demonstrate the existence of the essential ingredients of a criminal offence in order to succeed on her claim. Thus, the standard of proof is nearly equivalent to a criminal standard, the major difference being that the proceedings themselves do not follow criminal rules of procedure, but rather civil rules.

A TORT OF FAILURE TO ARREST IN CANADA

The development of civil actions for failure to arrest has induced many police departments to ameliorate both their arrest policies and the enforcement of protection orders. This essay proposes that such causes of action be introduced in Canada either through legislative enactment or judicial activism.

The emergence of pro-arrest policies among American police departments is partly related to a handful of successful civil suits launched by battered women against the police for "failure to protect." The leading case in this regard is *Thurman v. City of Torrington*.[145] It involved a Connecticut woman who, during a domestic assault, called the police. The police arrived on the scene yet did not arrest the abuser. After they left, he further assaulted her, resulting in permanent disability and disfigurement. She successfully won a tort claim in negligence against the police for "failure to protect domestic violence victims based on a non-arrest policy, or lack of a formal policy." Ms. Thurman relied on section 1983 of the *Civil Rights Act*, which provides citizens with a private remedy when state officials deprive individuals of their constitutional rights. There was clear evidence that the police responded less effectively to the Thurman call due to its domestic nature. The fall-out of the *Torrington* decision was widespread. Police departments across the U.S.A. were placed on the alert, and the state of Connecticut passed a mandatory arrest policy.

In Canada, the ambit of the duty of care that is to be imposed on the police (and the question of whether individual officers can be subject to personal liability) is naturally subject to legislative will and judicial interpretation. However, in determining the scope of the duty, provincial *Police Acts* shall have to be taken into consideration, since in most provinces, such legislation imposes affirmative duties upon the police to protect the public. In conclusion, the existence of these civil tort claims can thus help ensure that all Canadian police forces develop some sort of arrest policy, exercise diligence when deciding not to arrest an alleged abuser, and ensure that calls related to alleged violations of protection orders receive prompt responses.

THE INTERSECTION OF CRIMINAL AND FAMILY LAW

Since female partner abuse often occurs at the point of separation of the parties, family law should also have a role to play in the fight against womanbeating.[146] For example, the *Divorce Act*[147] should be amended so as to allow domestic violence civil claims in battery to be allowed to be grafted onto no-fault divorce claims. On another note, s. 46 of the Ontario *Family Law Act* and s. 36.1 of the British Columbia *Family Relations Act* permit restraining orders to be readily available through family law statutes. However, these statutes are sparingly used as mechanisms to secure these types of protective orders. Furthermore, sections 19 and 24 of the Ontario *Act* permit orders of exclusive possession to be given for the matrimonial home — this can be used in cases of domestic violence to allow the victim to safely stay with the children in the home. This section is only available to married couples, not common law spouses. The situation is different in British Columbia, where s. 79 of the *Family Relations Act*, empowering the court to order one spouse not to enter the premises occupied by the other spouse, applies by virtue of s. 1 to married couples as well as unmarried couples "living together as husband and wife for a period of not less than two years."[148] All of these family law provisions should be more purposively applied in the fight against womanbeating in Canada.

REDESIGNING COURTROOMS AND PROCEDURES

The possibility of creating special courtrooms for domestic violence cases with separate judges and prosecutors should be investigated.[149] These courts would cover civil and criminal matters related to female partner abuse as well as violence against women outside the home. These would not form a self-contained court system, but a separate structure within existing Criminal and Unified Family Courts.[150] A battered woman would thus be potentially able to obtain a temporary order of protection, sue the abuser civilly, divorce him, obtain maintenance, and help prosecute him criminally in the same court. Tort matters involving the police's failure to protect adequately would also be brought within this same court.

The creation of such an internal system could help co-ordinate the legal response to female partner abuse. An additional element in this co-ordination process is the gathering of information: a separate set of records for all violence against women crimes should be kept.[151] At present, womanbeating offences are not separately classified outside of the penal code provisions under which they are prosecuted. Domestic violence cases also need to be recorded separately in the law reporters. At present, in the vast majority of cases involving wife abuse, judicial dispositions are made without any written decisions. This must also change so as to create a solid series of precedents clarifying the state of the law. All restraining orders should be registered in the Canadian Police Information Computer to assist officers in obtaining immediate information when attending at a call.

Different rules of procedure should facilitate the introduction of expert witnesses and prior victim statements to the police as well as evidence related to prior assaults. The fact that it will be mandatory in every case for the police to fill out a report means that less responsibility shall fall on the shoulders of the victim in order to testify as a witness for the prosecution. Judges and lawyers should be educated on the sensitive nature of female partner abuse and should be instructed to inquire about whether the economic and housing needs of the victim and her children are being met.

In terms of courtroom design, the victims ought to be provided with separate waiting rooms so that the perpetrators do not have the opportunity to intimidate or threaten them prior to the trial, either verbally or simply through eye contact. Even the mere presence of the abuser in the same room prior to the trial might be enough to dissuade a victim from cogently presenting her case. The Minneapolis Court has even redesigned the actual courtroom to promote an informal environment: victim and abuser sit at a table with lawyers and referees.[152] Staffed daycare (found in the New York City Family Court) should be provided so as to allow victims greater flexibility in dealing with any delays that may arise in the disposition of the case. The availability of legal aid and advocacy groups to beaten women must also be increased. These new courtrooms should contain a woman's advocacy centre offering *pro bono* representation to all petitioners as well as witness assistance for victims in criminal matters. Experience reveals that victims accompanied by advocates have a better chance of success and are more confident in themselves.[153] These legal services should also be made available to accuseds and defendants so as to ensure the fairness of the proceedings.

A lesson can be learned from the "accelerated docket" approach taken by the Westminster (Colorado) Municipal Court. This Court hears all domestic violence cases during certain periods of the day. All trials occur within twenty-one days of the incident. The fact that trial is often by jury helps educate the public on the seriousness with which female partner abuse ought to be treated. The main advantage of the accelerated docket is that it allows the court to quickly intervene so as to bring services to the victim and therapy to the perpetrator before additional harm may be done within the nexus of the violent relationship. Although there is a risk that the accelerated docket could endanger the fairness of the trial or heighten the powerlessness felt by the woman, it also recognizes that overly long delays are to the benefit of no-one.

INCREASED USE OF VICTIM IMPACT STATEMENTS

Victims should also be involved in the sentencing process. They can assist the judge in determining the length and nature of a sentence through the use of Victim Impact Statements. These statements allow the victim to indicate, among other things, whether she feels incarceration is necessary, or what type of therapy could best help the batterer.

Judges should retain a certain element of discretion in terms of deciding whether to follow the suggestions in the Victim Impact Statement. For example, in a 1993 decision, the Alberta Court of Appeal approved a trial judge's decision to impose a three-month intermittent sentence upon a wife-beater (instead of the twenty-month jail term he would normally have imposed) at the behest of the accused's wife, who implored the court's leniency so that she could reconcile with the accused.[154] The majority decision was accompanied by the dissent of Bielby J., who pointed out that the use of Victim Impact Statements can invite situations in which the accused unduly influences the victim with regard to the making of submissions to the sentencing judge. A careful balance needs to be drawn so that the potential empowerment that can arise from Victim Impact Statements does not turn into a liability.

REFORMS TO AND CO-ORDINATION WITH THE SOCIAL SERVICES INFRASTRUCTURE

"Sensitive pro-arrest," a "concurrent two-track system," and *Criminal Code* amendments are not panaceas to an endemic problem. They are merely significant changes the justice system should consider if it wishes to improve its response to female part-ner abuse. It must be emphasized that the justice system is only one part in a broad constellation of services that should be attentive to the needs of battered women. There must be a broader community response. In fact, many victims of domestic violence prioritize needs such as counselling, housing, and emotional support above legal advice. Particular attention must be paid to the provision of these services (or, in the least, information thereon) in rural areas.[155] Moreover, in many areas, such information must be made available in a wide array of languages so that all batter-ing victims — not only those proficient in English or French — can learn about their rights and options.[156] This information should be made available in commu-nity centres as well as by police officers whenever called to appear at the scene of a domestic dispute.

The economic needs of victims must be taken into account. Most victims have children and are financially dependent on their abusers. This creates what the London Battered Woman's Advocacy Clinic labels "economic entrapment." Since the "entrapping" factor is the relative drop in the standard of living a woman faces when she leaves her abusive husband, this phenomenon affects *all* women, whether rich or poor. Economic independence is necessary if victims are to have alternatives to their battering relationship. Refresher courses should be available to permit these women easier entry into a labour market from which they may have been excluded for years.

The medical profession must be called upon to play a special role. At present in Ontario, if a doctor treats a patient whom she strongly believes to be injured as a result of domestic violence, she is under no obligation to report the incident. Nevertheless, despite the confidentiality of the doctor/patient relationship, doctors are under a duty to report perceived child abuse to the Children's Aid Society. Should doctors not be under a similar duty to report domestic violence? At the least, they should perhaps be mandated to inform the patient of her options.

One particular area in considerable need of attention is temporary housing for battering victims. In New York State, up to 40% of homeless women are homeless due to domestic violence.[157] Twenty to 40% of domestic violence victims return to their batterers due to a lack of alternative housing. Both first-stage (immediate post-assault) housing as well as second-stage (extended transition accommodation available for up to two years after the assault) housing must be developed. The Metro Toronto Committee Against Wife Assault feels that " ... once suitable housing is secured, the possibility of women returning to a violent relationship is greatly reduced."[158]

CONCLUSION

As long as the politicization of wife battering is resisted and the role of patriarchy remains unrecognized, the public response to wife battering cannot be adequately effective against the problem.[159]

Womanbeating is the most blatant form of sex-discrimination in Canadian soci-ety. It constitutes the most blunt mechanism with which women are deprived of their civil rights. The placing of female partner abuse in this context indicates the need for, and justifies the wide array of, reforms suggested by this paper. The ques-tion is not one of penetrating into the bedrooms of the nation; it is, rather, of safe-guarding human dignity and freedom.

The comparison between Buffalo and Toronto/London indicates that pro-arrest policies are much more effective than the absence of any policy in changing attitudes and charging abusers. Yet it is equally clear that the criminal law is not the only part of the entire justice system that should attack the problem of female partner abuse. Complementary civil remedies outside the sphere of the criminal law can, if well designed, also play an important role in addressing female partner abuse.

Just as the criminal law can only play a part in reducing female partner abuse, so too can reducing female partner abuse only play a part in the creation of a more egalitarian society. The fight for equality in the home must proceed hand in hand with the fight for equality in the workplace and the political arena.

Female partner abuse is only one form of family violence. We should not lose sight of the fact that child and elder abuse is also commonplace in homes throughout North America. Lessons learned from the law's attempt to curb female partner abuse could help to inform attacks on these other forms of equally insidious violence within the family.

QUESTIONS TO CONSIDER

1. Review arguments for using criminal and civil powers in cases of violence against women. What are the drawbacks and advantages of each approach?
2. Some analysts argue that violence by men against women is pervasive in our society. Moreover, such violence is often not taken seriously by authorities, and strong measures need to be taken to protect women. Others protest that there is a tendency to highlight physical and sexual violence against women and to downplay or ignore other forms of violence, including violence experienced by men. Using outside readings and Drumbl's review, weigh the evidence concerning the impact of violence against women and, briefly, which legal responses you think are best suited to addressing such violence.
3. Debate whether mandatory arrest policies in cases of alleged female partner abuse serve the principles of public safety and due process of law. What limitations does Drumbl outline in his essay? Do you favour implementation of such arrest policies? Explain how these policies, or other policies, might best address abuse of female partners or other victims.

NOTES

1. Surveys conclude that 50% of all women over the age of 18 in Canada (a total of 5 000 000 individuals) have been victims of family violence at some point in their lives: Statistics Canada Report on Violence against Women in Canada, cited in A. Mitchell, "50% of Women Report Assaults," *The Globe & Mail* (19 November 1993) A1. American surveys arrive at a similar percentage: New York Senate Committee on Investigations, Taxation, and Government, *Domestic Violence: The Hidden Crime* by R.M. Goodman (24 February 1992) at 4 [hereinafter *Domestic Violence: The Hidden Crime*]. M. Roy, ed., *The Abusive Partner: An Analysis of Domestic Battering* (New York: Van Nostrand Reinhold, 1982) at 259, estimates that violence occurs at least once in two-thirds of all marriages.
2. This term was developed by Caroline Forell in a recent article: "Stopping the Violence: Mandatory Arrest and Police Tort Liability for Failure to Assist Battered Women," (1990–91) 6 *Berkeley Women's Law Journal* 215. It applies to domestic as

well as public violence, and shows how wife assault is a subset of violence against women more generally — a conceptual approach adopted by this paper.

3. Under a pro-arrest policy, when the police arrive at the scene of a battering incident, a presumption of arrest applies to any person the police have reasonable grounds to believe was the perpetrator; the police officer can choose not to arrest if she feels there to be "probable cause" that such an arrest will be counter-productive to, for example, the interests of the victim or children. A mandatory arrest policy, on the other hand, requires in its purest form that the police officer arrest in every situation where there are reasonable grounds to believe a domestic assault took place. The differences between these two forms of policing practices as well as their respective merits is further discussed in section IV(B), *infra*.

4. U.S. Department of Justice, *Report to the Nation on Crime and Justice* (October 1983) at 21.

5. W.C. DeKeseredy & R. Hinch, *Woman Abuse: Sociological Perspectives* (Toronto: Thompson Educational Publishing Inc., 1991) at 11.

6. *Domestic Violence: The Hidden Crime, supra*, note 1 at 11.

7. Nevertheless, in using this term, one must not close one's eyes to two facts: (1) serious abuse can occur in male and female same-sex relationships; and (2) men are very occasionally physically abused by their female partners.

8. *R. v. Hutton* (1992), 76 C.C.C (3d) 476 at 477.

9. "Canada: Wife Battering Myths and Realities" (1991) 17 *Women's International Network News* 42. Twenty-five to 35% of women in emergency rooms are there because of injuries inflicted by a batterer.

10. *Regina v. Whynot* (1983), 9 C.C.C. (3d) 449 (N.S.S.C.) indicates how women who killed their abusers after being forced to engage in bestiality with the household dog were, as late as 1983, not able to use the *Criminal Code* self-defence provisions. The accused spent 6 months in a Nova Scotia jail after a plea bargain. The more recent Supreme Court decision in *R. v. Lavallee* (1990), 55 C.C.C. (3d) 97 has implicitly overturned *Whynot*.

11. Psychologists such as Lenore Walker, author of *The Battered Woman* (New York: Harper & Row, 1979), feel that instances of humiliation, emotional abuse, and verbal harassment can be just as painful as, if not more painful than, physical battery. There is debate as to whether such activity should amount to "violence" of sufficient nature as to be criminalized. Although criminalizing such activity might carry the justice system too deeply into the personal relationships of Canadians, it is interesting to note that there is some indication that Ontario courts are moving in the direction of accepting that "domestic violence" can be psychological in nature: *Hill v. Hill* (1987), 10 R.F.L. (3d) 225 (Ont. Dist. Ct.). The *Criminal Code* guards against intimidation (s. 423) and harassment (sections 264(1) and 372(3)). Although many women are both intimidated and harassed by their abusers, these sections have been rarely used to protect them. Nevertheless, if this harassment involves threats of murder or sexual assault (and is accompanied by acts or gestures of violence), then the abuser can be found to have engaged in criminal activity: *Criminal Code*, s. 745, *R. v. McCraw* (1989), 35 O.A.C. 144.

12. Statistics Canada Report on Violence against Women in Canada, cited in Mitchell, *supra*, note 1. Furthermore, Bowker's 1983 American survey, cited in E.J. Peters, ed., *Second Stage Housing for Battered Women in Canada* (Queen's University, 1990) at 5, shows that 70% of wife-beaters with families abused the children. Linda MacLeod found that 26% of battered women said their assaulters abused their children physically, 48% said they abused the children emotionally, and 7% said they abused the children sexually: cited in Peters at 6. This indicates that section 16(9) of the *Divorce Act*, S.C. 1991, c. D-3.4, should be amended so as to create a presumption that

custody shall be precluded from being awarded to a parent convicted of intimate assault. At present, the court is mandated not to take into consideration the past conduct of any person unless the conduct is relevant to that person's ability to act as a parent of a child. Given the link between female partner abuse and the propensity to commit child abuse, the statute should be amended so as to explicitly refer to this link.

13. Batterers often continue to harass the victim over an extended period of time well after the termination of the relationship or the laying of charges. Victims know this: the Canadian Urban Victimization Survey found that 50% of all women who did not report their abuse failed to do so out of "fear of revenge by the offender": Solicitor General (Canada), *Canadian Urban Victimization Survey: Female Victims of Crime* (Ottawa: Minister of Supply and Services, 1985) at 5. *Ex post* abuse rates are very high even when the victim *never* returns to the home or man after the incident: 44% of such women reported at least one violent incident after the break-up: Peters, *ibid.*, at 8.

14. L.W. Sherman & R.A. Berk, "The Specific Deterrent Effects of Arrest for Domestic Assault" (1984) 49 *Am. Soc. Rev.* 261 at 266. Within the Canadian context, the study of the Ontario Women's Directorate referred to in *R. v. Hutton* (1992), 76 C.C.C. (3d) 476 at 478 concluded that many incidents of femicide were committed by persons either on parole, probation, a peace bond, or some form of restraining order.

15. The November 1993 Statistics Canada survey of violence against women in Canada found that neither income nor education affected rates of wife battering. The only statistical correlation that was found related to whether the batterer had a history of battering in his family. In fact, women with violent fathers-in-law were three times more likely to be assaulted than other women. It is for this reason, as suggested in section V.A.(3) of this essay, that therapy must form an integral part of sentencing policy.

16. See DeKeseredy & Hinch, *supra*, note 5 at 28.

17. R. Tong, *Women, Sex, and the Law* (New Jersey: Rowman & Allanheld, 1984) at 170.

18. An example of this is found in Canada's aboriginal communities: it is common knowledge among such communities that " ... police are less apt to press charges in cases where the victim is aboriginal": M.G. Brown, *Gender Equality in the Courts: Criminal Law* (Ottawa: National Association of Women and the Law, 1991) at 2–7.

19. M. Steinman, "Lowering Recidivism Among Men Who Batter Women," (1990) 17 *Journal of Police Science and Administration* 124.

20. Buffalo Police Department Training Bulletin No. 86-3.

21. C. Cerulli, *The Need to Co-ordinate the Buffalo Legal Community's Response to Family Violence* (Buffalo Public Interest Law Program, 1990) at 13 [hereinafter *The Need to Co-ordinate*].

22. Personal Interview, 9 November 1992. According to Tomkins, there are two explanations for this behaviour: (1) the increased scope given to the Family Court since 1986; and (2) the fact that, due to the absence of a mandatory arrest policy, police arrive at the scene without a strategy or mandate and are thus less willing to take charge of the situation, placing the responsibility on the victim.

23. *The Need to Co-ordinate*, *supra*, note 21 at 4.

24. Even if the police arrest, the victim can arrange with the prosecutor that charges be dropped and she can then sue civilly.

25. The only exception to this is paragraph 813 of the *Family Court Act*, which permits for a case proceeding in Family Court to be transferred to Criminal Court at the discretion of the judge. This happens rarely.

26. Interestingly enough, New York remains the only jurisdiction in the United States that requires victims to "select" a court — it is for this reason that New York is a useful choice for a comparative analysis. The New York Senate Committee on

Investigations, Taxations, and Government Operations recommended in 1992 that this coerced choice be repealed. It is seen as unfair for it forces a choice at a moment when the woman is particularly vulnerable and has not yet been able to assess her own needs or which court could better address them. An abuser can effectively avoid criminal responsibility by pressuring the victim to file in civil court if she is to file at all. Aggressors are known to have enormous moral suasion over their victims.

27. *McKinney's Consolidated Law of New York* (1909), Book 39. Criminal law in the United States falls within the competence of the state legislatures. The *New York Penal Law* divides offences into special categories. Paragraph 60.01 prescribes penalties for each category of offence. There are four categories: felonies, misdemeanours, violations, and traffic infractions. A felony is any offence which carries a possible custodial term of one year or more, a misdemeanour can carry a custodial term of up to one year, and a violation 15 days. Both felonies and misdemeanours are further subdivided into different classes identified by letters (A, B, C, D, E for felonies and A, B, and "unclassified" for misdemeanours). Class A felonies, the most serious, are further subdivided into two classifications (A-I and A-II). Every sentence is related to the classification of the offence in question and can be an indeterminate amount between a statutorily fixed maximum and minimum. The lengths of sentences are thus more consistent than in Canada. There is a tendency to classify serious domestic violence cases as Class D felonies or Class A misdemeanours. This means that imprisonment is never mandatory unless the accused is a repeat offender and commits an assault causing grievous bodily harm.

28. However, unlike the civil remedies, criminal courts cannot decide property or money disagreements or give the victim support for her children.

29. *McKinney's Consolidated Laws of New York* (1989), Book 11A.

30. A divorced parent can also apply to the New York Supreme Court for an order of protection to form part of a custody/visitation order. This usually requires the help of a lawyer and is more procedurally complicated and encompasses more delays than a Family Court application.

31. There does not seem to be a valid reason why Family Court action is limited to those who are married, formerly married, or have a child in common. If anything, this fails to acknowledge the nature of many modern families.

32. Catherine Cerulli recounts one incident: "After one woman's account of how her husband broke down her bedroom door, climbed over a bureau she had placed in front of it, sat on top of her and started beating her, the judge responded, 'Oh, that's all he did?'": *The Need to Co-ordinate, supra*, note 21 at 21.

33. M.D. Fields & E. Lehman, *Handbook for Abused Women* (New York State Department of Social Services, 1989) at 10. As affirmed in *Owre v. Owre* (1977), 400 N.Y.S. 2d 131, the court will not issue a temporary order of protection without a full inquiry concerning the need to do so.

34. This last situation is the most frequent outcome. In fact, it is often the case in Erie County Family Court that the woman-beater will have to fail to appear several times before an *ex parte* order is issued. Up and until any order is issued, the victim is at high risk and is not legally protected unless she has been given a Temporary Order of Protection.

35. D.J. Besharov, "Practice Commentary," *Family Court Act, McKinney's Consolidated Laws of New York* (1989), Book 29A, Part 1.

36. Victim's statement cited in K. Fahnestock, "Not in My County," (1992) 31(3) *The Judges' Journal* 10 at 17.

37. As noted in N.Z. Hilton, "One in Ten: The Struggle and Disempowerment of the Battered Women's Movement" (1989) 7 *Can. J. Fam. L.* 313 at 331, "[n]on-enforcement of the law may convey the message that wife assault is acceptable." Moreover,

American surveys indicate that 10% of battered women were beaten *because* they had obtained a civil restraining order: Sue Tomkins, Personal Interview, 9 November 1992.

38. S.O. 1986, c. 4, as amended.

39. R.S.B.C. 1979, c. 121, as amended by the *Family Law Reform Amendments Act*, S.B.C. 1985, c. 72.

40. These parts of the *Act* only apply to married spouses.

41. Section 24(5) of the *Act* allows imprisonment for a willful breach of the order for exclusive possession.

42. Barbra Schlifer Clinic, *Your Rights: An Assaulted Woman's Guide to the Law* (Toronto: Ontario Women's Directorate, 1991) at 24.

43. R.S.C. 1985, c. C-46 [hereinafter the *Criminal Code* or simply the *Code*].

44. There are four kinds of assault: simple assault (s. 265 and 266), assault with a weapon or causing bodily harm (s. 267), aggravated assault (s. 268), or assault unlawfully causing bodily harm (s. 269). The Crown must proceed by indictment in all cases of assault except simple assault. If the Crown elects to proceed summarily under s. 266, the maximum sentence (as for many summary offences in Canada) is six months incarceration plus a fine of $2000.00. In terms of indictable offences, the maximum charges are as follows: 5 years for simple assault, 10 years for assault with a weapon, 14 years for aggravated assault, and 10 years for unlawfully causing bodily harm.

45. Sexual assault involving a weapon (s. 272) is punishable by indictment only and involves a maximum of 14 years. Aggravated sexual assault (that which maims, wounds, disfigures, or endangers life) is also an indictable offence and, as stated in section 273, can result in life imprisonment.

46. Brown, *supra*, note 18 at 1–42. Although the statistics specifically relate to Winnipeg, Manitoba, they are indicative of the national Canadian average.

47. *Supra*, note 42 at 63.

48. Hilton, *supra*, note 37 at 328.

49. P. Jaffe, D.A. Wolfe, A. Telford & G. Austin, "The Impact of Police Charges in Incidents of Wife Abuse" (1986) 1 *Journal of Family Violence* 37 at 37.

50. "Laying Charges Saves Wives" *The Globe and Mail* (5 July 1991).

51. Endorsed by the Attorney-General of Ontario on 20 August 1982.

52. Personal interview with B. Paskoff, 2 November 1992.

53. Ministry of the Solicitor General, *Law Enforcement Activity in Relation to Spousal Assault in Ontario* (Toronto, 1988) at 11.

54. "New Police Policy on Domestic Violence Praised" *The Globe and Mail* (12 September 1992) A9.

55. Personal interview with B. Paskoff, 2 November 1992.

56. "Laying Charges Saves Wives," *supra*, note 50 at 59.

57. Personal interview with B. Paskoff, 2 November 1992. There is also an indication that the police will be placed under a positive duty not only to arrest but also to help get the woman to a shelter.

58. B. Farge & B. Rahder, *Police Response to Incidents of Wife Assault* (Toronto: Assaulted Woman's Helpline, 1991).

59. *Ibid.* at 253.

60. B. Leighton, *Spousal Abuse in Metropolitan Toronto: Research Report on the Responses of the Criminal Justice System* (Toronto: Ministry of the Solicitor General, 1989) at 258.

61. M. Taylor, *For Abused Women: A Legal Rights Handbook* (Belleville, ON: Hastings and Prince Edward Legal Services, 1989) at 28.

62. Brown, *supra*, note 18 at 1–42. See note 47.

63. Personal interview with B. Paskoff, 2 November 1992. In general, the type of counselling imposed exclusively involved reducing drug or alcohol dependency.

64. L. MacLeod, *Battered But Not Beaten ... Preventing Wife Battering in Canada* (Ottawa: Canadian Advisory Council on the Status of Women, 1987).

65. *Ibid.* at 227.

66. (1984), 13 C.C.C. (3d) 416.

67. *Petrovic, ibid.* at 419.

68. *Ibid.*

69. A subsequent decision of the Supreme Court of Canada, *R. v. Lavallee, supra,* note 10 (further discussed *infra*), squarely places battered women into such a class of persons.

70. (1989), 69 C.R. (3d) 181.

71. The transcript of the trial reveals to what extent women can be victimized on the stand when they testify as witnesses. Defence counsel's gruelling cross-examination of the victim, Tanya Sidorova, led protestors outside the courtroom to chant "who's on trial?" In effect, a parallel can be drawn between the trauma inflicted by court-room procedures on battering victims to that of sexual assault victims when called upon to testify against the accused. These latter effects were discussed by L'Heureux-Dubé J. in her dissenting judgement in *R. v. Seaboyer* (1991), 66 C.C.C. (3d) 321 at 329 (S.C.C.).

72. *Inwood, supra,* note 71 at 181.

73. 74 N.S.R. (2d) 23 at 24.

74. (1990), 55 C.C.C. 97 (S.C.C.).

75. Walker also identified the cyclical nature of domestic violence: first there is a phase of tension build-up, then actual violence, and then, immediately thereafter, a honey-moon phase in which the man expresses remorse and induces the woman into believ-ing things will change. The fact that the honeymoon phase occurs so soon after the battering incident explains the difficulty many women face in going to the police at that time.

76. *The Globe and Mail* (21 December 1991).

77. *Ibid.*

78. *The Toronto Star* (20 November 1991).

79. Brown, *supra,* note 18 at 3–28.

80. *The Toronto Star* (25 October 1991), reproduced in J. Mosher, *Wife Abuse: Assessing the Interventions of Law and Social Work* (Faculty of Law, University of Toronto, 1992) at 339.

81. *Ibid.*

82. *Ibid.*

83. Both examples taken from Brown, *supra,* note 18 at 3–29 and 3–31.

84. C. Cornacchia, "It's Time to Lay Down the Law," *The [Montreal] Gazette* (10 January 1994) C2.

85. Forell, *supra,* note 2 at 224.

86. This discretion is better exercised when the officer has received training on how to deal with situations of female partner abuse and is thus better prepared to make value judgements.

87. *Wife Assault as a Crime* (London Family Court Clinic, June 1991) at 1. This was the rate in 1990. In 1987 it was 18%, over four times higher.

88. MacLeod, *supra,* note 64 at 227.

89. P. Jaffe, D. Reitzel, S. Kaye Wilson & E. Hastings, "Wife Assault as a Crime" (1991) 12 *Canadian Woman Studies* 113 at 113.

90. *Ibid.*

91. P. Jaffe & C. Burris, "Wife Abuse as a Crime: The Impact of Police Laying Charges" (1983) 25 *Can. J. Crim.* 309.

92. MacLeod, *supra,* note 64 at 225.

93. Moreover, human rights legislation can preclude discrimination in the employment context due to a record of offences: *Ontario Human Rights Code*, R.S.O. 1990, c. H-19. This provision is especially useful in battering situations due to the extent to which the financial well-being of the convicted accused is often tied to that of the victim.

94. Research by Jaffe & Burris, *supra*, note 91 yields similar results. In London, Ontario, the police arrested six wife-beaters in a six-month period in 1979; in a four-month period in 1981 (after the issuance of the mandatory arrest policy), the police laid 68 charges.

95. *Ibid.*

96. *Ibid.*

97. This revives another debate: is punishment itself an effective deterrent? The Durkheim school of sociology, viewing punishment as a very effective mechanism to control human behaviour, no longer holds a hegemonic position among psychologists.

98. Early anecdotal evidence revealed that middle-class batterers with no prior criminal record were strongly influenced by a night in jail: one therapist recalled the "deeply affected nature" of "an international banker in a three-piece suit" she interviewed in a Miami jail cell: L.G. Lerman, "Enforcing the Law Against Wife Abusers: The Role of Mental Health Professionals" in L.J. Dickstein and Carol C. Nadelson, eds., *Family Violence: Emerging Issues of a National Crisis* (Washington, D.C.: American Psychiatric Press, 1989) at 145.

99. *Supra*, note 14. They also found that arrest and initial incarceration alone may produce a deterrent effect, regardless of how the courts treat such cases.

100. J.D. Hirschel, I.W. Hutchison & C.W. Dean, "The Failure of Arrest to Deter Spouse Abuse" (1992) 29 *Journal of Research in Crime and Delinquency* 7.

101. Steinman, *supra*, note 19 at 131.

102. *Wife Assault as a Crime*, *supra*, note 87 at 1.

103. *Your Rights: An Assaulted Woman's Guide to the Law*, *supra*, note 42 at 42.

104. "Canada: Wife Battering Myths and Realities," *supra*, note 9.

105. Tong, *supra*, note 17 at 170–71.

106. *Ibid.* at 172.

107. Forell, *supra*, note 2.

108. *Ibid.* at 221. The Duluth survey also indicates that mandatory arrest creates better protection for Caucasian women.

109. Brown, *supra*, note 18 at 3–40.

110. MacLeod, *supra*, note 64 at 228.

111. *Ibid.*

112. M.D.A. Freeman, "Violence Against Women: Does the Legal System Provide Solutions or Itself Constitute the Problem?" (1980) 3 *Can. J. Fam. L.* 377.

113. Brown, *supra*, note 18 at v.

114. L. MacLeod, "Helping the Victims" (1988) 12 *Perception* 30.

115. MacLeod, *supra*, note 64 at 225.

116. See J. Mucalov, "Victims Twice Over: Women and Justice in B.C." (Dec. 1992) 16(9) *Canadian Lawyer* 19.

117. Steinman, *supra*, note 19 at 125.

118. *The Need to Co-ordinate*, *supra*, note 21 at 1.

119. *Andrews v. Law Society of British Columbia*, [1989] 1 S.C.R. 143. Other disempowered groups (such as children) are accorded special protection by the criminal law. Why not women?

120. This ties into the concept of "hate crimes." Several scholars have discussed the merits in instituting criminal provisions that specifically address crimes motivated by racism or homophobia: C. Petersen, "A Queer Response to Bashing: Legislating Against Hate"

(1991) 16 *Queen's L.J.* 237. The "crimes against women" provisions proposed by this paper also respond to an endemic "hate crime" — namely that of male misogynist violence against women.

121. (1993), 83 C.C.C. (3d) 1 at 4.

122. Or female–female intimate violence.

123. The need to address same-sex intimate violence is an important one and is consequently not collapsible within the scope of this paper.

124. Since this distinction does not involve an enumerated ground listed in s. 15, it would have to be demonstrated that this distinction between different "assaulters" touched on a ground analogous to those listed in s. 15.

125. *Andrews, supra*, note 119 at 152.

126. 739 F. Supp. 257 at 263–64 (ED Pa, 1990).

127. *Thurman v. City of Torrington*, 595 F. Supp. 1521 (D.C. Conn. 1984); *Hynson v. City of Chester* (1988), 864 F. 2d 1026 (3d Cir.).

128. Brown, *supra*, note 18 at 1–42.

129. *Regina v. Mullin* (1990), 56 C.C.C. (3d) 476 (P.E.I.S.C.).

130. *The Globe & Mail* (16 July 1990), cited in Mosher, *supra*, note 81 at 343 and Brown, *supra*, note 18 at 1–31. Mr. Justice Mark de Weerdt of the Northwest Territories Supreme Court said that the T-shirt implied "at least the possibility if not the actual promise of sexual perversity and promiscuity" and this "could be understood by the other spouse as an immediate threat ... since she refused to change into something else when he demanded she do so."

131. Fortunately, some Canadian courts have taken a more restrictive approach to the admission of provocation as a defence or mitigating factor in cases of femicide. For example, in *R. v. Hanna* (1993), 80 C.C.C. (3d) 289, the British Columbia Court of Appeal refused to allow an individual accused of the murder of his common law spouse to plead that he was provoked into the attack because he thought (with some extrinsic justification) that his wife was "being unfaithful" to him. In *R. v. Young* (1993), 78 C.C.C. (3d) 538 at 542, the Nova Scotia Court of Appeal held that " ... it would set a dangerous precedent to characterize terminating a relationship as an insult or wrong act capable of constituting provocation to kill."

132. Such as self-defence.

133. E. Schollenberg & B. Gibbons, "Domestic Violence Protection Orders: A Comparative Review" (1992) 10 *Can. J. Fam. L.* 191.

134. MacLeod, *supra*, note 64 at 230.

135. F.B. Rodgers, "Develop an Accelerated Docket for Domestic Violence Cases" (1992) 31 *The Judges' Journal* 1 at 8. There was a 33% increase in the number of petitions filed in the Westminster Colorado Municipal Court after the introduction of the "fast-track" system with treatment as the preferred sentence.

136. Steinman, *supra*, note 19.

137. MacLeod, *supra*, note 64 at 226.

138. C. Cerulli, *You Have a Long, Long Way to Go* (University of Buffalo School of Law, 1991) at 21.

139. Domestic violence costs North America $3 billion to $5 billion annually due to work absenteeism and medical expenses: Legal Defense and Education Fund, *Campaign to End Violence Against Women* (New York, 1992) at 3.

140. Personal interview, B. Paskoff, 2 November 1992.

141. However, being in treatment sessions could arouse significantly less hostility than imprisonment or other state retributive sanctions.

142. Personal interview with B. Paskoff, 2 November 1992.

143. *Wife Assault in Canada* (Toronto: Education Wife Assault, 1985).

144. *R. v. Wholesale Travel*, [1991] 3 S.C.R. 154.

145. 595 F. Supp. 1521 (D.C. Conn. 1984).
146. In *R. v. Hutton* (1992), 76 C.C.C. (3d) 476 at 477, Langdon J. discussed the findings of a 1992 study initiated by the Ontario Women's Directorate that homicides are five times more likely to occur at the point of separation than at other periods during the relationship or after it.
147. S.C. 1991, c. D-3.4.
148. R.S.B.C. 1979, c. 121, as amended.
149. Manitoba has headed in this direction in a series of reforms initiated in September 1990. The cities of Minneapolis, Chicago, and Los Angeles have also established semi-autonomous domestic violence courts. These have been praised for "reducing case and participant confusion, and increasing efficiency, sensitivity, and expertise": *The Need to Co-ordinate, supra,* note 21 at 17.
150. Another approach would be to actually develop a separate court system for all matters involving violence against women, in a manner similar to way in which the Unified Family Court was developed to address all issues pertaining to family law. Although the Unified Family Court pilot project launched in Hamilton-Wentworth (Ontario) has generally been a success, it is not without its critics. One principal objection is that creating separate court systems depending on the type of offence committed fractures the judicial system. Another concern is that these separate courts systems are less respected. These objections helped shape the reforms proposed by this paper, which are a compromise between separate "violence against women courts" and the status quo, in which female victims of gendered crimes are obliged to proceed within the general court system.
151. These are also necessary for police officers to quickly determine whether, in responding to a "domestic" call, there has been a history of assault in the family.
152. *The Need to Co-ordinate, supra,* note 21 at 17.
153. Personal interview with S. Tomkins, 9 November 1992. More specifically, Suzanne Tomkins indicates that her own personal experience in Erie County Family Court reveals that those victims accompanied by counsel have more credibility in the eyes of the court.
154. "Alta. C.A. Upholds 3-month Term for Man Who Beat Wife," *The Lawyers Weekly* (3 December 1993) 14.
155. Personal interview with B. Paskoff, 2 November 1992. The issue of domestic violence in rural areas is still largely taboo. Women live in greater isolation from services and each other. Poorer regions have fewer resources to assist battered women. Moreover, as pointed out by Bob Paskoff of Man-to-Man Counselling Services, rural judges have a greater tendency to believe that it is "normal" for a man to use physical force on his wife. For added information on the special concerns affecting domestic violence in rural areas, consult Fahnestock, *supra,* note 36.
156. A comprehensive description of the particularly precarious situation of abused immigrant women is found in L. Pope, "Immigration Law and Wife Assault," *DIVA Special Edition — Wife Assault: South Asian Perspective,* reproduced in Mosher, *supra,* note 80 at 271. A problem in this area is language barriers. The man may issue death threats to the woman in front of police officers and they may be unable to understand them. Moreover, it must be noted that battered women who are waiting for their sponsorship to become official do not even have any legal status in Canada. To this end, they are often more scared of leaving their abuser than they are of staying with him. Addressing the needs of battered women who have neither permanent residence status nor functional command of English is a pressing need worthy of thorough consideration.
157. *Domestic Violence: The Hidden Crime, supra,* note 1 at 2.
158. Peters, *supra,* note 12 at 10.
159. Hilton, *supra,* note 37 at 331–32.

ELEVEN

The Battered Woman Syndrome Revisited: Some Complicating Thoughts Five Years after R. v. Lavallee

MARTHA SHAFFER

In 1990, the Supreme Court of Canada released its ground-breaking decision in *R. v. Lavallee*,[1] in which it held that evidence of wife battering[2] could be relevant in establishing self-defence for women charged with murdering their abusive intimate partners. While feminists heralded the decision as an example of judicial sensitivity to gender difference,[3] they also raised concerns about the potential misuse of the so-called "battered woman syndrome" in the courts. Drawing upon problems identified by feminists in the United States, who had the benefit of a decade of experience with the use of battered woman syndrome in the courts, I, for one, cautioned that *Lavallee* could have negative consequences for women if it led to the view that women who live in domestic relationships marked by violence suffered from a "syndrome" and were thus pathological.[4] I also expressed concern that *Lavallee* could lead to a stereotype of battered women, such that only those women whose behaviour conformed to a narrow vision of what battered women should look like would be able to benefit from the expansion of self-defence.

In this paper, I seek to determine whether either of these concerns has been borne out. First, I provide an overview of *Lavallee* as a way of showing why feminists advocated the use of battered woman syndrome in self-defence cases, as well as the problems of using battered woman syndrome to explain women's behaviour. Then, I analyze the post-*Lavallee* cases in which women charged with a criminal offence have raised the "battered woman syndrome" as part of their defence or as a factor to be considered in sentencing. I conclude that while any definitive statements on the impact of *Lavallee* would be premature, there are indications that battered woman syndrome is being developed in ways that feminists will find troubling.

R. V. *LAVALLEE* AND THE LEGAL RECOGNITION OF THE BATTERED WOMAN SYNDROME

Angelique Lyn Lavallee was charged with the second degree murder of her common law husband, Kevin Rust. That she killed Rust was not disputed. Lavallee admitted to shooting Rust in the back of the head as he was leaving her bedroom to return

Source: Martha Shaffer, "The Battered Woman Syndrome Revisited: Some Complicating Thoughts Five Years after *R. v. Lavallee*," *University of Toronto Law Journal* 47, no. 1 (1997): 1–33.

to a party going on elsewhere in their house, although she said that she was aiming to shoot over his head to scare him. What was not clear was whether Lavallee could lead expert evidence of the battering Rust had inflicted upon her in order to support her claim that she acted in self-defence, or even whether self-defence could be made out in the circumstances. While the evidence at trial revealed that Rust had abused Lavallee throughout their relationship[5] and that immediately before the shooting Rust had beaten Lavallee and threatened to kill her after the party if she didn't kill him first, Lavallee's actions in shooting Rust as he was leaving the room arguably did not fall within the traditional doctrine of self-defence.

Lavallee relied on the form of self-defence found in section 34(2) of the *Criminal Code*, which applies where a person who in repelling an assault intends to cause death or grievous bodily harm to the assailant. Section 34(2) imposes two requirements on those seeking to claim self-defence: (1) accused persons must have acted under a reasonable apprehension of suffering death or grievous bodily harm at the hands of their assailant; and (2) they must believe, on reasonable grounds, that they cannot otherwise preserve themselves from death or grievous bodily harm. These conditions created two problems with viewing Lavallee's actions as taken in self-defence. First, the courts had interpreted the requirement that the accused act under a reasonable apprehension of death or grievous bodily harm as requiring the threat to the accused to be imminent. In other words, to invoke self-defence, the accused had to be responding to an attack that was actually under way or about to occur. This interpretation limited the scope of self-defence by making it unavailable to people who used violence in *anticipation* of an assault. On one reading of the facts, Lavallee could be said to have acted before the threat to her was imminent by shooting Rust as he was returning to the party.

Second, one could argue that Lavallee had trouble meeting the requirement that the accused believe, on reasonable grounds, that there was no way other than to use violence to avoid suffering death or grievous bodily harm. This requirement seeks to ensure that self-defence is not available to persons who respond to an attack with deadly force when other less extreme options for self-preservation were possible. The standard here is not whether the accused *subjectively* believed that he or she had alternative courses of action, but whether a reasonable person would have perceived other options. On one view, since Rust's attack on her was not imminent, Lavallee had other options: she could have preserved herself from Rust by leaving the house, by calling the police, or by simply seeking assistance from one of the guests at the party.

At trial, defence counsel called a psychiatrist, Dr. Fred Shane, as an expert witness. The purpose of Dr. Shane's evidence was to overcome the problems with Lavallee's self-defence claim by providing the jury with information about the effects on women of prolonged battering. The essence of his testimony was that Lavallee demonstrated a pattern of behaviour that abused women frequently exhibit, known as the "battered woman syndrome." Two characteristics of this "syndrome" were important in understanding Lavallee's defence. First, many women in abusive relationships are able to predict when the next violent episode will occur and how severe it is likely to be. This is so because wife abuse tends to follow a cyclical pattern starting with a "tension building phase" which escalates into an "acute battering phase" which is then followed by a phase characterized by "loving contrition" on the part of the batterer.[6] The cyclical nature of the violence means that women are often able to sense when the tension building phase is about to end and the acute battering to begin. It also means that women may be able to "detect changes or signs of novelty in the pattern of normal violence that connote increased danger" such that they can sense that they are facing a life-threatening attack.

Second, women who experience the syndrome often feel "trapped" by, and unable to leave, the relationship. Dr. Shane described this phenomenon, usually referred to as "learned helplessness," in the following way:

> ... the spouse gets beaten so badly ... that he or she loses the motivation to react and becomes helpless and becomes powerless. And it's been shown, sometimes, you know in — not that you can compare animals to human beings, but in laboratories, what you do if you shock an animal, after a while it can't respond to a threat of its life. It becomes just helpless and lies there in an amotivational state ... where it feels there's no power and there's no energy to do anything.... It happens in human beings as well. It's almost like being in a concentration camp ... you get paralyzed with fear.[7]

While leaving the relationship might seem to be an obvious means of avoiding further violence, the feelings of being trapped and helpless prevent battered women from perceiving this as an option.

Dr. Shane also gave his view on the circumstances in which Lavallee killed Rust. His view was that Lavallee was a battered woman who had been "terrorized by Rust to the point [of] feeling trapped, vulnerable, worthless, and unable to escape the relationship."[8] Dr. Shane also opined that Lavallee genuinely feared for her life when she shot Rust: " ... I think she felt, she felt in the final tragic moment that her life was on the line, that unless she defended herself, unless she reacted in a violent way, she would die."[9] The thrust of Dr. Shane's testimony was that Lavallee was able to sense that a fatal attack was imminent and perceived that her only means of protection was to take Rust's life first. Lavallee did not testify in her defence.

Lavallee was acquitted at trial, but the acquittal was overturned by the Manitoba Court of Appeal on the ground that Dr. Shane's testimony should not have been admitted. The majority of the Court of Appeal also raised doubts as to whether Lavallee's actions constituted self-defence:

> This was an unusual case. The accused shot Rust in the back of the head when he was leaving the bedroom. The accused says Rust loaded the rifle and handed it to her. Friends of the accused and Rust, including the couple who had planned to stay overnight, were present in another part of the residence. In these circumstances, absent the evidence of Dr. Shane, it is unlikely that the jury, properly instructed, would have accepted the accused's plea of self-defence.[10]

The Court of Appeal concluded with the suggestion that the Crown proceed with a manslaughter charge since a properly instructed jury would not convict Lavallee of second degree murder.

The Supreme Court of Canada restored Lavallee's acquittal, holding that the trial judge had correctly admitted Dr. Shane's evidence. Expert evidence could, in Wilson J.'s view, assist the jury in fairly assessing a battered woman's plea of self-defence in several ways. First, it could dispel myths and stereotypes about battered women that might adversely affect a woman's claim to have acted in self-defence. These include the myths that battered women are masochistic and enjoy the violence or that the violence could not have been as severe as the woman claimed, since she would have left if it had been.[11] Second, expert evidence could explain how a battered woman's perception that she faced a threat of death or grievous bodily harm might be reasonable, even where an outside observer might not perceive an attack to be imminent. Such evidence could also explain why women often remain in abusive relationships and thus why battered women might not perceive leaving as a reasonable alternative to striking out with deadly force against their abusers. In essence, Wilson J. was of the view that expert evidence could assist the jury in viewing the accused as a reasonable actor by explaining how a battered woman could — to return to the language of section 34(2) — reasonably apprehend a threat of death or grievous bodily harm, and reasonably believe that she had no option other than to use deadly force against her abuser.[12]

A CONUNDRUM FOR FEMINISTS: THE DUAL NATURE OF THE BATTERED WOMAN SYNDROME

While feminist responses to *Lavallee* were generally favourable, many feminists saw the judicial recognition of the battered woman syndrome as a double-edged sword. On the one hand, feminists believed that expert evidence on the "battered woman syndrome" was essential to securing fair trials for women accused of murdering abusive partners. Based on notorious cases in which women's claims to self-defence had been rejected by juries, feminists shared the view that the law of self-defence did not work for women who killed their partners. One explanation for this failure was that women did not kill in self-defence in the same way as men. Women might, for example, kill an abuser while he slept rather than during an attack or when an attack was looming. Such was the case in *R. v. Whynot*,[13] in which Jane (Whynot) Stafford was charged with first degree murder for shooting her abusive partner while he was passed out in the front seat of his pick-up truck. Although the evidence revealed that Billy Stafford had brutally abused Ms. Stafford for five years and that she acted only after he had threatened to kill her son, the Nova Scotia Court of Appeal held that the trial judge had erred by allowing self-defence to be put to the jury when no attack against either Ms. Stafford or her son was imminent. On this view, the substantive law of self-defence did not work for women like Jane Stafford because it was based on the forms of violence in which men typically engage, the "one off" confrontation, or the bar room brawl. While requiring an assault to be imminent might make sense in that context to ensure that an accused does not retaliate prematurely, it makes less sense in the context of relationships of cyclical violence in which the victim may be able to anticipate when the violence will recur. Thus, one explanation for the failure of courts to accept women's self-defence claims was that the doctrine was based on a male standard that could not accommodate women's violent responses to repeated abuse.

Other explanations for the failure to recognize women's self-defence claims stemmed from the inability of the jury to view battered women as reasonable actors, for the reasons Wilson J. identified in *Lavallee*. Although recent studies reveal wife abuse to be remarkably prevalent and thus a form of violence with which many people may have some familiarity, misconceptions about battered women continue to abound. Most of these misconceptions arise from an inability to comprehend why women would remain in violent relationships. Thus, as Wilson J. noted, many people deny the extent of the abuse a woman has suffered, preferring to believe that if the violence had really been as severe as she claimed, the woman would have left the relationship. Alternatively, if the woman is believed, people may explain her failure to leave by saying that she must have enjoyed the violence. In either case, negative qualities are attributed to the woman: either she is a liar or a masochist. In neither case would the woman's decision to stay in the relationship or to use deadly force against her batterer be reasonable.

The battered woman syndrome provided a way of disputing the prevailing stereotypes of battered women. The concepts of "learned helplessness" and "traumatic bonding" provided ways of answering the question "why didn't she simply leave?" that did not make the woman into a masochist or a liar. Instead, they made the woman's decision to stay understandable in light of a psychological state induced by repeated abuse. The battered woman syndrome also went some distance towards forcing a reconsideration of the imminence requirement by suggesting that a strict view of imminence may not apply to situations of recurring violence. For these reasons, feminists believed that the battered woman syndrome could make women's self-defence claims comprehensible to juries and provide them with a way of viewing battered women as reasonable and rational actors.

Nevertheless, from the earliest use of battered woman syndrome in the legal realm, feminists also recognized that relying on a syndrome to explain women's behaviour was problematic on many levels. Simply put, by implying that women who stayed in abusive relationships were "afflicted" with a "syndrome" — a word usually associated with a disease or disorder — battered woman's syndrome threatened to portray battered women as dysfunctional and to undermine their claim to being rational and reasonable actors. In addition, by requiring women to exhibit a specific set of clinical traits, battered woman's syndrome threatened to establish a stereotype of the "authentic" battered woman which might prevent some women from making legitimate use of the defence.

Battered woman syndrome ran the risk of depicting women as dysfunctional because it attempted to provide a psychological explanation for the "failure" of women to leave violent relationships.[14] The theory posited that repeated violence induced a state of helplessness in women which prevented them from taking effective action against their abusers. In this model, "helplessness" was not an innate condition of battered women, but a learned response to repeated trauma. In addition, helplessness was not a pathological response but a common — and perhaps even a "normal" — reaction to prolonged abuse.

Drawing upon studies that psychologist Martin Seligman had conducted on animals, Lenore Walker, the U.S. psychologist who first identified the "battered woman syndrome," explained the development of helplessness in battered women in the following way:

> Seligman and his researchers placed dogs in cages and administered electrical shocks at random and varied intervals. These dogs quickly learned that no matter what response they made, they could not control the shock. At first the dogs attempted to escape through various voluntary movements. When nothing they did stopped the shocks, the dogs ceased any further voluntary activity and became compliant, passive, and submissive. When the researchers attempted to change this procedure and teach the dogs that they could escape by crossing to the other side of the cage, the dogs would

still not respond. In fact, even when the door was left open and the dogs were shown the way out, they remained passive, refused to leave, and did not avoid the shock.[15]

In the case of battered women, Walker posited that abuse performed the same function as the shocks and taught women that they could do nothing to prevent the violence:

> [I]n applying the learned helplessness concept to battered women, the process of how the battered woman becomes victimized grows clearer. Repeated batterings, like electrical shocks, diminish the woman's motivation to respond. She becomes passive. Secondly, her cognitive ability to perceive success is changed. She does not believe her response will result in a favorable outcome, whether or not it might. Next, having generalized her helplessness, the battered woman does not believe anything she does will alter any outcome, not just the specific situation that has occurred. She says, "No matter what I do, I have no influence." She cannot think of alternatives. She says, "I am incapable and too stupid to learn how to change things."[16]

Nonetheless, at the same time as this theory attempted to show how helplessness was an expected response to the conditions in which battered women found themselves, it also depicted battered women as psychologically damaged individuals whose perceptions did not necessarily correspond to reality. According to Walker, helplessness impaired women's cognitive state, making them unable to perceive their "real" options and limiting their problem-solving abilities. It led women to believe they were incapable of leaving their relationships or of ending the violence, even though this was not the case:

> Once we believe we cannot control what happens to us, it is difficult to believe we can ever influence it, even if later we experience a favorable outcome. This concept is important for understanding why battered women do not attempt to free themselves from a battering relationship. Once the women are operating from a belief of helplessness, the perception becomes reality and they become passive, submissive, "helpless." *They allow things that appear to them to be out of control actually to get out of their control. When one listens to descriptions of battering incidents from battered women, it often seems as if these women were not as helpless as they perceived themselves to be. However, their behavior was determined by their negative cognitive set, or their perceptions of what they could or could not do, not by what actually existed.* The battered woman's behavior appears similar to Seligman's dogs, rats, and people (emphasis added).[17]

In suggesting that women's perceptions that they could not escape the violence were irrational and imaginary, battered woman's syndrome implied that women remained in abusive relationships because they were too emotionally damaged to react in a "normal" way.

Battered woman's syndrome also evoked deviance by implying that women remained in abusive relationships for mere psychological reasons, rather than because of "real" constraints. This obscured the fact that quite apart from any psychological damage, women may find leaving an abusive relationship difficult for numerous "external" reasons. These include the difficulty many women face in locating safe and affordable housing, concerns about the ability to provide financially for themselves and their children, and the inability of the police to ensure the safety of the woman, her children, and other family members if the woman does leave. Cultural, religious, and social pressures to keep the family intact may also discourage women from leaving abusive relationships. Many of these considerations may be more acute for women living in rural communities which lack services for abused women and for immigrant women who may not have a good enough command of the English language to gain access to whatever services are available. For aboriginal women living on reserves, leaving a violent relationship may mean leaving the reserve entirely and, as a result, leaving their family and community.[18]

These factors are important for a full understanding of the reasons women remain in abusive relationships because they show that leaving is not as simple as it may first appear. They also explain women's behaviour without implying psychological deviance on their part. If jurors understand that women may not have any place to go or that they may be subject to considerable pressure to try to make the relationship work, jurors may be more likely to view a woman's decision to stay in a violent relationship as a rational decision in the context of limited options.

Jurors may also be more likely to comprehend the decision to remain with an abusive partner if they are told that leaving the relationship will not automatically end the violence. Recent studies have shown that the belief that the violence ends when the relationship ends is as much a myth as the notion that battered women like to be beaten. Battered women are often stalked, harassed, beaten, and killed after they have ceased living with their abuser. For example, a 1986 study conducted in Australia revealed that 46 percent of women who were killed by their male partners had separated or were in the process of separating.[19] Other studies suggest that at the point of separation, the batterer's violence becomes more acute and potentially lethal.[20] These studies indicate that for many women, leaving a relationship may pose more dangers than staying in it and suggest that *leaving* is not always a rational response to abuse. By making it seem as if staying in an abusive relationship is a faulty decision resulting from psychological deficits, battered woman syndrome deprives jurors of important information that would allow them to view battered women as reasonable actors rather than as dysfunctional victims.

Perhaps most importantly, this image of deviance potentially undercuts the very purpose the battered woman syndrome was meant to serve. Battered woman syndrome was developed to show how a woman's actions in taking lethal self-help against her abuser were reasonable, yet by emphasizing the cognitive limitations that stem from learned helplessness, battered woman syndrome depicts a person who is not capable of reasonable action and, thus, is not capable of exercising self-defence. Elizabeth Schneider, one of the most active supporters of the use of expert testimony on battered woman syndrome, described the problem in the following way:

> From the standpoint of the jury's determination of whether the woman acted reasonably in self-defense, the explanation of the "battered woman syndrome" is only partial. Giving commonality to an individual woman's experience can make it seem less aberrational and more reasonable. *Yet to the degree that it is perceived to focus on her suffering from a "syndrome," a term which suggests a loss of control and passivity, the testimony seems to be inconsistent with the notion of reasonableness, and the substance of the testimony seems to focus on incapacity* (emphasis added).[21]

The danger here is that the more juries equate battered woman syndrome with deviance, the less likely they will be to accept the claim that a battered woman acted rationally in self-defence.[22] As a result, it may become more difficult for women's self-defence claims based on the battered woman syndrome to succeed.

Feminists also expressed concern that by making helplessness its defining trait, the battered woman syndrome also ran the risk of establishing a stereotype whereby battered women would be expected to exhibit submissive or helpless behaviour towards their abusers and in all other facets of their lives. The problem with this image is that it is unidimensional whereas battered woman are not. Women in abusive relationships can and do act in ways that demonstrate strength and ingenuity, rather than helplessness and passivity. For example, many battered women engage in resourceful attempts to stop, or at least control, their partner's violence.[23] Many have also taken aggressive action against their batterers, either in defending themselves from acts of abuse or in precipitating an abusive episode as a way of controlling when the battering occurs. Lavallee herself had acted violently against Rust on at least one occasion before the killing.[24] Finally, being battered in an intimate relationship does not mean that a woman will be unable to act competently in other facets of her life. Nonetheless, because battered woman syndrome puts so great a premium on helplessness, jurors may regard women who act aggressively or who show any measure of autonomy as not helpless enough to be "real" battered women.

Jurors may also expect battered women to be "deserving" victims, much like the archetypal "damsel in distress." As a result, the more a woman departs from an ideal of virtuous womanhood, the more difficult it may be to convince jurors that she was a "helpless" "victim" of abuse. Women with alcohol or drug problems, who use profane language, or who are involved in illegal activities may thus have less success using the battered woman syndrome, not because their self-defence claims are less valid, but because juries may be less likely to view them as deserving battered wives. This stereotype may work more harshly against women of colour, aboriginal women, and poor women.

Despite these problems with the battered women syndrome, feminists hoped that its overall effect would be positive in that it would make the doctrine of self-defence more accessible to women. They also hoped that battered woman syndrome would be presented by defence counsel and by the experts called to testify about the "syndrome" in a way that stressed rationality rather than deviance. The case law since *Lavallee* indicates, however, that this has not always been the case.

THE CASES[25]

To ascertain the effect of *Lavallee* on women's self-defence claims, I researched 35 cases in which women had raised the battered woman's syndrome either as a defence or as a factor in sentencing. Of these cases, 16 women had been charged with killing their abusive partners. These cases proved difficult to analyze for several reasons, and, as a result, it is premature to draw any firm conclusions about the impact of Lavallee for women's self-defence claims. Nonetheless, I believe the cases support two tentative observations. First, *Lavallee* does not appear to have led to a dramatic increase in successful self-defence claims by women. Of the 16 women charged with murder or manslaughter of an abusive partner, only three were ultimately acquitted.

In two other cases where it was clear that the women had acted in self-defence in the course of an attack by their batterer, the Crown dropped murder charges. The remaining 11 women were found guilty of manslaughter, nine of them pleading guilty to the offence.[26]

These results can support a number of explanations. One is that the women in most of these homicide cases did not kill in self-defence and, therefore, that *Lavallee* simply did not assist them. While it is impossible to assess this hypothesis in light of the limited information available in most of the cases in which women were convicted of manslaughter, there is at least some basis for questioning whether some of the women might have been able to establish a plea of self-defence. A second possibility is that *Lavallee* has had an impact on prosecutorial discretion, with the result that prosecutors are dropping charges in cases which clearly fall within the scope of *Lavallee*. The two instances I found in which this had occurred provide some evidence to suggest that this is happening, at least to a limited degree. Finally, it is also possible that the main effect of *Lavallee* in cases in which women killed a batterer may be a greater willingness on the part of the Crown to accept a guilty plea to manslaughter coupled with a greater willingness on the part of the judiciary to impose sentences at the low end of the sentencing range. In 6 of the 11 cases in which women were convicted of manslaughter, the sentencing judge declined to impose a term of incarceration, imposing probation with terms instead. In four of the remaining five cases, the maximum sentence was two years less a day. Whatever the explanation, it seems clear that, so far, *Lavallee* has not meant that women charged with killing their batterers are securing acquittals in great numbers.

Second, my analysis of all the reported cases, *including* those that did not raise self-defence, suggests that the feminist concerns about the battered woman syndrome are being borne out, at least to some degree. Some of the cases suggest that the key institutional players in the criminal justice system — judges, defence counsel, and Crown prosecutors — view battered women as dysfunctional and expect them to be utterly incapable of rational or autonomous action. Other cases raise the possibility that a stereotype of the "authentic" battered woman is operating, making it difficult for women who do not fit the mould to make use of self-defence. Each of these concerns will be discussed in greater detail.

BATTERED WOMEN AS DYSFUNCTIONAL: WOMEN INCAPABLE
OF AUTONOMOUS, RATIONAL ACTION

Some of the cases describe battered women in terms which suggest that at least some judges expect battered women to be devoid of autonomy, and thus incapable of taking any independent action. Comments of this sort appear in the case of *Fournier*,[27] a sentencing decision of de Weert J. of the Supreme Court of the Northwest Territories. Fournier had been convicted of five counts of uttering forged documents. She admitted that over a four-month period, she had forged cheques on her employer's bank account totalling roughly $3000 and explained that she had done so to obtain money for her common law partner, Joseph Catholique. At trial, she raised the defence of duress under section 17 of the *Criminal Code*. Presumably, although this is not clear from the decision, Fournier attempted to use the "battered woman syndrome" to substantiate her duress defence as a means of showing that she forged the cheques as a result of threats by her abusive partner.[28] The jury accepted her defence in relation to four other counts which are not specified in the decision, but rejected the defence on the remaining five counts. In considering the sentence to impose on Fournier, de Weert J. held: "the jury rejected [Fournier's] defence of compulsion under s. 17 of the Criminal Code, and I find myself in complete agreement with the jury in concluding that *she acted as an independent and autonomous individual in committing these offences, and not as a 'battered woman' with no will of her own at the times in question*" (emphasis added).[29] Justice de Weert reinforced this point later in the decision. While noting that Fournier had fled to a battered woman's shelter in Yellowknife in April 1989, de Weert J. stated: "I am less well satisfied that [Fournier] in fact was subjected to the horrors that are the accepted lot of the 'battered woman' who has fallen into *a state of virtual slavery and subjection* to a man."[30]

These statements may be nothing more than examples of imprecise use of language, attempts by de Weert J. to say that Fournier was not compelled to forge the cheques as a result of threats on the part of her abusive partner. On the other hand, they may be illustrative of de Weert J.'s image of battered women. It is one thing to say that a battered woman was not acting under compulsion; it is another to liken the living conditions of battered women to states of virtual slavery or to draw a sharp dichotomy between "independent and autonomous individuals" and battered women lacking any will of their own. Taken at face value, Justice de Weert's words threaten to conjure up a harmful caricature of battered women as dominated by their partners to such an extent that they are incapable of any measure of independent action.

From the facts, it is hard to tell whether such an image animated de Weert J.'s decision. Justice de Weert clearly rejected the argument that pressure from her violent spouse could have any bearing on the sentence to be imposed on Ms. Fournier. In fact, while acknowledging Mr. Catholique "was capable of violence"[31] against Ms. Fournier, he questioned the extent of the violence. Noting that Fournier had a "record of dishonesty" with a previous employer[32] — a record in which Mr. Catholique was also implicated — de Weert J. suggested that Ms. Fournier's claims of having been battered were less than truthful. He stated that he felt "less than fully confident in the validity of her assertions of compulsion." He also discounted the significance of Fournier's stay in the battered woman's shelter because he had "no evidence before me as to the basis of that admission other than the testimony of the offender."[33] These reasons fail to indicate whether judge de Weert agreed with the jury's conclusion that Ms. Fournier had not acted under compulsion because he believed that there was insufficient evidence to show that she had been beaten or because he believed that she demonstrated too much autonomy to be a real battered woman. Whatever his reasoning, de Weert J. imposed a suspended sentence of three years, primarily because Ms. Fournier had developed a "healthy and supportive mother–daughter relationship" with an older woman.[34]

The image of battered women as devoid of autonomy emerges more starkly from *R. v. Eagles*,[35] a decision of the Yukon Territorial Court. Dora Eagles was charged with uttering a threat against her husband, Darryl "Red" Eagles. About two months before the incident, the two had entered into a separation agreement in which Mr. Eagles had agreed to pay Ms. Eagles $2000 for furniture he had kept. On the day in question, Ms. Eagles telephoned Mr. Eagles three times over the noon-hour period. In the first call, she asked about the possibility of reconciling for a few weeks over the Christmas period, then about a month and a half away. He refused and hung up. Ms. Eagles called again, this time to ask for money Mr. Eagles owed her under the separation agreement.[36] She admitted to swearing at him during this call.[37] According to Ms. Eagles's testimony, Mr. Eagles responded by saying that he didn't have the money and that he wasn't going to get it.[38] A short time later, Ms. Eagles made the final call in which she told Mr. Eagles that he would be lucky if he lived through the night.[39] As a result of this statement, Ms. Eagles was charged with uttering a threat contrary to section 264.1 of the *Criminal Code*.

At trial, defence counsel argued that Ms. Eagles lacked the *mens rea* to commit the offence because she suffered from the battered woman syndrome. The evidence established that Mr. Eagles had abused Ms. Eagles both physically and emotionally over the course of their 25-year marriage. The physical abuse started when she was 2 months pregnant with their first child and occurred on average once a week. Ms. Eagles was frequently left with bruises and black eyes, her nose was broken on several occasions, and once her injuries were severe enough to require surgery.[40] Towards the end of the marriage, the physical abuse lessened, but the emotional abuse increased. According to the testimony of Alexis Eagles, the couple's 24-year-old daughter, Mr. Eagles would frequently insult her mother, would call her a "no-good alcoholic," a "good-for-nothing" and would constantly berate her for having a criminal record.[41] He expected Ms. Eagles to serve him at all times and humiliated her when she asserted herself. Alexis Eagles also testified that she had witnessed hundreds of incidents of violence by her father against her mother.[42] On some of these occasions, her mother would pick up a knife to defend herself. The criminal record for which Mr. Eagles castigated Ms. Eagles arose from these attempts at self-defence.[43]

For reasons that are deeply problematic, the trial judge accepted Ms. Eagles's claim that she lacked the necessary *mens rea* to commit the offence of uttering a threat. After noting that *mens rea* is related to moral fault, Lilles Terr. Ct. J. quoted the following passage from H.L.A. Hart:

> What is crucial is that those whom we punish should have had, when they acted, *the normal capacities, physical and mental, for doing what the law requires and abstaining from what it forbids, and a fair opportunity to exercise these capacities.* Where these capacities and opportunities are absent, as they are in the varied cases of *accident, mistake, paralysis, reflex action, coercion, insanity,* etc.; the moral protest is that it is morally wrong to punish because, *"he could not have helped it"* or *"he could not have done otherwise"* or *"he had no real choice"* (emphasis added).[44]

Lilles Terr. Ct. J. applied this concept of blameworthiness to the facts and concluded that Ms. Eagles could not be seen as exercising choice when she threatened Mr. Eagles:

> Listening to Mrs. Eagles give her evidence, it was apparent that her act was that of a desperate woman, cornered, and barely hanging on to threads of self-esteem and self-worth. She was powerless. Even while separated from her husband, he was significantly impacting, if not controlling her life. In the result, *I am not satisfied that she was in the position of making or exercising any real choice as contemplated by H.L.A. Hart.* The facts conjure up elements of reflex action, provocation, and self-defence while not clearly being any of the three.[45]

Judge Lilles maintained the view that Ms. Eagles lacked the necessary *mens rea* even though she admitted she had uttered the threat because: "In my own sick way, I guess I was trying to scare him."[46]

While at first blush this decision may seem to be sensitive to the life circumstances of battered women, on further analysis, it may actually be more harmful than helpful. Judge Lilles's reasoning absolves Ms. Eagles of responsibility for her behaviour because she, *as a battered woman*, lacked the normal physical or mental capacities to abide by the law. This suggests that as a result of the abuse she had suffered, Ms. Eagles had ceased to be a rational actor and no longer had the very minimal mental capacity to intend to intimidate her husband or to be taken seriously by him.[47] Thus, we cannot attribute Ms. Eagles's words to an understandable desire to lash out against her husband, a response that would be completely "normal" in light of the harms he had done her. Instead, Ms. Eagles's words must be taken to be akin to reflex action and beyond her conscious control. Judge Lilles's refusal to accept Ms. Eagles's admission that she was trying to alarm her husband further underscores this image of Ms. Eagles's irrationality. In rejecting the Crown's submission that Ms. Eagles had admitted that she had acted with the requisite *mens rea*, Judge Lilles said: "What Ms. Eagles was trying to say was: today, looking back in retrospect, I guess I was trying to scare him. [The statement] represented an attempt by her to explain, after the fact, why she did what she did."[48] In characterizing this statement as an *ex post facto* rationalization, Judge Lilles implies that at the time Ms. Eagles made the threat, she had no rational explanation for the words she uttered to her husband. Only by viewing Ms. Eagles as incapable of rational action is it possible to say that she did not mean to threaten her husband and to so totally discount her explanation for her behaviour.

In slightly different ways, *Fournier* and *Eagles* both interpret battered woman syndrome to portray battered women as deviant rather than as rational actors. In *Fournier*, it is hard to see how women who are virtual slaves and who lack any will of their own — as judge de Weert construes battered women — could be capable of reasonable and informed action. *Eagles* is more troubling. In *Eagles*, the entire reasoning proceeds on the basis that battered women may no longer be fully rational. As a result, *Eagles* uses the battered woman syndrome in a very different way from *Lavallee*. Lyn Lavallee was entitled to invoke self-defence *precisely because* her actions were *reasonable*; had she acted unreasonably, self-defence would not have been available. Instead of using battered woman syndrome to show how Ms. Eagles acted reasonably, *Eagles* uses it to show the opposite, namely that Ms. Eagles was not a fully competent actor and should be relieved of criminal responsibility on that basis.

While *Eagles* is not a self-defence case, its use of the battered woman syndrome to diminish women's competence will have implications for women's self-defence claims. By failing to distinguish between using battered woman syndrome to prove *reasonableness* and using it to prove *irrationality*, *Eagles* implies that battered woman syndrome encompasses everything from completely reasonable to utterly unreasonable behaviour. In so doing, it threatens to stretch the battered woman syndrome to the breaking point. The more battered woman syndrome becomes engulfed by associations of irrationality, the more difficult it will become to view battered women as reasonable actors and, as a result, the more difficult it will become to accept battered women's claims to have acted in self-defence.

This is not to suggest that wife abuse can never affect a woman's mental state or impair her ability to form the *mens rea* for criminal action. It may be the case that it is possible for abuse to cause such profound psychological damage that a woman's ability to make rational choices is undermined. It is, however, to suggest that this kind of psychological damage is very different from what is at issue in the battered woman syndrome and that it is important to keep the two distinct.

A STEREOTYPE OF THE AUTHENTIC BATTERED WOMAN

The feminist concern that the battered woman syndrome will lead to the creation of a stereotype of the "deserving" or "authentic" battered woman may explain, at least in part, the guilty pleas entered in some of the cases in which women were charged with killing their abuser. In these cases, the facts relied upon in sentencing suggest that the women may have had complete defences which were not pursued because of their decision to plead guilty. Although many considerations may factor into a person's decision to enter a guilty plea rather than to go to trial, two reasons may be especially important in this context. First, the stakes may be too high to go to trial when the Crown has offered a plea bargain, particularly where the accused has been charged with murder. As between a possible murder conviction with a mandatory sentence of life imprisonment and a guilty plea to manslaughter with no minimum sentence, many people may be inclined to take the manslaughter plea rather than risk an adverse decision at trial. Second, the stakes may get even higher when a battered woman deviates from the ideal of the "deserving" victim/battered woman who has "faultlessly" and passively endured vicious abuse. The more a woman may have displayed anger or aggressive tendencies, have experienced problems with alcohol or drug abuse, have been involved in criminal activities, or have demonstrated autonomous behaviour in other spheres of her life, the more risky a defence based on battered woman syndrome may become. It is also possible that the more a woman departs from the stereotype, her own defence counsel may be unable to perceive that "battered woman syndrome" could found a complete defence. Since any attempt to discern why a woman might have chosen to enter a guilty plea is highly speculative, it is extremely difficult to draw any firm conclusions from the cases as to whether a stereotype of this sort is operating. Nonetheless, two of the cases provide at least some basis for questioning whether a stereotype of the deserving battered woman is influencing women's decisions to plead guilty to manslaughter.

In the first of these cases, *R. v. Whitten*,[49] the accused was a 51-year-old woman who had been charged with the second degree murder of her common law spouse, Gerald Sampson. Whitten's personal history was tragic in the extreme. She came from a large Newfoundland family and only acquired a Grade 4 education. At the age of 16, she became pregnant, married the father of her child, and then had eight more children with him. At the time of her last pregnancy, her husband had become involved with her sister, who was also pregnant with his child. Mr. Whitten became abusive to Ms. Whitten and the marriage disintegrated. Following the end of the marriage, Ms. Whitten attempted to commit suicide. She developed psychiatric problems and as a result, lost custody of her children to Mr. Whitten. Mr. Whitten subsequently married Ms. Whitten's sister.

Ms. Whitten spent the next several years in and out of psychiatric facilities. She also developed a severe drinking problem. She eventually met Mr. Sampson, who was also an alcoholic, and by 1977 had entered into a common law relationship with him. The relationship was extremely violent and was characterized by both the Crown and defence counsel as "violent drunken hell."[50] According to Ms. Whitten's testimony, Mr. Sampson beat her every time he was drunk, and he would drink whenever he had any money to buy alcohol.[51] She was regularly kicked and punched, and her injuries routinely consisted of bruising, broken ribs, and a broken nose.[52] When Ms. Whitten sought medical treatment for her injuries, Mr. Sampson would sometimes accompany her to ensure that she did not reveal their true cause. When he did not accompany her, he would warn her that she had better say she had fallen.[53] Ms. Whitten also testified that she was afraid of Mr. Sampson,[54] and that he had threatened to "get a gun and blow her head off" if she ever left him.[55]

On the night of the killing — November 10, 1990 — the two were having dinner and consuming a fair bit of wine. According to Ms. Whitten's testimony, Mr. Sampson began verbally abusing and insulting her and repeatedly calling her a whore. A physical struggle ensued, during which Mr. Sampson became very angry and kicked the coffee table across the room. Both Mr. Sampson and Ms. Whitten had steak knives in their hands; she stabbed her knife into his side. Ms. Whitten testified that she was not intending to harm Mr. Sampson, but simply to stop his verbal abuse. She did not believe the wound she inflicted was serious. The knife had, however, pierced Mr. Sampson's lung.

After the stabbing, Ms. Whitten tried to convince Mr. Sampson to seek medical attention at the hospital. He refused and remained at home. The next day, Ms. Whitten asked Mr. Sampson's uncle to persuade Mr. Sampson to go to the hospital. The uncle was unsuccessful but left without any grave concern for Mr. Sampson, who was up and about, able to eat, and even able to attend a doctor's appointment with Ms. Whitten. Four days after the stabbing, after he had developed difficulty breathing, Mr. Sampson agreed to seek medical help. Ms. Whitten took him to the hospital by bus. Mr. Sampson died five days later, nine days after the stabbing. The cause of death was Adult Respiratory Distress Syndrome resulting from the stab wound.

These facts would appear to support a claim of self-defence on the grounds that Ms. Whitten had used reasonable force in repelling an attack by her abusive partner, who was verbally abusing her and brandishing a knife in his hand. In light of the history of abuse in the relationship, Ms. Whitten could reasonably have interpreted Mr. Sampson's verbal behaviour as antecedent to a physical assault and might reasonably have interpreted the knife as an actual threat. Although the assault was largely verbal at the time Ms. Whitten retaliated, as Madame Justice Glube noted in her sentencing decision, Mr. Sampson's verbal assaults had culminated in physical attacks on Ms. Whitten in the past.[56] Stabbing Mr. Sampson might be seen as a reasonable use of force in response to an imminent (or actual) attack.

Despite the possibility of securing a full acquittal on the basis of self-defence, Ms. Whitten pleaded guilty to manslaughter. Although any attempt to discern why she chose to forgo the possibility of an acquittal is necessarily speculative, Whitten's decision may have resulted in part from the fact that she deviated from the stereotype of the helpless but virtuous battered woman. Ms. Whitten had a severe alcohol problem. She had been violent towards the deceased on at least two previous occasions, although she stated she had acted in self-defence. In one of these incidents, Ms. Whitten had stabbed Mr. Sampson in the shoulder.[57] Finally, Ms. Whitten had a long history of psychiatric problems. Her diagnoses included reactive depression, alcohol abuse, withdrawal psychosis, passive dependent personality, and suicidal ideation.[58] She had been admitted to psychiatric hospitals on numerous occasions. Once she had been admitted for lying on the street in front of her house while praying and expressing paranoid ideas.[59]

These three factors — Whitten's alcoholism, her previous violence and in particular the previous knife attack, and her psychiatric history — may have made a self-defence claim too risky for Whitten to pursue. Specifically, Whitten's alcoholism and her psychiatric problems may have made it difficult for a jury to view Whitten as the kind of battered woman capable of taking reasonable action in self-defence.[60] These factors may at least partially account for the decision not to raise self-defence, a defence which appears strong on the facts.[61]

The second case which raises the prospect that a stereotype of the deserving battered woman may be operating is the case of *R. v. Bennett* (No. 1).[62] Jocelyn Bennett was charged with first degree murder in the stabbing death of her common law partner, Lonnie Shaw.[63] Like Geraldine Whitten, Jocelyne Bennett chose to plead guilty to manslaughter rather than to raise a self-defence plea. The evidence revealed that Lonnie Shaw had abused Ms. Bennett both physically and emotionally over the course of their relationship, the length of which is not specified in the decision. Ms. Bennett's injuries included a broken jaw, a black eye suffered while she was pregnant, and numerous cuts and welts to the head. A police report filed after an assault in December 1989 described Bennett as being covered in blood, her clothes full of blood, and as having black eyes.[64] Mr. Shaw also choked Ms. Bennett on at least two occasions, one of which, witnessed by a 14-year-old babysitter, involved Mr. Shaw choking Ms. Bennett against a car.[65] In three of these incidents, Mr. Shaw was charged with assault, but it is not clear from the decision whether convictions resulted.

Mr. Shaw had also threatened to kill Bennett at least twice. Once, when Ms. Bennett threw Mr. Shaw's clothes outside of the house in an attempt to end the relationship, he became enraged and began to strangle her. He reportedly told her "put my fucking clothes back or you'll leave in a body bag ... if they're not back when I return, I'll kill you."[66] The weekend before the killing, Mr. Shaw had grabbed Ms. Bennett by the throat and told her that this time he would not be jailed for assault but for murder.[67]

There was also strong psychological evidence of battered woman syndrome. Ms. Bennett had been assessed by Dr. Fred Shane, the same psychiatrist who had testified on behalf of Lyn Lavallee. In Dr. Shane's opinion, Ms. Bennett exhibited the battered woman syndrome in a "very dramatic manner."[68] It was also his view that Ms. Bennett killed Mr. Shaw in circumstances that could legally amount to self-defence. He described Shaw's death as "precipitated by Ms. Bennett's profound need to defend herself against what she perceived as an imminent sense of severe bodily harm or, possibly, death."[69] The evidence of battered woman syndrome arising from both Dr. Shane's testimony and the history of the relationship was strong enough to prompt Ratushny Prov. Ct. J. to consider striking out Ms. Bennett's guilty plea.[70]

One of the reasons why Bennett might have chosen to plead guilty to manslaughter notwithstanding the strong evidence of battered woman syndrome is that, even more so than Whitten, she departed from the image of the meek and helpless victim. Ms. Bennett had an alcohol problem and made liberal use of profane language. She was also belligerent and aggressive. A number of times when the police responded to calls of a domestic dispute at Bennett's residence, it was the opinion of attending officers that it was Bennett, not Shaw, who was behaving belligerently or strangely.[71] Ms. Bennett had once threatened a woman at a party by banging on the door of her washroom cubicle and yelling, "open the fucking door, its Jocelyne, if you come within 10 feet of my husband, I'll string you up."[72] One witness testified that when he first met Bennett, she looked past him and said, "I'm going to kick or punch that fucking bitch's teeth right down her throat."[73] Finally, Ms. Bennett had once publicly assaulted Mr. Shaw by slapping him five or six times across the face.[74]

In addition, Ms. Bennett was, as the judge in her subsequent criminal case called her, "one tough woman by anyone's standards" and a player in her own right in the "criminal underworld."[75] While on bail awaiting trial for Shaw's murder, Ms. Bennett was charged with robbery and conspiracy to commit robbery.[76] She later pleaded guilty to these offences. Although Ratushny Prov. Ct. J. does not refer to Bennett as tough or street wise, the sentencing decision for the subsequent robbery charges suggests that these characteristics would have been apparent to a jury had the murder charges proceeded to trial.

All of these characteristics — the alcohol abuse, the belligerence and aggression, the tough demeanour, and the profane language — might have made it difficult to convince a jury that Bennett was a battered woman legitimately exercising self-defence. In fact, at Bennett's sentencing hearing for manslaughter, the Crown relied upon these traits to argue vigorously that Bennett was not a victim suffering from the battered woman syndrome: "The Crown argues that the evidence reveals Ms. Bennett was, in her life with Mr. Shaw, often drunk, profane, verbally abusive, physically aggressive, prone to lying and exaggeration, that she was not in fact the submissive, passive, vulnerable woman who lived in a state of learned helplessness that Dr. Shane found her to be and that she was not, in her stabbing of Mr. Shaw, defending her life but was acting in drunken revenge."[77] Although Ratushny Prov. Ct. J. rejected this argument, it is possible that many prospective jurors would not have, but would instead have viewed Bennett as too tough and independent to be an "authentic" battered woman.[78]

While the guilty pleas in both *Whitten* and *Bennett* (No. 1) give rise to legitimate concerns about the operation of a stereotype, it is important not to overstate the case. The case of *Eagles*, in which the accused was acquitted despite her long-standing alcoholism, indicates that not all courts will require battered women to adhere to a particular ideal. In addition, there are statements in both *Bennett* (No. 1) and (No. 2) explicitly cautioning against the establishment of a stereotype. In *Bennett* (No. 1), Ratushny Prov. Ct. J. quotes *Lavallee* on the importance of using expert evidence of battered woman syndrome to dispel negative stereotypes about battered women and adds: "it could also be added, in my opinion, that society, in the process of becoming more enlightened and accepting that women do find themselves in these situations, nevertheless could fall back into stereotyping these women as having to be *credible, sweet, and helpless victims* who are brutalized by tyrannical men. With this, I disagree."[79] Nicholas Prov. Ct. J.'s discussion when sentencing Ms. Bennett on the robbery charges is more eloquent. Although it is lengthy, I quote it in its entirety because it is the best judicial articulation I have found of both the dangers of stereotyping and the impoverished understanding that wife battering stereotyping implies:

Lastly, I want to comment on the cynicism repeatedly expressed by the Crown, about Ms. Bennett's experience as a battered woman, belittling and trivializing that trauma by stating, on a number of occasions, that she is no longer a victim and is not the same person as portrayed in the manslaughter sentencing hearing. The tapes speak volumes of the abuse reaped on this accused by Shaw. They also reveal the accused to be verbally aggressive and abusive and one tough woman by most people's standard. *One does not negate the other, in my opinion. I have no difficulty accepting that the real Jocelyne Bennett is both; a woman who for reasons of emotional dependence, love, and low self-esteem was brutally abused by Lonnie Shaw, yet also a woman who is a player in the criminal underworld of this city, capable of being aggressive and reckless. Those who would disregard or mock her portrayal as a victim in her intimate relationships given her subsequent violent criminal behaviour for which she is being severely punished, suffer, in my opinion, from a rather myopic view of what is a victim, and fail to fully appreciate the battered woman syndrome.* In this case, it certainly does not excuse her behaviour, but it does go a long way in explaining how her life took a wrong turn with the result that she stands before me today. *All victims of abuse, not only those who are sweet, meek, and conform to the stereotyped acceptable behaviour for a female, are deserving of some compassion and the opportunity to break the cycle through rehabilitation and counselling* (emphasis added).[80]

Both of these statements, especially that of Nicholas Prov. Ct. J., demonstrate a commendable understanding of the complexities of wife abuse. Nonetheless, there is no reason to believe that all judges, defence counsel, Crown attorneys, or potential jurors share this more nuanced vision. In fact, the arguments by the Crown in both Bennett cases suggest that any significant departure from the ideal of the sweet and meek battered woman might be used by the Crown to dispute the claim that the accused's actions may be explained by her history of surviving wife abuse.

CONCLUSION

My assessment of the criminal cases that have invoked the battered woman syndrome since *Lavallee* leads me to conclude that battered woman syndrome may be developing in ways that should concern feminists. The cases indicate that at least some of the players in the criminal justice system understand battered woman syndrome as deviance and expect battered women to exhibit a purely passive demeanour. In part, this may explain why, in cases in which women killed their violent partners, *Lavallee* does not yet appear to have widened the doctrine of self-defence to the degree that feminists had hoped.

There are, however, ways of attempting to counter these tendencies. Lawyers who represent battered women can strive to ensure that testimony on the battered woman syndrome is not limited to an explanation of the psychological effects of suffering repeated abuse. They should ensure that experts explain to juries how leaving a violent relationship may not be an easy option because of external constraints, and how, in any event, leaving will not necessarily stem the violence. Lawyers should also scrutinize their own views to determine if they subscribe to stereotypes about battered women that might make them unable to see the strength of a woman's defence. If it may be difficult for a jury to view their client as a "legitimate" battered woman, lawyers should be sure that the expert testimony debunks stereotypes about what battered women should look like. Finally, lawyers should be clear about what they believe battered woman syndrome can do for their clients. If they wish to establish that battering has so greatly harmed a woman that she is no longer fully capable of rational action, they should clearly distinguish their argument from the battered woman syndrome invoked in *Lavallee*. While these suggestions cannot guarantee that battered woman syndrome will develop in a way that will serve the interests of women, they may at least point it in the right direction.

QUESTIONS TO CONSIDER

1. Review arguments for and against battered woman syndrome as set out by Shaffer. In what respects is recognition of the syndrome a victory for women? In what ways might it be a setback? Does BWS stand as a victory for feminism? Be specific.
2. Shaffer reviews battered woman syndrome as a specific defence for women subjected to abuse. What other groups might construct a similar defence — e.g., the elderly, racial or sexual minorities, male schoolchildren, or older males subject to bullying? Debate whether BWS might be extended to help us understand and protect other groups in Canada. Do you think extending this kind of defence would be a progressive step in law? Explain why or why not.
3. Using a database search and/or other sources, provide a detailed analysis of two legal cases where BWS was introduced. How has your initial reading of Shaffer's essay changed, if at all, after your analysis?

NOTES

1. [1990] 1 S.C.R. 852; 55 C.C.C. (3d) 97 [hereinafter *Lavallee* cited to S.C.R.].
2. I use the term wife abuse to refer to violence perpetrated by men against their intimate female partners. I include within this term male violence within marital relationships, within relationships in which the parties cohabit but are not married, and within intimate relationships in which the parties do not cohabit. I do not include abuse that occurs within lesbian relationships. While abuse in lesbian relationships may share some of features of abuse of women by men, I do not wish to generalize from the heterosexual context to violence between lesbians.
3. See *e.g.*, Donna Martinson *et al.*, "A Forum on *Lavallee* v. *R.*: Women and Self-Defence" (1991) 25 *U.B.C. L. Rev.* 23; and Christine Boyle, "The Battered Wife Syndrome and Self-Defence" (1990) 9 *Can. J. Fam. L.* 171.
4. Martha Shaffer, "*R. v. Lavallee*: A Review Essay" (1990) 22 *Ottawa L. Rev.* 607; see also Isabel Grant, "The 'Syndromization' of Women's Experience" (1991) 25 *U.B.C. L. Rev.* 51.
5. *Supra* note 1 at 857. Wilson J. notes that Lavallee's relationship with Rust was "volatile and punctuated by frequent arguments and violence" which often occurred several times a week. She also notes that between 1983 and 1986, Lavallee made several trips to the hospital for the treatment of injuries resulting from the abuse.
6. These three phases were first described by Dr. Lenore Walker, a pioneer in the field of wife abuse. They are known as the Walker Cycle Theory of Violence. See Lenore Walker, *The Battered Woman* (New York: Harper & Row, 1979).
7. As quoted by Wilson J., *supra* note 1 at 884.
8. As summarized by Wilson J., *ibid.* at 859.
9. As cited by Wilson J., *ibid.* at 859.

10. (1988), 52 Man. R. (2d) 274 at 281 (Man. C.A.)
11. *Ibid.* at 872–3.
12. One can argue that Wilson J. also changed the substantive law of self-defence by holding that the requirement of imminence should not apply in cases involving abused women who kill their batterers. Quoting from the American case of *State* v. *Gallegos*, 719 P.2d 1268 (N.M. 1986), Wilson J. held that requiring a battered woman to wait until an attack was under way before striking back would be "tantamount to sentencing her to 'murder by installment,'" *ibid.* at 883.
13. (1983), 9 C.C.C. (3d) 449.
14. Lenore Walker, the psychologist who coined the term "battered woman syndrome," realized that psychological factors did not provide a complete explanation for women's decisions to remain in abusive relationships: "A combination of sociological and psychological variables better explains the battered woman syndrome.... The sociological variables have been well documented by others. Del Martin, in her book *Battered Wives*, presents detailed evidence how a sexist society facilitates, if not actually encourages, the beating of women. Her research indicates, as does mine, that these women do not remain in the relationship because they basically like to be beaten. They have difficulty leaving because of complex psychological reasons. Many stay because of economic, social, and legal dependence. Others are afraid to leave because they have no safe place to go.... " (*supra* note 6 at 43). Walker describes her theory as a psychological rationale rooted in the social learning theory called learned helplessness, *ibid.*
15. *Ibid.* at 46.
16. *Ibid.* at 49–50.
17. *Ibid.* at 47–8.
18. See Mary-Ellen Turpel, 'Home/Land' (1991) 10 *Can. J. Fam. L.* 17.
19. As cited in Elizabeth Sheehy, Julie Stubbs & Julie Tolmie, "Defending Battered Women on Trial: The Battered Woman Syndrome and Its Limitations" (1992) 16 *Crim. L.J.* 369 at note 4.
20. Desmond Ellis, "Post-Separation Abuse: The Contribution of Lawyers as 'Barracudas,' 'Advocates,' and 'Counsellors'" (1987) 10 *Int. J. L. & Psy.* 403 at 408.
21. Elizabeth Schneider, "Describing and Changing: Women's Self-Defense Work and the Problem of Expert Testimony on Battering" (1986) 9 *Women's Rts. L. Rep.* 195 at 216.
22. For example, D'Arcy DePoe, the lawyer representing Theresa Kneiss, an Alberta woman acquitted of murdering her abusive husband, stated that as a result of learned helplessness, a battered woman "ceases to think like a rational person would." Marilyn Moysa, "Murder Case Takes Women Step Forward," *The Calgary Herald* (5 June 1992) C15.
23. See Martha Mahoney, "Legal Images of Battered Women: Redefining the Issue of Separation" (1991) 90 *Mich. L. Rev.* 1; Edward Gondolf and Ellen Fisher, *Battered Women as Survivors: An Alternative to Treating Learned Helplessness* (Lexington MA: Lexington Books, 1988).
24. The evidence revealed that Lavallee had pointed a gun at Rust once before the fatal shooting. Dr. Shane's testimony also referred to other aggressive acts: "And what would happen from time to time is that there would be moments where she would attempt to hit back to defend herself in order to prevent herself from being harmed or even, when the underlying rage may accumulate, if you will, the feeling that she had to do something to him in order to survive, in order to defend herself" (*Lavallee*, *supra* note 1 at 887–8). To her credit, Wilson J. did not view Lavallee's prior act of violence against Rust as discrediting her claim to having been battered. Wilson J. explicitly stated that the battered woman syndrome should not be understood as

requiring "that in the course of a battering relationship, a woman may never attempt to leave her partner or try to defend herself from assault," *ibid.*

25. This section has been abridged. Interested students should consult the original article for details of the exact cases.

26. The only two women who went to trial were Myrtle Trimble, see *R.* v. *Trimble*, [1992] O.J. No. 3287 (QL), and Jean Millar.

27. *R.* v. *Fournier*, [1991] N.W.T.R. 377 (N.W.T.S.C.).

28. Using the "battered woman syndrome" in a duress defence is a logical extension of the decision in *Lavallee*. According to s. 17 of the *Criminal Code*, to claim duress, the accused must show that she was acting under "compulsion by threats of immediate death or serious bodily harm" and that she believed the threats would be carried out.

29. *Fournier*, supra note 27.

30. *Ibid.* at 370.

31. *Ibid.*

32. Fournier had been convicted of theft over a thousand dollars from her previous employer. Her partner, Joseph Catholique, was also implicated in that conviction, although the nature of his role is not clear, *ibid.* at 271.

33. *Ibid.*

34. *Ibid.* at 372–3.

35. *R.* v. *Eagles*, [1991] Y.J. No. 147 (Q.L.).

36. *Ibid.* at 3. Mr. Eagles had paid about half the money.

37. *Ibid.*

38. *Ibid.*

39. Mr. Eagles's recollection was slightly different. He claimed that Ms. Eagles said "you won't live through the night," *ibid.* at 1.

40. *Ibid.* at 2.

41. *Ibid.*

42. *Ibid.*

43. Ms. Eagles's criminal record is described in the case as consisting of three weapons charges. She testified that she had pled guilty to the charges and not raised self-defence because she was "an alcoholic and nobody is going to believe an alcoholic," *ibid.*

44. *Ibid.* at 4.

45. *Ibid.* at 5.

46. *Ibid.*

47. The *mens rea* for a charge of threatening requires that the accused intend the threat to intimidate or to be taken seriously. It does not include the requirement that the accused intend to carry out the threat. See *R.* v. *Clemente* (1994), 91 C.C.C. (3d) 1 (S.C.C.).

48. *Eagles*, supra note 35 at 5.

49. *R.* v. *Whitten* (1992), 110 N.S.R. (2d) 148 (N.S.S.C.).

50. *Ibid.* at 151.

51. *Ibid.* at 150–1.

52. *Ibid.* at 151.

53. *Ibid.*

54. *Ibid.* at 150.

55. *Ibid.* at 151.

56. *Ibid.* at 157.

57. On this occasion, Ms. Whitten was charged with aggravated assault and possession of a weapon dangerous to the public peace, but the charges were dropped after the two resumed cohabitation (*supra* note 49 at 151). The other incident mentioned in the

case is described simply as the "incident with the iron bar," *ibid.* It is unclear whether Ms. Whitten had used violence against Mr. Sampson on other occasions, although Glube C.J.T.D. does refer to "several" instances during which Ms. Whitten acted physically against him, *ibid.*

58. *Ibid.* at 151.

59. *Ibid.*

60. This may not be attributable simply to a stereotype created by the battered woman syndrome. Whitten's alcoholism and mental illnesses may have weakened her credibility as a witness and might have dissuaded defence counsel from raising a defence that required calling Whitten to the stand. It is also possible that, quite apart from the battered woman syndrome, it will be difficult to make a self-defence claim where the accused has a history of mental illness. Juries may be less inclined to view such people as taking the kind of reasonable action which the defence of self-defence demands.

61. Whitten received a three-year suspended sentence. Glube C.J.T.D. decided a suspended sentence was appropriate based on her assessment that Ms. Whitten did not pose a danger to the public and that general deterrence "is meaningless if the person is in the circumstances in which Ms. Whitten was in" (*supra* note 49 at 157).

62. *R. v. Bennett,* (1993) O.J. No. 1011 (Q.L.) [hereinafter referred to as "*Bennett* (No. 1)"].

63. After the preliminary inquiry the charge was reduced to second degree murder.

64. *Bennett, supra,* note 62.

65. *Ibid.* at 16.

66. *Ibid.* at 12.

67. *Ibid.*

68. *Ibid.* at 2.

69. *Ibid.* at 6.

70. Ratushny Prov. Ct. J. began her decision by posing the following question: "In light of the evidence before me, which if believed could provide the accused with the defence of self-defence as a battered woman ... what is my duty with respect to Ms. Bennett's plea?" She decided to allow the plea to stand because Ms. Bennett had had the benefit of "experienced and competent counsel," *ibid.* at 5.

71. *Ibid.* at 13–4.

72. *Ibid.* at 13.

73. *Ibid.*

74. *Ibid.*

75. *Ibid.* at 15.

76. See *R. v. Bennett,* [1993] O.J. No. 892 (Q.L.) [hereinafter referred to as "*Bennett* (No. 2)"].

77. *Supra* note 62 at 9. The Crown in the armed robbery case made similar statements. See *infra* note 80 and accompanying text.

78. Any attempt to ascertain the degree to which a stereotype of the deserving battered woman motivated Bennett's decision to plead to manslaughter is hampered by the absence from the decision of a comprehensive recitation of the events of the night in question. It appears that shortly before the killing, Bennett called a friend, saying that she had a knife and that she was going to kill Mr. Shaw. In response to questions about Shaw's whereabouts, Bennett said he was asleep. A few minutes later, Bennett called a neighbour to say she had killed Shaw, *ibid.* at 16. There is no discussion of whether anything had led Bennett to believe that fatal attack against her was imminent.

79. *Supra* note 76 at 19.

80. *Ibid.* at 15–6.

TWELVE

Private Troubles, Private Solutions: Poverty among Divorced Women and the Politics of Support Enforcement and Child Custody Determination

JANE PULKINGHAM

To give a name to a thing is gratifying ... but it is also dangerous: the danger consists in one's becoming convinced that all is taken care of and that once named, the phenomenon has also been explained.

— Primo Levi, *Other People's Trades*

INTRODUCTION

The financial circumstances of divorced parents is a significant contemporary pol- icy issue, one that receives much attention from the media, the general public, government and academic quarters alike.[1] Typically, the problem is framed as the negative economic consequences of divorce; a plight largely preserved for custodial mothers who, at best, receive intermittent child and/or spousal support payments. Feminist scholars in particular focus on the subject of the negative economic con- sequences of divorce for mothers, many of whom live in or on the margins of poverty. In most analyses, the problem of women and divorce is defined in two ways; first, women's experience of divorce is encapsulated by the "feminization of poverty" thesis; second, maternal custody is said to be in jeopardy because of the operation of gender neutral standards in child custody determination, giving rise to the emer- gence of joint custody as a legal presumption, which is seen to undermine women's autonomy. As an alternative, a "primary caregiver presumption" is proposed.

In this paper, I will critique recent feminist analyses of the feminization of poverty thesis and arguments for a primary caregiver presumption. In its applica- tion to divorce, the feminization of poverty thesis is often deployed to suggest that: the economic consequences of divorce are devastating for women; divorce is the cause of the high incidence and risk of poverty among divorced women; women's

Source: Jane Pulkingham, "Private Troubles, Private Solutions: Poverty among Divorced Women and the Politics of Support Enforcement and Child Custody Determination," *Canadian Journal of Law and Society* 9, no. 2 (1994): 73–97.

poverty is largely an artifact of divorce; and the solution to the problem lies in a legal remedy, specifically, child support[2] enforcement legislation and programs. The primary caregiver presumption is presented as an alternative guideline to that of the "best interests of the child" that informs existing judicial and legal practice in determining post-divorce custody arrangements. The alternative guideline would establish that the parent with primary responsibility for child care and performing the majority of child care tasks before the separation/divorce, usually the mother, should be awarded sole custody.

Supporters of the primary caregiver presumption begin with the fact that mothers are primarily responsible for the day-to-day care of children, and as such, the mother–child relationship must be recognized and preserved. Ultimately, arguments for a primary caregiver presumption come down to the fact that mothers are perceived to be losing sole custody to joint custody arrangements. In these circumstances, fathers gain rights while women continue to *de facto* shoulder responsibility for child care. Joint custody is also seen to undermine an already precarious financial settlement. It is argued that the primary caregiver presumption would equip judges with clear guidelines by which to award custody. Arguing for the need to preserve the mother-custody norm, because anything else (especially joint custody) moves into uncharted territory, Fineman, for example, claims that "reform is occurring with the exception, rather than the norm, providing the prototype for change."[3]

An analysis of contested and uncontested child custody determinations in Canada suggests, however, that to the extent that there has been any increase in joint legal custody, it is very small and at the expense of sole paternal custody. Moreover, in setting out the "primary caregiver presumption" which is in fact equivalent to a maternal deference standard, the "solution" remains at the level of juxtaposing women's individual rights against those of men. This individualization of the problem is exacerbated further by reliance on the private provision of financial support (support enforcement).

Rather than starting within the discursive framework that relies on the "feminization of poverty" thesis to describe the problem of women and divorce, and that seeks resolution through family law reform, specifically support enforcement (spousal and/or child) — and where children are involved, a primary caretaker presumption — I will explore the relationship between the way in which the problem is understood and defined and the institution which has been accorded primary responsibility for its resolution. The professions are centrally implicated in the production of knowledge and the social construction of reality. As Walker argues, "conceptual practices used by professionals ... provide us with ways of understanding and organizing our experiences of the world."[4] Of particular concern is the location of these conceptual practices within the broader social relations of society, and how they become integrated into political practices more generally. "In themselves, concepts provide for particular courses of action. Understood in this way, concepts can be seen to do more than name a phenomenon. They are part of a social relation (used here to signify an ongoing and concerted course of action) that organizes the particular phenomena in specific ways and provides for response to what has been thus identified."[5]

Terms such as the "feminization of poverty" and "primary caregiver" principle point to the fact that the risk of poverty is greater for women than men, especially lone mothers, and that women continue to shoulder the responsibility for housework and childcare. But the dilemma faced by feminist activists is that simply naming the experience does not explain it, and often naming represents a double-edged weapon. The problem with these constructs is not simply semantic. The primary caregiver presumption, for example, may shore up power for individual women at the expense of individual men in gaining control over children. But, together with an established program of family maintenance enforcement, it will entrench an essentialist gender-based division of labour, further privatizing domestic and financial responsibilities that will exacerbate women's unequal position. What is needed is a more profound questioning of the way in which the issues have been constructed, primarily by feminist legal scholars who, as Morton argues, largely ignore any historical materialist conception of social reproduction.[6] Family law concerns the legal relationship among individual family members, but the starting point for any analysis of gender bias is in social relations, not the law. Similarly, solutions lie largely outside the scope of family law reform.

THE FEMINIZATION OF POVERTY THESIS
AND THE POLITICS OF SUPPORT ENFORCEMENT

"The social and economic consequences of marriage breakdown may be described as the 'feminization of poverty' or, in other words, the increasing numbers of poor, working women with children."[7] The above quote reflects a pervasive assumption about the causes of women's poverty and its apparent increase in the past 20 years. One of the most frequently identified factors said to contribute to women's poverty and decline in living standards after divorce is the operation of the principle of gender neutrality. Even though gender-neutral rules were introduced[8] ostensibly to eliminate gender-specific legislation that perpetuated women's inequality by preserving different roles for men and women in property division and support awards, *application* of gender-neutral rules translated into an assumption of *individual responsibility for self-sufficiency*,[9] without regard for the ways in which years of caregiving generally penalized divorced women in terms of their future access to resources (employment, income, pensions, etc.). As Fineman[10] argues, "what is surprising is not the negative economic consequences to women and children of equality-based divorce reform, but the fact that people ... are surprised when they discover them." This argument is echoed in the recent report of the Law Society of British Columbia Gender Bias Committee which states that: "The relationship between the feminization of poverty and marriage breakdown is, we believe, the court's misapplication and over-emphasis of spousal equality in its interpretation of the maintenance provisions in the *Divorce Act*, RSC (1985) and the *Family Relations Act*, RSBC c.121 (1979)."[11] However, the main factor contributing to women's poverty appears to be divorce itself, and consequently the inadequate level of support (maintenance) provided through divorce agreements. Thus Rogerson argues: "There is increasing evidence that the rising divorce rate is having dire consequences for women and children, leaving them, at best, with a substantially lower standard of living than that which they enjoyed during the marriage and, at worst, impoverishment. Social commentators have begun to refer to the 'feminization of poverty'; to the extent that women remain linked to children after divorce, the phenomenon also involves the impoverishment of children."[12]

These kinds of statements abound in the literature on women and divorce.[13] Many commentators also point to the unequal economic consequences of divorce in which serious income inequalities arise after breakup of the marriage. These analyses assume that husbands and wives are equally situated, in terms of their access to resources, within the pre-divorce household. Yet on average, wives have incomes equal to 46% of husbands in the pre-divorce family, yet the incidence of "secondary poverty" is not explored. What these analyses fail to recognize is that it is the visibility of women's unequal access to independent resources, primarily employment income, that divorce reveals. There is, then, an elision of women's financial position and that of the household in which they resided pre-divorce.[14]

Diana Pearce claims to have coined the term the "feminization of poverty" in the late 1970s to describe women's experience of the relationship between work and welfare in the United States. But as Eichler suggests,[15] this term became wedded to the notion that poverty among women and children is caused by divorce through the work of Lenore Weitzman. Weitzman's main study,[16] published as *The Divorce Revolution*, perhaps more than any other, cemented social and legal concern and approaches to the question of women, poverty, and divorce.

Not only has the problem of poverty among women come to be defined in a particular way, this definition implies and leads to a particular course of action. This direction is clearly enunciated by Mossman and McLean who argue that, "[i]f it is accepted that one of the consequences of the escalating divorce rate is the 'feminization of poverty,' it may be appropriate to try to alleviate such financial hardships for women through legal intervention."[17] Similarly, Rogerson argues that "one area in which law does play a role ... and which may have a significant impact on children's well-being after divorce, is the economic arrangements which follow marriage breakdown."[18] Across Canada over the past decade, family law reform measures — legislation to enforce support and custody orders — have proliferated and have been touted as the way to reverse the problem. The Ontario Advisory Council on Women's Issues captures this conviction in its brief to the Ontario Government on Access Orders when, in the opening paragraph, it states that the enactment of the Support and Custody Enforcement Orders Act represented "a significant step in reversing the trend towards the impoverishment of women and children as an economic consequence of marital breakdown."[19]

What we have, then, is a rather simple equation that dominates discussions about women and poverty, women and divorce:

Women and Divorce = Feminization of Poverty = Legal Remedies = Support Enforcement

But this equation is misleading and inaccurate. Not only is the feminization of poverty thesis in itself flawed, its application to the circumstances of divorced women is problematic.[20] There is no question that women are disproportionately represented among the ranks of the poor. In 1988, 60.4% of poor adults in Canada were women. But as research by Evans suggests,[21] the risk of poverty has *always* been greater for women than men. We tend to lose sight of this fact, however, when discussing women's poverty, especially when it is subsumed under the rubric of the feminization of poverty thesis. The popular version of this thesis suggests that the incidence of poverty among women is increasing rapidly and that recent trends (in family formation, employment, welfare state provisions, etc.) are making things much worse. Whereas it is true (in absolute terms) that the number of women who are poor is increasing, and women's share of poverty has remained higher than that of men over the past couple of decades (ranging between 57% and 60%), the *proportion* of women (as a percentage of the total population) who are poor has *fallen*, reflecting a decrease in the incidence of poverty in the general population.[22]

On the other hand, what *has* changed significantly is the *profile* of women who are poor. Whereas married women constituted more than half of poor women in 1971,[23] this situation has since changed dramatically; conversely, the *proportion of poor women* who are single or single mothers has increased considerably. In 1971, married women represented 55% of poor women, compared to 29% in 1988. In 1988, single women under the age of 65 represented 27% of poor women; single women over the age of 65 represented 21%; and single mothers represented 18%. The equivalent 1970 figures for these categories of women are 10%, 10%, and 7% respectively.[24] Thus, one of the reasons that women's poverty has become more visible is because the *majority of poor women are now single* (with and without dependent children) and have to rely on one income, when they used to be married and generally "hidden in the household." Marriage obscured their poverty for a number of reasons. First of all, whereas information about all income earners was collected, only information about the male "head of household" was published, therefore information about married women's status was neglected. Secondly, poverty measures typically ignore circumstances of "secondary poverty"; it was (and still is) assumed that if the income of the "head of household" or total household income is above the poverty line, no one in the family experiences poverty. However, research on the distribution of income within marriage suggests otherwise.[25] Thus, whereas there are increasing numbers of poor single women, to the extent that the feminization of poverty thesis does capture a trend, it is one of the *increasing visibility and recognition of the existence* of poverty among women generally.

Even though poor single women, especially single mothers, are increasing in absolute numbers, and their share of *women's poverty* has expanded, the incidence of poverty among single mothers has actually declined. In 1970, 62% of single mothers with children under the age of 18 were poor, compared to 48% in 1988.[26] Nevertheless, because the number and proportion of single-parent families headed by women have risen dramatically, and an increasing share of *poor women* are single mothers (the majority, divorced), the situation of divorced women is typically summed up by the feminization of poverty concept, which is employed to suggest that divorce is a major cause of women's poverty. But divorce is not the *cause* of women's economic insecurity: the disparity in income between ex-spouses, specifically married women's low income, has become more visible than when marriage previously obscured their unequal position. Divorced mothers, then, are not more vulnerable to poverty now than before. Their poverty has simply become more visible because of their growing numbers and expanding share of *women's* poverty (offset by married women's contracting share).

Another difficulty with the way that women's poverty is addressed is that their "deserving" status is usually tied to their status as mothers. Poverty among women is not usually heralded by itself. Rather, women and children tend to be lumped together, as a single category. The legitimacy of feminist demands on behalf of women tends to be established by evoking the moral claim of women *and* children, whose security, it would appear, has been jeopardized by the willful negligence and mean-spiritedness of their former husbands. Single never-married mothers will not necessarily benefit by the emphasis placed upon the plight of divorced and separated mothers. Claims to state support are legitimated in very different ways for different categories of men and women because of their particular relationship to the welfare state. Because women's dependence is assumed, they have to prove that they are morally deserving. In contrast, men's independence is assumed, and thus men have to prove that their dependence is legitimate.[27] Whereas the majority of lone-parent mothers are separated or divorced (58%),[28] an increasing proportion (18%) are never-married single parents.[29] And while the rate of poverty among children living in single-parent families is very high (66% were poor in 1990), the majority (55%) of all children who are poor live in two-parent households.[30] As Brenner argues:

> [p]ortraying poor women as innocent victims of men's irresponsibility may win sym-
> pathy for the plight of poor women but at the cost of failing to challenge deeply held
> notions about feminine dependence on a male breadwinner and distinctions between
> the deserving and the nondeserving poor, in particular between the "good" woman
> who is poor because her husband refuses support and the "bad" woman who is poor
> because she has had a child outside of marriage or has married a poor man who can-
> not provide.[31]

Thus the "rediscovery" of poverty among single-parent families headed by women in the 1980s raises a number of questions about the way in which income inequalities and poverty are explained and how to respond to them.[32]

Contrasting three models of the family, Eichler suggests that the problem with most family law reforms targeting poverty among women and children is that: "they point us towards the individual responsibility model of the family, which although ideologically premised on the notion of sex equality, shares with the patriarchal model of the family the view that the economic status of wives and children is the individual responsibility of the spouses and parents (in fact, often of the man)."[33]

On the other hand, the social responsibility model places the onus on the state for ensuring economic well-being where an individual is unable to fulfill this obligation. Family law, however, remains largely impervious to this alternative, enforcing a system of individual and privatized responsibility. Although most legislation is no longer premised upon an explicitly patriarchal model — spouses are generally *defined* as economically interdependent (the individual responsibility model) — family law *practice* remains firmly grounded upon the assumption that it is the wife who has to be taken care of economically[34] by the husband, not the state. This is demonstrated most clearly in Fudge's analysis of several challenges brought by fathers in the mid-to-late 1980s to financial support legislation designed to help custodial mothers.[35] In one case,[36] the British Columbia Court of Appeal defended legislation that provided for coercive measures to enforce child support obligations for natural mothers, measures that were not extended to natural (custodial) fathers seeking financial support from non-custodial mothers. Although the Court agreed that the *Child Paternity and Support Act* treated women and men differentially (thus violating the general principle of formal equality between men and women), it argued that: "The obligations of the father and mother to support the child, and the means of establishing the quantum of maintenance, are subsidiary to the broad public purpose of the legislation, namely, to establish paternity and therefore provide a basis for shifting the financial responsibility for the child from the public to the private domain."[37]

This decision underscores the interplay of the individual and patriarchal models informing assumptions about responsibility for economic well-being. Not only is the state attempting to privatize financial responsibility for childrearing, its intention is to reinforce a particular economic relationship between mothers and fathers, and between mothers, fathers, and their children. Underlying the judge's rationale is an assumption and prescription that the male breadwinner "family wage" system remain intact, and that it is sufficient to meet the financial needs of all families. Unfortunately, it seems that most feminist contributors to the debate also broadly endorse, or inadvertently perpetuate, this viewpoint. This is certainly the case for those who champion the cause of support enforcement programs in order to "make fathers pay," and who have been instrumental in bringing about legislative changes to child support provisions through family maintenance enforcement programs.

At both the federal and provincial levels, support enforcement is the preferred policy mechanism adopted to deal with the visible impoverishment of custodial mothers upon marital breakdown. Although research on family, marriage, and divorce has tended to be based on extremely small and unrepresentative samples[38] and minimal research has been conducted on child support orders in Canada,[39] the few studies that do address these issues suggest that the support quantum is entirely inadequate and usually amounts to a consistent dollar figure, regardless of the income of the parents; it also tends to be related to the amount of earnings permitted through income assistance programs. While 75% of custodial mothers with support orders in place receive support payments, only 50% receive their payments in full and on time.[40] Political concern about the inadequacy of child support provisions has led to an examination of the issue by the Federal/Provincial/Territorial Family Law Committee, which has been charged with the task of reviewing the Canadian system of determining child support quantum and providing information on alternatives for its determination.[41] Notwithstanding the fact that the governments concerned claim to be "seriously committed to resolving the problems of child support in Canada,"[42] the way in which the issue of post-divorce family poverty is conceptualized is problematic, as are the social policy implications.

The state is ostensibly in the business of "making fathers pay" in order to reduce pressure on the public purse and, coincidentally, to alleviate the financial hardship of custodial mothers and their children. However, maintenance enforcement is not an inexpensive endeavour, nor are the other more covert fiscal mechanisms used to encourage this family wage system. Child support order or agreements put into place prior to May 1997 allow non-custodial parents (primarily fathers) to receive greater tax recognition through the deductibility of child support than do living-together families and custodial mothers in child-related tax credits and allowances. Thus the state subsidizes non-residential fathers who support their children more than it does other parents.[43] Importantly, however, child support deductions are an "upside down benefit," worth more to high income earning non-custodial fathers than others. The deductibility of child support costs the federal government approximately $250 million per year.[44]

On the one hand, the federal government refuses to implement a national daycare program, on the grounds that it cannot afford to do so, and has also introduced a more restrictive system of child benefits. On the other hand, the same government spends almost as much on subsidies to non-custodial fathers to try and bolster a particular family form — the male breadwinner model — as it does on transfers to provinces through the Canada Assistance Plan (CAP) for child care ($275 million in 1992-1993). Non-custodial parents receive financial support equivalent to almost 50% of total federal government spending on child care through transfers and child care income tax deductions ($300 million in 1992–1993), and almost a third of total federal and provincial spending on child care ($840 million in 1992–1993). This, then, is the epitome of what Mary Ruggie refers to as the "paradox of liberal non-interventionism."

Recourse to notions of the feminization of poverty and demands for increased state action to enforce support orders rest on a liberal political discourse. But as Brenner argues,[45] we need to distinguish between demands that men take responsibility for their children and antifeminist demands that oblige men to be the family breadwinner. Women's poverty and economic insecurity cannot be addressed through family law reform alone. They have to be dealt with through a broader program of social and economic change where collective responsibility is recognized and undertaken.

THE PRIMARY CAREGIVER PRESUMPTION

Mirroring concerns about the misapplication of the principle of gender neutrality in the determination of maintenance provisions, calls for a primary caregiver presumption have emerged in the context of concern about the unintended consequences of the principle of gender neutrality in custody cases.[46] The *rules* of gender neutrality here are said to rest on the assertion of parental equality in parenting potential and practice, moving away from mother custody and the maternal preference ideal characterizing family law over this century. The maternal preference ideal operating this century is a relatively new development. Until the mid-19th century, custody and guardianship of children was a paternal right, protected in Judeo Christian and English common law through *patria potestas* (paternal power) in which children were viewed as property and fathers as the determiners of lineage, power, and wealth. However, in the mid-19th century, a new doctrine — *parens patriae* — was established, giving the court jurisdiction over the welfare of children under seven years, including the power to decide custody. Jurisdiction over all minors was extended to the court by the end of the century. In the first decades of the 20th century, courts began to reverse their practice of regarding fathers as the preferred parent. In particular, mothers were perceived as the more appropriate caretaker if the child was very young and the mother herself was deemed to be "morally fit" and not responsible for breach of the marriage contract. In the early 1920s, the presumption that children of "tender years" (12 and under) should be awarded to the mother, with the father paying support, began to be written into civil codes. This shift in child custody determination emerged in the context of industrialization and the child welfare reform legislation and "child-saving" movement that ensued, all of which was influenced, and in some instances initiated, by the women's movement and welfare feminists.[47]

Throughout this century, then, child custody *practice* in the field of divorce was guided largely by a maternal preference. It is important to recognize, however, that the tender years doctrine and maternal preference emerged through judicial *preference* rather than by statute.[48] Under the *Divorce Act*, the court still has ultimate jurisdiction over the welfare of children, the sole criterion being "the best interests of the child." Parental status (maternal or paternal) does not confer any *statutory* right to custody of children.[49] Gender neutrality, however, has come to be associated with an attack on the mother-custody norm, the disassociation between mothering and nurturing, a devaluation of mothering *per se*, and support for fathers' rights at the expense of mothers. In critiquing the ideal of equality (gender neutrality), feminist commentators have argued for the need to recognize gender differences in caretaking responsibilities during the marriage/union, and employment participation and future opportunities.[50] Part of the difficulty with the concept of gender neutrality has been in the way in which legislation and legal interpretation have presented this principle — something accomplished rather than a goal yet to be achieved. "Equality," interpreted in a formalistic manner as sameness of treatment, is widely criticized by feminist legal scholars on the grounds that it "renders invisible important differences, whether biological or sociological or a combination thereof, between women and men."[51]

The assumption that women and men are similarly situated ignores the reality of women's disadvantaged position and consequently denies special rights to those who bear the burden of inequality. "The ideology of equality is arguably by its very nature incapable of recognizing and adjusting to structural inequalities shaping the lives of women; by producing this ideology, the legal system diverts attention away from these inequalities."[52] In terms of child custody issues, Boyd suggests that application of the ideal of equality is reflected in the move to establish "the best interests of the child" as the basis for determining custody outcomes. This principle, she argues, attempts to avoid a "gendered preference" and presumes equal *parenting potential*, such that the judiciary awards custody to the parent(s) who can best provide for the welfare of the child. Fineman suggests that the ideal of equality places greater value on the biological, rather than the nurturing, relationship in determining custody.[53] In her view, joint custody "represents the paradigmatic expression of this biologically defined right."[54]

In recognition of women's primary responsibility for child care, a primary caregiver presumption is proposed to replace the "best interests of the child" principle. Boyd, for example, argues in support of "a legal presumption in favour of the primary caretaker, which could of course be rebutted by evidence that that parent was not carrying out primary caretaker responsibilities adequately.... "[55] Not only would the primary caregiver presumption formally recognize the role of the nurturing caretaker, but it would also represent compensation[56] for the "sacrifices" caregivers have had to make in the course of their lives. Sole maternal custody is thus being constructed, not simply as a reward, but as an "earned" right of mothers who have performed the majority of child care functions in the family. This is reflected in Fineman's comment that where the ideal of equality operates, custody determinations "have not taken the form of assessing whether men had adopted a 'mothering' or caretaking attitude toward their children and have therefore 'earned' equal consideration as the parent who will best provide for the child."[57]

There are a number of problems, however, with the "primary caregiver" solution.[58] First, it may be questioned whether establishing a primary caregiver presumption actually represents a departure from the *status quo*. Arguments for implementing a primary caregiver presumption are marshalled on the basis that the mother-custody norm is under siege. Fineman argues that mother-custody is overwhelmed by a "dominant discourse that controls all the terms of the modern custody debate ... and effectively excludes or minimizes contrary ideologies and concepts."[59] The "dominant discourse" referred to is the "best interests of the child" principle in determining child custody, a principle that is said to undermine sole maternal custody, bolster fathers' rights to sole paternal and joint custody, and deny women a meaningful political voice.

However, there is a serious problem with this position because it misleads as to the ongoing *practice* of child custody determination. To begin with, the cases used to support the contention that the ideal of motherhood and the associated "tender years doctrine" have been "successfully challenged," rest on analyses of unrepresentative samples and child custody cases that are clearly in the minority. Boyd's sample, for example, "consists of custody decisions decided in the 1980s [read pre-1986] and reported in the Reports of Family Law which involve mothers who were employed during the cohabitation period."[60] In an earlier article, Boyd provides a footnoted caveat that "[w]hile reported decisions do not completely represent reality, particularly for lower income groups who cannot afford litigation costs, they do reflect the attitudes of the judiciary and constitute the precedents most often referred to by practising lawyers and other courts."[61] Notably, Boyd chose to restrict her analysis to situations of legally contested cases only, and to cases which ultimately resulted in sole paternal custody awards.[62] Yet, contested custody cases are in the minority; less than 4% of divorces involving dependent children are finalized by a contested hearing. Moreover, of contested custody cases (where there is a counter-petition or trial), 75% result in sole maternal custody and only 8% in sole paternal custody.[63]

Furthermore, sole custody awards to fathers in Canada in this century have always been and remain a relatively unusual phenomenon. According to Central Divorce Registry data, in 1970, 14.6% of fathers were awarded sole custody, compared to 15.3% in 1986. However, this slight upward trend appears to have reversed. According to Statistics Canada data, in 1990, 12.2% of fathers were awarded sole custody.[64] Over the same period, sole custody awards to mothers have followed a curvilinear pattern: in 1973, approximately 73% of mothers were awarded sole custody, compared to 78.7% in 1979, 72% in 1986, and 73.3% in 1990. In fact, the likelihood of fathers who petition for sole custody obtaining this custody outcome appears to be decreasing.[65] In 1988, mothers who petitioned for sole custody were successful in 95.6% of cases; in contrast, fathers who petitioned for sole custody were successful in 17.5% of cases. These rates are down considerably from those obtained in a 1983 Statistics Canada study that found that between 1969 and 1979, male petitioners received sole custody in 43% of cases (compared to an overall rate of paternal sole custody of 14%).

But there is another perceived threat to sole maternal custody in the form of legal joint custody arrangements.[66] The concern is that mothers are losing (and will lose, in increasing proportions) sole custody to joint custody arrangements. This trend is criticized for several reasons: not only do women continue to *de facto* shoulder responsibility for child care where these arrangements exist, joint custody reinforces the devaluation of mothers' primary caring work in the home because the disproportionate work mothers do is obscured by the "joint custody" label. This is argued to undermine an already precarious financial settlement. The primary caregiver presumption, in contrast, would equip judges with clear guidelines by which to award custody and would promote recognition of the disparity between women's and men's involvement in family work tasks. It would allow women autonomy to continue to bear this responsibility.[67]

Canadian statistics, however, do not indicate the kind of revolution and magnitude of change intimated above in the actual award of joint custody. Based on Central Divorce Registry data for 1986, and its own data for 1988, the Department of Justice study of the *Divorce Act* indicates that in 1986, 11.6% of child custody awards were joint, compared to 12.6% in 1988.[68] More recent figures provided by Statistics Canada show that in 1990, 14.3% of custody awards were joint.[69] While there does appear to be a small upward trend in the award of joint legal custody, this increase is at the expense of sole paternal custody, not sole maternal custody. What appears to be happening is that fathers who may have previously been awarded sole custody are now being awarded joint legal custody. The proportion of mothers receiving sole maternal custody is not on the decline. Between 1986 (when information about joint custody began to be identified as an independent category) and 1990, sole maternal custody awards increased by 1.3%, sole paternal custody awards decreased by 3.1%, and joint custody awards increased by 2.7%. Furthermore, concerns about fathers' use of joint custody to negotiate reduced child support payments do not appear to be warranted. The Department of Justice study[70] found that on average, the amount (aggregate) of support paid by joint custodial fathers is *greater* than that paid by non-custodial fathers. When the number of dependent children is taken into account, there is *no difference* in the amount of support paid by joint and non-custodial fathers.

A second difficulty with the primary caregiver presumption, as it is presently conceptualized, is that it may represent a dangerous precedent and direction in which to move. Despite the fact that the feminist movement has pointed to the artificial separation of public and private realms, a device that serves to perpetuate women's subordination, calls for the primary caregiver presumption appear to be perilously close to suggesting that relationships *within* the family are and should remain off-limits to social intervention.[71] In arguing for the necessity of the primary caregiver principle in custody determinations, Boyd's argument is typical: "It is beyond the law to radically restructure relationships impacting custody arrangements. We can't legislate equal parenting."[72] But this assertion is problematic given that the primary caregiver presumption is posited as an alternative *legal* remedy to current legal practices (the best interests of the child standard/joint custody presumption) that are supposedly restructuring post-divorce custody (parenting) arrangements.[73]

Although it is the case that judges have acted to check other institutions of the state from intruding into the private sphere, the system of "checks" is fundamentally class- and race-specific. The courts, through child welfare law, do in fact intrude into the so-called "private sphere" of many families, a disproportionate number of whom are First Nations.[74] Child welfare law defines and legislates "good parenting," as many Native and poor families in particular know and experience.[75] What is less common is for middle- and upper-class families to be subject to the same kind of scrutiny and explicit pressure. And while family law *per se* may be an inappropriate tool for bringing about the kind of change that is necessary, parenting is a political issue open to social determination. The critical question in this instance, however, is where the boundaries of the political will be drawn, and by whom.

The importance of feminist activities in the construction of contemporary forms of social control must be recognized. As Gordon argues: "[t]he obstacles to perceiving and describing women's own power have been particularly great in issues relating to social policy and to family violence, because of the legacy of victim blaming."[76] It is because of the complexities of the situation of parenting — mothers and fathers are both empowered and disempowered — that there is such urgency in defending mothers against fathers. This stems from the fear of a loss of women's status as deserving, political "victims," if we acknowledge any degree of power, as reflected in sole maternal custody awards. And given the lack of advance in broader social measures, individual women do stand to lose ground:

> For all the oppressive and debilitating effects of the institution of motherhood, a woman does get social credit for being a "good" mother. She also accrues for herself some sense of control and authority in the growth and development of her children.... The myth of motherhood remains ideologically entrenched far beyond the point when its structural underpinnings have begun to crumble. She is giving up power in the domestic sphere, historically her domain, with little compensation from increased power in the public sphere.[77]

Boyd underscores the contradictory ways in which the ideologies of motherhood and equality often operate to disadvantage women.[78] The perverse way in which the concept of equality is interpreted by the judiciary, protecting fathers' "rights," placing undue emphasis on ways in which fathers participated in child care, and dismissing mothers' responsibilities, past and ongoing, clearly resounds with individual women's lived experience of divorce.[79] Responsibility, rather than "rights," is the crux of the matter. Thus, to the extent that reform focuses on joint (legal) custody, as distinct from shared parenting, it is imperative that patterns of custody and the fashioning of legal status be viewed critically.

Most feminist legal scholars do not make a distinction between joint custody and shared parenting.[80] Such a distinction, however, may be helpful. Joint custody, as it is recognized in the law, refers to a legal relationship but carries with it no obligation to share equally in the day-to-day caring and responsibility for children. Consequently, joint custody may be used by fathers to control the lives of their children and thereby custodial mothers, without having to assume responsibility for the actual physical care of the children. This, of course, can perpetuate the most egregious forms of patriarchal control and abuse of mothers and their children. Shared parenting, on the other hand, does not refer to the nominal legal status of the parents in respect of their children, but to the legal responsibilities and obligations for the actual physical and emotional care of the children.[81]

Joint legal custody is no remedy to a situation in which mothers continue to bear the primary responsibility for caring, and face financial insecurity and poverty. At the same time, neither is the primary caregiver presumption an adequate response or solution.[82] The premise for, and expectations of, the primary parent rule are seriously flawed. What is needed is a reorganization of parenting, one that involves more than the parents themselves. This is no longer a choice, but a necessity.

Given the demonstrable failure of the principle of gender neutrality in reversing the economic insecurities and inequalities experienced by women in the legal system and society at large, feminists are attempting to repoliticize the issue by reformulating it in stronger terms through the primary caregiver presumption. Although some are critical of the tendency to define women in terms of their children rather than as individuals, the primary caretaker presumption does precisely this. Moreover, even though the presumption is touted as a gender neutral standard, mothers will enjoy the same benefits and, more importantly, will be constrained by the same burdens they experienced within the "tender years doctrine" interpretation of the "best interests of the child." In short, it is unlikely that this proposed presumption would help "de-centre the law" as its proponents predict.[83] As Walker argues: "[w]hen we take up such terms ... we are participating in the bringing into being of the very phenomenon we seek to name and make visible. The language of abstraction is part of the making of ideology that transforms our understanding of our daily experience and implicates us in our own regulation. It does this by shaping our concern into 'issues' organized on the grounds and with the relevancies and imperatives of the institutions and practices of ruling."[84] Though unwittingly, those who promote the primary caregiver panacea are implicated in the construction and perpetuation of women's dependency.

CONCLUSION

The question of women's subordination in the context of child custody outcomes is of fundamental importance to the issue of financial support for raising children, and women's economic position in general. With respect to custody decisions, feminist legal scholars argue that the unintended consequences of "the best interests of the child" principle is to shore up the legal rights of fathers at the expense of mothers' rights in regard to custody and access, even when fathers are clearly not the "better" parent. It is also argued that giving fathers equal custodial status undermines their post-divorce financial obligations. Consequently, most feminist legal scholars argue for the principle of a primary caregiver presumption to replace "the best interests of the child" (a "gender neutral" principle) in order to recognize and give benefits (child custody and financial support) to those who have been primarily responsible for child care in the pre-divorce family. Thus, concerns about the "feminization of poverty," and mechanisms to enforce support, are intimately linked to the concept of the "primary caregiver presumption."

Yet the complexity and dialectical nature of this relationship does not appear to be fully appreciated in most analyses. Whereas custodial mothers are often identified as financially disadvantaged and non-custodial mothers as dispossessed, what often is ignored is the way in which "maternal custody" and "motherhood" itself are implicated in processes structuring women's disadvantaged economic position.

My concern is with the potential consequences of a primary caregiver presumption in determining custodial arrangements in concert with increasingly aggressive systems of paternal support enforcement. Whereas it may be countered that many who would advocate a primary caregiver presumption do not necessarily favour the more aggressive systems of support enforcement, the potential consequences of a primary caregiver principle must be considered in light of the context in which it will operate. And, for the time being at least, various levels of government are strengthening their support enforcement programs. It is important not to lose sight of what Gordon[85] refers to as the "larger irony" in understanding contemporary forms of gender inequality and oppression. This "larger irony" is the way in which male domination was itself "modernized" in the late 19th and early 20th centuries partly by the demands and actions of (first wave) feminists. A similar scenario confronts us today regarding how (second and third wave) feminist demands for post-divorce family relations are constructed. As Gordon argues, mothers themselves and feminist activists have been instrumental in *shaping and redefining* the nature of social control: "one central aspect of feminism's significance for capitalism has been omitted in [most] formulations — its role in redefining family norms and particularly norms of mothering."[86]

In focusing on rights for women as the goal, whether they be equality rights through gender neutral legislation (1970s style) or gender specific rights based on women's actual and/or "special" role as nurturers (1980s–1990s style), the implications of the interaction of feminist demands and state action in structuring women's subordination have been overlooked. Failure to carefully document and assess "solutions" such as the primary caregiver presumption may unwittingly reinforce both the privatization of social reproduction and paternal control over children.

Some would argue that the fortification of paternal rights and control is well under way, evidenced in the link between the amount of support paid by non-custodial fathers and the amount of access (or "visitation") they negotiate. Although no equivalent Canadian research has been conducted, United States research[87] points to a relationship between changes in custodial arrangements and *formal* compliance with support orders: fathers who subsequently receive more custody than specified in the original formal court order pay significantly less than fathers in cases where there has been no change in custodial arrangement; the situation is reversed for fathers who receive less custody than originally specified. In addition, the research underscores the importance of informal agreements to alter child support obligations reached by both parents that are not filed in court. Anywhere from 15 to 30% of cases had reached informal (mutual) agreements to alter the amount of support paid by the non-custodial parent either because the frequency of contact was changed or because of the changed financial circumstances. Whether these findings can be construed as evidence of a *trend* toward matching paternal financial responsibilities with legally enforceable "access" (visitation) rights for these same fathers is debatable. Nevertheless, the research clearly demonstrates that the amount of support paid changes when the frequency of contact changes, and provides support for the concern that the amount of visitation (or "access") may be used to influence the amount of support paid.

This *quid pro quo* approach reflects the prevalence of the male breadwinner family wage model; moreover, it flourishes in an environment primarily focused on strengthening individual rights. Consequently, as long as it is individual women's (maternal) rights that remain the object of attention for reform, rather than societal responsibility and paternal obligations and responsibilities *within* and beyond marriage, paternal rights will be fortified. This situation will do nothing to shift the burden of obligation and responsibility for day-to-day caring and the long-term costs from individual carers, primarily mothers, to fathers and society at large.

QUESTIONS TO CONSIDER

1. Feminist critics of family law argue that the impact of legal decisions surrounding child support often works to the disadvantage of women and dependent children. Consider how recent federal support guidelines might

affect support patterns. Is there an argument that state involvement in this area will benefit women and dependent children?

2. Discuss whether family law decisions in the area of custody and child support reinforce or undermine gendered relations — that is, women as primary parents and nurturers, men as paid workers who are marginally involved in child rearing. Refer to specific cases and studies, where possible.

3. Child custody decisions can be extremely difficult for estranged couples as well as for judges and lawyers. Debate whether there should be legal presumptions of (a) maternal custody or (b) shared custody/shared parenting. Critically assess child custody decisions using outside readings concerning separation, divorce, and remarriage in Canada.

4. Compose a position statement on reforms you believe are warranted in family law legislation and procedures. Identify which specific reforms are necessary, in your opinion, and articulate a rationale for these reforms. Make reference to available studies, statistics, and theoretical positions to support your suggestions.

NOTES

1. Apart from developments in the area of family law itself — the introduction of maintenance enforcement programs in most provinces and changes in federal and provincial enforcement legislation and deliberations over child support guidelines — government awareness and response to the issue of divorced custodial mothers' financial plight is reflected in the child tax benefit introduced in 1992. In abandoning the previous family allowance system and introducing the new child tax benefit, the government claimed one of its aims was to increase the responsiveness of the benefit to variations in family income. Notably, the only variation in family income that the new child tax benefit in fact recognizes is income changes resulting from marriage breakdown. On the other hand, the responsiveness of the new benefit will be worse than the previous system for income changes due to other circumstances such as unemployment or a move to a lower paying job.

2. In this paper, "support" and "maintenance" are used interchangeably. Whereas divorce legislation refers to "support," some provinces and territories still use the term "maintenance."

3. M. Fineman, "Dominant Discourse, Professional Language, and Legal Change in Child Custody Decisionmaking" (1988) 101:4 *Harvard Law Review* 727 at 769.

4. G. Walker, *Family Violence and the Women's Movement: The Conceptual Politics of Struggle* (Toronto: University of Toronto Press, 1990) at 10.

5. *Ibid.* at 12.

6. M. Morton, "The Cost of Sharing, the Price of Caring: Problems in the Determination of 'Equity' in Family Maintenance and Support" in J. Brockman & D. Chunn, eds., *Investigating Gender Bias: Law Courts, and the Legal Profession* (Toronto: Thompson Educational Publishing, 1993) 191.

7. Law Society of British Columbia Gender Bias Committee, *Gender Equality in the Justice System, vols. 1 & 2* (Vancouver: Law Society of British Columbia, 1992) at 5-2.

8. A requirement of s.15 of the *Charter*.

9. In fact, the recent landmark decision of the Supreme Court of Canada in *Moge* v. *Moge* overturns the idea that all women can and should be entirely "self-sufficient" and states that the *1985 Divorce Act* requires that any economic disadvantage suffered by women because of child care and housework responsibilities undertaken during

the marriage be recognized. It also establishes that the causal connection between a mother's obligation for childbearing and rearing, homemaking, and age and any consequent disadvantages to employment opportunities is a common-sense, non-technical matter.

10. M. Fineman, "Custody Determination at Divorce: The Limits of Social Science Research and the Fallacy of the Liberal Ideology of Equality" (1989) 3:1 *Canadian Journal of Women and the Law* 88.

11. *Supra* note 7 at 5-3.

12. C.J. Rogerson, "Winning the Battle, Losing the War: The Plight of the Custodial Mother" in M.E. Hughes & E.D. Pask, eds., *National Themes in Family Law* (Toronto: Carswell, 1988) 21.

13. *Cf.* D. Pask, "Family Law and Policy in Canada: Economic Implications for Single Custodial Mothers and their Children" in J. Hudson & B. Galaway, eds., *Single Parent Families: Perspectives on Research and Policy* (Toronto: Thompson Educational Publishing, 1993) 185; R. Finnie, "Women, Men, and the Economic Consequences of Divorce: Evidence from Canadian Longitudinal Data" (1993) 30:2 *Canadian Review of Sociology and Anthropology* 205; The Law Society of British Columbia Gender Bias Committee, *supra* note 7; Department of Justice, *Evaluation of the Divorce Act, Phase II: Monitoring and Evaluation* (Canada: Bureau of Review, 1990); E.D. Pask & M.L. McCall, *How Much and Why? The Economic Implications of Marriage Breakdown: Spousal and Child Support* (Calgary: Canadian Research Institute for Law and the Family, 1989); J. Fudge, "The Privatization of the Costs of Social Reproduction: Some Recent Charter Cases" (1989) 3:1 *Canadian Journal of Women and the Law* 246; Rogerson, *ibid.*; J. Mossman & M. McLean, "Family Law and Social Welfare: Toward a New Equality" (1986) 5 *Can. J. Fam. L.* 79; L. Weitzman, *The Divorce Revolution: The Unexpected Social and Economic Consequences for Women and Children in America* (New York: Free Press, 1985); K.L. Bridge, *An International Survey of Private and Public Law Maintenance of Single-Parent Families: Summary and Recommendations* (Ottawa: Documentation Centre, Status of Women, 1995); Canadian Institute of Law Research and Law Reform, *Matrimonial Support Failures: Reasons, Profiles and Perceptions of Individuals Involved* (Edmonton: Canadian Institute of Law Research and Law Reform, 1981); D. Chamber, *Making Fathers Pay* (Chicago: University of Chicago Press, 1979).

14. See below for a further discussion of these issues and J. Pulkingham, "Investigating the Economic Circumstances of Divorced Parents: Implications for Family Law Reform" (unpublished paper, available from the author on request).

15. M. Eichler, "The Limits of Family Law Reform or the Privatization of Female and Child Poverty" (1990) 7:1 *Canadian Family Law Quarterly* 59.

16. Weitzman, *supra* note 13.

17. Mossman & McLean, *supra* note 13 at 89.

18. Rogerson, *supra* note 12 at 21.

19. The Ontario Advisory Council on Women's Issues, *Brief to the Ontario Government on Access Orders* (1991) at 3.

20. Although the concept of the feminization of poverty is typically used in an unqualified way within the literature on women and divorce, commentators concerned with women and poverty more generally point to the shortcomings of this particular label. *Cf.* B. Kitchen, "Framing the Issues: The Political Economy of Poor Mothers" (1992) 12:4 *Canadian Woman Studies/Les Cahiers de la Femme* 10; P. Evans, "The Sexual Division of Poverty: The Consequences of Gendered Caring" in C. Baines, P. Evans & S. Neysmith, eds., *Women's Caring: Feminist Perspectives on Social Welfare* (Toronto: McClelland & Stewart, 1991); Eichler, *supra* note 15; J. Millar & C. Glendinning, "Invisible Women, Invisible Poverty" in C. Glendinning & J. Millar, eds., *Women and Poverty in Britain* (Sussex: Wheatsheaf Book, 1987); J. Millar & C.

Glendinning, "Gender and Poverty" (1989) 18:3 *Journal of Social Policy* 363; J. Brenner, "Feminist Political Discourses: Radical Versus Liberal Approaches to the Feminization of Poverty and Comparable Worth" (1987) 1:4 *Gender & Society* 447.

21. Evans, *ibid.* at 172.

22. *Ibid.* at 173 and 198 (note 3).

23. Even though Statistics Canada collected information that enabled this figure to be produced, it only began to publish and make publicly available information about the incidence of poverty for *married* women from 1980 onwards. For a more detailed discussion of this issue, see Evans, *ibid.*

24. *Ibid.* at 172–73.

25. *Cf.* J. Pahl, *Money and Marriage* (London: Macmillan, 1989); J. Pahl, "The Allocation of Money and the Structuring of Inequality Within Marriage" (1983) 31:2 *Sociological Review* 237; C. Vogler & J. Pahl, "Social and Economic Change and the Organization of Money Within Marriage" (1993) 7:1 *Work, Employment and Society* 71.

26. Evans, *supra* note 20 at 198 (note 3). Research by Dooley also points to the decline in the incidence of "low income" experienced by most family types, the exceptions being lone mothers and couples under the age of 25. M.D. Dooley, "Recent Changes in the Economic Welfare of Lone Mother Families in Canada: The Roles of Market Work, Earnings and Transfers" in Hudson & Galaway, eds., *supra* note 13, 115.

27. Brenner, *supra* note 20 at 450.

28. M. Moore, "Women Parenting Alone" in C. McKie & K. Thompson, eds., *Canadian Social Trends* (Toronto: Thompson Educational, 1990).

29. Evans, *supra* note 20.

30. K. Battle, "Policy Initiatives Related to the Well-Being of Women and Children" (Presentation to the Critical Review of Child Support Guidelines Workshop, Canadian Advisory Council on the Status of Women, Ottawa, 22–24 May 1992) [unpublished] at 52.

31. Brenner, *supra* note 20 at 452.

32. Evans, *supra* note 20; Eichler, *supra* note 15; C. Foote, "Recent State Responses to Separation and Divorce in Canada: Implications for Families and Social Welfare" (Winter 1988) 5 *Canadian Social Work Review* 28; Brenner, *supra* note 20.

33. Eichler, *supra* note 15 at 66–69. The three models are the patriarchal model, the individual responsibility model, and the social responsibility model. In the patriarchal model of the family, no distinction is made between the household and the family unit; the family is the unit of analysis; the father/husband is responsible economically; the mother/wife is responsible for nurturing and care; respective responsibilities are clearly delineated and mutually exclusive; and where the father and mother are alive, the state assumes no responsibility for economic or physical support. The individual model of the family parts company with the patriarchal model in terms of the issue of who is responsible for support and care. In the individual model, both parents are seen to be equally responsible for financial support and care of each other and offspring. Again, however, the society is not responsible for supporting families in any way where parents are present. The social responsibility model of the family is premised upon the assumption that all adults are responsible for their own economic well-being, unless this is impossible, in which case responsibility shifts to the state, not the family. Individuals in need should have this financed by the state, not the family. Childcare costs are borne by the parents and the state, regardless of the marital status of the parents.

34. *Ibid.* at 70.

35. J. Fudge, "The Privatization of the Costs of Social Reproduction: Some Recent Charter Cases" (1989) 3:1 *C.J.W.L.* 246.

36. *Shewchuk v. Ricard* (1986), 24 C.R.R. 45, 2 B.C.L.R. (2d) 324 (B.C.C.A.)

37. *Ibid.* quoted in Fudge, *supra* note 35 at 250.
38. *Cf.* Department of Justice, *supra* note 13.
39. Pask & McCall, *supra* note 13.
40. Department of Justice, *supra* note 13. Using Revenue Canada tax data, Diane Galarneau found that 21% of single-parent tax filers reported having received "alimony" (child and/or spousal support) in 1988. These figures exclude divorced custodial mothers who are now re-partnered and who may be receiving support payments. The average monthly amount of alimony tax filers reported receiving was $383. There are no data sources available that contain complete information on all those who receive or make support payments. D. Galarneau, "Alimony and Child Support" (1992) *Summer Perspectives* 8.
41. Federal/Provincial/Territorial Family Law Committee, *Child Support: Public Discussion Paper* (Ottawa: Department of Justice, 1991).
42. *Ibid.* at 1.
43. E.B. Zweibel. "Canadian Income Tax Policy on Child Support Payments: Old Rationales Applied to New Realities" in Hudson & Galaway, eds., *supra* note 13, 157.
44. Federal/Provincial/Territorial Committee on Child Support Guidelines, *The Financial Implications of Child Support Guidelines, Research Report* (Ottawa: Department of Justice, 1992).
45. Brenner, *supra* note 20 at 454.
46. *Cf.* S. Boyd, "Child Custody and Working Mothers" in S.L. Martin & K.E. Mahoney, eds., *Equality and Judicial Neutrality* (Toronto: Carswell, 1987) 168; S. Boyd, "From Gender Specificity to Gender Neutrality? Ideologies in Canadian Child Custody Law" in C. Smart & S. Sevenhuijsen, eds., *Child Custody and the Politics of Gender* (London: Routledge, 1989) 126; S. Boyd, "Child Custody, Ideologies and Employment" (1989) 3:1 *Canadian Journal of Women and the Law* 111; S. Boyd, "Potentialities and Perils of the Primary Caregiver Presumption" (1990) 7 *Canadian Family Law Quarterly* 1; Fineman, "Dominant Discourse," *supra* note 3; Fineman, "Custody Determination," *supra* note 10; M. Eichler, "Lone Parent Families: An Instable Category in Search of Stable Policies" in Hudson & Galaway, eds., *supra* note 13.
47. L. Gordon, "Family Violence, Feminism, and Social Control" in L. Gordon, ed., *Women, the State and Welfare* (Madison, WI.: The University of Wisconsin Press, 1990); Fineman, "Custody Determination," *ibid.*; J. Ursel, *Private Lives, Public Policy: 100 Years of State Intervention in the Family* (Toronto: Women's Press, 1988).
48. Weitzman, *supra* note 13.
49. Some would argue, however, that despite recent legal reform and the new rhetoric, judges are still guided by a maternal preference.
50. *Cf.* C. Smart, "Power and the Politics of Child Custody" in Smart & Sevenhuijsen, eds., *supra* note 46; Boyd, "Child Custody and Working Mothers," *supra* note 46; Boyd, "From Gender Specificity to Gender Neutrality," *supra* note 46; Boyd, "Child Custody, Ideologies and Employment," *supra* note 46; Boyd, "Potentialities and Perils," *supra* note 46; S. Boyd, "Investigating Gender Bias in Canadian Child Custody Law: Reflections on Questions and Methods" in Brockman & Chunn, eds., *supra* note 6; J. Brophy, "Custody Law, Child Care and Inequality in Britain" in Smart & Sevenhuijsen, eds., *supra* note 46 at 217; Fineman, "Dominant Discourse," *supra* note 3; Fineman, "Custody Determination," *supra* note 10; Eichler, "The Limits of Family Law Reform," *supra* note 15; Rogerson, *supra* note 12; J. Drakich, "In Search of the Better Parent: The Social Construction of Ideologies of Fatherhood" (1989) 3:1 *Canadian Journal of Women and the Law* 69.
51. Boyd, "Child Custody, Ideologies and Employment," *ibid.* at 112.
52. *Ibid.* at 117.
53. Fineman, "Custody Determination," *supra* note 10.

54. *Ibid.* at 99. Ironically, it is the same feminists who support more stringent maintenance enforcement programs which, particularly in the United States, but also in Canada, are focusing on establishing paternity in order to legally hold responsible biological fathers for financial support.

55. Boyd, "Child Custody, Ideologies and Employment," *supra* note 46 at 133.

56. *Ibid.*

57. Fineman, "Custody Determination," *supra* note 10 at 98.

58. In her paper, "Potentialities and Perils of the Primary Caregiver Presumption," Boyd examines several arguments against the primary caregiver presumption (*supra* note 46). Most of these deal with disputes about the psychological importance to children of a primary caregiver and loss of same to a secondary caregiver. The question of judicial capacity to assess the evidence is also examined. While Boyd concedes that the primary caregiver presumption cannot solve all the problems that attend custody disputes and the limits of legal reform are acknowledged, the primary caregiver presumption is nevertheless endorsed as a way of using the law to recognize current parenting patterns.

59. Fineman, *supra* note 3 at 730. Whereas Fineman is discussing the situation in the United States, she is frequently quoted by leading Canadian feminist legal scholars to substantiate their critique of the "best interests of the child" principle as it operates in Canada.

60. Boyd, "Child Custody, Ideologies and Employment," *supra* note 46 at 113.

61. Boyd, "Child Custody and Working Mothers," *supra* note 46 at 169.

62. *Ibid.*

63. Department of Justice, *supra* note 13 at 104.

64. L. Lapierre, "Divorces, Canada and the Provinces, 1990" (1991) 3:4 *Health Reports* 380.

65. Department of Justice, *supra* note 13 at 102.

66. Joint custody is associated with the ongoing "revolution" in the divorce process in which reforms in process (the use of mediation rather than litigation) are accompanied by a different outcome (joint rather than sole maternal custody).

67. *Cf.* S. Boyd, "'She Wants to Have Her Cake and Eat it Too': Child Custody Law and the Construction of Women's Work in Canada" (Lecture presented to the Feminist Institute for Studies on Law and Society, Simon Fraser University, 21 October 1992); Boyd, "Child Custody, Ideologies and Employment," *supra* note 46; Boyd, "Investigating Gender Bias," *supra* note 50; Fineman, "Dominant Discourse," *supra* note 3; Fineman, "Custody Determination," *supra* note 46.

68. Department of Justice, *supra* note 13 at 101.

69. Lapierre, *supra* note 64.

70. Department of Justice, *supra* note 13 at 82.

71. As Morton suggests, most feminist legal scholars involved in this debate are informed by radical feminist thought (*supra* note 6). Although Susan Boyd and Judy Fudge are exceptions to this categorization, the argument Boyd presents in defence of the primary caregiver presumption shares much ground with radical feminist thinking.

72. Boyd, *supra* note 67. Here Boyd is in fact echoing the sentiments of Julia Brophy, who argued that it "is beyond the scope of family law radically to transform structural differences in child care." Brophy, *supra* note 50. This is a position that Boyd endorsed in her 1990 article, "Potentialities and Perils of the Primary Caregiver Presumption," *supra* note 46.

73. Another problem with the primary caregiver presumption is that, ironically, even though the principle of gender neutrality is criticized strongly, the primary caregiver presumption is promoted as a gender neutral rule because it does not "prefer" one gender over the other. See Smart, *supra* note 46 at 24; Boyd, "Child Custody, Ideologies and Employment," *supra* note 46; Fineman, *supra* note 46; Brophy, *ibid.*

Boyd, for example, argues that the primary caregiver principle will give greater profile to the economic plight of caregivers and will signify recognition of "basic feminist goals *(equality through gender neutrality)* ...," Boyd, "Child Custody, Ideologies and Employment" *ibid.* at 124. That the primary caregiver presumption is not a gender neutral proposal is more readily proclaimed by Mary Becker (Professor of Law, Chicago) who advocates dropping the pretence of the primary caregiver presumption altogether and renaming it the maternal deference standard. Canadian feminist legal scholars are at pains, however, to retain the primary caregiver presumption label and defend it as a gender neutral standard. In part, this stems from the fact that adoption of an explicit maternal deference standard would be in breach of the Canadian *Charter of Rights and Freedoms.*

74. P. Monture, "A Vicious Circle: Child Welfare and the First Nations" (1989) 3:1 *Canadian Journal of Women and the Law* 1.
75. The recent custody dispute over David, foster child of the Tearoes, a "middle class," white, Victoria, B.C. couple, and natural child of Cecilia Sawan, a young single native "grade 10 drop-out" living in Northern Alberta, poignantly demonstrates this fact. Although Sawan gave up David for adoption a few months after his birth, she soon changed her mind, within the time period allowed by Alberta Family and Social Services. But Sawan, unable to get the agency to return her son when she requested, began legal proceedings in the fall of 1992. Although the British Columbia Supreme Court ordered David to be returned to his natural mother in June 1993 (an order the Tearoes defied), in August, the British Columbia Court of Appeal overturned the Supreme Court ruling and ordered that he remain with the Tearoes.
76. L. Gordon, *supra* note 47 at 182.
77. D. Ehrensaft, "When Women and Men Mother" (1983) 49 *Socialist Review* 48.
78. Boyd, "From Gender Specificity to Gender Neutrality," *supra* note 46; Boyd, "Child Custody, Ideologies and Employment," *supra* note 46.
79. *Cf.* J. Gordon, "Multiple Meanings of Equality: A Case Study in Custody Litigation" (1989) 3:1 *Canadian Journal of Women and the Law* 256; E. Faulkner, "The Case of 'Baby M'" (1989) 3:1 *Canadian Journal of Women and the Law* 239; P. Chesler, *Mothers on Trial* (New York: McGraw-Hill, 1991); G. Taylor, *In Whose Best Interests? A Working Report on Women's Experiences in Custody and Access Disputes* (B.C. Ministry of Women's Equality, 1992).
80. Fineman, for example, uses the terms interchangeably, *supra* note 3.
81. True shared parenting would, of course, require a fundamental restructuring of our economy, as Segal suggests, and a very different, and lower, standard of living among such families. But divorce occasions a lower standard of living anyway, for most women and many men, unless or until remarriage. L. Segal, *Is the Future Female: Troubled Thoughts on Contemporary Feminism* (London: Virago Press. 1987).
82. Another problem with the emphasis on the primary caregiver presumption as the answer to custodial mothers' problems, is that this solution is silent about the situation of custodial mothers where there is abuse, and the rights of abusive fathers to access. Whereas a minority of abusive husbands or fathers may obtain sole or joint custody, the majority are non-custodial and continue their abuse through their rights to visit the children.
83. Boyd, *supra* note 67.
84. Walker, *supra* note 4 at 108.
85. L. Gordon, *supra* note 47 at 187–88.
86. *Ibid.* at 198.
87. H.E. Peters et al., "Enforcing Divorce Settlements: Evidence from Child Support Compliance and Award Modifications" (1993) 30:4 *Demography* 719.

PART FIVE

Future Directions in Law and Society

We began this text by noting that legal conflict and legal debates have become increasingly common in contemporary Canadian society. The articles included in this collection represent some of the most important examples of current debates occupying the attention of Canadian academics, politicians, and the media. Limitations of space made it impossible to include all of the important topics facing Canadian society, and we were forced to exclude many excellent articles and several important topics. In this concluding section, we would like to outline briefly several topics that were not included and discuss several important themes that we feel will become increasingly important to the law and society field in Canada. This section will conclude with three articles that discuss the issues of hate crimes and restorative justice.

THE CONTINUING CHALLENGE OF THE FEMINIST MOVEMENT

Feminism has had an enormous impact on sociology generally and the field of socio-legal studies more specifically. Early feminist scholarship was almost exclusively concerned with drawing attention to the inequities facing women and identifying the most pressing areas of discrimination. This attention has not been without effect, both in academia and within the wider society. Early Canadian law and society texts contained little discussion of feminist issues. In contrast, over half of the articles included in this reader deal explicitly with feminist issues and concerns. Similar changes are evident in other recent Canadian texts, and there are many specialized texts dealing explicitly with women and the law. As well, universities are increasingly offering women and the law courses, and women's studies programs have become common. Further, many universities have established feminist-oriented research institutes, and there are several specialized journals dealing with feminist issues (e.g., *Women and Criminal Justice* and *Canadian Journal of Women and the Law*).

Increased attention to feminist issues in the academic world has been paralleled by similar attention in the wider society. Many organizations have instituted employment equity policies aimed at increasing the numbers of female professionals and other executives. Women have fought for and gained increasing acceptance in occupations previously closed to them, including medicine, police work, and the legal profession. These changes might prompt many people to conclude that the feminist battle for equality in the workplace has been won. Other writers, however, are more cautious, arguing that many of the professional successes achieved by women are partial at best, and that women still face significant barriers in many occupations. There is evidence, for example, that women are leaving Canadian police forces at significantly higher rates than males, and that this trend is due at least partially to issues such as sexual harassment, sexual discrimination, and unequal family responsibilities. Other researchers argue that, despite the gains made in the last few decades, women are still denied access to the highest echelons of Canadian society, and that simply increasing the number of women in the professions does not necessarily change entrenched patterns of domination and oppression.

It is clear that the feminist movement is maturing and becoming more discerning in its critique of male oppression. Recent analyses of prostitution by postmodern feminists have challenged the radical-feminist argument that patriarchal exploitation and oppression universally characterize prostitution. Similar arguments have been made regarding pornography. Some postmodern feminists are beginning to argue that the elites of the feminist movement have lost touch with the concerns of lesbians, racial minorities, and other marginalized groups of women. This leads to a more general point: to what extent do feminist perspectives reflect, or clash with, values and interests of women as a whole?

Regardless of the position one takes, feminist concerns will continue to influence and occupy law and society scholars well into the future. Although it is difficult to predict the exact direction that feminist analyses will take, we can predict that they will become increasingly multidimensional as they revisit issues such as reproductive rights and the transformation of families. These two issues will become particularly important in future law and society research inasmuch as birth control, affordable child care, and access to abortion are considered key factors in the ability of women to narrow the gap in wealth and power between women and males.

THE CHANGING MORAL AND POLITICAL LANDSCAPE IN CANADA

Canadian attitudes toward many previously sacrosanct moral values are changing rapidly due to several interrelated factors. The decline in the influence of religion as the primary moral order, combined with an increase in libertarian attitudes on both the left and the right, has lead many Canadians to question long-held beliefs about right and wrong. From a left-wing perspective, the practical implications of these moral shifts can be seen in the growing acceptance of many previously disparaged moral choices, including same-sex relationships, abortion, and even euthanasia. On the other side of the spectrum, the shift in moral values is evidenced by increasing public resentment toward the beneficiaries of Canada's welfare state and a retreat from Canadians' traditional tolerance of official policies of bilingualism and multiculturalism. Although seemingly contradictory, both of these shifts are consistent with the broad libertarian approach to individualism, in which individual autonomy is accepted as long as it does not impinge on the rights of others. In this context, libertarians view welfare programs as infringements of the rights of taxpayers who have to pay for the programs, but who may not benefit directly from them. Such thinking has also changed the political landscape, as political parties attempt to capitalize on the growing distrust of "big government," and have begun to rethink the social programs that have been considered an indispensable part of the Canadian social fabric.

The effects of these moral shifts have not occurred without disagreement, and Canadian legal and political institutions have recently become embroiled in contentious and passionate debates over several issues. A recent Ontario court ruling that insurance companies must recognize same-sex partners as legal spouses can be used to illustrate the degree to which the legal climate is changing with regard to moral and social issues. Justice Douglas Coo ruled that Ontario's Insurance Act must be amended to include same-sex couples because its current definition of "spouse" is out of touch with contemporary conjugal relationships. The emphatic tone of the judge's comments constitutes a startling affirmation of the degree to which the judicial climate has shifted from the "family values" approach still pre-eminent in the United States. Thus, although the Sanders article in Part Three of this reader suggests that there is considerable room for legislative improvement in this area, it seems clear that the courts are now starting to pressure governments to amend the relevant legislation. This being the case, it is likely that developments in the area of same-sex relationships will constitute an important area of socio-legal analysis for the foreseeable future.

A second area of moral discourse that has recently dominated political and legal debates involves the dual questions of euthanasia and assisted suicide. Several recent court cases have attracted media attention and public debate over such key issues as the right to die and the ethics of assisted suicide. A recent Canadian case involving active euthanasia illustrates the degree to which mercy killing has entered a legal "grey area" in Canadian society. The Latimer case arose when Saskatchewan farmer Robert Latimer asphyxiated his twelve-year-old daughter, Tracy, in the cab of his truck. Tracy, who was afflicted with cerebral palsy, was in excruciating pain, and Latimer claimed that his only motive was to end her suffering. Although he was twice convicted of murder, Latimer ultimately was sentenced to two years less a day in jail. This sentence is astounding, since the mandatory minimum sentence for murder is life in prison with no eligibility for parole for at least ten years. However, Judge Ted Noble of the Saskatchewan Supreme Court ruled that the minimum sentence would constitute cruel and unusual punishment, and he invoked a rarely used constitutional exemption in imposing this extremely light sentence.

The Latimer case has engendered a huge public debate in Canada. Advocates of disabled people argue that Latimer's light sentence sends a signal that the lives of disabled people are less valuable than the lives of other people. They argue that this signal may well precipitate a deluge of similar cases, as other caregivers decide to end their patients' suffering without their consent. On the other side of the debate, many people argue that compassion, rather than malice, motivated Robert Latimer, and that the real crime would have been to prolong Tracy Latimer's suffering. There have been several academic articles discussing this case, and one Canadian law professor has publicly argued in favour of a "compassionate homicide defence," which would reduce murder to manslaughter in cases motivated by the desire to end suffering. Although this debate is far from over, it is clear that a large segment of the Canadian public sympathized with Robert Latimer, even though they disagreed with his actions. For this reason, it can be expected that assisted suicide and euthanasia will become even more prominent in future Canadian socio-legal debates.

THE CASE FOR HATE-CRIME LEGISLATION IN CANADA

Three articles are contained in this concluding section, which discuss two further areas that are becoming increasingly important to the field of law and society. The first of these articles deals with the legislative responses to hate crimes. In "Criminal Responses to Hate-Motivated Violence: Is Bill C-41 Tough Enough?" Martha Shaffer conducts a critical assessment of Bill C-41, which was passed by the Canadian Parliament in 1995. She notes that this law was passed in response to a drastic increase in violence that appeared to be motivated by hatred for particular groups. Although Shaffer agrees that Bill C-41 is a step in the right direction, she argues that it does not go far enough because it allows hate motivation to be treated as an aggravating factor only during sentencing. She compares this procedure to the approach taken in the United States, where legislation creates distinct offences for hate-motivated violence and prescribes sentences that exceed those for similar acts that are not motivated by group hatred. She argues that this latter approach is necessary to reinforce the message that hate-motivated violence is different from other types of violence because it traumatizes the entire targeted group.

Inasmuch as racism and homophobia motivate most hate crimes, this topic is particularly important in contemporary Canadian society for at least two reasons. First, there is some evidence to suggest that the increasingly high profile accorded to gay rights groups is starting to trigger a backlash from certain segments of society. A similar argument can be made regarding violence committed against racial and ethnic groups. The fact that the Canadian population is increasingly descended from non-European groups, combined with a growing intolerance for employment equity and other diversity-oriented programs, may trigger increased resentment against racial and ethnic minorities. Although the link between resentment against such groups and actual violence is not completely clear, it is important to have legislation in place to deal with the problem as it develops. It can also be argued that it is important to continue research into all aspects of hate-motivated violence to gain a better understanding of the phenomenon.

THE CASE FOR A RESTORATIVE JUSTICE APPROACH TO LAW AND JUSTICE

The final two articles in this section focus on a different type of value change. In "An Introduction to Restorative Justice," Joe Hudson and Burt Galaway outline a very different approach to law and justice, which questions the entire philosophical underpinnings of our current legal and criminal justice systems. The authors propose an approach that views crime as "a conflict between individuals that results in injuries to individuals, communities, and the offenders themselves." The solution, according to the restorative justice model, is to reconcile all parties and repair all injuries through the active participation of all affected parties, as well as the community. This is very different from the adversarial view of crimes as offences against the state, which are dealt with through punishment and deterrence. The adversarial approach fails to address the root causes of the conflict, and thus the underlying problems are not really solved. Hudson and Galaway propose a three-step model for achieving restorative justice: premediation, mediation, and follow-up. The primary objective of restorative justice is to facilitate reconciliation between the offender and the victim through mutual discussion and an explanation of the events that constitute the offence. All participation is voluntary, and the offender must admit responsibility and apologize for his or her actions. The victim, in return, must be willing to forgive the offender if appropriate redress is made.

The final article in this section is entitled "Restorative Justice through Mediation: The Impact of Programs in Four Canadian Provinces." Professor Mark Umbreit evaluates mediation programs in Ontario, Manitoba, Alberta, and British Columbia. He describes the implementation of specific mediation programs serving both adult and juvenile offenders. The goal of the study was to determine the degree to which mediation resulted in an agreement and the level of participant satisfaction with the results. The results were extremely high on both points, with an agreement being reached in 93% of the cases, and 90% of the participants expressing satisfaction with their agreement. Further, 80% of all participants, including those who did not reach an agreement, reported that they had been treated fairly by the process. Finally, most of the victims noted that receiving explanations and apologies were important parts of the process for them. Thus, the results of this study appear to validate many of the major tenets of restorative justice, as outlined by Hudson and Galaway. However, two cautionary notes must be made about the results of this study. First, mediation is one of the least radical aspects of restorative justice and is frequently used as part of mainstream criminal justice. Therefore, it is not clear whether these findings can be used to predict the success of more radical restorative justice initiatives such as victim–offender reconciliation programs (VORP), conferencing, and healing circles. Further, no data were provided on recidivism rates, and thus we have no means of assessing whether restorative justice initiatives will reduce crime rates.

The articles in this collection help to define new directions in law and society studies, relying on new theoretical and methodological approaches, while exploring old, unsettled questions of law, social inequality, and social change. We can see a reflection of social values and conflicts in legal institutions and legal battles, including long-standing concerns over exclusion of certain groups through law and social conventions, and the difficult process of including more groups and individuals within the legal framework. We hope that these articles, and discussions that will accompany your reading of them, will prompt new ways of thinking and acting with respect to the much-contested and elusive ideal of social justice.

THIRTEEN

Criminal Responses to Hate-Motivated Violence: Is Bill C-41 Tough Enough?

MARTHA SHAFFER

INTRODUCTION

Canada appears to be witnessing an upsurge[1] in hate-motivated violence.[2] This raises the question — is the criminal justice system responding adequately to the problem of violence motivated by hate? At present, although the *Criminal Code* contains provisions dealing with hate propaganda,[3] it does not specifically address hate-motivated violence. Hate-motivated violence is prosecuted instead under the standard criminal provisions governing violent acts, such as assault, manslaughter, or mischief. The bigoted nature of any incident, assuming it enters into the process at all, is considered only as a factor in sentencing.

Source: The content of this article has been modified from its original version, appearing in Martha Shaffer, "Criminal Responses to Hate-Motivated Violence: Is Bill C-41 Tough Enough?" *McGill Law Journal* 41 (1995): 199–250.

In June 1994, the Canadian government announced its intention to take an aggressive stand against hate crime. Minister of Justice Allan Rock introduced legislation[4] to amend the *Criminal Code* to require judges, when passing sentence, to consider an offender's biased motive as a factor tending to increase the severity of the offence. Although the media portrayed Bill C-41 as a significant change and as a potential interference with the independence of the judiciary, the Bill actually does little to alter the current law. Under the Bill, hate crimes would continue to be prosecuted under existing *Criminal Code* provisions, and the accused's bigoted motive would only be considered at sentencing. The only significant difference between existing sentencing principles and the proposed amendments is that, under the latter, the *Criminal Code* would explicitly require consideration of an accused's biased motive as an element in sentencing.

In contrast to the existing Canadian approach to hate crime and to Parliament's codification of it, many jurisdictions in the United States have enacted provisions directed specifically at the problem of hate-motivated violence. These provisions increase the criminal penalties for offences involving violence motivated by hatred above those that attach to offences where group-based hatred is not an issue. Many also create a civil cause of action for victims of such violence. Despite considerable dispute over the constitutional validity of these statutes, the Supreme Court of the United States recently held that Wisconsin's hate-crime law[5] did not violate the United States Constitution.[6]

In light of the increase in hate crimes Canada appears to be witnessing, the time is ripe to consider how the criminal law should respond to this type of violence, and specifically, whether Bill C-41 is the best approach our criminal law has to offer. In this paper, I advance an argument in support of adopting U.S.-style hate-crime provisions. I suggest first that Bill C-41 does not represent a strong enough commitment to denouncing hate-motivated violence and to ensuring that perpetrators of such violence receive sufficient disapprobation. Then I draw upon the experience of the United States to canvass potential weaknesses of hate-crime legislation, both in terms of practical difficulties of enforcement and in terms of potential constitutional hurdles. Throughout this discussion, I attempt to show that there are no constitutional obstacles to enacting U.S.-style hate-crime provisions in Canada, and further, that even though U.S.-style hate-crime provisions may have some practical limitations, Bill C-41 does not appear to offer any advantages over the United States's approach. I conclude by arguing that, if we are serious about our commitment to harmonious inter-group relations, hate-crime provisions present a better use of the criminal law than does Bill C-41.

My argument in support of U.S.-style hate-crime provisions is qualified, however, by a number of concerns. First, although at first glance hate-crime legislation may appear to be a progressive measure offering protection and a means of redress for groups which have been victimized by hatemongers, upon greater reflection, it may not be as constructive. Like many other criminal law reforms, hate-crime provisions may be little more than symbolic gestures, incapable of contributing to the solution of deeply entrenched social problems. Second, if the hate-crime provisions turn out to be ineffective in yielding convictions — as seems to have been the case in the United States — they may do more harm than good. Rather than signalling that hate crime will be treated seriously, they may, in fact, send the opposite message. Third, once hate-crime legislation is in place, we may be tempted to believe that, because we have taken measures to combat hate-motivated violence, no further action is needed. Notwithstanding these problems, I believe that the creation of strong hate-crime legislation is important in a society that prides itself on its ethics of tolerance and multiculturalism and, yet, is plagued by deep undercurrents of hate.

Throughout the ensuing discussion, it is important to keep in mind the limited parameters of the debate, namely, the response of the criminal justice system to the problem of hate-motivated violence. The criminal-justice system is only one of many possible mechanisms for addressing hate-motivated violence, and, arguably, it has only a very small role to play in rooting out the causes of such violence. Hate-crime legislation should not, therefore, be seen as a panacea for eradicating hate crime, as should be clear from the experience of the United States where high levels of hate crime persist. This paper focuses on the limited question of whether the criminal justice system is making the best contribution it can to deterring racist violence and to ensuring that those who commit hate-motivated crime receive appropriate disapprobation.

THE CASE FOR STRONG HATE-CRIME LEGISLATION

THE DEVELOPMENT OF HATE-CRIME LEGISLATION IN THE UNITED STATES AND ITS APPLICABILITY TO CANADA

A brief overview of the hate-crime legislation that has proliferated in the United States over the last decade serves as a useful way to begin discussing the nature of such provisions and the reasons in favour of their enactment. During the late 1970s and the early 1980s, the United States experienced an upsurge in violence against members of racial and religious minorities as well as an increase in other hate-group activities such as cross burnings and the defacing of synagogues.[7] In response, several state legislatures began to consider legislation to deter racist violence, provide mechanisms of redress for victims of such violence, and express social disapproval of racist activities. In 1981, Oregon became the first state to enact criminal provisions specifically directed at hate-motivated violence.[8] Other states quickly followed suit, and by 1991, well over one-half of the states had enacted criminal provisions against hate-motivated violence. If civil remedies are also taken into account, forty-seven states had passed some form of legislation to combat hate-motivated violence by 1993.[9]

Many of the states based their criminal provisions, at least, in part, on model legislation drafted by the Anti-Defamation League of B'nai B'rith (A.D.L.). Having documented rising anti-Semitism in the late 1970s, the A.D.L. began to advocate the creation of hate-crime legislation and, in 1981, it released a model statute which it hoped would form the basis of legislation at the state level. The A.D.L. recommended the creation of two criminal offences: institutional vandalism and intimidation. Institutional vandalism prohibited the vandalism of cemeteries, places of worship, community centres, or schools, all of which are common forms of anti-Semitic activity. The offence of intimidation was based on the principle that crimes motivated by racial or religious hatred are more heinous than those which are not and provided that certain offences could be punished more harshly when motivated by hatred. Since the initial release of its model legislation, the A.D.L. has broadened its intimidation provision to include crimes committed because of the victim's sexual orientation. The provision, thus, now addresses gay and lesbian bashing, crimes which have become increasingly prevalent over the last few years.[10] The A.D.L. model now provides the following definition of intimidation:

A. A person commits the crime of intimidation if, by reason of the actual or perceived race, color, religion, national origin or sexual orientation of another individual or group of individuals, he violates Section _____ of the Penal Code (insert code provision for criminal trespass, criminal mischief, harassment, menacing, assault and/or other appropriate statutorily proscribed criminal conduct).
B. Intimidation is a _____ misdemeanor/felony (the degree of the criminal liability should be at least one degree more serious than that imposed for the commission of the offense).[11]

According to A.D.L. statistics, by 1991, twenty-eight states had passed legislation akin to the offence of intimidation.[12]

The offence of intimidation alters the criminal law's traditional response to hate-motivated violence in two ways. First, it creates a distinct criminal offence focused on the hatred precipitating the accused's action. In the absence of a provision of this sort, prosecution would proceed under one of the generic offences included within the crime of intimidation — for example, assault — and the accused's hateful motive would be considered only at the point of sentencing. Intimidation, thus, emphasizes the bigoted nature of the accused's actions rather than the particular violent act by which the accused expressed his or her antipathies. Second, intimidation increases the maximum penalty for hate-motivated violence *above* that available for the underlying violent offence. Thus, while in a particular jurisdiction assault might carry a maximum penalty of five years' imprisonment, by deeming intimidation to be "one degree more serious" than the underlying offence of assault, the provision increases the penalty that can be imposed on a person who commits an assault because of hatred of a group to which the victim belongs.

Four aspects of the A.D.L.'s intimidation provision merit further discussion. First, although the offence will generally involve inter-group violence, intimidation is not intended to penalize inter-group violence *per se* but is, instead, designed to cover instances in which the violence is *caused* by group hatred. The A.D.L. explained the scope of the offence in the following way:

The conduct targeted by the legislation ... is distinct from other criminal behavior. These are not incidents where the victim is coincidentally the member of a group different from the criminal's, or where the criminal — in the course of a burglary or a mugging — realizes his victim's status and utters a racist or anti-Semitic remark. These crimes occur *because* of the victim's actual or perceived status; where race, religion, ethnicity or sexual orientation is the *reason* for the crime. In the vast majority of these cases, but for this personal characteristic, no crime would occur.[13]

Thus, intimidation deals only with a specific kind of inter-group violence and would not apply simply because the accused and the victim happen to belong to different racial, ethnic, or religious groups, or have different sexual orientations.

Second, it is the accused's *perception* of the victim's race, religion, or sexual orientation, rather than the victim's *actual* identity, that is relevant to the offence. Thus, individuals will be guilty of intimidation if they assault a person they believe to be, for example, Jewish, whether or not that person is *in fact* Jewish. What matters is the accused's intention to assault a Jewish person to express hatred of Jewish people, not whether the accused was correct in his or her belief that the victim was Jewish. The crime of intimidation, therefore, can be made out even where the accused's ascription of characteristics to the victim was completely erroneous.

Third, although initially conceived as a response to violence by racist groups against racial and religious minorities, the A.D.L. provision is drafted to be race and religion neutral, with the result that it punishes crimes motivated by group hatred regardless of the identity of the accused or of the victim. Thus, people of colour can be convicted of intimidation if by reason of racial hatred, they assault someone of a different racial group. In fact, in *Mitchell*, where the United States Supreme Court upheld Wisconsin's intimidation provision, the accused was an African-American man and the victim was a white youth.[14] Since the condemnation of hate-based violence embodied in intimidation statutes works to the benefit of members of the majority, as well as to the benefit of members of minority groups, intimidation statutes cannot be said to offer "special" protection to minorities.

Finally, the A.D.L. provision is broad enough to cover not only violence directed at persons whom the accused perceives as members of the hated group, but also includes violence directed at members of the *accused's* own group who are targeted because of their association with the hated group. Thus, white supremacists could be convicted of a hate crime for assaulting a white man who is part of an inter-racial couple if the assault was motivated by an abhorrence of inter-racial dating or miscegenation. While the non-white member of the couple would not be the direct target of the violence, the assault would still have been perpetrated "by reason of" his or her race and association with the immediate victim.

There are two principal ways in which a provision analogous to the A.D.L. intimidation provision could be drafted in Canada. The first and most obvious course would be to enact an omnibus hate-crime provision akin to the A.D.L.'s model. Such a provision could set out the violent offences that, when coupled with a hateful motive, would constitute "intimidation." This provision could either specify the penalty increase for each underlying offence (as the A.D.L. model does) or simply impose a penalty distinct from that of the underlying offence. Alternatively, a provision analogous to section 85 of the *Criminal Code* could be enacted. Section 85 states that a person who uses a firearm while committing an indictable offence or while fleeing from committing or attempting to commit an indictable offence is guilty of a separate offence and is liable to imprisonment for a minimum of one year and a maximum of fourteen years. Since section 85 also stipulates that the sentence for this offence is to be served consecutively to the sentence for the underlying indictable offence, its effect is to increase the sentence for indictable offences committed with a firearm. A crime of ethnic intimidation could be drafted along these lines to provide that a person who has committed a specific violent offence and who was motivated by group hatred would be guilty of the offence of intimidation in addition to the underlying violent offence. That person would then be subject to a statutorily mandated minimum sentence to be served consecutively to the sentence for the underlying violent crime.

Second, the sentencing provisions of the *Criminal Code* could be amended to provide for an increased sentence where a person has been found guilty of specified violent offences and has been shown to have been motivated by group hatred. In other words, rather than creating a distinct offence of intimidation, Parliament could simply increase the maximum sentence for designated offences when these offences were motivated by group hatred. Since it would focus on sentencing, this approach would differ from Bill C-41 in only one key respect: it would permit the *maximum penalty to be increased beyond* the maximum available for an offence not motivated by hatred. This approach has been adopted in several U.S. states.

For reasons which I will discuss below, the first of these two options is more appealing. While both proposals would have the effect of increasing sentences for hate-motivated violence,[15] recognizing this form of violence as a distinct offence is a more powerful way of condemning such behaviour than simply providing for the possibility of an increased sentence for the underlying crime. Either approach would, however, be a stronger denunciation of hate-motivated violence than is Bill C-41.

THE ARGUMENTS IN FAVOUR OF ENACTING U.S.-STYLE HATE-CRIME LEGISLATION IN CANADA

Under Canada's current law, the fact that an accused acted with a biased motive in committing an offence does enter into the criminal process but only at the point of sentencing. According to accepted sentencing principles, hatred acts as an aggravating factor which increases the severity of the accused's crime and, hence, the sentence to be imposed. This principle was articulated in 1977 in *R. v. Ingram*,[16] a case involving a vicious assault of a Tanzanian man by two young white men. In increasing the sentence imposed by the trial court, the Court of Appeal held that the presence of racist hatred renders an assault particularly abhorrent:

> It is a fundamental principle of our society that every member must respect the dignity, privacy, and person of the other. Crimes of violence increase when respect for the rights of others decreases, and in that manner, assaults such as occurred in this case attack the very fabric of our society. Parliament's concern for the incitement of racial hatred is reflected in s. 281 [now s. 319] of the *Criminal Code*. An assault which is racially motivated renders the offence more heinous. Such assaults, unfortunately, invite imitation and repetition by others and incite retaliation. The danger is even greater in a multicultural, pluralistic urban society. The sentence imposed must be one which expresses the public's abhorrence for such conduct and their [sic] refusal to countenance it.[17]

A year later, in *R. v. Atkinson*,[18] the Ontario Court of Appeal applied this reasoning to homophobic assaults against gay men. In 1991, the Attorney General of Ontario issued guidelines to Crown Attorneys, quoting the *Ingram* and *Atkinson* decisions and stating that prosecutors should bring the presence of a racial motive to the attention of the sentencing judge. The Attorney General re-issued these guidelines in March 1993, following several widely publicized incidents of racist violence. Thus, it appears to be accepted within Canadian criminal law that the presence of a hate-based motive renders violent conduct more serious, with the result that a more severe sentence should be imposed.

The provisions of Bill C-41 concerned with hate crime would simply codify this practice. Section 718.2 of the Bill provides that a court imposing a sentence shall consider "evidence that the offence was motivated by bias, prejudice or hate based on race, national or ethnic origin, language, colour, religion, sex, age, mental or physical disability, sexual orientation, or any other similar factor" as aggravating factors.[19] The fact that an accused was motivated by group hatred would thus lead courts to impose a sentence towards the harsher end of the existing sentencing range but would *not* permit the courts to *increase* the sentence beyond the maximum currently available.

Four arguments suggest that the law's current treatment of hate crime — and, by implication, the provisions contained in Bill C-41 — may be inadequate and support the creation of a distinct hate-crime offence. First, making hate-motivated violence into a distinct crime is recognition that such violence constitutes a specific form of harm that differs in significant ways from other types of violence. Hate-motivated violence is not simply an attack on the individual who happens to be the immediate target of the assault, but also constitutes an affront to minority communities and runs counter to Canada's core values of equality and multiculturalism. The accused's selection of a victim by reason of race, religion, ethnicity, or sexual orientation demonstrates that the violent conduct is directed not only at the immediate victim, but also at the entire group of which the victim is — or is perceived by the perpetrator to be — a member. Thus, hate-motivated violence is, in effect, a form of group intimidation intended to express loathing towards a particular group and to instil fear among that group as a whole.[20] As a result, hate-motivated violence affects entire minority communities, because they know that they are all potential targets of such violence. Moreover, the harmful effects of hate-motivated violence directed at members of one minority community may spill over to other minority groups. Bigots seldom limit their hatred to one group, and many members of minority groups know that, although they were not targeted this time, they could be next on the list.

In addition, research in the United States indicates that hate-motivated violence may be more brutal and result in greater physical and psychological injury to the victim than other forms of violent conduct. In its brief to the United States Supreme Court, the A.D.L. summarized one study in the following way:

> Research on bias-motivated crimes is in its infancy, but the available evidence indicates that these crimes are generally much more violent and have a significantly greater community impact than other crimes. One researcher, for example, analyzed 452 hate-crime cases in Boston during the period between 1983 and 1987. The data revealed that 74% of bias-motivated assault incidents (including assault and battery and assault with a dangerous weapon) involved some physical injury to the victim. The national figure for all assault cases was 29%. Remarkably, these bias-motivated assault incidents involved hospitalization of their victims over four times more often than is the case with other assaults.[21]

According to a 1989 study conducted by the National Institute Against Prejudice and Violence, also cited by the A.D.L., the psychological effects experienced by victims of hate-motivated violence also tend to be more severe than for victims of violence that is not hate inspired. The study found that victims of hate-motivated violence experience on average "21% more of the standard psychophysiological symptoms of stress than did victims of similar acts of ordinary violence or abuse."[22] These results provide additional support for viewing hate-motivated violence as different from, and more severe than, other forms of violence.

By requiring judges to consider the accused's hateful motive at the time of sentencing, Bill C-41 implicitly recognizes the harmful effects of hate-motivated violence on minority communities and on Canadian society as a whole. However, Bill C-41's approach of redressing biased motives through the sentencing process may not sufficiently underscore the distinctive nature of hate-motivated crime. Prosecuting the accused with a standard, non-hate-specific offence may fail to emphasize the extent to which the accused's action was an expression of hatred of an entire group as effectively as would a prosecution under a specific hate-crime provision. Furthermore, under Bill C-41, the accused's hateful motive can *at most* increase his or her penalty to the existing maximum for the underlying offence. To account fully for the extent of the individual and social harms caused by hate crime, it is, I would argue, necessary to augment the penalties available for such crimes.

The second argument in favour of enacting provisions specifically directed at hate crime derives from the role the criminal law plays in demarcating the boundaries between acceptable and unacceptable conduct. By deeming certain activities to be subject to state sanction, the criminal law plays a normative or symbolic role in instructing citizens about the types of conduct that give rise to social disapprobation. The symbolic aspect of the criminal law has featured prominently in feminist scholarship. For example, in advocating law reform to abolish the rule that a man could not, by definition, rape his wife, and to ensure that spousal abuse is treated seriously by police and prosecutors, many feminist scholars have argued that legal rules or their selective implementation has created a cultural climate that condones violence against women. The premise behind feminist arguments for changing the law and for improving enforcement is that the messages enshrined in the criminal law can be a powerful force in shaping attitudes and altering behaviour.[23] The symbolic aspect of the criminal law also has a role to play in combatting racism and hate-motivated violence. Making hate-motivated violence into a distinct criminal offence sends a strong normative message that such violence is unacceptable and will not be tolerated in a society committed to pluralism. Considering motive in the sentencing process is not as powerful a statement, since it does not constitute an explicit denunciation of hate-motivated violence but treats hatred as only one of the many factors going to the severity of the crime.

Third, one can argue that absent an explicit criminal provision condemning hate-motivated violence, the criminal law fails to serve the needs of groups who are most likely to be the victims of hate crime. The argument here is that the criminal law has been formulated primarily by white men and reflects their views about the type of behaviour that ought to be subject to criminal sanction. As white male lawmakers are far less likely to view themselves as potential victims of hate crime than are members of minority groups, they may never have contemplated the criminal law's role in responding to hate crimes, nor viewed these crimes as requiring specific action. Although hate-motivated violence is not new to Canada, the fact that hate crime has not been the subject of significant public disapproval until recently supports this analysis. Since minorities are more likely to be targets of hate-motivated violence than members of the majority group, the absence of provisions designed specifically to address such violence raises the question of whether the criminal law confers equal protection on all citizens given the different types of harm they are likely to face. If one accepts the previous arguments concerning the distinctive nature of hate crime and the importance of the normative messages embodied in the criminal law, the answer — even after Bill C-41 — is that it does not.[24]

Finally, the creation of a crime of intimidation may make it easier for authorities to compile statistics on the incidence of hate crime. Assuming assiduous charging and prosecution of conduct giving rise to intimidation, the level of hate-motivated violence could be tracked by following the conviction rate for the offence of intimidation as well as for any other hate-specific offence. Determining the frequency of hate-motivated violence under the current system is, however, more complicated since it requires scrutiny of all violence-related offences. In addition, since the hateful nature of the offence will not be apparent from the charge itself, compilation of hate-crime statistics requires a recording and retrieval system that takes into account the facts of the case and the factors considered in sentencing and does not focus simply on the disposition. While this argument for creating a specific hate crime is, perhaps, less compelling than the others, it is, nonetheless, worthy of consideration.

ARGUMENTS AGAINST U.S.-STYLE HATE-CRIME LEGISLATION

An examination of the criticism that U.S. hate-crime provisions have attracted provides valuable insight into the potential pitfalls of enacting such provisions. Despite widespread agreement — at least on the rhetorical level — that hate crime is deplorable, many commentators question the wisdom of enacting A.D.L.-style hate-crime provisions. The most vociferous criticism has focused on the constitutional validity of these provisions and, in particular, on their potential conflict with free speech. Critics also question the effectiveness of hate-crime legislation, often pointing to the fact that few convictions have been entered under such laws. Finally, some critics question the appropriateness of using the criminal law to tackle problems as complex as group hatred. I will examine each of these objections to assess if they assist in determining whether Canadians should eschew U.S.-style hate-crime legislation in favour of the Bill C-41 approach. My analysis of these criticisms suggests that there are no serious reasons why A.D.L.-style hate-crime legislation should not be enacted in Canada.

CONSTITUTIONAL CONCERNS

Until the Supreme Court of the United States declared that Wisconsin's hate-crime provision did not violate the United States Constitution, concern that hate-crime provisions were unconstitutional was widespread. Hate-crime provisions were thought to violate the constitution in three ways: (1) by infringing the freedom of speech and thought protected by the First Amendment; (2) by violating the guarantee of equal protection; and (3) by violating the due process clause of the Fourteenth Amendment through vagueness. Of these, the freedom of speech challenge was viewed as the most damaging in light of the stringent protection courts in the United States have accorded to speech.

Although the constitutional validity of hate-crime statutes is settled in the United States, similar arguments could be made in Canada were U.S.-style hate-crime legislation to be enacted. Thus, I will explore each of the above challenges, as well as arguments against hate-crime legislation that could be brought under section 7 of the *Canadian Charter of Rights and Freedoms*. My focus throughout this discussion will be to demonstrate that the *Charter* poses no impediments to the enactment of U.S.-style hate-crime legislation in Canada.

FREEDOM OF SPEECH AND FREEDOM OF EXPRESSION

Until *Mitchell*, hate-crime statutes were viewed as violating free speech in two ways: (1) they were seen to constitute a thought crime; and (2) they were regarded as violating the doctrine of overbreadth. On the basis of these arguments, hate-crime provisions had been struck down by the supreme courts of Wisconsin and Ohio.[25]

Hate crimes as "thought crimes" and the doctrine of overbreadth The argument that hate-crime provisions punish thoughts derives from the fact that the violent actions forming the basis of hate crimes are already criminal offences. According to this argument, the only element differentiating hate-based offences from "simple" offences is the accused's expression of group hatred. Hate-crime provisions, therefore, do nothing more than punish an accused's hateful motive for engaging in what is already a criminal offence. This amounts to creating a thought crime in which the accused is punished more severely for subscribing to racist beliefs and for expressing them through violent conduct. While such beliefs are undoubtedly heinous, the First Amendment prohibits the state from choosing among competing viewpoints, thereby dictating to its citizens which opinions they may hold. This protection is most important where the beliefs in question are "reviled by society" and are, consequently, more easily suppressed. Thus, while the state is legitimately entitled to punish the accused's violent conduct, it may not increase the punishment on the basis of the discriminatory thought that motivated the conduct.

The overbreadth argument is slightly more complicated. Unlike in Canada, where overbreadth forms part of the proportionality analysis within section 1 of the *Charter* or falls within a section 7 analysis,[26] in the United States, overbreadth exists as an independent basis for challenging legislation under the First Amendment. The overbreadth doctrine refers to laws which, though directed at an activity that the government is entitled to control, sweep within their grasp activity protected by the First Amendment. Where a protected activity is a significant part of the law's target, and no satisfactory way of separating constitutional from unconstitutional applications of the law exists, the law will be void for overbreadth.[27] Invalidating the entire law is appropriate because a gradual removal of the law's unconstitutional aspects would result in a chill on free speech; to avoid running afoul of the law, individuals would engage in self-censorship and refrain from validly exercising their right to free speech. The importance of free speech within the constitutional framework of the United States renders this situation unacceptable.

In the case of hate-crime statutes, the overbreadth argument stems from the use of the accused's statements as evidence that his or her crimes were inspired by hate. The accused's speech, uttered either during the incident or before it occurred, will often be the most compelling — if not the only — evidence that the accused committed a hate crime. Relevant statements would clearly include blatantly racist comments but, the argument goes, might also include less heinous speech, such as ethnic jokes or remarks made in the course of serious intellectual inquiry. All of these forms of speech are protected by the First Amendment. Thus, hate-crime provisions are said to be overbroad because, by permitting the accused's statements to be used to prove an element of the offence, they sweep constitutionally protected speech within their ambit. Susan Gellman, a vigorous opponent of hate-crime legislation, puts this argument in the following way: "Anyone charged with one of the underlying offenses could be charged with ... [a hate crime] as well, and face the possibility of public scrutiny of a lifetime of ... ethnic jokes to serious intellectual inquiry. Awareness of this possibility could lead to habitual self-censorship of ... one's ideas, and reluctance to read or listen publicly to the ideas of others, whenever one fears that those ideas might run contrary to popular sentiment on the subject of ethnic relations."[28] In other words, hate-crime legislation might have a chilling effect on speech as people would be forced to censor themselves in order to avoid prosecution for a hate crime should they, at some future point, commit a violent act.

For reasons which Canadian courts would likely find instructive, the Supreme Court of the United States rejected both the thought-crime and overbreadth arguments in *Mitchell*. That case involved the prosecution of an African-American man for an assault on a white youth under Wisconsin's hate-crime statute. Mitchell and a number of other African-American men and youths had been discussing a scene from the movie *Mississippi Burning*, in which a group of white men beat a young African-American boy who was praying. In the course of this discussion, Mitchell asked the group whether they felt "hyped up to move on some white people."[29] Shortly after, a white youth walked by and Mitchell said, "You all want to fuck somebody up? There goes a white boy; go get him."[30] Mitchell then counted to three and pointed in the youth's direction. The group beat the boy so severely that he was in a coma for four days. Mitchell was convicted of aggravated battery. Although the maximum penalty for aggravated battery is normally imprisonment for two years, Wisconsin's hate-crime provision increased the maximum to seven years where the offence had been motivated by group hatred. The court sentenced Mitchell to four years imprisonment because his actions had been motivated by racial hatred. Mitchell appealed the increase of his sentence, arguing that Wisconsin's hate-crime provision violated the United States Constitution, and in particular, that it violated his constitutional guarantee of free speech.

The Supreme Court of the United States gave three principal reasons for rejecting Mitchell's "thought crime" challenge. First, the Court stressed that judges passing sentence have traditionally considered the accused's motive for acting, and that using motive as either a mitigating or aggravating factor in sentencing was entirely appropriate.[31] Even where the accused's motive could be said to consist of discriminatory thoughts or beliefs, nothing in First Amendment jurisprudence prevented courts from taking these motives into account. While it would be impermissible to increase an accused's sentence *simply because* he or she held offensive beliefs, where the beliefs related directly to the crime, the guarantee of free speech *did not* prohibit consideration of the reasons the accused acted.

Second, the Court noted that intimidation provisions simply formalize existing judicial practice by providing, as a matter of policy, that hate crimes merit stiffer sentences. There was nothing wrong in legislating an increase in the maximum sentence available for crimes motivated by hatred since "the primary responsibility for fixing criminal penalties lies with the legislature."[32] In the Court's view, the State's justification for this increase — that hate-inspired violence inflicts greater individual and societal harm — provided "an adequate explanation for its penalty-enhancement provision over and above mere disagreement with offenders' beliefs and biases."[33] In accepting the validity of this justification, the Court quoted Blackstone: "[I]t is but reasonable that among crimes of different natures those should be most severely punished, which are the most destructive of the public safety and happiness."[34]

Finally, the Court drew an analogy between the use of motive in hate-crime provisions and the use of motive in anti-discrimination laws: both types of statutes use motive in the same way, namely, to prove that a person acted in a discriminatory fashion. Citing an earlier decision[35] that established that anti-discrimination laws comport with the First Amendment, the Court held that the guarantee of free speech posed no constitutional impediment to the use of motive in hate-crime provisions. Thus, primarily on the basis that courts may legitimately consider motive in sentencing, the United States Supreme Court rejected the argument that Wisconsin's hate-crime provision created a thought crime and, thereby, violated the First Amendment.

The Court rejected Mitchell's overbreadth argument with only summary consideration. The chill argument, the Court noted, depended on "the prospect of a citizen suppressing his bigoted beliefs for fear that evidence of such beliefs will be introduced against him at trial" should he or she in the future commit a serious offence. The Court deemed this prospect too speculative to sustain an overbreadth claim.[36] In addition, the Court noted that the First Amendment does not prevent the introduction into evidence of an accused's speech to establish the existence of a motive to commit an offence or of the mental state required for criminal culpability. On the contrary, accused persons' statements are routinely used for these purposes so long as they comport with evidentiary rules of relevance and admissibility. Use of the accused's speech as evidence that his or her actions were hate inspired did not, the Court concluded, render hate-crime provisions invalid on the basis of overbreadth.

Hate-crime provisions and section 2(b) of the *Charter* While arguments similar to the thought crime and overbreadth challenges could be made under section 2(b) of the *Charter*, differences in wording between the Canadian and U.S. constitutional guarantees as well as differences in constitutional doctrine would result in the arguments taking a different form. In the United States, it is necessary to argue that hate-crime provisions punish *thought* rather than *conduct* to receive protection under the constitutional guarantee of free speech. No such manoeuvering need occur in Canada, however, under the more broadly framed constitutional guarantee of freedom of *expression*, which protects most forms of expressive conduct. To separate the "thought" aspect of hate crime from the "conduct" aspect would, in fact, be at odds with the Canadian approach to freedom of expression, which considers both the form and content of the expression in question. The Canadian equivalent of the thought-crime argument would focus squarely on hate-motivated violence as a form of expressive activity that conveys messages about particular groups. The argument would be as follows: because hate crime is expressive activity, punishing it more severely than other forms of criminal activity restricts the accused's right to express certain ideas in a violent form.

The overbreadth argument would be recast in a similar fashion. As in the United States, the argument in Canada would be that the prosecution might use statements the accused made before the violent act to prove that the accused acted out of hatred. So long as these statements did not fall afoul of the hate-propaganda provisions of the *Criminal Code*, they might well be protected under section 2(b) of the *Charter*. Allowing the accused's speech to be used in evidence could be said to have a chilling effect on constitutionally acceptable expression if there is a risk that people will desist from making bigoted statements as a result of the enactment of hate-crime provisions. Thus, by permitting the accused's *non-violent* expressions of group hatred — and perhaps even the accused's associations with groups known to espouse bigoted ideas — to be used as evidence of his or her hateful motive, hate-crime provisions could be said to have the *effect* of violating section 2(b), and potentially section 2(d) (freedom of association).

Before subjecting each of these arguments to a formal section 2(b) analysis, some general comments on their persuasiveness should be made. For both political and jurisprudential reasons, the Canadian equivalents of the thought-crime and overbreadth arguments would not prove as vexing to hate-crime legislation as their counterparts have in the United States. First, as a general matter, there is greater social tolerance for measures designed to combat discrimination in Canada than in the United States. Although Canada, like the United States, has experienced its share of historical racism, and bigotry continues to be a pressing concern, Canadians, rightly or wrongly, pride themselves on being an accommodating and tolerant nation in which newcomers can celebrate their ethnicity, rather than feeling that they have to shed their cultural identity at the border. Canadians are also less likely than those in the U.S. to conceive of violent expressions of group hatred as implicating a constitutional right, much less a right to expression. Within the Canadian social and political context, hate-crime provisions are apt to be seen as one of many available tools to eradicate racism and promote congenial ethnic relations, rather than as illegitimate government intrusion on free expression.

The Canadian equivalent of the thought-crime argument While the Supreme Court has never specifically considered whether violent forms of expression are protected under section 2(b), its decisions clearly imply that expression taking a violent form will not be constitutionally protected. Despite embracing a wide and inclusive interpretation of expression within section 2(b), the Supreme Court has, from its earliest pronouncement on freedom of expression in *R. W.D.S.U. v. Dolphin Delivery Ltd.*,[37] clearly stated that violence is a *form* of expression that will not be given constitutional protection. The Court has reiterated the exclusion of violence from section 2(b) in subsequent cases. For example, in *Irwin Toy Ltd. v. Quebec (A.G.)*,[38] in which the Supreme Court established the framework for analyzing freedom of expression claims, the Court drew a distinction between regulating expression based on its form and regulation based on content. While section 2(b) protects the content or substance of expression regardless of the meaning conveyed, it does not protect all forms of expression. Physical violence is an unprotected form. Thus, although freedom of expression will *prima facie* protect any attempt to convey meaning, and although violence may have expressive content, expressive activity that takes a violent form will lose its constitutional protection. Hate-motivated violence would seem to fit squarely within what the Court described in *Keegstra* as the "rare cases" in which an activity with expressive content is not protected by section 2(b) because it is "communicated in a physically violent form."[39]

This conclusion may give rise to the concern that exempting all violent forms of expression from scrutiny under section 2(b) of the *Charter* would allow the state to punish certain messages expressed through violence more harshly than others *based on the content* of the message being conveyed. For example, one might argue that if violent messages are not protected by section 2(b), nothing prevents Parliament from amending the *Criminal Code* to provide that violence deemed "political" should be subject to twice the normal penalties of "non-political" violence. To prevent this, one could argue that it is necessary to confer section 2(b) protection on expression of a violent nature. This argument, however, fails to take into account the presence of other rights in the *Charter* that limit the state's ability to enact restrictive provisions in the criminal realm.

Assuming that courts continue to adhere to the distinction between restrictions on the form of expression and restrictions on its content, I am of the view that the Canadian equivalent of the thought-crime argument would be rejected. In the event that a court were to depart from this analysis and hold that a hate-crime statute did violate section 2(b), however, I believe that the violation would be justified under section 1.

Section 1 of the Charter The Supreme Court's analysis in *Keegstra* provides a useful basis for predicting the fate of hate-crime provisions under a section 1 analysis. *Keegstra* involved a challenge to one of the hate-propaganda provisions of the *Criminal Code* — section 319(2) — under section 2(b) of the *Charter*. Section 319(2) made it an offence to communicate statements, other than in private conversation, to willfully promote hatred of a group identifiable by colour, race, religion, or ethnic origin. The Supreme Court agreed that this provision violated freedom of expression because it restricted the *non-violent* expression of ideas, but held — by a five-to-four majority — that the violation could be justified under section 1. Given the similarity between the expression prohibited by the hate-propaganda provisions and the expressive aspect of hate-inspired violence, the *Keegstra* analysis would have a direct bearing on a determination of the validity of hate-crime legislation under section 1.

Three aspects of the Court's reasoning in *Keegstra* are of particular relevance. The first concerns the Court's discussion of the government's objective in seeking to curtail hate propaganda. Both the majority and the dissent characterized this objective as twofold: (1) preventing harm to members of groups targeted by hate propaganda and, thus, safeguarding individual dignity; and (2) protecting society from the social discord, including violence, that might result from the acceptance of hateful messages.[40] Both judgements stressed the importance of this objective and agreed that it satisfied the first hurdle of the *Oakes*[41] test. The objective of hate-crime legislation would closely parallel that of section 319(2). It could be described as recognizing the distinct harm which hate-motivated violence poses to the individual victims of that violence, to the group(s) to which the individual belongs, to other minority groups, and to Canadian society generally. The similarity between the objectives suggests that hate-crime legislation would satisfy the first branch of the *Oakes* test.

Second, the majority regarded the message contained in hate propaganda as tenuously linked to the three core values which are protected by freedom of expression: (1) the search for truth; (2) participation in the political process; and (3) individual self-fulfilment. This is significant since the Supreme Court has repeatedly held that restrictions on types of expression that lie on the periphery of freedom of expression will be easier to justify under the proportionality part of the *Oakes* test than limitations on types of expression which are close to the core.[42] In the majority's view, hate propaganda failed to promote the search for truth since there was very little chance that statements intended to promote hatred would be true or that the vision of society implicit within such statements would lead to a better world.[43] Hate propaganda also failed to advance the value of individual fulfilment since the articulation of hatred conflicts with the individual fulfilment of members of a targeted group.[44] Finally, the willful promotion of hatred against an identifiable group could not be seen to foster participation in the political process since the view that not all persons are entitled to equal dignity and respect, inherent within statements promoting hatred, is inimical to the democratic participation of all persons.

All these arguments could be made even more strongly in the case of expression curtailed by hate-crime provisions. Violent expressions of group hatred are even more tenuously related to the values underlying freedom of expression than the promotion of group hatred through non-violent means. While it is possible to reject the majority's view and to argue that non-violent expressions of group hatred have some social value, it is much more difficult to claim that violent expressions of hatred have any redeeming social value worthy of constitutional protection.

Finally, there is much to suggest that even the dissenting justices in *Keegstra* would have an easier time upholding hate-crime provisions under section 1. The dissent found that the hate-propaganda provisions failed all three components of the *Oakes* proportionality test based on flaws from which hate-crime provisions, arguably, do not suffer. They found that the provision lacked a rational connection to the government's objective because it potentially promoted, rather than curtailed, racist speech through the media coverage given the accused's message during his or her prosecution.[45] The provision failed the minimal-impairment test because it was overbroad, catching more expressive conduct than could be justified by the objectives of promoting social harmony and individual dignity, and because non-criminal remedies were available to combat hate propaganda. Finally, the provision failed the last element of the *Oakes* test; in the dissent's view, non-violent hate propaganda implicated all three values at the core of freedom of expression — the search for truth, participation in the democratic process, and individual self-fulfilment — and, therefore, the benefit derived from the legislation did not outweigh the magnitude of the violation.

It would be difficult to argue that hate-crime provisions are not rationally connected to the objective of recognizing and redressing the harms that hate-motivated violence causes. Increasing the maximum penalty available for violent crimes motivated by hatred is rationally linked to the desire to acknowledge that such conduct inflicts great harm on individual victims, on minority groups, and on the larger society. As a result, hate-crime provisions are not prone to the rational connection criticism that McLachlin J., writing for the dissent in *Keegstra*, levied against section 319(2). McLachlin J. was of the view that criminal hate-propaganda laws are not rationally connected to the objective of protecting minority groups from harm because the criminal prosecution of persons accused of willfully spreading hatred serves to give hatemongers a public platform they otherwise would not have. This concern would be far less compelling in the case of hate-motivated violence. While prosecutions under section 319(2) would focus on the *content* of the accused's statements and whether the accused intended to foment hatred, trials for hate-motivated violence would focus on the *violent act* of the accused, and whether it was motivated by racial animosity. Since proof of racial enmity would not generally involve detailed scrutiny of an accused's non-violent writings or statements but would, instead, focus on statements the accused made at the time of the assault, hate-crime prosecutions are unlikely to provide the accused with a platform for articulating and defending racist beliefs.

Hate-crime provisions also do not suffer from the same minimal-impairment concerns McLachlin J. perceived in section 319(2). Although her reasons were not altogether clear, she appeared to hold the view that the section failed the minimal-impairment part of the *Oakes* test because, through a combination of overbreadth and vagueness, it caught more expressive activity than its objective warranted. Section 319(2) was overbroad, according to McLachlin J., because it potentially covered a wide range of expression with the result that people who made statements "primarily for non-nefarious reasons" could be subject to criminal conviction. McLachlin J.'s concern stemmed primarily from her view that the term "hatred" was vague and subjective and, therefore, capable of denoting a broad spectrum of emotions ranging from "the most powerful of virulent emotions lying beyond the bounds of human decency," on the one hand, to "active dislike," on the other.[46] Thus, people could be convicted under section 319(2) for making statements designed to contribute to political or social debate where they knew that their statements would have the *effect* of promoting dislike of a group, even if they did not actually desire to promote hatred. In addition, because section 319(2) applied to all statements *other than* those made in private conversation, McLachlin J. expressed concern that "the circumstances in which the offending statements are prohibited [are] virtually unlimited."[47] Thus, forms of expression on which society places a high value could conceivably fall afoul of section 319(2): "Speeches are caught. The corner soapbox is no longer open. Books, films, and works of art — all these fall under the censor's scrutiny because of s. 319(2) of the *Criminal Code*."

It is difficult to see how a hate-crime provision would be vulnerable to McLachlin J.'s overbreadth concerns. Whereas it was possible to argue that the legislation in *Keegstra* would capture too much non-violent expression because it specifically targeted non-violent statements in a broad and undefined fashion, the same argument does not arise in hate-crime provisions. Hate-crime provisions restrict a narrow and clearly delineated form of expression, namely, violent expressions of group hatred. Since there could be no prosecution without an act of violence, under no circumstances could hate-crime provisions sweep non-violent expressions of bigotry — however heinous these may be — within their ambit. Hate-crime provisions could only be said to be overbroad insofar as they risked encompassing too much violence — that is, violent acts that are not, in fact, motivated by group hatred. Since the prosecution would be required to prove the accused's hate-based motivation beyond a reasonable doubt, this is not likely to be a problem.

Finally, hate-crime provisions would not be vulnerable to the concerns McLachlin J. raised under the last part of the *Oakes* test — that of proportionality between the objective of the legislation and its effects. McLachlin J.'s reasoning in *Keegstra* was based on her view that the kind of non-violent expression prohibited by section 319(2) of the *Criminal Code* implicated the values on which freedom of expression was founded. In the context of hate-motivated violence, this argument is difficult to sustain since the expression of hatred through violence can hardly be said to strike at the heart of section 2(b). The highly tenuous nature of the expression involved in hate-motivated violence could hardly outweigh the benefit that hate-crime provisions would seek to confer.

Keegstra, therefore, suggests that even if hate-crime provisions were found to violate section 2(b) of the *Charter* because they impose a higher penalty on violence intended to promote group hatred than on other forms of violence, they would still be sustained under section 1. Further support for this view can be derived from

Butler, in which the Supreme Court unanimously held that the obscenity provisions of the *Criminal Code* could be justified under section 1 even though these provisions violated section 2(b). As in *Keegstra*, the Court's reasoning was based on an assessment of the importance of the expression in fostering the values underlying section 2(b). Both *Keegstra* and *Butler* indicate the Supreme Court's willingness to uphold restrictions on freedom of expression in circumstances where the expression lies far from the core of section 2(b) and causes or threatens significant social harm.

The Canadian version of the overbreadth argument The argument that hate-crime provisions violate section 2(b) of the *Charter* by allowing into evidence the accused's non-violent statements is based on the effects of the provisions rather than their *purpose*. The purpose of hate-crime provisions is not to infringe on non-violent expressions of group hatred. Nonetheless, hate-crime provisions could have this effect by chilling non-violent speech if people avoid commenting on controversial issues for fear of being charged, in the future, with a hate crime.

Since *R. v. Big M Drug Mart Ltd.*,[48] it has been clear that legislation with a valid purpose may be found to violate the *Charter* if it has the *effect* of infringing *Charter* rights. However, as the Court indicated in *R. v. Edwards Books and Art Ltd.*,[49] for an effects-based challenge to succeed, the impugned law must have more than a trivial or insubstantial effect but must reasonably or actually threaten[50] the right in question. Thus, not every law that potentially affects freedom of expression will violate section 2(b).

There are two reasons why it will be difficult to establish that hate-crime provisions have the effect of violating free speech. First, the chill which may potentially arise from the use of the accused's speech as evidence in the prosecution of hate crime is, as the United States Supreme Court noted in *Mitchell*, highly speculative. To consider the chill as a serious threat, one would have to assume that people wishing to relate racist jokes or to explore ethnic differences through scientific or artistic inquiry would refrain from doing so, contemplating that they may at some later date attack, maim, or even kill a member of an identifiable group. This scenario is highly unrealistic. Further, not all of the accused's prior statements would be admissible, since statements introduced at trial must comply with the rules of evidence. For example, racist jokes told by an accused are not likely to be highly probative of the issue of whether he or she committed a violent act to express racial hatred, unless they are accompanied by additional evidence that the accused harboured racist views. Thus, it is not at all clear that hate-crime provisions would "reasonably or actually" threaten freedom of expression.

Second, as the United States Supreme Court noted in *Mitchell*, use of the accused's prior statements in the case against him or her is not unique to the prosecution of hate crime. The rules of evidence allow the use of an accused person's statements in criminal trials to prove various aspects of the Crown's case, including motive and *mens rea*. For example, in a murder trial, the accused's declarations of animosity towards the deceased could be admissible to demonstrate motive. Use of these comments could be said to have a chilling effect on free expression because people might refrain from expressing their resentment of particular individuals, knowing that these statements could be used against them in the future. More to the point, statements evincing bigoted attitudes on the part of the defendant are used in human rights complaints to establish discrimination. These statements are used in much the same way as in hate-crime prosecutions. To suggest that use of the accused's prior speech violates free expression is to cast doubt on the use of speech in all of these contexts. It is difficult to imagine courts accepting an argument that evidentiary use of speech — even if it could be said to have a chilling effect — violates section 2(b).

Even if courts were to accept the argument that hate-crime provisions chill free expression, this violation would be justified with little difficulty under section 1. The analysis here would, to a large degree, mirror that conducted for the claim that the purpose of hate-crime legislation violates free expression. However, because the analysis would focus on the *effect* of hate-crime provisions on non-violent *expression*, some differences would arise under the minimal impairment and balancing aspects of the *Oakes* test. The courts would have to determine whether hate-crime legislation impairs non-violent expression as little as possible, and if so, whether the effects on non-violent expression are nonetheless so grievous that they outweigh the benefits of the provision. Hate-crime legislation should clear the first of these hurdles since, given the distinct harms posed by hate-motivated violence, there is no less restrictive way of attaining the objective underlying hate-crime provisions. The approach proposed in Bill C-41 is no less restrictive, since it gives rise to the same "chill" arguments as do U.S.-style hate-crime provisions. Finally, having established that it is highly unrealistic that hate-crime provisions would create any substantial chill on free expression, the requirement of balancing the effects of the legislation against its objective would not pose an obstacle to the validity of the provisions.

EFFECTIVENESS CONCERNS

The second set of concerns regarding hate-crime provisions relates to their effectiveness. Although such provisions have existed in various states for some time, there have been few charges laid and even fewer successful prosecutions. Further, given the level of racial animosity and racial violence that persists throughout the United States, it is hard to make a compelling case that hate-crime provisions have had much of an impact in combatting violent expressions of group hatred, let alone in reducing prejudice and racism in that country. Examining these problems of effectiveness is important to determine the degree to which they are peculiar to the United States or are inherent in hate-crime provisions, as well as the extent to which they would be circumvented by adopting the Bill C-41 approach.

The paucity of convictions under hate-crime statutes may be due to a combination of several factors. It may, in part, result from the reluctance of prosecutors to lay charges under legislation of questionable constitutional validity. The volatility of race trials in the United States may also be a factor. Because highly visible prosecutions risk bringing strained racial tensions to the boiling point, prosecutors may either consciously or unconsciously attempt to avoid making race central to the trial. Overt racism by key players in the justice system may also account for the low prosecution and conviction rates. Racist police officers, for example, might not investigate hate-crime vigorously and might even resist laying a charge under a hate-crime provision. Discussion of these considerations is conspicuously absent from the literature in the United States, which has, instead, focused on two explanations of the provisions' poor track record: (1) the need to prove racial motivation beyond a reasonable doubt; and (2) the operation of unconscious racism in the prosecution of hate crime.

PROBLEMS OF PROOF: PROOF BEYOND A REASONABLE DOUBT AND THE USE OF SIMILAR FACT EVIDENCE

Since hate-crime provisions make biased motivation an element of the offence, the prosecution is required to prove racial motivation beyond a reasonable doubt. Commentators have argued that this burden will be next to impossible to meet and consequently that it will yield few convictions. The difficulty in obtaining convictions, it is contended, will dissuade prosecutors from proceeding with hate-crime charges, prosecuting the accused, instead, with the violent offence underlying the hate-crime charge. Requiring the prosecution to prove motive will, therefore, make hate-crime provisions unenforceable and, thereby, undermine the objective of the provisions.

Commentators have offered two principal reasons as to why motive may be difficult to prove beyond a reasonable doubt. First, they argue that motive differs from other mental states that figure in the criminal process because it lies more deeply within the accused's sole knowledge and, thus, is not susceptible to standard techniques of proof. For example, in determining whether the accused committed a crime requiring intention, the trier of fact may be assisted by the inference that a person normally intends the natural and probable consequences of his or her actions. While the triers of fact would still have to decide, on the evidence, whether the accused did act intentionally, the availability of a simple inference would assist them in reaching a conclusion. In contrast, it is more difficult to infer an accused's motive from the actions themselves. For example, a jury might easily infer that an accused who, without provocation, assaulted a stranger standing alone at a bus stop acted intentionally. In the absence of other evidence, however, the accused's motive is less clear. The accused could have been motivated by a fear of strangers, by homophobia, by racism, or by some combination of the three. Without considerably more evidence, it will be difficult to prove beyond a reasonable doubt which of these factors motivated the accused. Thus, the argument goes, motive is much more elusive than other mental states, and it may be virtually incapable of being proved.

Second, commentators argue that the evidence necessary to prove a biased motive may often be inadmissible. Unless the accused's motive is clear from statements uttered during the commission of the crime or from demonstrative acts, such as painting swastikas, proof of motive will require evidence showing that the accused has made bigoted remarks in the past, belongs to racist organizations, or has been involved in prior incidents of hate-motivated violence. The problem with this evidence is that it relates to the accused's character and, thus, raises problems of admissibility. As a general rule, the prosecution cannot seek to admit evidence of the accused's bad character unless the accused has first placed his or her character in issue. Character evidence is, *prima facie*, inadmissible because it invites the trier of fact to convict on the ground that the accused is a bad person, not because they are convinced that the accused committed the offence.

The rules of evidence in both the United States and Canada permit some exceptions to this general exclusionary rule. Under the similar fact evidence rule, evidence of the accused's bad character or disposition can be tendered by the prosecution if it is relevant to an issue in the case beyond showing that the accused is the sort of person likely to commit a criminal offence. On the traditional view of the rule, character evidence establishing identity, motive, intent, the presence of a system or plan, or evidence tending to rebut the defences of accident, mistake, or innocent association would be admissible since it would not be used merely to infer guilt from the accused's past misconduct. Although this would appear to allow the introduction of character evidence tending to show the accused's motive, according to one U.S. commentator, courts have been extremely wary of admitting evidence of the accused's bigoted character and have done so "only where the evidence involves statements made at the time of alleged criminal activity which reasonably explain the defendant's behavior."

Neither argument regarding the difficulty of proving motive provides a persuasive explanation for the scarcity of convictions under hate-crime statutes. The first argument is convincing only to the extent that proving motive is significantly different from proving the other mental states that routinely appear in criminal trials. While motive may sometimes be more difficult to establish than intention or recklessness, the method of proof remains the same regardless of the state of mind at issue. In each case, the trier of fact must infer the accused's subjective state of mind from the actions the accused is alleged to have performed as well as the statements the accused is alleged to have made.[51]

The motive argument also assumes that in the vast majority of cases of hate-inspired violence, there will be insufficient evidence to prove motive beyond a reasonable doubt. This, however, is unlikely. While there will certainly be hard cases where the evidence is ambiguous, there will also be many cases in which there will be ample evidence of the accused's biased motive. For example, if a group of youths belonging to a white-supremacist organization assault a person of colour waiting at a bus stop, it is not difficult to infer that the assault was motivated by racial hatred. Further, since hate crimes are seldom perpetrated in silence, evidence of bigoted remarks uttered in the course of the violence will frequently be available. By using statements made at the time of the offence, prior racist statements, and evidence of membership in racist groups — evidence which may well be available in many cases of racist violence — the prosecution should be able to establish motive beyond a reasonable doubt.

The need to rely on character evidence is also not likely to constitute a fatal impediment to hate-crime prosecutions in Canada, where, as in the United States, character evidence is admissible to prove the accused's motive or intent so long as its probative value outweighs its prejudicial effect. Although the probative value would have to be balanced with the prejudice in each case, evidence establishing the accused's membership in — or support of — bigoted groups, past racist activities, or a history of making bigoted statements should generally be admissible; evidence of this sort is highly probative of the accused's motive when considered in conjunction with the circumstances of the violent act. In contrast, evidence that an accused had a penchant for racist jokes would not in itself be admissible because racist jokes are regrettably all too common to be highly probative of bias. Similarly, bigoted statements uttered years before the offence might be inadmissible if there is nothing to suggest continued animosity.

Finally, it is worth considering whether either of these alleged impediments to proving motive in a hate-crime provision would be alleviated by Bill C-41. In my view, Bill C-41 does not appear to possess any significant advantage over the creation of an independent hate crime. Since the standard of proof at sentencing is the same as during the trial, under Bill C-41, the Crown would still have to prove biased motive beyond a reasonable doubt before it could be considered an aggravating factor in sentencing. The Crown may derive some benefit under the Bill from the fact that rules of evidence are relaxed at sentencing, permitting the introduction of evidence that would be inadmissible at trial. It is unlikely however, that this benefit would be significant enough to outweigh the advantages of enacting a separate hate-crime offence.

UNCONSCIOUS RACISM OR BIGOTRY

Commentators have also posited that unconscious racism on the part of prosecutors prevents them from effectively prosecuting hate crimes and even of perceiving hate crimes when they occur. Unconscious racism refers to racist attitudes and beliefs that are so deeply ingrained within a culture that, for the most part, they go unrecognized.[52] Lawrence describes this phenomenon in the following way:

> Americans share a common historical and cultural heritage in which racism has played and still plays a dominant role. Because of this shared experience, we also inevitably share many ideas, attitudes, and beliefs that attach significance to an individual's race and induce negative feelings and opinions about non-whites. To the extent that this cultural belief system has influenced all of us, we are all racists. At the same time, most of us are unaware of our racism. We do not recognize the ways in which our cultural experience has influenced our beliefs about race or the occasions on which those beliefs affect our actions. In other words, a large part of the behavior that produces racial discrimination is influenced by unconscious racial motivation.

On this theory, even though most prosecutors are not overtly racist,[53] they (like the rest of us) will approach their jobs with socially condoned beliefs, which may impair their ability to handle hate-motivated violence.

Unconscious racism may hinder prosecutors from acknowledging violence as racially motivated by causing them to deny the existence of racism in all but the most egregious cases. In other words, prosecutors may be willing to attribute violence to causes other than group hatred. Further, unconscious racism may affect the vigour with which prosecutors approach cases in which the victim is a member of a minority group. Hernández, for example, cites evidence indicating that prosecutors in the United States have been more willing to accept the "decisions of minority assault victims to forego prosecution rather than those of white assault victims."[54] She also points to research on the death penalty which demonstrates that "prosecutors are more rigorous in their investigation of cases involving white victims than they are of cases involving Black victims."[55] In the context of hate crimes, these tendencies may lead prosecutors to accept plea bargains to lesser offences rather than embark upon the onerous task of prosecuting the hate crime. Prosecutors may also be willing to accept plea bargains if, because of unconscious racism, they believe that the accused's motive will be difficult to prove.

Although the literature in the United States focuses specifically on racism, the unconscious acceptance and transmission of stereotypes also occurs in other forms of bigotry such as sexism and homophobia. The Supreme Court of Canada tacitly recognized this in the context of gender when it held in R. v. Lavallee[56] that expert evidence on the psychology of wife battering was admissible to explain how a woman who killed her batterer could have been acting in self-defence. The Court recognized that jurors might be prone to stereotypes about battered women — including the claim that battered women enjoy the violence inflicted upon them —

and that expert evidence was needed to offset these misconceptions. The stereotypes may be said to be examples of unconscious sexism. In a similar vein, Cynthia Petersen provides startling examples of deeply ingrained hetero-sexism in her discussion of the widespread refusal to recognize homophobic animus in two well-publicized incidents of gay bashing. In the first case, a gay activist was brutally murdered by a gang of fifteen youths while sitting in a bus stopped outside a Montreal subway station. Even though the youths repeatedly shouted "faggot" during the assault, the police refused to recognize the murder as an instance of anti-gay violence.[57] The denial of hetero-sexism in the murder of Kenneth Zeller is even more glaring. Zeller was murdered in a Toronto park by five male youths. Petersen relates:

> Trial testimony revealed that members of the gang had agreed to go to the park to "beat up a fag." Yet the media and the public at large denied that anti-gay sentiment was involved in the crime. At the sentencing hearing, defence counsel presented some 20 character witnesses who suggested explanations for the murderous assault. These included the disinhibiting effect of alcohol and the force of adolescent peer pressure, but did *not* include homophobia. The hockey coach of three of the accused admitted that they would occasionally call opposing players "gay," but only if the players were perceived to be "clumsy" athletes. He added: "Never was the term spoken with any hostility." A clinical psychiatrist called to give expert testimony stated that the fact that one of the boys yelled "you fucking faggot" while he chased then beat Kenneth Zeller to death "did not indicate hostility toward homosexuals." The phrase, he opined, was used only to please the group.[58]

As these examples illustrate, the concern with unconscious bigotry should apply not only to prosecutors, but also to the police who lay the initial charge, conduct the investigation, and provide the prosecution with the evidence for trial. Unconscious bigotry on the part of police officers may affect their decision to charge the accused with a hate crime as well as the zeal with which they proceed with the investigation. Similarly, the unconscious bigotry which hinders police and prosecutors from perceiving the hateful motive behind particular acts of violence may also make judges and juries reluctant to convict an accused of a hate crime unless the evidence is overwhelming.

It is hard to accept, as some commentators in the United States have suggested, that prosecutors' unconscious bigotry, alone, accounts for the low number of convictions under hate-crime statutes. It is, however, possible that unconscious bigotry on the part of all of the main players in the criminal-justice system diminishes the effectiveness of hate-crime legislation. This raises two questions: is the presence of unconscious bigotry a reason to eschew the creation of U.S.-style hate-crime legislation in favour of the Bill C-41 approach, and, further, is it a reason for rejecting any attempt to address the special nature of hate-motivated violence? The answer to both of these questions is clearly no. For the same reasons that unconscious bigotry may undermine the efficacy of U.S.-style hate-crime provisions, it would also impede the effectiveness of Bill C-41. Furthermore, it can be no excuse to say that we will not attempt to confront hate-motivated violence because deeply ingrained bigotry makes this process difficult.

The problem of unconscious bigotry underscores the limitations inherent in relying solely upon the criminal law to solve social problems and points to the need for education. Until we become more aware of the ways in which bigoted attitudes shape our culture, the legal initiatives aimed at addressing hate crime will not be as effective as they could be. While there is no easy or short-term solution to unconscious bigotry, any lasting solution will require a greater social consciousness of the ways in which bigoted beliefs shape our culture.

THE LIMITATIONS OF THE CRIMINAL LAW: POLITICAL CONCERNS

The final set of objections to hate-crime provisions questions the wisdom of using the criminal law to attempt to eradicate or reduce hate-motivated violence. Commentators in the United States have raised two main concerns in this regard. First, critics speculate that hate-crime charges will be laid more often against members of minority groups who lash out against white victims than against white offenders.[59] The prevalence of unconscious bigotry suggests this may, indeed, be a problem. White police officers, who still constitute the majority in police forces across the country, may be more willing to attribute a hateful motive to a minority offender than to a white offender. Officers may, for example, be better able to identify with white victims and, therefore, might be more likely to perceive violence against white victims as motivated by hate. However, to the extent that unconscious bigotry may determine who is charged with hate crimes, it will also be a problem in sentencing. Police officers may be more likely to furnish prosecutors with evidence of a hateful motive when the offender is a member of a minority group, with the result that minorities will disproportionately face stiffer sentences. Thus, regardless of whether Bill C-41 or U.S.-style hate-crime legislation is adopted, vigilance will be required to ensure that the law is not being applied in a discriminatory manner.

Second, critics query whether hate-crime legislation can have any significant effect in reducing hate crime or whether it is largely a symbolic gesture. Although a symbolic denunciation of hate crime may be valuable in itself by performing an educative function, it is clearly an insufficient response to the problem of hate-motivated violence. Passing a hate-crime provision may, however, end up being the only response that is implemented because it allows people to believe they have taken effective action and may lessen their inclination to do more. As Gellman warns:

> Notwithstanding the self-affirming and educative value of such [symbolic] gestures, however, there is the danger of their distracting us from taking action that would be more than merely symbolic. A purely symbolic action *may* stimulate us to take further, substantive action. But to the extent that ... [symbolic action] *satisfies* our desire to "do something," we will be that much less likely to contact our elected officials to press for more effective action. In the same way, if enacting a largely ineffective ethnic intimidation statute allows us to feel that we have taken steps to eliminate bigotry and bias-related crime and thus reduces somewhat or even entirely our feeling of the urgency of doing more, the enactment of that law ultimately *slows* the process of combatting bigotry.[60]

A more radical version of this criticism focuses on three reasons for which the state may find criminal responses to hate crime appealing. First, enacting criminal legislation is often a relatively easy way for government to claim that it is addressing a social problem. For example, it is much easier to pass a criminal law condemning hate-motivated violence than it is to devise and implement the multiple strategies that a more comprehensive response would demand.

Second, criminal legislation may be comparatively inexpensive. Although creating additional criminal offences or increasing criminal penalties may increase the costs associated with law enforcement and incarceration, the government may avoid the cost of the development and implementation of educational programs aimed at curbing bigotry. At times, use of the criminal law may be false economy since the costs to the justice system may be greater than the costs of social programs which might avoid engagement with the criminal process. For example, to the extent that improving the economic conditions of lower-income Canadians might reduce the rate of addiction to illegal drugs, paying for economic and social programs may be a more cost-effective allocation of resources than paying for the personnel necessary to combat the drug problem through the criminal justice system.

Third, the process of enacting criminal provisions regarding hate crime attracts considerable media attention, as do trials conducted under hate-crime provisions. The publicity provides the government with free political mileage in a way that less-visible educational strategies do not. This is particularly significant when, as now, the electorate perceives crime to be a serious problem and, accordingly, "law and order" responses are politically popular.

Finally, as numerous critical scholars have noted, the criminal justice system is rarely an instrument of progressive social change.[61] Changes in the criminal law do not tend to bring about fundamental social reform, nor do they normally empower those whom they seek to protect. According to this critique, the criminal law will do little to dismantle the social power structure that gives rise to hate-motivated violence. The symbolic effect of hate-crime provisions will be largely illusory.

These concerns with the limitations of the criminal law are important. They are useful reminders that the criminal law alone is not a sufficient response to social problems, and that non-criminal avenues must be explored. These criticisms, however, do not offer much guidance on the question of which criminal-law remedy should be adopted where a number of responses are available. Given that violence — including violence motivated by group hatred — is conduct that should be subject to criminal sanction, the appropriate question is not *whether* criminal remedies should be pursued, but *which* of the criminal remedies can best contribute to the solution of this problem. These concerns do not help us to determine whether the bigoted motivation behind violent crimes should be a factor in sentencing, whether it should be the subject of a specific criminal offence, or even further, whether it should be considered at all in the criminal process.

CONCLUSION

My assessment of the arguments for and against U.S.-style hate-crime provisions leads me to conclude that we should adopt similar legislation in Canada. Hate-crime laws constitute a powerful statement that hate-motivated violence is unacceptable and will not be tolerated in a society committed to equality and multiculturalism. While Bill C-41 conveys a similar message, it fails to do so as forcefully. Since there seem to be no compelling reasons for adopting the weaker denunciation of hate crime over the stronger, I believe that we should embrace the United States approach and permit penalty enhancement when violent crime is motivated by group hatred.

I do have some hesitation, however, in making this recommendation. First, hate-crime provisions, if enacted, might not be vigorously enforced. Such provisions will only contribute to reducing hate crime to the extent that they are enforced in a non-discriminatory manner, and that they yield convictions where warranted. If they fail on either of these scores, hate-crime provisions may be counter-productive because they will send a message that our opposition to hate crime is purely rhetorical. Once enacted, hate-crime provisions must be carefully monitored to ensure that they are not doing more harm than good.

Second, the enactment of hate-crime legislation may provide Parliament with an excuse to avoid enacting other, potentially more effective, measures against hate crime. The enactment of hate-crime legislation — whether in the form of Bill C-41 or in the form of U.S.-style intimidation provisions — cannot be the only response to hate-motivated violence. As discussed above, the criminal law can play only a small role in eliminating the underlying causes of group hatred. Educational strategies aimed at preventing the development of bigoted attitudes must also be pursued. Economic measures may also be needed given the role that economic factors play in the marginalization and stigmatization of many minority groups and given the increase of inter-group tension during tough economic times. The passage of hate-crime legislation may provide Parliament with an excuse to avoid undertaking more difficult and more costly measures to combat group hatred, yet may offer the weakest prospect of bringing about significant social change.

Despite these concerns, however, I believe that U.S.-style hate-crime provisions should be enacted. Even if the provisions can make only a modest contribution to the reduction of violence motivated by group hatred, they play a part in a broader solution. To this end, it may be helpful to offer some brief observations on the policy decisions involved in drafting a hate-crime provision and some thoughts as to what, in broad terms, a Canadian provision might look like.

The enactment of U.S.-style hate-crime provisions in Canada presents five main policy questions. The first question relates to the forms of group hatred to be proscribed. Most intimidation statutes in the United States prohibit violence motivated by the victim's race, religion, or national origin. Some, however, go further and add sexual orientation, disability, age, and gender to this list. Bill C-41 takes an even more inclusive approach by listing hatred on the basis of race, national or ethnic origin, language, religion, sex, age, mental or physical disability, sexual orientation, or *other similar factors* as aggravating factors in sentencing.

A second question concerns the offences to which hate-crime legislation would apply. Most U.S. statutes, following the A.D.L. model, list a number of specific offences that, when committed with a hateful motive, constitute the offence of intimidation. Such a list usually includes assault and often includes the offences of harassment and menacing. Again, Bill C-41 adopts a broader approach. Rather than curtailing its application to a number of specified offences, Bill C-41 provides that evidence that an offence was motivated by bias, prejudice, or hate is a consideration in sentencing in any case. Parliament would have to decide whether to retain this broad approach or to limit hate-crime legislation to a number of specified acts of violence.

Third, Parliament must decide whether to limit the ambit of a hate-crime provision to inter-group violence or whether to extend the legislation to situations in which the accused attacks a member of his or her own group because of that member's association with members of a disliked group. The language of the A.D.L. provision sustains the broader approach. Bill C-41 is ambiguous on this point but could, arguably, be interpreted as also supporting the broader interpretation since it does not expressly limit consideration of the accused's hateful motive to circumstances in which the accused and the victim are members of different groups.[62]

The fourth issue relates to the necessity of choosing between creating a substantive offence to proscribe hate-motivated violence or simply amending the *Criminal Code*'s sentencing provisions to enhance sentences beyond the existing maximum where an offence is motivated by group hatred. Both of these approaches are in use in the United States.

Finally, the degree to which the maximum penalty for committing a hate-motivated crime should be increased beyond the existing maximum for the underlying violent offence will have to be determined. Parliament must also decide whether to impose a mandatory minimum-sentence for the presence of a hate-based motive.

In my view, a vigorous response to hate-motivated violence would entail the creation of a separate offence of intimidation that would explicitly recognize hate crime as a distinct form of violence and, therefore, as a distinct offence. Creating a separate offence acknowledges, in a more direct and forceful way than a response focused simply on sentencing, that hate crime causes distinct harms to its victims, to minority groups, and to the fabric of Canadian society. This offence could be modelled along the lines of section 85 of the *Criminal Code*, which, by requiring the imposition of a minimum term of imprisonment for indictable offences committed with a firearm, has the effect of deeming offences committed with a firearm to be more heinous than those committed without. Like section 85, which is charged along with the underlying offence, an accused would be charged with the offence of intimidation in addition to the generic offence of violence. An offence of intimidation would also — like section 85 — impose a mandatory term of imprisonment to be served consecutively to the sentence for the underlying violent offence. While the sentencing range for the offence of intimidation would be determined by Parliament and would depend on whether the offence was indictable or punishable solely upon summary conviction, I suggest that for indictable offences, a minimum sentence of imprisonment for six months and a maximum of five years might be appropriate.[63]

I also favour a broad approach to the policy questions involving the scope of the offence of intimidation. In this respect, some of the features of Bill C-41 are laudable. The grounds of hatred to be proscribed should be broadly defined — as they are in Bill C-41 — so as to include sexual orientation, language, disability, and gender in addition to the standard grounds of race, ethnic or national origin, and religion. All of these denote forms of group hatred that a pluralistic society should condemn. While the inclusion of sexual orientation within Bill C-41 sparked considerable opposition, particularly from members of the Reform Party,[64] it is, in my view, crucial that sexual orientation be a prohibited ground of hatred within any hate-crime provision, given the well-documented level of homophobic violence.[65] The offences to which intimidation can apply should also be defined inclusively, as they are in Bill C-41. Rather than restricting the crime to a specific set of violent offences, intimidation could he drafted to apply to all offences.[66] Finally, I support the view that intimidation should not be limited to inter-group violence, but should also apply where members of one group harm another member of their own group to express dislike for a different group. To my mind, violence of this sort is clearly hate-motivated violence and should be covered by hate-crime provisions.

Legislation of this type would, in my view, make a better contribution to redressing hate-motivated violence than does Bill C-41. As one element of a broader strategy aimed at eliminating group hatred and promoting congenial inter-group relations, such a provision merits serious consideration.

QUESTIONS TO CONSIDER

1. Outline several arguments that Shaffer makes in favour of and against enacting American-style hate-crime legislation in Canada. Discuss which side of the argument you find most persuasive.
2. Critically compare the "freedom of expression" argument with the "thought crime" argument discussed in Shaffer's article. Do you feel that hate-crime legislation represents a genuine threat to freedom of expression?
3. Discuss several concerns outlined by Shaffer regarding the effectiveness of hate-crime legislation. Do these concerns appear to have been remedied by Bill C-41?

NOTES

1. Since police forces in Canada have not kept accurate statistics on hate-motivated violence, it is unclear whether there has been a real upsurge or whether there is greater media attention focused on the problem and greater social recognition that racist violence is unacceptable. However, given that scapegoating and racist actions tend to increase during periods of economic downturn, an increase in racist violence would not be surprising. Statistics released by the Toronto Police force, which began to compile bias crime statistics in January 1993, appear to support this hypothesis. During the first six months of that year, police identified "a definite bias" as the motive in 75 criminal assaults, with the annual total reaching 155. Figures released by the Metropolitan Toronto Police Hate Crime Unit for the first six months of 1994 refer to 112 bias crimes (see G. Swainson, "Hate Crimes on Increase Among Teens Figures Show" *The Toronto Star* (23 June 1994) N.Y. 4).
2. I use the term "hate-motivated violence" to refer to violence based on a person's racial, religious, or ethnic identification, as well as on the victim's sexual orientation or disability. See *infra* notes 10 and 11 and accompanying text.
3. R.S.C. 1985, c. C–A6 [hereinafter *Criminal Code*] ss. 318–19.
4. Bill C-41, *An Act to Amend the Criminal Code (Sentencing) and Other Acts in Consequence Thereof*, 1st Sess., 35th Parl., 1995 (assented to 13 July 1995, S.C. 1995, c. 22) [hereinafter Bill C-41].
5. Wis. Stat. Ann. § 939.645 (West Supp. 1992) [hereinafter Wisconsin Statute].
6. See *Wisconsin v. Mitchell*, 113 S. Ct. 2194, 124 L. Ed. (2d) (1993) [hereinafter *Mitchell* cited to S. Ct.].
7. See H. Mazur-Hart, "Racial and Religious Intimidation: An Analysis of Oregon's 1981 Law" (1982) 18 Willamette L. Rev. 198; S. Gellman, "Sticks and Stones Can Put You in Jail, but Can Words Increase Your Sentence? Constitutional and Policy Dilemmas of Ethnic Intimidation Laws" (1991) 39 *U.C.L.A. L. Rev.* 333.
8. G. Padgett, "Racially-Motivated Violence and Intimidation: Inadequate State Enforcement and Federal Civil Rights Remedies" (1984) 75 *J. Crim. L. & Criminology* 103.
9. See J. Levin & J. McDevitt, *Hate Crimes* (New York: Plenum Press, 1993) at c. 13.

10. See C. Petersen, "A Queer Response to Bashing: Legislating Against Hate" (1991) 16 *Queen's* L.J. 237.

11. Anti-Defamation League, *Hate Crimes Statutes: A 1991 Status Report* (New York: A.D.L., 1992) at 4. The A.D.L. also expanded its model legislation to include two additional components: a civil action for institutional vandalism and intimidation; and provisions requiring states to keep records of hate crime and to train police officers to identify and to respond effectively to hate crime (see *ibid.* at 4–5). Although the four components may be seen to constitute a comprehensive package of legislative action to respond to hate crime, a discussion of the non-criminal provisions is beyond the scope of this paper (but is explored *ibid.* at 2–3).

12. See *ibid.* at 22–23.

13. Brief of *Amici Curiae* the Anti-Defamation League et al., in *Mitchell*, at 7 [hereinafter A.D.L. Brief in *Mitchell*].

14. See *ibid.* For a discussion of this case, see text accompanying notes 29–36.

15. The second option might not be as effective in increasing sentences, since it does not compel judges to impose a higher sentence where a crime is motivated by group hatred. Nonetheless, the experience in the United States has shown that, where provisions of this sort are invoked, they have led to the imposition of a higher penalty. See *e.g.*, the trial court's reasoning in *Mitchell* as described in the United States Supreme Court's judgment (*Mitchell, supra* note 6).

16. (1977), 35 C.C.C. (2d) 376 (Ont. C.A.) [hereinafter *Ingram*].

17. *Ingram, ibid.* at 379.

18. (1978), 43 C.C.C. (2d) 342, 5 C.R. (3d) S-30 [hereinafter *Atkinson* cited to C.C.C.].

19. Bill C-41, *An Act to Amend the Criminal Code (Sentencing) and Other Acts in Consequence Thereof*, 1st Sess., 35 Parl., 1994–1995, (as passed by the House of Commons 15 June 1995), cl. 178. 2(a)(i).

20. This goal is often achieved. For instance, following a vicious beating of a Tamil man, his friends told the media that "everybody in the Tamil community" was afraid not only of the attacks but of retaliation for reporting them (R. DiManno, "The Quiet Dignity of a Tamil Beaten by Racists" *The Toronto Star* (16 June 1993) A7).

21. A.D.L. Brief in *Mitchell, supra* note 13 at 7

22. Quoted in the A.D.L. Brief in *Mitchell, ibid.* at 8.

23. See S. Edwards, "Violence Against Women: Feminism and the Law" in L. Gelsthorpe & A. Morris, eds., *Feminist Perspectives in Criminology* (Philadelphia: Open University Press, 1990) 145.

24. Hate-crime offences may be seen as an anti-discrimination measure within the criminal law. Just as the goal of human-rights legislation is to ensure that minorities receive equal protection of the law, hate-crime legislation would attempt to ensure that the criminal law addresses the harms minorities are likely to suffer.

25. See: *State v. Mitchell*, 485 N.W.2d 807 (Wis. 1992) [hereinafter *Mitchell* (Wis. S.C.)]; *State v. Wyant*, 64 Ohio St.3d 566, 597 N.E.2d 450 (1992) [hereinafter *Wyant I* cited to NE.2d]. See *contra State v. Wyant*, 68 Ohio St.3d 162, 624 N.E.2d 722 (1994) [hereinafter *Wyant II* cited to N.E.2d].

26. In *R. v. Nova Scotia Pharmaceutical Society*, [1992] 2 S.C.R. 606, 93 D.L.R. (4th) 36 [hereinafter *N.S. Pharmaceutical* cited to S.C.R.], the Supreme Court held that overbreadth was not an independent constitutional doctrine in Canada but, instead, is part of the minimal impairment component of the section 1 proportionality test (*ibid.* at 629). However, two years later, in *R. v. Heywood*, [1994] 3 S.C.R. 761, 120 D.L.R. (4th) 348, the Court held that overbreadth can be considered in determining whether legislation conforms to the principles of fundamental justice in section 7.

27. See L.H. Tribe, *American Constitutional Law*, 2d ed. (Mineola, NY: Foundation Press, 1988) at 1022.

28. Gellman, *supra* note 7 at 360–61.
29. *Mitchell, supra* note 6 at 2196.
30. *Ibid.* at 2196–197.
31. *Ibid.* at 2199.
32. *Ibid.* at 2200.
33. *Ibid.* at 2201.
34. W. Blackstone, *Commentaries on the Laws of England*, C.M. Haar, ed., vol. 4 (Boston: Beacon Press, 1962) at 14, cited *ibid.*
35. See *Hishon v. King & Spalding*, 467 U.S. 69, 104 S. Ct. 2229 (1984).
36. See *Mitchell, supra* note 6 at 2201.
37. [1986] 2 S.C.R. 573, 33 D.L.R. (4th) 174.
38. [1989] 1 S.C.R. 927, 58 D.L.R. (4th) 577 [hereinafter *Irwin Toy* cited to S.C.R.].
39. *R. v. Keegstra*, [1990] 3 S.C.R. 697, 61 C.C.C. (3d) 1 [hereinafter *Keegstra* cited to S.C.R.].
40. *Ibid.* at 736–37, Dickson C.J.; and at 811–12, McLachlin J.
41. *R. v. Oakes*, [1986] 1 S.C.R. 103, 53 O.R. (2d) 719 [hereinafter *Oakes*].
42. Wilson J. (concurring) in *Edmonton Journal v. Alberta (A.G.)*, [1989] 2 S.C.R. 1326, 64 D.L.R. (4th) 174 [hereinafter *Edmonton Journal* cited to S.C.R.] stated: "One virtue of the contextual approach, it seems to me, is that it recognizes that a particular right or freedom may have a different value depending on the context. It may be, for example, that freedom of expression has greater value in a political context than it does in the context of disclosure of the details of a matrimonial dispute. The contextual approach attempts to bring into sharp relief the aspect of the right or freedom which is truly at stake in the case as well as the relevant aspects of any values in competition with it" (*Edmonton Journal, ibid.* at 1355–356).
43. See *Keegstra, supra* note 39 at 762–63.
44. See *ibid.* at 763.
45. McLachlin J. also questioned the effectiveness of section 319(2) on the basis that the hate-propaganda laws existing in Germany in the 1930s did not prevent the Nazi rise to power and the subsequent atrocities (see *Keegstra, ibid.* at 854).
46. *Ibid.* at 855–56.
47. *Ibid.* at 858–59.
48. [1985] 1 S.C.R. 295, 18 D.L.R. (4th) 321.
49. [1986] 2 S.C.R. 713, 35 D.L.R. (4th) 1.
50. *Ibid.*
51. Although the difficulties in proving motive do not appear to be nearly as arduous as commentators have claimed, it is worth briefly considering the proposals that have been advanced to circumvent them. Some commentators have argued for a presumption of racial motivation in all cases of inter-group violence such that accused persons who attack a member of another group would have the onus of establishing that their conduct was not racially motivated (see: M.L. Fleischauer, "Teeth for a Paper Tiger: A Proposal to Add Enforceability to Florida's Hate Crimes Act" (1990) 17 *Fla. St. U. L. Rev.* 697; Note, "Combatting Racial Violence: A Legislative Proposal" (1988) 101 *Harv. L. Rev.* 1270 [hereinafter "Combatting Racial Violence"]. Other commentators go further, arguing that this presumption should only apply where the victim is a member of a racial minority and the accused is white (see e.g. "Combatting Racial Violence," *ibid.*). While these measures would undoubtedly increase the number of convictions for inter-group violence, they conflict with the presumption of innocence and would not likely withstand challenge under section 11(d) of the *Charter*. The proposal limiting the presumption to white persons who attack non-white victims might also conflict with section 15 of the *Charter*.
52. See C.R. Lawrence III, "The Id, the Ego, and Equal Protection: Reckoning with Unconscious Racism" (1987) 39 *Stan. L. Rev.* 317.

53. This discussion of unconscious bigotry is not meant to ignore the extent to which overt racism, sexism, and homophobia operate within the criminal justice system, generally, and will hamper hate-crime statutes, specifically. Overtly racist police officers may intentionally investigate hate crimes less thoroughly, giving a well-meaning prosecutor insufficient evidence on which to build a case. Similarly, overtly racist judges and jurors may be less likely to convict of hate crime.

54. T.K. Hernández, Note, "Bias Crimes: Unconscious Racism in the Prosecution of 'Racially-Motivated Violence'" (1990) 99 *Yale L.J.* 845 at 854, citing F.W. Miller, *Prosecution: The Decision to Charge a Suspect with a Crime* (Boston: Little, Brown, 1969) at 175–76.

55. Hernández, *ibid.* at 853, citing M.L. Radelet & G.L. Pierce, "Race and Prosecutorial Discretion in Homicide Cases" (1985) 19 *Law & Soc. Rev.* 587. This research was introduced in *McKlesky* v. *Kemp*, 481 U.S. 279, 107 S. Ct. 1756 (1987) in which the accused challenged the constitutional validity of the death penalty on the basis of racial discrimination.

56. [1990] 1 S.C.R. 852, 55 C.C.C. (3d) 97.

57. Petersen, *supra* note 10 at 246.

58. *Ibid.*

59. See *e.g.* Gellman, *supra* note 7.

60. *Ibid.* at 389.

61. 9 *Cdn. J. of L. & Soc.* 75; M. Mandel, *The Great Repression: Criminal Punishment in the Nineteen-Eighties* (Toronto: Garamond Press, 1991).

62. The exact wording of the relevant provision of Bill C-41 is as follows:

> **718.2** A court that imposes a sentence shall also take into consideration the following principles:
>   (a) a sentence should be increased or reduced to account for any relevant aggravating or mitigating circumstances relating to the offence or the offender, and, without limiting the generality of the foregoing,
>   (i) evidence that the offence was motivated by bias, prejudice, or hate based on race, national or ethnic origin, language, colour, religion, sex, age, mental or physical disability, sexual orientation, or any other similar factor ...

> For the purposes of this argument, it is significant that the final wording of this provision, shown here, was changed from earlier versions. The previous wording could have been interpreted to preclude application of this section where the offence was not motivated by the race of the victim. When the Bill was presented for first reading, clause 718.2(a)(i) provided that the sentencing judge had to consider "evidence that the offence was motivated by bias, prejudice, or hate based on the race, nationality, colour, religion, sex, age, mental or physical disability, or sexual orientation *of the victim.*" It is also worth noting that this earlier incarnation did not include reference to language or ethnic origin as grounds of hatred, nor did it include the generic catch-all "any other similar factor" (Bill C-41, *An Act to Amend the Criminal Code (Sentencing) and Other Acts in Consequence Thereof,* 1st Sess., 35th Parl., 1994 (1st reading 13 June 1994) [emphasis added]).

63. Drafting intimidation in this way might lead to problems with the *Kienapple* principle, prohibiting multiple convictions for the same delicts (see: *R.* v. *Kienapple* (1974), [1975] 1 S.C.R. 729, 44 D.L.R. (3d) 351 [hereinafter *Kienapple*]; *R.* v. *Prince*, [1986] 2 S.C.R. 480, 33 D.L.R. (4th) 724 [hereinafter *Prince* cited to S.C.R.]. It could be argued that the subject matter of intimidation is not sufficiently different from the

subject matter of the related violent offence to warrant convictions for two offences. The outcome of this argument is not certain, however, given that in both *Kienapple* and *Prince*, the Supreme Court appears to leave scope for multiple convictions where Parliament clearly intends to abrogate the *Kienapple* rule. For example, in *Prince*, the court stated: "It has been a consistent theme in the jurisprudence from *Quon*, through *Kienapple* and *Krug* that the rule against multiple convictions in respect of the same cause, matter or delict is subject to an expression of Parliamentary intent that more than one conviction be entered when offences overlap ..." (*Prince, ibid.* at 498). If, however, my proposed offence of intimidation is objectionable based on *Kienapple*, I would favour drafting intimidation to look very much like the A.D.L. offence such that offences of violence coupled with a hateful motive would constitute the offence. On this model, charges for the offences of violence would not be laid in addition to charges of intimidation and these offences would be lesser included offences for which convictions could be registered if the greater offence of intimidation were not established.

64. Four Liberal M.Ps — Tom Wappel, Daniel McTeague, Paul Steckle, and Roseanne Skoke — also voted against the Bill. Opponents expressed the view that the inclusion of sexual orientation would be a backhanded way of creating "special rights" for gays and lesbians under other statutes and would give protection to pedophiles for their actions (see T.T. Ha, "Sex Orientation Dispute Hounds Justice Minister" *The [Toronto] Globe and Mail* (16 June 1995) A4). In my view, these arguments are completely without merit.

65. See *e.g.* Petersen, *supra* note 10.

66. Although intimidation will have no relevance to many offences listed in the *Criminal Code*, I believe it is better to draft a provision to apply to all offences, rather than to attempt to list offences beforehand and risk omissions. An alternative option would be to denote a group of offences by using the language Parliament has used in Bill C-72, which provides that the "drunkenness defence" will not apply to any offence "that includes as an element an assault or any other interference or threat of interference by a person with the bodily integrity of another person" (Bill C-72, *An Act to Amend the Criminal Code (Self-induced Intoxication)*, 1st Sess., 35th Parl., 1994–1995, cl. 1 (assented to 13 July 1995, S.C. 1995, c. 32, and in force 15 September 1995)).

FOURTEEN

An Introduction to Restorative Justice

JOE HUDSON AND BURT GALAWAY

This article introduces the theory, research, and practice of restorative justice. Current restorative justice approaches mirror ancient ways of settling disputes.

Source: Joe Hudson and Burt Galaway, Introduction, in *Restorative Justice: International Perspectives*, ed. Galaway and Hudson (Monsey, NY: Criminal Justice Press, 1996), 1–14.

ELEMENTS OF A RESTORATIVE JUSTICE APPROACH

Three elements are fundamental to any restorative justice definition and practice. First, crime is viewed primarily as a conflict between individuals that results in injuries to victims, communities, and the offenders themselves, and only secondarily as a violation against the state. Second, the aim of the criminal justice process should be to create peace in communities by reconciling the parties and repairing the injuries caused by the dispute. Third, the criminal justice process should facilitate active participation by victims, offenders, and their communities in order to find solutions to the conflict.

High value is placed on direct involvement by the relevant parties — victims, offenders, and community members. All parties have responsibilities associated with participation in the dispute settlement process. Offenders are responsible for acknowledging the wrong done, making apology, expressing remorse, and being willing to compensate or make reparation. The responsibilities of victims are to accept the expressions of remorse made by the offender and to express a willingness to forgive. Community members participate by providing necessary support and encouragement to the parties to arrive at a settlement and provide opportunities to carry out the agreement. Restorative justice is based on the key principles of reparation and mediation. Historically, reparation was incorporated in a process aimed at settling the dispute and reconciling the parties. Reparation, whether in material or symbolic forms, and victim and offender involvement in settling the dispute are key elements of a restorative justice approach. This personal involvement distinguishes the restorative justice approach. Some argue that the state and its criminal justice system cannot stand in as a fictitious surrogate for real people who have been personally afflicted by a crime. The debts offenders owe are not to an abstract entity called "the state" but to their victims and actual communities.

The notion of direct participation by victims and offenders, rather than through the state as a surrogate, has been well developed by the proponents of restorative justice. Less well developed, however, is the idea of how the community, or more correctly the communities of victims and the offenders, can be active participants in the process. The matter is also addressed, although in examining conditions for creating peaceful communities; in the involvement of Aboriginal communities in circle sentencing; and in family group conferences and views about extending this practice to community conferences for adults. The involvement of the communities will require that restorative justice processes be decentralized — located in the neighborhoods of the victims and offenders — and that the processes be open and public. This may run counter to notions of privacy and confidentiality, especially in juvenile proceedings.

Another aspect of community participation, and one which is only implicit in these papers, is the likely deprofessionalization of the process. Empowering communities, as well as victims and offenders, may require placing the process in the hands of non-professional community members. By their very nature, professions remove power from others and concentrate it in their own alleged area of expertise. Some see the possibility for representatives from social agencies and law enforcement to participate with community residents in dealing with offenses in a restorative justice program. Local communities are responsible for acting immediately to protect victims and offenders, holding offenders accountable, and insisting on active involvement of the interested parties in the resolution process.

The idea of family and community involvement may extend to families and communities sharing responsibility for the offense and for peacemaking. In traditional Maori customs, kin and clan groups took responsibility for accepting punishment and paying compensation: this notion of collective responsibility was very foreign to the individual responsibility notion of the British. McElrea (1996) notes that in family group conferences, families and extended kin may take responsibility for the behavior of their youthful offender and that this idea might also be extended to adults where responsibility for compensation might be made by a broader group. Yazzie and Zion (1996) note that family and clan members often make payment on a relative's behalf in the peacemaking processes of the Navajo.

PROCESS OF RESTORATIVE JUSTICE

Restorative justice programs operate in different settings and in different ways. All agree, however, on the central role played by the mediator or facilitator. How this role is played out, particularly in terms of relations between victims and offenders, differs from one setting to another. The neutrality of the mediator is seen as important by some, while others report that Navajo community peacemakers are not expected to be neutral but to offer opinions on what should be done to settle the dispute. In this, they act more as guides or teachers than neutral mediators.

Several researchers favor formal mediator training, while others raise the more fundamental question of whether we want a new profession of mediators or want to retain the informal character of mediation by relying largely on community volunteers. Is there danger of a new bureaucracy arising, composed of formally trained professionals who take over the process from victims, offenders, and local community representatives? What is appropriate training if volunteers from the community are to be relied upon to serve as mediators? Other jurisdictions, such as a New Zealand neighborhood that runs a community supervisor service, rely on trained criminal justice professionals to carry out the mediation role. Harding (1996) notes, however, that such initiatives are time-consuming and will require extra financing for probation services to do more than a very limited amount of work.

Key operations carried out in restorative justice programs can be identified in three phases — the pre-mediation phase, the mediation phase, and the follow-up phase. Most programs carry out similar tasks and activities within each phase.

PRE-MEDIATION PHASE

The restorative justice program must have procedures established for intake and a set of activities to be carried out in preparing for mediation. Intake activities include collecting and recording information on cases assigned or referred to the program, and making decisions about program eligibility and admission. Many programs have intake criteria requiring the offender to have admitted guilt and agreed to participate in meetings with the victim and other interested parties. Victim willingness to participate is almost always an eligibility condition.

Several writers emphasize the importance of adequate preparation for mediation. Preparation is critical for circle sentencing, and investing more time and effort in the pre-hearing work with offenders, victims, families, and support groups will lead to more successful outcomes. Research shows that preparation for mediation is the most important variable for a successful mediation. Key tasks involved in preparing for mediation or conferencing are contacting the parties; securing a willingness to participate; and agreeing on the date, time, and place to hold the meeting. Some emphasize the importance of the facilitator not delegating responsibility to others to prepare for conferences. Instead, they see the importance of facilitators convening their own conferences by telephoning each participant to invite them; this is the beginning of a bond or relationship between the facilitator and participants. These authors also emphasize the importance of holding conferences as soon as possible after the offense. At the same time, they argue for maximizing the number of participants in the sessions but fail to appreciate that maximizing participation may conflict with the timeliness of the meeting.

Mediators usually have discretion to decide which parties to contact first, and they exercise this discretion depending on the circumstances of each case. Most programs emphasize voluntary participation by both victims and offenders; this is often a criteria for program admission. The job of the facilitator is to communicate clearly the purpose of the planned meeting and the process to be followed to potential participants. Some facilitators engage in several meetings with victims and offenders to assist them in preparing questions, practicing responses, and providing more detailed information about the process.

Participants must see the mediation setting as being safe. This may mean holding meetings in settings familiar to participants, such as schools, churches, or community centers in the local neighborhood.

While victim and offender meetings are often seen as central to a restorative justice approach, many programs involve relatively little formal contact between the parties. Jervis (1996) notes that face-to-face negotiations are bypassed in New Zealand probation services if both parties agreed on the amount of reparation and the schedule. Netzig and Trenczek (1996) report that only approximately one-third of German victim–offender mediation cases involved face-to-face meetings; the other two-thirds involved no contact between the parties except through a mediator who carried out a form of shuttle negotiation. Jervis's research in New Zealand shows that face-to-face meetings between victims and offenders occurred in only 4% of court cases, largely because judges and probation officers underestimated the willingness of victims to meet their offenders.

MEDIATION PHASE

Practices vary, but mediation sessions usually involve ceremonies, welcomes, and introductions; clarification of the process to be followed and meeting guidelines; discussion by each of the parties ending in an agreement; and closing comments. Mediation sessions begin with prayers or other cultural ceremonies. Welcoming comments are then made by the mediator, followed by participant introductions and statements about why they are participating in the meeting. The mediator explains the process to be followed and the ground rules for the meeting. Each party is provided an opportunity to participate, discuss, and ask questions. In many programs, victims are offered an opportunity to explain the personal impact of the offense and share their feelings about it. Offenders explain and apologize for their behavior; other parties such as family members and friends who are also participating in the meeting have opportunities to speak, ask questions, and provide information. The focus then turns to what the offender is prepared to do to restore victim losses. Victims respond to the offenders' proposal, and agreement is usually reached on how the losses will be restored and how the other concerns expressed by victims and other parties are to be addressed.

There are two other key outcomes, which Retzinger and Scheff (1996) call symbolic reparation. The first is that the offender clearly expresses genuine shame and remorse for his or her actions. The second is that victims take at least a first step toward forgiving the offender for the incident. These two outcomes are referred to as the core sequence, are seen as generating repair and restoration of the bond between victim and offender, and serve as the key toward reconciliation. Restorative justice programs must shame offenders by having victims tell of the effects of crime on them, as well as provide offenders with a way back from the shame and into acceptance. Some believe that no additional shaming is necessary beyond that which is experienced by the offender as a result of a victim's recounting the personal impact of the crime. Time must be provided for victims to receive answers from offenders about why they committed the offense and their current feelings about it, for victims to tell offenders about the effects the offense had on them, for offenders to make apologies, for victims to accept apologies and consider forgiveness, and for victims and offenders to negotiate a reparation agreement.

FOLLOW-UP PHASE AND OUTCOMES

A variety of outcomes exist for restorative justice programs, including those relating to the offender, victim, community, and formal justice system. Outcomes or objectives held for offenders in mediation programs include:

- restoring or reintegrating the offender back into the community,
- providing offenders with an understanding of the human impact of what they have done,
- holding offenders accountable,
- reducing future criminal behavior,
- giving offenders a sense of having been treated fairly, and
- increasing social competence.

Victim outcomes include:

- providing an opportunity for participation in the justice process,
- receiving answers to their questions and a better understanding of why they were chosen to be victimized,
- restoring the emotional and material losses to victims,
- reducing their fears, and
- giving them a sense of having been treated fairly.

For both parties, the aim is to achieve a sense of closure and improve their ability to move on with their lives.

Increased citizen participation in victim–offender mediation programs is seen as leading to improved citizen understanding of crime and criminal justice, and to safer communities. Participants in sentencing circles often address the underlying contributors to crime in their communities. Outcomes of restorative justice programs for the criminal justice system include improving or enhancing the quality of justice as perceived by crime victims, reducing caseload pressures felt by the courts, and humanizing the justice system.

Umbreit [see chapter fifteen] reports research showing that victims are less likely to remain upset about the crime as a result of having participated in mediation meetings, and report less fear of being re-victimized by the same offender. While restorative justice programs strive to achieve a variety of outcomes, little rigorous evidence is available to support the extent to which these are actually achieved. Expectations for program outcomes should be kept realistic and modest to prevent a major disappointment if they are not met.

SIGNIFICANT ISSUES

There are a number of issues associated with restorative justice practices. Among these are the extent to which restorative justice practices can be incorporated in the formal criminal justice system; the spread of social control; the extent to which programs operate fairly; and public support for restorative justice.

Should restorative justice programs be separate from, or part of, the criminal justice system? The essential question is whether the key concepts of restorative justice are so incompatible with the essentially retributive nature of the criminal justice system that criminal justice organizations cannot be expected to operate in a restorative manner. Pranis (1996), however, suggests that restorative justice practices can be introduced into criminal justice, and she is working to expand restorative justice practices within the criminal justice system in Minnesota. Walter and Wagner (1996) describe a study of how police officers manage difficult situations, noting that many of these situations — although certainly not all — are managed in a restorative manner. Some note that the family group conference approach in New Zealand has the potential for converting the entire youth justice system to a restorative approach. Family group conferences are supported by legislation and are uniformly used across the country to respond to juvenile offenders. Gordon Bazemore (1996) outlines a detailed set of programmatic principles for implementing a restorative justice policy. He stresses, however, that to transform an agency from either a retributive or individual treatment paradigm to one of restorative justice necessarily involves getting staff involved in the process of making the transformation as they figure out how to implement a restorative justice approach within their own setting. The support must grow throughout the organization and cannot be imposed top-down.

Efforts to incorporate restorative justice in the formal criminal justice system have the potential for cooptation, in which the offender is seen as offending against both the victim and the state. In turn, this can lead to additional punishments. Bringing a wide variety of participants into the restorative process and opening it to public view may have the effect of recharging the emotional atmosphere originally surrounding the offense. Minor and Morrison (1996) identify three options that could be pursued. First is the option of gradually substituting restorative justice programming for traditional criminal justice practices; this trend is likely to be strongly resisted by established agencies and criminal justice professionals. Further, the great risk in pursuing this option is that the existing system, with its overwhelming orientation to offenders, will be unable to shift to a truly victim- and offender-centered approach to resolving crime. The second option is to allow restorative and traditional criminal justice programs to coexist independently of one another. This means that decisions would have to be made about cases that are appropriate for restorative justice programs and those that are more suitable for the more traditional justice system. The third option, also raised by Minor and Morrison (1996), is to graft restorative justice onto established agencies in the justice system. They note that this may lead to undermining restorative justice by goal displacement, another form of cooptation by the criminal justice system, and may lead to more specialized and bureaucratized forms of restorative justice.

This issue of the manner and extent to which restorative justice practices can sit within the formal justice system is particularly significant with Aboriginal programming efforts. In New Zealand, there have been strong calls for a separate adult justice system for Aboriginal persons. New Zealand has legislated restorative justice for young offenders, and Japan has historically placed restorative approaches in a central place in the administration of justice.

Proponents of reform in the criminal justice system have been concerned about the tendency of many reforms to extend the net of social control. This occurs when an innovative program designed to serve as an alternative to other interventions receives offenders who would have been given less or no actions against them in the formal system. Programs have attempted to avoid spreading the net of social control by setting clear admission criteria, applying admission criteria consistently, and monitoring their application. Restorative justice, however, may require a rethinking of this concern. For example, is the victim of a home burglary by a first-time, naive offender any less deserving of an opportunity to participate in the system than the victim of a burglary carried out by a sophisticated, repeat offender? Should the process go forward even if the first-time burglar may experience sanctions that he or she would not normally have experienced in the formal system? Expanding the system of social control to ensure that reasonable actions are taken in regard to all offenders may not be undesirable. The key questions are what is reasonable, who decides, and what is the degree of formality or informality in the process. Rather than debating widening or narrowing the network, it may be more useful to debate which offenses should be dealt with by the state through the formal system of justice, which should be dealt with more informally by community processes, and how victims and offenders can be involved in the decisions as to what are reasonable requirements.

Research on implementation of the family group conference approach in the New Zealand youth justice system found that the net had been widened in the sense that many more youngsters were receiving sanctions, but that these were sanctions determined by the youngsters, their families, and the victims rather than the courts; further, the use of both formal court processes as well as incarceration was significantly decreased (Maxwell and Morris, 1995). Is expanding social control necessarily an undesirable thing, if it is informal with key decisions being made by the participants, including families, and when there is a concomitant reduction in both the more formal processes and the use of the more severe sanctions? The matter may hinge on the extent of control exercised by the state through formal organizations, compared to more informal social control exercised by families and neighborhoods.

Griffiths and Hamilton (1996) make the same point about the importance of ensuring that the rights of victims are adequately protected and appropriate sanctions imposed. They caution against particular people within communities exercising considerable power over the restorative practices and compromising the administration of justice. Netzig and Trenczek (1996) emphasize the importance of protecting victims from being misused in the role of helping offenders within a restorative justice program. They argue for national standards for programs and, along with McElrea, suggest a role for the judiciary in overseeing restorative justice programs. Wright (1996) notes that defendants might also feel induced to plead guilty and participate in a restorative justice program when they may have had a valid defense against the charges. Prosecutors may overcharge defendants and then agree to reduce charges given the defendants' willingness to admit guilt and participate in a restorative justice program.

The debate about fairness and proportional sentences or requirements may illustrate a potential incompatibility between a restorative and retributive justice approach. The concept of proportionality is essentially a retributive justice notion that comes into play when the state is imposing punishment to ensure that offenders who committed like offenses are handled the same way. If one rejects the notion of state-imposed punishment, a common theme among the restorative justice writers, then the matter of proportionality and fairness is less important than reconciliation and creating peace in neighborhoods, so long as victims and offenders believe they have been handled fairly even though the requirements and responses may be very different across a group of offenders who have committed similar offenses. Fairness is not uniformity but satisfaction. Several of the authors have addressed the need for safeguards for victims, but none have addressed the need for safeguards for offenders. Historically, one of the reasons for the development of the more formal criminal justice system was to protect offenders from the unmitigated vengeance of victims and their families and, as the system developed, to secure some reasonable balance between the penalties the state could impose and the seriousness of the offense. Advocates of restorative justice will need to give some careful attention about how to avoid vigilantism. There is no assurance that all victims and communities are interested in reconciliation and peace; some may be interested in carefully nurturing and preserving anger and hatred that can be vented by overly harsh and cruel responses to offenders.

Will the public support movement toward a system based on the philosophy of restorative justice with emphasis on reconciliation and peacemaking? Public support will be essential if the political will is to be developed to make this transition. Most authors report considerable public support for restorative justice principles. Alan Harland (1996) is optimistic about the future of restorative justice, but notes that proponents must overcome two challenges if the concept is to gain the political and public support necessary to flourish. The first is to reconcile differences among the supporters, and the second is to define and clarify the most essential aims and related mechanisms.

QUESTION TO CONSIDER

1. Compare how the principles of the restorative justice model differ from the adversarial model currently used by the Canadian legal system. What major advantages are offered by the restorative justice model?

REFERENCES

Bazemore, G. (1996). Three paradigms for juvenile justice. In B. Galloway and J. Hudson (Eds.). *Restorative justice: International perspectives* (pp. 37–68). Monsey, NY: Criminal Justice Press.

Griffiths, C.T. & Hamilton, R. (1996). Sanctioning and healing: Restorative justice in Canadian aboriginal communities. In B. Galloway and J. Hudson (Eds.). *Restorative justice: International perspectives* (pp. 175–192). Monsey, NY: Criminal Justice Press.

Harding, J. (1996). Whither restorative justice in England and Wales? A probation perspective. In B. Galloway and J. Hudson (Eds.). *Restorative justice: International perspectives* (pp. 261–270). Monsey, NY: Criminal Justice Press.

Harland, A. (1996). Towards a restorative justice future. In B. Galloway and J. Hudson (Eds.). *Restorative justice: International perspectives* (pp. 505–516). Monsey, NY: Criminal Justice Press.

Jervis, B. (1996). Developing reparation plans through victim-offender mediation by New Zealand probation officers. In B. Galloway and J. Hudson (Eds.). *Restorative justice: International perspectives* (pp. 417–430). Monsey, NY: Criminal Justice Press.

Maxwell, G., & Morris, A. (1995). Deciding about justice for young people in New Zealand: The involvement of families, victims and culture. In J. Hudson & B. Galaway (Eds.). *Child welfare in Canada: Research and policy implications.* Toronto: Thompson Educational Publishing.

McElrea, F.W.M. (1996). The New Zealand youth court: A model for use with adults. In B. Galloway and J. Hudson (Eds.). *Restorative justice: International perspectives* (pp. 69–84). Monsey, NY: Criminal Justice Press.

Minor, K.I. & Morrison, J.T. (1996) A theoretical study and critique of restorative justice. In B. Galloway and J. Hudson (Eds.). *Restorative justice: International perspectives* (pp. 117–136). Monsey, NY: Criminal Justice Press.

Netzig, L. & Trenczek, T. (1996). Restorative justice as participation: Theory, law, experience, and research. In B. Galloway and J. Hudson (Eds.). *Restorative justice: International perspectives* (pp. 241–260). Monsey, NY: Criminal Justice Press.

Pranis, K. (1996) A state initiative toward restorative justice: The Minnesota experience. In B. Galloway and J. Hudson (Eds.). *Restorative justice: International perspectives* (pp. 493–504). Monsey, NY: Criminal Justice Press.

Retzinger, S.M. & Scheff, T.J. (1996). Strategy for community conferences: Emotions and social bonds. In B. Galloway and J. Hudson (Eds.). *Restorative justice: International perspectives* (pp. 315–336). Monsey, NY: Criminal Justice Press.

Walter, M. & Wagner, A. (1996). How police officers manage difficult situations: The predominance of soothing and smoothing strategies. In B. Galloway and J. Hudson (Eds.). *Restorative justice: International perspectives* (pp. 271–282). Monsey, NY: Criminal Justice Press.

Wright, M. (1996). Can mediation be an alternative to criminal justice? In B. Galloway and J. Hudson (Eds.). *Restorative justice: International perspectives* (pp. 227–240). Monsey, NY: Criminal Justice Press.

Yazzie, R. & Zion, J.W. (1996). Navajo restorative justice: The law of equality and justice. In B. Galloway and J. Hudson (Eds.). *Restorative justice: International perspectives* (pp. 157–174). Monsey, NY: Criminal Justice Press.

FIFTEEN

Restorative Justice through Mediation: The Impact of Programs in Four Canadian Provinces

MARK S. UMBREIT

Mediation of criminal conflicts is a powerful expression of restorative justice which emphasizes that crime is relational (not just against the state), that the role of victims in the justice process should be elevated, and that the focus of justice should be upon restoring emotional and material losses left in the wake of crime, and upon building safer communities through active citizen participation (Zehr, 1990). High levels of client satisfaction with the mediation process and outcome have consistently been found over the years in studies throughout North America and Europe (Coates and Gehm, 1989; Collins, 1984; Dignan, 1990; Fischer and Jeune, 1987; Galaway, 1988; Galaway and Hudson, 1990; Gehm, 1990; Marshall and Merry, 1990; Perry *et al.*, 1987; Umbreit, 1989, 1991, 1993, 1994, 1995; Umbreit and Coates, 1993; Wright and Galaway, 1989). Studies have found higher restitution completion rates (Umbreit, 1994), reduced fear among victims (Umbreit and Coates, 1993; Umbreit, 1995), and reduced future criminal behavior (Butts and Snyder, 1991; Schneider, 1986; Umbreit, 1994). Multi-site studies have been completed in England (Marshall and Merry, 1990) and the U.S. (Coates and Gehm, 1989; Umbreit, 1994). This chapter reports findings from four victim–offender mediation programs in Canada.

Most victim–offender mediation programs employ a process of intake, preparation for mediation, mediation, and follow up. Two of the programs (Winnipeg and Ottawa) refer to their clients as the accused, since no formal admissions of guilt have occurred. Similarly, these two programs refer to complainants rather than to victims.

During the intake phase, case information is logged, and the case is assigned to a mediator. The preparation for the mediation phase involves a considerable amount

Source: Mark S. Umbreit, "Restorative Justice through Mediation: The Impact of Programs in Four Canadian Provinces," in *Restorative Justice: International Perspectives*, ed. Burt Galaway and Joe Hudson (Monsey, NY: Criminal Justice Press, 1996) 373–85.

of work. The parties involved in the conflict will be contacted separately and interviewed. In most victim–offender mediation programs, the mediator will call and then later meet separately with the victim and the offender. In two of the programs in this study, however, the mediator had no prior contact with the parties. Staff in the agency contact the parties by letter and most often interview them by phone. An in-person interview will occasionally be conducted when deemed appropriate. The mediation phase consists of the joint victim–offender meeting. The agenda usually focuses first on clarifying information about the alleged or actual criminal behavior and on expressing concerns that one or both parties may have. The second part of the mediation session addresses the issues related to the impact that the conflict had on the parties, usually culminating in a discussion of the losses experienced by the victim and the potential for the offender to compensate the victim. This often results in the parties negotiating an agreement to restore losses incurred or to address other concerns. Mediation sessions tend to range in length from one to two hours. The follow-up phase consists of monitoring completion of any negotiated restitution that was agreed upon, intervening if additional issues arise or conflict develops between the parties, and scheduling follow-up joint meetings between the involved parties when appropriate, although this is not frequently done.

METHODOLOGY

Community-based non-profit organizations, providing mediation services for referrals from the criminal justice system, were examined in Langley, British Columbia; Calgary, Alberta; Winnipeg, Manitoba; and Ottawa, Ontario. The programs in Langley, Calgary, and Winnipeg identify themselves as victim–offender mediation programs, whereas the program in Ottawa identifies itself as a criminal court mediation program.

The four program sites are diverse in program design, community acceptance, caseload size, history, case management procedures, and impact on the criminal justice system; the diversity is summarized in Table 15.1. The programs in Winnipeg and Ottawa accept primarily adult cases. Both staff and community volunteers serve as mediators. Some programs also accept referrals from defense counsel, police, and either party involved in the incident. The Victim Offender Reconciliation Program in Langley and the Victim Young Offender Reconciliation Program in Calgary are more similar than the other two sites. The Victim Offender Mediation Program of Mediation Services in Winnipeg and the Criminal Pretrial Mediation Programme of the Dispute Resolution Centre for Ottawa-Carleton are also more similar to each other than to the Calgary and Langley sites.

The Youth Advocacy and Mediation Services Program in Calgary was initiated by the Calgary John Howard Society. This program assists victims to better understand their feelings about being victimized and presents an opportunity to become more involved in the criminal justice system. The young people who choose to participate are given the opportunity to discuss the offense with the victim and decide upon a restitution agreement. From 1991 through 1993, 258 cases were referred to this victim–offender mediation program.

The Victim Offender Reconciliation Program (VORP) in Langley, British Columbia, was initially developed in 1982 by the Langley Mennonite Fellowship and later became one of several programs of the Fraser Region Community Justice

TABLE 15.1 *Program Characteristics by Site*

	Calgary	Langley	Ottawa	Winnipeg
Program start	1985	1982	1989	1979
Organization type	Private non-profit	Private non-profit	Private non-profit	Private non-profit
Total budget, 1993	$55 000	$55 000	$85 000	$122 000
Staff (FTEs), 1993	1.5	2	1.6	4.5
No. of volunteer mediators, 1993	1	25	10	55
Mediation training length	40 hrs.+ apprenticeship	30 hrs. class +3 observations	3 days + apprenticeship	4.5 days apprenticeship
Co-mediators routinely used	No	No	No	Yes
Primary referral source	Probation	Probation	Crown	Crown
Point of case referral	Post-sentencing	Pretrial/ court order	Postcharge/ pretrial	Postcharge /pre-plea/ pretrial
Most frequent offense	B & E	Mischief	Assault	Assault

Initiatives, which was founded in 1985. The VORP is a community-based alternative that empowers participants to devise their own solutions in face-to-face encounters guided by trained community mediators. This program serves courts in both Langley and Surrey. From 1991 through 1993, a total of 851 cases were referred to the VORP.

The Dispute Resolution Centre for Ottawa-Carleton was established in 1986 as a community-based non-profit agency with the mandate to demonstrate and facilitate the practice of conflict resolution techniques within the community. The Centre works closely with Crown attorneys. Mediation is conducted in selected cases after a charge has been laid by the police, but generally, before the case has been set for trial. From 1991 through 1993, a total of 689 cases were referred to the Dispute Resolution Centre.

The criminal court program of the Mediation Services in Winnipeg was established in 1979 as a victim–offender mediation project of the Mennonite Central Committee of Manitoba. In 1992, Mediation Services became independent of the Mennonite Central Committee, partly to establish a broader base of community support and involvement in the organization. The purpose of Mediation Services is to promote peace and restorative justice within the community by empowering people, through education and mediation, to resolve conflict using non-violent conflict resolution processes. From 1991 through 1993, a total of 2647 cases were referred,

TABLE 15.2 *Program Outcomes by Site*

	Calgary	Langley	Ottawa	Winnipeg	Combined
Case referrals, 1991	40	317	178	725	1260
Case referrals, 1992	79	349	200	963	1591
Case referrals, 1993	139	185	311	959	1594
Total case referrals, 1991–93	258	851	689	2647	4445
Mediations, 1991	12	142	60	335	549
Mediations, 1992	28	107	85	393	613
Mediations, 1993	51	82	114	327	574
Total mediations, 1991–93	91	331	259	1055	1736
Successfully negotiated agreements, 1991–93	83 (91%)	327 (99%)	243 (94%)	947 (90%)	1600 (93)
Proportion of mediations to case referrals, 1991–93	35%	39%	38%	40%	39%

representing the largest volume of case referrals to a single victim–offender mediation program in Canada.

Both quantitative and qualitative data were collected and analyzed. Phone interviews with victims and offenders were conducted two months following either the mediation session (experimental group) or the date that the prosecutor, court, or related agency disposed of the case (comparison group). Twenty-four mediation sessions were observed. Interviews with court officials, program staff, and volunteer mediators, as well as reviews of records, were used to examine how the process of mediation with offenders and their victims was being applied, and to identify any public policy implications. Emphasis was placed upon understanding the application of the mediation process and the outcomes in differing programmatic and cultural settings. A total of 610 interviews were conducted with participants referred to mediation, involving 323 victims and 287 offenders. Fifty-nine percent of the victims were male, with an average age of 33 years; 86% were white. There were no significant differences between the mediation and no-mediation samples for victims. Eighty percent of offenders were male, with an average age of 24 years; 80% were white. Most offenders from the Ottawa and Winnipeg sites were adults. Aboriginals were the most frequent minority race for both victims and offenders. The most common offense referred was assault, followed by property crimes such as vandalism, theft, and burglary. The sub-samples within program sites are identified in Table 15.3.

FINDINGS

The programs received 4445 referrals from 1991 through 1993. Referrals were primarily adult cases. The Winnipeg program received a total of 2647 cases during this three-year period. Langley had 851 cases referred, followed by the Ottawa-Carleton program with 689 referrals and the Calgary program with 258. Nearly all referrals in Winnipeg and Ottawa were adult cases, while in Langley and Calgary, most referrals were youth. Mediation sessions between the involved parties were held in 39%

TABLE 15.3 *Canadian Cross-site Program Sub-samples*

	Experimental groups participating in mediation samples		Comparison groups referred but no-mediation samples		Total sample
	Victims	*Offenders*	*Victims*	*Offenders*	
Calgary Program	7	7	2	5	21
Langley Program	42	41	37	42	162
Ottawa Program	42	16	22	12	92
Winnipeg Program	92	95	79	69	335
Totals	183	159	140	128	610

of the cases referred. Mediation rates were 35% in Calgary, 38% in Ottawa, 39% in Langley, and 40% in Winnipeg. Successfully negotiated agreements which were acceptable to both parties were reached in 93% of the cases that were mediated: 90% in Winnipeg, 91% in Calgary, 94% in Ottawa, and 99% in Langley.

Seventy-eight percent of victims and 74% of offenders who participated in the mediation reported satisfaction with the manner in which the justice system responded to their case, compared to 48% of victims and 53% of offenders who were referred but never participated in mediation. Satisfaction with the outcome of the mediation session was reported by 89% of the victims and 91% of the offenders.

Perception of participating voluntarily in mediation was reported by 90% of victims and 83% of offenders at the combined sites; 91% of the victims and 93% of the offenders would participate in mediation again. Being fairly treated by the justice system was expressed by 80% of victims and 80% of offenders who participated in mediation, compared to 43% of victims and 56% of the offenders who were referred but who never participated in mediation. The mediated agreement was viewed as fair by 92% of the victims and by 93% of offenders.

The importance of the victim receiving answers from the offender about what happened was more likely to be found among victims (87%) who participated in a mediation session with the offender, at the combined sites, than among victims (51%) who were referred but who never participated in mediation. The importance

TABLE 15.4 *Victim Satisfaction with Criminal Justice System Comparing Mediated to Non-mediated Case*

	Combined sites*		Calgary		Langley		Ottawa*		Winnipeg*	
	Med.	*Non-med.*	*Med.*	*Non-med.*	*Med.*	*Non-med.*	*Med.*	*Non-med.*	*Med.*	*Non-med.*
Satisfied (%)	78.0	48.0	86.0	100.0	58.0	57.0	85.0	52.0	82.0	41.0
Dissatisfied (%)	22.0	52.0	14.0	0.0	42.0	43.0	15.0	48.0	18.0	59.0
n =	178	134	7	2	40	37	41	21	90	74

*FINDING OF SIGNIFICANT DIFFERENCE BETWEEN MEDIATION AND NON-MEDIATION SAMPLES (P = 0.05 OR LESS).

TABLE 15.5 *Offender Satisfaction with Criminal Justice System Comparing Mediated to Non-mediated Cases*

	Combined sites*		Calgary		Langley		Ottawa*		Winnipeg*	
	Med.	Non-med.	Med.	Non-med.	Med.	Non-med.	Med.	Non-med.	Med.	Non-med.
Satisfied (%)	73.9	53.2	28.6	100.0	83.0	59.5	68.8	41.7	74.2	47.8
Dissatisfied (%)	26.1	46.8	71.4	0.0	17.0	40.5	31.2	58.3	25.8	52.2
n = 157	126	7	5	41	42	16	12	93	67	

*FINDING OF SIGNIFICANT DIFFERENCE BETWEEN SAMPLES (P = 0.05 OR LESS).

of the victim telling the offender the impact the event had upon him or her was more likely to be found among victims (89%) who participated in a mediation session with the offender than among victims (51%) who were referred to mediation but who never participated in it.

The importance of the victim receiving an apology from the offender was more likely to be found among victims (74%) who participated in a mediation session with the offender than among victims (40%) who were referred but who never participated in mediation. The importance of the victim having been able to negotiate restitution with the offender was more likely to be found among victims (88%) who participated in a mediation session with the offender than among victims (52%) who were referred but who never participated in mediation. The importance of the offender being able to tell the victim about what happened was more likely to be found among offenders (84%) who participated in a mediation session with the victim than among offenders (68%) who were referred but who never participated in mediation. The importance of the offender having been able to negotiate a restitution settlement with the victim was more likely to be found among offenders (98%) who participated in a mediation session with the victim than among offenders (77%) who were referred but who never participated in mediation. The importance of the offender apologizing to the victim was more likely to be found among offenders (78%) who participated in a mediation session with the victim than offenders (67%) who were referred but who never participated in mediation.

An apology by the offender was more likely to have been seen among offenders (84%) who participated in a mediation session with the victim than among offenders (30%) who were referred but who never participated in mediation. Fear

TABLE 15.6 *Victim Satisfaction with Outcome of Mediation*

	Combined		Calgary		Langley		Ottawa		Winnipeg	
Satisfied	(188)	89%	(7)	100%	(31)	82%	(39)	93%	(81)	90%
Dissatisfied	(19)	11%	(0)	—	(7)	18%	(3)	7%	(9)	10%
Totals	(177)	100%	(7)	100%	(38)	100%	(42)	100%	(90)	100%

TABLE 15.7 *Offender Satisfaction with Outcome of Mediation*

	Combined		Calgary		Langley		Ottawa		Winnipeg	
Satisfied	(139)	91%	(7)	100%	(37)	97%	(14)	93%	(82)	88%
Dissatisfied	(13)	9%	(0)	—	(1)	3%	(1)	7%	(11)	12%
Totals	(152)	100%	(7)	100%	(38)	100%	(15)	100%	(93)	100%

of being revictimized by the same offender was less likely to be expressed among victims (11%) who participated in a mediation session with the offender than among victims (31%) who were referred but who never participated in mediation. Remaining upset about the crime was less likely to be expressed by victims (53%) who participated in a mediation session with the offender than among offenders (66%) who were referred but never participated in mediation.

The vast majority of criminal justice officials ($n = 45$) (police constables, Crown attorneys, defense attorneys, judges, probation officers) were supportive of mediating in appropriate criminal conflicts; they indicated an awareness that the major benefit provided by mediation was to address the emotional and informational needs facing the parties. Criminal justice officials at three of the four program sites indicated a high degree of satisfaction with the services provided by the local mediation program. They emphasized highly dedicated and committed program staff, competent and professional staff, and effective management and resolution of cases that are referred to the program.

SUMMARY AND CONCLUSIONS

Data were collected from four Canadian victim–offender mediation programs, two serving primarily adult offenders and their victims and two serving primarily juvenile offenders and their victims. Post-program interviews were held with victims and offenders as well as with a comparison group of victims and offenders, who were referred to the programs but who chose not to participate; mediation sessions were observed, and interviews were conducted with criminal justice officials.

From 1991 through 1993, 4445 offenders were referred to the programs, the majority of whom were adults. Thirty-nine percent of the referrals resulted in a

TABLE 15.8 *Victim's Perception of Fairness in Justice System*

Perceived:	Combined*		Calgary		Langley		Ottawa*		Winnipeg*	
	Med.	Non-med.	Med.	Non-med.	Med.	Non-med.	Med.	Non-med.	Med.	Non-med.
Fair	79.9	42.7	42.9	50.0	63.2	48.6	87.8	42.1	86.4	39.7
Unfair	20.1	57.3	57.1	50.0	36.8	51.4	12.2	57.9	13.6	60.3
n =	174	124	7	2	38	35	41	19	88	68

*FINDING OF SIGNIFICANT DIFFERENCE BETWEEN MEDIATION AND NON-MEDIATION SAMPLES (P = 0.05 OR LESS).

TABLE 15.9 *Offenders' Perception of Fairness in Justice System*

Perceived:	Combined*		Calgary		Langley		Ottawa		Winnipeg*	
	Med.	Non-med.	Med.	Non-med.	Med.	Non-med.	Med.	Non-med.	Med.	Non-med.
Fair (%)	80.1	56.2	57.1	100.0	81.0	69.2	68.8	47.0	83.3	47.0
Unfair (%)	19.9	43.8	42.9	0.0	19.0	30.8	31.2	53.0	16.7	53.0
n =	156	121	7	5	37	39	16	11	96	66

*FINDING OF SIGNIFICANT DIFFERENCE BETWEEN MEDIATION AND NON-MEDIATION SAMPLES (P = 0.05 OR LESS).

face-to-face meeting with the victim and, when mediation occurred, 93% resulted in an agreement. Both victims and offenders who participated in mediation were significantly more likely to be satisfied (78% for victims and 74% for offenders) than those who were referred but did not participate. Ninety percent of both victims and offenders reported satisfaction with the terms of the mediated agreement. Eighty percent of both victims and offenders who participated in mediation reported that they had been treated fairly by the justice system: there is a significant difference between this group and those who did not participate in mediation.

Victims who participated in mediation were significantly more likely than victims who did not participate in mediation to report that it was important for them to receive answers to questions from the offender, important for them to tell the offender the impact the event had had on them, important to receive an apology from the offender, and important to receive restitution from the offender. Offenders who participated in mediation were more likely than those who did not participate to report that it was important to them to tell the victim about what had happened, important to them to be able to apologize to the victim, and important to them to negotiate an agreement with the victim. Victims who participated in mediation were significantly less likely than those who did not to report fear of subsequently being revictimized by the same offender. The findings from this Canadian study are strikingly similar to earlier reported findings from an American study which used the same methodology and data elements.

1. The findings relating to high levels of client satisfaction and perceptions of fairness with mediation in four Canadian provinces are consistent with prior research in the U.S. which used a similar methodology, including common data elements and instruments (Umbreit, 1994; Umbreit and Coates, 1993). These similarities are summarized in Table 15.10. These findings were also consistent with a number of other studies conducted in the U.S. (Coates and Gehm, 1989; Galaway, 1988; Gehm, 1990; Umbreit, 1989, 1991) and in Europe (Dignan, 1990; Marshall and Merry, 1990).
2. The quality of justice experienced by victims and offenders can be significantly enhanced by expanded use of mediation in criminal conflicts.
3. Mediation can provide an opportunity for victims to become actively involved in the process of holding the offender accountable and of gaining a greater sense of closure.

TABLE 15.10 *Comparison of Canadian and U.S. Studies*

	Combined Canadian victim–offender mediation program sites (4)	Combined American victim–offender mediation program sites (4)
Victim satisfaction with mediation process	78%	79%
Offender satisfaction with mediation process	74%	87%
Victim satisfaction with mediation outcome	89%	90%
Offender satisfaction with mediation outcome	91%	91%
Victim perceptions of fairness in mediation	80%	83%
Offender perceptions of fairness in mediation	80%	89%

QUESTION TO CONSIDER

1. Discuss the degree to which Umbreit's evaluation of mediation programs in four provinces validates the principles of restorative justice. Also discuss whether there were any weaknesses of the study itself that affect its usefulness in assessing restorative justice.

REFERENCES

Butts, J.A., & Snyder, H.N. (1991). *Restitution and juvenile recidivism.* Pittsburgh, PA: National Center for Juvenile Justice.

Coates, R.B., & Gehm, J. (1989). An empirical assessment. In M. Wright & B. Galaway (Eds.). *Mediation and criminal justice.* London: Sage Publications.

Collins, J.P. (1984). *Evaluation report: Grande Prairie reconciliation project for young offenders.* Ottawa: Ministry of the Solicitor General of Canada, Consultation Centre (Prairies).

Dignan, J. (1990). *Repairing the damage.* Sheffield, UK: Centre for Criminological and Legal Research, University of Sheffield.

Fischer, D.G., & Jeune, R. (1987). Juvenile diversion: A process analysis. *Canadian Psychology, 28,* 60–70.

Galaway, B. (1988). Crime victim and offender mediation as a social work strategy. *Social Service Review, 62,* 668–683.

Galaway, B., & Hudson, J. (1990). *Criminal justice, restitution, and reconciliation.* Monsey, NY: Criminal Justice Press.

Gehm, J. (1990). Mediated victim–offender restitution agreements: An exploratory analysis of factors related to victim participation. In B. Galaway & J. Hudson (Eds.). *Criminal justice, restitution and reconciliation.* Monsey, NY: Criminal Justice Press.

Marshall, T.F., & Merry, S. (1990). *Crime and accountability.* London: Home Office.

Perry, L., Lajeunesse, T., & Woods, A. (1987). *Mediation services: An evaluation.* Winnipeg: Research, Planning and Evaluation Office of the Attorney General.

Schneider, A.L. (1986). Restitution and recidivism rates of juvenile offenders: Results from four experimental studies. *Criminology, 24*(3), 533–552.

Umbreit, M.S. (1989). Victims seeking fairness, not revenge: Toward restorative justice. *Federal Probation 53*(3), 52–57.

Umbreit, M.S. (1991). Minnesota mediation center gets positive results. *Corrections Today Journal* (August), 194–197.

Umbreit, M.S. (1993). Juvenile offenders meet their victims: The impact of mediation in Albuquerque, New Mexico. *Family and Conciliation Courts Review, 31*(1), 90–100.

Umbreit, M.S. (1994). *Victim meets offender: The impact of restorative justice & mediation.* Monsey, NY: Criminal Justice Press.

Umbreit, M.S. (1995). *Mediating interpersonal conflicts: A pathway to peace.* West Concord, MN: CPI Publishing.

Umbreit, M.S., & Coates, R.B. (1993). Cross-site analysis of victim offender mediation in four states. *Crime and Delinquency 39*(4), 565–585.

Wright, M., & Galaway, B. (1989). *Mediation and criminal justice.* London: Sage.

Zehr, H. (1990). *Changing lenses: A new focus for crime and justice.* Scottsdale, PA: Herald Press.

READER REPLY CARD

We are interested in your reaction to *Law in Society: A Canadian Reader* by Nick Larsen and Brian Burtch. You can help us to improve this book in future editions by completing this questionnaire.

1. What was your reason for using this book?

   ❏ university course   ❏ college course   ❏ continuing education course

   ❏ professional   ❏ personal   ❏ other _____
      development   interest   _____

2. If you are a student, please identify your school and the course in which you used this book.

   _____

   _____

3. Which chapters or parts of this book did you use? Which did you omit?

   _____

   _____

4. What did you like best about this book? What did you like least?

   _____

   _____

5. Please identify any topics you think should be added to future editions.

   _____

   _____

6. Please add any comments or suggestions.

   _____

   _____

7. May we contact you for further information?

   _____

   _____

   Name: _____

   Address: _____

   _____

   Phone: _____

   E-Mail: _____

(fold here and tape shut)

MAIL ≫ POSTE

Canada Post Corporation / Société canadienne des postes

Postage paid
If mailed in Canada

Port payé
si posté au Canada

Business Reply

Réponse d'affaires

0116870399   01

0116870399-M8Z4X6-BR01

Larry Gillevet
Director of Product Development
HARCOURT BRACE & COMPANY, CANADA
55 HORNER AVENUE
TORONTO, ONTARIO
M8Z 9Z9